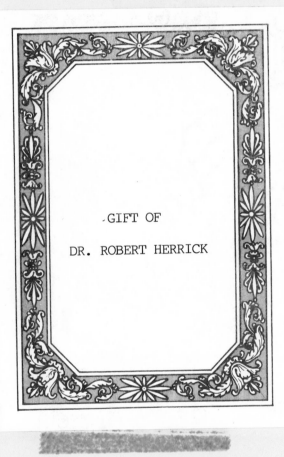

THE DEVELOPMENT OF
SOCIAL THOUGHT

THE DEVELOPMENT OF
SOCIAL THOUGHT

BY

EMORY S. BOGARDUS

PROFESSOR OF SOCIOLOGY
UNIVERSITY OF SOUTHERN CALIFORNIA
EDITOR, *Sociology and Social Research*

Fourth Edition

LONGMANS, GREEN AND CO.
NEW YORK · LONDON · TORONTO

LONGMANS, GREEN AND CO., INC.
119 WEST 40TH STREET, NEW YORK 18

LONGMANS, GREEN AND CO. LTD.
48 GROSVENOR STREET, LONDON W 1

LONGMANS, GREEN AND CO.
137 BOND STREET, TORONTO 2

BOGARDUS
THE DEVELOPMENT OF SOCIAL THOUGHT

First edition January 1940
Reprinted November 1942
January 1944, December 1945
July 1946
Second edition November 1947
September 1948, May 1949
June 1950, May 1952
Third edition May 1955
Reprinted August 1957
Fourth edition April 1960
Reprinted June 1961

PRINTED IN THE UNITED STATES OF AMERICA

PREFACE

This book is written for the world of students. In it any serious-minded person should find a fundamental background for understanding the central themes of human progress, a substantial basis for attacking the most important problems of the day, and a call to renew his faith in the soundness of human aspirations.

Inasmuch as this treatise is written for students, it is intended to be not the last word on the subject, but simply a first word. The theme of each chapter is in itself a subject for further investigation. In fact, the student with an alert mind will find in each chapter many subjects concerning which he will want to learn more. If the discussions in this book stimulate the student to make inquiries on his own initiative, they will have accomplished more than the author could have expected.

This book is designed as an introduction to the field of social thought for college students, irrespective of the fields in which their special interests lie. It is planned to give any college student a broad background for orienting himself and his life work in this human world.

Perhaps some students will have their mental appetites aroused in such a way that they will continue further studies in the field of social thought. Perhaps some will be stimulated to pursue research in this broad realm of knowledge.

The book is designed also to meet the needs of the reading public which has not made an acquaintance in a systematic and historical way with the social thought of the leaders of mankind in all ages and all cultures. The materials are presented in a descriptive manner. It is not the purpose to write a critique, or to enter into a discussion of fine points or of abstract and theoretical doctrines. Other studies are available for these purposes.

Important source materials have been listed at the close of each chapter. They may well be given primary consideration. They will serve to introduce the student to further readings in the sources, and at the same time help to make clear the main context of each chapter.

Topics for discussion have been appended to each chapter. These may be assigned as the basis of a discussion period at the beginning of each class meeting. It is important that these discussions be conducted in terms of facts and their meanings rather than on the level of opinions and arguments.

In the titles of many chapters the name of a particular social thinker, not now living, is included, either as a point of departure, or as a central point of discussion around which to consider the thinking of a number of significant contributors to a given phase of social thought. The name of the noteworthy figure together with the related concept or theme is the basis of the title of each chapter.

This analysis of the history of social thought is presented first in terms of the social life that is represented by each theme. Social thought is considered here both as an expression of the times in which it appears and as a stimulus to its day and age. Second, this history of social thought has unlimited possibilities for throwing light on the solution of social problems today. An attempt is made to point out some of the connections between human experience as revealed in the history of social thought and the possible treatment of the baffling social problems of the hour. It is self-evident that anyone who would become a leader in solving current social problems needs as a minimum background an acquaintance with the salient phases of the history of social thought.

EMORY S. BOGARDUS

PREFACE TO THE FOURTH EDITION

Among the new developments that appear in the Fourth Edition, besides new references that have been added to the "Readings" at the close of the chapters, and minor revisions, are two new chapters, one on Odum and folk sociology and another on Mukerjee and social values.

While Odum received his graduate school training at Columbia and at Clark University and came directly under the influence of Giddings, he became an outstanding representative of social thinking based on the history of the South in the United States. In fact he is the first representative of the South to be given major attention in this book. He compiled a rich collection of folk lore and did perhaps more than any other person to create a folk sociology. His contributions in this connection fill a large gap in the development of social thought.

The new chapter on Mukerjee and social values marks the rounding out of a cycle in the history of social thought that came into being centuries ago. It is a cycle whose beginning is emphasized by the first chapters of this book which deal with East Indian, Chinese, Japanese, and Hebrew social thought. Then came major contributions to social thinking in Europe and America, accompanied in recent decades by important developments in this field in the Orient, particularly as represented by the writings of Radhakamal Mukerjee of India. Mukerjee received a part of his education in Europe and America and hence has been in an excellent position to integrate Eastern and Western social ideas. He comes close to positing in an introductory way what might be called a universal system of social thought. In fact a new, master social science is being intimated today that will include not only the findings of the social sciences but will utilize within its synthetic process all scientific knowledge, in short, all knowledge.

E. S. B.

January, 1960

CONTENTS

THE DEVELOPMENT OF
SOCIAL THOUGHT

THE DEVELOPMENT OF
SOCIAL THOUGHT

CHAPTER I

THE NATURE OF SOCIAL THOUGHT

Man faces a world of complex social problems. As a result he is perplexed beyond description; his thinking often ends in confusion. Inasmuch as the average person, for the first time in the world's history, is beginning to attack social problems, he is entitled to all the aid that can be made available. Upon the success of the common man and woman in mastering the intricacies of social thinking, the further development if not the very life of civilization depends. Upon a similar basis rests the advance if not the survival of democracy. Democratic adjustment of problems calls for democratic thinking, which in turn means that the rank and file of group membership must think clearly about the nature and solution of social problems. Thus, social thought, or thinking about the nature and solution of the problems of any society, large or small, needs to be widespread if not universal. Socially minded leaders cannot proceed in their activities very far beyond the level of the social thinking of the common people.

Hitherto a large proportion of the analyses of social questions has been academic. These discussions have terminated in either quibbles or erudite generalities. Insofar as social theories have been correct they have been reserved largely for the theorists alone. The large majority of any social group have not understood the nature of social thought; neither have they benefited. Hence, they have held social thought in contempt. Sound social thought needs to be democratized, that is, made available for all the people.

In thinking about social problems, the so-called practical

person has proceeded in his own way. He has had personal experience, which to him has been sufficient. Often he has been motivated by a sense of injustice, and stung into fervid thought by circumstances which he has judged to be unfair. As a result, he has concocted a makeshift remedy, or impulsively accepted a ready-made program. Perhaps he has believed in a single cause for all social ills and in consequence has prescribed a single remedy for all social diseases. Usually he has been very limited in his observations, untrained in making accurate deductions, and hence, narrow and intolerant in his conclusions. Either he has been entirely nonplussed or else he has felt cocksure.

The practicalist is often a poor theorist. He may be even the most dangerous type of theorist. He has scoffed at genuine theory so long that he has fallen into the pit of unsound theory. He has failed to see, for example, that a bridge does not project itself across a chasm, or that just anyone cannot build a substantial bridge. He is blind to the role of scientific engineering in bridge-building. With social practicalists calling theorists names instead of respecting sound theory and putting their shoulders to the wheels of broad-minded and scientifically derived theories of social development, civilization has floundered and social problems have piled up, mountain high.

Another difficulty in the pathway of sound social thinking is found in the absence of proper intellectual backgrounds. People are prone to offer solutions for social questions without first equipping themselves with a knowledge of social processes and laws. Moreover, they are often unwilling to acquaint themselves with this necessary knowledge. Only by accident, however, can current social problems be understood unless the historical sequences of social cause and effect are perceived. Nearly all social questions today are essentially the outcroppings of tendencies which have had a long human history. A current social maladjustment is generally indicative of a long line of antecedent factors. A knowledge of societary processes is essential to sound thinking about present-day evils. A history of social thought furnishes a minimum of background materials for the understanding of today's baffling social dilemmas.

While social action may be greatly needed, yet social action that does not emerge from thorough-going social thinking is dangerous. Social action that springs from blind desire or irritated convictions is as likely to do harm as it is to do good. A knowledge of the history of social experiences and of the social thought which grows out of social experiences is basic to wise social action.

SOCIAL THOUGHT DEFINED

In the strict sense, social thought is the product of the thinking together of *socii* or of associates. Most social thought is of the ordinary dinner table variety, that is, casual and desultory. Most social thought in the sense of group thought about social questions has contributed little to knowledge. Discussion-group thinking illustrates social thinking on its higher levels, but discussion-group thinking is not yet extensive.[1] However, a great deal may be expected from it in the future. In fact, in countries that preserve freedom of speech, it promises to become ultimately the main type of thought.

As far as the past and the present are concerned, social thought amounts, as a rule, to the thought about social questions by individual persons. In this sense, social thought is thinking about societary problems by one or a few persons here and there in human history or at the present. This book as a history of social thought will deal for the most part with the thinking of certain persons about associative life and its problems. With this meaning the term *social thought* will hereafter be used, unless otherwise indicated.

The thinking of persons about social life falls into three categories: (1) that involving the advancement of human groups as groups; (2) that referring to the manipulation of human beings to the gain of a special clique or group; and (3) that which aims to analyze the underlying social processes and laws irrespective of the effects of such analyses or the uses to which they are put.

[1] A practical exposition of social group thinking may be found in Harrison S. Elliott, *The Process of Group Thinking*. An introduction to the theory underlying social thinking has been advanced by M. P. Follette, *Creative Experience*.

The first-mentioned type is connected in one way or another with social planning. The concept of social planning, however, is extensively misunderstood. Some of its opponents have interpreted it to mean a type of thinking that is designed to establish socialism or communism, or fascism. This interpretation, however, often has no foundation. Some of the friends of social planning have done their cause harm by being unwilling to think deeply first and plan afterward. Some have been guided chiefly by wishful thinking. In its essence social planning is the proposing of carefully thought-out procedures by expert and practical students of community life in behalf of the development of human communities, large or small.

The second-mentioned type of social thinking may be in reality anti-social thinking. It usually starts from individualistic thinking and emerges in schemes that work to the gain of the few but to the disadvantage of the many. When its harmful effects are discovered by the larger group who are involved it is sooner or later repudiated.

The third-mentioned phase of social thinking seeks out the processes underlying both pro-social and anti-social thinking. It penetrates to the nature of social processes and it undertakes to formulate social laws. It gives analyses that are fundamental to any program of social improvement. Unfortunately, unscrupulous persons may appropriate its findings in the direction of social manipulation. However, as larger and larger numbers of persons grow versed in scientific social thinking, the more difficult will the anti-social uses of propaganda become.

In recent decades scientific social thinking has made commanding strides. A definitely technical or sociological vocabulary has been developing. A number of useful social-thought concepts have been defined and some agreement regarding the meanings of these concepts has been achieved. In this book the account of basic social thought of outstanding persons here and there naturally shades into a description of the sociological type of social thinking.

Social thought is abstract. It is complementary to practical thought about social matters, and at times contrasts sharply with popular thinking. Practical thinking rarely goes deep.

It asks few basic questions, raises few underlying doubts, and perceives few far-reaching connections. On the other hand, abstract thinking seeks causal explanations, classifies concreteness, penetrates into relationships, and leads to well-balanced procedures. Practical thinking is characteristic of every normal person, but abstract reasoning is uncommon. The ability to do abstract thinking, to grasp the deeper meanings of phenomena, and to penetrate the mysteries of life is rare. Practical thinking, based on a few experiences, constitutes the major sector of the thought life of every person, nearly all of his thinking time.

Here and there in human history, however, we find persons who have been freed or who have freed themselves from the daily struggle for a living, from the race to make money, or from the useless enticements of lifelong loafing, and have joined the company of scholars, past and present, seeking primarily to know the truth, the truth which makes men and women free — free to develop constructive personalities in a vast, changing complex of human living. When scholars have had leisure to think in abstract terms, to analyze and to sympathize, to evolve creative generalizations, their minds have ventured along one or more of five intellectual pathways.

FIVE LINES OF HUMAN THOUGHT

(1) Man has given considerable attention to his relation to the universe. Primitive man conceived of a personal universe, peopled with spirits. Throughout human history man has been a religious being, trying to solve the problems of a universe ruled by spirits or gods or by one Supreme God. This type of thinking has produced polytheisms, monotheisms, and theocracies. It has formulated theological creeds and resulted in bitter ecclesiastical controversies. It has created fears, hopes, faiths, social ideals, and sacrificial living.

(2) Irrespective of religious needs, man has endeavored to think out his relations to the whole universe, animate and inanimate. He has philosophized. He has tried to reduce to a few far-reaching concepts this baffling, intangible as well as tangible, universal environment. He has searched for reliable grounds for explaining his relationship to the universe.

He has sought unity in change and monism in multiplicity. He has proclaimed that blind change itself is lord of all, or he has found solace in a creative evolution. He has put man at the apex of all creation or he has asserted that all is vanity. At any rate he has sought ultimate meanings in as unbiased an interpretation of which he is capable.

(3) From the far-flung horizons of religious and philosophic systems of thought, man has directed his concentrated and prolonged attention in an opposite direction. He has turned his thought upon itself. He has maneuvered his thought processes introspectively. He has puzzled long and diligently upon the structure and functions of thinking and behaving. These series of studies have led on the one hand to treatises such as Kant's *Critique of Pure Reason,* and on the other hand to the current expressions of behavioristic or of gestaltistic psychology.

(4) Man has sought to fathom the material secrets of the earth. Since the Industrial Revolution in England, inquiring minds have focused tremendous energies upon attempts to understand and harness the physical elements. Rocks and strata of rocks have been caused to yield a wealth of ores, and subterranean caverns have been made to pour forth reservoirs of gas and oil. Modern transportation has been made possible by man's knowledge about steam, gasoline, and electricity. Mechanical inventions have followed one another in unanticipated fashion, paying awe-inspiring tribute to the thought power of man. Abstract thinking has given man a marvelous degree of control over the material side of life. In other words, science has become the god of mankind in many fields. Scientific thought has added immeasurably to the conveniences and comforts of life.

(5) Recently, the problem of man's adjustment to his fellow men has received worthy attention at the bar of scientific thought. Socially scientific thinking has acquired increasing accuracy during the present century. For millenniums man has pondered hard over his relation and obligation to his God, as well as to his universe, over the nature of his thought processes and of his mind, over ways and means of acquiring individual success through a manipulation of the material resources of the earth. Incomprehensible as it may seem, it

is true, however, that man has neglected almost wholly until recent decades the very heart of all truly successful living, namely, his relation and obligation to his fellow men and to society. Social thinking, or the analytical thinking about the nature of social life, its trends, and its problems, has been largely ignored. Social thinking, the center of all complete thinking, has been so little perfected that the world today is suffering beneath a staggering load of ills that few seem able to diagnose accurately. In the present age, however, the need is great for scientific social thinking about the whole gamut of social ills.

Today religious thought is seeking revitalization through socialized thinking. In their modern endeavors to re-define their purposes two religions in particular, Christianity and Judaism, are appropriating to good advantage current knowledge about social processes. A remarkable step has been taken in the United States within the last ten years toward co-operative thinking, at least about social and economic problems, by Catholics, Jews, and Protestants.

After many vain searches among false theories and impersonal elements, philosophy is seeking to find itself in a social universe. Psychology, likewise, is no longer individual, structural, and formal. It is now trying to interpret the world in terms of human behavior and of gestaltistic patterns. Group processes are being searched for the origins of stimuli that will explain personal behavior.

Science, maintaining objective methods, is plunging into the measurement of the influence of material and social factors alike upon behavior. Science, with all the aid that it has given to creating better and better instrumentalities of life, is raising questions about the relation of these instrumentalities to the values of life. Science, however, turns over this problem to the non-quantitative disciplines and to evaluative studies.

The phase of social thought known as economic thought is particularly important in its influence. It is seeking to measure and re-evaluate industrial and business enterprise in terms of their societary significance. The ownership of the material resources of the earth, the management of technological enterprise, the distribution of economic gain and surplus

— these are concepts that the economist is now endeavoring to re-define in terms of their societary meanings. Industrial procedures are being subjected to the test of human welfare standards. Likewise, educational systems are being held up to the light of societary evaluation. Political regimes are so fearful of democratic standards of thinking that some governments have denied freedom of speech to their subjects.

Social thought results in part from the nature of social conditions. To understand it, the student must know the times which furnish the setting for it. A thorough-going knowledge of the culture and of the social, economic, political, and religious standards of a people is a minimum essential for studying social thought. In the chapters that follow some hints will be given in each regarding the social situations which have served as bases for the ensuing social thought.

The history of social thought rises out of the beginnings of human struggle on earth and with jagged edges extends along the full sweep of the changing historical horizon. It finds expression through some of the world's best minds. Our quest will bring us in contact with the most vital moments of the world's most valuable thinkers.

Social thought usually finds its initial expression during social crises. When "prosperity" reigns and people are in general satisfied, new social thought is at ebb tide. But when social conditions are marked by gross injustices or when social changes come rapidly due to inventions, wars, or other basic disturbances, then thinking about social life and problems is highly stimulated and new ideas or systems of ideas, that is, ideologies, are originated.

However, the developing and perfecting of new social ideologies are usually the work of scholars somewhat removed from the turmoil of the hour. Social thought thus is the product of social crises and of scholarly analysis and synthesis.

DISCUSSION GROUP TOPICS

1. The nature of human thought.
2. The main lines or subdivisions of thought.
3. The different types of social thought.
4. The marks of sociological thought.
5. The nature of group thinking.
6. The reasons for the lack of group thinking.
7. The basic requirements for discussion-group thinking.
8. The distinctions between practical thinking and abstract thinking.
9. The dangers of doing practical thinking regarding social situations.
10. Weaknesses in the thinking of the "self-made man."
11. Extent of and danger in particularistic thinking.
12. The nature and abuses of propagandist thinking.
13. The essential traits of a social situation.
14. The relation of social and economic conditions to social thought.
15. The present need for social thought.

READINGS

Beach, Walter G., *The Growth of Social Thought* (New York : Charles Scribner's Sons 1939).

Elliott, Harrison S., *The Process of Group Thinking* (New York : Association Press 1928).

Ellwood, Charles A., *A History of Social Philosophy* (New York : Prentice-Hall, Inc. 1938).

Follette, Mary P., *Creative Experience* (New York : Longmans, Green and Co. 1924).

Furfey, Paul H., *A History of Social Thought* (New York : The Macmillan Company, 1942), Ch. I.

House, Floyd N., *The Development of Sociology* (New York : McGraw-Hill Book Company 1936), Ch. I.

MacIver, Robert M., "Social Philosophy," *American Journal of Sociology,* 39:835-841.

Odum, Howard W., *Man's Quest for Social Guidance* (New York : Henry Holt and Company 1922) Chs. I-IV, XXXIII.

Walser, Frank, *The Art of Conference* (New York : Harper and Brothers 1933).

CHAPTER II

EARLIEST SOCIAL THOUGHT

Pre-literate people were inquisitive. They thought about the dramatic phases of life, and they sought explanations. Their attention was centered on the tangibles of life. Their sense of observation was often well developed. Their imagination worked out fantastic and supernatural explanations. They reasoned about the daily occurrences of life in concrete, graphic, and personal terms.

In a piecemeal and microscopic way pre-literate people everywhere sensed some of the meanings of social relationships. Archeological records indicate an awareness by pre-literate people of simple, crude, but nevertheless genuine social implications. Early mythologies recognize the importance of social bonds. Out of the dim dawn of tribal life there appeared a rough-hewn concept of social property. The proverbs of primitive people include definite implications of social responsibility.

In their group behavior pre-literate people exemplified some of the simplest phases of social thought. The loose forms of family life harbored a degree of social consideration. Wherever ancestor worship developed, the family group assumed large proportions and manifested strong social ties. The clan, or *gens,* betokened social fealty. Throughout this phase of social organization an elementary conception of social thinking was implied.

Communal property testified to communal thinking. The existence of common hunting grounds and tribal flocks was indicative of folkthought. Group dances, feasts, building enterprises, celebrations, delineated a social spirit. Even warfare produced bursts of tribal loyalty. An examination of the folkways reveals indistinct but incipient notions of societal welfare. Such a treatise as Sumner's *Folkways* chronicles a vast amount of elemental folk thinking.

FOLK THINKING

Folk thinking permeated primitive religions. The earliest forms of religion presupposed societies of spirits or gods. The behavior of a person was regulated by his ideas concerning the ways in which he had pleased or offended the spirits or gods. An infant was born into a society peopled with human and spirit beings. The latter were often more numerous than the former; frequently they were more feared, and hence were more powerful. The living people, the departed spirits, and the gods in a hierarchal order constituted an effective society for the exercise of many vigorous forms of social control.

If pestilence came, it was because the gods had been offended by some person. As a result of the offense of one person, the whole tribe was considered to be liable to punishment. Consequently, the tribe in turn would punish the offending member, and through the use of force and fear it would exert a tremendous power over personal behavior and thought.

Primitive people were dominated by custom and transition. They were subject to the autocracy of the past. They were hopelessly caught between ancestral ascendance and current fears. They threaded their way, mentally, through tantalizingly uncertain and narrow apertures. They learned the meaning of obedience, but obedience to a harsh and rigorous past and to a fickle and disconcerting future. Leadership was drastic and capricious; followership was frantic and tremulous.

Some of the incipient social concepts of primitive peoples have been preserved in the form of proverbs. Many of the subtler social relationships of life were recognized by early man. His limited thinking drifted into simple formulae. His vocabulary was scanty; his ideas were few. He thought in terms of conventional sayings. "Primitive man spoke in proverbs."

Many folkthoughts, or primitive conceptions of social obligations, have been preserved. The early proverbs of man reveal the beginnings of social thought. Equally valuable and similar materials are found in the sayings of the tribes which today are in a state of arrested development. Many living Americans can quote at least a few social proverbs which they learned as children from their parents. Selected illustrations of embryonic social thought of this type will be given here.

AFRICAN FOLKTHOUGHT

The first examples will be selected from the folkthoughts of the Africans of the Guinea Coast.[1] The proverb, "Ashes fly back in the face of him who throws them," recognizes that evil deeds return upon the doer, or as moderns declare, "Curses come home to roost." In the saying, "Cowries are men," primitive man roughly but succinctly stated the theory of the economic determination of human history. It is cowries, or money, which molds human thought, determines human attitudes, and gives social power. An age-long conception, indicative of a low sense of social feeling but possessing great force in society, is revealed in the dictum, "Full-belly child says to hungry-belly child 'Keep good cheer.'" Throughout human history, the fortunate glutton has always recommended patience and tranquillity to the unfortunate, hard-working brother. An eminent American financier of the multi-millionaire class expressed pity for girls who work long hours, but declared that their harsh conditions were what the good Lord had made them for. But how far has this well-groomed citizen of our century advanced beyond the "full-belly" social philosophy of pre-literate man?

In the observation, "A fool of Ika and an idiot of Iluka meet together to make friends," the African has noted that friends are persons of similar types, of similar minds, of similar prejudices, and that "birds of a feather flock together." Whether consciously or unconsciously, close association usually occurs among persons of a kind, among fools of Ika and idiots of Iluka, blind to each other's foolishness.

Romantic love, evidently, has always been fickle, for the African has discovered that "quick loving a woman means quick not-loving a woman." If this naïve but shrewd reflection concerning love-making were taken at its probable worth

[1] W. I. Thomas, *Source Book for Social Origins*, p. 162.

at the present time, it would be crystallized into a marriage law requiring that a license to marry should be obtained as a rule at least fifteen or thirty days before the marriage could be celebrated.

A rather keen sense of social injustice is expressed in the monologue: "The ground-pig said: 'I do not feel so angry with the man who killed me as with the man who dashed me on the ground afterward.'" Here the injustice of striking a person when he is down is depicted. Even pre-literate people have a sense of sympathy for the defeated and helpless.

"Three elders cannot all fail to pronounce the word *ekulu* (antelope); one may say ekúlu; another ekulú; but the third will say, ékulu (which is correct)." In other words, several heads are better than one; or, in a multitude of counsellors, there is safety. It was this simple social precept which an individualistic leader like Theodore Roosevelt used frequently to the advantage of himself and the nation. When a perplexing national problem would confront him, he was wont to invite to the White House persons whose beliefs varied in different ways from his own in order to secure their opinions. He acted independently, but first he took counsel with several "elders."

Current social thought, however, emphasizes the importance of arriving at decisions while the "elders" are present, not as individuals but in a group. It points out the significance of arriving at decisions affecting human welfare in a consensus fashion, that is, by the leaders and representative advisers, thinking aloud in the presence of all and arriving at new thought procedures by a consensus or near-consensus of judgments.

In *Thinking Black,* Daniel Crawford has presented certain phases of the African's philosophy. While much is individual philosophy, more is social philosophy. Custom imitation prevails. The social thought of the African Negro is summarized in the rule: "Follow your leader." Social precedent, not principle, is the guide to behavior. If you are a follower, follow patiently; if you are a leader, lead drastically. "If thou are an anvil, be patient . . . but if thou are a hammer, strike hard."

The African understands the social psychology of language.

He watches the eyes more carefully than he listens to the voice. To him the human eye speaks all languages under the sun. Mr. Crawford reports that the wary eye of the African "can easily fish news out of the two liquid pools of your eyeballs." If your eye says one thing and your tongue another, then the African "will plump for the verdict of the eye."

The aphorism, "There is no pocket in a shroud," warns a person against the possibility of taking his material goods into the next world. To share with other persons is rated a higher act than to store for self. He is richest who shares most. Among the Africans with whom Mr. Crawford worked, the word for criminal was not applied to the person who had stolen property or who had taken life, but to one who eats alone. "The high crime and misdemeanor of the town is to dine alone"; the criminal above all other persons is Mr. Eat-Alone. He who refuses to share his food with those who are less fortunate than himself is an arch devil. Such a vice is common among beasts; it is beneath the dignity of man, according to the African. When several primitive people were taken to London and shown the wealthy and the poor sections of that city, they were dumbfounded. They were utterly unable to understand how any persons with the slightest spark of human nature in them could endure to live to themselves in wealth when in the same city there were the wretched and prostrated multitudes of Whitechapel and of the other cheerless slums.

"What baby lion ever trembled at his father's roaring?" Some time ago I heard an angry parent in a high-pitched voice yelling at his son, but the disobedient child kept on in his own way. I wondered how far this father had advanced in parental influence and discipline beyond the stage represented by the African seer who drew his social images from a lion-frequented environment. "If a tree has grown up crooked, it is because no one straightened it when young." This statement postulates social responsibility for juvenile delinquency and even for adult crime. The underlying principle is the same as that in the Hebraic injunction: "Train up a child in the way he should go; and when he is old, he will not depart from it." The principle has received current recognition in the doctrine of contributory negligence. The modern observation, full of socially dangerous implications, that parents are blind to the weaknesses of their children, has its African counterpart: "The beetle is a beauty in the eyes of its mother." A gleam of light is thrown upon the current discussions concerning social parasitism by the African's assertion: "The parasite has no roots." [2]

This discussion may be concluded by a group of Kaffir proverbs. Most of them are more or less self-explanatory and all are highly significant expressions of important generalizations:

"Height is not reached in a hurry."
"There is no path that won't go homeward."
"The monkey cannot see his own eyebrow."
"One link of a chain cannot ring alone."
"If you are patient you will see the eyes of a snail."
"Sleep has no friendship."
"A chicken is not taught to scratch up the ground."
"He who follows all paths will lose his way home."

ORIENTAL FOLKTHOUGHT

Let us turn next to ancient Chinese folkthought. Some of the primeval sayings purporting to emanate from China may have been borrowed from other countries. Others may have originated in China but have been borrowed by other countries. Many will be recognized because of their distinctive Chinese atmosphere. The concept of filial relationship will be recognized in, "To forget one's ancestors is to be a brook without a source, a tree without a root." A basis for the doctrine of "old roguery" that Lin Yutang has made well known in his *My Country and My People* is found in, "When old men are not upright, they teach their sons and grandsons to be rogues."

It would be a people who continually faced dire necessity who would advise, "Better sell for small profits than fail in business." The misery of always being in debt is realized by the author of, "Rather check your appetite than get in debt,"

[2] For a study of the social and economic life in Africa that will furnish a background for understanding social thought in different regions of that continent, see Richard C. Thurnwald, *Black and White in East Africa*.

and "Though penniless be patient." Living close to bare need, however, produces endurance and sturdiness of character, as reflected in, "He is equal to any task who can subsist on cabbage stalks." You must not expect too much of life, for, "Every day cannot be a feast of lanterns."

A tax-ridden people cry out against the system where "The big fish eat the little ones, the little fish eat the shrimps, and the shrimps are forced to eat mud." Where else can you find such a severe indictment of economic exploitation? There is a degree beyond which one cannot go in exploitation, because "You cannot strip two skins from one cow."

A crude but shrewd sense of business psychology is revealed in a proverb such as, "A man without a smiling face must not open a shop." Likewise, "In business one must be perfectly affable." Not only the Chinese but people of other cultures have followed the injunction, "He who would rise in the world should veil his ambition with the forms of humanity."

That scholarship and learning are prized among the Chinese and that books are treasured, are attested to, as follows: "Something is learned every time a book is opened." Conversation with a wise person likewise is even more valuable, for, "A single conversation across the table with a wise man is better than ten years' study of books." However, beware of being merely wise, for, "It is easier to know how to do a thing than it is to do it." The way to wisdom is limited, for, "Without climbing mountains, no one can know the height of heaven." A realistic and pragmatic view of wisdom born of an overwhelming environment is suggested by, "A wise man adapts himself to circumstances as water shapes itself to the vessel that contains it."

The influence of the group over the individual member was well stated by the Chinese in the observation, "One takes the color of one's company." Closely related is the generalization, "Keep company with good men and good men you will learn to be." The susceptibility of children to this law is found in the Chinese proverb, "A young branch takes on all the bends that one gives it."

The greatest personality traits are kindness, forbearance, and good will. The Chinese say, "Kindness is more binding than a loan." They put the idea this way, "An unkind word

falls easily from the tongue, but a coach with six horses cannot bring it back." They even go so far as to declare, "The
hearts of the people are the only legitimate foundations of
empire."

The need for elemental personality traits is expressed in,
"If you don't succeed with one blow, don't hesitate to deliver two." Again, "To perfect diligence nothing is difficult" ;
or, "In a hurry is error." The counterpart of a well-known
Hebrew saying is found in, "Govern thyself and you will be
able to govern the world." On the other hand, beware of
small evils, because, "A mole can undermine the strongest
wall."

Something of eugenic significance is suggested by, "Ivory
is not taken from the mouth of a rat." Defective superiority
is more to be desired than mediocrity or, "A diamond with a
flaw is better than a common stone." Was it a sage who said,
"Drunkenness does not produce faults; it uncovers them,"
or who declared, "The best cure for drunkenness is while
sober to see a drunken man" ? Another weakness of human
nature is artfully expressed in these words, "A fool never
admires himself so much as when he has committed a folly."
Penetrating likewise is the charge that, "He who laughs at an
impertinence makes himself an accomplice." The powerful
influence that social environment plays in human life is
shrewdly stated : "By nature men are nearly alike, but by
practice they get to be wide apart."

Shall we turn next to the pre-literate Australian Blackfel-
lows ? Not black, but brown ; and not Negroid so much as
something else ; yet, very near the beginning of human culture — such is the Australian Blackfellow. When he goes upon
a day's journey, he sometimes takes a handful of Mother Earth
with him. In this way he testifies to his loyalty to home, and
provides against the rise of lonesomeness which he may experience during tribal hunts. His act crudely represents the
essence of the concept of patriotism. A sense of justice is
common to pre-literate Australians. Among the Whayook of
Australia a man who has wounded a fellow tribesman is required to present himself to the injured in order to receive
a similar wound.[3] Among the Wumbias, a person who is

3 E. M. Carr, *The Australian Race.*

absent when a relative dies must not speak to anyone on his return to camp until he has had spears thrown at him.[4]   On good authority, it is reported that the Australian primitive regards any offense as wiped out by a suitable offer of atonement.

The Filipino declares: "A piece of green wood will burn if placed near the fire."   In other words, temptation is a subtle element that ultimately may destroy even persons who are supposedly temptation-proof.   In the proverb, "Boastfulness drives away wisdom," the Filipino has pointed out that the desire to make a strong impression upon associates hinders intellectual progress.   The chief danger of luxury is stated in the saying: "He who is raised in ease, is usually destitute."   The leading result of being financially fortunate is summarized thus: "Easy earning means quick spending."   The evils of hypercriticism are bluntly phrased: "The fault-finder has the biggest faults."

The law of social compensation is stated as follows: "You laugh today; I laugh tomorrow."   The organic nature of society is implied in the truism: "The pain of a finger is the suffering of the whole body."   The need for independent thinking is urged in the declaration: "Whoever believes everything said, has no mind of his own."   On the other hand, the egocentric mind receives solemn warning in the dictum: "He who despises counsel is on the way to misfortune."   The value of helpful attitudes is proclaimed as follows: "Kindness is a great capital"; and again, "Good deeds are more precious than gold or silver."   A gentle hint of social importance is given in the formula: "Kindness is with kindness to be paid; not with gold or silver."   The force of rumor is vividly indicated: "A whisper is louder than a shout."   A vital criticism is found in: "He who is always preparing to do something never does anything."   A direct hint is offered: "A lazy dog does not get even bones."   Too much caution is disastrous: "If you are afraid of every dog bark, you will never reach your destination."   Littleness is often deceived: "The fly on the carabao thinks it is taller than the carabao."   Do not be too particular: "If you want eggs, put up with the cackling of the hen."   Some goals are

[4] A. M. Howitt, *The Organization of Australian Tribes.*

won by being naïve : "If you want to fool, pretend to be a fool."

Japanese axioms like those of other countries have had a long history, and doubtless some of them have originated in other countries, particularly in China and Korea. You do not study proverbs long before you discover similarities in meaning if not in similar wording of statements. Perhaps this situation indicates similarity in experience more than it does anything else.

Social psychological insight is shown in the saying, perhaps of Chinese origin, "The mouth of the mass melts gold." Perhaps the reference is to the fundamental force of public opinion, or possibly to the significance of a highly integrated social order, such as Japan developed long ago. In the observation, "The world is like a looking-glass ; if you smile, others also smile," may be found the elemental nature of indirect suggestion, or what used to be called unconscious imitation. The assertion, "What the ruler wants, the ruled also wants," is another testimony to the force of indirect suggestion. Stated differently it means that what the upper classes desire, the lower classes will also want ; or as Tarde has said, "The superior are imitated by the inferior." The saying, "Three men get together and have knowledge equivalent to that of the Monju" (a famous Buddhist thinker), clearly refers to the wisdom which comes from taking counsel with others. "The net of Heaven is rough, but will never miss one victim," has an equivalent in a European and American proverb, "The mills of the Gods grind slowly, but they grind exceedingly small." "Evil brings its own reward, sooner or later." The law of retribution, in other words, cannot be overcome. Notice this, "If one tells a falsehood, ten thousand others spread it as a truth." Gossip is portrayed, and the humanity-wide tendency of hearsay reports to gain social force is pictured. Likewise, "The tongue is but three inches long, but it can kill a man six feet high," shows the vicious nature of gossip. Moreover, the severest punishment is not always physical ; it may come from a human tongue. The tendency of the Japanese to conceal their feelings may partially explain the saying, "Applause is the root of abuse." Perhaps there are such serious evils in applauding that its value may be questioned.

The dramatic description, "A man takes a drink, then the drink takes the man," warns against the evils in the consumption of liquor.

Judged by their proverbs, the ancient Japanese possessed a greater understanding of human nature than is usually accorded them. As practical students of social psychology, their conclusions bear many elements of far-reaching generalizations.

In Ceylon there has been a prevalence of proverbs relating to economic life, implying the presence of the extremes of poverty and of wealth. For example, there is the philanthropic injunction: "When you eat, think of the poor." The Cingalese, however, recognize the importance of maintaining the scientific attitude in regard to charity, for they have a saying: "He who gives alms must do it with discretion."

On the other hand, the blighting influence of wealth is recognized: "A covetous man has two sources of iniquity — how to amass money, and how to use it." The importance of giving with a joyous spirit is indirectly enjoined: "He who gives grudgingly shall be taught better by adversity."

A simple concept of the need for co-operative thinking and acting is found in the observation: "The poverty of the poor shall be at an end when they learn to minister to the wants of each other." The importance of industry is made plain: "He who follows idleness shall find it the path to distress."

The significance of character is appreciated: "A man who is wise and learned, but without virtue, is despised." More striking is the saying: "Garlic will not lose its smell even if it is enveloped in perfume." Bold and scathing is the indictment: "The conversation of the wicked is a fountain of mischief."

Self-restraint is urged: "Immoderate sorrow causes great mischief." That humility has its own reward is recognized: "Sorrow felt by a man conscious of his ignorance is like the joy of heaven." For woman, modesty is proclaimed: "The ornament of a woman is her modesty." Learning puts people in a class by themselves, it would appear: "A learned man can only be appreciated by another learned man."

Arabia has its unique statements of social proverbs. A law of intersocial stimulation is stated simply: "A wise man associating with the vicious becomes an idiot; a dog traveling with good men becomes a rational being." The strength which comes from unity is forcibly phrased: "Three if they unite against a town will ruin it." The transforming power of love is recognized: "Love can make any place agreeable." An idealistic social standard is set for the individual in the aphorism: "It is more noble to pardon than to punish."

On the other hand, mercy may be misplaced: "Mercy to the criminal may be cruelty to the people." A person must beware of being an ingrate and prevent his egoistic desires from crushing out the spirit of gratitude: "A tree that affords thee shade, do not order it cut down." The omnipresence of envy is understood: "Envy assails the noblest; the winds howl around the highest peaks." The anti-social tendency of a vicious habit is well described: "A hand accustomed to take is far from giving." Perhaps the Malthusian advocate will find solace in the simple description: "If the sailors become too numerous, the boat will sink." He who pleases everybody has done so at the expense of his own character, or as the Arabs say: "He deserves no man's good will of whom all men speak well." A Persian proverb of far-reaching social meaning may be added: "The wise man can understand the foolish; but the foolish cannot comprehend the wise because he has never been wise."

EUROPEAN FOLKTHOUGHT

Some of the following social proverbs as found in the writings of Spenser, Shakespeare, and other English scholars well represent the large field of European folkthought. Some go back either to Teutonic or to Roman and Greek origins. A number are found in the sayings of such writers as the Stoic philosophers; for example, Seneca, Aurelius, and Epictetus.

The role of friendship is a noticeable theme. Who would not agree: "That is not lost which a friend gets"? A homely bit of sound psychology is voiced: "A man who has friends must show himself friendly." The experience of everyone would testify that: "The shortest road is where the company is good." A true and vital test of friendship is suggested: "A

friend is never known till a man have need." The precious-
ness of friendship is declared. We may have many acquaint-
ances, but we can have few friends. On the other hand, it is
necessary to distinguish between friends: "Nothing is more
dangerous than an imprudent friend."

Closely related are the maxims regarding the importance
not only of doing good in the world, but of doing good sincerely. The essence of the principle is found in: "Bare is
the gift without the giver." A vivid contrast is found in this
comparison: "Charity gives itself; covetousness hoards itself
poor." Another comparison that contains a contrast which
speaks louder than words is: "He who receives a good turn
should never forget it; but he who does it, should never remember it." The double returns that are yielded by good
behavior are well put: "He that does good to another does
good also to himself."

An awareness of group psychology is indicated in many
axioms. From watching the bees comes the generalization:
"What is not good for the swarm is not good for the bee."
The world as a group and the human race as one is suggested
by: "The universe is but one great city, full of beloved ones,
divine and human, by nature endeared to each other." A
note on gossip and on the way that many listeners become
many talkers is offered: "There would not be so many mouths
if there were not so many open ears."

"He is happiest, be he king or peasant, who finds peace in
his home": here is revealed a bit of basic social psychology.
An unattainable standard is set forth for a happy marriage:
"To make a happy couple, the husband must be deaf, and
the wife, blind." A knowledge of parent-child relationships
is revealed, for, "It is a wise father who knows his own son."

An elemental knowledge of human nature is found in:
"He who has never known adversity is but half-acquainted
with others, or with himself." The relation of language to
personality is proclaimed: "Language most shows the man,
speak that I may see thee." The significance of being genuine and sincere is recognized: "Study to be what you wish
to seem." Self-control is advised: "He is richest who is content with the least." One's personality includes that which
he loves; therefore: "Love me, love my dog."

A little more complicated aspect of human nature is suggested by: "A slave has but one master; the ambitious man
has as many masters as there are persons whose aid may contribute to the advancement of his fortune." A social aspect
of religion and of ethics is made plain: "It is to be doubted
whether he will ever find the way to heaven who desires to
go thither alone." Praise has a socially quantitative aspect:
"Praise like gold and diamonds owes its value only to its
scarcity." Another important aspect of praise, and of its
opposite, is the source: "The slander of some people is as
great a recommendation as the praise of others." A serious
indictment of mankind is proclaimed: "Thirst teaches all
animals to drink but drunkenness belongs only to man."
Change and progress must be considered by anyone who is
jealous of maintaining his standing: "To be as good as our
fathers we must be better."

"The closed hand gets the shut fist," says an Irish proverb;
and illustrates a psycho-social law to the effect that a gesture
is met by an appropriate response. A good neighbor is closer
than a brother, according to a maxim of Greek origin, and
again, "In selecting a house, consider first the neighbors."
Here the intimacy and the influence exerted by neighbors is
well stated.

Old Russian proverbs give considerable attention to economic problems. Many of them emerged from oppression at
the hands of a dominant wealthy class:

"When money speaks, truth keeps silence."

"The kindness of the landlord is as fleeting as the dew."

"A nobleman is always in the right when the peasant sues."

"The big thieves hang the little thieves."

"Our souls are God's, our bodies the Tsar's."

The adverse effects of gossip, the tendency to say unkind
things, the meanness of an erstwhile friend, the unruly
tongue, these human frailties are played up in Russian
proverbs:

"Man is caught by his tongue, and an ox by its horns."

"Ravens do not tear each other's eyes out."

"To know a friend it is necessary to eat several bushels of
salt with him."

"A friend turned hostile is the worst enemy."

"A thousand friends are few, one enemy is too many."

"A good reputation sits still, a bad one runs about."

"If two dogs are quarreling, let the third beware."

"Love, friendship, worthy companions are lasting and invaluable. The most enduring and effective trait of all is a mother's love."

"A mother's love will draw up from the depths of the sea."

"A present is cheap, but love is dear."

"A wise companion is half the journey."

"Treasure is not always a friend, but a friend is always a treasure."

Wholesome advice runs through Russian as well as other proverbs. The importance of a worthy character, the danger in bad companions, the risk in untried friends, the impossibility of recalling words once spoken, and the role of Death, the chief leveler, these are some of the basic ideas to be found in the historic proverbs of Russia:

"Make peace with man and quarrel with your sins."

"Lie down with dogs and you will get up with fleas."

"An untried friend is like an uncracked nut."

"An empty sack cannot stand up."

"The spoken word cannot be swallowed."

"The greatest king must at last be put to bed with a shovel."

EARLY AMERICAN, INDIAN, AND MEXICAN FOLKTHOUGHT

Most of the proverbs that were passed from person to person in American colonial days doubtless came from England and other European sources. Some originated in the sayings of writers like Benjamin Franklin. Nearly all were exceedingly practical. Close observation regarding elementary social relationships was reflected in maxims, such as: (1) "A man is known by the company he keeps," (2) "Birds of a feather flock together," (3) "One bad example spoils many precepts," (4) "One good turn deserves another," (5) "Misery loves company," (6) "Faint heart never won fair lady," (7) "Many hands make light work," (8) "Too many cooks spoil the broth," (9) "There is no fool like an old fool," and (10) "Honesty is the best policy."

Related social thinking that is a little more subtle and more complicated in all of its implications is reflected in such sayings as these: (1) "People who live in glass houses mustn't throw stones," (2) "Little pitchers have big ears," (3) "He laughs best who laughs last," (4) "The good will of a dog is better than the ill will," and (5) "Uneasy lies the head that wears the crown."

Much early American social thought deals with personality organization: (1) "There is no use crying over spilt milk," (2) "Better let well enough alone," (3) "Practice makes perfect," (4) "Where there's a will, there is a way," (5) "Time and tide wait for no man," (6) "Don't cut off your nose to spite your face," (7) "Don't jump out of the frying pan into the fire," and (8) "You can't have your cake and eat it too."

American Indian proverbs reveal both careful observation and shrewd generalization. Experience is a great teacher in training one to be on his guard against what was once trickery but now has become chicanery: "When the fox walks lame, old rabbit jumps." The universal nature of gossip is again attested in this vivid analogy: "A squaw's tongue runs faster than the wind's legs." The problems of primitive life are reduced to three: "There are three things it takes a strong man to hold—a young warrior, a wild horse, and a handsome squaw."

Among Mexican proverbs, social ideas are not missing. The reader will catch the significance of the following: (1) "A howling cat is not a good hunter," (2) "Everybody can climb up the limbs of the fallen tree," (3) "A rich widow cries with one eye and rings the wedding bells with the other," (4) "The tongue slow; the eyes quick," and (5) "From January to January the bankers have all the money."

SUMMARY

The nature of the primitive social thought that has been preserved through proverbs and sayings justifies the following observations: (1) Primitive social thought was on the whole exceedingly simple, crude, and undeveloped. (2) It was uncorrelated, unsystematic, and fugitive. (3) A classification of the proverbs of any primitive people into individual and social types shows that not more than a small per cent are social. Primitive thinking was done primarily in terms of the individual himself. The social thinking was commonly of individualistic origin. A social idea was originally suggested not for its own sake or disinterestedly, but for the reason that its observance was to the advantage of a number of individuals who were living together. (4) Likewise, social thinking was exceedingly practical. It pertained to daily life. It did not originate in an abstract thought life. (5) The phraseology of many proverbs is hortatory. They are didactic and in the form of advice. (6) Social proverbs employ figures of speech extensively. Similes from nature are frequent; physical analogies are not uncommon. Many of these figures disclose a rural or bucolic life. Many indicate how close primitive people lived to the poverty line, and how rigor in livelihood was essential. (7) Frequently, the social proverbs of the various races pertain to family and small group relationships. The sense of social responsibility does not penetrate, as a rule, beyond primary groups. The responsibility of group to group is rarely expressed or implied. Ordinarily, the social vision does not extend to a whole race or to mankind.

(8) A comparative study of primitive social sayings reveals countless similarities, and testifies to the uniformity of human experiences and social needs, irrespective of racial distinctions. These resemblances do not imply collaboration, collusion, or imitation. They mean that the needs of primitive persons in various and unrelated parts of the world have everywhere led the human mind out in search of socially significant explanations. Primitive thinking supports the theory of independent origins more extensively than it does the doctrine of cultural diffusion. Primitive thought produced fundamental social concepts, such as kinship, authority, dependence, and tribal loyalty.

DISCUSSION GROUP TOPICS

1. The range of primitive social thought.
2. The forms in which earliest social thought are preserved.
3. The independent origins of primitive social thought.
4. Comparisons of the social thought of any two primitive peoples.
5. A rating of social proverbs in terms of their depth of insight.
6. The most significant conclusions concerning the nature of primitive social thought.
7. Distinctions between proverbs, maxims, sayings, injunctions, and axioms as vehicles of social thought.
8. The most important of the eight final observations concerning the nature of primitive social thought.
9. Additional conclusions concerning the nature of primitive social thought.
10. New proverbs that are being originated today. Illustrations.
11. The chief merit of a proverb as a vehicle of social thought.

READINGS

Becker, Howard, and Harry E. Barnes, *Social Thought from Lore to Science* (Washington: Harren Press 1952), Vol. I, Ch. 1.

Champion, Selwyn G., *Racial Proverbs* (New York: The Macmillan Company 1938).

Crawford, Daniel, *Thinking Black* (New York: George H. Doran Company 1913).

Furfey, Paul H., *A History of Social Thought* (New York: The Macmillan Company 1942), Ch. 2.

Hertzler, Joyce O., *The Social Thought of the Ancient Civilizations* (New York: McGraw-Hill Book Company 1936), Ch. I.

Herzog, G., *Jabo Proverbs from Liberia* (New York: Oxford University Press 1936).

Howitt, A. M., *The Native Tribes of Southeast Australia* (New York: The Macmillan Company 1904).

Proverbs, Book of, *Old Testament*.

Stephens, Thomas A., *Proverb Literature; a Bibliography of Works Relating to Proverbs* (edited by W. Bouser. London: Folklore Society 1930).

Sumner, William G., *Folkways* (Boston: Ginn and Company 1907).

Thurnwald, Richard C., *Black and White in East Africa* (London: Routledge and Sons 1935).

CHAPTER III

EGYPTIAN AND BABYLONIAN SOCIAL THOUGHT

The evidences of social thought in early Egypt are meager and inchoate. Inferential evidence must be utilized. A strong hand ruled in ancient Egypt. The chieftains were supreme. With the rise of the Theban hierarchy, the priestly class came into power and established a theocratic regime. Then military leaders became prominent and dominant. Later, they overthrew the theocracy of the priests.

With the historical rise of Egypt about 4000 B.C., the emphasis upon law as the basis of the social order stands out. The books of laws early acquired sacred or religious significance. They were reputed to be of divine origins; they provided for courts of justice; and they prescribed punishments for offenses.

The social ideas are to be gleaned from inscriptions in tombs, from legal and religious documents, and they sometimes appear in the form of proverbs. Egyptian scholars refer to collections of moral precepts as being of a practical rather than of a systematic philosophical nature. Well known are the Proverbs of Ptah-Hotep, and the Prescriptions of Ani.

EGYPTIAN SOCIAL THOUGHT

Earliest Egyptian social thought was colored by the kingly and divine form of structure of society that prevailed. The social order was dominated by a ruler who was supposed to be divine. The king and a small number of nobles owned the land. A large percentage of the people were serfs or slaves. The middle class must have been small in numbers and weak. When the temple authorities were in control, the social conditions of the masses were no better. The priests shared the authority with their auxiliaries, the soldiers. The underprivileged classes included the farmers, boatmen, mechanics, tradespeople, besides the slaves.[1]

[1] Translated by Griffith, "Boulak Papyrus," *La Moral Egyptienne,* p. 534.

The social thought of the oppressed occasionally burst forth in the form of protests. Sometimes there were prophets who spoke for the oppressed. Occasionally a somewhat self-righteous ruler developed and proclaimed a doctrine of paternalistic social thought. Henku, who lived about 2850 B.C., announced his good behavior and called attention to the fine example that he had set. He gave bread to the hungry, clothed the naked, and appointed serfs to be officials. Moreover, he did not oppress the weak and did not cause the helpless to fear him. He was a benefactor to rural people.[2]

A voice that sounds like many a Hebrew prophet is found in the words of him who declared: "Hearts are shameless; every man seizeth the goods of his neighbor."[3] Something of the harshness and hopelessness of the times is reflected in the indictment: "There is no righteous man left; the earth is an example of those who do evil."[4]

Egyptian life was largely rural. There was little commerce. Higher education was reserved for a very few, although elementary education was less confined. The priests often used their educational advantages to prey upon and excite the superstitions of the people, thereby strengthening the social control which they enjoyed.

An anomalous phase of the Egyptian mind was that it shifted back and forth from a hedonistic enjoyment of the moment to a serious contemplation of the future life. Amusements were fostered, the drinking of intoxicating liquor was extensive, and the emphasis on music was widespread. The game of draughts was perhaps the national pastime. The people were not warriors. Mercenaries were employed to do the fighting; ultimately they became socially powerful.

Polygyny was countenanced and practiced, but only of course among the wealthy. A relative degree of freedom was granted the women among the privileged classes. They appeared in public with their husbands; they publicly engaged in religious ceremonies; and they were given unusual property rights. It is reported that at one time some Egyptian

[2] Translated by Breasted, *Ancient Records*,
[3] E. A. W. Budge, *The Literature of the Egyptians*, p. 232.
[4] *Loc. cit.*

women could not only own property, but could dispose of it as they wished, or could loan money at interest to their husbands. At another time the following injunction seems to have been issued: "Thou shalt not forget thy mother, and what she has done for thee, that she bore thee, and nurtured thee in all ways."[5] Children were enjoined to obey their parents, to be respectful to their superiors, and to be reserved. Greatness was identified with kindness. Justice was urged upon the leaders.

Proverbs disclose a social thought that revolves around the noble conduct of the moral individual. The negative nature of these claims to good behavior suggests the Ten Commandments of the Hebrews. Selected protestations read: "I have not committed theft; I have not slain man or woman; I have not uttered falsehood; I have not acted deceitfully; I have not sought for distinctions."[6]

At the other pole is the belief in the future world. As a result sculpture flourished. It was believed that if the human figure were copied and the copy preserved, the spirit and the body of the departed person could be more easily reunited. Architecture developed, but with the tombs or pyramids and other monuments as the chief forms. Urban mural works are still to be found, affording evidences of Egyptian social thought.

It was taught that in the next world a person would be held accountable for his deeds in this life. This belief acted as a powerful social control; it involved specific social obligations. A person must deal openly with his fellow men. He must observe the rights of the weaker members of society. For example, he must not make false charges against a slave to the master of the slave. He must show that he has respected the social rights that were invested in property. From the moral and social writings of the Egyptian scribes it is apparent that in religious matters a person was moved to give thought to his duties as a citizen and a neighbor.

After an extensive study of the documents that give some idea about the social thought of the early Egyptians, J. O.

[5] Translated by Gunn, *The Instruction of Ptah-Hotep* (Wisdom of the East Series).

[6] W. M. F. Petrie, *Social Life in Ancient Egypt.*

Hertzler mentions five main though overlapping sources of
Egyptian social thought : (1) the precepts or admonitions in
effect among the upper classes that denote the social obligations of these classes. (2) The expressions of social discontent and unrest that reveal a considerable degree of social
injustice and the resultant misery. (3) The ideals for observance by administrative officials that disclose formal social standards. (4) The prophetic utterances that indicate
the coming of an ideal ruler and that suggest a criticism of
the present rulers. (5) The list of anti-social actions of
which religious persons declare themselves to be innocent.[7]
All told, the results, if viewed merely as elemental social
literature, are impressive.

BABYLONIAN SOCIAL THOUGHT

The ancient Babylonian social order was similar in many
ways to Egyptian civilization in its beginning stages. The
Babylonian description of a great flood resembles the account of the Flood that is given in the Old Testament, and
indicates thought about morals and social life. Both Babylon
and Assyria developed a religion which was expressed in
terms of the nation group. The boundaries of one, with
Merodach at the head, and of the other with Assur in supreme control, marked the national group divisions. It was
believed that Merodach accompanied the king in wars and
fought for the nation. In other words, he was a very partial
and serviceable god, working for Babylonia and against all
other worthy peoples. According to tradition he was concerned entirely with the welfare of Babylonia as a population group.

The attitude in Babylonian society toward the institution
of slavery was distinctly different from that in Rome, but
similar to Egyptian practices. The slave was considered in
a more social light than by the Romans. He was frequently
regarded as one of the family ; he could even become a free
member of society. "Slavery was no bar to his promotion."
Moreover, slavery did not necessarily imprint a social stigma
upon the slave.

7 Joyce O. Hertzler, *Social Thought of the Ancient Civilizations*, pp. 73, 74.

The social rights of women were similar to the Egyptian customs. The married woman of the ruling classes possessed definite property rights. She could use the property that she owned as she saw fit; she could even bequeath it as she chose. Her dowry gave her economic independence; it was her absolute property, which she could bequeath by will in any way that she desired.

CODE OF HAMMURABI

The earliest well-known Babylonian ruler was Hammurabi (2124–2083 B.C.). He is probably the same as Amraphel, referred to in the Old Testament, a king who invaded Canaan shortly after the arrival of Abraham. While the literary and scientific work accomplished during his reign seems to have been slight, he became famous as an administrator and the Code of Hammurabi bespeaks for the author or authors the desire to rule Babylonian society with justice. His name includes, Hammu, which means uncle, and rabi (shortened form of rabbi) which means great. "The uncle is great," a literal translation, implies that his work was appreciated probably in his own time.

A text of the Code was found at Susa in Persia in 1902. It is inscribed on a black diorite stela about eight feet in height and contains some 3600 lines. It is seven feet in circumference at the bottom but is somewhat less at the top. This text is now in Paris in the Louvre. Part of the laws have been defaced but some of these appear on sections of an Assyrian copy found in Nineveh.

In the Prologue a eulogy of Hammurabi is given. It suggests the tribute that is paid to Job. Hammurabi is described as one who stood for justice and who destroyed the unjust. The conclusion is long and pays tribute to Hammurabi's achievements as a promoter of peace. There is little doubt that Hammurabi was a notable leader in the Tigris and Euphrates Valley and that his social thought was remarkable for his time and place.

The Code is characterized by its strong humanitarian emphasis. The author was determined to defend the helpless.

So strong was his aim in this direction that he became re-
tributive in his theory of punishment, holding literally to
the "eye for an eye" doctrine. "If a man has caused the loss
of a patrician's eye, his eye shall one cause to be lost." [8]

Justice, however, was subject to the law of social gradation. An offense against a man of lower rank might be
atoned by paying money. "If a man has caused a poor man
to lose his eye, he shall pay one mina of silver." [9] The idea
of social gradation may be illustrated by another law: "If a
builder has built a house for a man and has not made strong
his work and the house he has built has fallen, and he has
caused the death of the owner of the house, that builder
shall be put to death." [10] If in the falling of the house, a
slave is killed, then the builder must present the owner with
a slave. If a son is killed in the falling of the house, then a
son of the builder is to be killed. Again, an expression of
the law of social gradation will be noted.

There are minute regulations of labor conditions and of
private business which give the Code some of the characteristics of eighteenth-century mercantilistic thought. The
Code contains one of the earliest statements of labor legislation that is known. Through laws Hammurabi sought to
determine wages for different classes of labor. The Code
prescribed severe punishment for anyone who sheltered a
runaway slave. In this and other ways property rights were
protected and human considerations subordinated.

The Code gives considerable attention to the family as a
social institution. A legal marriage is required. Divorce
is recognized. A form of alimony is announced. If a woman
who has borne her husband children is divorced, she may
claim the return of her dowry and a portion of the family
property in order that she may care for the children. If a
man's wife runs her house into debt through extravagance
and neglect, her husband may take legal proceedings against
her. If "she gad about" and "belittle her husband" she may
be thrown "into the water." On the other hand, if her husband shall "have been tramping around, belittling her very

8 *Code of Hammurabi*, Section 196.
9 *Ibid.*, Section 198.
10 *Ibid.*, Section 229.

much," she shall be considered blameless and "take her dowry and return to the house of her father." [11]

The adoption of children is provided for in eight sections. Adultery is punishable on a graduated basis, depending upon the conditions under which it occurred.

The intellectual progress and the inventions of the Babylonians are indicative of social status. The development along artistic lines, particularly in architecture and sculpture, must have exerted an indirect but important social influence. Fragmentary evidences point to the development of a Wisdom literature similar to that of the Old Testament. As in the case of the Egyptians, Hebrews, and similar peoples, the admonitions and prohibitions take the form of proverbs. Some advances in surgery doubtless had been made before the reign of Hammurabi. In medicine, however, the demonic theory of the causes of disease enslaved the people.

HITTITE CODE

Closely related to the Code of Hammurabi was the Hittite Code. The Hittites were people who seemed to have flourished from perhaps 2000 B.C. to 700 B.C. Their best known center was Boghazkeui in Cappadocia, and the height of their power came about 1200 B.C. Their downfall was finally accomplished about 700 B.C. It is from Boghazkeui that most of the archeological finds have come regarding the social thought of the Hittites. The compilation of laws and decisions, sometimes called the Hittite Code, is similar to other Western Asiatic codes. It relates to slaves, to the taking of life, to marriage, to the rights of private property, and particularly to stealing. Architecture and sculpture were developed extensively by the Hittites, but religious thought seems to have been neglected. A cosmopolitan range of culture is revealed by the archeological discoveries, showing that the Hittites had a relatively wide range of contacts. Several languages were used by them.

Another related Code is that of the Assyrians, whose early capital was Assur, which was located in the upper Tigris

[11] *Ibid.*, Section 142.

Valley, and which preceded Nineveh as the Assyrian capital. Their Code dates back to about 1400 B.C. The Assyrians early showed an interest in books. They developed the remarkable library of Assurbani-pal at Nineveh. Geography, history, and government received their attention. Religion was relatively undeveloped. The early regulations as represented in the so-called Assyrian Code cover the usual themes of private property, sex relations, marriage and widowhood, and assault.

The Assyrian artists seem to have given their attention chiefly to the king, the court, and to war. The Assyrian palaces were elaborately decorated. Stoic human figures are found on the bas-reliefs. Their gods assumed animal types that at times portrayed violence in the guise of symbolism.

On the whole, Egyptian and Babylonian social thought is concrete, specific, and practical. It bears a legalistic imprint. It gives an ethical import to daily behavior. It utters injunctions regarding personal conduct. It laid the foundations of human conduct in precepts for current living.

DISCUSSION GROUP TOPICS

1. The most important phases of social thought among the Egyptians.
2. Origins of Egyptian social thought.
3. The Code of Hammurabi as an expression of social thought.
4. Origins of the social thought in the Code of Hammurabi.
5. The law of social gradation.
6. Social thought concerning women and slaves in Babylonia.
7. Social thought in the Hittite Code.
8. Relation of social thought in the Code of Hammurabi to the social thought in the Hittite Code.
9. Comparisons of Egyptian social thought with Babylonian social thought.
10. Contributions of Egyptian and Babylonian social thought to present-day thinking.

READINGS

Breasted, J. H., *Development of Religion and Thought in Ancient Egypt* (New York : Charles Scribner's Sons 1912).
———, *The Dawn of Conscience* (New York : Charles Scribner's Sons 1934).
Budge, E. A. W., *The Teaching of Amen-enapt* (London : Hopkinson 1924).
———, *The Literature of the Eygptians* (London : K. Paul 1914).
Chambliss, Rollin, *Social Thought* (New York: The Dryden Press, 1954), Ch. 3.
Furfey, Paul H., *A History of Social Thought* (New York: The Macmillan Company 1942), Ch. 3.
Hertzler, Joyce O., *The Social Thought of the Ancient Civilizations* (New York: McGraw-Hill Company 1936), Chs. II-VI.
Harper, F. R., *The Code of Hammurabi* (Chicago: University of Chicago Press 1904).
Jastrow, Morris, "An Assyrian Law Code," *Journal of the American Oriental Society,* 44:1-59.
Langdon, S. H., *Babylonian Wisdom* (London: Luzac and Company 1923).
Müller, Frederick Max, *The Sacred Books of the East* (Oxford: Clarendon Press 1879–1910).
Peet, Thomas E., *A Comparative Study of the Literatures of Egypt, Palestine, and Mesopotamia* (London: Oxford University Press 1931).
Petrie, W. M. F., *Religion and Conscience in Ancient Egypt* (London: Methuen and Company 1920).
Vincent, George E., "The Laws of Hammurabi," *American Journal of Sociology,* 9:737-54.

CHAPTER IV

EAST INDIAN AND PERSIAN SOCIAL THOUGHT

When we turn to East Indian records we find a longer and higher development of social thought than in Egypt or Babylonia. The span from the early Vedic hymns to the writings of present-day Indian scholars is a long one, filled with a rich literature. While Indian thought has been built largely on the pattern of the negation of the world and life, yet it has definite and real social implications. There is a unique sweep to Indian thought, for it takes in the relation of man not simply to other human beings but to all life.

India is composed of peoples of many origins. Dravidians arrived in prehistoric times. Aryans were arriving in considerable numbers in Afghanistan by 1500 B.C. Mongoloid peoples came from the northeast; Turkish and Iranian types have immigrated to India. In recent decades North Europeans entered and India came under the control of Great Britain. Queen Victoria was proclaimed Empress of India in 1876, but now an independence movement is under way.

To complicate still further the thought life of the peoples of India, the land has been an active theater of various religious movements characterized by deep convictions and animosities. Hinduism, Brahmanism, Buddhism, Mohammedanism, Parseeism, Christianity—this list does not begin to tell the story, but is sufficient to indicate how social thought is entangled in religious thinking.

The Vedic hymns, which go back to about 1500 B.C., reveal a simple joy in living and a serene attitude on the part of those who have succeeded in rising above worldly sin. Veda means knowledge and Rig-Veda, the title of the best known of the early Vedas, means song-knowledge. The Vedas, which were the product of early Indo-Aryans, reveal leaders or Shamans who attained release from the sins of the flesh and of the world and thereby reached a state of ecstasy and mysticism. Here is the beginning of a theory of world negation and of attainment of oneness with a Divine power.

37

Among the early Vedic believers, sacrifice acquired a positive social function as far as the relationship of the individual and his god was concerned. Sacrifice was a social act in which the worshiper and his god took part. The food strengthened the god and the spiritual contact strengthened the worshiper and lifted him out of this life of trouble while still living in it.

In an early East Indian account of a deluge, similar to the deluge that is described in Genesis, there is a conception of punishment that falls upon the group because of the sins of individuals. Hence, a sense of group responsibility on the part of the individual was not only present but fostered.

Life must have seemed unduly harsh to the early Indo-Aryans. They sought release from it through a system of religious thought and action, but it was a system of life-negation. Climatic conditions of a humid, semi-tropical nature possibly played a role in developing a negation theory as contrasted with the ideas of world affirmation and participation which have been so prominent in Europe and America.

Shall we affirm, or escape from, this life? Both tendencies are evidently in human nature. Sometimes one predominates and sometimes the other, depending on the age of the individual and on the ease or harshness of personal circumstances. Thus, two life theories underlie all concepts of social thought. The people of India challenge the world of thought with one of these two major theories.

BRAHMAN THOUGHT

When the Aryans reached the Ganges region they had developed a strong priestly class, or Brahmans, whose thought had developed several special phases. Ceremonies and rituals gave a definite fixation to the teachings of the Brahman priests. The Vedic doctrine of becoming one with the supra-worldly forces has been expressed in considerable detail. As in an individualistic system of thought, for example, in Western individualism, good behavior was practiced by a person with reference to his fellows on a ground that was chiefly self-centered and for individual gain. The concept of genuine social responsibility has always been and still is exceedingly slow in developing in the life of man.

With the rise of Brahmanism the caste system developed and a social gradation of status was evolved. Brahmanism divided society. It gave structure to the concept that some people are naturally, and artificially, superior to other people. As might be expected the Brahmans, or priests, put themselves first. Their protectors and defenders came second, the Kshatriyas, or warriors. Third place in social status was assigned to the Vaisyas, or craftsmen and farmers, the producers. After dividing themselves into these three castes, the Indo-Aryans put the aborigines and others into still other castes. The Sudras, or fourth caste, were those who did menial labor for the other three groups. Then there were various other groups known as outcasts, of which today the "untouchables" are the lowest.

The Brahmans developed a doctrine of supermen. They were the supermen and they claimed, as the word *Brahman* indicates, "sacred power." They seemed to have developed the idea that they were human gods. This priestly class illustrates the dangers of over-specialization. The priests failed to show any interest in anything except how they and their followers might identify themselves with the supra-worldly Power.

By the eighth century B.C. the Upanishads were written. These documents followed the Brahmanas and developed the Brahmanic doctrine still further. Upani-shad means confidential instruction, and represents special ways in which the individual can become identified with the universal Self or Power. Mysticism developed as an expression of the thought that the individual carries the essence of the supreme Power in himself.

The later Upanishads divided life into four Asramas, or stages: (1) schooldays under the tutelage of a teacher, (2) head of a household, (3) outdoor retirement, and (4) complete solitary living. It will be noted here that the individual could not start out on his search for universal Oneness until after he had fulfilled certain worldly duties. In the second stage he assumed the duties of fatherhood and paternal responsibility in order that his kind might not die out. The

Brahman faith thus required for its own functioning the necessity of preparing and making sacrifices, and for its continuance the raising of children.

The Upanishads emphasize the doctrine of reincarnation or transmigration of souls. The souls of plants, animals, and men are assumed to be related. The soul of a man after his death wanders. It is seeking absorption in the universal Soul, but it must merit this achievement, and this it may do by being born again and living again, and so on. If his evil deeds outweigh his good ones, then he is born again as an animal. Thus, a person must give very careful attention to his behavior.

JAINISM

Jinism, or Jainism, raises a practical question about reincarnation. It dates from Vardhamana, who lived about 500 B.C. Vardhamana spent a dozen years as an ascetic and finally achieved soul-victory. He is known as Mahavira, the "Great Hero" and as Jina, the "Victor." He lived at about the same time as did Buddha. Jainism has about a million adherents.

Vardhamana emphasized the doctrine of reincarnation to the point that one's consciousness is maintained throughout all his reincarnations, which normally are eight, before he attains perfect bliss or Nirvana. Special consideration was given to animals because in them the spirits of human beings might be living. An early commandment, therefore, of Jainism is: "Do not kill and do not harm any living creature." The social thought here is negative, that is, the responsibility which is assumed rests not on genuine social attitudes but on the desire to keep one's self sinless.

Jainism prohibits one from farming or from working in the soil. It is not possible to work in the earth without harming animal life, hence one cannot become a good Jainist. The adherents of this belief, therefore, have specialized in trade and become merchants.

Jainism leaps the bonds of caste. It draws no caste distinctions as is done in the Brahmanas and Upanishads. A new breadth to social thought thus is attained. In the development of asylums or homes for diseased and disabled ani mals the Jainists developed a new application of their sense of universal responsibility for living creatures.

BUDDHIST THOUGHT

Buddhism arose as a protest against earlier thought. A prince whose family name was Gautama, who lived about 500 B.C., became disturbed over the doctrine of reincarnation and sought a better interpretation. He renounced his paternal family and his own family, and after years of wandering and fasting he received a dream about a better way. He became known as the Buddha, or "enlightened one," and his influence has extended far and wide.

Buddha built up a system of thought based on law, and a belief in power that emanates from the individual. Evidence of a pure life is found in a radiation of kindliness. Here is a positive social doctrine of great moment, based as it is on indirect influences. By the development of kindly attitudes one can stop the incarnation series and enter into Nirvana. It is a curious but significant doctrine that by being most kindly toward the world of suffering one can escape from it the most quickly.

This kindliness doctrine has another negative social meaning. It checks all anger. It eradicates and prevents all enmity in the world. It suggests the Christian doctrine of overcoming evil with good.

The belief in compassion is of course negative and implies no responsibility for any positive action. It lays no bases for a constructive and widespread welfare program. It builds a world of individually kind souls, who drop out of the world as soon as they attain complete perfection.

Closely related is the absence of the caste concept. According to the Buddhist, it is not necessary to draw and maintain distinctions between classes of people on the basis of their birth or occupation. The Buddhist rises above such petty distinctions.

Another belief of social importance is found in the injunction to exercise self-control. In reality, kindliness requires self-control. Not only must one not kill any living creatures or not hate another being, but he must refrain from drinking intoxicating liquor, from unchastity, and from dishonesty. Inner perfection requires impervious attitudes toward all worldly temptations. Even the mind must be kept off these things, which is a belief that is related to a principle of current social psychology. If it is true that one tends to go where he thinks, even where he thinks adversely, then it is important to keep one's mind only on those ideas that one would follow.

A positive social principle is found in Buddha's emphasis on gratitude. Ingratitude is deplored. Gratitude to parents is especially encouraged. If one were to live to the age of a hundred, "carrying around his mother on one shoulder and his father on the other," he could not have rendered adequate appreciation to his parents.[1] Still, this is not the doctrine of positive love of Christianity which Buddha taught. This belief does not go much further than building rest-houses and digging wells for weary travelers.[2] Of course love and marriage and the raising of children are all permitted.

Buddhism inaugurated a whole set of "noble truths." Commendation is extended to "right speech," which requires that speech be friendly and sincere toward others. The requirements include "right conduct" which is conduct that is peaceful and honorable toward other persons. Stress is placed upon "right" means of securing livelihood; that is, on means that do not involve the injury or the taking of life.

Additional light is thrown on the social thought of Buddha by the following sayings which are credited to him:

"Pity and sympathy is the Buddha's mind."

"Pity to his parents is the supreme law."

"Even a strong man cannot lift himself."

"The picture which is painted by ten fingers (men) is accurate." (In a multitude of counsellors there is safety.)

"Nursing a sick man is the great field where the righteous tree of the mind grows."

"If there is no Buddha in the world, be good to your parents; for to be good to one's parents is to minister unto Buddha."

Among Buddha's Ten Commandments there are several

[1] *Auguttara-Nikaya*, ii-4, p. 1.
[2] Albert Schweitzer, *Indian Thought and Its Development*, p. 112.

that are distinctly social. Each of these is stated not only
negatively, but also positively. Each conveys a constructive
suggestion. (1) "Kill not, but have regard for life." (2)
"Steal not, neither do ye rob; but help everybody to be master of the fruits of his labor." (3) "Abstain from impur-
ity, and lead a life of chastity." (4) "Lie not, but be truthful.
Speak the truth with discretion, fearlessly, and in a loving
heart." (5) "Invent not evil reports, neither do ye repeat
them. Carp not, but look for the good sides of your fellow-
beings, so that you may with sincerity defend them against
their enemies." (6) "Swear not, but speak decently and with
dignity." (7) "Waste not the time with gossip, but speak to
the purpose or keep silence." (8) "Covet not, nor envy, but
rejoice at the fortunes of other people." (9) "Cleanse your
heart of malice and cherish no hatred, not even against your
enemies; but embrace all living things with kindness." (10)
"Free your mind of ignorance and be anxious to learn the
truth, especially in the one thing that is needed, lest you fall
a prey either to scepticism or to errors." [3]

Other source thoughts of Buddha that reveal the early emphasis of Buddhism are:

"Our good or evil deeds follow us continually like shad-
ows."

"Love and compassion he gives with reverence and he ban-
ishes all hatred, envy, and anger."

"The immortal can be reached only by continuous acts of
kindliness."

In the East Indian systems of early religious thought, such
as Brahmanism, Jainism, and early Buddhism there runs a
common thread of negation of this world, and yet there is
in each another common emphasis, namely, of hopefulness
based on the escape or emancipation doctrine peculiar to all.
Each has a method whereby the individual may escape the
evils of this world.

The next major development of East Indian thought is
found in the *Laws of Manu* which appeared perhaps about
200 B.C., and which represents a codified treatment of Brahmanism. Much of the material is very old and differs little
from the Vedic literature. However, new ideas occur. If

[3] Paul Carus, editor, *The Gospel of Buddha*, pp. 106-107.

the Brahmans or priests are to be venerated as gods, they must live like gods. The Laws of Manu show that the super-man must maintain superior attitudes of forbearance, of modesty, of gentleness — how different from Nietzsche's concept of a superman, and how like early Christian teachings! Three types of personalities are described. One is based on feelings and is the mystical, poetic, artistic type, deeply devoted to his religion. A second is the active type of personality, a leader, but one whose actions are motivated by "disinterested service, the pursuit of the Good." The third is the thinking type of personality, that which penetrates philosophically or scientifically into the nature of nature and of human nature. The first type seeks the Beautiful; the second, the Good; and the third, the True.[4]

According to the Laws of Manu, there are four major social institutions. These are: education, the family-economic system, the political, and the religious. The purpose of education is to sublimate desire, control action, train the intellect, and direct the spirit of man. Meditation plays a definite role in the training program.[5] The purpose of the family-economic institution is to satisfy biological and livelihood needs "but with an eye to the development of the highest personality." Woman is to be protected, but her best protection is self-protection. She can go astray, however, and may fall before temptations, such as: "Drinking, associating with immoral people, separating from her husband, roaming around, sleeping late, and dwelling with other men."[6] Romance is mere "desire." Marriage should be arranged by people who can keep the best interests of both parties in mind. Then love should follow. Endogamy, or marriage with the same group, is urged. Marriage of persons on the same status levels is enjoined. The family involves a three-fold spiritual unity of man, woman, and child.

Livelihood should be found in a socially useful occupation. Not in work that undermines his own or the group's welfare. "Competition is a law of the jungle, not of human society."

[4] For this analysis the author is especially indebted to Kewal Motwani, *A Study in Hindu Social Theory*, Chapter III.
[5] *Ibid.*, Chapter V.
[6] *Ibid.*, p. 126.

The third institution, or the civic one, involves partial withdrawal from the family, and service outside the family. If a person stays in the family, he may work without personal gain; or he may live in the open and "by meditation and prayer send out a continuous stream of good-will to his fellow men." [7]

The fourth institution is the one through which one may obtain his "final liberation." Solitude, life in the forest, absence from society, these are some of the conditions. Without property, he begs. He relaxes, breathes properly, meditates, returns good for evil, thinks kindly of everything. [8]

Social progress consists in the moving of society in "the desired direction." A perfected society is one in which the virtues of the good man function everywhere. No hatred, no greed, no unchastity — this is the direction of desired progress.

A noteworthy variation from and development of Brahmanic teachings is found in the philosophical poem known as the Bhagavad-Gita, a composite work that has been extensively read and idealized. A leading spokesman is Krishna, who announces the doctrine: "My interest shall only be directed to the deed, never to the fruits thereof." [9] Not an aim but a pure sense of duty is made paramount. The wise man is "unknown to that triumvirate called fear and anger and anxieties, which e'er were bred by that vile harlot hate." [10] Self-control is urged in these words: "Be glad, but never over-glad in happiness; encounter grief, and be not over-sad"; [11] and again in these: "I am never known to fools or base and evil men; nor to those imbeciles who plume themselves with feathers fine and choose the fickle, rapid goddess of the styles." [12]

Kindness and love must be wholehearted, for "half-kindness and half-selfishness won't make a man of thee." Moreover, "Love's gentle light shines in all hearts however hard they seem." [13]

---

[7] *Ibid.*, p. 158.
[8] *Ibid.*, Chapter VIII.
[9] Albert Schweitzer, *op. cit.*, p. 188.
[10] Richard Carlyle, *The Psalms of Krishna*, p. 14
[11] *Ibid.*, p. 43.
[12] *Ibid.*, p. 51.
[13] *Ibid.*, p. 57.

CURRENT INDIAN THOUGHT

We turn now briefly to modern East Indian thought. Ram Mohan Ray (1772–1833) was a social reformer who urged the abolition of the custom of the burning of widows, until the British government forbade the practice in 1829.[14] He also opposed the caste system.

Mahatma Gandhi, born in 1869, studied law in London, and went in 1893 to South Africa as a lawyer, where he learned how the East Indians living in the Province of Natal had almost no rights. He was treated as one of them and cast out of the train on which he was traveling. There and then he developed the doctrine of passive resistance. His Hindu religion would not permit him to take a more active stand. His passive resistance methods succeeded. He was a forerunner of the sit-down striker.

Conscientious objecting acquired a powerful advocate in Gandhi. To anyone who puts the inner life foremost, and who has achieved great personality strength as a result of long years of sacrificial living and careful meditation, the role of conscientious objecting comes very naturally.

Gandhi has given many years to a number of social reforms. He has worked for the removal of prejudices against the untouchables. He has labored in behalf of children in order to protect them from early marriage. He has urged the recognition of women's rights. He has sought to control the use of alcohol and harmful drugs in India. "Never before has any Indian taken so much interest in concrete realities as has Gandhi." [15]

Gandhi lives simply, enters on long fasts, and seeks to achieve inner perfection by withdrawing for stated intervals from the "world," for rest, meditation, and inspiration. The "Ashram," or place of retreat from the world, is a vital phase of his life. Great strength of personality is a secret of his social power. The ancient doctrine of non-violence secures powerful expression through him. It becomes a far-reaching social force that worries even the throne of Britain. Passive resistance can be exerted without giving way to hatred.

[14] Albert Schweitzer, *op. cit.*, p. 211.
[15] *Ibid.*, p. 227.

Gandhi's social strength illustrates the surprising effectiveness that can be achieved under theories of life and world negation. Gandhi's "satyagraha" or "non-violent direct action" has been defined at length recently by Shridharani, one of Gandhi's followers.

In Rabindranath Tagore, born in 1861, India has a representative who is trying to reconcile the two doctrines of world negation and world affirmation.[16] He criticizes both the Eastern ascetics and the Western leaders who have lost inner spiritual strength. "He demands both things together: that man should belong to God with his soul and serve Him actively in his world."[17] Material gains are nothing unless subordinated to spiritual and human advancement. Well-being is for all; wisdom and justice shall reign everywhere; art and poetry shall ennoble all men's minds.[18] Here is a thought-symphony, originating in ancient Vedic struggles toward inner perfection that has incorporated in itself the Western doctrine of life and world affirmation. The goal of becoming united with God through deeds will make this a more wholesome world for all who live in it.

INDIAN SOCIOLOGY

A current sociological view as expressed by Radhakamal Mukerjee of Lucknow University is "that social interests and experiences must express our conceptions of the nature and functions of divinity."[19] Moreover, universal law as affecting human beings "is something which is molded by the interaction of classes and interests within the state."[20] Furthermore, it is in "groups and associations which conflict or co-operate with one another" that human values are molded. Man's ethical problem today is that of deciding what to do about his myriads of conflicting loyalties and hence of conflicting values. How can he interweave these together into "an ideal Person"?

According to Mukerjee the building of a personality is

[16] *Ibid.*, 238 ff.
[17] *Ibid.*, p. 239.
[18] *Loc. cit.*
[19] Radhakamal Mukerjee, "The Social Conception of Religion," *Sociology and Social Research*, 13:519.
[20] *Loc. cit.*

much more difficult today than formerly. "Personality develops out of a process of interweaving of group interests and values with clearly marked out and even stereotyped loyalties." [21]   This organization of impulses will be furthered and completed by religion.   The essence of self, according to Hindu religion, is love and justice.   God is "the All-True, the All-Good and the All-Beautiful, present now and yet eternal, the original of the life and love in human beings." Persons seek to achieve their highest goals by establishing "harmony and communion with all sentient beings." [22]   Professor Mukerjee goes still further and indicates the necessity for man to establish a balance with the inorganic as well as the organic world around him.[23]

Professor Mukerjee's thinking is testimony to the rise of sociology in India.   His thought ranges from ecological studies and observations to religion and mysticism.   Not only that but he endeavors to integrate such extremes as ecology and mysticism into one grand whole.

D. P. Mukerji of India, who has recently (1932) made an analysis of concepts in sociology, has emphasized such concepts as personality, progress, equality, social forces, and social control.   He possesses both a knowledge of Western sociology and an Eastern background.   He finds progress in three principles.   (1) The principle of harmony "sustains the universe amidst all its incessant changes, movements, and conflicts."   (2) The principle of co-ordination is found in the social environment.   (3) The principle of unity transcends all and permeates all.   The three ultimate values are : Peace, Welfare, and Unity.

Equality consists in variety.   "There can be no equality in uniformity."   The necessary variety for progress and for growth of personality is found in different abilities and psychological equipments "working out different adjustments with dissimilar stimuli in their respective environments." [24] To this end both a caste system and a Russian communist system are fatal.

[21] *Loc. cit.*
[22] *Ibid.*, p. 525.
[23] Radhakamal Mukerjee, "Social Ecology of a River Valley," *Sociology and Social Research*, 12:347.
[24] D. P. Mukerji, *Basic Concepts in Sociology*, p. 51.

The problem, then, of progress is the growth of personality. This growth depends on the four factors of "variety, change, directivity, and purpose." There are four conditioning phenomena in social life that postulate variety, change, directivity, and purpose. These are geographic factors, technic factors, psycho-physical factors, and social (ideas and sentiments) factors. The first and third are relatively fixed, but the technic and the social elements are subject to social control and constitute social forces.

The factors in social force are also four, namely, perseveration, feelings, meaning, and the interplay of the first three factors. These are all psychological in character. Closely related is valuation, whose nature is revealed in the conflict between "old habits and new experiences."

Social control, according to Mukerji, involves (1) the need for order, (2) controlling authority that has its own scheme of order, (3) and some type of accommodation or acceptance by a large part of the people controlled.[25] Social control means that a majority identify their interests with the welfare of the whole society. The controlling authority may be the militarist, the priestly class, the capitalist, or the communist.

Two types of control have existed in the world, namely, control by classes and control by castes. Neither is satisfactory. "The first principle of control is to prepare for its own demise." Self-culture and "a strictly objective and disinterested attitude towards other individuals as ends by themselves," is the second principle. Not communistic social planning nor "the cracking caste-system," nor any other type of control imposed from without is satisfactory to personality. Control needs to be transferred from without to within.

A contribution to group psychology has been made by Radhakamal Mukerjee and N. N. Sen-Gupta in their *Introduction to Social Psychology*. The sub-title, "The Mind in Society" is significant. Through culture patterns the group shapes the patterns of personality. The individual is normally engaged in adjusting himself to the physical world. Activity, not reason or sympathy, is the best of social groups.[26]

[25] *Ibid.*, p. 151.
[26] *Introduction to Social Psychology*, p. VIII.

Group life offers man what he needs in making his adjustments. If the proper groups are not in operation, then new groups will arise to meet human needs in the adjustment process. Myths and faiths arise to meet the same needs. Regional factors are basic in determining to what factors man must adjust. Mukerjee and Sen-Gupta suggest a psychoanalytic analogy when they compare social maladjustments with the individual's neuroses. However, they are cautious in their use of the term *social neuroses*.

East Indian social thought is unique. Its cultural backgrounds, particularly its underlying religious and philosophical principles, are distinctive. The outcropping of social thinking even in a world negation theory is significant. The arrival in India in recent years of Western sociological concepts has made an impression, and the new social thought in India is showing signs of noteworthy developments and integrations. Out of this process may arise markedly original ideas of sociological significance.

PERSIAN THOUGHT

The Persians deserve special mention at this point. After their defeat by Alexander the Great in 331 B.C. they are alleged to have turned over the torch of civilization to the Greeks. However, they had already made a contribution to social thought somewhat similar to that credited to other ancient peoples. Under Cyrus the Great, Darius, and Xerxes a system of state education was fostered which was designed chiefly to train soldiers. It did not stress social and intellectual development, although it existed in a land that produced the Magi. The persons who were not in the army nor favored by the officials received slight educational benefits.

In the teachings of Zoroaster of the seventh century B.C. we first find the main trend of Persian social thought. The *Avesta,* the document from which Zoroastrianism and the modern Parsee religion have evolved, emphasizes the principle of kindliness in all human relationships. Sanitation, business honesty, and chastity in family relationships are sought.

Spitama Zarathustra, as Zoroaster has been called, had a

series of visions. The *Avesta*, or Law, contains liturgies, hymns, and a legal code. Zoroaster made over the natural religion of agricultural Iran into a religion of good and evil, with Ahura-Mazdah reigning over the good forces of the world. He was aided by certain personified forces, such as good thinking, righteous doing, steadfast devotion, perfect attainment, and immortal living. Ahriman was the chief of the evil forces. Man, occupying an intermediate position, aided the forces of good by his good behavior and the forces of evil by his bad behavior. Ultimately Ahura-Mazdah and the good in the world and good people would win and achieve immortality.

In the *Avesta* the "Yasna" presents the liturgies; the "Gathas," the hymns said to have been composed by Zoroaster and perhaps the oldest part of the *Avesta;* the "Yashts," a later group of hymns; and the "Vendidad," which is historical and homiletical, and which contains most of the social thought of the *Avesta*.

Certain virtues are emphasized as means of combatting the forces of evil. Purity is placed foremost and includes "good thoughts, good words, and good deeds." Truth ranks high as a social virtue. Lying is deprecated. The good for one's self is made the yardstick in Zoroaster's negative Golden Rule: "That nature alone is good which shall not do unto another whatever is not good for its own self." Likewise, Zoroaster or his followers are credited with having enunciated a set of Ten Commandments, for instance:

1. Commit no slander.
2. Form no covetous desire.
3. Indulge in no wrathfulness.
4. Suffer no anxiety.
5. Commit no lustfulness.
6. Bear no improper envy.
7. Practice no sloth.
8. Be diligent.
9. Do not extort from the wealth of others.
10. Abstain from the wives of others.[27]

27 "Dina-i Mainog-i Khirad," 20:3-7, in *Sacred Books of the East*, Vol. XXIV.

Persian social thought reached the end of its creative period when Mohammedanism overran Iran in A.D. 651. The
influence of Persian thought, however, was considerable on
Greek and Hebrew thought, and its effect upon early Christian thinking was by no means insignificant.[28]

GROUP DISCUSSION TOPICS

1. The origins of Vedic social thought.
2. The later changes in Vedic social thought.
3. Brahmanism's social significance.
4. The distinctive social elements in Jainism.
5. The social implications of early Buddhism.
6. Contrasts in social thought in Hinduism and Buddhism.
7. Comparisons of Buddha's Ten Commandments and the Decalogue of the Old Testament.
8. New social emphases in the Laws of Manu.
9. Krishna as a symbol of social thought.
10. Gandhi's social thought evaluated.
11. Contrasts in Gandhi's and Tagore's social thinking.
12. The rise of sociology in India.
13. Distinctive aspects of East Indian social thought.
14. Origins of Zoroaster's social precepts.
15. An evaluation of social thought in the *Avesta*.

READINGS

Becker, Howard, and Harry E. Barnes, *Social Thought from Lore to Science* (Washington : Harren Press 1952), Vol. I, Ch. 3.
Buddha, Dialogues of, translated by T. W. R. Davids (London: Frowde 1899).
Chambliss, Rollin, *Social Thought* (New York: The Dryden Press 1954), Ch. 5.
Carus, Paul, editor, *The Gospel of Buddha* (Chicago : The Open Court Publishing Company 1909).
Dasgupta, S., *A History of Indian Philosophy* (Cambridge : University Press 1922).
Dawson, M. M., *The Ethical Religion of Zoroaster* (New York : The Macmillan Company 1931).
Davids, T. W. R., *Buddhism, Its History and Literature* (New York : G. P. Putnam's Sons 1896).
Frazer, R. W., *Indian Thought, Past and Present* (London : Unwin 1915).

[28] A modern remnant of Zoroastrianism are the Parsees of Bombay and its environs in India. They preserve the ancient Pahlivi ritual, and are of course fire-worshipers. They are a merchant class numbering about 100,000.

Hume, R. E., *The Thirteen Principal Upanishads* (London: Oxford University Press 1931).

Motwani, Kewal, *Manu, A Study in Hindu Social Theory* (Madras, India: Ganesh and Company 1934).

Mukerjee, Radhakamal, "The Social Conception of Religion," *Sociology and Social Research*, 13:517-25.

Mukerjee, Radhakamal, and N. N. Sen-Gupta, *An Introduction to Social Psychology* (Boston: D. C. Heath and Company 1928).

————, "A General Theory of Society," in B. Singh, editor, *The Frontiers of Social Science* (London: Macmillan and Company 1956), pp. 21-74.

Mukerji, D. P., *Basic Concepts in Sociology* (London: Paul Trench, Trubner and Company 1932).

Müller, Frederick Max, *The Sacred Books of the East* (London: Clarendon Press 1879–1910).

Northrop, F. S. C., *The Meeting of East and West* (New York: The Macmillan Company 1946), Chs. IX-XI.

Risley, H. R. *The People of India* (London: Thacker and Company 1915).

Saunders, Kenneth, *The Ideals of East and West* (New York: The Macmillan Company 1934), Ch. I.

Schweitzer, Albert, *Indian Thought and Its Development* (New York: Henry Holt and Company 1936).

Shridharani, K., *War Without Violence* (New York: Harcourt, Brace and Company 1939).

Sirar, Mahendra N., "Social and Moral Ideas in the Upanishads," *International Journal of Ethics*, 44:94-105.

Springett, B. H., *Zoroaster the Great Teacher* (London: W. Rider 1923).

Swami, Shree P., and W. B. Yeats, *The Ten Principal Upanishads* (New York: The Macmillan Company 1937).

CHAPTER V

CHINESE SOCIAL THOUGHT

By the fifth century B.C., Chinese thought began to secure formulation in a number of important directions. The gamut of Chinese social thought is extensive; the variety is amazing. The various systems of social thought now prevalent in the world had very early beginnings in China. In fact, many of them developed and matured in China before they were thought of elsewhere.

Earliest Chinese thought developed in the third or Chou Dynasty. This seems to have been a period of intellectual unrest, social disturbances, and violence. Out of these changes came at least four major systems of social thought.

TAOISM

The first that will be discussed will be Taoism. Its founder is reputed to be Lao-tzu, born as early possibly as 600 B.C. His doctrines, found in the Tao Teh King, are deeply philosophical and difficult to interpret. Tao is usually translated to mean "the Way," or the way of life. Basically, it is a religious "way," but it has social meanings.

Taoism is a form of nature worship. It draws its adherents away from human life and the turmoil of the world toward a worship of nature. While many different and conflicting ideas have become bound up with Taoism, the withdrawal emphasis is clear.

A reflection of Taoism is seen today in Chinese paintings. Nature is dominant, and human life is secondary. A mountain, trees, a bridge, a path, and then one or a few people can be found if you look close enough. They are subordinated to the total effect, and are following one of the paths and speculating on the beauties of nature.

Another major idea in Taoism is the individualistic, which at times becomes anarchistic. It is closely related to the withdrawal concept. The individual finds his major satisfaction in life, not as a member of society, but by himself, and by being a law unto himself. Social institutions and laws cramp the style of man.

Taoism means a type of personality in which there is no sense of pride. Likewise, selfishness is absent. No claims to ownership of anything are involved. Ambitions would be prevented from arising. On the negative side there is some resemblance to Buddhism, and hence the rapid spread of Buddhism in China, especially among the near-Taoists, Buddhism, which reached its height in China during the T'ang Dynasty (A.D. 618–907), developed numerous abuses, and lost most of its social value.

On its positive side, Taoism gave freedom to personality. It aimed to offer complete freedom. Unhampered by ambition, selfishness, pride, personality acts entirely in a spontaneous way. It soars on endless wings. But such a condition meant getting away from society, from the family, and from any social obligations whatsoever. Primitive simplicity, childhood simplicity, no desires, no knowledge, were the goals. While on the way toward the goals, one was to repay injury with kindness, to maintain attitudes of complete humility, to treat everyone as a complete equal.

CONFUCIANISM

Another system of thought also originated about the same time that Lao-tzu was formulating the original concepts of Taoism. The name of Confucius (551–478 B.C.) suggests a philosophy with definite social elements. Confucius faced a day of social unrest. It was evident that social turmoil, conflict, and violence were not to be accepted as final solutions to the human problem. The Taoist plan of escape might have merit for a small percentage of the people. It was entirely irrational and fantastic to think of a whole people or race splitting up into individual units with each one living more or less to himself and with nature.

The logical conclusion to be drawn to the dilemma represented by social turmoil on the one hand, and the Taoistic answer of individual escape on the other, was some form or degree of social organization. Confucius sought to work out this answer in terms of definite social organization for the smallest unit possible, namely, the family. This unit, of course, naturally grew to include a clan of families or a village of families, most of whom were related at least distantly.

Confucius was a practical man of affairs as well as a philosopher. He did not lay claim to being original and a creator of ideas. He wished to conserve the best of the past, and so centered his writings on concepts of personal virtue, related chiefly to the family members. Rituals to further these principles were developed.

Confucius constructed his social thought around five human relationships, four of which were related to the family : (1) between father and son, (2) between husband and wife, (3) between brother and brother, and (4) between members of one family and of another family. Obedience of the younger to the older was the dominant rule of conduct. Ritual enforced the rule.

The family was supposed to be self-sufficient economically and became the economic unit of society. All worked for the family. Thus the people became above all else family-minded.

The last (5) type of human relationship that Confucius emphasized was that between king and subject. Again obedience of subject to ruler was enjoined, but as in the case of the family, obedience became a blind relationship, encrusted in ceremonies.

Confucius lived in a feudal age of society. There were three classes, the rulers or lords, the scholars, and the rural peasants who constituted the vast majority, and who according to the Confucian thought remained peasants and blind subjects. Their attention was taken from their condition by their actions in behalf of the members of the family, their elders, and their ancestors. Instead of urging the individual to get out of society, as Taoism taught, the doctrine of Confucius suggested that he remain in even an abject social order and submit to it.

The teachings of Confucius left the peasants in ignorance and encouraged their obedience to their grasping and greedy overlords and the vested interests of the day. Conservation rather than change was the result. Looking backward (to ancestors) rather than forward (to new ideas) was fostered, if not required. Acquiescence in, rather than ambitious efforts to get out of, social misery was put at a premium. Individualism, as known in America, was killed by the ethics of Confucius. Submission to dictatorships was virtually made the rule.

Confucius talked a great deal about the "superior man" and the "gentleman," and the duties and behavior of such an ideal person. These desired traits are largely of a personal nature, and relate to good manners and morals of the individual. Quiet, exemplary conduct is praised and made the goal. All is to take place within the framework of social institutions, particularly the political and the economic.

Confucius had no doctrine of social institutions, and he did not perceive that a peaceful and gentle person, living within a bad political or economic institution, plays into the hands of such an institution, and indirectly promotes badness.

Confucius enunciated a Golden Rule. That it was stated negatively is no adequate reason for calling it "a Silver Rule." He said: "Do not unto others what you would not they should do unto you." The full benefit of this maxim comes only when those in authority in a social institution put it into effect for themselves first of all. Unfortunately, the rulers, lords, and bosses usually preach this doctrine for their underlings to follow, while many of them give it only lip service. It was this problem that Confucius did not solve.

Confucius was a realistic sort of philosopher, who himself held political office and tried to put into practice some of his own teachings, but it seems that he ultimately gave up the task because he could not get the "higher-ups" to practice the ethical principles in which he so sincerely believed. As long as he was in charge of a district he was highly successful and people moved into this district so that they could live under his jurisdiction. But finally the duke or lord above him refused to follow the principles in which Confucius believed, and no other lords in an equally high position would use his services. He would not compromise himself or his principles and spent his closing years in disappointment. Not only would the lords or rulers not change to his way of

thinking, but their subjects, who were benefactors of corruption, refused to listen to him.

Confucius appreciated the importance of a just government and of just rulers, but his statements were weak in
meeting the actual situation. He said that the business of
government is "to rectify." [1] He argued that a good ruler
would be a parent to his people. His rules for governing
include "dealing with the mass of the people as children."
With reference to stimulating the common people, the ruler
will demonstrate his ability by "employing them only at the
regular times and making the imposts light." Again, Confucius states that it is supremely important that the ruler
maintain the "confidence" of his people. In one connection
he rises to a far-sighted social position, for in describing the
qualities of a certain ruler the following summary is made:
"By his generosity he won all. By his sincerity, he made the
people repose trust in him. By his earnest activity, his
achievements were great. By his justice, all were delighted." [2]

Confucius was a good student of human nature. His concepts of personality were full of insight. In his statement:
"A man and his faults are of a piece," [3] he perceives something of the gestalt nature of personality. Shrewd indeed is
the observation: "I have met no one who can see his own
faults and arraign himself within." [4] Perhaps one of the most
far-sighted and far-reaching observations is his generalization: "By nature men are nearly all alike; by practice they
get to be wide apart." [5] In this generalization Confucius recognizes a common human nature that is characteristic of all
mankind, and the role of differences in environmental stimuli in creating divisions among people.

Confucius was not a reformer nor a religious leader, but
primarily a conserver. His writings reflect not his own ideas,
for his originality was not great. He brought together many
concepts which had been worked out before his day. In the
Lo Ki, or Record of Rites, there are many social, domestic,
and individualistic precepts. In a way the *Lo Ki* is one of

[1] *Analects,* 12:17.
[2] *Ibid.,* 20:1.
[3] *Ibid.,* 4:25.
[4] *Ibid.,* 5:27.
[5] *Ibid.,* 17:2.

the most influential manuals of conduct that has ever been written.

Confucius believed in the efficacy of setting good examples. Imitation would then operate to accomplish the desired results. By such a method Confucius expected that society at large would be improved. He urged that a person should strive for perfection. According to the Confucian concept of the Superior Man, a person should master his own desires and passions, substituting an enjoyment of music, ceremony, and of friendship, for the enjoyment that comes from the exercise of bodily desires. He should seek salvation through the study of nature and of things. Morals and intelligence, if accompanied by bravery, will produce the highest type of personality.

Confucius did much to promulgate stable family life among the Chinese. Around the family group he caused his social ideas to revolve. On the death of his mother, Confucius went into seclusion for twenty-seven months. On sacrificial occasions the living members and the departed spirits of the household were accustomed to gather in one filial communal group. The welfare of the individual was completely subordinated to the interests of the family groups of spirits and living members, with the former being in the vast majority. This worship of the past paralyzed new thought.

Marriage received special attention, but the arrangements were made by relatives or other "go-betweens," with the view to selecting marriage mates who would be wisely suited to each other. Although polygamy as such was discountenanced, concubinage was permitted, particularly with a view to enabling sons to carry on the family rituals and to maintain the lineage. The sexes dress much alike (except for headgear and footgear) and the style is kept simple and æsthetic with an added emphasis "on minimizing the visible distinctions of sex."

Confucius objected to the maintenance of a government by the use of fear and of coercive measures. He predicted that capital punishment (even in a land ruled by customs) would be abolished in a hundred years. Because the ancient laws were elaborate the judges exercised an unusual degree of power. Contrary to Western procedure, the Chinese considered an accused man guilty until proved otherwise. Excessive corporal punishment was deplored.[6] Although customs ruled, the judges often possessed a liberal margin of freedom in determining the nature of punishment.

Obedience to authority has been for centuries a cardinal social principle of the Chinese. It was enunciated by Confucius who spoke as a representative of the upper classes. On stressing obedience to temporal authorities and in shunning the gods, Confucius has been accused of fostering a materialistic philosophy. This charge is offset by his ethical teachings. He was a humanitarian rather than a materialist; an utilitarian or a pragmatist rather than an idealist. In these ideas, he reflects not his own opinions so much as the thought of the generations which preceded him.

A local form of social organization in which Confucius was much interested and in which he participated was the "hsien." The hsien or local district has been pronounced "the real unit of Chinese corporate life" for centuries, and the hsien magistrate, "the heart and soul of all official life." Since this magistrate keeps in touch with the peasants, he has been called "the father and mother officer."

Confucius was unfavorable to militarism. One tended to lose status if he joined the army. The concepts of peace and harmonious social relationships were made paramount by Confucius. He held war in contempt and scorned militarism. It is ironical that as China begins to function as a world power she must change her age-old policy, and become a militarist nation.

MENCIUS

Mencius (372–289 B.C.) is considered Confucius' most distinguished follower. In the *Book of Mencius,* we recognize the ideas of Confucius with modifications and improvements. Mencius lived in the declining years of the long Chou Dynasty. Social and political conditions were deplorable. After a short trial, Mencius withdrew from public life in disgust. He was an environmentalist in the sense that he believed that external evil influences have corrupted man's original

[6] *Shoo King,* 27:3

good nature. Only personal regeneration could withstand and overcome social corruption. Mencius was a more thorough-going humanist than was Confucius, for he made the happiness of the people the supreme goal for the individual. He condemned war and soldiers and declared that generals are criminals. He asserted that it is wrong to conquer a territory against the wishes of the people of that territory.

Five personal evils, according to Mencius, are: (1) laziness, and failure to support one's parents; (2) gambling and drinking wine; (3) prizing goods and money; (4) falling before physical temptations; and (5) reckless bravery and fighting and quarreling.[7] The concept of the Superior Individual is developed at length, and teaching is considered more efficient than government and force.

MO TI

While the name of Mo Ti (575–525 B.C.), is not well known in Western countries, it is nevertheless one of the most important in the entire field of Chinese social thought. In some ways his contributions to social thought might be ranked ahead of all other Chinese thinkers. He was a younger contemporary of Confucius. Dr. C. F. Lung calls him the founder of Chinese utilitarianism, although distinguishing sharply between Mo Ti and Jeremy Bentham in this regard.[8]

Mo Ti's (or Motse's) ideas are found in *The Ethical and Political Works of Motse,* translated by Yi-Pao Mei.[9] They appear in the form of fifteen "books" which include fifty-three essays, not all of which, however, were written by Mo Ti. He definitely attacked the problem of social conflict. He could not accept conflict as normal, neither could he agree with the Lao-tzu that the "way out" was "back to nature." He evidently felt that the emphasis by Confucius on filial duty was too limited. His mind undertook a larger

---

[7] *Book of Mencius,* Book IV, Part II, Chapter XXX, p. 2.

[8] Chieng Fu Lung, "The Evolution of Chinese Social Thought" (unpublished doctoral dissertation, University of Southern California, Los Angeles 1935). For the accompanying description of Mo Ti's thought the writer acknowledges his indebtedness to the unpublished doctoral dissertation by Dr. C. F. Lung.

[9] Yi-Pao Mei, *The Ethical and Political Works of Motse* (London: Probsthain 1929).

swing. He sought out the causes of human misery and social contention and disintegration and advanced remedial and preventive procedures. He opposed war, corruption, and greed.

Mo Ti developed a concept of the Universal Good. What is useful is good, and what is good is desirable. What is both useful and desirable can be carried into action for the welfare of all.

The problem, then, is to determine, what is the useful? And the answer? Three tests: First, it is to be based on past experience. Second, it is to be tested by present experience. Third, it is to be judged by its effects on the people. What can meet these three tests is useful.

Mo Ti gave expression to the social principle of conduct of "loving all," thus identifying himself with the teachings of Jesus. His thought has a cast to it similar to the Buddhist doctrine of treating all with kindness. He was idealistic when compared with Confucius' practical idea of love gradation, that is, of letting love diminish in its strength as human relationships grow attenuated.

Instead of making a fetish out of loyalty within the family, Mo Ti promulgated the doctrine of universal brotherhood on a religious basis. He believed in individual telesis, or in the ability of each individual to set himself a useful goal and barring accident to achieve it. Here is universalism in love and indeterminism in personal growth and achievement. The thought is broad, sweeping, dynamic, and personal.

Mo Ti must have been a first-class logician. He was a kind of Socrates, for he enjoyed engaging the followers of Confucius in an argument and then flooring them. He was merciless in exposing the weaknesses of applied Confucianism. The tendency of Confucianism to stress very elaborate and expensive funerals as a result of family loyalty and enslavement to ritual and custom was satirized.[10] In fact, Mo Ti sums up the situation by pointing out that the followers of Confucius tend to give so much attention to the rituals regarding family life that they have no time on the one hand to attend to government; and on the other hand they will not attend to their daily work. In other words, here is fam-

[10] Yi-Pao Mei, *op. cit.*, Section 48.

ily ritualism gone mad. It is exactly this same contention that is vividly portrayed by Richard LaPiere in *The Son of Han,* a current novel on old Chinese life. The leading character has ambitions to become a scholar, and tries time and again to carry them to successful completion but each time is interrupted by filial duties. His son is born, and the question is raised: Is the son condemned to a similar round of defeats in attempting to make intellectual headway?

Mo Ti believed in the validity of social institutions and claimed that they came into existence in response to human needs. The abuse of institutions, however, is a real problem. The trouble lies in the attitudes of the individual, or in the lack of responsible attitudes. What has been called the principle of "the identification with the superior" is Mo Ti's way of pointing out the duty of each individual to report all infractions of rules to superiors and also all benefactions as well. The basic cause of social disorder "lies in the want of mutual love."

Mo Ti took the essence of the teaching of Confucius about the family and gave it universal meaning. Let everyone really love universally. His doctrines not only suggest the religious teachings of Christ but also the ideas of Kropotkin, who by concrete references to animal and human life arrived at a concept of mutual aid.

Social order ranks high. It is based on love to superior, and the ultimate superior becomes Heaven or the will of Heaven. The resultant system is a kind of social theocracy.

Social justice comes next. The big state shall not oppress the small one. The crowd or group shall not crush the individual member. The strong or wealthy man shall not grind down the poor. Social justice will prevail when all are "affectionate and filial."

Social economy is also vital. Many expenditures are unnecessary and hence wasteful. "What is the purpose?" is the question that Mo Ti would have everyone apply to all that he does. If constructive answers cannot be given to questions like this one, then a proposed action should be abandoned.

War is the most uneconomical of all activities. It consumes men. It brings about widespread neglect of useful occupations. The equipment required by war is either destroyed in war or else it becomes useless as soon as the war is over. Viewed purely as a eugenic and an economic problem, war is to be condemned. Moreover, Mo Ti seems to have traveled extensively, attempting to persuade rulers to desist from war. He sought to practice what he preached. Mo Ti's doctrine of universal brotherhood and related social concepts have never received the recognition that they deserved. Only now, in the twentieth century, are they beginning to receive attention.[11] They have been too far ahead of their times.

LEGALISTS

Han Fei, who lived in the third century B.C., will be treated as a representative of a fourth school of Chinese social thought. He was no advocate of an individualistic Taoism. He saw merit in the teachings of Confucius but he felt that they were entirely inadequate for a nation such as his people might become. He appreciated some of the teachings of Lao-tzu, Confucius, and Mo Ti. But each of these doctrines centered attention on the individual. Even a state such as Mo Ti envisioned would fall of the weight of its multiple individualisms.

Social salvation is to be found in another direction. Individuals tend to ask too much of each other. Persons expect special favors from their friends who are in authority. A state cannot rest for its guidance on the good will of its countless members. A personal state will become a state of too many personal interpretations of what to do next. With everybody in authority nobody will be in authority. Han Fei's ideas run counter to democracy and point to some of the practical weaknesses in a democracy.

Han Fei's ideas belonged to what has been called the Legalistic system of social thought, and more recently the Fascist. At any rate, he believed that the supreme authority should be objective laws. Here is an authority that will treat everyone impersonally, not on the basis of partiality or of subjectively developed variations. Law shall be inexorable. It will hold individuals to a more rigid style of behavior and hence develop a more effective government than can a demo-

[11] Hu Shih, *The Development of the Logical Method in Ancient China.*

cratic state with all its fluctuations in opinions and parties in control.

In Han Fei and those who believed as he did the state dominates the individual. The state and its spokesman become everything and the individual nothing. This is totalitarianism of the Fascist variety.

Han Fei was a thinker who believed in acting in the light of current circumstances. He must have possessed the courageous spirit of the reformer to have attacked the customs and traditions of the past in this ruthless manner. "The sage aims neither at the cultivation of what is ancient, nor at the observance of what is usual. He studies the conditions of the time and provides remedy for them." [12]

Han Fei thus would have one set of laws for one period and another set for a succeeding era. He was a relativist. Carried to a logical extreme, he would favor laws that "would work," and his teachings would approach those found in *The Prince* by Machiavelli.

Love will lead to a fool's paradise; but law to happiness in the end, although at the beginning there will be hardships.[13] This sounds like doctrines that have been taught at the outset in modern Fascist countries. Law will be inexorable in the punishment of offenders. It will eliminate corruption and graft. It will regulate work. The ultimate result, however, will be a well-ordered, happy people.

Leave people alone, announce a doctrine of love, and what will come to pass? Some will not respond nobly, but will take advantage of the guileless. Some in high places will do evil rather than good, and thus wreck the whole state. But let laws be announced and punishments meted out without favoritism, and a law-abiding and a self-respecting people will be developed. The ruler of a state therefore should rule with an impersonal if not an iron hand. Regulation is his watchword: "Let everything be in its place and every talent be put to its most appropriate use."

"Let the cock watch for the dawn, let the cat watch for the rats, and the sovereign need do nothing at all." Give more emphasis to prohibitions than to rewards. The best prohibi-

---

[12] Han Fei Tsu, Chapter XLIX (quoted by C. F. Lung, *op. cit.*, p. 141).
[13] *Cf.* C. F. Lung, *op. cit.*, p. 144.

tion is to curb thinking; the next best, is to prohibit speech; and the third is to prohibit deed. It was a Ch'in emperor Shih Huang Ti who tried to put this legalist philosophy into practice; he collected many of the best books of his time, Confucian classics, and had them burned, about 213 B.C. By setting up his own laws and allowing no one to read or think about any other doctrines, he hoped to control the people and maintain social order.[14]

Han Fei gave thought to the nature of social evolution. He pointed out, according to C. F. Lung, three stages in social evolution: (1) man's conquest of animals and disease; (2) his conquest of the more overt forces of nature; and (3) his conquest of social obstacles. He thought that the use of the same techniques in these three different types of conquest would be folly. Moreover, each age or period has its own problems. The solution of these does not lie in using the methods of yesterday. The solution consists in adjusting methods of yesterday to particular circumstances. His was in part the principle of expediency; and in a way he was thus a forerunner of Machiavelli.

Regulation put into complete force means the elimination of personal freedom. In fact Han Fei is credited with urging the restriction of thought, the limiting of speech, and even the prohibiting of all actions contrary to law. Again, the upshot of the matter is something akin to what occurs in totalitarian states.

Other founders of legalistic social thought were Shang Tang and Kuan-tsu. The former advocated that a strong legalistic state should engage in war and conquest. He favored an imperialist social order. Virtue, filial duty, morals, integrity are in his list of evils. Let the laws be made, and let everyone live up to them. Ethics in the personal sense is not needed. Reward lightly and punish heavily.

"Punishment produces force, force produces strength, strength produces awe, awe produces virtue."[15] The final arrival at a condition of virtue is the same as in the totalitarian state. High and low, rank and file, all should be treated alike for similar offenses. Shang Tang's goal was a

[14] *Loc. cit.*
[15] *Cf.* C. F. Lung, *op. cit.*, p. 131.

strong nation. Land and population are to be kept in balance. If your country is overpopulated, get more land. If
your country is but partly occupied, increase your population.

Earlier than Shang Tang was Kuan-tsu, or Kuan Chung.
He maintained the ethical viewpoint in his legalistic thinking. His attention centered in part on building a nationalism. He wished to make his country powerful. To the nation he assigned four corner stones, namely: rites, justice,
uprightness, and sense of shame. "Through rite people learn
not to be excessive. Through justice people learn not to be
aggressive. Through uprightness people learn not to conceal evil. And through the sense of shame people learn not
to associate with the socially undesirable." [16]

Kuan-tsu was something of a social psychologist, for he
pointed out that when the granaries of the people are full,
the people are easiest governed. Poverty leads to dissatisfaction, and dissatisfaction leads to rebellion.[17] Therefore, see
to it that all the people of your country are economically
prosperous and you can put any political theory into practice
that you wish.

Kuan-tsu advocated a system of community organization
so that a strong state might develop. "Efficiency" was his
watchword as a means of building a powerful nationalism.
Everyone is taught both to fight and to work.[18]

The social and personal philosophy of the Legalists has
been summed up by Marcel Granet in his *Chinese Civilization* in a threefold way: (1) man is naturally bad; (2) he
seeks pleasure and escape from pain; and (3) law, the guide
to all conduct, has its sources in an absolute state as represented by the ruler or emperor. Rules and regulations, thus,
were elaborately prescribed. They could be learned and
obeyed, and peace would exist in the land.

YANG AND YIN

The principle of Yang and Yin, of light and darkness, of
two similar symbols within a common circle, is basic to Chi-

---

[16] Quoted by C. F. Lung, *op. cit.*, p. 103, from *Kuan-tsu*, Chapter 29.
[17] *Ibid.*, p. 108.
[18] *Ibid.*, p. 118.

nese philosophy. Yang and Yin represent the two-in-one principle of all life and creation. Yang is active and Yin is passive. Alice T. Hobart, in the foreword to her novel, *Yang and Yin,* suggests that Yang is motion and Yin is repose ; one is energy and the other inertia ; one is light, the other is darkness ; one is spiritual and the other is material ; one is heaven and the other is earth. Yang and Yin are "forever opposed, forever united." Beneath all humanity is this striving and uniting, this disunity in unity. The underlying need of mankind is to maintain the harmony of Yang and Yin, and all will be well.

What has held China together during the centuries? Many factors, but apparently the emphasis is to be placed on a unified culture. Of the various culture elements that known as Confucianism is perhaps most important. No other term has received so wide a recognition. On the whole, Confucianism has been conservative. It has had a backward look — toward ancestors and the past. Stability amid turmoil has been the result.

Today the stage is being re-arranged. Change is in the saddle. At last the impact of Western science is being not only felt but heeded. China is "going modern" in politics, in economics, in military measures, in religion. One result is to discount Confucianism, if not to throw it overboard. New China considers Confucius' emphasis on the past, on aristocratic life, on *laissez faire* as being outmoded. She is changing her course. But what will take the place of the stabilizing role of Confucianism? What will be the spiritual cement that will hold four hundred million people together?

SUN YAT-SEN

One answer is found in the teachings of Sun Yat-sen. It is the philosophy of Sun Yat-sen, according to many, that will supplant Confucianism and that will keep the people united as they establish for the first time a nation in which the people themselves take part and assume responsibilities.

Sun Yat-sen, born in 1866, in a humble home near Canton, grew to manhood greatly influenced by the T'aiping Rebellion. He grasped its original essence, namely, the attempt to overthrow foreign domination as represented by the Manchus. He went further, and planned not only to overthrow the Manchus but to relieve China from foreign economic domination as represented by the Great Powers. He perceived that if the people of China were really to have a chance to develop they must eliminate all foreign domination, economic as well as political. Moreover, he reacted against the control of warlords, and saw only one way of salvation, namely, that the people of China must take an interest in governing themselves.

According to Dr. Leonard S. Hsu, the life of Sun Yat-sen was divided into four parts. The first extended from birth until he was nineteen and was marked by "growing up and getting revolutionary inspiration." The second covered the twenty years from the age of nineteen to thirty-nine. During this time he was engaged in "crudely organized revolutionary activities" and in attempts to formulate a program. During the third period, from the age of thirty-nine to fifty-three, Sun Yat-sen participated in revolutionary activities and in getting the new republic started. During the fourth period of six years extending to his death, he formulated and developed his thought about the "Three Principles" as a means of freeing China from her ills.[19]

Sun Yat-sen's thought was wrapped up in securing freedom for China, both within China, and from enemies without. According to his formula "the present spheres of influence can be abolished; the international commercial war can be done away with; the internecine capitalistic competition can be got rid of; and last, but not least, the class struggle between capital and labor can be avoided. Thus the root of war will be forever exterminated so far as China is concerned."[20] In these words Sun Yat-sen's basic desire for a peaceful development of China may be seen.

An excellent summary of twelve major factors that influenced Sun Yat-sen and that help to explain his social thought is given by Dr. Hsu. These factors are:

(1) The control of China by an alien race and the corruption of the Manchu regime; (2) the intervention in or invasion of

---

[19] Leonard S. Hsu, *Sun Yat-sen, His Ethical and Political Ideals*, p. 25.
[20] Sun Yat-sen, *The International Development of China.*

China by imperialistic powers; (3) the rise of the school of higher criticism in Chinese philosophy; (4) his peasant parentage and his early association with ex-T'aiping soldiers; (5) militarism in China; (6) the reform movement of 1897–1898; (7) the growth of nationalism and imperialism in the West and in Japan; (8) the establishment of republican government in the United States, in France, and in other countries; (9) the social democratic movements in the West; (10) his knowledge of Rousseau, Lincoln, and Marx, and his friendship with Lenin; (11) the student movement and other social movements in China since 1919; and (12) his foreign education and his long residence in foreign countries.[21]

THE THREE PRINCIPLES

Sun Yat-sen's social thought is bound up in the Three Principles. Into the San Min doctrine Sun Yat-sen put his reflections concerning the welfare of China, based first on extensive studies at home, and widespread contacts in the United States, England, France, Germany, and elsewhere, for he traveled around the globe twice. Not only did he know the history of his own country well, but he thought about it long and hard, particularly in the light of perspectives which he obtained while sojourning or moving about in Western countries. His social thought is limited largely to the development of a new social organization for his people. As a reformer he ranks high; as an administrator, low. His philosophy is not that of a scholar but of a person deeply concerned about the welfare of his people and country. There is nothing of the armchair in his social thought. It arose out of stimuli gained in moving to and fro in China and in the West.

While China has made no cult out of Sun Yat-senism, the name of Sun Yat-sen is honored today in China above every other name. Doubtless many leaders are doing lip-service to his name, as a means of furthering their own gain, yet behind and beneath all this the Three Principles represent China's major thought-pattern. The Three Principles are parallel in a way, suggests Sun Yat-sen, to Abraham Lincoln's threefold analysis of democracy, namely, *of* the people, *by* the people, and *for* the people. The first principle is that of

[21] *Ibid.*, pp. 36-37.

Nationalism, which is a government based on the loyalty of the people; the second is Democracy, which is a government carried on by the people themselves; and the third is Livelihood, by which government promotes comfort and happiness for the people.[22] Put in another way, the Three Principles mean: (1) the people are to have national loyalty; (2) the people are to govern; and (3) the people are to enjoy life. "The people must be able to govern themselves before they can enjoy the blessings of government." [23] Hence the second principle, namely, of Democracy, is made primary in importance.

NATIONALISM

In developing his concept of Min Ts'u, or Nationalism, Sun Yat-sen pointed out two extremes to be avoided. One is represented by China in the past; that is, a China in which the people have lived and moved in small, local groups, and have been content to leave the rulership of China largely to emperors and others remotely removed. The chief evil of this system has been that China has fallen a prey to militarists within her boundaries and to the imperialistic powers, or nations, of the world. Within, the people have suffered civil wars due to conflicts between military leaders. "China is suffering from militarists, and the greatest enemies of our country are our own militarists," who keep the country divided "and prolong civil war purely to satisfy their own ambitions." [24] From without, the country has suffered "economic exploitation by foreign imperialists." She has become a sub-colony not only "of one power, but a sub-colony of all the powers. China is the slave of ten or more masters." She has suffered not only from Chinese capitalists, "but even more so from foreign capitalists." [25]

The other extreme is known variously as cosmopolitanism or universalism. When China became interested in cosmopolitanism, she lost interest in nationalism, and fell a victim of her foes. Moreover, some people advocate cosmopolitanism in order to take advantage of China. The great

22 *Ibid.*, p. 108.
23 *Loc. cit.*
24 *Ibid.*, p. 326.
25 *Ibid.*, p. 22.

powers have urged cosmopolitanism upon small states in order to keep them small. "Their doctrine of cosmopolitanism is in fact the doctrine of imperialism in disguise." [26]

China needs to develop a strong nationalism in order to protect herself against three enemies: (1) the increase of foreign populations, which will eventually outnumber China with her stationary population; (2) political force of the diplomats of the other nations; and (3) the economic penetration of foreigners. [27]

Sun Yat-sen criticized Lao-tzu's description of a nation with no ruler and no law. Lao-tzu's state, where the people would live "in a state of nature," is an anarchistic utopia. But the Chinese people through their political experience "have found no use for anarchism." [28] Lao-tzu's kingdom of *Hua Hsu* will never do for China.

A serious difficulty facing China has been her lack of power of organization; but some way must be found to build up a national organization, or China is lost. It is necessary that the Chinese be made "conscious of the present crisis and of the danger to come if they do not develop a nationalism." After they become conscious of the dangers facing them because of a lack of national unity in a world of imperialists, the Chinese must proceed "to teach nationalism through family loyalty." By beginning with the clans and by organizing them into province-wide organizations, it will be possible to create a nation-wide organization. [29] Then, nationalism can be taught from families up through the clans, the province-organizations of clans, and the national grouping of province-organizations of clans.

Moreover, let this new nationalism be based on principles of peace in its attitudes toward the rest of the world. Do not let the fact that other nations are warlike and imperialistic set an example for China. "Our people are by nature peacelovers!" Let this spirit not only be preserved but developed "to its highest excellence." [30]

In his last will and testament Sun Yat-sen relates how he

[26] *Ibid.,* p. 221.
[27] *Ibid.,* pp. 213, 233.
[28] *Ibid.,* p. 106.
[29] *Ibid.,* p. 242.
[30] *Ibid.,* p. 252.

has served his people for forty years and then calls upon his followers to finish the tasks he has been unable to see brought to their fruition: "to awaken the masses of our people, and to join hands with those countries which are prepared to treat us as equals in our fight for the common cause of humanity." [31]

DEMOCRACY

Min Ch'uan, or the doctrine of Democracy, relates to the form and practice of the new Nationalism that is being developed in China. The state is recognized "as the most powerful of all social organizations." [32] It shall steer between freedom and autocracy. One leads to disintegration, the other to static consolidation. If liberty means to act without restraint, it is dangerous. The Chinese know the meaning of liberty, for they have had a great deal, having been allowed to live as they wished in their local communities. [33]

At this point the socio-political ideas of Jefferson and Hamilton are considered. Jefferson's idea that men are innately good and that government is a necessary evil is put over against Hamilton's belief that human beings are innately selfish and that "the rights of the masses should be limited and checked." [34] A middle ground is urged by Sun Yat-sen. Beware of mob rule on one hand, and of autocratic militarism on the other.

A government having five sets of powers is defined: executive, legislative, judicial, examining, and supervisory. The last two call for special comment. Sun Yat-sen, following custom in China, would have an elaborate examination system maintained and permit only "experts" to become candidates for office. In a democracy it is not possible for the people to know who is qualified for office and who is not. Sun Yat-sen advocated a system which he believed is vastly superior to that in the United States. He cited an instance where a well-trained man ran for office against a chauffeur,

[31] *Ibid.,* p. 43.
[32] *Ibid.,* p. 216.
[33] *Ibid.,* pp. 291 ff.
[34] *Ibid.,* p. 321.

and the latter won because of his greater ability to appeal to the feelings of the people.[35]

The fifth power is that of impeachment, which is to rest in a separate group of people. In this way legislators or others will not be subjected to special influences.

To offset the five sets of governmental powers, the people are to be guaranteed four rights, namely, suffrage, initiative, referendum, and recall. Thus, the defects in the government can be remedied from time to time.

Sun Yat-sen distinguished at length between power and ability, that is, between "ch'uan" and "neng." He would have "the people control the political power" and the government assume the political responsibility through its corps of experts. The two, the power and the administrative ability, are to be kept separate.[36]

The democratic state is the last of four evolutionary stages of social control. The first or primeval period may be called "the stage of great wilderness." It was the time when man contended with animals for supremacy. The second stage, or that of theocracy, was the age when the gods ruled man. Man fought with natural forces. This grew into the stage of monocracy, or the rulership by autocrats, when nations fought with nations. Its evils were many and it was followed by democracy, which is to govern by principles of peaceful cooperation, and in which the masses are deeply interested in public affairs or the welfare of all.[37]

Democracy is to be achieved by three stages. First comes military dictatorship, as a prelude to a period of political tutelage or training. Finally, when the people are educated for it, constitutional government will be inaugurated.[38]

The problem of democracy involves the inequality of persons by birth. This inequality has usually been promoted by autocratic social and political systems. As a result conditions have gone from bad to worse and revolutions have broken out. Sun Yat-sen's theory of revolution is thought-

[35] Ibid., p. 111.
[36] Ibid., pp. 342, 360, 362, 376.
[37] Ibid., p. 263.
[38] Ibid., p. 139.

provoking. He held that revolutions break forth "for the purpose of abolishing inequalities among men." [39]

Sun Yat-sen criticizes Rousseau. Freedom and equality are not innate rights. Neither has man entered into any contract with his superiors to give them the innate rights that man does not have.

There are three classes of people : (1) The geniuses are the inventors and creators. (2) The intelligent followers are the spreaders of new ideas through the process of adoption. (3) Then there are the "unthinkable majority," who blindly act or react to the ideas of the geniuses. These three are inventors, propagators, and practicians. Moreover, ethically there are two classes: the selfish, who often aim at raiding others' enjoyment for their own good,[40] and the unselfish, who are sincerely interested in the welfare of others.

Since the rights of the people are not inborn but created, it is important to train even the "unthinking majority" in the use of certain rights of liberty and democracy. Everyone is entitled to free and equal opportunity "to develop his own natural endowment." All should have opportunity to develop the best qualities in them without hindrance. Moreover, "the moral consciousness of all should be equalized, and all be made to work for the same moral ideals." [41]

Sun Yat-sen disagrees with Mencius' doctrine that "the mental workers govern and the manual workers are governed." He points out that in human society it is possible to invent ways and means to overcome this class division.

LIVELIHOOD

The doctrine of the People's Livelihood, or of *Min Sheng,* is designed to enrich the social existence of the masses and to raise their level of activity and thought. Especially do the masses suffer during a period of industrialization, or when a change from a rural to an industrial economy is taking place. The first step in social reconstruction is "to promote the economic well-being of the people."

[39] *Ibid.,* p. 301.
[40] *Ibid.,* p. 317.
[41] *Ibid.,* pp. 301, 310, 317, 352.

Sun Yat-sen discussed the teachings of Karl Marx at length. He dissented from Marx's materialistic interpretation of history on the ground that human history cannot be explained chiefly by changes in the physical environment. He held that the problem of livelihood is the central factor in social progress.[42] It is the level of subsistence which determines one's economic and social ideas.

Sun Yat-sen minimized the class struggle idea. Serious as may be the fact that many capitalists take by far the larger share of the profits, while labor receives a very insignificant portion, and while "unearned increment" robs the poor and enriches the rich, class struggle is a social disease and not an underlying cause. The basic cause of misery is found in the fact that a social group lacks the means of livelihood and resolves to use abnormal means of obtaining its livelihood. The problems of livelihood and of obtaining the means of livelihood are basic. They lead to a socially pathological condition or to class struggle.

Marx is also mistaken in his doctrine of "surplus value" and in his contention that capitalists obtain this surplus value by robbery from labor. Sun Yat-sen held that surplus value is created by everyone "who is doing useful work, whether he is a producer or a consumer." The class conflict between labor and capital is a misnomer. The real conflict is between society as a whole, producers and consumers together, and "the class of selfish capitalists."[43] Sun Yat-sen arrives at the conclusion that neither capitalism nor communism of the Russian type is suited for China, with her own special set of conditions.

But something must be done for the workers, or else they will start revolutions. When the workers had little education they did not recognize "the tyranny that the capitalists imposed on them" and that they were being "treated as commodities rather than as human beings." When the workers became educated and "wise," they organized. They used the passive policy of non-co-operation, or the strike. They went too far and revolted against their intellectual

[42] *Ibid.,* p. 401.
[43] *Ibid.,* p. 407.

guides and became the enemies of law and order. They were exploited by some of their own self-centered leaders. Hence a governmental program is needed.

Two programs are outlined in behalf of the livelihood of the people: one of giving the masses adequate opportunities for land ownership; the other of the regulation of capital, for "the capitalists are becoming unbearably autocratic toward the common people."

Land speculation, which is "a very popular gambling game in China," is to be met by a system of taxation and purchase. The large landowner is to be asked to set a value on his holdings. He will be taxed according to this, and his land may be purchased at any time by the government at the price he has set. Reasonable figures thus will be determined by the owner himself. "Any increment to the value of the land shall go to the public." [44] Thus increment will come to the community and ownership will tend toward a wider and needed distribution. This increasing distribution of land will promote livelihood and decrease the dangers of revolution.

China needs the development of national capital as well as the regulation of private capitalists. State industries are needed. Capital concentrated in private hands is a source of misery to the masses, but capital controlled by a wise government will be a "a source of blessing to all the people."

A good government will provide a normal development of the livelihood of the people. A lack of such development is abnormal. Evils follow in its train, such as: (1) growth of culture is checked; (2) reform of economic organization is prevented; (3) moral degeneration of individuals occurs; (4) social inequality is continued; (5) labor is oppressed; and (6) class struggle is encouraged.

In summary of the social thought of Sun Yat-sen, it may be said that while many of his statements lack polish, while many do not have depth, and while contradictions occur, yet his social ideas are: (1) novel for China, being based on Western experience; (2) designed to meet the Chinese situation and need; (3) more practical than theoretical, and yet

[44] *Ibid.*, p. 433.

idealistic; (4) evolutionary rather than revolutionary; and (5) representative of a new departure for a very ancient culture.

Modern sociological thought has developed considerably in China since 1920. Chinese sociologists for the most part have been trained in the United States and represent the points of view that have been developed in the West. A few of the texts in sociology written in the United States have been translated into Chinese and used in Chinese universities. A small number of important monographic studies have been made in China, chiefly by Chinese investigators. As a rule these are valuable examples of Chinese social research. Survey and local studies have been developing in China since about 1925. A number of articles dealing with social conditions and movements in China have appeared in journals published there, in both the Chinese and the English languages. Closely related has been the growth of sociological periodicals. The Chinese Sociological Society which was organized at Shanghai in 1930 testifies to the growth of Chinese sociology.[45]

The growth of sociological courses in Chinese universities has been extensive since about 1920, with the institutions in Shanghai, Peiping, Nanking, and Canton having led in the new movement. Yenching University, Peiping, at one time offered the largest number of courses in sociology.

The emphasis on social welfare has been closely tied up with the growth of sociology. In fact modern Chinese sociology has tended toward concrete studies of social conditions. Chinese sociologists have taken part in public welfare activities of many kinds, thus insuring to sociology a theory based on experience.

[45] Leonard S. Hsu, "The Sociological Movement in China," *Pacific Affairs*, 4:283-307.

GROUP DISCUSSION TOPICS

1. Reasons for the early development of Chinese social thought.
2. Origins of Lao-tzu's "back to nature" ideas.
3. Taoism as a social concept.
4. Backgrounds and early training of Confucius.
5. The filial doctrines of Confucius.
6. The backward look of Confucianism.
7. Confucius' "gentlemen."
8. Confucius as a student of human nature.
9. Confucius' doctrine of the "hsien."
10. Relation of the social thought of Mencius to that of Confucius.
11. An evaluation of the "personal evils" of Mencius.
12. Origins of Mo Ti's brotherhood-of-man doctrine.
13. The Universal Good according to Mo Ti.
14. Mo Ti's concept of war.
15. Origins of Legalist doctrines.
16. Han Fei's reasons for deifying law.
17. Comparison of social thought of Han Fei, Kuan-tsu and Shang Tang.
18. Comparison of the Legalists' doctrine and modern Fascist ideas.
19. Social thought in China from Han Fei to Sun Yat-sen.
20. Origins of the social thought of Sun Yat-sen.
21. Evaluation of Sun Yat-sen's concept of "nationalism."
22. Evaluation of Sun Yat-sen's concept of "democracy."
23. Evaluation of Sun Yat-sen's concept of "livelihood."
24. The rise of sociology in China.

READINGS

Becker, Howard, and Harry E. Barnes, *Social Thought from Lore to Science* (Washington : Harren Press 1952), Vol. I, Ch. 2.

Buck, Pearl, *House of Earth* (New York: John Day 1936).

Chambliss, Rollin, *Social Thought* (New York: The Dryden Press 1954), Ch. 4.

Chen, Theodore H. E., and Wen-hui Chen, "Attitudes toward Parents in China," *Sociology and Social Research,* 43:175-82.

Clark, Grover, *The Great Wall Crumbles* (New York: The Macmillan Company 1935).

Ethics of Confucius, comments by M. M. Dawson (New York: G. P. Putnam's Sons 1915).

Granet, Marcel, *Chinese Civilization* (New York: A. A. Knopf 1930).

Hsu, Leonard S., *Sun Yat-sen, His Political and Social Ideals* (Los Angeles: University of Southern California Press 1933).

———, "Sociological Training in China," *Sociology and Social Research*, 14:211-20.

———, "The Sociological Movement in China," *Pacific Affairs*, 4:283-307.

LaPiere, Richard, *Son of Han* (New York: Harper & Brothers 1937).

Latourette, Kenneth S., *The Chinese, Their History and Culture* (New York: The Macmillan Company 1934).

Legge, James, *The Four Books* (Confucian Analects, The Great Learning, The Doctrine of the Mean, The Works of Mencius) (Shanghai: Shanghai Book Company 1930).

Lin Yutang, *My Country and My People* (New York: John Day 1935).

———, *The Wisdom of China and India* (New York: Modern Library 1955).

Linebarger, Paul M., *Sun Yat-sen and the Chinese Republic* (New York: Century Company 1925).

Lung, Chieng Fu, "The Evolution of Chinese Social Thought," (unpublished doctoral dissertation, University of Southern California, Los Angeles, 1935).

Mei, Yi-Pao, *The Ethical and Political Works of Motse* (London: Probsthain 1929).

Northrop, F. S. C., *The Meeting of East and West* (New York: The Macmillan Company 1946), Ch. XI.

Pratt, Helen, *China and Her Unfinished Revolution* (New York: American Council, Institute of Pacific Relations 1937).

Restavich, H. B., *Sun Yat-sen, Liberator of China* (New Haven: Yale University Press 1931).

Rudd, Herbert F., *Chinese Social Origins* (Chicago: University of Chicago Press 1928).

Saunders, Kenneth, *The Ideals of East and West* (New York: The Macmillan Company 1934), Ch. II.

Sun Yat-sen, *San Min Chu I, The Three Principles of People* (Shanghai: China Committee, Institute of Pacific Relations 1927).

———, *The International Development of China* (New York: G. P. Putnam's Sons 1922).

T'ang Leang-Li, *The New Social Order in China* (Shanghai: China United Press 1936).

Wang, Gung-hsing, *The Chinese Mind* (New York: John Day Company 1946).

CHAPTER VI

JAPANESE SOCIAL THOUGHT

The origins of Japanese social thought are found in early mythology and they extend to modern political and economic life. With the emperor tracing his ancestry back to the Sun Goddess, Amaterasu, we find a central figure around which the thought of the Japanese people has revolved from legendary days. This divine basis of the Imperial House of Japan, which reaches back through 124 generations to a date alleged to have been 660 B.C., is very significant, for it furnishes throughout Japanese life a sacred axis around which the life and thought, even the social thought of the people, have persistently evolved.

The belief in the divine nature of the emperor has not only made his name sacred but has given him tremendous power over the thinking of his people and made his edicts widely respected. Americans often cannot understand why the Japanese objected so strenuously when an American newspaper once caricatured their emperor. But to the Japanese the emperor holds the same relation as do the Stars and Stripes to the American people. Let a Japanese cartoonist drag the American flag in the mire of caricature, and protests would go up all over the United States. The emperor is viewed as being the essence of all that is good for the Japanese nation.

RELIGIOUS ORIGINS

Another early origin of Japanese social thought is found in religion. Shintoism was not only the earliest religion of the Japanese, but it has maintained itself during the centuries, and today despite its many divisions it stands out prominently. As one writer has suggested: "If you find a hydro-electric plant at the bottom of a hill, at the top will be a Shinto shrine, and not only that, but at the shrine you will find people worshipping."

Amaterasu is not only a lineal ancestor of the ruling house but she is also a founder of the Shinto faith. Religion and the crown are thus one in origins. To maintain one is to maintain the other. Moreover, Shintoism has maintained a worship not only of nature but also of ancestors. Again its long life and current recognition have a foundation in basic sentiments.

Shintoism's emphasis on ancestor worship has meant that each generation is tied up closely not only with yesterday's generation but with the generations of twenty centuries ago. Social thought thus is bound up in perpendicular bundles of loyalty extending back through the centuries. Since all these threads of filial loyalty are themselves oriented around the emperor, the thinking of the people thus has two age-old foci, ancestors and emperor, or family and state. Individuals today, ancestors, emperor, religion, state, all are parts of one big family relationship.

When Buddhism was introduced into Japan in the sixth century A.D., Shintoism accepted it as a form of inner essence. Religion took on a "double aspect" quality. Buddhism's spirit of resignation, obedience, meekness was interpreted to represent the inner character of religion and to be complementary to the outer or objective evidence as found in the Shinto gods. Although Buddhism has developed into many sects and has at times degenerated, yet its presence has not created any serious conflict. Its spiritual elements of resignation and obedience have been added to the social thought of the Japanese and led large numbers to become more devoted than ever to ancestors, emperor, religion, and state.

The teachings of Emperor Monmu in the eighth century A.D. may be noticed. One emphasis is upon "etiquette." There can be no peaceful development of a people "without etiquette among the king and his subjects, parents and their children, brother and sister, and so on down the line." [1] By etiquette the emperor of course meant much more than do Americans today. Etiquette was more than forms or

[1] Tasaku Miura, *Nippon Riuri Gakushi*, p. 27. Quoted by Y. Sugimachi, in his master's thesis, University of Southern California 1937, "The Social Thought of Ancient Japan," p. 28.

manners; it included deference and respect with appropriate accompaniments in behavior.

Moreover, the emperor issued the edict: "Restrain anger." An old folksong runs: "When my angry passions arise, I wish there to be a stream in the garden, so I may lave my heart in water pure." [2] It will be noted again that these teachings fit into the Buddhist doctrines of obedience to the familial and political doctrines. In addition there is the emphasis on self-control. Feelings are to be subordinated along with the suppression of self-centered desire. Another link thus is added to the chain of Japanese unity through personal obedience to family and state.

Patriarchal thought has prevailed throughout the centuries in Japan (barring a current change among a few in the cities) in the family. It has been a thorough-going patriarchalism too. The parents have had complete power over the children, and the father or eldest son (in case the father is not living) over all. Even in current years suffrage has been withheld from women because, as one Japanese leader explained to the writer: "The women aren't ready for it."

Moreover, large families and especially sons have been and are considered desirable. The reason is twofold: to strengthen the family and to insure parents that the family line will be kept intact; and also to strengthen the state, for numbers are considered a measure of effectiveness. In a closely-knit family system, production of goods or the raising of a food supply has depended in Japan upon having a large number of working units. Again, we see how the social concept of unity upon which Japan is founded and moves is furthered by the ideas concerning the family.

The ideas concerning property are also vital. The emperor in a way virtually owns all. A strong central system of government not only has vast properties of its own, but, because of its omnipotent rights of control, it virtually owns the property of the people. It was a totalitarian type of ownership which was expressed in Japan centuries before Italy and Germany evolved their Fascist systems. In the re-

[2] Iwao Matsuhara, *Minyo Folk Song of Japan*, p. 191. Quoted by Y. Sugimachi, *op. cit.*, p. 29.

formation of the *Taika* in the seventh century the "land was all confiscated by the central government, and the people became direct subjects or citizens of the emperor." Land was then given out to the people in small lots to be held as long as farmed or until the holder died. "The registration was renewed every sixth year."[3] The Mexican system, represented by the *Ejida* and the plan of distributing communal land for use, thus has a semi-counterpart in Japan twelve or more centuries ago.

Feudalism and the samurai and powerful financial groups have developed in Japan alongside of a rural peasantry of tenant-farmers, and of owner-farmers who are slaves to constant indebtedness. Household industry has been maintained and the factory system has only recently begun to develop. Paternalism in industry has permitted the rise of powerful business houses. Capitalistic thought has become intrenched in government, and communistic thought has been rigidly suppressed. It is dangerous to express "dangerous thoughts," or thought about the overthrow of the present economic system in Japan.

Japan has deified "regulation" until individual freedom has been unduly hampered. When nearly everything in life is subject to "regulations," the people have little freedom of thought on economic and political matters. As far back as A.D. 701 the Suiko Code was promulgated. Altogether it contains some thirty sections and 1260 articles of a regulatory nature. These relate to the protection of the imperial family, to rules for the military and civil officials, to criminal procedure and methods of punishment, to religious observances, to family registration, to marriage regulation, and to the building of houses, to land usages and the breeding of animals, to taxation, to school administration. These all stand for efficiency and scientific management that began to develop over a thousand years ago. They also mean that individual freedom is hampered. On these bases it has been said that the Japanese have become convention-minded and custom-minded. They think not in terms of the individual but habitually in terms of the conventions and customs which have been handed down from family to family.

[3] Y. Sukimachi, *op. cit.*, p. 58.

During the Tokugawa Shogunate (1603–1867), when Japan was closed to the outside world, the country experienced one very important gain, viewed nationally. As an offset to the loss of stimulation from outside contacts, the country developed a remarkable degree of integration and unity. The self-segregation period was used for unifying purposes. One of the elements in this process was the fact that every family in Japan was officially joined to Buddhism, giving everyone a kind of sacred relationship to everyone else and all to the emperor as the head of Shintoism. However, this result was brought about by the use of force and dictatorial action.

ATTITUDES TOWARD LABOR

Attitudes toward labor in Japan have been paternalistic. No strong labor consciousness has developed. A number of factors account for the current attitudes regarding labor.

(1) Hand industry still obtains in Japan. Handicraft activities are carried on largely in homes, where labor is employed extensively in small units. Employer and employees work together, and as in American pre-factory days, they tend to understand each other's problems.

It is only when the factory system develops and thousands of workers labor together that they lose their employer's point of view. The industrialization of Japan that is now taking place means that employer and employee will drift apart more and more and that a greater social consciousness among laborers will develop unless offset by other tendencies. However, small industries are being encouraged to remain small, and thus a large-scale labor movement is being checked.

(2) The average laborer is so much a part of the family organization of life that he does not have much time for or interest in unionization. If he breaks loose from the family organization that connects him not only with his own immediate family, but with family after family extending back through generations, he will doubtless learn to think more extensively in labor union concepts.

(3) National loyalty is so strong that it diverts the laborer's attention from the labor union. When the Japanese goes

to work in the morning it is said that he thinks first of the way in which his work will help his nation in building it up and in increasing its strength, and then of the way that his labor will help himself. This attitude may be contrasted with the individualistic emphasis in the United States which leads many Americans to think chiefly of the day's work in terms of getting ahead. Only secondarily or not at all do many Americans think of their activities as contributing to the well-being of the nation.

(4) The Japanese government is more or less unfavorable to the growth of labor unions. Its opposition keeps large numbers of workers from joining the unions. The government's policy has unintentionally, but to a notable degree, limited the labor union movement to the more courageous and at the same time to the more radical workers. The latter dare to oppose the government. In turn, the government views them with increasing alarm. They are likely to be charged with harboring "dangerous thoughts." An observer gains the impression that there is a great deal of unrest and radicalism in Japan, but that these forces have been driven underground.

Japanese labor is in the bicycle stage. It has given up the rickshaw. The man-power pattern of transportation is still extensive. The number of workers who pull heavy loads on carts or other vehicles is still large, but more and more in the cities you see the laborer adopting the bicycle pattern. Sometimes he attaches a small trailer to his bicycle in order to haul a large load. He is beginning to acquire trucks but is still far removed from the automobile stage of travel. These facts concerning the Japanese laborer explain his social thinking, which is in an elemental stage. It is controlled largely by the integrated socio-political and economic universe of which he is a functioning unit.

The number of women and children in industry is on the increase. Paternalistic attitudes prevail and the apprentice system persists. Young and unmarried women often live in dormitories provided by the factory owners. Conditions are being improved slowly. The economic pressure upon many families, notably rural, is so great that many daughters are sent to the cities to earn money by being employed as geisha girls and as mistresses. The outlook for many of these young women is depressing. This abject condition is accepted blindly by the girls, and condoned by their elders on the ground of necessity.

The farm laborer is in a dilemma. His wages are exceedingly low, but his wants however are few and simple. Rents and interest rates are so high that he seems condemned to be a "hired hand" or a tenant for life. Like farm laborers elsewhere he does not organize. The chief ray of light for him today comes from the co-operatives that have been developing extensively in rural Japan. The co-operatives are an economic boon and receive government approval and financial aid. Dr. Toyohiko Kagawa's plan, which analyzes life into seven sets of values and which provides seven kinds of co-operatives, retains an emphasis on personal initiative and profits, but the latter are distributed in the form of savings to all who participate.

The thought life of the masses of the people of Japan is much simpler than that of similar persons in the United States. Simplicity is a universal trait among Japan's millions. They are not only satisfied with less, but because of their social philosophy probably are happier with less than are Americans who live on higher economic levels.

In the *Tanomoshi* the Japanese have put a unique concept of co-operation into effect. Tanomoshiko as used in Western Japan comes from "tanomui" which means "dependable." The procedure seems to have originated in pooling contributions to a given fund and drawing lots to see who might go on pilgrimages to the shrines and temples. During the early part of the Tokugawa Period Tanomoshi took on a definite economic meaning. A number of persons would contribute small amounts monthly toward paying for one item of a needed article each month. Instead of drawing by lot to see which member of the "ko," or association of persons, might obtain the particular article that is purchased by the ko month by month, the procedure has developed of giving the purchased article each month to the one who offers to pay the highest interest.

Special emphasis is placed on social responsibility. If Mr. A obtains the desired article the first month, he continues to pay for the stipulated period. If anyone runs away and fails to fulfill his agreement, "all friendship bonds are broken and the individual becomes an outcast from the group thereafter." [4] He is branded as not worthy of human association.

The development of sociological thought in Japan has lagged. German and French models have been followed, rather than English and American.[5] Hence Japanese sociology is little known to readers in the English language. Early Japanese sociology was formal, abstract, and philosophical. Dr. Yasuma Takata of Kyoto Imperial University was one of the first to break away from a formal concept of sociology. About 1920, he developed a theory of social groups in terms of their formation, causes, and effects, and "built upon the two complementary principles of aggregation and separation." [6]

Since 1925, Japanese sociology has shifted away from its origins in Comte and German philosophy and has taken on something of a distinctive color growing out of studies of social problems in Japan. For example, Professor Junichiro Matsumoto of Hosei University, Tokyo, has attempted to combine formal sociology with cultural sociology and with concrete research. The cultural sociology follows Durkheim somewhat, while the research emphases have followed American methods and have dealt with studies of the family, and of urban conditions. The Japanese Sociological Society, organized in 1925, has tended to build on distinctive studies of Japanese life.

In an analysis of "the fundamental conception of Buddhist Sociology," Ken Assano has outlined a generalizing science in which French sociological thought predominates. Buddhist sociology is more of a promise than a realization. It treats of (1) Buddhism and family phenomena, (2) Buddhism and moral phenomena, (3) Buddhism and juridical phenomena, (4) Buddhism and political phenomena, (5) Buddhism and economic phenomena, (6) Buddhism and

---

[4] Ruth N. Masuda, "The Japanese 'Tanomoshi,'" *Social Process in Hawaii*, pp. 16-19.

[5] Jesse F. Steiner, "The Development and Present Status of Sociology in Japanese Universities," *American Journal of Sociology*, 41:707-722.

[6] *Ibid.*, p. 713.

esthetic phenomena, and (7) Buddhism and linguistic, scientific, and educational phenomena.[7] The treatment is of an elementary, descriptive nature, deserving mention here, but not a presentation. It assumes a set of philosophical beliefs, and interprets life in terms of these beliefs. It cannot lay claim to being scientific.

A recent summary by J. Matsumoto and other sociological writers shows that general sociology patterned after European thought has developed further in Japan than has sociology as a science. Next in emphasis are studies of the family, of rural life, and of population problems. Many fields have been neglected, such as folk and class, the city, socio-political problems, and socio-religious questions.[8]

A current presentation of leading sociological books shows that Japanese writers are still in the stage of asking what is sociology and what are its chief centers of attention.[9] They are still utilizing European sociological studies and are not closely in touch with American sociology. However, they are making progress in research methods. For example, T. Toda classifies social research into (1) "total," or census and population studies of a whole country, (2) "partial," or studies of phases of culture or of community life, and (3) "individual," or examination of personal growth and development.[10]

In final review, it may be said that Japanese sociologists have given promise of making original contributions of scientific worth. Unfortunately, war conditions and totalitarian influences have been inimical to sociological thinking.

[7] Ken Assano, *The Fundamental Conception of Buddhist Sociology.*
[8] *Cf.* Earle Eubank, "Sociology, Past and Present, in Japan," *Sociology and Social Research*, XXII:347-356.
[9] Ken Imai and Earle Eubank, "Japanese Sociology: An Outline and Summary," *Sociology and Social Research*, XXIII:568-577.
[10] *Ibid.*, p. 575.

GROUP DISCUSSION TOPICS

1. Reasons for the slowness of development of Japanese social thought.
2. The central concept in Japanese social and political life.
3. The concept of "etiquette."
4. The concept of Tanomoshi.
5. Social effects of Shinto.
6. Social implications of Buddhism in Japan.
7. Slowness of changes in social attitudes of labor.
8. The origins of Japanese sociology.
9. Handicaps of sociology.
10. Fascist social thought in Japan.
11. Effect of war conditions on sociology in Japan.

READINGS

Assano, Ken, *The Fundamental Conception of Buddhist Sociology* (Tokyo : Kanda, Hitotsubashi 1936).

Barnes, Harry E., and Howard Becker, *Social Thought from Lore to Science* (Boston : D. C. Heath and Company 1938), pp. 1156-1174.

Becker, Howard, "Sociology in Japan," *American Sociological Review,* 1:455-474.

Benedict, Ruth, *The Chrysanthemum and the Sword* (Boston : Houghton Mifflin Company 1946).

Eubank, Earle, "Sociology, Past and Present, in Japan," *Sociology and Social Research,* 22:347-357.

Imai, Ken and Earle Eubank, "Japanese Sociology : An Outline and Summary," *Sociology and Social Research:* 23: 568-577.

Imori, R., *Rural Sociology* (Tokyo : Meguro Book Company 1929, in Japanese).

Masuda, Ruth N., "The Japanese 'Tanomoshi,'" *Social Process in Hawaii* (Honolulu : University of Hawaii 1937).

Matsumoto, J., *Japanese Sociology* (Tokyo : Jicho Company 1937, in Japanese).

———, *The Principles of Sociology* (Tokyo : Jicho Company 1937, in Japanese).

———, editor, *Sociology, Past and Present, in Japan* (Tokyo : Sansyusya Press 1937, in English).

Maurette, Fernand, *Social Aspects of Industrial Development in Japan* (London : King and Son 1934).

———, "Trends of Thought in Present Japan," *Open Court,* 47: 181-196.

Nitobe, Inazo O., *Japan* (New York : Charles Scribner's Sons 1931).

Robertson-Scott, J. W., *The Foundations of Japan* (New York : Appleton and Company 1922).

Pratt, Helen, *Japan, Where Ancient Loyalties Survive* (New York : American Council, Institute of Pacific Relations 1937).

Saunders, Kenneth, *The Ideals of East and West* (New York : The Macmillan Company 1934), Ch. III.

Sansom, G. B., *Japan, A Short Cultural History* (New York : Century Company 1931).

Shimmei, Seido, *The Essentials of Sociology* (Tokyo : Kobundo 1935, in Japanese).

Steiner, Jesse F., "The Development and Present Status of Sociology in Japanese Universities," *American Journal of Sociology*, 41:707-722.

Sugimachi, Y., "The Social Thought of Ancient Japan" (unpublished master's thesis, University of Southern California, Los Angeles 1937).

Toda, T., *Social Research* (Tokyo : Jichocho 1933, in Japanese).

CHAPTER VII

SOCIAL THOUGHT OF THE HEBREWS

Ancient Egyptian, Babylonian and Assyrian, East Indian, and Persian records disclose a set of elemental and yet more or less passive social backgrounds against which the social ideals of the Hebrew prophets shine forth like stars of the first magnitude. The Pentateuch and the writings of the Hebrew wise men are rich in gleams of a social spirit, while the Hebrew prophets, notably Amos, Hosea, Isaiah, and Jeremiah, uttered flaming indictments of social evils.

If we go back as far as the third or fourth century B.C., we find three great sets of social thought, namely, the Chinese, the Hebrew, and the Greek. The Chinese and the Greek social thought leans toward the intellectual side of life, while the Hebrew expresses the feelings and sympathies born of conflict. Only the Chinese philosopher Mo Ti may be compared with the Hebrew spokesmen. His ideas, however, are broader in scope than those of the Hebrew writers, approximating the broad sweep of the early Christian doctrines of universal love.

The Hebrews left a series of historical documents, covering several centuries and revealing a specific evolution in social concepts. They expressed the fundamentals from which Christian social thought developed, and from which much of the ethical and social thinking of Western civilization on its practical side has evolved.

ORIGINS OF SOCIAL THOUGHT

The social thought of the Hebrews was born of group suffering. Through the mists of the earliest Hebrew traditions we discern that conflicts occurred in the Euphrates Valley which sent Abraham out on his perilous journey toward unknown and hostile Canaan. The gaunt specter, famine, brought distress to the household of the domestic-loving Abraham and drove him on to Egypt where he sojourned for a time. Abram, exalted father, or Abraham, father of a multitude, became the founder, in a sense, of three world religions, for to him Judaism, Christianity, and Mohammedanism trace their origins.

Throughout the years of migration, exile, and suffering, Abraham maintained his religious faith and belief. By means of his simple religion he was able to interpret sanely the troubles and conflicts of life. Out of suffering interpreted religiously, Abraham developed a remarkably well-balanced and social personality. From this beginning, Hebrew social thought evolved. Ultimately, Israel created social concepts which have won for her the distinction of being "the leading social teacher of the human race." [1]

As a social entity the Hebrews were the result of "a titanic social struggle"; they arose out of an industrial crisis. The scene was laid in Egypt. The descendants of Jacob were working long hours with little pay, as slaves, and under harsh social conditions. One of their number, more favored than the rest by heredity and environment, saw a Hebrew workman being beaten by an Egyptian "boss." The favored one, Moses, felt the surging passions of social injustice rising within his breast — and he slew the boss. By an act of violence in the impassioned days of youth, Moses became "a social agitator"; by years of patient service of his people in the name of Jehovah, he became one of the world's great social seers.

Rameses II was "an unprincipled captain of industry." He was haughty, hard-hearted, and without social conscience. Moses was sympathetic, socially sensitive, and keenly religious. Rameses II was a leading representative of an ancient aristocracy; Moses was one of the first great exponents of an incipient democracy, and one of the first men in history "with a well-developed social consciousness."

According to the Exodus record, Moses, as the murderer of an Egyptian boss, felt no qualms of conscience, but he did fear the mighty Pharaoh. At that time it was a minor matter to kill a slave; but to have killed a boss was vastly different. The slave represented weakness; the boss was the official representative of political and financial power. Consequently,

[1] Charles F. Kent, *The Social Teachings of the Prophets and Jesus*, p. 4.

Moses fled from the country. In Egypt he was helpless, and in danger of losing his life. He fled to Midian.

In Midian Moses pondered over the economic and social injustices to which his people were being subjected. He communed with God, from whom he received the motive power to correct a gigantic social wrong. His vision of Jehovah gave him the conviction that Jehovah is a God of justice and mercy who understands social and industrial evils and sympathizes with the socially-defeated classes. Moses reports this remarkable social message from Jehovah:

"I have surely seen the affliction of my people that are in Egypt, and have heard their cry of anguish because of their taskmasters, and I am come down to deliver them out of the power of the Egyptians." [2]

In other words, against the union of great wealth and political power in the hands of an unjust man, God revolted, and God said to Moses: "Rescue this Israelitish people from the heels of autocracy." Moses conceived of Jehovah as a God who is "full of sympathy for the afflicted and dependent, and ever eager to champion their cause against cruel oppression." Moses' conception of Jehovah as a socially-spirited God is unique for that day in human history. God is described as a lover of justice and even a lover of mankind. When God speaks, it is usually in terms of social sympathy. The first social teachings of the Old Testament, considered chronologically, are those against social and industrial oppression.

A momentous conflict ensued. Fired by the promises and presence and power of Jehovah, Moses journeyed back to Egypt. He proceeded to organize the first labor strike known to mankind. Thereupon, the angry Pharaoh commanded the workers to make bricks without straw. And when the workers cried out against the impositions and burdens, the agents of "the first great captains of industry" taunted the workers and cried at them: "Ye are idle, ye are idle." But God and Moses won against the hosts of autocracy and plutocracy. The workers were freed.

Out of these struggles the Hebrew nation took form. Group loyalty, or patriotism, became a conscious Hebrew concept. The idea of kinship was supplemented by an appreciation of

[2] *Exodus*, 3:7, 8.

the meaning of national life. Furthermore, a sense of social and economic justice received a clear-cut and positive human expression and divine approval. For the first time the social problem was defined.

The major social chord which the Hebrew prophets kept vibrating was justice. Some of the recurring interpretations of the needs of the hour were: Let justice roll down like waters. Rulers shall govern in justice. Hear, I pray you, ye heads of Israel, is it not for you to know justice?

The Hebrew word for the English "justice" is *mishpat*. It is used in various senses, such as: justice, order, law, right, legal right. Amos wanted *mishpat* established in the land. Micah asserted that Jehovah requires the individual to do *mishpat,* and to love kindness, and to walk humbly with his God. Isaiah urged the people to do well and to seek *mishpat;* he pronounced woe upon those who turned aside the needy from *mishpat;* he declared Jehovah to be a God of *mishpat.* Jeremiah made plain that Jehovah exercises mercy and *mishpat* among the people.

Amos protested vigorously against special class privileges. He denounced the wealthy classes because of their social arrogance and economic injustice. In describing them he points out a fundamental principle of social revolution. By their repression of those who are protesting, they "are heaping up violence"; that is, autocratic repression will never right injustice, but will foster ultimate revolution. Amos charged the rulers and all persons in positions of social power with the primary obligation of seeing that the poor and the outcast are protected from exploitation. What satire in a day when rulers were noted for their exploitation of the weak social classes!

A special responsibility rests upon judges. Amos severely arraigned all who turn judgment to wormwood and cast righteousness to the ground. Anathemas were heaped upon the takers of bribes, especially if they sit in places of public authority and wear the robes of law and patriotism. Hot denunciation fell also upon the private doer of injustice; upon the merchant who makes smaller the measure and perverts the false balances; upon all who trample in any way upon the needy, who trample on the head of the poor, who sell the righteous for silver, who turn aside the way of the humble.[3] The concept of justice was vividly defined by Amos. Moreover, the shepherd-prophet of Tekoa had the courage and ability to make the concept clear to all who would listen to him. Amos spoke for justice on the throne, on the judge's bench, in the activities of the wealthy, in the transactions of merchants, and in the daily dealings of persons with one another.

The campaign against injustice is carried forward by the first Isaiah, the statesman and orator. In the Kingdom of Judah, Isaiah found the same social evils that Amos had earlier preached against in the Northern kingdom. The boldness of his attack is startling:

"Thy princes are rebellious, and companions of thieves: everyone loveth gifts, and followeth after rewards: they judge not the fatherless, neither does the cause of the widow come unto them." [4]

Then Isaiah enters upon perhaps the most open, daring, and indignant challenge to doers of social iniquity that is to be found anywhere:

"Ye have eaten of the vineyard; the spoil of the poor is in your houses. What mean ye that ye beat my people to pieces, and grind the faces of the poor?" [5]

After the manner of Amos, Isaiah protested vigorously against the judges and officers of the law who for a bribe vindicate the wicked and deprive the innocent man of his innocence. He denounced in no doubtful language the scribes who devote themselves to writing oppression, who turn aside the dependent from securing justice, who prevent Jehovah's followers from receiving honest treatment, who prey upon widows and despoil orphans. Special condemnation was heaped upon those who set up iniquitous decrees.

Isaiah was a forerunner in an indirect sense of Henry George, for he vehemently rebuked land monopolists. His

[3] *Amos*, 2:6, 3:10, 4:1, 2; 5:7, 15; 6:4.
[4] *Isaiah*, 1:23.
[5] *Isaiah*, 3:14, 15.

new principle is contained in a pronouncement of woes upon the persons who join house to house and add field to field, until there is no land left except for the monopolist who dwells as a lord over all. Isaiah protested against social injustice not only because of the harmful effects upon persons, but also because of the destructive and enervating national results.

After the manner of Amos and Isaiah, Micah conceived of Jehovah as a just God. Micah depicts the social injustice of his day in terms of the persons who hate the good and love the evil, who pluck off the skin of the weak; "who also eat the flesh of my people, and flay their skin from off them; and they break their bones, and chop them to pieces, as for the pot, and as flesh within the caldron." [6]

Micah unhesitatingly condemns the priests who are giving oracles for a reward, and the prophets who are divining for silver and who are trusting in Jehovah to protect them. Micah was perhaps the first person to describe the activities of the criminaloid which have been so carefully analyzed by Edward A. Ross.[7] He grasped the concept of the social sinner who keeps within the law. He attacked wealthy landowners who crush the small holders; he spared neither high officials nor priests. He presented his social concepts with precision and effectiveness.

The invectives against social injustice are carried into the teachings of Jeremiah. They appear later in the Deuteronomic Code. The Psalmists deprecated injustice. The wisdom teachers uttered profound warnings on the subject. The writer of Job deplored injustice. Throughout the Old Testament the almost countless references justify the conclusion that social justice is the leading concept which is presented by ancient Hebrew thought.

DIATRIBES AGAINST LUXURY

The Old Testament parallels its denunciation of unjust social relationships with diatribes against luxury. The evil effects of great riches are again and again described. Amos

[6] *Micah*, 3:2, 3.
[7] Edward A. Ross, in *Sin and Society*.

boldly pointed the finger of scorn at the idle rich, and at those who "lie upon beds of ivory and stretch themselves upon their couches."

The possession of vast wealth has usually been considered by those persons who are immediately concerned as an expression of divine favor. Amos exposed the fallacies in this belief, commanded the owners of wealth to assume social responsibility, and instantly to cease their unholy practices of securing gain.

Isaiah united with Amos in treating the possession of wealth not as a matter of favor or luck, but as a social trust. With one stroke Jeremiah tore off the gilded frame from about the life of the self-indulgent, luxury-loving King Jehoiakim. What powerful and autocratic monarch was ever charged with indulging in luxury in such relentless and uncompromising language as this?

Woe unto him that buildeth his house by unrighteousness, and his chambers by injustice. . .
Shalt thou reign, because thou closest thyself in cedar? . . .
But thine eyes and thine heart are not but for thy covetousness, and for to shed innocent blood, and for oppression, and for violence, to do it.[8]

The ways of the dishonest rich are vividly described by Jeremiah. They set snares and catch people with lying. Their houses are full of evidences of their crooked dealings. They maintain themselves in luxury despite wanton expenditures by violating the needs of the fatherless and the needy.

Zephaniah was no less direct in pointing out the dangers in wealth. He declared that ill-gotten gains shall themselves become a prey and that the houses of the sinful rich shall become desolate. All their silver and their gold shall not be able to deliver them from their ultimate desolation.

In a beautiful and effective style the Wisdom writer in Proverbs, 23:4, 5, unconsciously sums up the Old Testament philosophy concerning wealth:

Labor not to become rich; cease from thine own wisdom. Wilt thou set thine eyes upon that which is not? For riches certainly make themselves wings; they fly as an eagle toward heaven.

[8] *Jeremiah*, 22:13, 15, 17 (*Modern Reader's Bible*).

The Old Testament with surprising uniformity supports the cause of labor. The welfare of the slave is frequently espoused. According to the Deuteronomic Code a runaway slave who was caught did not necessarily need to be returned to his owner. In fact, a person who harbored such a slave was expressly enjoined not to return him. By this injunction the rights of property and vested interests in slaves were ignored. Such an attitude was in opposition to the Code of Hammurabi and to the codes of vested interests throughout history. Slavery, however, was a well-established institution among the ancient Hebrews.[9]

Although the law book of Hammurabi fixed the wages of laborers, the Old Testament law book restricted the hours of labor. Not only is the master to limit his labor to six days a week, but he is commanded to see that his slaves, male and female, do not work more than six days. Modern industry, even twentieth-century manufacturing enterprise in the United States, has been persistently violating the labor rules of the Hebrew law-givers. Employers are commanded not to take advantage of poor and needy hired servants. They shall not oppress labor simply because they are powerful and labor is weak. Even the poor immigrant laborer is not to be exploited!

The first legislation in behalf of immigrants is found in Deuteronomy. Employers must respect the needs of alien workers. The foreigner shall not be oppressed. In the ordinary dealing between citizens and foreigners, justice must not be perverted. The Hebrew lawmakers even went so far as to issue the command: "Love ye therefore the strangers, for ye were strangers in the land of Egypt."

MARRIAGE AND THE FAMILY

The institution of marriage is early accented in the Old Testament. In the second chapter of Genesis divine approval is placed upon marriage. In accordance with biological and social needs the institution of marriage is made sacred. Although the Hebrews are noted for their emphasis upon the responsibility of children to parents, the husband is ordered

[9] Louis Wallis, *Sociological Study of the Bible*, Chapter VII.

to forsake his father and his mother and cleave unto his wife. A man's obligations to his helpmate exceed even his obligations to his father and mother.

The concept of a long-suffering, patient husband is extensively elaborated in the teachings of Hosea. This prophet of the eighth century B.C. demonstrated the sanctity of the marriage relation by remaining true to it even after the wife bore children of whom he was not the father. It is remarkable that Hosea should not have divorced his wife at once when he learned of her unfaithfulness to the marriage vow. Hosea taught, by example, that divorce should be the last resort only when all the means of love have been used in trying to win back the erring partner.

The description of Hosea's domestic difficulties, whether allegorical or not, is an early protest against the double standard of morals for man and woman. The attitude of people in modern society who blame and shun the fallen woman but permit the guilty man to continue to enjoy the company of respectable men and women is vigorously challenged by Hosea.

The last word against sex immorality was pronounced by Hosea. His description of the effects of widespread sex immorality is brief but incisive:

Whoredom and wine and new wine take away the heart.
Their glory shall fly like a bird, from the birth, and from the womb, and from the conception.
Their root is dried up, they shall bear no fruit.[10]

In the Deuteronomic laws we find the duties of parents to children and of children to parents carefully outlined. Parents, primarily, are made responsible for moral and religious education in the home; and children are under obligations to obey their parents. This teaching is summed up in the injunction: "Honor thy father and thy mother, that thy days may be long upon the land which the Lord thy God giveth thee"; [11] and in the imprecation: "Whoso curseth his father or his mother, his lamp shall be put out in obscure darkness." [12]

---

[10] *Hosea*, 4:11; 9:11, 16.
[11] *Exodus*, 20:12.
[12] *Proverbs*, 20:20.

The Wisdom writers dwell at considerable length upon the proper relationships of husbands and wives and of parents and children. They point the finger of shame at the quarrelsome woman. They warn against the woman whose chief asset is her beauty. "A virtuous wife is a crown to her husband, but an immoral wife is as rottenness in his bones."[13]

The Wisdom teachers do not minimize the importance of parental discipline. On occasion parents must act with force. Correction of children is commanded. The situation is pictured in the following language:

The word and reproof bring wisdom; but a child left to himself bringeth his mother to shame.[14]

In other words, it is necessary that parents assume a positive, definite attitude in regard to child nurture. They must see that their children are actually trained in the ways in which they should go. Even the loving parent must sometimes show his affection for his child by chastising the child. Only by such a procedure do children grow up to be a comfort to parents in their old age.

On the other hand, the child must assume his share of responsibility. It is the part of wisdom for children to receive willingly the instruction that parents can give. The wise son loves parental advice. He listens gladly to his father; he does not despise his mother's counsels.

> Train a child the way he should go,
> When he is old he will not depart from it.
> Correct your son, and he will bring you comfort,
> And give you exquisite delight.
> Better is open rebuke
> Than love that is hidden.[15]

It has already been intimated that the Old Testament writers frequently stress the importance of high standards of conduct for women. Amos rebuked the wives of nobles and the wealthy who fritter away their best impulses in idleness and sinful living and who dissipate their deepest impulses in debauchery. Amos and Isaiah agreed, apparently, that a na-

13 *Proverbs*, 12:4.
14 *Proverbs*, 29:15.
15 Charles F. Kent, *The Old Testament* (Shorter Bible), p. 539.

tion's welfare depends on the attitudes of its women. The wrath of God will fall upon women who are haughty, who walk with heads held high and with wanton glances, who go tripping along, "making a tinkling with their feet."

SOCIAL SIN

The antisocial character of sin was pointed out in Genesis. Cain was the first to raise naïvely and blandly the question: "Am I my brother's keeper?" Sinful living narrows the soul, increases selfishness, and vitiates a genuine social attitude. Sinning is repudiating social responsibility. Amos advanced the idea that selfish living was nothing less than disloyalty to one's own country. To dissipate one's energy is to undermine one's usefulness to his nation.

Intemperance was deplored. Isaiah has been called the first temperance reformer of the world. His impassioned and classic utterances are well represented by the following lines:

Woe unto them that rise up early in the morning that they may follow strong drink; that continue until night, till wine inflame them.[16]

Isaiah warned especially the priests and the prophets of the evils of intemperance. Wine will swallow them up, it will put them out of the way, it will cause them to err in wisdom and to stumble in judgment.

In both Leviticus and Numbers the danger that lurks in the wine cup is recognized. The special servants of Jehovah are commanded to separate themselves from wine and strong drink. In Proverbs the Wisdom writer declares:

Wine is a mocker, strong drink is turbulent,
And whoever is misled by it is not wise. . .
So look not on wine when it is red.
When it sparkles in the cup,
And glides down smoothly.
At last it bites like a snake,
And stings like an adder.[17]

[16] *Isaiah*, 5:11.
[17] Charles F. Kent, *op. cit.*, p. 550.

The same authority admonishes rulers and judges not to drink wine lest they forget the law and pervert judgment of the afflicted. On the other hand, a reversion to a lower standard is made in Proverbs when the legitimacy of giving strong drink to the poor and miserable is recognized, so that they may forget their poverty and misery.[18] The general teaching, however, is that strong drink leads to social inefficiency and the disintegration of human personalities.

The cities of refuge represent a new social idea. A person who has taken life without intention may flee to and find protection in the cities of refuge. The altar and the sanctuary are designated as places to which persons may flee who are not wilful murderers.[19]

Of the ten commandments six were distinctly social. It is startling to compare these with the "commandments" of the Oriental religious leaders. The similarity raises a number of interesting questions, including one relative to culture diffusion versus independent origins of ethical ideas.

SOCIAL DEMOCRACY

The social concept of democracy occupies an interesting plane in the Old Testament literature. In the days of Abraham the kinship group prevailed. Within this group there were many households, ruled by patriarchs. Within the kinship groups standards of honor were maintained, but antisocial attitudes toward foreign groups were encouraged. It was justifiable, for example, to lie to foreign groups and even to kill the representatives of such peoples.

The concept of social democracy developed *pari passu* with the evolution of the idea of Jehovah. In the minds of the Hebrews, Jehovah, or Jahweh, was first a tribal god, then a national god; and finally, a universal God, that is, a being who is interested in the welfare of all peoples, and not simply in the welfare of "the chosen people."

The Hebrew conception of the state contained several democratic elements. The fundamental purpose of the state was declared to be the welfare not of an irresponsible mon-

[18] *Proverbs*, 31:7.
[19] *Exodus*, 21:13; *I Kings*, 1:50; 2:28.

arch, but of the people themselves. This idea stands out in marked contradiction to the practices of the Canaanites, who submitted themselves helplessly to capricious and autocratic rulers.

The Hebrews treated the state as a part of a theocracy. But when Jehovah spoke, he usually arraigned ill-gotten wealth, arbitrary political power, selfish ambition of kings, luxurious living, and special privileges. Jehovah spoke for the oppressed, the poor, the defeated, the laborer, in short, for humanity.

Consequently, loyalty to the nation was positive and persistent. Consider this statement from Psalm 137 of Hebrew patriotism on the part of exiled Hebrews who longed for their native land:

By the rivers of Babylon, there we sat down, yea, we wept, when we remembered Zion.
We hanged our harps upon the willows in the midst thereof. . .
If I forgot thee, O Jerusalem, let my right hand forget her cunning.
If I do not remember thee, let my tongue cleave to the roof of my mouth ; if I prefer not Jerusalem above my chief joy.[20]

According to Hosea, Jehovah charged the citizens of the land to deal with one another on the basis of fidelity and true love, and to stamp out all social evils, such as perjury, stealing, committing adultery, and mob violence. The writer of the Book of Job portrayed a good citizen as one who delivers the poor, who helps those about to perish, who causes the widow's heart to sing for joy.[21] He defends the blameless. He does not put his confidence in gold or rejoice at his enemies when evils beset them or they are destroyed. It may be truly said Hebrew thinkers made valuable contributions at an early date to the concept of democracy.

INTERNATIONALISM AND PEACE

Amos pronounced Jehovah the God of other peoples besides the Israelites. "Have not I brought up Israel out of the land of Egypt?" said Jehovah, "and the Philistines from Caph-

---

[20] *King James Version.*
[21] *Job,* 21.

tor, and the Syrians from Kir?"[22]   The day would come, according to Isaiah and Micah, when Jehovah would judge over many peoples and rebuke strong nations.   The conception of Jehovah as a Being who transcends both time and space gave to the Hebrew mind at its best a broader cast and a more universal comprehension than the peoples of contemporary tribes and nations possessed.

The concept of universal peace was invented by the Hebrews.   Isaiah and Micah share the honor of being the first persons to advocate world peace, and to predict the day when all nations shall worship a just God and thereby be enabled to beat their swords into plowshares and their spears into pruning-hooks, when nation shall not stand against nation, and when the methods of warfare shall no longer be taught. The spirit of hatred and of blind, egoistic antagonism shall pass away.   No modern writer has ever spoken the doom of militarism so trenchantly as the Old Testament prophet, Isaiah, who said, according to the translation by Charles Foster Kent:

> For every boot of the warrior with noisy tread,
> And every war-cloak drenched in the blood of the slain
> Will be completely burned up as fuel for the flame.[23]

The Hebrews strongly emphasized love as a social dynamic. Love will make socialized individuals.   It will demonstrate to a person his responsibilities as a member of society and his duties to his fellow human beings.   It will stifle hatred. It will even return good for evil.   It is the cardinal virtue and an eternal principle of right living.

The Old Testament teaches social salvation.   Jehovah is fundamentally interested in the improvement of social and living conditions.   He commanded the socialization of all human relationships.   His teachings, as given by the prophets and Wisdom writers, take cognizance of the influence of environment upon character.

Hebrew social thought deals largely with social injustice. Social evils are vividly described and evil-doers, chiefly kings

---

[22] *Amos*, 9:7.
[23] *Isaiah*, 9:5; *cf.* Kent, *The Social Teachings of the Prophets and Jesus*, p. 112.

and judges, are vigorously and fearlessly arraigned. The family is made the chief social institution, and love is crowned servant of all. Education is centered in the home, and moral discipline is made the keynote of education; hence the Hebrews survived the Greeks and Romans. A new and perfect social order, directed by a just Jehovah and motivated throughout all its individual and social relationships by love, is prophesied.

GROUP DISCUSSION TOPICS

1. Origins of Hebrew social thought.
2. Abraham's role as a world personality.
3. The first labor strike in history.
4. Moses as a radical.
5. The type of social consciousness possessed by Moses.
6. The keynote of Amos' social thought.
7. Labor legislation in the Old Testament.
8. Isaiah as a forerunner of Henry George.
9. Isaiah as a precursor of prohibition.
10. Micah as an advance spokesman for E. A. Ross in his *Sin and Society*.
11. The "social duet" of Isaiah and Micah.
12. Comparison of the social thought of Jeremiah and Zephaniah.
13. The social theme of the Book of Hosea.
14. The social thought of the story of Cain.
15. Social thought themes in the Book of Job.
16. Main phases of Old Testament labor legislation.
17. Old Testament attitudes toward marriage.
18. The filial-duty concept of Old Testament writers.
19. Comparisons of Chinese and Hebrew social thought for similar periods.
20. A comparative rating of the Hebrew writers in terms of the importance of their social ideas.
21. A summary of Hebrew social thought in three words.

READINGS

Barton, G. A., *A History of the Hebrew People* (New York: Century Company 1930).

Chambliss, Rollin, *Social Thought* (New York: The Dryden Press 1954), Ch. 6.

Driver, Samuel R., *The Ideals of the Prophets* (Edinburgh: Clark 1915).

Furfey, Paul H., *A History of Social Thought* (New York: The Macmillan Company 1942), Ch. 4.

Kent, Charles F., *The Social Teachings of the Prophets and Jesus* (New York: Charles Scribner's Sons 1917).

——, *The Old Testament* (Shorter Bible) (New York: Charles Scribner's Sons 1925).

Kilzer, E., and E. J. Ross, *Western Social Thought* (Milwaukee: The Bruce Publishing Company 1954), Ch. 5.

Noyes, Charleton E., *The Genius of Israel* (Boston: Houghton Mifflin 1924).

Saunders, Kenneth, *The Ideals of East and West* (New York: The Macmillan Company 1934), Ch. V.

Soares, T. G., *The Social Institutions and Ideals of the Bible* (New York: Abington Press 1915).

Wallis, Louis, *Sociological Study of the Bible* (Chicago: University of Chicago Press 1912).

Willett, Herbert L., *The Moral Leaders of Israel* (Chicago: University of Chicago Press 1916).

CHAPTER VIII

PLATO AND GRECIAN SOCIAL THOUGHT

In turning to a study of Grecian civilization we find a development of social thought which on the rational side excels in many particulars the social thinking of the Chinese and the Hebrews, but which in its affective elements falls far below the quality of Hebrew social thought. Grecian social thought compares favorably with an equally important development in the fourth and fifth centuries in China. We may expect to find, therefore, in Grecian social thought important new contributions which are complementary to the legacies from the Hebrews, and which, when taken in conjunction with Chinese social thought and with the early Christian forms of Hebrew social thought, constitute the main foundations of modern social thought.

The thought life of the Greeks reached the crescendo in the idealism of Plato (427–347 B.C.) and in the opportunism of Aristotle (384–322 B.C.). After studying 158 constitutions, Aristotle formulated rules of practical social procedure. Plato's *Republic* and Aristotle's *Politics* are the two leading source-books of Grecian social thought.

Plato and Aristotle were the first two Western thinkers in history who left definitely organized analyses of societary life. Although in point of time they stand close together, in content of social thought they are at many places antagonistic. However, their high rank as thinkers need not blind anyone to the fact that their social thought was in part an outgrowth of theories held by predecessors. Antecedent to Plato were Socrates and the Sophists; antecedent to these scholars were many thinkers who, incidentally to their main intellectual efforts, gave expression to isolated but significant social ideas.

How can we account for the remarkable development of social thought in the Hellenic cities in the fourth and fifth centuries B.C.? There are many factors. These cities occupied a strategic position. They were near the main lines of trade of that time and hence there occurred the sharpening of idea upon idea. They were on or near the main lines of adventure and exploration. Conflicts and wars were common, and unrest was in the air. The old superstitions were being proved inadequate. As the cities grew and dominated the rural economy, they produced young men who were critics and sceptics and who challenged outworn customs. The cities produced emancipated minds. Hence the rise of the Sophists was natural. With the decline of the Grecian democracy many attempts were made to analyze the causal factors and to outline a revised social order that would prove desirable and stable. Plato and Aristotle were the two outstanding thinkers who faced disturbed social conditions and tried to think through the social difficulties of the troubled times in which they lived.

EARLIEST GREEK THOUGHT

As early as the ninth century B.C., Lycurgus declared that the state owned the child, and urged a system of education which would prepare the child for the state. In spite, however, of a similar emphasis by many later Greek leaders, "Hellas" never developed a genuine national unity. She experienced a temporary national patriotism only when attacked by the Persians, and at the seasons when the national games were at their height.

It was Hesiod, the founder of Greek didactic poetry, who, about 700 B.C., described the Golden Age and the subsequent ages of society. Hesiod protested mildly against the social injustice of his time.[1] In the following century, Anaximander, the philosopher, and Theognis, the elegiac poet,[2] discussed the value to society of providing that children should be well born and well trained — the fundamental concepts of current eugenics and euthenics.

Solon, the Athenian lawgiver, about 590 B.C., began to put into legislative practice certain ideas of social reform, thereby preventing revolution. At that time it was customary to sell into slavery persons who could not pay their debts — a pro-

[1] Hesiod, *Work and Days,* translated by A. W. Mains.
[2] *The Works of Hesiod, Calimachus, and Theognis,* translated by Banks, Bohn's Classical Library, p. 227.

cedure which Solon ended. The cost of living was very high, consequently Solon forbade the export of food products and thereby reduced prices for the consumer. He introduced a measure which today would be considered revolutionary, namely, the limiting of the amount of land which a person might hold. For the classification of people on the basis of wealth, he substituted a classification on the basis of income. He lessened the severity of the laws of Draco, and in other ways increased the freedom of the individual. Although Solon's regime was followed by a tyranny, Solon is credited with initiating certain essential ideas of democracy.

BEGINNINGS OF DEMOCRATIC THOUGHT

After the Tyrants, Athens under the leadership of men like Cleisthenes became "a pure democracy." Cleisthenes democ ratized the Athenian Constitution. For the four phylae he substituted ten phylae, or units of government, thus securing a new and better distribution of authority. He is credited with introducing ostracism as a mode of punishment; he, it is alleged, was the first person to be ostracized by his government.

The fifth-century precursors of Plato and Aristotle were numerous. Aeschylus (525–456 B.C.), the first of the famous Athenian tragic poets, described in general terms the evolution of civilized society.[3] The artistic historian, Herodotus, developed through his imagination a world point of view. From an almost unlimited store of legendary and ethnological materials, he elaborated a planetary theme which had its beginning in the Trojan War and its culmination in the conflict between Eastern and Western civilizations. The basic social principle in the writings of Herodotus is that downfall awaits the insolent autocrats of earth. Herodotus describes the customs and habits of the peoples whom he visited on his numerous foreign travels in such a detailed and elaborate fashion that he has been styled the world's first descriptive sociologist.[4]

Pericles (495 ?–429 B.C.), perhaps the greatest statesman of

---

[3] Botsford and Sihler, *Hellenic Civilization*, p. 64.
[4] George Rawlinson, translator, *History of Herodotus*, 4 vols.

Greece, furthered the cause of democracy. His conception of democracy led him to make the entire body of citizens eligible for officeholding. Pericles initiated a social program which in certain aspects was paternalistic. He instituted the plan of granting allowances for performing public duties. As a result, true public service was minimized and political morale was weakened. Pericles was led into this error [5] by the desire to compete for public esteem with Cimon, who made extensive gifts to the poor in the form of dinners and clothes.

In his tragedies, Euripides (480–406 B.C.) aroused interest in the experiences, not of legendary characters as many of his predecessors had done, but of the ordinary members of Athenian society. He was a spokesman for the emancipation of woman ; [6] his writings reveal the social changes that were occurring in the fifth century in Athens. Likewise, the comedies of Aristophanes reflected social changes, and, in addition, caricatured social conditions.

Hippocrates, the so-called father of medical science, wrote several works which attracted the studious attention of Plato. He gave as the first of two chief causes of disease, the influence of climate, seasons, weather, on the individual. [7] He might be called the first anthropo-geographer. At any rate, he opened the field which has been so well covered by Ellen C. Semple in the *Influences of Geographic Environment,* and by Ellsworth Huntington in his recent studies on civilization in relation to climate.

By their disconcerting and sceptical teachings the Sophists, who also lived in the fifth century B.C. stimulated the intellectual activities of Socrates. The influence of the Sophist leaders, such as Protagoras, Gorgas, Callicles, Thrasymachus, brought forward the problem of training pupils to solve civic questions rather than scientific or philosophical questions. According to Plato, Callicles believed that government was an instrument for exploiting the masses. Thrasymachus argued that so-called justice is that type of activity which favors the interest of the strongest members of society, and that

5 Plutarch's *Pericles,* revised by Clough, 1:234 ff.
6 Botsford and Sihler, *op. cit.,* p. 340.
7 *On Airs, Waters, and Places,* in the genuine Works of Hippocrates, translated by Adams, Vol. I.

might determines what is called right.[8] Epaminondas, the Theban statesman, personified in his own career an unusually high interpretation of the concept of patriotism, perhaps a broader expression of patriotism than is represented by any other political spokesman of the Hellenic states.

SOCRATIC THOUGHT

The argument of the Sophists that what is best for the individual is best for society aroused the antagonism of Socrates (469–399 B.C.), whose ideas are reported by Plato and Xenophon. Socrates, the son of an Athenian sculptor, asserted that the qualities of justice, wisdom, temperance, and courage which make an individual a good member of society and which increase social welfare, are the same qualities which make an individual a good person and secure his personal advancement. Socrates spent many years at the market places, on the streets where people congregate, and at the public resorts in studying the actions of persons and in engaging them in conversation concerning their moral life. As a result Socrates evolved a significant social philosophy. The heart of this philosophy is found in the statement that "virtue is knowledge," not in the sense of mere memorized facts but of a thorough understanding. If a person understands completely the good and evil phases of a proposed act, he will choose the right. For example, when one is completely convinced of the harmful effects of poor teeth, he will employ the regular services of a dentist to keep his teeth in good condition. When he perceives the evil effects of dishonesty, he will establish honest habits. The conclusion might be drawn that social virtue rests upon societary knowledge.

Socrates was convinced that something was fundamentally wrong with Athenian society. Everywhere he saw that ignorance led to vice. Only in the mechanical and professional activities did he discover correct action, but this was preceded by correct knowledge.[9]

---

[8] *Plato* I, 338 B.C. (All references to Plato's *Dialogues* in this chapter or in later chapters are to Jowett's translation.)

[9] Adela M. Adam, *Plato, Moral and Political Ideals*, p. 10.

A good carpenter is an individual who thoroughly understands carpentry; a good man is an individual who truly knows the value of good actions. Similarly, it might be said that a good urban resident is a person who deeply appreciates what it means to have a city of mutually developing people.

Socrates wished to make all men intelligent. His teachings raised the deep-seated social question: How can social organization be made highly advantageous to a person, and a person made so aware of these advantages that he will always act socially?[10] Inasmuch as Socrates left no writings, it is impossible to explain with certainty his teachings. Fortunately, he left a permanent impress of his personality on the lives of his associates, and particularly, upon his able and brilliant pupil, Plato.

In the fundamental dictum that virtue is knowledge, Socrates is theoretically correct, but practically he ignores the overpowering influence that oftentimes is exerted by the inherited and acquired behavior patterns. He underestimates the power that is represented by behavior patterns deeply ingrained in the feelings, for these are firmly established neurologically, whereas knowledge is often new to a person and merely a veneer on the surface of his life. The acquisition of knowledge is no guarantee that instinctive tendencies centuries old will be promptly overcome or redirected.

Furthermore, with a young child the instinctive tendencies begin to assert themselves and to give direction to the growth of the character of the child, long before his mentality has unfolded and developed to the point where he is capable of genuinely understanding the real meaning of many forms of activity, and where many phases of knowledge are entirely beyond his ability to comprehend.

PLATO'S SOCIAL THOUGHT

Little is known concerning Plato's early life and training. The most influential factors were the life and teachings of Socrates. The strong Socratic personality left its indelible impress upon the thought-life of Plato. As a young man,

---

[10] The reader will find in Will Durant's *Philosophy and the Social Problem*, Chapter I, a unique interpretation of Socrates.

Plato became greatly interested in Athenian social and civic life. When he was perhaps twenty-three years of age, the self-styled "Fair and Good" rulers came into control of Athens. The failure of these men, whom history calls the Thirty Tyrants, to govern wisely, produced an attitude of thorough disgust in the mind of Plato. Further, the legalized murder of Socrates by the restored democracy in 399 B.C. aroused the bitter antagonism of Plato to the existing forms of government. In the years which followed the death of Socrates, popular rule produced loose and licentious social conditions. As a consequence, Plato turned to the realms of the thought world in order to find a perfect society. As a result of his contact with everyday life and government, Plato evolved in his mind an ideal republic.

The Socratic principle that virtue is knowledge was accepted by Plato. In Plato's thinking this proposition led to the generalization that education is the most important thing in the world. Upon this doctrine more than any other, Plato's twentieth-century influence thrives.

What shall be the nature of a world-molding education? Theoretically, Plato gives his answer in his epistemology. Ideas are the ruling forces in life. Over against the uncertain fluctuating sense world, Plato set up a realm of eternal, changeless ideas. An individual man is simply an ephemeral expression of Man. Plato created a concept of unchangeable reality which he found in Ideas. These, alone, are the permanent, worth-while elements which man must seek to know and understand.

Because of his aristocratic attitudes and of his early disgust with the experiments in democracy in his day, Plato turned away in his social philosophy from the direct study of the people, such as had engaged the attention of Socrates, to a search for a just society in the world of ideas. This line of thinking found expression chiefly in the *Republic,* written during Plato's mature manhood. A discussion of these idealistic concepts is found in the *Laws* and the *Politicus,* the latter being written in Plato's old age and representing a partial reaction from the idealism of the *Republic.* Because of its consideration of nearly every aspect of social life from a specific viewpoint, the *Republic* may be called the first treatise in social philosophy. While it falls below the social writings of the Hebrews in its dynamic and practical phases, it excels them in its unity, its profundity, and its philosophic quality.[11]

Plato's idea of the origin of human society is interesting though unduly simplified. However, he is doubtless sound, for he begins with human needs. To meet these elemental needs individuals band together into a group for mutual aid. They learn to see the advantages of exchanging services and goods. "When these partners and helpers are gathered together in one habitation the body of inhabitants is called a state." The true creator of a state is necessity.[12]

Plato's concept of temperance is related to his ideas concerning self-control. His analysis of personality is not psychological but ethical. There are two sets of forces contending for the control of personality, a better and a worse principle. One leads to mastery of self; the other to self-slavery and unprincipled behavior.[13]

AN IDEAL SOCIETY

Inasmuch as Plato had turned away from an inviting though strenuous public career to a private life of scholarly thought, his perfect society assumed characteristics that were far from mundane. Because Plato lived in a day of small political groups and in a country of limited size, he limited his ideal society to a group represented by 5040 heads of families.[14] Consequently it is impossible to apply Plato's social ideas with accuracy to a modern metropolitan center of 5,000,000 people, or to a nation-state of 100,000,000 people. Several phases of Plato's thought, however, were given a practical turn in the *Laws*. In revealing Plato's social philosophy, the *Politicus,* or *Statesman* ranks third.[15]

In Plato's ideal society there is a hierarchy of rank, which includes three classes of people: the rulers, or true guardians; the soldiers, or auxiliaries; and the artisans, or the in-

[11] The *Republic* is also to be considered as ranking first in point of time among the outstanding descriptions of a utopian society.
[12] The *Republic*, by Plato, translated by Jowett, third edition, 369 B, C.
[13] *Ibid.*, 431 A, B.
[14] *Laws*, 738.
[15] The beginning student of Plato's social thought should first read the *Republic*, especially 5:472 A to 7:541 B.

dustrial and agricultural workers. In introducing the ideal state Plato uses mature individuals.[16] Out of the needs and through the activities of fully developed persons, Plato builds an ideal commonwealth.

SOCIAL CLASSES

No individual is self-sufficing. Each has his peculiar bias, or ability. By uniting, all will profit. There are not only specialized classes, but there is specialization within the occupational groups. An essential rule for the building of a just society is that each person shall find his place in the social order and shall fulfill his special function. Plato recognized the need for correlating the diversities of nature and the different types of occupation.[17]

The common people are engaged in the foundational occupations as skilled artisans. The advantages of a special education are not open to them. They receive the common education, including gymnastic and music training. But, in accordance with the aristocratic strain in Plato's social philosophy, it is useless to try to give a higher education to that large proportion of the people who are mentally incapable of profiting by higher education. The logic is good but the major premise is faulty in this pedagogical rule.

The second class, the soldiers, will maintain order at home, repel invaders, and conduct territorial wars. The growth of population will create a demand for more territory. Other states likewise will need more territory, and war will become inevitable.[18] Plato frankly admits the territorial basis of wars. From this factor he sees no escape, although he declares peace to be better than war.[19] In his *Timæus* and *Critias* he pictured a peace-state, "Atlantis."

The soldier's occupation is an art which requires years of training. The chief physical trait of a true soldier is courage. The social psychological significance of a military regime is that soldiers are continually inciting their country to go to war. Such a regime raises up enemies against itself, many

[16] *Republic*, 369 B.
[17] *Ibid.*, 370 B.
[18] *Laws*, 803.
[19] *Loc. cit.*

and mighty, and results either in ruining the specific people or in enslaving the foes of these people.[20] On the other hand, the non-soldier classes, since they prefer to lead a peaceful life and seek to conduct their affairs quietly, unduly endeavor to avoid war. By degrees, they become unwarlike; their children develop a like attitude. Eventually, they find themselves at the mercy of their enemies and are enslaved.[21]

Among the members of the state there will be a few especially able persons, destined by birth and reinforced by training to be rulers and true guardians of the welfare of all.[22] They are lovers of wisdom and philosophy. Flabbiness of character, drunkenness, selfishness, are unbecoming to them.[23] Egoistic living is condemned.[24] The guardians are characterized, according to Plato, by the greatest eagerness to do what is for the good of their country. They show utter repugnance to anything that is contrary to the best interests of the state.[25]

The guardians, however, rule aristocratically.[26] They do not inquire of the citizens the kind of laws which they want passed, for the same reason that a physician does not ask the patient the kind of medicine which he wants. In the *Republic*, the *Laws*, and the other dialogues where the nature of rulers and philosophers is discussed, Plato's "best men" show an indifference to earthly or material things and uniformly seek righteousness, even social righteousness. The three classes, those seeking honor, those who are soldiers, and the philosophers, develop an occupational psychology. Each class develops attitudes that are occupationally conditioned.

LEADERSHIP TESTS

The candidates for guardianship receive first the elements of education. At twenty years of age they must pass a general education test, in order that they may go on with a special course, including arithmetic, geometry, and astronomy.[27]

---

[20] *Statesman*, 308.
[21] *Ibid.*, 307.
[22] *Ibid.*, 297.
[23] *Republic*, 398 E, 412.
[24] *Laws*, 731, 732.
[25] *Republic*, 412.
[26] *Statesman*, 303.
[27] *Republic*, 525; *cf. Laws*. 818.

At thirty they are subjected to a further examination, after which the successful individuals devote five years to the study of philosophy. At thirty-five they enter practical life, hold minor offices, balance their theoretical training by practical studies, and submit to diverse temptations.[28]

They undergo a civil service examination which extends over a period of years. At the close they are subjected to a final series of threefold tests. The first test is that of logic; they must argue successfully that it pays an individual, especially a guardian, to serve society. The second test is that of fear; they are faced with dangers, for example, the dangers to life, which beset those who undertake to rule without favoritism and without compromising their principles when confronted with the ambitions and desires of powerful vested interests. The third test is that of pleasure; they are submitted to all the pleasures which thrill the heart of man.

In other words, they must show proof that the highest interest of the state is to be the ruling interest of their lives.[29] Neither pain nor threats must affect their loyalty. The temptations which come from pleasures and enchantments must not disturb their self-control nor weaken their qualities of guardianship. From these requirements it will be seen that Plato provided for a long period of intensive and extensive training for the rulers. His idea varied greatly from the ancient theory of the divine right of kings and from the current practice of distributing political spoils to friends.

Plato saw that the rulers once selected and installed in office would be tempted to become avaricious at the expense of the state. Instead of becoming and remaining democratic they will be prone to become tyrannical.[30] Plato perceived that it would be difficult, after good rulers had been selected, to keep them on the plane of good rulership. In order to preserve their virtue as guardians and to remove the powerful temptation to wink at exploitation that is carried on by the economically powerful, Plato indicated certain protective devices. The guardians shall be permitted no private property beyond a few incidentals. They shall not live in

[28] *Ibid.*, 537, 539, 540.
[29] *Ibid.*, 413.
[30] *Ibid.*, 416.

private houses, but shall dwell and eat together. They shall receive a fixed salary, sufficient to meet necessary expenses, but no more. They shall not be allowed to touch gold and silver or to wear gold and silver ornaments. They shall be taught that they are made of divine gold and silver, and therefore shall have no need of the earthly dross. They shall not be subject to pollution from any earthly contacts. If the guardians should acquire lands or moneys or homes of their own, they would be unable to give their undivided attention to the state, and they would become not guardians of the welfare of the citizens, but tyrants, plotting and being plotted against.[31] In his zealous care that the rulers might not be distracted from guarding with undivided attention the interests of the state, Plato advocated community of wives and children of the rulers.[32]

PUBLIC OPINION AND EDUCATION

The question arose : Will the people be content to accept the division of the population into hierarchal classes ? In reply, Plato suggested that the power of public opinion be utilized, and that all the inhabitants of the state be taught that they are brothers, that is, children of their common Mother Earth. This instruction will serve to keep the masses in a humble attitude. Further, they are to be told that different metals have been used by Mother Earth in making different individuals. Those persons in whose make-up gold has been mingled have the power of command and may become rulers. Others who are made of silver may become auxiliaries, or soldiers; while the masses, being made of brass and iron, are destined to become artisans.[33]

The objection is raised that people will not believe this "audacious fiction." The truth of the objection is admitted, and a solution of the problem is offered. Teach the children the gold, silver, brass, and iron fiction ; and they will believe it. When they grow to maturity, they will tell their children, who in turn will teach it. Posterity, thus, will accept it.[34] In

[31] *Republic,* 416, 417.
[32] *Ibid.,* 457 C, 464 C.
[33] *Ibid.,* 414, 415.
[34] *Ibid.,* 415.

this way Plato founded his social philosophy upon propaganda. Plato made clear that any kind of social or economic theory can be foisted upon a whole people through the utilization of the educational processes. A few antisocial exploiters, by controlling the educational system, can ruin a nation in a generation.

VOCATIONAL SELECTION

The guardians are instructed to examine the children in order to discover of what metals they are made. Plato admitted a democracy of talent in the sense that talent is likely to appear in the children of brass and iron parents, while gold parents may beget brass and iron children. If a gold child is found among the children of the artisans, he is to be encouraged and trained to become a guardian. If a brass and iron child is found among the children of the gold parents, he must descend the social scale and be trained for husbandry or artisanship.[35] Plato foresaw the fact, now scientifically established, that geniuses are born indiscriminately among all classes of society from the highest to the lowest. They are just as likely to be born in the hovel or overcrowded tenement as in the spacious and luxurious palace. Consequently, society should seek out potential genius and give it opportunities commensurate with its possibilities and not allow its dynamic and divine spark to be snuffed out in a heavy-laden tenement atmosphere.

Furthermore, according to Plato, the guardians are to seek out the imperfect children and put them out of the way as easily as possible and without attracting public attention.[36] If the capable must devote their energies to the care of imperfect children, they would presumably be wasting their ability and would be prevented from devoting themselves to upbuilding the state. This doctrine neglects the consideration of the harsh, unsympathetic attitude which it would engender.

The guardians are to supervise marriage. Plato especially deplores the fact that almost all persons choose their

[35] Loc. cit.
[36] Republic, 460 C, 461 C.

life-partners in marriage without proper regard to the kind
of children that will be procreated.[37]   The marriage relationship should not be primarily an individual affair, but
should be governed by the thought of the children that are
not yet born and by due regard to the welfare of the state
and society.[38]   The true purpose of marriage is not found in
wealth or power or rank, but in the procreation of healthy-
minded children.   Marriage is sacred in the highest degree
because it is socially necessary.   Plato deplores class marriages, that is, marriage within temperamentally similar
groups.   Persons of gentle nature seek persons of gentle nature ; the courageous seek the courageous.   It would be better if the gentle would seek the courageous in marriage, and
vice versa.[39]   Marriage is sacred, and hence should be subjected to strict eugenic safeguards.

POVERTY AND WEALTH

The guardians shall prevent the extremes of poverty and
riches.   With farsighted social wisdom Plato points out that
poverty is the parent of meanness and viciousness, and that
wealth leads to luxury and indolence.[40]   Both result in discontent and both cause the deterioration of the arts.   The
poor man cannot properly equip or train himself, nor enter
into his work painstakingly ; the rich man will grow careless and no longer act diligently when he comes into the
possession of unlimited wealth.[41]

In the acquisition of wealth the laws of imitation function
powerfully.   One person accumulates property ; others are
immediately stimulated to do likewise.   In consequence, all
the citizens may become lovers of money.[42]   But a money-
loving public would be disastrous to the state.

The larger amount of wealth that a person accumulates,
the more he will want to accumulate.   The momentum of
the desire for money-getting is socially destructive.   The
more a person is hypnotized by the wealth-getting delusion,

---

[37] *Statesman*, 310.
[38] *Laws*, 773.
[39] *Statesman*, 310.
[40] *Republic*, 422 A; *Laws*, 744, 745.
[41] *Ibid.*, 421.
[42] *Ibid.*, D, E; *Laws*, 742, 791.

the less attention does he give to the maintenance of virtue. When the desire for virtue is in competition with the desire for riches, the former decreases as the latter increases.[43]

When the state becomes established on a property basis, the rich exercise power and the poor are deprived of it.[44] In ordinary times the rich are as indifferent to the welfare of the poor as to the development of virtue, but in times of group crises they will not despise the poor. In the days of prosperity and peace the poor man is given the hindmost position, but when war comes, "the wiry, sunburnt poor man" is placed in battle at the side of the wealthy man [45] — and social democracy obtains. But in battle the poor man fights longer and better than the rich man "who has never spoilt his complexion and has plenty of superfluous flesh." In the words of the poor man Plato draws the astounding conclusion that many persons are rich because no one has the courage to despoil them.[46] At this point Plato has given a striking explanation of the rise of socialism, and economic radicalism.

When you see paupers, according to Plato, you may safely conclude that somewhere there are also present thieves, rob- bers of temples, and malefactors.[47] The causes of pauperism are given as (1) a lack of proper education, (2) ill-training, and (3) unjust social laws and an unjust constitution of the state.[48]

Plato's statement of the two major economic evils is suc- cinct and to the point; wealth and poverty: "One is the parent of luxury and indolence, and the other of meanness and viciousness, and both of discontent." [49]

Plato suggested two instruments for preventing extreme wealth and poverty, legislation and education. Each person is to be guaranteed a minimum amount of property. He may acquire as much as four times this amount, but above the maximum a one hundred per cent excess tax operates.[50]

[43] Ibid., 550.
[44] Ibid., 550 C.
[45] Ibid., 556.
[46] Republic, 556.
[47] Ibid., 552 D.
[48] Ibid., 552 E.
[49] Ibid., 421 D, 422 B.
[50] Laws, 744, 745.

Plato planned a form of communism, not primarily to secure the material well-being of the state, but to safeguard the rulers against falling before selfish temptations. Plato also wanted to protect the state from splitting asunder because of the distractions that arise from labor-capital controversies. By educational means the children are to be trained to be satisfied with the necessaries of life [51] — at least some children are to be so trained. Parents should bequeath to their children not riches but the spirit of reverence,[52] an injunction which the Chinese have succeeded in observing better than any other people on a large scale.

CENSORSHIP

The guardians shall be censors. They shall establish a censorship over the arts in order to protect the children from seeing indecent sights and hearing vulgar sounds. The works of fiction shall be censored in order to prevent the children from reading and adopting bad ideas. The creative artists shall be prevented from exhibiting forms of vice and intemperance, in order that the future guardians may not grow up in an atmosphere contaminated by images of moral deformity, and in order that all children may develop in an environment of fair sights and may receive unhindered and unhampered the good in everything.[53]

The guardians shall protect the *mores*. Since Plato described a perfect state, any change in the established customs would mean retrogression.[54] Hence, the rulers should jealously guard the customs, allowing no insidious innovations. Further, if any change is permitted to take place in small things, there may be no stopping the spirit of change.

Plato rested his argument for an ideal society upon the education of wise leaders. Their judgment is better even than government by law. Law is too rigid and inflexible. In view of the changeable character of human conditions, which Plato recognized, no final nor absolute laws can be laid down.[55] The chief advantage of laws, however, is not

[51] *Ibid.*, 729.
[52] *Loc. cit.*
[53] *Republic*, 377, 401.
[54] *Laws*, 772.
[55] *Statesman*, 294.

that they make men honest but that they make men act uniformly, and hence in a socially reliable way. Laws are to be
respected because they represent the ripe fruits of long experience.[56]

Considerable attention is given to penology in the *Laws*.[57]
In view of the sanctity of custom and of the necessity of law,
obedience is a highly important social virtue. In theory
Plato is modern and scientific, for he advocated punishment,
not as a vindictive but as a preventive and reformatory
measure.[58] Reformation is the true aim of punishment.[59]
In practice Plato is rigid and harsh. For example, beggars
are simply to be sent out of the city and out of the country.[60]
The death penalty is utilized freely.[61]

Plato opened occupations to women as well as men, even
the highest, that of ruling.[62] The only difference between
the sexes that needs to be recognized occupationally is that
men are stronger physically than women.[63] One individual is fitted for one kind of vocation ; another for some other
type of work.

Although the fundamental importance of bearing children is appreciated, Plato observed that it is unnecessary
that a woman devote her whole life to the rearing of children. All women should have opportunities for the development of their personalities. Those women who have
special talent for public service should enter thereupon. Although a social conservative, Plato admits an innovation in
the ideal republic — universal woman suffrage.

Since women have the same duties as men, they receive
the same opportunities for training. Women must share in
the toils of war, and the defense of their country.[64] Women
may be priestesses ;[65] they serve on committees for the regulation of marriage, and for deciding divorce cases.[66]

[56] *Ibid.*, 300.
[57] In books IX-XII.
[58] *Laws*, 934.
[59] *Ibid.*, 862 ff.
[60] *Laws*, 936.
[61] *Ibid.*, 955.
[62] *Republic*, 455, 456; *Laws*, 805.
[63] *Ibid.*, 451.
[34] *Ibid.*, 475 A; *Laws*, 814.
[65] *Laws*, 759.
[66] *Ibid.*, 929, 930.

ROLE OF EDUCATION

Although Plato was averse to change, he advocated a dynamic type of education. This educational system, however, is to be definitely controlled by the guardians. It is also paternalistic. Common education shall be of two kinds: gymnastic for the body; music for the soul.[67] Gymnastic training will produce a temper of hardness, and music will lead to gentleness. The extreme of the one is ferocity and brutality; the extreme of the other is softness and effeminacy.[68] When taken together, they produce a well-ordered personality. The one sustains and makes bold the reason; the second moderates and civilizes the wildness of passion.[69] Gymnastic exercises provide for the care and training of the body through childhood and youth so that in maturity the body may best serve the soul.[70] Music, including literature, trains through the influence of its qualities of harmony and rhythm. For example, through exercises in harmony the child develops a harmonious temperament.

Education is not a process of acquisition, but of the development of the powers within the individual.[71] It is a life-long process; it begins with birth and continues until death. However, it slows up as the individual grows old. An aged person cannot learn much, any more than he can run much.[72] Education in the early years of life is the most important. As a child is educated, so will his future be determined.[73] A child should be taught early to respect his parents. Great care should be given to the first years of life. From three to six years of age the children in Plato's republic come under the supervision of chosen matrons and nurses.

Education shall be universal, but not compulsory; that is, all shall be taught, but not compelled to learn. Education shall be made attractive, almost a form of government.[74]

---

67 *Republic*, 457 A; *Laws*, 795 ff., 813 ff., 830 ff.
68 *Republic*, 410.
69 *Ibid.*, 441.
70 *Ibid.*, 498 B.
71 *Ibid.*, 518.
72 *Ibid.*, 536.
73 *Ibid.*, 425; *Laws*, 643.
74 *Republic*, 537.

The laws of imitation shall be utilized. The tutor shall carry out his teachings in practice.

A well-trained individual is a replica of a just society. Plato draws a parallelism, which is inaccurate, between the three classes in society and three traits of the individual. The rulers, soldiers, and artisans are compared respectively to the reason, the spirit, and the passions of the individual. The passions must be subordinated to the spirit, and both must be controlled by reason. The result will be a just person. In society a similar hierarchal relation shall hold between the rulers, soldiers, and artisans. The fundamental aim in education shall be to secure a change in the attitudes of people. Such changes are more important than modification in external matters.

Religion plays a basic role in the ideal republic. Plato held that belief in God superseded in importance the doctrine that might is right. Impiety undermines the strength of the social kingdom. God created the individual for the whole, but not the whole for the individual. The worship of God is necessary for a person in order to prevent him from reverting to swinishness and from making his humanitarian beliefs purely egoistic phenomena.[75]

SOCIAL CHANGE

Inasmuch as Plato outlined at the start a perfect republic, any change would likely constitute a deterioration. But even an ideal state is not immune to the entry of destructive ideas. The wise men, the rulers, are not proof against the temptations of absolute power. To remove the stirrings of self-interest in the minds of the guardians, Plato planned a communistic order. He overlooked, however, the weaknesses of communism, but these were pointed out at a later time by Aristotle.

In spite of excellent safeguards the wisdom of the best rulers will occasionally fail them. Sooner or later they will err. In examining the youth they will allow warrior youth to be trained for the guardian class. With their spirit of contention and of ambition for honor these adventitious

[75] *Laws,* 903.

guardians will start the perfect state upon the downward road.[76] When the rulers seek personal power and honor, the ideal republic will be superseded by a timocracy.

In a timocracy the ruler with the most private wealth will possess the greatest personal power and receive the highest honor. Moreover, other persons will be stimulated, thereby, to acquire wealth and power. In the meantime the masses will lose nearly everything. The result is an oligarchy in which the wealthy are honored and made rulers.[77] The poor are treated with dishonor and deprived of position.

In such an oligarchic state there is a fundamental division; there are two states instead of one. In spirit, the rich and the poor comprise separate states. They live in the same territory but are conspiring against one another.[78] Social stability is destroyed by the conflicts between the extremes of countless riches and utter poverty. The property-less hate and conspire against the propertied.[79] Civil war ensues. Because the wealthy have fallen into carelessness and extravagance, and because the poor possess superior numbers, the poor are the victors. A democracy — the rule of *Demos* — comes into being. Everyone rules.

But the populace is not fitted to rule. They are without experience. Since the drones are numerous among the common people, the drones manage almost everything in a democracy.[80] Excess of liberty among people untrained for liberty leads to anarchy. Persons will set themselves up as the special friends of the common people. These self-appointed friends of the people will prove to be self-seeking tyrants; the democracy will be transformed into a tyranny — the lowest state of all in Plato's fivefold devolution.

With distrust of the masses and with a paternalistic government, Plato coupled a belief that a person must participate in the life of society. Social injustice does not consist in doing good to one's friends and ill to one's enemies, or in catering to the interests of the most powerful. The theory that might is right is repudiated.[81] A just society is one in

76 *Republic*, 545-549.
77 *Ibid.*, 550, 551.
78 *Loc. cit.*
79 *Ibid.*, 555.
80 *Ibid.*, 564.
81 *Republic*, 339 ; *Laws*, 714.

which every person has found his place of greatest usefulness to the state and fulfills his entire obligations in that place. On the whole Plato exhibited an impassioned faith in the moral and social order.

Plato believed that Ideas are real and that they are the tools with which the world is made over. He perceived perfect Forms, even a perfect Social Form. Through intellectual control, Plato planned a new social order.

GROUP DISCUSSION TOPICS

1. The meaning of Socrates' dictum : Virtue is knowledge.
2. Plato's application of the Socratic dictum.
3. Plato as an idealist.
4. Socrates and Plato as complementary exponents of social thought.
5. Plato and the Hebrew prophets as complementary social thought representatives.
6. The differences between a utopian leader and a prophet.
7. An ideal society according to Plato.
8. Plato's reactions to war.
9. Plato's concept of an aristocratic rulership.
10. Plato's plan to keep rulers efficient.
11. Plato's attitude toward wealth and poverty.
12. Plato's view of censorship.
13. The place of law in society according to Plato.
14. The complementary role of gymnastics and music in personality training.
15. The place of education in an ideal society.
16. The nature of a timocracy.
17. Plato's idea of democracy.
18. A comparison of the social thought of Confucius and of Plato.
19. A summary of Plato's social thought.

READINGS

Adam, Adela M., *Plato, Moral and Political Ideals* (London: Macmillan and Company 1913).

Barker, Ernest, *Greek Political Theory, Plato and His Predecessors* (London: Methuen 1918).

Beach, Walter G., *The Growth of Social Thought* (New York: Charles Scribner's Sons 1939), Ch. III.

Becker, Howard, and Harry E. Barnes, *Social Thought from Lore to Science* (Washington: Harren Press 1952), Vol. I, Ch. 4.

Botsford and Sihler, *Hellenic Civilization* (New York: Columbia University Press 1915).

Chambliss, R., *Social Thought* (New York: Dryden Press 1954), Ch. 7.

Dealey, James Q., "Plato's Course in Social Problems," *Sociology and Social Research*, 12:203-207.

Durant, Will, *Philosophy and the Social Problem* (New York: The Macmillan Company 1913).

Ellwood, Charles A., *A History of Social Philosophy* (New York: Prentice-Hall, Inc. 1938), Ch. II.

Furfey, Paul H., *A History of Social Thought* (New York: The Macmillan Company 1942), Ch. 6.

Gitler, Joseph B., *Social Thought Among the Early Greeks* (Athens: University of Georgia 1941).

Grote, George, *Plato and the Other Companions of Socrates* (London: Murray 1867).

Hesiod, *Work and Days* (London: Oxford University Press 1908, translated by A. W. Mains).

Hesiod, Calimachus, and Theognis, *The Works of,* translated by Adams (London: Wyman and Sons 1881).

Hippocrates, *On Airs, Waters, and Places,* translated by J. Banks (London: Bohn 1856).

Lichtenberger, James P., *Development of Social Theory* (New York: Century Company 1923), Ch. I.

Nettleship, R. L., *Lectures on the Republic of Plato* (New York: The Macmillan Company 1921).

Plutarch's Lives (New York: The Macmillan Company 1914).

Plato, *Dialogues,* translated by Jowett (London: Oxford University Press 1892).

Plato, *Laws,* translated by Jowett (London: Oxford University Press 1892).

Plato, *Statesman,* translated by Jowett (London: Oxford University Press 1892).

CHAPTER IX

ARISTOTLE AND GRECIAN SOCIAL THOUGHT

Aristotle (384–322 B.C.), the distinguished pupil of Plato, did not make, like his master, a unified contribution to social thought. He sacrificed unity for the examination of parts. Aristotle was an opportunist, a pragmatist, and a practical student of conditions and constitutions. Unlike Plato, Aristotle did not look for Ideas separate from but in things.

Aristotle studied 158 constitutions inductively and comparatively. His primary attention was given to what is, rather than to what ought to be. His eyes were directed first of all to the parts, and then to the whole. In this examination he found that the parts are related and, further, that they hold a developmental relation. Instead of Plato's perfection, we shall now consider Aristotle's process of becoming. Although unsystematic, the social ideas of Aristotle reveal the concepts of process and progress.

VIRTUE AS A MEAN

In Aristotle's *Ethics* the discussion of virtue is socially valuable. Virtue is a mean. Virtue is an impulse which is expressed neither in excess nor in deficiency. It is an impulse expressed temperately until it becomes habitual. Excess and deficiency are equally fatal. The coward is he who avoids and fears anything; the foolhardy he who rushes into danger anywhere.[1] Liberality is the mean between prodigality and avarice; civility is the mean between obsequiousness and insolence. Virtue itself is the mean between self-indulgence and asceticism. In virtue lies happiness, man's *summum bonum.*

Aristotle's *Politics* affords a searching analysis of many phases of societary life. The family and the state are by nature prior to the individual, since the whole must exist before any individual part.[2] When isolated, the individual is

[1] *Ethics,* translation by Welldon, II, 2.
[2] *Politics,* translation by Jowett, I, 2.

not self-sufficient. Thus, the state is founded on the social needs of the individual. By virtue of these social needs, man possesses the gregarious, or social instinct. By nature, man is a political animal,[3] that is, he is a being who by nature or necessity lives in association with his kind. Man can attain his highest good only as a member of society.

Property is accorded by Aristotle a fundamental social position. Physical necessities can best be provided through the efforts of individuals. Communal ownership of property on a large scale will fail. In referring to Plato's communism, Aristotle declared: "For that which is common to the greatest number has the least care bestowed upon it."[4] Further, when one feels a thing to be his own, how much greater is his pleasure in it.[5] Then, if one has private property, he may have the great pleasure which comes from making gifts to others. Moreover, communism will lead to an unusual amount of quarreling; those who work faithfully will feel aggrieved when they see that those who work dilettantishly receive and consume a full portion.[6]

Aristotle deprecated land equalization. Equalization of the desire for land is urged. Instead of dividing land equally or of establishing communism in land, Aristotle advocated that the higher classes be trained not to desire more land. He also stated that speculators and land schemers should be prevented from getting more land.[7]

The communism in wives and children that Plato suggested Aristotle denounced as impracticable and foolish. Such a procedure will weaken friendship and destroy love. Moreover, it will break up the unity of the state.[8]

Aristotle held the prevalent disdainful attitude toward manual labor, and theoretically justified slavery. A slave is a person who by nature is a slave, a person who by nature expresses himself through bodily action. He is unable to guide himself by means of reason.[9]

[3] *Loc. cit.*
[4] *Ibid.*, II, 3.
[5] *Ibid.*, II, 5.
[6] *Loc. cit.*
[7] *Politics*, Jowett, 8, 9.
[8] *Ibid.*, II, 4.
[9] *Ibid.*, I, 4.

SOCIAL CONTROL

The subject of social control and government received extended treatment from Aristotle. After considering a great variety of forms of government, he avoided a dogmatic choice of any particular form. He arrived at what is the modern, scientific conclusion, namely, that no one form of government is to be worshiped to the exclusion of all other types. A successful, or virtuous, government depends on the attitude of the people. Human nature must be changed. All people must become socially virtuous before a perfected government can be established.

Theoretically, Aristotle believed that the best government would come through the absolute rulership of one man, provided that there is available a man pre-eminently wise and virtuous. But practically, Aristotle held that in choosing a form of government which will succeed, it is necessary to consider the actual social conditions, the state of development of the people, and the attitude of the ruler or rulers. It does not matter whether one person, or a few persons, or a large number of persons perform the function of ruler so long as the best interests of the state are kept uppermost. If the interests of the entire group are the guiding principles, then royalty, aristocracy, or constitutionalism is commendable. The one, the few, or the many are good rulers, providing they are dominated by the common interests. In these declarations Aristotle overlooked the fact that participation in government by the governed is essential. He also neglected the fact that a "best" ruler would be subjected to very many temptations as a result of personifying in himself all the forms of political, economic, and social power that exist within the state. After a time he would probably yield to some interests which are inimical to the welfare of the whole.[10]

When private interests control the government, the resultant forms of government are either tyranny, oligarchy, or democracy. According to Aristotle the chief difference between oligarchy and democracy is that an oligarchy is the

[10] *Politics*, III, 7.

rule of the rich and a democracy is the rule of the poor.
Evidently he believed that the poor are as egoistic as the
rich and that the poor are incapable of being trained to the
levels of virtuous citizenship.

Although Aristotle was aristocratic in his political science
and advocated frequently the rule of the best few, he endorsed a constitutional republic. Such a form of government will succeed where there are many wise and virtuous
persons. He admitted that in large numbers there is stability of judgment and that common sense bulks large. Under
constitutional government, the extremes will cancel one
another, and the virtuous mean will rule. Large numbers
of persons are less likely to be corrupted than a few persons
or even the one best person.[11]

There are two fundamentals in a good government: first,
actual obedience to the laws by the citizens; second, the social goodness of the laws. Aristotle's formula for an ideal
society is this: virtuous people and good laws, both judged
by the common welfare. And practically, the form of political organization — a monarchy, an aristocracy, or a constitutional republic — depends upon the place of the members of
the social order on the incline of socialization.

If a constitutional republic is established, then rotation
in office should be practiced. The tenure of office should
be restricted to six months.[12] An office should rarely be
held more than once by the same person.

On the other hand, the laws should be changed slowly.[13]
Law has no power to make people obey in spirit, except
through force of habit. The state must guard itself against
small changes in laws. Any apparently slight neglect or disregard of law is insidious; transgression creeps in unper-
ceived.[14] At first, small transgressions may not be observed;
then, they may gain such momentum that they will ruin the
state. Hence, there should be at all times strict observance
of laws.

11 *Ibid.*, III, 15.
12 *Ibid.*, V, 8 ; VII, 2.
13 *Ibid.*, II, 8.
14 *Ibid.*, V, 8.

THE SOCIAL MEAN

The major chord in Aristotle's ideal society is the social mean. The existence of two classes only, the very rich and the very poor, will bring disaster to the state. The very wealthy consider themselves above legalistic or social authority; the very poor are too degraded to understand the necessity and the reason for authority.[15] In fact, all who possess, not simply an unusual degree of wealth, but great beauty, great strength, or a "noble" birth feel that they should be accorded special privileges. Further, not only those who are very poor, but also the persons who are very weak, or very disgraced find it difficult to follow the dictates of law or of social reason.

With the privileged characters who possess a superabundance of advantages, arrogant attitudes developed when they were yet children. At home, they received special considerations; they did not learn obedience within the small family group. In consequence, how could they be expected to be obedient citizens within the larger nation-group? The rich are likely to become insolent and avaricious; they will rule despotically.[16] Not everyone can bear either prosperity or adversity. An increase in prosperity in any part of society should be carefully noted, and that part of society should be placed under surveillance. No one should receive extraordinary power, either from friends or through money.

A society is safest when the middle class is in control.[17] The states will likely be well administered in which the middle class is numerous. Persons of about equal condition do not plot against others; neither are they plotted against. A middle class prevents both the arrogant wealthy and the impetuous proletariat from dominating the state. "Inequality is the source of all revolutions."

CAUSES OF REVOLUTION

Poverty is a cause of revolution and crime.[18] In time of war it is important that the poor be well fed, else they will

[15] *Ibid.*, IV, 11.
[16] *Ibid.*, V, 7.
[17] *Politics*, IV, 11.
[18] *Ibid.*, II, 6.

cause disturbances. Aristotle might have added that in time of peace the poor should be able to feed themselves well, else they will in due season cause revolution.

But poverty is not the only cause of crime. Riches often lead to crime. Wealth causes the commitment of greater crimes than does poverty. The greatest offenses are not occasioned by necessity but by excess.[19] In order to gratify some passion or desire, crime is often committed. Of the passions ambition and avarice are the chief causes of crime.[20] Intoxication produces crime.[21]

The causes of social revolution are manifold. The desire for equality and the desire for inequality are common factors.[22] Inferiors revolt in order that they may attain a state of equality with other persons. Equals revolt in order that they may gain superior levels of honor and status. Aristotle cited a long list of additional factors in social revolution: insolence, fear, political graft, a disproportionate increase of wealth in some part of the state, neglect of trifles in the observance of laws, dissimilarity in elements, such as racial. The fundamental cause, however, of social revolution is love of gain and honor.

Aristotle relies on the middle class to keep the ship of state from being rocked unduly. Its membership is most likely to act according to principles of common sense. The middle class, therefore, should be kept in the majority.

In fact it is fortunate for a state to have all its citizens belong to the middle class in beauty, physical strength, birth, and wealth.

The reasons why people at either extreme of society are not likely to be good citizens are found either in a refusal to respond to law or in unreasonable demands for what they do not have. Again social salvation lies in the middle class.

Aristotle was not a militarist, for he believed that war in itself is not a social good. No people should be trained to conquer and obtain dominion over neighboring states.[23] Military states are safe only when they are at war. After

[19] *Loc. cit.*
[20] *Ibid.*, II, 9.
[21] *Ibid.*, II, 12.
[22] *Ibid.*, V 1.
[23] *Ibid.*, VII, 14.

they declare peace the weight of their military burdens brings about their downfall.[24]

Aristotle was a public health advocate. The location for an ideal city should be carefully chosen. It should be selected, first of all, with reference to the health of the citizens. This point is of greater importance than that of locating a city wisely for the purpose of public administration or war.[25] The importance of a pure water supply is given almost a modern emphasis.

The question of eugenics received the attention of Aristotle. In order that children may be as physically sound as possible, legislators should give special attention to the institution of marriage. Youthful marriages are condemned because the children that are born of such unions will be wanting in respect for their parents.[26] Late marriages will be unsatisfactory because there will be too great differences between the ages of the parents and their children. The marriage of a man and a woman whose ages are widely disproportionate will lead to misunderstandings and quarrels. According to the rigorous dictum of Aristotle, no deformed child shall be permitted to live.[27] Even the advocates of modern birth control may turn for encouragement to Aristotle.

In the marriage relation there is inequality. The man is by nature better fitted to command than the woman.[28] The chief characteristic of a good wife is obedience to her husband—a doctrine which is patriarchal. Unfaithfulness of either sex in marriage is disgraceful.[29]

Aristotle, like Plato, considers education the leading social force. There is a fundamental educational problem: Shall youth be trained primarily (1) to do useful work, (2) to be virtuous, or (3) to gain higher knowledge?[30] No final answer is given. Aristotle's conception of education, however, is paternalistic.

Utilitarian education possesses a danger line. To be seek-

[24] *Loc. cit.*
[25] *Ibid.*, VII.
[26] *Ibid.*, VII, 15.
[27] *Ibid.*, VII, 16.
[28] *Politics*, I, 12.
[29] *Ibid.*, VII, 16.
[30] *Ibid.*, VIII, 2.

ing always after the useful prevents one from developing a free and exalted soul.[31]   Utilitarian education should cease when it cramps the body and spirit and makes either less fit for the practice of virtue.

Gymnastic education should never be professionalized or allowed to hinder a person's higher education.[32]   The excessive training which leads to Olympic victories is antisocial, because the constitution of the given person is exhausted.   Music is valuable inasmuch as it has the power of forming character.[33]   The persons who are engaged in serious-minded occupations need amusements which will give relaxation.

In summary of Aristotle's social thought it may be said that the Stagirite introduced the comparative method of studying human institutions.   He demonstrated the relative value of institutions, showing that those which are best for one age of society will be worthless for a later period.   In order to meet changing social needs and conditions, institutions must change.   There is a fundamental evolution in social changes.

A communistic social organization, according to Aristotle, is psycho-sociologically untenable.   The importance of the middle classes is socially inestimable.   Laws should be respected in small particulars.   The attitudes of the members of society toward their social organizations are more important than the type of organization itself.   Human conduct in the mass is to a degree predictable.

POST-ARISTOTELIAN THOUGHT

After the time of Aristotle, Hellenic life degenerated. Political corruption, military intrigue, and intellectual scepticism vitiated the Hellenic morality that was founded on custom.   The ideal, held by Plato and Aristotle, of man as an integral part of a constructive social order was supplanted by a philosophy of pure individualism.

In Athens, Epicurus (342–270 B.C.) became the leader of the popular hedonistic philosophy with its emphasis upon

[31] *Ibid.*, VII, 3.
[32] *Ibid.*, VIII, 4
[33] *Ibid.*, VIII, 5.

pleasure. Self-sacrifice and noble conduct in the social sense are foreign to Epicureanism. Friends should be sought, not for the sake of cultivating their friendship, but for the pleasure of the seeker. If you treat other persons unjustly, they will retaliate; therefore, treat others justly.

Stoicism, which was founded in Athens by Zeno, reached its culmination among the Romans and hence will be discussed in the following chapter. Polybius (205–123 B.C.), known as the last Hellenic social philosopher, developed a theory of social evolution, based on the belief that people associate because of the selfish benefits that accrue, and on the fact that group approval and disapproval play a leading part in the development of human attitudes. The social process begins in war and conflict and shades over into toleration, argument, and consent.

Grecian social thought is noteworthy because of its intellectual foundations. It ignored many affective elements, and for that reason it became one-sided and unbalanced. It was rational rather than affective or supernatural. It was designed to meet the needs of this life. It moved away from authority and toward opportunism.

Economically, Hellenic social thought assumed or justified slavery. It postulated a democracy, but a democracy builded on the backs of thousands of slaves. In practice, at the zenith of the Athenian democracy, there were only about 25,000 free Athenians as against 300,000 slaves. Women were not enfranchised. The governments put slaves into armies, and ultimately attempted to throw out a commercial net over the other Mediterranean states. As a result they lost the spirit of democracy. The whole system and concept of democracy was undermined by the debilitating influences of an industrial autocracy. The social thought of the Greek was limited in its actual application largely to the privileged few, who aristocratically ignored the needs of the helpless many.

Grecian social thought at the height of the Athenian democracy did achieve, however, for its day and epoch, a unique degree of expression among the free citizens. For example, in the matter of athletics and recreation, the Athenians worked together in furnishing themselves organized group activities. Their athletic contests were of a free community nature untrammeled by commercialized motives. In furnishing recreation for themselves, they co-operated; they acted as community units. Moreover, in these community activities they generated in themselves the spirit of a genuine democratic consciousness.

The fundamentals of Grecian social thought were preserved by the Romans, without being augmented by them. Together with the Chinese, the Hebrew, and the early Christian social thought, Grecian social thought laid the foundations for the rise of modern social science, and even of sociology.

GROUP DISCUSSION TOPICS

1. Aristotle's concept of virtue.
2. Aristotle's most famous dictum.
3. Aristotle's estimate of Plato's attitude toward communism
4. Land equalization according to Aristotle.
5. Aristotle's theory of government.
6. The "social mean" as expressed by Aristotle.
7. Aristotle's "middle class" concept.
8. Aristotle's theory of crime.
9. Causes of social revolution.
10. The fundamental educational problem.
11. Aristotle's contribution to methods of making social science studies.
12. Comparisons of Aristotle's and Plato's social thought.
13. The chief contributions of Grecian social thought.

READINGS

Aristotle, *Politics,* translated by B. Jowett (London : Oxford University Press 1905).

———, *Nicomachean Ethics,* translated by H. Rackham (New York : G. P. Putnam's Sons 1926).

Barker, Ernest, *The Political Thought of Plato and Aristotle* (New York : G. P. Putnam's Sons 1906).

Beach, Walter G., *The Growth of Social Thought* (New York: Charles Scribner's Sons 1939), Ch. III.

Becker, Howard, and Harry E. Barnes, *Social Thought from Lore to Science* (Washington : Harren Press 1952), Vol. I, Ch. 4.

Chambliss, R., *Social Thought* (New York : Dryden Press 1954), Ch. 8.

Ellwood, Charles A., "Aristotle as a Sociologist," *Annals of the American Academy of Political and Social Science,* 19:228-238.

Lichtenberger, James P., *Development of Social Theory* (New York : Century Company 1923), Ch. II.

Loos, Isaac R., *Studies in the Politics of Aristotle and the Republic of Plato* (Iowa City : University Press 1889).

Saunders, Kenneth, *The Ideals of East and West* (New York : The Macmillan Company 1934), Ch. IV.

CHAPTER X

AURELIUS AND ROMAN SOCIAL THOUGHT

Roman social thought is an outgrowth of Hellenic philosophic movements. It is represented in part by the codification of social rules and laws; it was the product to a degree of the legalistic genius of the Romans. It was Stoicism, however, which greatly affected and conditioned the relatively meager social thinking of the Roman scholars. Although no one person made a far-reaching contribution to social thought, there were scholars who made valuable social observations or analyses.

Lucretius (96–55 B.C.), was the chief Roman exponent of Epicureanism. In his story of social evolution he began with the various phases of the biological struggle for existence, and proceeded to depict in a remarkably significant fashion the origins of social practices and customs.[1] Although his data are of questionable value, his descriptions of social origins often run strangely parallel to modern findings.

CICERO

The ideal commonwealth of Marcus Tullius Cicero (106–43 B.C.) is founded on the belief that Rome has the possibility of becoming an ideal state.[2] The best ideas in this connection were selected by Cicero from the Aristotelian, Epicurean, and Stoic philosophies. Cicero was apparently an exponent of honest statesmanship and finally gave his life for civic efficiency. He argued that a child should not be punished by either a parent or a teacher in a fit of anger. Corporal punishment should be considered only when other methods fail to discipline.

Cicero followed Plato's example and described the principles on which a republic should be established, in terms,

[1] Lucretius, *De rerum natura*, translated by Muno, in Bohn's Libraries, V 335 ff., 778 ff.
[2] *De officiis*, translated by Edmonds, Bohn's Libraries, I, XVII, XIV; *De republica*, translated by Younge, Bohn's Libraries, I, XXV-XXVI, XIV.

however, of the Roman situation. In *The Laws,* he discusses the application of his political principles. Community of interest and the practice of justice laid the foundation for a strong commonwealth. Human beings are naturally gregarious and naturally seek association. A state develops by a slow evolutionary process in which many leaders have participated. The universality of human traits, the similarity of human nature underneath divergent customs, and the widespread exhibition of mental ability irrespective of race are proclaimed. Moreover, there is even a natural equality in morals, in learning, and in responsiveness to kindly treatment. Cicero offered the world a far-reaching set of social doctrines based on the common elements in human nature ; they forecast the doctrine of peace on earth to all people of good will. Cicero brought together a great many ideas regarding social life and outlined an ideal state.

Julius Cæsar (100–44 B.C.) in his *Commentaries* presents social studies of contemporary conditions ; they possess modern value. In a large number of instances the accuracy of Cæsar's social notes has been verified.

STOIC SOCIAL THOUGHT

The teachings of the Roman Stoics may be traced back to the Socratic formula : Virtue is knowledge. Virtue is knowledge which grows out of practical human conduct. Unlike Aristotle, the Stoics believed that sympathy is a disease. It is pathological and hence must be overcome. In helping other people, the wise person does not allow the emotion of pity to appear.

Contrary to the theory of the Epicureans, the Stoics taught that pleasure is a tiresome and sickly goal. Seneca (4 B.C.–A.D. 65), a leading Roman Stoic, declared that he was "seeking to find what is good for a man, not for his belly." Virtue, according to Stoic philosophy, consists in living a free and undisturbed life. A line was drawn between the virtuous and the non-virtuous, between a few virtuous and a multitude of fools. This doctrine tends to engender in the few virtuous a contemptuous regard for the pig-trough philosophy of the many.

This tendency, however, was offset by the Stoic belief that all persons originally possess the same nature and that all are children of the same universal Spirit. Social differences, hence, are external and superficial. Beneath the surface of human nature there is a cosmopolitanism which constitutes a passive brotherhood of man. Brotherly love should rule, according to the Stoics, but it should rule temperately, and not in such a way as to disturb the individual's self-control. Brotherly love should be not a passionate but an intellectual element.

In his treatise on *Benefits,* Seneca makes benevolence the most social of all virtues and ingratitude the most venal of all crimes. Seneca defines a benefit as "the act of a well-wisher who bestows joy and derives joy from the bestowal of it, and is inclined to do what he does from the prompting of his own will."[3] The phase of it that counts is "the spirit of the action." Intention exalts small gifts and discredits great ones. Moreover, "generosity moves swiftly," for if its benefits are given tardily, heartiness has gone out of them. "Tardy goodwill smacks of illwill."[4]

Moreover, the giver of a benefit must not tell others of it. "Let the giver of a benefit hold his tongue."[5] If one expects gain or pleasure from a benefit, then it is not a benefit. "He who has given a benefit in order that he may get something back has really not given it."[6] In other words, "To transfer something from the left hand to the right hand is neither to give nor to receive."[7] A friend is found not in a reception hall or on display, but in the heart. In the heart he must be admitted, retained, and enshrined. Moreover, it is persistent goodness which finally "wins over bad men."[8]

Proper giving is very difficult. It must be just and reasonable. Wrong giving "is no other than a shameful waste." The reasons for correct giving are manifold: (1) to do a service, (2) to make a return, (3) to give succor, and (4) to give so as to keep a deserving person from being dragged down

[3] Seneca, "On Benefits," I, VI, 1.
[4] *Ibid.,* II, V, 4.
[5] *Ibid.,* II, XI, 2.
[6] *Ibid.,* IV, XIV, 3.
[7] *Ibid.,* V, VIII, 1.
[8] *Ibid.,* VII, XXXI, 1.

by poverty. To some in need Seneca would not give help, for it might pauperize them. To others he would thrust gifts upon them, because their pride perhaps keeps them from accepting or from asking.[9]

MARCUS AURELIUS AND SOCIAL PRACTICE

Marcus Aurelius (A.D. 121–180), even as emperor, practiced the Stoic principles and yet took a full and active part in the rulership of his country. He was a humanitarian; he cut down the taxes to be paid by the poor; he practiced individualization of punishment for lawbreakers; he opposed some of the brutalities in public punishments and at the gladiatorial contests. He gave the social injunction: Love mankind.[10] Living should consist in passing from one social act to another.[11] This is a social world; men exist for the sake of one another.[12]

The Stoic emperor declared that God is social and that persons are part of God's universe. Each person is a component part of the social system, and hence every act of a person is an integral phase of social life.[13] Inasmuch as the Intelligence of the universe is social, human society functions as a phase of the cosmic co-ordination. We are all co-laborers and co-operators. Even the persons who find fault and who hinder what happens, are performing useful co-operative functions.[14] That which is harmful to the swarm is likewise harmful to the individual. Man is a citizen of the world.[15] The services of a good citizen are never lost. The good citizen does good chiefly by the example he sets.

Aurelius had a concept of the Good Community that is worthy of consideration. It is unnatural for people to work against each other. It was Aurelius who held to a rigid interpretation of each person's social responsibility. He urged that each individual know his relation to the whole social

[9] Seneca, "On the Happy Life," XXIV, 1.
[10] *Thoughts*, translated by Long, VII, 31.
[11] *Ibid.*, VI, 7.
[12] *Ibid.*, VII, 59.
[13] *Ibid.*, IX, 23.
[14] *Ibid.*, VI, 42.
[15] *Ibid.*, XII, 36.

system and not to allow any act to serve in any other relationship.

EPICTETUS

An other-worldly center for one's thinking is suggested by
Epictetus (A.D. 60–120), a slave who became an able Stoic phi
losopher. Epictetus, like Socrates, left no writings. His
ideas are known to us through his pupil, Arrian. Rise above
your enemies, was one of Epictetus' guiding principles. You
ought to rise above being offended and hating. You ought
to pity the one who is offensive. You ought to be sorry for
him inasmuch as he has allowed the brute nature that is in
us all to crop out.[16]
Epictetus had an exalted idea of the nature of human nature. He implies that what is ordinarily called bad nature
is really brute nature that is a phase of human nature.

PASSIVE COSMOPOLITANISM

But the cosmopolitanism of the Stoics never extended beyond a passive interest in the world of affairs. It meant that
a person should be agreeable with other persons, that he
should be tolerant of the weaknesses of others, and that he
should be constantly aware that others are watching him and
likely to copy the example he sets. Stoicism requires the
suppression of anger and the exercising of clemency toward
all human beings. While Stoicism does not extend so far in
its profession as Christianity's doctrine of brotherhood of
man, it represents a broader viewpoint of life than any code
of conduct which previously had developed in the non-
Christian world.
The purpose of punishment, according to the Stoic philosophy, is twofold: either to reform the evil-doer, or to prevent the operation of his evil influence and to stop him from
setting harmful examples. The social medicine must be determined, quantitatively and qualitatively, by the nature of
the offender and the offense. Above all things else, he who
administers punishment must not act in anger. Justice can-

16 Epictetus, *Discourses*, I, 73.

not be angry. Lynch procedure is entirely contrary to the teachings of Stoicism.

Seneca recounts an interesting proposal that was made in the Roman Senate, namely, that all the slaves should be dressed so as to distinguish them from the free men. The plan did not receive a hearing, for it was anticipated that when the slaves discovered how greatly they outnumbered the free men they might start a revolution.[17]

First of all, thieves and robbers should be instructed in the error of their ways. Obtain their point of view and administer punishment accordingly. Pity them. The person who understands why criminals commit offenses is prevented from becoming angry with them.[18] Aurelius, like Jesus,[19] gave the injunction: Love even those who do wrong. Aurelius, like Paul,[20] urged an attitude of charity toward wrongdoers.[21]

The Stoics condemned luxurious living and fashion racing. True riches consists not in augmenting one's fortune, but in abating the desires for securing material wealth.[22] The words of Emperor Aurelius regarding ostentatious living do not seem out of place when applied to the modern display of wealth. Seneca asserted that he would despise wealth as much when he has it as when he does not possess it.

Stoicism urged the Aristotelian social mean regarding property. Much property is a burden and a cause of worry and fear. It excites envy in others. The best society is that which is characterized by neither poverty nor plenty. The poor should not condemn riches, and the wealthy err in extolling the benefits of poverty — each is speaking of a situation which is objective to him and outside his sphere. Since it is objective to him, he is not qualified to speak concerning it. A person is great who is not corrupted by his wealth; but he is greater who is honestly poor in the midst of plenty. Riches constitute a power to do evil, hence mediocrity of fortune with a gentleness of mind represents the best status.

[17] "On Mercy," I, XXIV, 1.
[18] Epictetus, *Discourses,* Book I, Chapter XVIII.
[19] *Matthew,* 5:44.
[20] *Thoughts,* VII, 22.
[21] *Romans,* 12:17.
[22] *Thoughts,* VII, 26; III, 7.

SENECA

A happy life, according to Seneca, is one that is in harmony with its own nature.[23] A happy life can be attained through (1) a sound, sane mind, (2) a mind capable of "the noblest fortitude," "careful of the body," and (3) a user but not a slave "of the gifts of fortune." Happiness involves being reconciled to one's circumstances, and virtue is "something lofty, exalted and regal, unconquerable, and unwearied."[24] People who seek variety and special opportunities flock to the city, because the latter offers the satisfactions that the undifferentiated rural district does not afford.

There are three kinds of life. One is devoted to pleasures. A second is given over to contemplation. The third is characterized by action. Of the three, contemplation is most favored by the Stoics.[25]

Stoicism enunciated excellent social ideals, which were, however, passively intellectual. They were not effectively dynamic. Despite their implications, they begat social inertia. The teachings of the Stoics as a rule removed rather than instilled a sense of public responsibility. The doctrines are available to the few rather than to the masses, although Epictetus, a slave, attained freedom and rose to a full interpretation of Stoic principles. The social ideals and concepts of the Stoics did not possess enough power to regenerate a degenerate society. They had sufficient strength, however, to maintain themselves in a voluptuous and pleasure-seeking world. They performed the exceedingly useful function of preparing the way for the invasion of the Roman Empire by the new and active Christian propaganda. The teachings of the Stoics made easier the conquest of Rome by Christianity. They softened a little an otherwise hard-hearted world.

As a class the Romans were men of action. They were soldiers and administrators. The name of Rome is still synonymous with power. On the whole it must be said that the Romans made little contribution to societary thought.

[23] "On the Happy Life," III, 3.
[24] Ibid., VII, 3.
[25] Ibid., VII. 1-4.

LEGAL AND ADMINISTRATIVE THOUGHT

The constructive work of the Romans was legal and administrative. They built up a special social science — legal science. The legal genius of the Romans emphasized the rights of contract, of private property, of interest. Although this attention to the development of individualistic institutions was fatal to the rise of new social attitudes and to an increase in the sense of social responsibility, it nevertheless was instrumental in constructing a stable framework for the evolution of the social process.

The Romans preserved a portion of Hellenic culture. The teachings of Plato and Aristotle were saved to modern civilization. Credit is due the Romans for receiving, keeping, working over, and handing on a part of the best Hellenic civilization.

The dominant type of Roman thought accentuated military principles of authority, even to the point of autocracy. It tended to crush the unprivileged populace. It tried to keep the masses contented by generous state aid. It denied to personality its complete individual and social expressions. In building an individualistic framework which would provide an orderly *milieu* for the rise of the institution of private property, it ignored the needs of the uneducated and poverty-enslaved masses for a full measure of liberty.

Rome developed the concept of organized power. The organizing ability of the Romans was marvelous, an organizing power that lives today in and through the Catholic Church.

The greatest gift of Rome was its Stoic concepts. Although these originated in Hellas, they attained their maturity in Rome. They opened the way for the reception of the Christian social concepts of love, service, brotherhood of man.

GROUP DISCUSSION TOPICS

1. The attitude of the Stoics toward the concept of brotherly love.
2. The purpose of punishment according to the Stoics.
3. The Stoic view of wealth.
4. The Stoic concepts of virtue.
5. Comparison of the ideas of Aurelius, of Seneca, and of Epictetus.
6. Contrasts between Epicureanism and Stoicism.
7. Similarities in and differences between the social teachings of Stoicism and of Christianity.
8. Relation between Stoicism and early Hindu social thought.
9. The social values in Stoic philosophy.
10. The specific major contributions of the Romans to social thought.

READINGS

Abbott, F. F., *History and Description of Roman Political Institutions* (Boston : Ginn & Company 1901).

Aurelius, Marcus, *Thoughts* (London : Frowde, n.d.).

Barbour, Francis, *The Political Works of Marcus Tullius Cicero* (London : Spettigue 1841).

Bussell, F. W., *Marcus Aurelius and the Later Stoics* (Edinburgh : Clark 1910).

Davis, C. H. S., *Greek and Roman Stoicism* (Boston : Turner and Company 1903).

Ellwood, Charles A., *A History of Social Philosophy* (New York : Prentice-Hall, Inc. 1938), Ch. IV.

Epictetus, *Discourses of* (New York : Scott-Thaw 1903).

Gummere, Richard M., *Seneca the Philosopher and his Modern Message* (Boston : Marshall Jones 1922).

Holland, Francis, *Seneca* (New York : Longmans, Green & Co. 1920).

Lichtenberger, James P., *Development of Social Theory* (New York : Century Company 1923), Ch. III.

Seneca, *Moral Essays* (includes "Dialogues") (transl. by J. W. Bashore) (New York : G. P. Putnam's Sons 1928).

Zeller, Edward, *Stoics, Epicureans, and Sceptics* (London : Reichel, Longmans & Co. 1870).

———, *Meditations* (London : Dent and Company 1935).

CHAPTER XI

EARLY CHRISTIAN SOCIAL THOUGHT

Christian social thought is the direct outgrowth of Hebrew social concepts. Amos and Hosea and Isaiah paved the way for the social teachings of Jesus. The social commandments of the Old Testament were the progenitors of the modified social injunctions of the New Testament. Job, the social citizen, was not an unworthy precursor of Jesus, the lover of humanity. Out of the love and tender care for children which thrived in Hebrew homes there arose the concept of the brotherhood of man and the Fatherhood of God — the two cardinal principles of Christianity.

That the social teachings of the Chinese philosopher, Mo Ti, who lived in the fifth century B.C., are similar in their emphasis on universal love is remarkable. There is no evidence that Jesus was in touch in any way with the thought of Mo Ti.

SOCIAL BACKGROUNDS

Jesus gave expression to no system of social thought, but uttered social principles and concepts which, when put together, constituted the basis of a new social order. He dealt with personalities rather than with institutions. He looked to the individual rather than to the mass. He emphasized functions rather than structures. He proclaimed the elements of a new social order. He lived at a time of great social turmoil and uncertainty. Revolts against Roman authority were not uncommon. The Jews were divided into antagonistic parties or sects. Jesus was not in sympathy with Roman dictatorships and He found the Jewish sects, such as the Pharisees and the Sadducees, promoting selfish and mercenary activities. He spoke out freely against what He considered intolerable wrongs and sought a way out in terms of a new birth for the individual. His doctrines were considered "dangerous," and He was betrayed by one of the radical Zealots, seized, and executed, but not without maintaining

His poise and what was considered to be an unaccountable sense of forgiveness of His enemies. He analyzed the need for socio-religious personalities. If He could get these, He was sure of the ultimate societal results. He foresaw a perfect society — the Kingdom of God.

Unlike Plato and Aristotle, Jesus was a continual student of everyday life. Like Socrates, Jesus was fond of people. He was a student of personal and social affairs. He mixed with all types of human beings. Like Socrates, He wrote practically nothing. Unlike Socrates, Jesus had a dynamic element in His nature which forbade Him to remain content in a world of suffering (after the Socratic manner), but which drove Him to help and to heal. He went about doing good. The Gospel records are replete with instance after instance of His work in healing the sick of their infirmities. He was not, however, a physician but a teacher and a savior from sin and evil.

THE IDEAL SOCIETY

Behind all the teachings of Jesus, there is the concept of a perfect human order. This kingdom begins in the hearts of individuals.[1] It is a spirit or an attitude of mind which leads the individual toward co-operative living. The Kingdom may come on earth as well as in heaven. Consider the picture or a harmonious community life which Jesus gave when lamenting over Jerusalem: "How often would I have gathered thy children together, as a hen doth gather her brood together under her wings, and ye would not!"[2]

Jesus extended the concept of brotherhood. Whoever shall do the will of God is a brother to me.[3] The world, under God, is one family. The Kingdom, therefore, is to include all human beings who worship God in spirit and in truth and who at the same time love their fellow men in justice and co-operative living.

The ideal society is organic. It grows from good examples. Live so that other persons, seeing the helpfulness of your life, may live likewise. The Kingdom grows like a

[1] *Luke,* 17:20, 21.
[2] *Luke,* 13:34.
[3] *Matthew,* 12:48; *Mark,* 3:34.

grain of mustard seed, which finally becomes a tree in whose branches the birds find homes.[4]   Love grows, and like leaven, permeates and transforms the whole mass — the result is a perfect Kingdom.

God is the spiritual leader of the new society, to whom Jesus prayed in the social term, *Our Father.*   God is the personification of love.   God loved the sinful world so much that He gave His beloved son to the task of saving not simply the Jews or modern Europeans, but the whole world from all sins.   The Star which guided the Magi was God's service Star, announcing that He had given His beloved son in the war against sin.

THE SOCIAL PRINCIPLE OF LOVE

Love is the new note that is to reform the world.[5]   Love is the scientific principle from which all other true sociological concepts are derived.   Love received the most perfect human expression in the personality and life of Jesus, who came not for self-glory but to save people from hate and sin ; who sought not the sheep in order to oppress and slay them for his own gratification, but to direct them, when lost, back to safe living; who sought not to weigh down the burdened with unjust taxes and harsh living conditions, but to relieve and give rest to the heavy-laden ; who cared less for the upper Four Hundred than for the lower Four Million.

The principle of love compels the members of the Kingdom to show mercy.   God is full of mercy, therefore, let His followers show mercy.   Love forgives.   The Christian citizen is instructed to become reconciled with his brother citizen before worshiping at the altar of God.[6]   If a person would be forgiven for his sins, he must acquire the habit of forgiving other persons.   He must be careful not to judge harshly, lest other persons judge him harshly.   He should forgive others seventy times seven, that is, without stint or measure.

St. Luke, the physician, recites the story of a loving father. The prodigal son impetuously demanded his share of the in-

---

[4] *Matthew,* 13:31, 32; *Mark,* 4:30; *Luke,* 13:18, 19.
[5] *John,* 3:16.
[6] *Matthew,* 5:23; 18:15; *Luke,* 6:41, 42.

heritance and, going into a far country, wasted his substance in riotous living. But upon showing true remorse for these exceedingly grave offenses, his father received him back with a loving, forgiving heart, a feast, the best robes, and music, and dancing. One of the malefactors who was crucified with Christ showed a penitent heart at the last moment and received forgiveness from the loving, dying Christ. Since no one is without sin, no one has a right to be unforgiving. Even the woman taken in adultery came within the law of forgiving love.

The societary principle of love is the major chord of Christianity. It is Christianity's non-scientific but greatest gift to social ethics. It has become the fundamental concept of social ethics. To the Old Testament type of love which urged persons to love their neighbors and to love the alien and stranger, Jesus repeatedly insisted upon a love that is still greater, namely, a love which will include enemies. Love your enemies.[7] Jesus Himself exemplified this form of love. He made no idle interpretation of an impossible love, but demonstrated and lived a love which forgave His enemies, even those who mockingly, shamelessly nailed Him to a cross. So great is the drawing power of this almost superhuman love which Jesus expressed in deeds that He himself predicted that if He were lifted up He would draw all people unto Him.

Love fills people with compassion. The Gospels are replete with references to the fact that wherever Jesus saw sickness, poverty, sin, He was moved with compassion. The illustrations range from the blind men by the wayside to the bread-hungry multitudes, from the unclean leper in Galilee to murderous Jerusalem.

Love is cosmopolitan. All peoples are entitled to know the meaning of Christian love.[8] Both Jew and Gentile shall feel its warming glow. The good Samaritan lives it. Loving neighborliness includes more than priestly and Levitical acts; it involves Samaritan kindness. The love in the heart of Jesus reached first to a few close friends, then to sinners and outcasts, then to the Samaritans and the Gentiles, and

[7] *Matthew*, 5:44, 46; *Luke*, 6:20, 35.
[8] *Matthew*, 28:20; 24:14.

finally to the whole world. It led ultimately to one of the most sacrificial of all human enterprises — the missionary movement.

Love leads to humility and self-sacrifice. Alms-giving is done in private, not for social plaudits. A person prays, not to be seen of men and to be accounted good.[9] He who seeks to save his life shall lose it; whoever loses his life for the sake of the Kingdom shall save it. He who stores up for himself the wealth of the world shall lose himself. Salutations in the market places and chief seats in the synagogues in themselves are unworthy. The poor in spirit are blessed.

Love shuns positions of worldly power, lest they be secured at the loss of one's soul.[10] The best positions in life are not to be seized; they are obtained through the exercise of love; they are bestowed in recognition of merit and worth. He who exalts himself will be abased; the humble will be exalted.

Love creates true greatness. The members of the society of perfect love are characterized by the sincerity, purity, humility of little children.[11] He who serves most is greatest. The Kingdom of God is an aristocracy, not of Might but of Service. The Son of God came to serve, not to be served. For the sake of those outside the Kingdom, Jesus sanctified Himself, sacrificing even His life in that cause.

Love makes the Golden Rule the best ethical proposition in Hebrew and Christian literature. "Whatsoever ye would that men should do to you, do ye even so to them." In reply to a lawyer of the Pharisees, Jesus enunciated a twofold commandment, the first part of which invoked complete love to God; the second part, to man. The love of a person for his fellow man as shown in both attitude and deeds is the test of the love of a person for God. Love means service. Love does not connote lip-service; neither does it mean divided service. No one can serve two masters, God and mammon.

SOCIAL SERVICE

Christian love implies definite and continued personal

[9] *John,* 12:43; *Matthew,* 6:5.
[10] *Matthew,* 4:8.
[11] *Luke,* 9:48; *Mark,* 10:14; *Matthew,* 12:1.

service.   Social service is the test of entrance to the Kingdom, and of the sincerity of a person's religious profession.[12]
On the judgment day those on the right hand will be blessed
and given life eternal, and to them the King of the judgment
will say:

> For I was hungry, and you fed me,
> I was thirsty and you gave me drink,
> I was a stranger and you welcomed me,
> I was without clothes and you clothed me,
> I was in prison, and you visited me.[13]

Then the righteous, with surprise, will inquire of the
Lord of the judgment: When did we see you hungry and
feed you; or thirsty, and give you drink?   When did we see
you a stranger and take you in?   Then the Lord of the judgment will answer them that when they had served the weak
and poor and the heavy-laden on earth, they had been serving Him and thereby had proved their loyalty to God and
earned the rewards of everlasting life.   And those who fail
to measure up to the social service test, whether professing
Christians or not, will be turned away.

The importance and nature of religio-social service is indicated by Jesus when He symbolizes the giving of a cup of
cold water in His name as a test for receiving eternal life.[14]
He who has two coats should give one to him who has none.
The sharing of food with those who have no food is commanded.   Give liberally; give all thou hast.   It is blessed to
give in all circumstances.   Material riches are insignificant
in value when compared with spiritual wealth.   To give the
things of this world is to receive the greater things of the
spirit.   He is richest who gives most, of both material and
spiritual goods.   As an expression of His love for God, Jesus
lived a life of social and human service.

Whenever Jesus mentioned the ten commandments — all
three synoptic writers agree on this point — He omitted the
four commandments of individual import and repeated only
the social rules, or principles, and revised one (the sixth
below):

[12] *Matthew,* 25:31-46.
[13] Charles F. Kent, *The Social Teachings of the Prophets and Jesus,* pp.
184-185.
[14] *Mark,* 9:41; *Matthew,* 10:42.

(1) Thou shalt do no murder,
(2) Thou shalt not commit adultery,
(3) Thou shalt not steal,
(4) Thou shalt not bear false witness,
(5) Honor thy father and thy mother,
(6) Thou shalt love thy neighbor as thyself.[15]

After the fashion of the major social prophets, Jesus cried out vehemently against social injustice. He denounced the persons who devour widows' houses, or who lay unnecessary economic burdens upon their fellow men.

SOCIAL JUSTICE

Antisocial religion, above all things, angered Jesus. He wanted no followers who were practicing social or political injustice. Cursed are those persons who appear righteous, who make long prayers, or who go about in long robes, but who inwardly are hypocrites, are full of dead men's bones, of uncleanness, of extortion and excess.[16] The shedding of innocent blood is condemned. The paying of money in order to expiate sin will avail nothing. Such money is tainted ; it is blood money.[17]

Antisocial and commercialized religion so angered Jesus that, contrary to his customary attitudes toward sinners, He committed violence on one occasion against offenders. He overthrew the tables of the money changers in the temple, and, making a scourge of small cords, He drove out the money changers. In so doing, He declared that the worship of God should not be commercialized.[18] He would not have the house of worship turned into a cultured den of thieves.

So furious were the scribes and the chief priests because of the attack of Jesus upon antisocial religious practices that they planned how they might kill Him.[19] It appears that, as a direct result of the antagonism of Jesus to the antisocial practices of the religious, or temple authorities, and of the other religious leaders, the conspiracy against Jesus finally brought about His death. Jesus went about stirring up the

[15] *Matthew*, 19:18, 19.
[16] *Matthew*, 23:23-33.
[17] *Loc. cit.*
[18] *John*, 2:13-17; *Matthew*, 21:12, 13.
[19] *Mark*, 11:18; *Luke*, 19:47.

common people in a democratic movement against the auto-cratic, hypocritical, antisocial, religious leaders among the Jews. He met His death while championing the need of the masses who were being exploited in the name of religion.

Jesus was the highest type of social democrat. The per-fected social order which He foresaw is democratic in spirit, and ruled by the principles of love and service in the name of God. Furthermore, no one shall be compelled to come into the Kingdom. The good tidings shall be presented to all, but the principle of voluntary assent, not compulsion or conscription, rules in recruiting for the Kingdom. More-over, within the Kingdom, compulsion is unknown. Love sufficeth.

Jesus hated sin. To Him sin was anything which over-comes love and which causes a person or society to disinte-grate. Sin is that which defeats or hinders the coming of the Kingdom of Love. Sin breaks up or holds back the so-cial process. Sin, like love, is organic. Sin grows. An evil tree brings forth evil fruit; grapes and figs are not gathered from thorns or thistle-bearing plants.

Jesus forgave sinners; even social sinners. By means of imagination, He put Himself in the place of the sinner and sought to understand the causes of the sinning. As His mind filled with an understanding of sin, His heart over-flowed with pity and forgiveness for the sinner. He sought primarily to reclaim; He thought secondarily of punish-ment. Even in the case of the adulterous woman, He sought to save what was left of the broken spirit rather than to punish. His cardinal penological principle was reformation.

THE FAMILY

It is significant that the social institution which Jesus sup-ported above all others, even above the church and the state, was the family. Jesus spoke frequently for the family. He commanded that children should unwaveringly act loyally toward parents; he used not only the clear-cut terms of the writer of Exodus but the included curse of death upon those who abuse their parents.[20]

20 *Matthew*, 15:4; 19:19; *Exodus*, 21:17.

An even stronger command was given by Jesus concerning loyalty to the marriage relation. A man's genuine loyalty to his parents, undiminished in intensity, must be subordinated to faithfulness to his wife.[21] This social theory is opposite in nature to that of Confucius concerning attitudes toward parents and wives. The conception which Jesus urged leads to social progress, while the teaching of Confucius leads to social stability.

A man and woman who have been spiritually joined together in wedlock are one flesh, above and beyond separation by civil authorities. Jesus uttered the stern and awe-inspiring sanction : What therefore God hath joined together, let not man put asunder.[22] The family as an institution is accorded a sacredly fundamental place in the social order.

Jesus recognized woman as equal with man spiritually. His attitude toward His mother and the other women of His day was one of respect, chivalry, and gentleness. He laid the foundations of a social order in which women function on terms of equality with men.

Honor to parents and honor to wife must be supplemented by honor to children. Jesus worshiped little children. In them He saw the innocence and purity of God. When He wished to describe the attributes of the Kingdom, He selected a little child and held him up as typifying the simple, natural spirit of perfect living. Although without children himself, Jesus loved little children, choosing them for special honors, and declaring that of such is the kingdom of God. It is not God's will that one of these little ones should perish ; it is stupidity of man and the lack of social conscience that cause a high mortality rate of little children. He who harms the trustful child shall be cursed. It were better for such a miscreant that a millstone were tied about his neck and that he were thrown into the sea.[23]

PROPERTY AND POVERTY

In regard to the influence of private property Jesus was fearful. His zeal for and whole-hearted loyalty to spiritual

[21] *Mark,* 10:7, 8; *Matthew,* 19:5.
[22] *Matthew,* 19:6; *Mark,* 10:9.
[23] *Mark,* 9:42.

values made Him suspicious of vested interests. He repeatedly warned in vigorous language against the lure of gold
and the baneful influences of material wealth upon the attitudes and acts of persons. He Himself showed no interest in
owning property. He lived without a home of His own and
without private means. If He had possessed these, His life-
work probably would have failed. He urged His disciples
to remain free from the desire for money; He even commanded them to rely for means of material subsistence upon
the people with whom they labored. Jesus believed that
private property hindered the realization of the principle of
brotherhood of man. He made a sharp distinction between
the interests of God and mammon. He believed that these
two sets of interests are diametrically opposed to each other.
To the extent that a person relies upon property, he separates himself from God and the things of the Spirit. The
disciples were instructed to scorn, not only the earning of
wealth, but if they possessed earthly goods, they were to sell
these and give the proceeds to the poor.[24] The disciple of
the spiritual life must divorce himself from the love of
monetary gain.

Toward the poor, Jesus was sympathetic. The Gospel
shall be preached chiefly to the poor, not because the poor,
per se, need it more than the rich, and not because the poor
should be specially favored, but because they recognize their
needs. They are in a receptive attitude, whereas the attitude of the rich has been calloused by their wealth. The
response to the Gospel is not likely to be wholehearted by
persons who value riches highly.

Jesus taught a spiritual socialism. He thought in terms
of spiritual love for all persons, not of material well-being
for the proletariat. But He seemed to prefer the company
of the poor. Blessed are the poor, was His attitude; for
they are in a frame of mind which makes them fit subjects
for the perfect Kingdom. The possession of property gives
a person a feeling of self-exaltation; poverty gives rise to
humility—a cardinal virtue of the Kingdom.

Jesus did not attack poverty with preventive measures.

24 *Matthew,* 19:21.

Poverty will continue to exist.[25]   Perhaps it is well that it should continue, for a nation of economically-satisfied people might not be religious-minded.   It is harder for a camel to go through a needle's eye than for a rich man to get into the swing of an untrammeled social process.   Woe unto the rich, because they are self-centered, materially inclined, and pleasure-loving.   The man who pulled down his barns in order to build larger barns, saying to himself: "Take thine ease, eat, drink, and be merry," is scathingly condemned by Jesus.[26]   He is ostracized from the ideal society.   In the story of Lazarus and the rich man, the former is carried to Abraham's bosom, but the latter, in torments, begs for a cup of water and the company of Lazarus.   He wanted Lazarus sent to Him; he longed for the company of him whom he once ignored.   The attention of Jesus was continually centered on the dangers of wealth.

Zacchaeus, a rich man, was called as a disciple of Jesus. But before the discipleship began, the superintendent not only came down from the mulberry tree and declared his allegiance to God, but he volunteered evidence of being social-minded as well by stating that he gave one half of his wealth to the poor, and that he restored falsely acquired possessions fourfold.

Then there was the rich young man who came to Jesus, asking how he might obtain admittance to the Kingdom, declaring that he observed the commandments.   One more thing, however, was required of him, namely, that he sell all his possessions and give the returns to the poor.   Only by so giving might he have treasure in the social Kingdom.

The teaching of Jesus concerning the Sabbath throws light on the exceedingly human element in His thought. The Sabbath is a special day for doing good deeds.[27]   The Sabbath is to be treated not primarily from the standpoint of religious rites but from the viewpoint of human welfare. Works of necessity, and deeds of mercy and kindness to man and beast are proper to the Sabbath.[28]   Man was not made

[25] John, 12:8; Mark, 14:7; Matthew, 26:11.
[26] Luke, 12:13-21.
[27] Luke, 13:14; Matthew, 12:2; 10:13.
[28] Mark, 2:27; 3:4.

for the Sabbath, but the day of rest and good deeds was designed for the benefit of man.

PEACE VERSUS WAR

The attitude of Jesus toward the problem of peace versus
war has aroused considerable controversy. There are certain of His sayings which seem to contradict each other.
But an analysis of all His teachings demonstrates that His
emphasis was on peace. The exceptions to the rule will be
stated first.[29] On one occasion He said: "I came not to
send peace but a sword." The context shows that Jesus was
speaking in an individual and not a national way. He had
in mind the conflicts which arise between persons who are
converted to the ideals of the Kingdom and those who are
not. Jesus explained that those who love Him must do so
even at the expense of forsaking father and mother.[30] Loyalty to the Kingdom may mean that the son will oppose the
practices of his father in business, the daughter will object
to the time wasted in the un-Christian practices of her
mother, the parents will protest the sowing of "wild oats"
by son or daughter.

In the temple, on one occasion, Jesus displayed anger and
used violence. He was dealing, however, with a group of
criminals, cultured criminals, who apparently would respond
to no treatment except violence. They would not cease
their nefarious practices except through compulsion.

On the other hand, the illustrations are many where Jesus
used love in order to change the ways of people. He never
used force in His own behalf, even to save His life. He rebuked Simon Peter for drawing his sword and cutting off the
right ear of the servant of the high priest who in company
with others was seeking Jesus in order to bind Him and kill
Him.[31] At another time Jesus specifically enjoined: "Resist not evil"; and instructed His followers when smitten
upon the right cheek to turn the left also.[32] Those who take

[29] *Matthew*, 10:34-39.
[30] *Luke*, 12:49-53.
[31] *John*, 18:10; *Matthew*, 26:50-56.
[32] *Matthew*, 5:39.

the sword shall perish by the sword; the nation that builds itself up by the sword shall be destroyed by it.

The birth of Jesus was accompanied by glad tidings and song, proclaiming peace on earth and good will toward men.[33] Blessed are the peacemakers. In the perfect society, good will by all to all will be shown, perfect love will reign, and permanent peace will prevail.

Jesus may or may not have expressed himself on several important issues of His day. The incomplete records do not indicate His attitude upon many vital social problems. It appears that Jesus usually spoke in remedial rather than preventive social terms. However, beneath this remedial terminology there are fundamental social principles, which, if put into common practice, would solve social problems. Jesus proposed to build an ideal society by remaking and regenerating persons. He dared to promulgate the radical program of remaking human nature itself. He commanded that all self-centered impulses and tendencies be completely subordinated to altruistic and socializing stimuli.

Throughout His life-work Jesus insisted upon the principle that material factors must be subjected to spiritual values. In order to make this principle clear He often took particular pains to treat material goods with the utmost insignificance. He perceived that persons are made slaves by the worship of wealth. He inaugurated a program of spiritualization which would free the world from the slavery which may come from the economic forces.

Although a religious leader above all things else, Jesus insisted upon the necessity of something more than a saving faith alone. He required a social attitude of mind, a heart of social love, and a spirit of service. Give freely to others. Serve others. By giving Himself for others, a person will function in the Kingdom of perfect love, and win other persons to that Kingdom.

Jesus required that love be substituted for hate. Unkind deeds must be supplanted by kind deeds. According to this principle, employers and employees must learn to love one another; and business must be put upon the basis of love and service. Government must be a series of mutual serv-

[33] *Luke*, 2:13, 14.

ices. Religion must harbor no narrowness. In all human relationships, Jesus reiterated the principle: Love, love, love. This is the spiritualizing and socializing dynamic by which Jesus proposed to make over the social order.

PAUL AS A SOCIAL THINKER

It remained for Paul, a tent-maker, a Jew who was also a Roman citizen, to give the teachings of Jesus a new universal significance. He elaborated the ideas relating to the importance of the individual and made prominent the belief in the dramatic coming of the Kingdom of Heaven. Although he was a social conservative in many ways, his religious ideas implied a far-reaching social idealism.

Paul, the apostle to the Gentiles, by virtue of unique experiences and many travels possessed a cosmopolitan attitude of mind. He gave a practical application of the teaching of Jesus concerning the brotherhood of man. He urged the equal treatment of Jews and Gentiles, bond and free.[34] He preached the essential unity of mankind. It was Paul who affirmed that "God hath made of one blood all nations of men." God is no respecter of persons; his Kingdom is a spiritual democracy. We are all — Jew and Gentile — children of the same Father, who gave His son in service for all.[35] To the call to come over into Macedonia for the purpose of rendering aid, Paul responded immediately and favorably. By so doing, he believed that he was carrying out the true implications of the love of God.

The greatest tribute that has ever been paid to love as a social force was that given by Paul.[36] Although possessing the highest educational qualifications and being able to speak with the greatest eloquence, any person leads a practically useless life unless that life is motivated by love. Giving one's possessions to the poor and sacrificing one's body count little if one does these things in any other spirit than that of love. Love protects a person from envying his neighbors, from becoming proud and haughty and boastful. Love is the greatest principle of life.

[34] *Acts*, 15:9; 10:28; *Galatians*, 3:28.
[35] *Romans*, 8:16; 32.
[36] *I Corinthians*, Chapter 13.

The members of the Kingdom of God should love one another under all circumstances.[37] They should bear one another's burdens.[38] They should do good to all men, even to those who persecute. Above all, they should not recompense any man with evil for evil, nor fail to feed their enemies if the latter hunger. Love is the law of God. Perfect love is more powerful than principalities and powers and even death.[39] Love conquers all evil. Love is more powerful than might. A practical, cosmopolitan brotherhood of man is one of the fundamental concepts of Paul's teachings.

Paul taught the organic unity of mankind. In the perfect Christian order each person has a specific function to perform which is a part of the whole process. Paul compares this situation to the human body in which there are many organs, each performing its individual but correlated function.[40] No one liveth to himself, no one dieth to himself.[41] Every person, even in dying, influences the social equilibrium and affects group progress. All individuals in the perfect Kingdom are co-laborers and co-operators. Whatever weakens an individual weakens society; whatever strengthens the individual strengthens society, provided that strength is used societarily.

Another fundamental element in the social thought of Paul was his concept of sin. Sin is socially and individually destructive. The wages of sin — a generic term — is death. Paul made a long list of social sins, namely: covetousness, maliciousness, drunkenness, wantonness, dishonesty, fraud, stealing, fornication, murder. In nearly all his letters, Paul warned his followers against the evils which beset mankind. He urged people to beware of the appearance of doing evil. Paul's rule of conduct was the Aristotelian mean: Be temperate in all things.

On the other hand, Paul cited long lists of virtues. Love is continually urged. Temperance, meekness, gentleness,

---

[37] *Galatians,* 5:13; *Romans,* 12:10.
[38] *Galatians,* 6:2; 6:10; *Acts,* 20:35.
[39] *Romans,* 8:35-39; 12:17; *Ephesians,* 1:21; 2:4; 3:17; 18.
[40] *Romans,* 12:4-8, cf. *I Corinthians,* 12:12.
[41] *Romans,* 14:7.

honesty, purity, and justice are repeatedly stressed. Paul's description of a good man and bishop is the delineation of the nature of a social citizen who is temperate, a good husband, not mercenary nor covetous, who ruleth well his household, and possesses a good reputation and character.

In all Paul's thought, righteous living was uppermost. Cheerful giving was recommended. The strong must bear the infirmities of the weak, not only for the sake of the week, but in order that the strong may not become self-centered.

Paul taught a gospel of peace. He deprecated strife between persons. He trusted in the operation of the law of love. Love will bring order out of confusion, and peace out of discord. The social Kingdom of God, motivated by love, moves orderly, harmoniously, and constructively.

Paul firmly supported the family as an essential institution of society. He admonished children to obey their parents, to honor their fathers and mothers. He commanded wives to obey their husbands, and husbands to love their wives even as Christ loved the church and as men love themselves.[42] He commanded men to remain true in the marriage relation, and to keep the single standard of morals inviolate.

The dangers of wealth were frequently pointed out by Paul. We brought no riches into this life; we can not take any riches out. Riches continually subject us to temptations, snares, and lusts. The love of money is the root of all evil.[43] The greatest wealth which any person can acquire is the wealth of good deeds done to other persons.

The thought of Paul concerning law is exceedingly modern. Law is not for the righteous; law is for the lawless and disobedient. The honest and righteous and just are above the law in the sense that a well-mated husband and wife are above the law of divorce. If there were none other than happily mated husbands and wives, there would be no need for divorce laws. In a similar way, if perfect love prevailed among all people, law could be discarded, except for "traffic regulations" of one type or another. The teachings of Paul run the gamut of brotherly love. Paul thought in terms of

42 *Ephesians*, 5:22-23; *Colossians*, 3:18, 19; *I Corinthians*, 11:0.
43 *I Timothy*, 6:7-10; 17:18.

concepts such as these : being well-grounded in love ; abound-
ing in love ; let brotherly love continue ; the love of Christ
constraineth us. Paul carried a message of love to all men,
and established the church as a home for all who would accept Christ's message of love.

<h2 style="text-align:center">OTHER SOCIAL APOSTLES</h2>

The apostle James spoke in no uncertain terms of the
democracy of God, the need of helping the weak, the dangers
of riches, the evils of strife, and the social commandments.
James made social service a fundamental test of religion.[44]

Peter attacked the same social sins that Jesus and Paul had
flayed, argued in behalf of the Justice of God, and proclaimed with new vigor the law of love.

John is the chief exponent of the principle of love : God
is love. The reign of God is a reign of love ; the Kingdom
of God is a kingdom of perfect love. In the Book of Revelations, the writer describes two cities: one wicked, and the
other perfect. The first is elegantly clothed in purple and
gold, bedecked with precious stones. But her heart is rotten.
Lust and vice have ruined her. Her dominating sins are
sex immorality and luxury. The perfect city is the New
Jerusalem, a community of happy people, motivated in all
things by love. Nothing that defileth is permitted in the
New Jerusalem, nor anything that worketh abomination, or
maketh a lie.[45]

The fundamentals of early Christian social thought may
now be summarized. The New Testament authorities
offered no system of sociology ; they did not submit a scientific program for the social reorganization of the world, but
made, however, substantial contributions.

(1) Early Christian social thought represented a system of
changing the attitudes of persons. By making over persons
the world can be improved. The person is exalted. The
person must be re-educated . The right sort of persons will
produce the right sort of social structure and the proper
type of social process and society. Christianity indicated so-

---

[44] *James*, 1:26, 27.
[45] *Revelations*, Chapter 21.

cialized principles of conduct which the disciples of Christianity must accept.[46]

(2) The Fatherhood of God is made a cardinal principle of the Kingdom. When all persons recognize the Fatherhood of God, they will have a strong tie binding them together and impelling them to regenerated living.

(3) The universal brotherhood of man is a natural corollary of the principle of the Fatherhood of God. When everyone recognizes the underlying brotherhood of all persons, the prejudices of race which now so bitterly divide mankind will begin to dissolve.

(4) Marriage is a divine rite, and husbands and wives shall work together in behalf of their children. The family is the chief social institution which the New Testament writers supported.

(5) Little children set examples of simple faith and trust. They call for sacrifice and transform parents into altruistic beings.

(6) Early Christian thought was missionary. It was not self-centered. It said: Go. It drove out its adherents into all forms of sacrificial living. It required that its followers help the sick, preach the gospel, travel into foreign lands. It was an activity religion. It defined in living terms the dynamic and driving principle of love.

[46] An excellent summary of the "Social Gospel" is given by A. C. Knudson in the *Personalist,* V:102-114, under the title of "The Social Gospel and Theology." Four main aspects are mentioned: (1) The Social Gospel's dominant interest in the present earthly life; (2) its democratic tendency; (3) its ethical emphasis; and (4) its stress on social solidarity.

GROUP DISCUSSION TOPICS

1. The bases of early Christian social thought.
2. The major contributions of the teachings of Jesus to social thought.
3. Dynamic principles enunciated by Jesus.
4. "Behavioristic" rules according to Jesus.
5. The greatest riches in the world in Jesus' estimation.
6. Social causes of the successful attack upon the life of Jesus.
7. The nature of a social sinner.
8. The early Christian attitude toward wealth.
9. In what sense will there always be poor people?
10. The meaning of a spiritual socialism.
11. The Christian attitude regarding war and peace.
12. The apostle Paul's contribution to the brotherhood-of-man principle.
13. The best wealth according to Paul.
14. The Christian concept of the organic unity of mankind.
15. The most meaningful of the social thought teachings of Christianity.

READINGS

Case, S. M., *The Social Origins of Christianity* (Chicago : University of Chicago Press 1923).

Furfey, Paul H., *A History of Social Thought* (New York : The Macmillan Company 1942), Ch. 7.

Kent, Charles F., *The Social Teachings of the Prophets and Jesus* (New York : Charles Scribner's Sons 1917).

——, *The New Testament* (Shorter Bible) (New York: Charles Scribner's Sons 1923).

——, *The Old Testament* (Shorter Bible) (New York: Charles Scribner's Sons 1925).

King, Henry C., *The Ethics of Jesus* (New York : The Macmillan Company 1910).

Knudson, A. C., "The Social Gospel and Theology," *Personalist,* V : 102-114.

Mathews, Shailer, *The Social Teachings of Jesus* (New York : The Macmillan Company 1909).

McCown, C. C., *The Genesis of the Social Gospel* (New York : The Macmillan Company 1929).

Peabody, Francis G., *Jesus Christ and the Social Question* (New York : The Macmillan Company 1900).

Saunders, Kenneth, *The Ideals of East and West* (New York : The Macmillan Company 1934), Ch. VI.

CHAPTER XII

SOCIAL THOUGHT IN THE MIDDLE AGES

The social thought of the Middle Ages was in part a reflection of the unsettled social conditions, and in part an outgrowth of the thought and life of the five centuries which intervened between the beginning of the Christian Era and the Fall of Rome. During these centuries the Church Fathers modified somewhat the pristine Christian teachings. While they accepted the underlying social nature of mankind and believed that government and social organization were necessary in order to curb evil tendencies, they taught that the authority of all just government was derived from God. Government is a natural institution, necessary to the welfare of society, and therefore every subject owed obedience and loyalty to justly constituted government. The authoritative rather than the revolutionary element in government received support. The essential unity of mankind was proclaimed.

The strong Roman bias for organization and administration was builded into the church — the result was the powerful Church of Rome with its hierarchal structure. After the Fall of Rome, the Roman proclivity for centralization of government lived on and produced within the Church a center of power that has been the marvel of church history.

The Church Fathers directed the attention of the people to the next world and to preparation therefor. Sacramental and sacrificial methods of salvation were elaborated. The importance of a changing social order was underrated. In fact, the injustices in the current social order were considered as disciplinary measures for the soul in its preparation for the next world.

By the third century, loyalty to creed had become a dominant note in Christianity. The poor constituted a decreasing influence in church life; wealth was exerting unChristian influences. The aristocratic elements in church organization began to transform the poor into a special class within the church. Poverty was not viewed preventively. By the time of the Fall of Rome the poor had become objects upon which to bestow alms as a means of expiating sin.

AUGUSTINE'S CONTRIBUTION

The greatest of the Latin Fathers was St. Augustine (354–430). Among other works, he wrote an important document under the title of *The City of God*. In this gigantic undertaking social thought was submerged beneath theological discussions. A part of the argument is devoted to an explanation of the Fall of Rome. The leading causal elements are described as economic factors, such as the rise of luxury; and religious unbelief, such as the worship of pagan gods. St. Augustine describes two cities, one of this world, materialistic and debasing; and one of the next world — the City of God — which through the will of God will finally triumph.

St. Augustine centered his attention upon the importance of a pure heart. He inveighed against the presence of evil thoughts in the human mind.

St. Augustine found four sources of personal action. One is connected with the pleasures of the body; a second, with the pleasures of the mind; a third source is found in the pleasures of the body and mind combined; the fourth is in God.

St. Augustine described two societies, one of men and the other of God. One is full of evil; the other, of good. One is temporal and at war with religion; the other is eternal and is controlled by religion. The "City of God" is socially conservative and ruled by a theocracy.

During the first half of the Middle Ages the dominant tendencies were Roman and Christian. The Roman power of organization gained increasing strength in its new form — the Church. The Christian influences were expressed in high ideals, new duties, and asceticism. The church acted as a soothing and quieting force in the centuries of unrest. It built elaborate monasteries and gathered together under its protecting wing large numbers of people, chiefly the poor. Under the supervision of the church, these religious believers lived in communal and sympathetic fashion. Along with these developments the church also manifested grave abuses.

Out of the period of social disorder which characterized the early Middle Ages there developed educational movements, such as that which Charlemagne sponsored, and the system of Feudalism, which gave to the Middle Ages its most distinctive set of characteristics. Feudalism made land the central institution of society. The ownership of land gave power; land constituted social and political power. Land was parceled out upon the receipt of oaths of homage and fealty. Under this land system there were three classes of people: the nobles, the clergy, and the peasants. The nobles were the rulers and exercised military prerogatives. The clergy were either the privileged subjects of the nobles, or else through the institution which they represented they acquired land power. The peasants often despised the nobles, although they worked for and supported them.

As an outgrowth of feudal industry various forms of guilds or industrial organizations flourished from the tenth to the fifteenth centuries. Sometimes the masters and workmen jointly belonged to guilds, as in the case of the merchant guilds. Sometimes the guilds became local monopolies. Always they possessed the aim of improving the conditions of the membership.

The religious wars, or Crusades, of the eleventh to the thirteenth centuries inaugurated many changes. They gave the restless nobility major themes of attention and even removed many nobles through death in battle from the European arena. They created intellectual unrest. They enlarged the horizons of many persons and gave rise to scepticism. They led to the contradictory types of social thought that were characteristic of the Reformation.

PERSONAL LIBERTY

Social thought in the Middle Ages received a considerable stimulus from Teutonic sources. The "barbarous Teutons" contributed ideas of freedom. They increased the emphasis upon the individual. They were rough, bold exponents of "personal liberty," and disregarded mere churchly procedure, social traditions, and some of the finer ideals of life and character. On the other hand, chivalry and knighthood were perhaps of Teutonic origin.

The church utilized chivalry. It became the duty of the knight to defend the church and that which belonged to the church. Chivalry became a form of social discipline which ruled in the latter part of the Middle Ages. It softened manners and became the sponsor for virtue. It remained, however, a modified military structure with military traditions.

The rise of scholasticism manifested many traits opposite to those of monasticism. In the ninth century the leading thinkers had not advanced beyond the conception of a natural social state characterized by chaotic conditions, and organized by political machinery. By the twelfth century only the faintest glimmerings of a doctrine of popular sovereignty had begun to appear. The thought of the day was largely theological.

The church through its system of monasteries had maintained centers where religious and intellectual traditions had been preserved. These centers were undoubtedly important factors in conserving much that was valuable in an age when ruthless disregard for civilized values prevailed.

Because of the abuses which sprang up in connection with the monasteries, certain positive reactions against the monasteries arose. St. Francis of Assisi (1182–1226) turned from the monastery to actual life. He inaugurated a method for the regeneration of society. He and his followers lived and spent themselves among the actual poor, subjecting themselves to the economic conditions of the poor. They helped the poor, not by giving alms as an expiation for sin and to secure self-salvation, but by the first-hand giving of their lives. St. Francis ignored the regular ecclesiastical conception of charity and gave it all the reality of a new and genuine social force. By renouncing the possession of property and living as the poor live, he obtained what he could secure in no other way — the poor man's point of view. In this way, also, he secured an entrance into the poor man's mind and heart that could not be had so well by any other method. By renouncing wealth and accepting literal poverty he reached the core of the problem of poverty. St. Francis was motivated by a desire to live a life of love. He spent not wealth but his life for the poor. In living among the poor on the same economic level as the poor live, St. Francis established a rapport with them that could be obtained in no other way. In living as they had to live, he gained insight into their attitudes of life.

SCHOLASTICISM

According to scholasticism a person should look to reason for the attainment of truths of the natural order, and to faith under the guidance and infallible authority of the Church for the attainment of revealed truth or truths of the supernatural order. In all matters affecting faith and morals the teaching authority of the Church was supreme: "Philosophy is the handmaid of theology, and reason is the foundation of faith."

Scholasticism, developing during four centuries, reached its highest expression in the teachings of Thomas Aquinas (1225–1274). He pushed forward the Aristotelian premises as follows: Man is a social being; he unites with other persons in a social organization in order to gain his own purposes. A person looks to able rulers for wise political guidance; he accords the requisite power to these rulers. Aquinas taught that man was by nature a social being, that he was ordained by nature to live in association with other men. As men have diverse thoughts, desires, and impulses, government as a unifying principle is necessary. Man cannot live happily except in society; society is impossible without government; and therefore man must of necessity establish some form of government.

"To live a life of pleasure, or to think only of getting rich, appears as good only to a sensual and grasping man." [1] Men are obliged to live in society; it must be morally good to help our fellows. Social justice rests upon "a solemn affirmation of solidarity and mutual assistance." [2] If the people are careful guardians of the common weal then they have

[1] M. De Wulf, *Mediaeval Philosophy*, p. 105.
[2] *Ibid.*, p. 125.

a right to choose their magistrates, but if they become so corrupt as to sell their votes then they forfeit their rights.[3]

Aquinas' thought is centered in his doctrine of law. First, there is eternal law which is divine reason in control of the universe. Second, there is natural law which is the increasing rationalization of eternal law by human beings. Third, there is human law which is eternal law expressed in the social order. Fourth, there is divine law, revealed in the Bible and supplementing the incompleteness of human law.[4] Thus, Aquinas outlined "a logical and progressive order of social analysis." A threefold and gradual "unfolding of the Divine purpose in Eternal law" is postulated, namely: "the natural history aspect of society in which social institutions have their natural origin, the organization of society into political form chiefly through conscious effort, and the final conformity of society and government to the will of God."[5]

In religion, scholasticism reduced religious mysticism to rational forms. It based religion on learning rather than on authority; it pursued the methods of reasoning rather than of contemplation.

Scholasticism furthered the advancement of learning; it aided and developed the life of the universities. It encouraged the growth of independent thinking, although its decline set in about the fourteenth century, before it had had a fair opportunity to inaugurate a movement which would lead to an inductive philosophy or to sociology.

Various other thought elements appeared in the closing centuries of the Middle Ages. As early as the ninth century a maritime code, a military code, and a rural code were formulated in the Byzantine Empire in order to meet new social needs. Until the fall of Constantinople the Byzantine influence was a deterrent against the forces from the East. Byzantium preserved and gave a new impetus to Grecian literature, art, architecture, and law.

Dante (1265–1321), the Italian literary genius, was interested in political and social life. He conceived a world society "ruled by one Supreme prince," not with reference to making trifling judgments for each particular town, but in

[3] M. De Wulf, *Philosophy and Civilization in the Middle Ages*, p. 256.
[4] J. P. Lichtenberger. *Development of Social Theory*, p. 110.
[5] *Ibid.*, p. 1..

those matters which are common to all men. In their peculiarities each town should be governed by special laws, but in commonalities the world should be governed by one person and by a rule common to them all, with a view to their peace.[6] "The proper work of the human race, taken as a whole, is to set in action the whole capacity of that understanding which is capable of achievement. . . . The condition requisite for the accomplishment of this purpose is universal peace."[7]

In Arabia the celebrated historian and philosopher Ibn Khaldun (1332–1406), made a detailed and surprisingly accurate description of the Arab. With the evolution of the individual, he compared the development of the successive stages in social life. This distinguished writer urged that history should consider not simply rulers, dynasties, and wars, but also racial factors, climatic forces, the laws of association, and the stages of associative life. He wished to make history scientific, even a social science. He formulated an evolutionary doctrine of social progress. He evolved a spiral theory of social evolution, beginning with the crudest primitive life and ending with civilized urban life.

PIERS THE PLOWMAN

In the latter part of the fourteenth century, England's great popular poet, William Langland, wrote an allegorical poem entitled, *Piers the Plowman*. In this work the oppressed laboring and peasant classes cry aloud their longings for improved conditions. They are personified in Piers the Plowman who, as a dignified laborer, plays for the first time the leading role in serious thought. He is a spokesman for all types of people who are laboring together and longing for a better social order. Along with the agricultural laborers we see weavers and tailors, friars and minstrels, merchants and knights. Labor of every sort is dignified. All living laborers who work with their hands and minds, truly earning, living in love and according to the laws of social order and progress, will become the pure and perfected leaders of truth.

[6] Dante's *De Monarchia*, translated by F. C. Church, Book I, Chapter 12.
[7] *Ibid.*, Book I, Chapter 4.

Langland depicted well the living and working conditions of the English laboring classes. Productive toil, he argued, will receive its crown of glory. But he did not indicate practical solutions. Langland was sure, however, that the service of labor to society is sacred. He pronounced patient poverty to be the prince of all virtues. He personified Jesus in the form of a working man. Langland's fourteenth-century social message was that the individual should renounce wealth, join the honest laboring poor, and follow Christ's example of living a life of labor and love.[8]

Piers developed a "do well" philosophy of life. To do well is to save one's soul, and to do evil is to lose one's soul. The problems of life are thus reduced to simplicity itself. The dramatic results, particularly, of doing evil are vividly portrayed. Again, the "do well" philosophy is the only escape from calamities.

Samples of social thought regarding property and material goods show how complete dedication to a spiritual goal tends indirectly to create socialized attitudes. Some of the scholars of the Middle Ages illustrate this fact vividly.

In one sense, social thought in the Middle Ages is fragmentary; but, on the other hand, there are the extensive social teachings of the scholastics, dealing with the family, the state, charity, social organization, institutions, social obligations. The scholastics had a teleological view of society and taught concerning the improvement of society through the improvement of persons. The scholastics anticipated Ward's "social telesis" although they would not have agreed with this modern sociologist on what constitutes social progress. While several centuries are included in the period known as the Middle Ages, new social ideas are few. The centuries of unrest and transition and the prevalent illiteracy of the masses did not conduce to new types of social thinking. There were, however, outstanding thinkers, such as Augustus Abelard, Albertus Magnus, Thomas Aquinas, Duns Scotus, not to mention leaders such as Charlemagne or Ibn Khaldun. The Middle Ages also has to its credit a number of enduring accomplishments which benefit mankind, such as the

[8] B test, Passus VIII. The manuscripts of *Piers Plowman* number more than forty and fall into three sets: A, B, and C.

Gothic cathedrals, the hospitals, organized charity, and the Magna Charta. A portion of the social thinking of earlier epochs was preserved, constituting another foundation for the renaissance of social thought that followed the Middle Ages. "The struggle of kings with vassals, the communes, the establishment of citizenship, the freedom of the serfs" [9]— all these social changes indicate that the Middle Ages possessed elements of dynamic social thinking.

[9] De Wulf, *Philosophy and Civilization in the Middle Ages*, p. 60.

GROUP DISCUSSION TOPICS

1. Augustine's contributions to social thought.
2. The social meaning of "personal liberty."
3. The social keynote of "chivalry."
4. The proposals of St. Francis to regenerate society.
5. Social thought in the writings of Ibn Khaldun.
6. The main social concept of Thomas Aquinas.
7. Social thought of Dante.
8. The social thought implication of the poem *Piers the Plow man*.
9. A summary of social thought in the Middle Ages.

READINGS

Augustine, St., *The City of God* (trans. by Watts) (New York : G. P. Putnam and Sons 1912).

Becker, Howard, and Harry E. Barnes, *Social Thought from Lore to Science* (Washington : Harren Press 1952), Vol. I, Ch. 6.

Browning, Oscar, *Dante, his Life and Writings* (London : Sonnenschein 1891).

De Wulf, M., *Mediaeval Philosophy* (Cambridge, Mass. : Harvard University Press 1924).

———, *Philosophy and Civilization in the Middle Ages* (London : Cambridge University Press 1900).

Dante, *De Monarchia* (transl. by Aurelia Henry) (Boston : Houghton Mifflin Company 1904).

———, *La Divina Commedia* (trans. by C. H. Grandgent) (Boston : D. C. Heath and Company 1909).

Dunning, W. A., *Political Theories, Ancient and Mediaeval* (New York The Macmillan Company 1902).

Ellwood, Charles A., *A History of Social Philosophy* (New York : Prentice-Hall, Inc. 1938), Ch. V.

Figgis, J. N., *The Political Aspects of Saint Augustine's 'City of God'* (New York : Longmans, Green & Co. 1921).

Furfey, Paul H., *A History of Social Thought* (New York : The Macmillan Company 1942), Chs. 8, 9.

Gierke, Otto F., *Political Theories of the Middle Ages* (London : Cambridge University Press 1900).

Langland, William, *The Vision of Piers the Plowman* (arranged by Arthur Burrill) (New York : E. P. Dutton and Company 1912).

Lichtenberger, James P., *Development of Social Theory* (New York : Century Company 1923), Ch. V.

Vaughn, R. B., *The Life and Labours of Thomas Aquinas* (London : Longmans, Green & Co. 1871).

CHAPTER XIII

MORE AND UTOPIAN SOCIAL THOUGHT

Of the more than one hundred social utopias or ideal societies that have been described, none equals, on the whole,
the Utopia by Thomas More, unless Plato's *Republic* be included in this class. Shortly after the close of the Middle
Ages, with its modicum of new social thinking, the idealism
of Plato appeared in the new form of descriptive utopias.
More's *Utopia* deserves a degree of attention which is not
customarily accorded it. It was written by one of England's
sane, shrewd, tolerant students of social conditions, at a time
when it was dangerous to suggest social changes.

More mediated Plato to modern social philosophy; he
moved in the field of Platonic ideas and ideals. He was also
indebted to Plutarch's account of Spartan life. At the dawn
of the Renaissance he presented the concept of a perfect
commonwealth.

If one would understand the social thought of More, a
contemporary of Columbus, he must put himself under the
spell of fifteenth- and sixteenth-century conditions in England. He must remind himself of Henry VII and Henry
VIII, two autocratic rulers whom it was difficult for any demo-
cratically-minded person to please. The living conditions
of the peasants were almost intolerable. Unemployment
was common. Punishments were severe and brutalizing.
Even thieves were subject to capital punishment. If an individual stole a loaf of bread, he might as well kill the person who saw him steal the bread. In fact, by so doing, he
might be better off — the only witness to his theft would thus
be unable to testify against him.

Sir Thomas More could not have openly criticized the unjust social conditions of his day, and long have escaped death.
It was necessary for him to put his radical ideas into the
mouth of a fictitious traveler, Raphael Hythloday, and
thereby disown them. At it was, More became a martyr to
his religious faith and to the cause of social freedom.

MORE'S UTOPIA

More wrote the *Utopia* in two parts. Part One was written as an explanation, or introduction, to Part Two. In Part One a conversation involving three persons is reported. A conservative Dutch citizen of Antwerp converses with Raphael Hythloday, an experienced traveler, and with More. Hythloday, however, is the chief speaker. He is well versed in Latin culture and especially in Greek culture. Moreover, he has traveled extensively, even with Amerigo Vespucci, the Florentine navigator. In this way he is given prestige in the mind of the reader. It is not impossible in Part One of *Utopia* to recognize a distinct resemblance to the dialogue form of Plato.

Part One describes certain factors in the political situation in England. The untoward phases of poverty and the vicious forms of punishment that prevailed are painted in gloomy colors. The reader is glad to turn from this unpleasant social picture to the description in Part Two of *Utopia,* where the people are living under well-ordered conditions.

The ideal commonwealth is located on the mystical island of Amaurote, where Raphael Hythloday lived for five years. On this island the economic and social life is communistic, somewhat after the manner of Plato's *Republic.* It is a fundamental communism which More postulates. Complete communism of goods exists on Amaurote.[1] All possess equal portions of wealth. The Utopian communistic state implies a radical change in human nature. More justifies communism on the grounds that it roots out that serious social evil, covetousness.[2] Likewise, the incentive for stealing and plundering is removed. If there is a scarcity of economic commodities in any part of Utopia, the surplus in any other part is immediately drawn upon to meet the need. Thus the whole land conducts itself as if it were one family or household.[3] The guiding principle in regard to economic goods is that of human needs.

[1] *The Utopia of Sir Thomas More,* edited by George Simpson in Bohn's Classical Libraries, p. 75.
[2] *Ibid.,* p. 104.
[3] *Ibid.,* p. 111.

CO-OPERATION

In Utopia everyone finds his greatest pleasure in giving to others. The strongest league of peoples or of nations is not that which is united chiefly by covenants or treaties, but one which is knit together by love and a benevolent attitude.[4] The strongest league in the world is that which is based on the fellowship of kindred natures — a genuine Christian brotherhood of nations.

In Utopia, agriculture is the most highly respected occupation. Agriculture is a science in which all Utopian men and women are expert. In the harvest days the urban people, both men and women (farmerettes), go out into the country and help gather in the crops.[5] Urban and rural co-operation at harvest time solves the farmer's employment problems to the pleasure, good feeling, and advantage of all concerned. The food question is considered of paramount national importance. The agriculturist is equipped with the best tools and follows intensive methods.[6]

In addition to agricultural science, every citizen of Utopia learns at least one trade or craft.[7] Even every woman learns a skilled trade. The advantages of learning a trade by every citizen are obvious — they include a great increase in the potential industrial resources of a people. The question may be raised here whether it would not be a worthwhile asset for every citizen in our modern days to learn a trade. Such an accomplishment would give a sense of economic independence to every individual; it would afford to everyone the point of view of the skilled workman; it would add a gigantic potential force to production.

In Utopia there is one leader, or syphogrant, to every thirty families. Although there are other officers, including a prince for each city and a king for the island, the syphogrants are in reality the leading officials. It is noteworthy that no public matters are to be decided until they have been carefully considered and debated. By this scientific

4 *Ibid.*, p. 153.
5 *Ibid.*, pp. 84, 93.
6 *Ibid.*, pp. 84, 135.
7 *Ibid.*, p. 93.

procedure the necessity of rescinding hasty legislative action is reduced to a minimum.

EMPLOYMENT PROBLEMS

An important duty of the syphogrants is to regulate employment. Not only is everyone in Utopia to have a trade, but all are to work. There are no idle poor nor idle rich. All rich men, commonly called "gentlemen," all women, priests, monks, and friars (except a few) engage in productive labor. Even the syphogrants, or officials, work spontaneously. All useless occupations are prohibited. In countries where the dollar rules, there are many vain occupations which serve only to augment riotous superfluities.[8] Thus, since all persons work and since only needed occupations are permitted in Utopia, the working day is shortened to six hours.

In the case of a season of unemployment, a simple device is adopted for shortening temporarily the labor day. By cutting down the hours of labor to four a day during an unemployment period, work is provided for all. When an individual, it may be added, visits his friends, he works the same as if he were at home. He sets himself to the task in which his friends are engaged. No one in Utopia is encumbered with visitors who sit about doing nothing and who at the same time hinder their hosts from engaging in productive activities.

Laws in Utopia are few in number. Inasmuch as all the people are well instructed and socially-minded, many laws are needless.[9] Each citizen is above the law in the same way that an honest person is above the law against stealing. In the case of those disputes which must necessarily arise, the plaintiff and defendant go before the judge and plead for themselves. Utopia is noted for its scarcity of laws and the absence of attorneys. Laws are few because of the socialized attitudes of all the people. Even lawyers are unnecessary, so able is each person to plead his own case before a judge. No crafty and subtle interpretation of laws by attorneys is permitted. Every man is his own attorney and

[8] *Ibid.*, p. 97.
[9] *Ibid.*, p. 92.

simply states the facts in the given dispute; the judge knows the law and decides the case.[10]

The organization of the cities is interesting. In the middle of each quarter of each city there is a market place for the exchange of all manner of goods. Public abattoirs are in operation. Splendidly appointed hospitals are located outside the cities in a quiet environment. Contagious wards are provided. So excellent is the care which is afforded the patients in the public hospitals that any person who falls sick prefers going to a hospital to being cared for by the kindly ministrations of relatives at home. It may be noted that every city is provided with a hall of fame.

Every urban community is a garden city; every house has a garden plot. Furthermore, the people take much pride in their gardens; they compete with one another, endeavoring to excel in the fruitage and in the beauty of the gardens.

City planning rules in Utopia.[11] Overcrowding is not permitted; whenever a city exceeds the norm, a new city is established. New urban communities are established by public action.

Social centers are common on the island of Amaurote. In the winter when the people cannot work in their gardens after the supper hour, they gather in their community halls, where they engage in music, wholesale conversation, and games. Dice-play and similar foolish and pernicious games are unknown.[12] Wine taverns, alehouses, "stewes," lurking corners, and places of wicked counsels are prohibited.[13]

Good health is a virtue in Amaurote; great pleasure is derived from possessing a well-ordered state of public health. Health is considered a sovereign pleasure in itself.[14] Preventive measures are substituted for remedial medicines.

FASHION AND ORNAMENTATION

Fashions are regulated rigidly. Fashion imitation is prevented. The garments for men are all of one mode; and for

[10] *Ibid.*, p. 88.
[11] *The Utopia of Sir Thomas More* (Simpson, editor), p. 90.
[12] *Ibid.*, p. 96.
[13] *Ibid.*, p. 110; *cf.* Bacon: *The New Atlantis,* in "Ideal Commonwealths," p. 125.
[14] *Utopia,* p. 131.

women, of another mode.[15] The married are distinguished
from the unmarried by the style of wearing apparel. Thus,
there are simply four sets of styles in Amaurote. Coats of
uniform colors — the natural color of wool — are worn. It is
argued that coats of many colors are no warmer and hence
no more practical than coats of the one natural color; they
are more expensive and hence more wasteful.

In Utopia, gold and silver are held in reproach. They
are considered to be not so useful as iron. Consequently,
the Utopians load down their slaves with gold and silver
ornaments and pearls.[16] In this connection the description
of the visit of a group of ambassadors to Amaurote is amus-
ing. The ambassadors from an adjoining country were
dressed in gorgeous apparel like the very gods. They came
to Amaurote wearing chains of gold and displaying peacock
feathers. The citizens of Amaurote, coming out to meet the
guests, rushed past the ambassadors and greeted the helpers
who were dressed in plain costumes. They mistook the ambassadors for fools and knaves.[17]

The ridiculous figures which the visitors made when
dressed in their robes and jewels are evident even to the children. The satire reaches its climax in the attitudes of the
children of Utopia toward such wanton displays.

Sudden changes in attitudes occur, however, as soon as
the ambassadors perceived the worth and the habits of the
people of Amaurote. They grew ashamed of their cheap
display of fashions. After being in Amaurote a short time,
the ambassadors perceived how foolish it was to set emphasis
on "the doubtful glistenings of trifling stones." They recognized that it is foolish to consider oneself nobler than
other selves because one can wear clothes that are spun
from finer wool than the clothes of other persons. After all,
whether the wool is coarse or fine, it may have come from
the self-same sheep.

Although in Utopia no man is wealthy, yet in a sense, all
men are wealthy. All live joyfully, without worrying, and
without fearing that they or their children will fall into

15 *Ibid.*, p. 93.
16 *Ibid.*, p. 115.
17 *Ibid.*, p. 117; *cf. Campanella. The City of the Sun,* in "Ideal Commonwealths." p. 157.

poverty. Amaurote is a gigantic household, wherein the more able take a personal interest in the less able and in the unfortunate. No one lives in idleness and no one lives by virtue of any form of unnecessary economic enterprise. Rich men are not permitted by either private fraud or common law to snatch away from the poor man some portion, great or small, of his daily earnings. There are no idle rich, conniving how they may keep their unearned wealth or how they may grind down the poor in order to get more wealth. Since the love of money is unknown in Amaurote, other passions are also absent. Since the people do not love money, they have lost the desire to perpetrate the money crimes, such as fraud, theft, murder, treason. Likewise, pride which measures its satisfaction, not in terms of its own merits, *per se,* but by comparison with the poverty of human beings, is destroyed. The Utopians have conquered materialism. They are not subject to the life and death struggles which are caused by the love of money. Luxuries have been suppressed and the leisure class has been eliminated. Social extremes are unknown.

People are honored, not for their wealth but for their serviceableness to the community.[18] In the halls of fame, to which allusion has already been made, benefactors of the commonwealth are rewarded by having images of themselves set up in perpetual memory of their good deeds to their fellows.

The family is the fundamental social unit, but it is of the patriarchal type. Pure monogamic love is idealized. Especial care is taken that neither of the parties of a marriage vow possesses any hidden vices. Adultery is the chief justification for breaking the marriage bond. A single standard of morals for both husband and wife is set. Love may be won by beauty, but it can be kept and preserved only by virtue and obedience.

EDUCATION

Because of freedom from long hours of monotonous labor, nearly everyone in Utopia is able to maintain his intellec-

[18] *Ibid.,* p. 174.

tual interests and to experience mental growth throughout life. It is the solemn custom to have daily lectures early every morning and it is the habit of multitudes of people of all types to attend. All of the time that it is possible to spare from the necessary occupations is devoted to the development and garnishing of the mind.[19] Nearly all the citizens devote their extra-occupational hours throughout their lives to the arts and sciences. The chief felicity of life is said to be found in learning. In training the mind, the Utopians never weary. As a matter of course, a common school education is provided for every individual. Classes for adults and adult education are made the outstanding features of the public school system in Amaurote. One must learn to live and must go on learning throughout life. Hence, the provisions of public education should be adequate for the adult as well as for the adolescent.

Religious education and practice are considered essential. More's tolerant attitude in an age of brutal intolerance is shown by the fact that the Utopians are permitted whatever religion they prefer. Superstitious beliefs are taboo. More makes a subtle thrust when he observes that the priests of Amaurote are possessed of great holiness and hence are few in number.[20] It is no esoteric or monastic religion which More endorses. Future happiness may be secured best by busy labors and social efforts in this life.[21] Public service, including the care of the sick, is religiously emphasized.

WAR

War is beastly. Contrary to the attitudes of the people in all other countries, the people of Amaurote count nothing so inglorious as the glory that is obtained in fighting and killing.[22] No imagination is necessary in order to understand the courage which More displayed in making a vigorous attack in the sixteenth century upon war.

Under limited conditions, however, war is justifiable. More gives three worthy reasons for declaring war: (1) the

[19] Ibid., p. 95.
[20] Ibid., p. 101.
[21] Ibid., p. 175.
[22] Ibid., p. 174.

defense of one's own country; (2) the defense of one's friendly neighbors; and (3) delivering oppressed peoples anywhere from the yoke and bondage of tyranny.[23]

These reasons are all "defense" factors — which is remarkable in view of the fact that they were enunciated in an age when "offensive" wars were common. The only reason for assuming the offensive in matters of war is the social one of taking land away from people who deliberately withhold land from cultivation and fail to produce food for the nourishment of mankind.[24] By this plan, More severely indicts the holders of large landed estates which are held chiefly for the personal gratification of the owners.

Hired or mercenary soldiers are employed in war. The people of Amaurote employ hideous, savage fighters from the wild woods and the high mountains to do their fighting for them. The larger the number of these impetuous barbarians who are killed in battle, the better off is the world.

More opposed conscription. Ordinarily, no one is forced to fight, because in such circumstances he will not fight well. In the case, however, of defending Amaurote, the cowards are distributed among the bold-hearted. In warfare, the people of Amaurote do not allow their warriors to lay waste or destroy the land of their enemies. Neither foraging nor the burning of food supplies is permitted. No one who is unarmed is to be hurt.

PUNISHMENT

More's penological ideas are modern. He points out the folly of making theft a capital offense the same as murder. The temptation will be to steal, or rob, and to kill also, whereas under a more reasonable law the temptation in many cases would be to steal only. A law which makes theft a capital offense is harsher than even the harsh Mosaic law of an eye for an eye, a life for a life, because the former justifies the government in taking the life of a person who is guilty of stealing money. In Utopia, the thief is compelled to restore the stolen goods to the person from whom he

23 *Ibid.*, p. 154.
24 *Ibid.*, p. 103.

stole, and not to the king, as in many lands in More's time. The thief is put at common labor, not thrown into a city or county jail and left in idleness. Compulsory labor is the common method of punishment.[25]

The fundamental penological principle which More developed was that crime should be prevented by taking away the occasion of offense.[26] He condemned the prevailing method of England of allowing wickedness to increase, and then punishing the sinners after they had been permitted to grow up in an environment of sin. He objected to taking men from the trades for war service and then later irresponsibly discharging them, leaving many of them industrially stranded, unemployed, and subject to the temptation of stealing. More's dictum was: Show people how to live; do not let them steal and then take their lives away. Life in Utopia is more or less equally divided between five factors; industry, study, music, travel, and domesticity.

In the *Utopia,* Sir Thomas More made an indirect criticism of conditions in England; he showed himself an able student of social problems; and his ideas are noted for their modernness. Altogether, the *Utopia* has made a remarkable impression, not simply upon social idealists but also upon practical thinkers. As a literary invention for shrewdly suggesting criticisms of vicious but entrenched social wrongs it has been followed by imitations, but remains unparalleled in quality.

OTHER UTOPIAS

In *The New Atlantis,* Sir Francis Bacon (1561–1626) wrote an unfinished description of a utopian island where there is a high degree of social welfare and where "social salvation by scientific education" obtains. An Order or Society of "Solomon's House" is established which sends out every twelve years merchants of light (intellectual) who travel for the following period of twelve years, gathering facts in all branches of science and art.[27] Upon being relieved by the next group of traveler scholars, they return home and contribute their knowledge to the acquired store, which in the meantime has

[25] *Ibid.,* pp. 140, 141.
[26] *Ibid.,* p. 67.
[27] Bacon, *The New Atlantis,* in "Ideal Commonwealths," pp. 135 ff.

been added unto by many trained experimenters and research scholars. Airplanes, horseless wagons, and submarines are not unknown in *The New Atlantis*. Superstition is banished. Social knowledge will lead to a nation of socialized persons — this is the Baconian implication.

Tommaso Campanella (1568–1639), a monk, a philosopher, and an Italian contemporary of Francis Bacon, urged that human nature should be studied rather than books. Because of so-called heretical ideas, he was imprisoned for twenty-seven years. Shortly after his release he fled to Paris, where he died. In prison he wrote *The City of the Sun,* a crude but significant psychological analysis of society. He describes a social order based on the balanced relations of the three principles of Power, Intelligence, and Love. These forces are equally expressed in the social process and produce a perfect society.

Oceana, "a Midsummer Night's Dream of Politics," is the title of a romance which was written by James Harrington (1611–1677). His social order rests on economic factors, chiefly landed estates. However, the author advocates the election of rulers by ballot every three years and the choosing of them from the intellectually élite.

In this chapter it is impossible to note all the "utopias" that have been written. The utopian and communistic systems of socialists, such as Fourier, Saint Simon, and Owen will be referred to in Chapter XVII. There are other important utopian contributions, such as those by William Morris and Edward Bellamy. In *News from Nowhere,* William Morris (1834–1896), an English artist and socialist, describes his native England as a perfected society under a regime of socialism. Because of its American setting, Bellamy's *Looking Backward* will be presented in some detail in the following paragraphs.

"LOOKING BACKWARD"

In recent decades the utopian postulates of Edward Bellamy (1850–1898) in *Looking Backward* and *Equality* have had a wide reading. The author was the first American to command attention in the field of utopian thought. Bellamy presents a plan of industrial organization on a national scale with individuals sharing equally in the products of labor, or in public income, in the same way that "men share equally in the free gifts of nature." Bellamy protests against an economic order whose chief evil is summed up in the following question: How can men be free who must ask the right to labor and to live from their fellows, and seek their bread from the hand of others?

Society is likened to a gigantic coach to which the masses of humanity are harnessed, toiling along a very hilly and sandy road. The best seats are on top of the coach. The occupants of the elegant seats are constantly in fear of falling from their cushions of ease, splendor, and power — and hence their interest in the toilers.

In *Looking Backward* the entire social process is made an expression of service. Service is a matter of course, not of compulsion. No business is so fundamentally the public's business as the industry and trade on which the livelihood of the public depends.[28] Therefore, to intrust industry and commerce to private persons to be managed for private profit is a folly "similar to that of surrendering the functions of political government to kings and nobles for their personal glorification."

Buying and selling are pronounced antisocial. They are an education in self-seeking at the expense of others.[29] Citizens who are so trained are unable to rise above a very low grade of civilization.[30] They are sensitive chiefly to such motives as fear of want and love of luxury. For buying and selling, credit books are substituted which are good at any public warehouse. In place of higher wages, the chief motives to activity are honor, men's gratitude, the inspiration of duty, patriotism, the satisfaction of doing one's work well — in other words, the same motives that now influence, for example, the members of the teaching profession.

The arduousness of the trades is equalized, so that all shall be equally attractive, by making the hours of labor in different trades to differ inversely according to the arduousness.[31]

[28] Bellamy, *Looking Backward,* p. 57.
[29] *Ibid.,* p. 88.
[30] *Ibid.,* p. 89.
[31] *Ibid.,* p. 67.

Everyone works as a common laborer for three years and then chooses an occupation — agriculture, mechanics, the professions, art. The working life is twenty-four years long, from the ages of twenty-one to forty-five, after which all may devote themselves to self-improvement and enjoyment, but subject to emergency calls along industrial and other social service lines.

Bellamy challenges an individualism which incapacitates people for co-operation. He builds his society upon solidarity of race and brotherhood of man. He does not fear corruption in a society "where there is neither poverty to be bribed nor wealth to bribe." [32]

All cases of criminal atavism are treated in hospitals. There are no jails. Under capitalism nineteen-twentieths of misdemeanors are due to economic inequality. The remainder are the outcropping of ancestral traits. In Bellamy's society there are no private property disputes and no lawyers.

The educational system in *Looking Backward* does not educate some persons highly and leave others untrained. [33] It gives everyone "the completest education that the nation can give," in order that persons may enjoy themselves, in order that they may enjoy one another, and in order that the unborn may be guaranteed an intelligent and refined parentage.

Bellamy holds that human nature in its essential quality is good, not bad, and that men are naturally generous, not selfish ; sympathetic, not cruel ; godlike in aspirations, moved by divine impulses of goodness, images of God and not the travesties upon Him which they have seemed. [34] It is our economic order which has fostered shameless self-assertion, mutual depreciation, "a stunning clamor of conflicting boasts," and a stupendous system of "brazen beggary."

In three utopias, H. G. Wells portrays societary conditions that are kinetic rather than static and worldwide rather than local in scope. [35] While the author provides a changed economic system, socialistic in nature, he urges that changed

[32] *Ibid.*, p. 192.
[33] *Ibid.*, pp. 220 ff.
[34] *Ibid.*, pp. 287 ff.
[35] H. G. Wells, *Anticipation, Mankind in the Making,* and *A Modern Utopia.* See *A Modern Utopia,* pp. 5, 11 ff.

social attitudes are also needed. Works such as Bellamy's *Looking Backward,* Wells' *A Modern Utopia,* and similar modern treatises are not strictly utopian. They are less unreal than the earlier utopias; they utilize evolutionary and developmental principles in part; they deal with human nature more as it really is.

MANNHEIM

Mannheim has defined a utopia as an idea "which seems to be unrealizable only from the point of view of a given social order which is already in existence."[36] A utopian thinker is in danger of seeing the desired society so strongly that he views the entire current social order in a negative way. In fact he may go to the extreme of wishing the destruction of the present social conditions.[37] The wish-fulfillment tendencies are outstanding characteristics of the utopian mentality.

The process by which utopian thinking arises, according to Mannheim, begins when a people allows to develop "those ideas and values in which are contained in condensed form the unrealized and the unfulfilled tendencies which represent the need of each age." These intellectual elements then become the explosive materials which burst "the limits of the existing order."[38]

The utopian mentality is characterized by several forms. The first is the chiliastic in which the Second Coming of Christ is thought of as ushering in the Millennium, and which is conceived as a theocratically-governed and ideal society on earth. A second utopian form of thinking is the liberal-humanitarian with an ethical tone dominant in social life. A third form is the conservative in which people are urged to let well enough alone. The conservative mind has no utopia, but because of attack is forced to set up a counter utopia to the utopias proposed by the reformers. A fourth utopia is the well-known socialist-communist type.[39]

Utopias have the advantages of being ideals, and without

[36] Karl Mannheim, *Ideology and Utopia,* p. 176.
[37] *Ibid.,* p. 36.
[38] *Ibid.,* p. 179.
[39] *Ibid.,* pp. 190-236.

ideals to work toward, man "becomes a mere creature of impulses."[40]   Utopias represent unfulfilled longings.   By indirection they denote social deficiencies and problems that need attention and solution.

In the utopian social thought that has been presented in this chapter and in the many utopias which are not mentioned here, there is generally displayed (1) a common weakness of impracticability in current circumstances, (2) an over-emphasis upon simply changing the economic order, and (3) static rather than dynamic principles.   As Hertzler has pointed out, the utopian writers fail in important ways: namely, to see the necessity in a broad way of "a sound physical basis of social advance," to start with things as they are, to perceive that life is and probably always will be a constant struggle, to see that their ideal states were not necessarily "the final goal in social endeavor," and to recognize that a state of social perfection is hardly possible.[41]

Utopias are to be viewed as "worlds of escape."   We live in two worlds, the real world with all its imperfections, and an ideal world, where the imperfections are all corrected. Utopias are the result of compensatory effort.   Our utopias make our real worlds tolerable to us.[42]   The nature of our utopias is indicative of the shortcomings of our real worlds. Utopias are mirrors, often exaggerated, of the times in which they are written.   Utopias, thus, are very real.

Important elements of reconstruction appear in all utopias.   It is rather remarkable that nearly all take the form of cities; and that modern town-planning should be frequently anticipated.   That a new economic order is developed in many utopias is quite natural.   Important new inventions are found in nearly all utopias.

The underlying utopian spirit is "that society is capable of improvement and can be made over to realize a rational ideal."[43]   Utopias are a laboratory wherein improvement through social ideals may be studies.   Utopias "look ahead." The writers of utopias have been characterized by Hertzler[44]

[40] *Ibid.*, p. 236.
[41] J. O. Hertzler, *The History of Utopian Thought*, pp. 301 ff.
[42] Lewis Mumford, *The Story of Utopias*, p. 11.
[43] J. O. Hertzler, *op. cit.*, p. 3.
[44] *Ibid.*, pp. 259 ff.

as persons who are filled with a divine discontent with things as they are; critics of their age who promulgate often "with sharp satire a happy ideal for the future"; individuals of constructive imagination and intellectual originality who have "a commendable faith," and who have been among our most important "carriers of social idealism."

The strength of utopian social thought is found (1) in its drastic criticism of current social evils, (2) in its relative harmlessness at the given time, (3) in the force of its indirect suggestion, (4) in the widespread hearing which it secures, and (5) in its social idealism.

GROUP DISCUSSION TOPICS

1. Major reasons for writing utopias.
2. Social conditions in England when More lived.
3. The technique, characters, and setting of More's *Utopia*.
4. Values in having every citizen learn a trade.
5. Safeguards against hasty legislation, according to More.
6. More's solutions of unemployment.
7. The Utopians' attitudes toward laws and lawyers.
8. More's housing ideas.
9. The Utopians' practice regarding fashions.
10. Attitudes toward ornamentation.
11. Reactions toward wealth-seeking.
12. The intellectual attitudes of Utopians.
13. The conditions under which Utopians go to war.
14. The reasons for the use of hired soldiers by the Utopians.
15. More's basic penological idea.
16. The chief merit of More's Utopia.
17. The social thought dictum of Bacon's *New Atlantis*.
18. The organization of Campanella's *City of the Sun*.
19. The fundamental question of Bellamy's *Looking Backward*.
20. The resemblance of society to a gigantic coach.
21. Bellamy's division of labor plan.
22. Educational standards in *Looking Backward*.
23. The weaknesses of utopias.
24. The strong points of utopian social thought.

READINGS

Bacon, Francis, *The New Atlantis* (New York : Collier 1901, in "Ideal Commonwealths").

Bellamy, Edward, *Looking Backward* (New York : Grosset and Dunlap 1898).

Bestor, Arthur E., Jr., *Backwoods Utopias* (Philadelphia: University of Pennsylvania Press 1950).

Campanella, Tommaso, *The City of the Sun* (New York : Collier 1901, in "Ideal Commonwealth").

Hertzler, Joyce O., *The History of Utopian Thought* (New York : The Macmillan Company 1923).

Mannheim, Karl, *Ideology and Utopia* (New York : Harcourt, Brace and Company 1936).

——, *Diagnosis of Our Time* (New York : Oxford University Press, 1944).

——, *Man and Society in an Age of Reconstruction* (New York : Harcourt, Brace and Company 1940).

Morgan, Arthur E., *Nowhere was Somewhere* (Chapel Hill : University of North Carolina Press 1946).

Mumford, Lewis, *The Story of Utopias* (New York : Boni and Liveright 1922).

Sinclair, Upton, *Co-op* (New York : Farrar and Rinehart 1936).

Smith, H. F. R., *Harrington and His Oceans* (London : Cambridge University Press 1914).

The Utopia of Sir Thomas More (edited by George Simpson) (London : Bell and Sons 1910).

Wells, H. G., *A Modern Utopia* (New York : Charles Scribner's Sons 1905).

——, *Mankind in the Making* (New York : Charles Scribner's Sons 1904).

CHAPTER XIV

INDIVIDUALISTIC SOCIAL THOUGHT

At the dawn of the Renaissance, tradition and dogmatism were ruling mankind. Here and there, however, certain persons were perceiving the nature of the bondage. Occasionally a cry for individual freedom was uttered. Petrarch dared to say that the world was made for man's enjoyment. The early Teutons crudely developed the idea of personal liberty. In France a movement arose which culminated in the doctrines of natural rights and "Back to Nature." Both Rousseau and Voltaire were promoting the cause of individualism. The stress upon individualism in England became so deeply ingrained that it exists today as a powerful form of traditionalism. The United States was founded, in part, upon a doctrine of natural rights.

MACHIAVELLI

Absolutely unlike Sir Thomas More in many ways, Niccolo Machiavelli (1469–1527), an Italian contemporary, broke with tradition and received the sobriquet, the Galileo of modern science. Unfortunately, many people think of the Italian writer in terms of the adjective which bears his name, Machiavellian, or political intrigue. While he deserves this reputation, he should be considered also in another light. He cut loose from the customary ways of thinking of his time and asserted that it is not necessary to take all things on fiat or alleged divine decree. Machiavelli was no idealist in the accepted sense of the term, but a man who mixed with people, traveled extensively, and studied actual conditions. He declared that people should be considered as they are, and not according to false teachings about them.

A century before the time of Sir Francis Bacon, the inaugurator of the so-called inductive or scientific method of study, Machiavelli was observing human conditions and upon the basis of these observations was drawing conclusions. He believed that it does not pay to be guided in one's conduct by abstract ethics or impracticable ideals — and said so, in an age when imprisonment, exile, or death awaited anyone who opposed the autocratic authorities.   From abstract ethics, Machiavelli swung to the extreme of concrete expediency. He lived and thought in the exigencies of the moment.   He is an example of one who reacts so strongly against the stress and strain of the hour that he cannot get the larger vision that is necessary for balanced thinking on fundamental issues.

Machiavelli wrote on the subject of leadership and government.   He advocated either an autocratic or a democratic form of government — according to the conditions of the time and place.   In *The Prince* he described with noteworthy accuracy the traits and methods of a leader whose constituents must be treated with absolute authority.   In the *Discourses* he dealt with a democratic-republican type of leadership and control.

The successful prince, or leader, in the egoistic sense, makes himself both beloved and feared by his people.[1]   On occasion he uses force and even fraud.   Sometimes he must either exterminate or be exterminated.   He must repeal or suppress old laws and make new ones to fit the social situation.   He seeks to be considered merciful rather than cruel. He exercises universal pity in order to prevent social disorders from occurring and producing rapine and murder.[2] He does not allow his mercy to be taken advantage of by ungrateful and hypocritical persons.   He is strong-minded; he is either a sincere friend or a generous foe.   He is paternalistic, urging that his subjects be well fed and have a good livelihood,[3] thus gaining and maintaining the affection of the people.   In international affairs he acts with a strong hand, fortifying well his city or nation, providing good laws for internal growth.[4]   Machiavelli errs grossly, however, in his fundamental philosophy that any plan or action that is for the welfare of the state, or nation, considered as a su-

[1] Machiavelli, *The Prince*, p. 53.
[2] *Ibid.*, pp. 104, 105.
[3] *Ibid.*, p. 71.
[4] *Ibid.*, p. 77.

preme unit of authority in itself, is socially sound. In many ways he is a forerunner of totalitarianism.

In giving special attention to Machiavellism, J. P. Lichtenberger noted that Machiavelli "withdrew social and political interpretation from the domain of hypothetical speculation and started it upon a course of inductive observation." His social philosophy resulted "in inductive researches in the fields of social analysis and social control." [5] Machiavelli's philosophy of expediency "deserves the censure it has received." It belongs to the period of savagery. It is based "upon natural impulses" rather than on "genuinely ethical foundations." "His ethical opportunism is that of a committee of public safety." [6] His emphasis on preserving "the purity of religious observances," even though they be false, is also opportunistic. He was not concerned with the spiritual benefits that the individual might derive from religion. His interest in religion was that of one who viewed it as aid to a ruler in maintaining himself in power. His outlook was limited to the nation-state and he failed to conceive of any larger social grouping.

FRANCIS BACON

Sir Francis Bacon, whose noteworthy contributions to utopian social thought have been indicated in the foregoing chapter, placed all social thinkers under deep obligations by his emphasis upon inductive reasoning. He helped to free persons from control by dogma and superstition. He provided them with a technique for securing a new sense of individual freedom. In freeing himself a person discards his irrational pre-judgments, whether socially inherited or individually developed. He protects himself from anthropomorphic judgments, i.e., from judgments which he makes because he looks upon life and the universe through human eyes. These pre-judgments are common to all mankind — they are "the idols of the tribe." On the other hand, a person avoids purely individual preferences, which he is likely to hold because of his own peculiar experiences, and which

[5] *Development of Social Theory*, p. 148.
[6] *Ibid.*, p. 148.

thus place him outside the pale of common experience — these are "the idols of the cave."

Then there are "the idols of the forum," which cause a person to give undue dependence to words and language. "The idols of the theater" are traditional systems of thought. Bacon's dictum has been stated as follows: Get as little of yourself and of other selves as possible in the way of the thing which you wish to see.

Having eliminated human predispositions, a person is ready to gather facts, arrange them in groups, draw conclusions from them, and act according to the resultant laws. Knowledge gives power. Social knowledge gives power to improve human conditions and makes possible wise social control. Thus, Bacon opened the road to personal growth.

Too much personal freedom, however, destroys government and the social order. If each person is a law unto himself, anarchy reigns and progress is prevented. Consequently, the question arises: How can individually free persons unite in a society without giving up their freedom? The answer to this question took the form of a controversy on the subject of the social contract, i.e., the contract or agreement of persons, as units, to form and maintain societies. This controversy arose in the seventeenth century and was waged vigorously in the eighteenth century.

HOBBES

Thomas Hobbes (1588–1679), the distinguished social philosopher of England, introduced his analysis of society with the idea that man was originally self-centered, egoistic, and pleasure-loving. He was an independent center. His interest in other people was based on their ability to cater to his own good. He and they desired the same things in life. His hand was thus raised, in competition, against every other man. This state of continual conflict became mutually destructive and unbearable. In consequence, each person agreed to give over some of his precious, inalienable rights to a central authority or sovereign, whose decrees should constitute law and serve as the guide for conduct. The war of each against all, with the concomitant state of fear, was thus supplanted by a mutual contract, conferring sovereignty by popular agreement upon the ruler. In this way Hobbes met the dilemma of supporting an absolute form of government in which he believed, and of denying the divine right of kings. He urged after all an undemocratic political absolutism. Hobbes conferred humanly derived but irrevocable authority upon the king. He, however, traced sovereignty back to the people rather than to a divine right.

In getting away from the conditions "of Warre of every one against every one" in the natural state where "every man has a Right to everything," Hobbes swung to an undemocratic extreme. His Puritanic training gave an undue severity to his social thought. The Puritans, however, believed in the complete eradication of savage human tendencies and also in the ultimate elimination of kings. Hobbes did not analyze deeply the instinctive bases of human nature. He built his *Leviathan* out of natural human qualities and tied its units together by means of a strong, central will — this was his perfect society.

Hobbes was asked why mankind could not live together peaceably in a natural way without creating artificial agreements. It was pointed out to him that if bees and wasps did not need to resort to artificial arrangements, why is man so compelled? He gave six reasons why man is different from the social bees and wasps, namely: (1) "Men are continually in competition for honor and dignity," and the bees and wasps are not. (2) Among men each seeks eminence, and hence the common good is not exactly the same as the private good. (3) Among men, some try to reform the social organization of their times. (4) Men have a special persuasive power of words. (5) Men distinguish between injury and damage. (6) Men come to agreements by covenants.[7]

SPINOZA

Baruch Spinoza (1632–1677), the Portuguese Jewish Philosopher of Holland, improved on the social contract idea. He believed that man was originally of an antisocial and a tooth-and-fang nature, possessing only incipient social im-

[7] Hobbes, *Leviathan*, Ch. XIII.

pulses. Hence, man is not naturally bad, but naturally anti-social. Social organization was effected for purposes of "in-dividual" gain and glory; it was promulgated and furthered by "individuals" in order that they might escape the miseries of unregulated conflict.

Agreements were made whereby sovereignty was embodied in a ruler, but if the ruler abused the sovereignty entrusted to him, it reverted immediately to the people. This demo-cratic conception was vastly superior to the idea of Hobbes, that sovereignty is delegated by the people to the king as an irresponsible monarch.

LOCKE

John Locke (1632–1704) strengthened the social contract theory, elaborating the idea that sovereignty reverts to the people whenever the king becomes a tyrant. He held that the natural state of "individuals" is a condition of perfect freedom to order their actions, not asking leave of any man.[8] This state of liberty is not a state of license to "individuals" to destroy themselves or their neighbors.[9] The state of lib-erty has the law of nature to govern it. Since all are equal, no one ought to harm another in his liberty or possessions.

Locke affirmed that men are in a state of nature until by their own consent they join in a political society. In order to meet their needs effectively, they join in societies. One of these important needs is the preservation of property. Locke defended private property on the ground that it is a normal expression of, and necessary to, "individuality."

Right and wrong are not determined by the ruler or the state; they existed before society developed. Here the Puri-tanism of Locke enters. He stressed moral values. He made the natural rights of "individuals" supreme; "individuals" may even overturn the government and still keep within their rights.

Locke's justification of revolution is his most startling doc-trine. Imagine the heart-throb of the common people who heard Locke's contention that the end of government is the

---

[8] Locke, *Two Treatises on Government,* p. 18.
[9] *Ibid.,* p. 193.

good of mankind, that people should not submit to tyranny, that whoever uses his force without right and law puts himself in a state of war with those against whom he uses it, and that in such a state the people have a right to resist and defend themselves.[10]   Further, the people have a right to act as the supreme social force and to put legislation into new forms and into the hands of new executives.   By these bold declarations Locke created a new public opinion, and aroused new moral power in the minds and hearts of the common people.

PHYSIOCRATS

By the middle of the eighteenth century the concept of "individual freedom" became crystallized in the doctrines of "the natural rights of the individual," the contractual societary relationships between independent "individuals," and the *laissez-faire* principle in governmental science.   The physiocrats, who took up the ideas of natural liberty and economic freedom, exercised a tremendous influence in France during the three decades following 1750.   Their leaders were Quesnay, de Gournay, Condorcet, and Turgot.[11]   They believed that there was a natural law ruling human lives, just as there is a natural law ruling the physical world. They chafed under the social restraints.   Under the natural law, every "individual" has natural rights, chief of which is the right to the free exercise of all his faculties as long as he does not infringe on the similar right of other "individuals." Unlike John Locke and other English thinkers who accepted the idea of "individual liberty," the physiocrats argued that this natural liberty could not be abridged by a social contract.

According to the physiocrats, the chief function of governmental control is to preserve the natural liberty of "individuals."   Industry and commerce must not be governmentally regulated, for by such regulation the rights of some men, chiefly employers, will be infringed upon.   Employees, on the other hand, who are being treated unjustly, will freely

[10] Locke, *op. cit.*, p. 315.
[11] See Charles A. Ellwood, "Turgot, A Neglected Social Philosopher of the Eighteenth Century," *Social Science*, 10:213-218.

quit a harsh employer and obtain employment with consid-
erate masters.   Thus, an unjust employer will be unable to
secure workers and be forced to discontinue his unjust practices—without government regulation.   Likewise, a dishonest merchant will lose his customers and be forced to
become honest or to close his shop—and again without government regulation.   The physiocrats became known by their
famous phrase, *laissez faire, laissez passer.*

Jean Jacques Rousseau (1712–1778), an able but baffling
character, is the best known champion of the social contract
idea.   Although he advocated the family as a social institution and praised fatherhood, he reports that he carried his
own children to a foundling asylum.   He deprecated the dis-
integrating elements in civilization and urged a return to
nature's simple ways.   In his chief works, the *Contrat social,*
and *Emile,* he attacked civilization vigorously.   He asserted
that civilization had almost destroyed the natural rights of
man.   His dictum was: Trust nature.

According to Rousseau the early life of mankind was
nearly ideal in its simplicity and pleasantness.   War and conflict were relatively unknown.   In his later writings, Rousseau
modified his belief and asserted that primitive confusion
made necessary some kind of social organization.   On the
other hand, it became the belief of Rousseau that civilization
generates social evils, and results sooner or later in social
deterioration.   Corruption in society has become notorious.
Social inequality is rampant and unbearable.   "Man is born
free, and is everywhere in chains."   People have become en-
grossed in the artificialities of social life and so bewildered
by its complexities that happiness has been lost.

Leave the "individual" free to carry out his own plans,
untrammeled by complex social rules, restrictions, and duties.
There is no social sanction at all; there is no authority except nature, which is necessary.   In *Emile,* Rousseau takes
his two leading characters to an island, where they live alone
—happily!   Liberty, not authority, reigns.   But Emile, who
has declared for liberty as opposed to authority, insists in

his discussions of domestic relationships that "woman is made to please man." The "unselfish unsocial life" of Emile and Sophie turns out to be more than purely individualistic — it is anarchic and sensual. *Emile* fails to demonstrate the merit of Rousseau's own theories, such as "Man is good naturally but by institutions he is made bad," and "Everything is good as it comes from the hands of the Author of Nature; everything degenerates in the hands of man." [12]

In explaining the nature of the "social pact" as Rousseau conceived the idea, he points out that the pact is a concomitant of a complex society. A small and simple group would not need to enter into an elaborate agreement.

The forming of an association of people or of society calls for the greatest degree of social understanding. How can a pact be developed so that each may "coalesce" with all and still be free as possible? [13] Rousseau believed that he had solved the dilemma and pointed out that in the social pact each gains the equivalent of the freedom that he signs away.

Slavery is wrong, according to Rousseau. [14] It is a contract or agreement, at the expense of the slave and for the profit of the slaveholder, in which the slaveholder asserts: I'll observe the agreement and you will observe it — as long as it pleases me.

Strength does not make right. Strength and moral force are not necessarily the same. Strength may often be ironically accepted in appearance and established in principle. By a social contract man loses his natural liberty and gains civil and moral liberty. [15] In this connection Rousseau was simply the spokesman of a point of view which found frequent expression in the seventeenth and eighteenth centuries. For example, in 1635, John Winthrop, the first governor of the Massachusetts colony, made a clear-cut distinction between natural liberties, and civil and moral liberties. Natural liberty is liberty to do what one lists, to do evil as well as good. Civil or moral liberty is liberty under the covenant between God and man, under the political covenants between men and men, and under the moral law.

---

[12] Rousseau, *Contrat social*, p. 240.
[13] *Loc. cit.*
[14] *Ibid.*, p. 246.
[15] *Ibid.*, p. 249.

It is a liberty to do only that which is good, just, and honest.[16]

It was Rousseau who contended that life, liberty, and the pursuit of happiness are man's inalienable rights. It was this doctrine which profoundly influenced Thomas Jefferson, as evidenced in the Declaration of Independence. Sovereignty rests not in a ruler or monarch but in the community of people — this was perhaps Rousseau's main contribution to social thought.

MONTESQUIEU

Before Rousseau wrote the *Contrat social,* however, the social contract theory had been overthrown. The writings of Montesquieu (1689–1755) offer an elaborate analysis of social and political processes. These analyses are similar, in some ways, to Aristotle's analyses of 158 constitutions. Montesquieu discussed the doctrine of natural rights, but did not believe that the natural state of mankind was one of conflict, in which social organization was forced as a means of meeting the needs of "individual" protection. He asserted that there was a natural, innate tendency in man toward association. In the support of his belief Montesquieu drew facts from the lives of the individual members of the primitive tribes which were extant in his day. The influence of Montesquieu was clearly inimical to the social contract doctrine.

According to Montesquieu's *Esprit des lois* there are four laws which account for the development of human associations. These are: (1) The need for peace, (2) hunger, (3) sex attraction, and (4) the need for one another's company. Montesquieu also analyzed four types of government: (1) Democracy, based on patriotism and the desire for equality; (2) aristocracy, which urges the best few to rule in behalf of the welfare of all; (3) monarchy, with its emphasis on class distinctions, and (4) despotism, which is the rule of one person by the use of fear.

In the *Esprit des lois,* Montesquieu dissected the laws of many nations and tried to show the relations between these

---

16 John Winthrop in *Selections from Early American Writers,* 1607–1800; edited by W. B. Cairns, p. 52.

laws and social and political conditions. The general implication is that laws are a natural outgrowth of life conditions rather than of formal contractual agreements. Hence, society is a natural evolution rather than a contract.

HUME

Perhaps the chief antagonist in the eighteenth century of the social contract theory was David Hume (1711–1776), the father of social psychology. According to Hume, the origin of society was not in a contract arrived at by intellectual processes; it was instinctive. Man is a social animal. His traits of good will, kindliness, and benevolence are irresistible.

At the basis of this sociability lies the sex instinct, which resulted in the establishment of the family. The sex instinct is strongly supported by the sentiment of sympathy which also is innate, and which may develop into intelligent cooperation. Man is not entirely self-centered; he takes pleasure in other people's pleasures and suffers when others are in pain, or the victims of disease, or are dying.

Sympathy, like the sex instinct, is a genuinely fundamental element in human nature and in society. However, the combination of sympathy and the sex instinct is not strong enough to support the family in either its simple or complex stages from the attacks upon it that are made by inherent human selfishness. Hence, social and political organizations are necessary to hold the selfish impulses and interests of mankind in check. Intellectual control of society thus becomes necessary and consciously recognized. Environment alone does not cause people in a given community to act alike.[17] It is imitation, primarily, which operates to bring about group conformity.

Hume indulges in a picture of society in which human affections are allowed to operate without conflict from evil impulses. The result is a society based on "enlarged affections" where law would be practically unnecessary.

Unfortunately, man does not allow his affections to govern his actions in the large aspects of social life. In the family,

[17] David Hume, *A Treatise of Human Nature, II*, pp. 77, 114, 140, 150.

however, is found a sample of what may be developed later in a larger way.

War has a degenerating influence. You are at a terrible disadvantage unless you resort to the same barbarous actions that warriors use. War is a violation of justice.

In actual experience man is in a large measure governed by "interest." It is impossible for men to consult their interests "in so effective a manner as by a universal and inflexible observance of the rules of justice by which alone they can preserve society, and keep themselves from falling into that wretched and savage condition, which is commonly represented as the state of nature." [18]

According to the contract theory, people expect protection and security. If they meet with tyranny and oppression, they are freed from their promises and return to that state of liberty which preceded the institution of government. But Hume maintained that if people entered into no contract and made no promises, government would still be necessary in all civilized societies. The obligation of submission to government is not derived from any promise of the subjects.[19]

Adam Ferguson (1723–1816) wrote *An Essay on the History of Civil Society* and *The History of the Progress and Termination of the Roman Republic.* He argued that social institutions and social convenience lead to inherent sociability, and pointed out that competition and conflict are vital to social development. In 1792 his *Principles of Moral and Political Science* was published.

In a summary of Ferguson's thought, W. C. Lehmann mentions seven contributions of importance. (1) Ferguson developed a concept of society and analyzed it in an empirical way. (2) He held to the organic nature of society, which he treated historically and to a degree psychologically. (3) His social thinking followed an evolutionary pattern. (4) He was one of the first writers to project a division of labor theory. (5) He recognized the independence of the various phases of social life. (6) He was one of the first to combine a psychological approach with the cultural viewpoint. (7)

[18] *Ibid.*, p. 534.
[19] *Ibid.*, p. 546.

He laid foundations for a conflict theory of society.[20] While most of Ferguson's social thought was of an introductory and philosophical nature, it doubtless played a real role in helping lay foundations for the science of sociology.

Thomas Paine (1737–1809) asserted that man is inherently social and that social organization is a natural development. He was an influence in promoting the ideas that are given prominence in the Declaration of Independence. He attacked those who criticized the French Revolution, and became known for his brilliant though at times impetuous arguments in behalf of the rule of reason in all things, even in the field of religion.

MERCANTILISM

The natural rights theory and the resultant individualism not only repudiated their false derivative, the social contract concept, but also wrestled with considerable success with the socio-economic concept of mercantilism. Mercantilism was a system of regulating industrial enterprise by governments in order to build up strong nation-states. Mercantilism reached its strictest form in France in the writings of Colbert (1619–1683). It prevailed in Europe during the sixteenth and seventeenth centuries, and the first four decades of the eighteenth century. It was a system which grew out of feudalism and the city-state type of society. It operated to bring together towns and cities into national unities. Under feudalism, the town had regulated industry for its own advancement and against the welfare, perchance, of neighboring towns. Mercantilism served to unite towns and to create in townspeople a national loyalty.

Under mercantilism the nation entered upon the task of regulating industry and finance so as to build a strong state. A favorable balance of trade was sought in order to add to the bullion within the state. High tariffs were enacted, which sometimes defeated the intended purposes. A dense population was favored as a means of securing cheap labor, and hence of furthering manufacture, which in turn would de-

[20] W. C. Lehmann, *Adam Ferguson and the Beginnings of Modern Sociology*, pp. 26, 27.

velop foreign trade and bring in the coveted bullion—the heralded strength of a nation.

In the eighteenth century mercantilism in France and England met defeat in the contest with the *laissez-faire* theory, with which the names of the physiocrats and of Adam Smith are inseparably connected. It often fathered too stringent regulations. Instead of supporting national ends, mercantilistic measures frequently furthered private interests. Mercantilism, however, played a strong part in building up the concepts of national unity and loyalty.

CAMERALISM

In the German states and Austria, Cameralism represented the ideas for which mercantilism stood in England, France, and elsewhere in western and southern Europe. Among the leading Cameralists were Von Osse, Seckendorf, Horing, Justi, and Sonnenfels. Cameralism obtained a far deeper hold upon the German states than mercantilism did, for example, in England. The *laissez-faire* philosophy was never able to make a deep inroad upon Cameralism. In fact, the *laissez-faire* philosophy did not receive serious consideration in the German states before 1880, and did not strike deep. National self-sufficiency, paternalistic control, minute regulation of internal affairs, rearing of large families, and subordination to the welfare of the state—these are the concepts which ruled in Germany.

Cameralism began in the German states about 1555 with the publication of Von Osse's *Testament*. The term came from the German word *Kammer*, meaning "treasury." At first the Cameralists were literally experts of the treasury. Soon the term took on a broader meaning and referred in an incipient way to the science of government, or broader still, of the state.

The basic question that the Cameralists asked was: "How can a strong state be built?" This movement in the latter part of the sixteenth century among the German states is closely similar to the one that has engaged Germany's attention since the World War. In an elaborated form, the question becomes: "How may a government be strong enough to resist other states, and to preserve order among its own peoples ?" [21]

The Cameralists answered the question in the strict and practical economic sense. They said that a strong state depends on having money with which to carry on governmental activities. The ruler was to exercise enough power to suppress restless subjects, and to be furnished enough money to conduct successful wars. The result is almost a current totalitarian concept. The individual is minimized and the state is exalted.

Cameralism reached its climax about 1765. At this time it emphasized (1) "internal security" of the state, (2) the development of commerce as a means of replenishing the treasury, and (3) fiscal science.[22] The concepts of a collectivistic philosophy were put on an economic basis. The welfare of the state, not of the individual, was made supreme. Germany thus has put the state first for two centuries. Albion W. Small points out that the progressive German asks : "Without disturbing public order, what additions are possible to individual freedom?" On the other hand, in the United States the primary question is : "Without diminishing individual freedom, what additions are possible to public order ?" [23]

ADAM SMITH

Adam Smith (1723–1790), primarily an economist and often referred to as the father of political economy, exerted a profound influence upon social thought. He coupled a modified natural rights theory with a doctrine of sympathy ; he spoke for the natural rights of the individual, of the poorer classes in society, and of the smaller nations. He vigorously attacked mercantilism with its system of minute regulation. He objected to promoting unduly the interests of one class of men in a country, for by so doing, the interests of all other classes in that country and of all persons in all other countries are harmed.[24] He pointed out the fallacy of building

[21] Albion W. Small, *Origins of Sociology,* p. 111.
[22] *Ibid.,* p. 117.
[23] *Ibid.,* p. 114. For a full description of *Cameralism,* see A. W. Small, *The Cameralists.*
[24] Adam Smith. *Wealth of Nations,* Ii:114.

a nation of shopkeepers, for in so doing the government of such a nation will be unduly influenced and controlled by the interests of shopkeepers. The interests of other classes will be more or less ignored. Adam Smith protested against Great Britain's methods of regulating the American colonies. To prohibit the American colonies from making all they could of every part of their own produce or from employing their stock and industry in the way that they judged most advantageous to themselves, was "a manifest violation of the most sacred rights of mankind."[25]

Mercantilism made use of monopoly of one kind or another, and hence is objectionable, according to Smith. Mercantilism is regulation, and regulation is often carried on for the benefit of the rich and powerful, thus neglecting and oppressing the poor.[26] Smith failed to note, however, that the *laissez-faire* policy likewise favored the rich and powerful and neglected the poor. Mercantilism, according to Smith, considers production and not consumption as the end of industry and commerce, and thus favors one class at the expense of other classes.

"Wherever there is great property," said Smith, "there is great inequality." For every very rich man there must be at least 500 poor men, and the affluence of the few supposes the indigence of the many.[27] But no society can be flourishing and happy wherein the greater part of the members are poor and miserable.[28] The laboring men should have "such a share of the produce of their own labor as to be themselves tolerably well fed, clothed, and lodged." "Poverty does not prevent the procreation of children, but is on the other hand extremely unfavorable to the rearing of children." [29]

Smith pointed out four causes of social inequality: [30] (1) Superiority in personal qualifications, such as strength, beauty, agility of body; or wisdom, virtue, prudence, justice, fortitude, moderation of mind. (2) Superiority of age and experience. (3) Superiority of fortune. Riches give social

---

[25] *Ibid.,* II:83.
[26] Adam Smith, *op cit.,* II:143.
[27] *Ibid.,* II:203.
[28] *Ibid.,* I:80.
[29] *Ibid.,* I:81.
[30] *Ibid.,* II:203-207.

authority; riches possess power to buy. (4) Superiority of birth, based on family prestige.

In putting the responsibility for social welfare upon voluntary activities of individuals, Smith expected too much of enlightened self-interest, or at least he did not take into account all the people who would not come up to this standard of enlightened self-interest. To the state he permitted the tasks of enforcing law and justice and also of providing education and of administering public works. In addition the state should defend its own borders against attack.

Smith extolled the merits of division of labor in industry with the resultant increase in the quantity of work. There are three sets of causal circumstances: [31] (1) the increase of dexterity; (2) the saving of time in passing from one kind of work to another; and (3) the invention of a large number of machines. Smith, however, deplored the deadening effect upon the individual of repeating over and over a simple process, hundreds or thousands of times daily. In summary, Adam Smith (1) applied the concept of natural rights to industrial conditions; (2) developed Hume's concept of sympathy into a theory of mutual aid between individuals, classes, and nations; and (3) supported the necessity of division of labor.

The natural rights and social contract theories affected in one way or another the thinking not only of the men who have already been considered in this chapter, but also of many other individuals. Blackstone (1723–1780) held that man's weakness in isolation led to association. The primary group was the patriarchal family. Blackstone was not an advocate of social regulation. His exposition of English law in the *Commentaries* stood for law itself, and became the bulwark at once of the doctrines of individual rights and property rights in both England and the American colonies. In the United States, its influence remained dominant for more than a century after the founding of the republic.

Although Edmund Burke (1729–1797) believed in a corporate unity of society, he became in his century the chief spokesman of humanity for humanity's sake. He pleaded for justice for and conciliation with the American colonies; he

[31] *Ibid.*, i:11.

spoke for the benighted Hindus who were being plundered by English stockholders; and he championed the rights of slaves. He failed, on the other hand, to appreciate the struggles of the French people which culminated in the French Revolution.

KANT

Immanuel Kant (1724–1804) declared man in a natural state is both social and unsocial and referred to the "unsocial sociableness" of man. "Man cannot get on with fellows and he cannot do without them." Man has an inclination to associate with others and also a great propensity to isolate himself from others. He wishes to direct things according to his own ideas and thus courts resistance and conflict. It is this conflict, however, which leads to "individual" advancement.

Kant laid great stress upon a good will.[32] The "individual" may have intelligence and sagacity, power and wealth, but he may still be a pernicious and hurtful member of society. He is not even worthy to be happy unless he possesses a good will. A man's will is good not because of the end he seeks, nor because of the results of his activities, but because he inherently wills the good. It is this "good will" of Kant which is in conflict with the utilitarianism of Bentham and Mill, and also with modern behavioristic psychology and objective sociology. To Kant, morality is subjective. Social laws may regulate and control man's conduct but they cannot control his motives.

Kant's famous dictum was: "Act as if the maxim from which you act were to become through your will a universal law of nature." The Königsberg philosopher opposed slavery and deplored exploitation of all kinds. He also argued in behalf of "eternal peace" and held that peace would not be assured until the people themselves should have freedom in deciding whether they want peace or war.

Johann Fichte (1762–1814) joined with Kant in the interpretation of a good will. He held that property is essential to the development of freedom. However, he pushed the social contract idea to an extreme and developed a doctrine

---

[32] Kant, *Theory of Ethics,* translated by Abbott, p. 9.

of an idealistic state socialism, including the superiority of Germany among the nations of the world.

Hegel (1770–1831) supported Cameralism by developing the State idea, with the implication that Germany would become the supreme State in the world. Hegel even asserted that man has his existence and his ethical status "only in being a member of the State." [33] Morality is not a matter of striving independently to realize one's inner self, but of living in accord with the traditions of one's State.

OTHER INDIVIDUALISTS

Perhaps the individual rights theory never manifested a greater aberration than in the mind of Friedrich Nietzsche (1844–1900). Power is supreme. The "individual" or the nation with the greatest power has the greatest right to live. Against this idea or the expressions of this idea, weaker persons tend to combine and to extol their weaknesses as virtues, even building a religion out of these glorified weaknesses, for example, Christianity. Nietzsche's doctrine of the superman and the superstate will be discussed in Chapter XXIV.

UTILITARIANISM

Closely related to the discussions concerning natural rights and the social contract is the doctrine of utilitarianism, a modified form of individualism with certain objective standards. Jeremy Bentham (1728–1832) made utilitarianism well known, and particularly the standard: The greatest good of the greatest number. In accordance with a formal idea of social change, Bentham urged that social improvements be made by legislation. He demanded objective standards as opposed to Kant's emphasis on the inner motive. Where Kant accented the "how" of conduct, Bentham insisted on the "what" of conduct. He pointed out the need for improved forms of government, apparently ignoring or at least greatly underestimating the fact that real progress comes chiefly through modifying organic processes. However, Bentham may be rated a virile social reformer, for he strongly

---

[33] Hegel, *Philosophy of Right,* translated by Dvde. Part III, p. 150.

advocated such measures as the secret ballot, woman suffrage, trained statesmancraft. He made social welfare a main goal.

The doctrine of utilitarianism was carried forward by James Mill (1773–1836) and was brought to its highest fruition by the son, John Stuart Mill (1806–1873). The elder Mill contended that utility is morality. Like Bentham, the elder Mill urged many social reforms.

John Stuart Mill adopted a modified form of the natural rights theory. He asserted that the "individual" should have all the rights that he can exercise without infringing upon the equal rights of other "individuals." Mill recognized a gradation in the pleasures which satisfy human beings. He declared that it is better to be a man dissatisfied than a pig satisfied ; he objected to the prevailing classification of people on the basis of poverty and wealth, and urged the substitution of standards of personal worth, honor, and true leadership as bases for social classification.

Sir Henry Maine (1832–1888) invented the phrase : From status to contract. He applied this phrase to a program of social welfare. There are many illustrations, he pointed out, in business and industrial life, and even in political and fraternal activities where people make social contracts. The marriage contract also has many of the characteristics of a genuine social contract. Maine pushed the social contract idea to its furthest practical point ; but deprecated the possibility that the masses might come into power. His individualism deprived him of a faith in the possible social development of the uneducated.

Frederic W. Maitland (1850–1906), English jurist and authority in the field of jurisprudence, was much interested in the social factors behind the development and changes in laws. His chief contribution, probably, was in his analysis of the rise of certain created groups as agencies of social conservation and experimentation. In the Middle Ages the law of primogeniture worked undue hardship upon those landlords who wished to do something in the way of bestowing property, or the use of it, upon their younger children. Thus it came about early in the fifteenth century that a law of trust developed whereby a trust could be created for the benefit of these other children. This trust idea, however. gradually developed into a group for holding property for the use of the churches and the labor unions. These trust-groups enabled religion and labor to acquire new and increased strength. Moreover, these trust-groups gave their sponsors a new degree of freedom and enabled them to become instruments for social experimentation. Hence, an agency created to help an individual ultimately becomes a social group in itself, serving a new and distinct social purpose.[34]

Herbert Spencer, whose ideas will be discussed more extensively in a subsequent chapter, became one of the chief exponents of the doctrine of *laissez faire* in governmental matters. He brought a vast reading knowledge and able arguments to the support of individualistic doctrines. He added very little that was new to individualistic and *laissez-faire* theories, although he was at one time perhaps their leading exponent. One of his chief contributions to social thought was indirect and unintentional, namely, the way in which his writings challenged the attention of an American paleontologist, Lester F. Ward, and led him to point out the psychical nature and hence telic possibilities of civilization. In consequence of this challenge Spencer fell, and Ward rose to the rank of dean of American sociologists. An entire chapter will be devoted to the sociology of Lester F. Ward.

William G. Sumner was one of the last noted champions of a governmental *laissez-faire* doctrine.[35] He held that the State owes nothing to anybody except peace, order, and the guarantee of rights. It is not true that the poor ought to care for each other, and that the churches ought to collect capital and spend it for the poor; it is not true that if you get wealth you should support others; and that if you do not get wealth others ought to support you. In a society based on contract there is no place for sentiment in public or common affairs.[36] Everyone will develop the self-reliance of a free person, if he is not taught that others will care for him in case he fails to care for himself. Sumner spoke vigorously as well as harshly

---

[34] See Ernest Barker, "Maitland as a Sociologist," *Sociological Review,* XXIX: 121-135.

[35] W. G. Sumner, *What Social Classes Owe to Each Other,* Harper 1920, p. 12.

[36] *Ibid.,* p. 25.

in support of liberty, contract, and private property. Al-though he took an extreme and untenable position, his ideas will bear careful, unbiased study, for they contain values that will be indicated at some length in another chapter.

A noteworthy statement which has come from a current American school of legal thinkers concerning individualistic social thought is found in the writings of Professor Roscoe Pound of Harvard Law School. In "A Theory of Social Interests" he has summed up the new point of view.[37] In the last century all interests were thought of in terms of individual interests; all were reduced to their purely individual elements and considered as rights.

In this century, Professor Pound indicates that law, for example, aims primarily to conserve some general social interest. It conserves the social interest in the general security, that is, in public health and in peace. It conserves the social interest in natural resources, preventing the waste of oil and gas and protecting water rights. It conserves the social interest in general progress, in economic, political, cultural progress, although its main contributions in other fields, such as promoting the esthetic interests, are yet to be made. It conserves the social interests in individual life and in seeing that people live humanly and that the will of the individual is not crushed. Legal processes have thus become types of social engineering.

Theories of natural rights have been supplanted by considerations of natural needs, both "individual" and social. Human needs are now considered the only imperatives, but even they are relative and changing. Frank Wilson Blackmar, a pioneer in sociology, sums up the whole matter in his book entitled *Justifiable Individualism* as follows: "The only individualism that is justifiable is that which is built up in the service of others." If individualism is essential to progress, then socialization of human attitudes is essential to individualism. Even the study of sociology requires broad foundations. Blackmar suggested that the study of sociology requires a broad foundation in the natural sciences, a cultural outlook, and a deep insight into human nature obtained

[37] Publications of the American Sociological Society, Vol. XV.

through "an acquaintanceship with psychology, history, po-litical science, economics." [38]

SUMMARY

The doctrine of natural rights reached its largest degree of acceptance in England, France, and the United States. It was not only reflected in the thought of Thomas Jefferson but in the fundamental principles upon which the United States was established. It suffered an aberration in the form of the social contract theory which in its extreme forms was later repudiated. Its greatest weaknesses were found in the exaggerated form which it assumed, especially in England and the United States. In the latter country it became greatly magnified through contact with the spirit of discovery, in-vention, and pioneering which prevailed for more than a century. Consequently, it dominated the thought life of the United States throughout the nineteenth century. It per-mitted captains of industry to exploit the helpless masses, and encouraged politicians to pursue selfish practices until governments became honeycombed with graft. It nearly capsized the good Ship of State — Democracy.

[38] Howard E. Jensen, "The Sociologist and his Training," *Social Science* 12:411-419.

GROUP DISCUSSION TOPICS

1. Machiavelli's main contribution to social thought.
2. The characteristics of a "prince," or leader.
3. The indebtedness of social thinking to Francis Bacon.
4. The idols of the tribe.
5. The idols of the cave.
6. The idols of the forum.
7. The idols of the theater.
8. The nature of the individual according to Thomas Hobbes.
9. Man's original nature according to Spinoza.
10. John Locke's justification of revolution.
11. The Physiocratic idea of *laissez faire*.
12. Inalienable rights according to Rousseau.
13. The evolutionary nature of society as developed by Montesquieu.
14. The justification for calling Hume the father of social psychology.
15. The meaning of Cameralism.
16. The causes of inequality as outlined by Adam Smith.
17. The meaning of Kant's phrase : "unsocial sociableness of man."
18. Social implications of Kant's "good will."
19. The social meaning of the statement : "It is better to be a man dissatisfied than a pig satisfied."
20. W. G. Sumner as a representative of individualistic social thought.
21. The nature of "social jurisprudence" according to Roscoe Pound.
22. Blackmar's concept of "justifiable individualism."
23. Weaknesses of individualistic social thought.

READINGS

Barker, Ernest, "Maitland as a Sociologist," *Sociological Review,* XXIX : 121-135.

Beach, Walter G., *The Growth of Social Thought* (New York : Charles Scribner's Sons 1939), Ch. V-IX.

Becker, Howard, and Harry E. Barnes, *Social Thought from Lore to Science* (Washington : Harren Press 1952), Vol. I, Ch. 12.

Blackmar, Frank W., *Justifiable Individualism* (New York : Thomas Y. Crowell Company 1922).

Bodin, Jean, *The Six Books of a Commonweale* (transl. by R. Knolles) (London : Bishop 1606).

Detmold, C. E., *The Writings of Niccolo Machiavelli* (Boston : Osgood 1882).

Ellwood, Charles A., *A History of Social Philosophy* (New York : Prentice-Hall, Inc. 1938), Chs. VI, VII.

Furfey, Paul H., *A History of Social Thought* (New York : The Macmillan Company 1942), Chs. 10, 11.

Hegel, G. W. F., *Philosophy of History* (trans. by Sibree) (London : Bell 1910).

Hobbes, Thomas, *Leviathan* (New York : G. P. Putnam's Sons 1904).

House, Floyd N., *The Development of Sociology* (New York : McGraw-Hill Book Company 1936), Ch. V.

Hudson, W. H., *Rousseau* (New York : Charles Scribner's Sons 1903).

Hume, David, *Enquiries Concerning the Human Understanding and Concerning the Principles of Morals* (Oxford : Clarendon Press 1902).

———, *A Treatise of Human Nature,* edited by Selby-Bigge (London : Oxford University Press 1896).

Kant, Immanuel, *Perpetual Peace* (Boston : American Peace Society 1897).

Lehman, W. C., *Adam Ferguson and the Beginnings of Modern Sociology* (New York : Columbia University Press 1930).

Lichtenberger, James P., *Development of Social Theory* (New York : Century Company 1923), Chs. VI-IX.

Locke, John. *Two Treatises on Government* (London : Routledge and Sons, n.d.).

Machiavelli, *The Prince* (London : Routledge and Sons, n.d.), p. 53.

Mill, John Stuart, *On Social Freedom* (New York : Columbia University Press 1941).

Montesquieu, Charles L., *The Spirit of Laws* (transl. by Nugent) (London : Bell & Sons 1894).

Rousseau, J. J., *Contrat social* (Paris : Garnier, n.d.).

Salomon, Albert, "Adam Smith as Sociologist," *Social Forces* 12:22-42.

Small, Albion W., *Origins of Sociology* (Chicago: University of Chicago Press, 1924).

———, *The Cameralists* (Chicago: University of Chicago Press 1909).

Smith, Adam, *Inquiry into the Nature and Causes of the Wealth of Nations* (New York: G. P. Putnam's Sons 1904).

Strauss, Leo, *Thoughts on Machiavelli* (Glencoe, Ill.: The Free Press 1958).

Von Martin, Alfred, *Sociology of the Renaissance* (New York: Oxford University Press 1944).

CHAPTER XV

MALTHUS AND POPULATION CONCEPTS

A unique and distinctive trend in social thought with important sociological implications developed in the closing years of the eighteenth century, namely, Malthusian thought regarding population. Malthusianism, however, was preceded by the ideas of William Godwin and Adam Smith. In 1775 Adam Smith had stated that "every species of animals naturally multiplies in proportion to the means of their subsistence, and no species can ever multiply beyond it."[1] Scanty subsistence, however, destroys a large percentage of offspring. Inasmuch as men, like all other animals, multiply naturally in proportion to the means of their subsistence, food is always, more or less, in demand; and food, or the cost of living, regulates population.[2] City people must depend upon the country for their subsistence, whereas seaport towns can command food resources from all parts of the earth.

The population ideas of William Godwin (1756–1836) were the immediate stimuli which set Malthus at work. In 1793 Godwin's *Enquiry Concerning Justice* was published. Godwin elaborated several radical social ideas of the French Physiocratic philosophers. He declared that human misery is caused by coercive institutions. Government, he asserted, is an evil, and should be abolished. He urged also the abolition of strict marriage relations, although he personally acquiesced in the custom and in his last days he commended marriage. He thought that no social group should be larger than a parish, and that there should be an equal distribution of property. Godwin thus carried the doctrine of natural rights to the verge of anarchy and licentiousness. His ideas furnished a basis for the nineteenth century experiments in communism. But what is more important, Godwin's ideas regarding the reconstruction of society stimulated Thomas Malthus, who developed what is commonly known as the Malthusian doctrine of population.

[1] Adam Smith, *Wealth of Nations*, I:81.
[2] *Ibid.*, p. 147.

MALTHUS AND THE SOCIAL PROBLEM

In 1798, under an assumed name, Thomas Robert Malthus (1766–1834) offered to the world the first carefully collected and elaborated body of data, dealing with what he called the social problem, namely: What is the underlying cause of human unhappiness? This study may be counted, in a sense, the beginning of modern sociological study. Early in life Malthus showed an interest in social questions. Godwin's ideas had centered Malthus' attention on population. Malthus' well-known treatise entitled, *An Essay on the Principle of Population as it Affects the Future Improvement of Society*, undertook two important tasks: (1) To investigate the causes that have impeded the progress of mankind toward happiness, and (2) to examine probabilities of a total or partial removal of these causes.[3]

Among both plants and animals there is a constant tendency to reproduce numerically beyond the subsistence level. Wherever there is liberty, this power of increase blindly asserts itself. Afterwards, a lack of nourishment and of room represses the superabundant numbers.[4] It appears, therefore, that the ultimate check to population is lack of food, since population increases faster than food supply. Nature in other words, sets a harsher law over the increase of subsistence than she does over the birth rate. Man fails to take cognizance of this law and brings untold misery upon himself. The lower economic classes are the chief victims, and the giants of poverty and pauperism rule over whole sections of human population. Malthus considers the question of population the fundamental social problem.

CHECKS ON POPULATION

Since population outruns food supply, dire human consequences naturally follow. Food supply, as a check upon population, operates harshly; it is but representative of an entire series of rigorous natural, or positive, checks upon population. In this list there are unwholesome occupations, forms

[3] *An Essay on the Principles of Population*, eighth edition, p. 1: *cf.* W. S. Thompson, *Population: A Study in Malthusianism*, Ch. I.
[4] *Ibid.*, p. 2.

of severe labor, extreme poverty, damp and wretched housing conditions, diseases, epidemics, plagues, poor nursing, intestine commotion, martial law, civil war, wars of all forms, excesses of all kinds.[5] These positive checks upon population are the results of two main causes, namely, vice and misery. As a result of the operation of these factors, population is being continually cut down and kept near the mere subsistence plane.

Malthus pointed out another check upon population, the preventive. The fear of falling into poverty causes many young people to postpone marriage until they can safely marry — economically. This check, so far as voluntary, is peculiar to man, and to the extent that it is not followed by irregular sex gratification, is prudential. The actual pressure of population upon food supply, or the fear of this impingement, prevents people from marrying earlier than they do and from reproducing their kind faster than they would do otherwise. The pressure, or the fear of it, cuts down the marriage rate in times of economic depression. But let prosperity come, and the marriage rate leaps upward, especially among the poorer classes.

The positive and preventive checks upon population hold a definite relation to each other. "In every country where the whole of the procreative power cannot be called into action, the preventive and the positive checks must vary inversely as each other."[6] That is to say, when positive checks, such as famine and war, slay large numbers of people, moral restraint is diminished and the population numbers rapidly increase. When the preventive check expresses itself strongly, the population is kept down numerically, and positive checks, such as famine or even war are defeated.

Malthus attempted to establish three propositions:

(1) That population is limited by the restriction of the means of subsistence.

(2) That there is an invariable increase of population whenever the means of subsistence increase, unless prevented by powerful checks.

(3) That the factors which keep population on a level with

[5] Malthus, *op. cit.*, p. 8.
[6] *Ibid.*, p. 9.

the means of subsistence are all resolvable into three : moral restraint, vice, and misery.[7]

POPULATION PROBLEMS

No one can gainsay the importance· ȯr the seriousness of the problem of population. Plato wrestled with it, and urged that procreation, when it goes on too fast or too slowly, should be regulated by the state — through a proper distribution of marks of ignominy or of honor. The number of marriages should be determined by the magistrates.

Aristotle suggested that the ages of marriages for both sexes should be regulated; he even advocated the regulation of the number of children for each marriage. Additional children should be aborted.

Malthus, however, was wiser than either Plato or Aristotle, for he observed that the cause which has the most lasting effect in improving the condition of the poorer classes is the conduct and prudence of the individuals themselves.[8] Malthus asserted that it is in the power of each individual to avoid all the evil consequences to himself and society which result from the principle of population, "by the practice of a virtue clearly dictated to him by the light of nature and expressly enjoined in revealed religion."[9]

Malthus demonstrated clearly the weakness of liberal poor laws. Give more food to the poor, and they will produce more children, and suffer more misery. Poor laws increase the numbers of children of the poor, and hence increase the amount of misery. Both private benevolence and poor laws increase the number of marriages and of children.[10]

Education is the solution which Malthus demanded.[11] Educate the poor to postpone marriage, to keep the birth rate down, and to practice economic thrift. To a great extent education will secure the operation of the prudential check upon population. The science of moral and political philosophy should not be confined within such narrow limits

[7] *Ibid.*, p. 13.
[8] *Ibid.*, p. 371.
[9] *Ibid.*, p. 402.
[10] *Ibid.*, p. 416.
[11] *Ibid.*, p. 437.

that it is unable to overcome in practical ways the obstacles to human happiness which arise from the law of population.[12]

NEW POPULATION PROBLEMS

There are factors in the population situation which did not exist in the time of Malthus, or which he did not see. Today there are additional preventive checks upon population; for example, the rise of democracy in the family whereby the wife and mother no longer is dominated by the husband and father, but has a voice of her own regarding domestic matters, such as the number of children. Closely related to this tendency is the feminist movement, or woman's rights movement, whereby women are demanding that they not be confined to the sphere of bearing and rearing children. Increasing intelligence and foresight have served as a powerful preventive check upon population. The current emphasis upon luxury is inimical to the birth rate. A higher economic status almost uniformly cuts down the birth rate. Within the last score of years the new science of eugenics has attracted widespread attention. Eugenics stresses quality of population. It would effect a decrease in the numbers of children born among the lower classes, among the poorer stocks, and prevent procreation among the mentally deficient. It would increase the birth rate among the cultured and the high-grade stocks.

Malthus appreciated the dependence of urban population upon rural districts, but he could not foresee the degree to which cities would grow in the nineteenth and twentieth centuries. The relative decrease of agricultural labor and the proportional increase in non-agricultural labor has thrown a burden upon the food supply which even Malthus could not forecast.

On the other hand, Malthus did not realize the extent to which new countries such as the United States, Canada, Australia, Argentina would contribute to the world's means of subsistence. He could not predict the way in which invention would be applied in solving agricultural problems, and

[12] *Ibid.*, p. 481.

how today one man with improved machinery and intensive methods can produce a hundred ears of corn where one was produced a century ago.

Moreover, the creation of synthetic food products in chemical laboratories may greatly affect the population in ways unanticipated by Malthus. Nevertheless, the "new country" argument against Malthus' principle of population is ultimately fallacious, for new countries soon become old, the supply of new countries becomes exhausted, and there is even a limit to soil productiveness. The very pressure of population against means of subsistence is, however, a cause of inventiveness, so that unanticipated increases in food supply may occur at any time.

Socialism has criticized Malthus severely. Socialism holds that at a given time the food supply is sufficient to meet human needs but that it is poorly or unjustly distributed. With just distribution of the returns from industry, food supply would not impinge strongly on population. But socialism might greatly endanger the prudential check on population, and hence result in an increased birth rate; which in turn would more than balance any release from human misery that a just distribution of the returns from industry would effect.

Another point which Malthus did not observe is that the increase in technical skill which comes with vocational education is overcome by the tendency of the world's population to overtake the world's food productiveness. With increase in population, the price of land rises, the rent for land increases, the cost of living mounts upward, and the purchasing power of the dollar, or its equivalent, declines.

NEO-MALTHUSIANISM

Some of the followers of Malthus have advocated birth control as an artificial means of regulating population. Birth control prevents by physical means the birth of children. It is a useful weapon against sexually brutal husbands. It does not provide for self-control or moral control of the sexual impulses. It may encourage rather than control gratification of the sexual desires. By it a gain is made in protecting

helpless women and in cutting down the birth rate among
the lower classes, whether wealthy or poor, but the gain may
be more than offset by the opportunity which birth control
gives to the irregular gratification of sexual impulses and by
the resultant weakening of moral fibre.

Many writers have pointed out, however, what a tremendous injury mankind does itself by allowing the more highly
developed members of various races to practice voluntary
parenthood, while the less developed reproduce at a more
natural and a far higher rate. The world must control its
population rate or face famine, argues E. M. East. Soon
there will be 3000 million people on the earth and then "a
sudden drop of 25 per cent in the grain crop, just such a
drop as has occurred time and again before . . . will make
what is left of them awaken to the folly of negligence." [13]
The world question, continues Professor East, is the question
"of reducing a swiftly increasing population to fit a rapidly
diminishing food reserve." This startling conclusion is a
stimulus for thought, although the situation may not be so
serious as implied.

Population experts now predict certain maximum limits
for the various nations. It is claimed, for example, that the
increase in the population of the United States will gradually slow up in the next few decades and that it will reach
a maximum of perhaps 175,000,000 or 200,000,000, where it
will remain for some time.

Thomas N. Carver, whose thinking will be referred to
again in subsequent chapters, has developed an interesting
population theory which is partly Malthusian.[14] The increase in population from both immigration sources and the
birth rate should be cut down, thereby decreasing the percentage of unskilled labor. Further, persons should be trained
out of the unskilled group into the skilled group and then
into the *entrepreneur* class. Thus, by greatly decreasing the
number of unskilled laborers and by increasing the number
of *entrepreneurs,* wages will advance and profits will be increasingly subdivided. The poor will become well-to-do, and

13 E. M. East, *Mankind at the Crossroads*, p. 349.
14 T. N. Carver, *Essays in Social Justice,* Harvard University Press 1915,
Ch. XIV.

poverty as it is now known will tend to disappear. This theory underestimates the role of psychological motives and of social attitudes under a system where a marked degree of competition is encouraged — certain persons will still take advantage of their fellows. In other words, if self-centered attitudes continue to operate, even Carver's plan will not keep some people from taking advantage of the many.

The totalitarian states, chiefly those which are militaristic, are putting a premium upon large families. They disfavor birth control in order that many young men may be raised up to fight for their country. Propaganda to this effect is widely put into operation.

The militaristic states thus create problems of over-population. Hunger results. In these circumstances the people are easily led to believe that they are justified in taking territory away by military force from weaker or "backward" states.

In Edward Alsworth Ross' book entitled *Standing Room Only,* the author contends that in Asia and Africa people breed thoughtlessly and have produced economic misery. He urges a program of adaptive fertility for mankind, or a birth rate adapted to the economic circumstances.[15]

Warren S. Thompson has diagnosed the important causes of friction between nations as arising from "the differential pressure of peoples on their resources." Population pressure leads people to look greedily toward countries where underpopulation exists. Immigration barriers have been put up. The tendency toward the rise of force in obtaining unused or misused lands is increasing.[16]

Thompson has defined three population policies that have prevailed or do prevail in the world. These are the restrictive, the expansive, and the eugenic. Where life has been harsh, restrictive policies, sometimes akin to Malthus' preventive checks, have operated. The nineteenth century saw a great expansion in the world's population, particularly in Europe. The population increased from 200 million to more than 500 million in 100 years. Some connection is to be noted between territorial expansion and increase in population. Thompson's eugenic concept includes compensa-

[15] Edward A. Ross, *Standing Room Only.*
[16] Warren S. Thompson, *Danger Spots in World Population.*

tion to certain selected parents for rearing children, up to five or six in numbers.[17]

In the birth control movement in the United States the outstanding name has been that of Margaret Sanger. This movement originated in the main among social reformers and general welfare workers. They saw how wives on the lower economic levels were continually engaged in the process of child-bearing and child-caring. As a result they were slaves to sex, bedraggled human beings unable to extricate themselves from undue burdens, bringing into the world more children than they could care for properly. Sometimes the husbands, failing to hold their jobs, would desert the family, leaving the wife and mother with the added burden of becoming a wage-earner. Sometimes mentally dull wives or mentally defective were the most prolific in bringing low-grade children into the world. Social workers pointed out that the wives on a low economic level should have the knowledge of birth control already known to, and put into practice by, those on the higher economic levels. In this way the population would not be replenished so largely as now by the lowest cultural and biological grades of men and women, and thus the eugenic cause would be promoted.

Neo-Malthusianism also includes the sterilization movement whereby the mentally defective, the criminally insane, and the lowest biological dregs would be prevented from becoming parents. Again, a eugenic population would be indirectly but definitely advanced.

POPULATION QUALITY

A. M. Carr-Saunders divides population problems into the quantitative and the qualitative. He then presents his theory of "germinal change." He believes that the quality of germplasm is subject to change by virtue of the operation of environmental factors. He sums up his population theory in terms both of germinal change and of changes in tradition.

Another major emphasis today in the study of population is "the control of population quality." [18] Such control, how-

---

[17] Warren S. Thompson, *Population Problems*, pp. 10 ff., 450 ff.
[18] See Edward B. Reuter, *Population Problems*, Ch. XIX.

ever, includes eugenics, to which a later chapter will be devoted. The present tendency in democratic countries is to cut down the increase in birth rate and to devise means for increasing the quality of the stock. Totalitarian countries still follow the policy of promoting quantity.

In conclusion, it may be stated that the principle of population as given by Malthus is fundamental to an understanding of the problems of social progress.[19] There is a positive relation between population and means of subsistence. Positive and preventive checks upon population are continually at work. Moral restraint and self-control tend to create a better moral fibre than birth control. The quality of personality is far more important than mere numbers of population. The struggle for equality in personality must be supplanted by justice in industrial and social processes before the population problem can be solved.

[19] Cf. W. S. Thompson, *Population: A Study in Malthusianism.*

GROUP DISCUSSION TOPICS

1. The two major tasks which Malthus set himself.
2. The basic Malthusian principle.
3. The positive checks upon population.
4. The preventive checks upon population.
5. The relation of the operation of these checks upon each other.
6. The solution to the population problem as suggested by Malthus.
7. Socialism's criticism of Malthus.
8. Carver's population plan.
9. Your reactions to Malthusianism.
10. Population problems not foreseen by Malthus.
11. E. A. Ross' "standing room only" theory.
12. Neo-Malthusian ideas.
13. The theories of Carr-Saunders.
14. Comparison of population concepts of Carr-Saunders and of Thompson.

READINGS

Carr-Saunders, A. M., *The Population Problem* (London : Oxford University Press 1922).

Carver, T. N., *Essays in Social Justice* (Cambridge, Mass. : Harvard University Press 1915).

East, E. M., *Mankind at the Crossroads* (New York : Charles Scribner's Sons 1923).

Malthus, Thomas, *An Essay on the Principle of Population* (London : Reeves and Turner 1878).

Reuter, E. B., *Population Problems* (Chicago : J. B. Lippincott Company 1937).

Ross, Edward A., *Standing Room Only* (New York : Century Company 1927).

Smith, Adam, *Wealth of Nations* (New York : G. P. Putnam's Sons 1901).

Thompson, W. S., *Population : A Study in Malthusianism* (New York : Columbia University Press 1915).

———, *Danger Spots in World Population* (New York : A. A. Knopf 1929).

———, *Population Problems* (New York : McGraw-Hill Book Company 1935).

CHAPTER XVI

COMTE AND POSITIVE SOCIAL THOUGHT

An organized foundation for the field of social thought was not laid until near the close of the first half of the nineteenth century. At that time Auguste Comte (1798–1857) gave at least an organized groundwork, if not a synthetic introduction to sociology. He was the first to stake out the territory of social thought, to show the relation of social thought to other fields of knowledge, and to separate social statics from social dynamics. He was the first important social philosopher, and his *Positive Philosophy* the first treatise roughly to propose the field of sociology.

About 1838, Auguste Comte invented the term *sociology*, by which he meant the science of human association. While he did not contribute much to the science itself, he laid important foundations. He reacted against all forms of loose thinking about man, rejected metaphysical and theological speculations, and insisted upon the observation and classification of social phenomena. He repudiated attempts to discover causes of social uniformities, and coined the name *positivism* for the philosophical system upon which he founded sociology. The bases of positivism may be discovered in the ideas of Bacon, Galileo, and Descartes. As each of these three men broke with tradition and sought observed facts in their respective fields, so Comte was likewise prompted to do in the field of social thought.

Auguste Comte was born at Montpelier, France, the son of humble and law-abiding Catholic parents. At the age of nine he displayed unusual mental ability, a strong character, and a tendency to defy authority. He is described as "brilliant and recalcitrant." He possessed a wonderful memory and a remarkable avidity for reading. In school he won many prizes, and took a position of leadership among his fellow students, who called him "the philosopher." At the age of sixteen he was devoting his energies and abilities to the study of mathematics.

As a youth Comte demanded the resignation of one of his instructors, criticized Napoleon, and disregarded both ecclesiastical and parental authority. He especially enjoyed pointing out the stupidity of his superiors and opposing tyranny.

At the age of nineteen Comte made the acquaintance of Saint-Simon, the well-known socialist. The friendship lasted for only a few years, but long enough to exert a deep influence upon the youthful mathematician. Saint-Simon (1760–1825) had indicated the need for a scientific classification of the sciences with political science at the head of the list, and had developed a new fraternalism under the name of *Le nouveau Christianisme*. This system was optimistic and humanitarian, but dreamy. Comte was dissatisfied with it, and undertook to work out a better scheme of social analysis and organization.

REORGANIZATION OF SOCIETY

In 1822, Comte's first important work was published. It contained an introduction by Saint-Simon, and was entitled *A Prospectus of the Scientific Works Required for the Reorganization of Society*. It represented an important beginning of the task on which Comte was to spend his life. Upon the problem Comte read and worked assiduously, save as he was interrupted by an unhappy married life and by mental aberrations due to overwork. He gave courses of public lectures, but insisted upon working gratuitously. He would not accept royalties from the sale of his books, despite the fact that he lived continually on the verge of starvation. His friends, however, made him gifts and established a subsidy. He insisted upon the rule that all his literary productions should be given to the public gratuitously.[1]

His method of composition has been commented upon by his biographers. As a result of his unusual memory and the high degree of mental concentration to which he attained, he was able to plan chapters and volumes in their smallest details, and then from memory to put them into written form. This method enabled him to secure "an extraordinary unity of conception and organic symmetry of plan."

Comte manifested an unusual regard for the truth. This

[1] Auguste Comte, *Positive Philosophy*, translated by Martineau, I:xviii.

attitude required him to modify and qualify statements of fundamental principles at great length. As a result his works are often tedious reading. He preferred, however, to write meticulously and thus to safeguard truth, rather than to speak in epigrams and sacrifice truth.

Comte's two leading works are the *Positive Philosophy* and the *Positive Polity*. The first appeared in six volumes during the years from 1830 to 1842. The second work, in four volumes, was published in the years from 1851 to 1854. It is not the equal of the *Positive Philosophy,* which was translated into English in 1853 by Harriet Martineau.

John Stuart Mill has referred to Comte as among the first of European thinkers; and, by his institution of a new social science, in some respects the first.[2] George Henry Lewes called Comte the greatest of modern thinkers. John Morley, the English statesman and author, says of Comte: "Neither Franklin, nor any man that has ever lived, could surpass him in the heroic tenacity with which, in the face of a thousand obstacles, he pursued his own ideal of a vocation." Harriet Martineau summarizes his methods as follows: "There can be no question but that his whole career was one of the most intense concentration of mind, gigantic industry, rigid economy, and singular punctuality and exactness in all his habits."[3]

TYPES OF THINKING

In laying the foundations for a new social science, Comte began with an analysis of types of thinking. Primitive and untrained persons everywhere think in supernatural terms. They suppose that all physical phenomena are caused by the immediate action of capricious supernatural beings. The primitive man believes in all kinds of fetishes in which spirits or supernatural beings live. Fetishism admitted of no priesthood, because its gods are individual, each residing in fixed objects.[4]

As the mind of primitive man became better organized, fetishism became cumbersome. Too many fetishes produced mental confusion. A coalescence of gods resulted

[2] *Ibid.,* I:XI.
[3] *Ibid.,* I:XV.
[4] *Ibid.,* III:13.

and polytheism arose. The polytheistic gods represented different phases of life. This state in human thought is well illustrated by the Homeric gods.

But a large number of capricious divinities are mentally unsatisfactory. They create mental contradictions. Consequently, the gods are arranged in a hierarchy. Finally, the idea of one God, or of monotheism, developed. The belief arose that every phenomenon is produced by the immediate action of the one God. As man's vision widened and his observations increased in scope and depth, the concept of a monotheistic universe became clarified. Monotheism is the climax of the theological stage of thinking.

But rationalism argues that God does not stand directly behind every phenomenon. Pure reason insists that God is a First Cause or an Abstract Being. Pure reason speaks in terms of inalienable rights; metaphysical explanations, however, are unsatisfactory to the mind.

Hence, Comte developed his concept of positivism, which is a purely intellectual way of looking at the world. Comte held that the mind should concentrate on the observation and classification of phenomena. He believed that both theological and metaphysical speculations, as he used the terms, were as likely to be fiction as truth, and that there is no way of determining which is the case. Thus it will be more profitable if a person would direct his thoughts to the lines of thinking which are most truly prolific, namely, to observation and classification of data. Comte even took the position that it is futile to try to determine causes. We can observe uniformities, or laws, but it is mere speculation to assign causes to these uniformities. Positivism deified observation and classification of data. Its weaknesses should not hinder the student, however, from seeing the importance of its emphasis upon the scientific procedure of observing and classifying data in an age when dogmatism and speculation were rife.

The three stages of thought which Comte described are not three levels of thought, as Comte contended, but, as Herbert Spencer indicated, they may represent the same plane of thinking. Each requires about the same degree of thinking ability. Moreover, as John Fiske argued, the three methods of approach to problems are often pursued simultaneously by a given person. Some phenomena are explained theologically; others, metaphysically; and others, positively.

SOCIAL ORGANIZATION

A second main contribution which Comte made to social thought is that each of the three modes of thinking determines and corresponds to a type of social organization. Speaking from the standpoint of his own religious contacts, he declared that theological thinking leads to a military and monarchical social organization, with God at the head of the hierarchy as King of kings and a mighty warrior, and with human beings arranged in a military organization. Divine sanction rules. As expressed through the human leaders, this divine sanction must not be questioned. Dogmatism must be meekly endured, or else its threatened punishments will be turned loose upon helpless offenders.

Metaphysical thinking produces a government dominated by doctrines of abstract rights. Natural rights are substituted for divine rights. A priesthood is furthered. Social organization becomes legalistic, formal, structural, without adequate content.

Positive thinking produces practical results in the form of industrial enterprises, and ushers in an industrial age. It inquires into the nature and utilization of natural forces. It transforms the material resources of the earth, and produces material inventions.

Comte failed to postulate a fourth mode of thinking, namely, socialized thinking, or a system of thought which would emphasize not simply the use of natural forces, but the use of natural forces for social ends, for the purpose of building constructive, just, and harmonious societies, and of developing persons who will evaluate life in terms of the welfare of other persons. Comte, however, should be credited with opening the way for the rise of socialized thinking.

CLASSIFICATION OF THE SCIENCES

A third phase of Comte's system was his classification of the sciences, with sociology as the latest and greatest of the group. The Greek thinkers, it will be recalled, undertook to classify all knowledge under three headings: physics, ethics, and politics. Bacon made the divisions correlative to the so-called mental faculties of memory, imagination, and reason, namely: history, poetry, and science.

Comte chose as his principle of classifying knowledge the order of increasing dependence. He arranged the sciences so that each category may be grounded on the principal laws of the preceding category, and serve as a basis for the next ensuing category.[5] The order, hence, is one of increasing complexity and decreasing generality. The most simple phenomena must be the most general — general in the sense of being everywhere present.[6]

Comte began with mathematics, the basic tool of the mind. With mathematics as its chief tool, the mind of man can go anywhere in its thinking. Mathematics is the most powerful instrument which the mind may use in the investigation of natural laws.[7]

Mathematics is not a constituent member of the group of sciences. It is the basis of them all. It holds the first place in the hierarchy of the sciences, and is the best point of departure in all education, whether general or special.[8] It is the oldest and most perfect of all the sciences.[9]

Mathematics is the science which measures precisely the relations between objects and ideas. It is *the* science.[10] Its function is that of ascertaining relationships, a process which is basic to scientific thinking in all fields. Education that is based on any other method is faulty, inexact, and unreliable. It is only through mathematics that we can understand science.

The highest form of mathematics is calculus. There is no scientific inquiry in which calculus is not used. Even the physician in prescribing for the cure of disease must provide for the mixing together of different quantities of different medicines, so that, when taken at determined intervals of

5 *Positive Philosophy*, I:26.
6 *Loc. cit.*
7 *Ibid.*, I:34.
8 *Ibid.*, I:35.
9 *Ibid.*, I:36.
10 *Ibid.*, I:41.

time, they will possess the right qualities for bringing the human body back to its normal state. Calculus is the branch of science which has the highest intellectual dignity.[11] In it the proportion of reasoning to observation is greater than elsewhere.

With mathematics as the tool, the classification of knowledge may proceed. All natural phenomena fall into two grand divisions: inorganic and organic. The inorganic are more general and should be considered first.

Inorganic phenomena are of two classes: astronomical and terrestrial. Astronomical phenomena are the most general of all. The stars and planets appear under the least varied aspects.[12] Astronomy is the science by which the movements of the heavenly bodies, including the earth, are measured. How can we thoroughly understand any terrestrial phenomena without considering the nature of the earth and its relation to the other units of the solar system?[13]

Terrestrial physics includes two fields: physics proper and chemistry. Material bodies may be regarded in either their physical or chemical aspects. Physics is more general than chemistry; it deals with masses rather than elements. Chemical phenomena depend upon the laws of physics, without being influenced by them in turn. Chemical action is conditioned by the laws of weight, heat, electricity. The study of inorganic phenomena thus falls under three scientific heads: astronomy, physics, and chemistry.

Organic phenomena include two types: individual and group. The first refers to the function and structure of all individual forms in the plant and animal worlds. It is general physiology, or, in modern terms, biology. It involves the study of all life and the general laws pertaining to the individual units of life.[14]

Biology rests upon chemistry, because in chemistry all reliable knowledge about nutrition or secretion is found. Biology is indebted to physics for knowledge concerning the weight of, temperature of, and related facts about living organisms. Biological laws are partially determined by astro-

[11] Ibid., I:27 ff.
[12] Ibid., I:149.
[13] Ibid., I:153, 154.
[14] Ibid., I:28, 29.

nomical factors.   If the earth were to rotate faster than it does, the course of physiological phenomena would be accelerated, and the length of life would be shortened.[15]   If the orbit of the earth were to become as eccentric as that of a comet, changes of a fatal nature would occur to all life on earth.   If there were no inclination of the earth's axis, the seasons would be unknown, and the geographical distribution of living species would be vastly different from the present situation.   All accurate work in biological studies is mathematical in character.   Thus biology, the science of organic phenomena, is dependent on all the preceding divisions on the scale of knowledge.   Social physics or sociology is the most dependent of all.

SOCIOLOGY

The study of gregarious or associative life is a special field. Comte called this science *social physics,* and for it invented the specific term *sociology.*   It rests in turn upon biological, chemical, physical, and astronomical knowledge and uses mathematics as its tool.   Comte virtually defines six sciences : mathematics, astronomy, physics, chemistry, biology, and sociology.   He treats of transcendental biology, which is the basis of modern psychology.   Comte urged that no science could be effectually studied without competent knowledge concerning the sciences on which it depends.   It is necessary not only to have a general knowledge of all the sciences but to study each of them in order — this is Comte's dictum to the student of sociology.   Comte insisted that one general science could not develop beyond a given point until the preceding science has passed a given stage.

Each of the six general sciences has passed through the three stages of thought.   Mathematics, which has advanced furthest into the positive stage, is still connected with superstition, such as that which hovers round the number 13. The other general sciences are less further along.   Sociology, the latest science to develop, Comte hoped by his works to push over into the positive stage.

Comte divided sociology, or social physics, into social

[15] *Ibid.,* II:30.

statics and social dynamics. Social statics is the study of the laws of action and reaction of the different parts of the social order, aside for the time being from the general social movements which are modifying them.[16] Social dynamics considers the laws of progress. Social statics inquires into the laws of coexistence of social phenomena ; social dynamics examines the laws of social succession. Sociology is the study of social organization and of social progress.

Society is in a state of anarchy. Individuals with the best of purposes are continually weakening the efforts of each other. Powerful persons are crushing the weak. The defeated are conniving against the strong. Why all this social anarchy? To Comte the answer is clear. Behind moral and social anarchy there is intellectual anarchy. People do not have a knowledge of the fundamental laws of social order and social progress.

Moreover, people fail to appreciate the necessity of knowledge of social laws. They are insensible to the value of sound social theory. They want nothing but the "practical," unmindful of the fact that the "practical" is as likely to be based on incorrect social theory as upon sound social conceptions.

The necessity of fundamental concepts concerning society underlies social organization. In the absence of these general ideas, there is "no other daily resource for the maintenance of even a rough and precarious social order than an appeal, more or less immediate, to personal interests." [17] In the absence of a moral authority, the material order requires the use of either terror or corruption ; the latter is less inconvenient and more in accordance with the nature of modern society.[18] Moreover, politicians and other public men work against the elaboration of the social theory which is necessary for the salvation of society. They sneer at the development of social science. Many of those who occupy the chief political stations regard with antipathy the true reorganization of society. Social principles are not even sought. On the other hand, social charlatanism attracts by the mag-

16 *Positive Philosophy,* II:219.
17 *Ibid.,* II:174.
18 *Ibid.,* I:176.

nificence of its promises and dazzles by its transient successes. Comte deplored attempts to remake society through institutionalism, regardless of social theory. He stressed the fundamental importance of social principles as the only means of guaranteeing a correct institutional procedure. As a practical principle of social adjustment, Comte endorsed the Catholic ideal: In necessary things, unity; in doubtful things, liberty; in all things, charity.

Comte protested vigorously against materialism. He pointed out that for three centuries the best minds had been devoted to material science and had neglected societary problems.[19] Material institutions should be modified and made to harmonize with the underlying laws of social evolution. A moral reorganization of society must precede and direct the material and political reorganization.[20]

Social improvement is a result of mental development. This development favors the preponderance of the noblest human tendencies. Prevision and science when applied to society will bring out the best phases of human nature, and thus result in social improvement. Although the lower instincts will continue to manifest themselves in modified action, their less sustained exercise will debilitate them by degrees.[21]

SOCIAL VARIATION

The three chief causes of social variation result from (1) race, (2) climate, and (3) political action in its whole scientific content. The first and second factors cannot be changed greatly, but the political influences are wide open to modification by social prevision. In this connection sociology finds its manifestation.

Comte argues strongly that *ennui,* the result of inactivity or of routine activity, is indirectly a factor in social progress. When one becomes aware of *ennui* he reacts against the state that has produced it, and thus is stimulated to new forms of activity.

With the development of society, intellectual activity and gregariousness slowly overcome the preponderance of the

19 *Ibid.,* II:180.
20 *Ibid.,* II:193.
21 *Ibid.,* II:234.

affective over the intellectual phases of life. But even in the best natures the personally affective elements are more powerful than the social affections. Real intellectual development, however, will strengthen man's empire over his passions, refine his gregariousness, and release his energies for social activities.

The direction of social evolution is toward further development of the noblest dispositions and the most generous feelings, and away from the expression of the animal appetites and the material desires.[22] The trend is from the satisfaction of the selfish impulses to the habitual exercise of the social impulses. Happiness depends on the presence of new stimuli in one's form of activity. A life of labor that is full of constructive stimuli is after all the fittest to develop personality.

The place of increase in population in social evolution is considered to be vital. A warning, however, is uttered. What is going to happen when population becomes so great that the whole earth is crowded?[23]

Comte makes the family the social unit. Man cannot survive in isolation, but the family can survive by itself.[24] The striking characteristic of domestic organization is its establishment of the elementary idea of social perpetuity, by directly and irresistibly connecting the future with the past.[25] Family life will always be the school of social life, both for obedience and for command. Comte failed to escape the logic of the patriarchal family life. He did credit women, however, with being superior to men in the spontaneous expression of sympathy and sociality, although being inferior in understanding and reason.

Comte was the friend of popular education.[26] He based his contention on the invariable homogeneity of the human mind. The minds of people of all races are potentially similar. All members of the race are capable of development to a common plane.

In his *Positive Polity,* Comte made important changes in

[22] *Ibid.,* II:304.
[23] *Ibid.,* II:306.
[24] *Ibid.,* II:292.
[25] *Ibid.,* II:287.
[26] *Ibid.,* III:320.

his thinking. This work was the product of his later years, and shows the effects of deprivation and struggle. It is inferior in quality to his earlier treatise on *Positive Philosophy*. It is a question, therefore, how far his later ideas should be permitted to supersede his thinking when he was in his prime. In his later thought he receded from his emphasis upon the intellectual nature and stressed the importance of the affections. He made affection the central point of life and developed the concept of love. We tire of thinking and even of acting, he asserted, but we never tire of loving.[27]

The Comtean ideal became a disinterested love of mankind. Comte developed a religion of humanity. His contact with Christianity gave him the belief that it is chiefly ecclesiastical. He did not see in Christianity a social keynote. Hence, he attempted to create a purely social religion. He made mankind an end in itself. He was "morality-intoxicated."[28] Although not a strict religionist, Comte considered the atheist "the most irrational of all theologians!" The atheist, while essaying to speak of God, begins "by denying the very things of which he is speaking."[29]

SUMMARY

The master-thoughts of Comte have been ably summarized by F. S. Marvin. (1) First is Humanity, the necessary ideal in any comprehensive system of thought. (2) Then comes Science as the directing force. (3) Synthesis is the next key-word, for Humanity and Science must be integrated. (4) Faith is needed as a necessary concomitant to the predictions of Science. Humanity, Science, Synthesis, Faith — these four are the essence of Comte's social thought.[30]

If we judge Comte by his own time and age, we shall see the importance of his contributions to social thought, which may be restated as follows: (1) There is need for accurate thinking about society. Mathematics is the best tool for obtaining social accuracy. (2) Comte developed positivism with its emphasis upon observation and classification of so-

[27] Comte, *Positive Polity*, I:1.
[28] F. S. Marvin, *Comte*, p. 120.
[29] Quoted by F. S. Marvin, *op. cit.*, p. 124.
[30] F. S. Marvin, *op. cit.*, p. 212.

cial data. (3) Knowledge has scientific divisions, according to the principles of increasing dependence and decreasing generality. This scale begins with mathematics and astronomy, includes physics, chemistry, biology, in order, and ends with the social sciences, particularly sociology. (4) Sociology deals with the static and dynamic phases of human association. (5) Comte developed a humanitarian philosophy. (6) Comte insisted on an intellectual understanding of social processes as the only true basis for overcoming social anarchy and for solving the problems of society.

GROUP DISCUSSION TOPICS

1. The derivation of the term *sociology*.
2. Significant personality traits of Auguste Comte.
3. The influence of socialism upon Comte.
4. The social significance of Comte's first book.
5. Three major types of human thinking.
6. Other types of thinking.
7. The culmination of the three types of thinking in types of social organization.
8. The nature of positivism.
9. Comte's principle of classifying knowledge.
10. Comte's classification of the sciences.
11. The relation of mathematics to social thought.
12. The differences between social statics and social dynamics.
13. The reasons for society being in a state of anarchy.
14. Comte's reactions concerning materialism.
15. The meaning of prevision.
16. The direction of social evolution.
17. Comte's outstanding contribution to social thought.

READINGS

Barnes, Harry E., Editor, *An Introduction to the History of Sociology* (Chicago: University of Chicago Press 1948), Ch. 3.

Beach, Walter G., *The Growth of Social Thought* (New York: Charles Scribner's Sons 1939), Ch. X.

Becker, Howard, "The Limits of Sociological Positivism," *Journal of Social Philosophy*, 6:362-369.

Becker, Howard, and Harry E. Barnes, *Social Thought from Lore to Science* (Washington: Harren Press 1952), Vol. I, Ch. 15.

Bernard, L. L., "The Significance of Comte," *Social Forces*, 21: 8-14.

Booth, A. J., *Saint-Simon and Saint-Simonism* (New York: Longmans, Green & Co. 1871).

Chambliss, Rollin, *Social Thought* (New York: The Dryden Press 1954), Ch. 16.

Comte, Auguste, *Positive Philosophy* (translated by H. Martineau) (London: Bell and Sons 1913).

———, *Positive Polity* (translated by H. Martineau) (London: Bell and Sons 1896).

DeGrange, McQuilkin, "Comte's Sociologies," *American Sociological Review*, 4:17-25.

Durkheim, Emile, *Socialism and Saint-Simon*, edited by A. W. Gouldner (Yellow Springs, Ohio: The Antioch Press 1958).

Ellwood, Charles A., *A History of Social Philosophy* (New York: Prentice-Hall, Inc. 1938), Chs. XXIII, XXIV.

Furfey, Paul H., *A History of Social Thought* (New York: The Macmillan Company 1942), Ch. XVI.

Hartung, Frank E., "The Sociology of Positivism," *Science and Society*, VIII:328-341.

House, Floyd N., *The Development of Sociology* (New York: McGraw-Hill Book Company 1936), Ch. X.

Lichtenberger, James P., *Development of Social Theory* (New York: Century Company 1923), Ch. X.

Lundberg, George, "Contemporary Positivism in Sociology," *American Sociological Review*, 4:42-55.

Marjohn, Robert, "French Sociology—Comte and Durkheim," *American Journal of Sociology*, XLII: 693-704.

Marvin, F. S., *Comte* (New York: John Wiley & Sons 1937).

Mihanovich, C. S., *Social Theorists* (Milwaukee: The Bruce Publishing Company 1953), Ch. 3.

Mill, John Stuart, *Auguste Comte and Positivism* (Philadelphia: J. B. Lippincott Company 1866).

CHAPTER XVII

MARX AND SOCIALISTIC THOUGHT

Socialism proper had its beginning in the second and third decades of the nineteenth century. It developed primarily in continental Europe and in England. Although Plato's communism and More's utopianism were forerunners of socialism, the social unrest in Europe in the early years of the nineteenth century was the direct causal factor. Socialism also represented a reaction against the prevailing *laissez-faire* thought regarding the evils of society and the suffering of the poorer classes.

Socialism began with the concepts and experiments of Saint-Simon and Fourier in France, of Robert Owen in England and of Rodbertus, Lassalle, Marx, and Engels in Germany. In France the movement was carried forward by Proudhon and Blanc; and in England by the Christian socialists, chiefly Maurice and Kingsley. In Germany Marx maintained the position of leadership for many decades, and finally became the best known exponent of socialist thought in the world.

In his *New Christianity*, Saint-Simon, who was referred to in the preceding chapter, made a unique contribution to social thought. His thinking was not deep, nor systematic, but ingenious. Saint-Simon advocated a society in which only useful things are produced. In this industrial order, men of science will be in control. Saint-Simon was greatly interested in the welfare of the poorest classes. His *New Christianity* was essentially a plea that the whole world devote itself to the improvement of the living conditions of the very poor. The influence which Saint-Simon had upon Comte has already been mentioned.

FOURIER

Another important socialistic ideal was developed by Fourier (1772–1837), who worked out a social system in which the *phalange* is the chief instrument in securing a perfect society. The phalange is composed of from twenty-four to thirty-two groups of people. Each group comprises from seven to nine persons. The unifying bond is natural attraction, or free elective love and sympathy. The members of each phalange live communistically in a large commodious structure called a *phalanstere*. The phalanges were to unite in one large world federation, with headquarters at Constantinople.

The people work according to their interests, frequently changing occupations. The products of labor are subdivided; a minimum goes equally to all, irrespective of any conditioning factors; of the remainder five-twelfths go to labor, three-twelfths to special ability, and four-twelfths to capital. Difficult common labor is paid the most, on the assumption that he who does pleasant labor receives pay in mental ways. Every person should have an opportunity to acquire wealth; and every woman should be enabled to become independent economically. These utopian plans of Fourier called for a sudden and complete transformation of human nature.

BLANC

Socialistic thought was carried into politics by Louis Blanc (1811–1882). He declared that no genuine reformation of society could take place until political machinery was organized democratically. The democratic state would endow national workshops. These workshops would be operated by industrial associations composed of workingmen who would elect their own officers, regulate their own industries, and provide for the distribution of the returns from industry. Once started by the state these industrial associations will expand and increase in number until the whole nation, and then the world, will be organized in this way.

Blanc participated in the French Revolution of 1848 and became a member of the provisional government. His national workshop idea failed in practice. His enemies were partly responsible for this defeat, because the essentials of productive work and guarantees of character which Blanc urged were disregarded. The fact, however, that these two essentials were considered necessary for the successful development of national workshops indicates that the system, under average conditions, might not be a success.

Nearly all the early socialists were evolutionists rather than revolutionists. They did not advocate class struggle theories. They developed bourgeois rather than proletariat ideas. An outstanding exception to these statements is found in the radical attitude of Babeuf (1760–1797), who was essentially a forerunner of Marxian socialism and also of the anarchistic philosophy of Proudhon and Bakunin. Babeuf vigorously proclaimed the sovereignty of the proletariat, and advocated the abolition of inheritance laws and of private property. He urged that the property of corporations be confiscated, and that a communistic state be established.

PROUDHON

The well-known principles of justice, liberty, and equality were utilized by Proudhon (1809–1865), a philosophic anarchist. He would have the same wages paid to an unskilled workman as to a successful business or professional man. He predicted that equalization of opportunity would bring about an equalization of ability.

Proudhon attacked property rights. He declared that property is theft. In itself property is lifeless, but it nevertheless demands rent, interest, or profits, or all three. It protects itself behind law, and in order to guarantee its alleged rights, it calls out the militia, evicts families, and takes bread from the mouths of little children. It robs labor of its just returns. "Property, after having robbed the laborer by usury, murders him by slow starvation."[1]

Proudhon urged the free development of individuals in society, whereby each would learn to govern himself so well in society that government in its usual sense would no longer be needed. He declared that individuals have no freedom; neither do they have security.

To remedy the unjust social order, Proudhon urged the establishment of "mutualist" groups. These would be based on "veracity, mutuality, rights," and hence liberty without

[1] Proudhon, *What Is Property?* p. 183.

license.   Individuals are not to lose their identity in large associations, but are to hold "equivalent" relationships toward one another.

The mutualist groups, work groups, or communes were to be federated.   Inter-group relations were to be established, and sovereignty would be sub-divided.   Each commune and mutual association, agricultural and work-group alike would have representation in a federated parliament.   This parliament would represent all the different work-interest groups. It would promote inter-group exchange of services and maintain a social balance.   Human dignity would be maintained. Proudhon, however, failed to foresee the future complexity of human relations, although his central theme of personal justice and dignity are vital elements in any developing and permanent social order.

ROBERT OWEN

In England, Robert Owen (1771–1858) became a founder of socialism.   As a factory manager, Owen developed social ideas.   Living in an age of long hours, woman and child labor of the worst forms, and deplorable housing conditions, Owen deserves the credit of inaugurating a twentieth-century campaign of welfare work.   It was Owen's theory that the workingman is so subject to his environment that even his character is determined for him.   Owen attempted in theory and practice to prevent the impingement of the economic environment upon the workers.   He believed in self-governing organizations of labor.   He had a part in inaugurating the co-operative movement as a means of securing industrial justice and of giving the workingman a chance at the free development of his personality.

Owen objected to Malthus' doctrine of population on the ground that it failed to consider the marvelous increase in the means of subsistence which might come from the application of inventive genius to the sources of food supply.   He also protested against the Malthusian argument for the restriction of population, because this argument did not give due weight to the unjust distribution of wealth and to the enslaving social organization to which labor is subject.

Owen's experiments, particularly at New Harmony, Indiana, indicated that a communistic organization in itself cannot save society. The strength of Owen's thought lay in its accentuation of the need for providing labor with opportunities of industrial initiative and co-operation.

During the middle of the nineteenth century in England the Christian socialists flourished. The founders of this movement were Frederick Maurice and Charles Kingsley. These men were clergymen who became greatly interested in the welfare of the working classes. They made clear the evils of the prevailing economic order and the formality of the Manchester school of economics; they proposed to apply the principles of Christianity to the economic system of the day. They opposed economic competition. For this method they urged the substitution of the ethical and spiritual principles of co-operation and love in industrial relationships — for both employer and employee in all their dealings with each other. Their socialism is essentially a vigorous application of Christian love to everyday relationships.

The influence of Christian socialism strengthened the experiment of the twenty-eight Rochdale weavers who in 1844 had organized a consumers' co-operative society. The concept of consumers' co-operation received its original impetus from the thought and practice of Robert Owen, achieved a measurable degree of concreteness under the efforts of the Rochdale weavers, and through Maurice and Kingsley won able support. However, in the democratic principles of the co-operative movement, as given in Chapter XXV of this book, are to be found the main reasons for the remarkable achievements that have followed the humble organization effected by the Rochdale Pioneers.

RODBERTUS

In Germany Rodbertus, Lassalle, Marx and Engels molded the thinking of socialists about the nature of human society. Rodbertus (1805–1875), the son of a university professor, was a quiet, deep thinker about social processes. According to his analysis of social development, three stages may be pointed out. The first was marked by slavery, or by private property in human beings. The second state is an indirect form of the first, namely, one of private property in land and capital. Through this type of ownership the economically fortunate or shrewd are able to exercise widespread power over the unfortunate and the uneducated. In the third state, toward which society is trending, the concept of service will rule, and private property as a dominant concept will be compelled to take a thoroughly subordinate place in human activities. The ultimate goal, according to Rodbertus, is a world communist society, with land and capital as national property, and with labor rewarded according to its productiveness.[2]

Rodbertus denied the validity of the wages fund theory and argued that wages are not paid by capital; it is that part of the productive earnings of labor which labor receives. His fundamental thesis is that labor is the source and measure of all value. He advocated an evolutionary procedure whereby the state should pass legislation that would guarantee just returns to labor. This form of state socialism is to be gradually developed, until a scientific socialism is reached with its emphasis upon a government of labor, for labor, and by labor.

LASSALLE

The founder of Social Democracy in Germany, Ferdinand Lassalle (1825–1864), wrote two significant treatises, the *Bastiat-Schulze* and the *Working Men's Programme*. Lassalle believed that natural conditions are productive of misery and vice, and that it is the chief business of the state to extricate men from this thraldom. The state should provide means for lifting the laboring man to a level of industrial freedom.

Lassalle objected to the theory known as the iron law of wages. He protested against the smallness of the share of his earnings which the laborer really receives. He advocated the establishment of productive associations wherein labor might perform the double function of workman and capitalist. In order that these productive associations might be started, the state should advance funds. After the produc-

---

[2] See Rodbertus, *Overproduction and Crises.*

tive associations have secured momentum they will continue by virtue of their own strength. Ultimately, industry will be conducted exclusively through productive associations; both industrial and social democracy will finally rule in political life. Lassalle became the founder of the Social Democratic party in Germany. Lassalle boldly denounced the reactionary classes that were in political power in his time and led the workers in a movement to overthrow the existing social order.[3]

KARL MARX

The name of Karl Marx (1818–1883) is supreme on the list of socialists. Marx was born in Germany of Jewish parents, and educated at the universities of Bonn and Berlin. He became a journalist, but the paper which he edited was considered too liberal and was suppressed. In 1842 Marx went to Paris, where he continued editorial work. At this time he was influenced by French socialism and its leader, Proudhon. In 1845, he was expelled from Paris at the request of the Prussian government. He went to Brussels. In the meantime a deep friendship with Friedrich Engels (1820–1895) had been established.

In 1847, Marx and Engels issued the Communist Manifesto.[4] This radical document was circulated widely and became extensively accepted by social revolutionists. Its doctrines were:

1. Abolition of property in lands; rents to be used for public purposes.
2. Abolition of all rights of inheritance.
3. Progressive income tax.
4. Nationalization of the means of transportation and commerce.
5. Extension of productive enterprises by the state.
6. Compulsory labor.
7. Free education; no child labor.
8. Elimination of the distrust between town and country.

Marx returned to Germany and established the *Neue Rheinische Zeitung* in Cologne in 1848. Engels served as

---

[3] See Lassalle, *Science and the Workingman.*
[4] Marx and Engels, *Manifesto of the Communist Party.*

editor. Because of revolutionary activity, Marx was forced to leave Germany in 1849. He went to Paris and then to London, where he became a newspaper correspondent, and where he lived until his death in 1883.

In 1859 the *Kritik der politischen Oekonomie* was published. It contains the essential principles of Marx's system of thought. In 1864 Marx found the opportunity for which he had long been seeking, namely, to organize the workers of the world into one large association. On September 28, in St. Martin's Hall, London, Marx, before a large concourse of people, initiated the "International Workingmen's Association." The fundamental idea was to organize the societies of workingmen which have a common purpose, namely, the emancipation of the working classes, into a world of international union for co-operative purposes. The International proposes that governments shall put the interests of the working classes to the forefront of national concern, and subordinate the present attention they give to war, diplomacy, and national jealousies.

In 1869, Marx, with Wilhelm Liebknecht (1826–1900), Engels, and others, organized in Germany the Social Democratic Labor party. The movement which Lassalle had started became united with the Marxian movement, and in 1875 the German Social Democracy presented a united front to capitalism. Marx, Engels, Liebknecht, and Bebel are its best known leaders. Bismarck was forced to acknowledge its power, and condescended to inaugurate a system of social insurance in order to appease its rank and file.

In 1867, 1885, and 1895, the three volumes of *Das Kapital* appeared, in chronological order.[5] By this work, Marx is known throughout the world. The style is laborious; the analyses are minute and in places difficult to follow. The method is historical. Marx analyzes social evolution. He traces the rise of capitalism from its humble beginnings to its autocratic fruition. In this development the instruments of capital showed a tendency to congregate in a decreasing number of hands. By this token it will be seen that the number of the propertyless ever increases. In this way the proletariat is developed, a result of capitalism.

[5] *Ibid.*, 1:673 ff., 834 ff.

THE CAPITALIST CLASS

A definite class, the capitalist, acquires increasing industrial, political, and social power. The proletariat suffer increasing misery. They own nothing except their ability to labor. They are forced to throw this human quality on the commercial market and sell it to the highest bidder. But capitalism increases the number of the proletariat. This tendency, together with the increase in population, creates a superabundance of labor. Laborers are forced to compete in the labor market. The laborers who will sell their labor for the least wages will be employed.

Capitalism thus forces wages to a mere subsistence level, with the result that the misery and suffering of the proletariat are greatly augmented. In this way the laborer is crushed by the operation of the iron law of wages.

By the operation of the iron law, the capitalist is enabled to appropriate to himself an increasing amount of the earnings of labor. This appropriated amount is called the surplus value. Marx developed at length the concept of surplus value. Capitalism exploits the laborer by taking possession of as large a proportion of the earnings of labor as it can obtain — through its might and shrewdness.

CLASS CONSCIOUSNESS

The growth of capitalism also causes a class consciousness to develop among the members of the proletariat. This class consciousness is increasing. It produces labor organizations; these organizations are acquiring vast power. The struggles between them and the capitalistic classes go on. By force of numbers the proletariat are bound finally to win, and to overthrow the capitalistic classes which are now in power; they will seize the means of production and manage them for the good of all, according to Marx.

Marx did not outline a utopia. He described the historical evolution of society as he saw it, and he participated in plans for the organization of all laborers for their common good. Inasmuch as Marx advocated compulsory labor, the laboring class under Marxian socialism would include all people. Marx advocated an equal distribution of wealth, not in the sense of the popular misconception of that term, but in the sense that the earnings from the industry shall be distributed to the workers in proportion to their achievements.

REVOLUTIONARY SOCIALISM

In Russia, Marxian socialism in 1917 came into power. The Bolsheviki represented the radical wing of the Marxian followers. They established essentially a dictatorship of the proletariat, substituting it for the dictatorship of capitalists which existed under the reign of the czars. Bolshevism substitutes occupation for geographic area as a basis of representative government. This program is deficient, because occupational groups do not encompass all phases of human personality. A government based on occupational-group needs is representative of only a portion of the elements of human life. When extensive illiteracy exists, in Russia or elsewhere for that matter, no form of government, whether democratic or not, can be other than a dictatorship.

Revolutionary socialism coincides, in part, with syndicalism, a movement which developed in France and England. Syndicalism is a radical form of trade unionism. It declares that workingmen cannot hope for genuine betterment through politics. They must organize and inaugurate a general strike. This universal strike will paralyze the present regime and render it helpless. As a result the workers will come into power. In the meantime, the workers must keep up a running warfare with capitalists and the government which supports capitalism.

Sabotage is a common concept among syndicalists. It implies a program of destroying machinery, hindering the production of economic goods, and creating inefficiency in capitalistic industry. In both England and the United States, the Industrial Workers of the World, or I.W.W., confessed to doctrines similar to those which have been espoused in Europe under the name of syndicalism. A leading philosophic exponent of syndicalism has been Georges Sorel.

Anarchism and socialism make similar attacks upon the evils of capitalism. Both are determined to overthrow capitalism. Both believe in revolt. They part company when they advocate a constructive program for the new order which will follow the violent overthrow of capitalism. Unlike socialism, anarchism holds that all government is an evil and that industry can go on without organization. It advocates a free communism.

HENRY GEORGE

One of the essentials in the Communist Manifesto was the appropriation of rents for public purposes. Starting from a viewpoint distinctly different from that of Karl Marx, Henry George (1839–1897) developed a single tax theory. In early life Henry George came to San Francisco and established a struggling newspaper. At once he found himself practically overwhelmed by the brutal competition of the metropolitan press and telegraphic news service. George was crushed by monopoly. It was this defeat which gave him a new idea — an idea that was to command the attention of the world.

George went about his search fearlessly. He sought to free his mind from any preconceptions. He proposed to speak without fear or favor. George proceeded by a process of elimination. He examined one possible cause of poverty after another in order to find the basic one. He was disappointed to discover that increase in productive power does not "extirpate poverty."

PROBLEM OF POVERTY

The new economic forces of production do not lift everybody to better levels of livelihood. They strike society "at a point between top and bottom," crushing those beneath its entering weight. George wondered why it is that as you move from rich to richer centers in the United States the poverty grows worse.

As George walked the streets of New York, N. Y., he puzzled over the existence of indescribable destitution and suffering in the shadow of the homes of the princely rich with their ostentatious luxuries.[6] Why in a land blessed with generous

[6] *Ibid.*, pp. 9, 10.

natural resources should there be such poverty? Although discovery has followed discovery and invention has followed invention, neither has lessened the toil of those who most need respite. With material progress poverty grows more serious. George set himself the task of finding out why poverty is associated with progress.

This cause George found in the land situation. As land increases in value, poverty increases. The price of land is an index of the disparity in the economic conditions of the people at the extremes of the social scale. Land is more valuable in New York than it is in San Francisco, and there is more squalor and misery in New York than in San Francisco. Land is more valuable in London than in New York, and likewise there is more squalor and destitution in London than in New York.

When increasing numbers of people live in a limited area under a system of private property in land, rents are raised and land values go up. The cost of living mounts, wages are kept to a minimum, overcongestion of population ensues; and again rents and land values are increased.[7]

Upon what does title to land rest? Where did it originate? In force. But has the first comer at a banquet the right to turn back all the chairs, and claim that none of the other guests shall partake of the food that has been provided? Does the first passenger who enters a railroad car thereby possess the right to keep out all other persons, or admit them only upon payment to him of sums of money?[8]

As a result of private property in land, the owner possesses power over the tenant, a power which is tantamount to slavery. There is nothing strange, therefore, about poverty. The Creator has not placed in the world the taint of injustice. Amid our highest civilization men faint and die with want, not because of the niggardliness of nature or the injustice of the Creator, but because of the injustice of man.[9] Since the owner of land receives wealth without labor to an increasing degree, so there is an increasing robbery of earnings of those who labor.

[7] *Ibid.*, pp. 286, 287.
[8] *Ibid.*, p. 342.
[9] *Ibid.*, p. 290.

George attacked Malthusianism, and pointed out the deficiencies in the proposed remedies for poverty, such as greater economy in government, diffusion of knowledge, and improved habits of industry. He then proceeded to give his own and well-known solution, namely, making land common property through a system of taxation of land values alone. Since land, not labor, is the source of all wealth, it is necessary to make land common property.

The weakness of Henry George's argument lies in his single panacea for securing justice. He overemphasized the importance of one line of procedure. He neglected important factors, such as self-centered human nature. He rendered a service, however, in showing the weaknesses in the system of private property in land.

In this discussion of the contributions of socialism to social thought, many types or expressions of socialism have not been presented. The educational propaganda of the Fabian socialists in England should be mentioned as being effective. Although small in number, this group of intellectuals, the best known being Sidney and Beatrice Webb, have exerted a constructive and practical influence upon social thought.

SOCIALISM SUMMARIZED

Socialism has assumed various phases. (1) It originated in utopianism and in a loose, broad type of communism. (2) It then took the form of associationism, urging the organization of groups of associated individuals, such as phalanges. As utopianism was in part the expression of a poetic imagination, so associationism represented a bourgeois philosophy. (3) In the next place socialism assumed political aspirations, and advocated a governmental program whereby the existing governments shall gradually extend their power until they exercise control over rent-producing land and interest-producing capital. (4) State socialism, however, was supplanted in many minds by ideas of more radical procedure. Marxian socialism holds that a class conflict is inevitable and that the workers must overthrow the capitalists, together with the governments which they control. (5) To the other radical extreme is philosophic anarchism, with its emphasis upon the abolition of all existing governments, and the establishment of individual autonomy.

Socialism has made several contributions to social thought. (1) It has called to the attention of civilized mankind, and particularly of the economically wealthy classes, to the needs of the weaker classes. (2) It has introduced humanitarian concepts into the minds of the socially unthinking, educated classes. (3) It has held social theory to a more practical course and to developing more immediate social solutions than otherwise would have been achieved. (4) In developing a recognition equal to that held by "individualism," it has helped to demonstrate the dualistic nature of social evolution, that is, that there are two poles to human life rather than one.

GROUP DISCUSSION TOPICS

1. Fourier's plan for the distribution of wealth.
2. Blanc's idea of national workshops.
3. Proudhon's concept of property.
4. Reasons for the lack of success of Robert Owen's co-operative societies.
5. An evaluation of the ideas of the Christian socialists.
6. Rodbertus' analysis of social development.
7. The nature of the Communist Manifesto.
8. The world movement inaugurated by Marx.
9. The chief theme of Marx's volumes entitled *Capital*.
10. Marx's meaning of "equal distribution of wealth."
11. The relation of bolshevism and sovietism to Marxianism.
12. The keynote of syndicalism.
13. Bakunin's major thought.
14. The underlying problem that Henry George attacked.
15. The cause of social injustice as seen by Henry George.
16. The weakness of George's proposed remedy.
17. The strongest point of socialistic social thought.
18. The greatest weakness of socialism.

READINGS

Beach, Walter G., *The Growth of Social Thought* (New York: Charles Scribner's Sons 1939), Ch. XIV.

Becker, Howard, and Harry E. Barnes, *Social Thought from Lore to Science* (Washington: Harren Press 1952), Vol. I, Ch. 17.

Douglas, Dorothy M., "P. J. Proudhon: A Prophet of 1848," *American Journal of Sociology*, XXXV:35-59.

Ellwood, Charles A., *A History of Social Philosophy* (New York: Prentice-Hall, Inc. 1938), Ch. XXI.

George, Henry, *Progress and Poverty* (Various editions).

———, *Social Problems* (London: Kegan 1884).

Guthrie, Elton F., "Sociological Theory and Historical Materialism," *Sociology and Social Research*, XXI: 339-342.

Kilzer, E., and E. J. Ross, *Western Social Thought* (Milwaukee: The Bruce Publishing Company 1954), Ch. 15.

Lassalle, Ferdinand, *Science and the Workingman* (Chicago: Kerr 1903).

Marx, Karl, *Das Kapital* (transl. by Moore and Aveling) (Chicago: Kerr 1909).

Marx and Engels, *Manifesto of the Communist Party* (Chicago: Kerr 1902).

Proudhon, Pierre J., *What is Property?* (transl. by B. R. Tucker) (Princeton, Mass., B. R. Tucker 1876).

Rodbertus, Karl J., *Overproduction and Crises* (New York: Charles Scribner's Sons 1906).

Seligman, E. R. A., *The Economic Interpretation of History* (New York: Columbia University Press 1902).

Sorokin, Pitirim A., *Contemporary Sociological Theories* (New York: Harper & Brothers 1928), Ch. X.

Spargo, John, *Karl Marx, his Life and Works* (New York: Huebsch 1910).

Venable, Herman, *Human Nature, The Marxian View* (New York: Alfred A. Knopf 1945).

CHAPTER XVIII

MIKHALOVSKY AND RUSSIAN SOCIAL THOUGHT

Perhaps the name of any one of four or five Russian social philosophers is as good as that of another in the heading of this chapter. Mikhalovsky is given the preference because of his originality and because of his leadership in the field of Russian sociology. He worked out a theory of Individualism to a greater extent than did any of his confreres.

It is interesting that the Russian School of the latter half of the nineteenth century centered their thought in individualistic concepts. They lived at a time when Russian autocracy in state and church was suppressing the individual who belonged to the masses and hence their thinking turned toward an emphasis on individual freedom.

The arguments in behalf of the individual doubtless contributed to the "incipient revolution" that was brewing at the time in Russia. Their theories led them as a class to support the strong man who would help the masses secure release from oppression. On the other hand their social theories led them to think extensively in terms of social solidarity.

When the Revolution of November 1917 occurred, Marxian thought came into power, and the Russian sociologists for the most part found themselves eclipsed if not exiled. Their doctrines in the main were antagonistic to the principles of dialectic materialism.

In his *Russian Sociology,* Dr. Julius Hecker critically reviews the history of social philosophy in Russia. He finds that in his country social philosophy is represented in part by the subjectivist school which includes Lavrov, Mikhalovsky, Youzhakov, and Kareyev. Lavrov (1823-1900) was an extremist in the development of subjective-teleological ideas. Lavrov defined sociology as "the science of solidarity of conscious individuals." [1] It studied the "formation, growth, weakening, and disintegration of this solidarity." Lavrov

1 Julius Hecker. *Russian Sociology,* p. 78.

developed three theories, one of social solidarity or social control, one of individuation or of personality, and one of social progress." [2]   According to Lavrov, solidarity developed among the lowest strata of organic life and has been helped on by association "which is pleasurable to congregated organisms." It is promoted by statecraft, by democracy, by the interests of individuals, and by social and geographic environment. Individuality is intrinsically related to solidarity. The individual is a product of the group and yet attacks groups, breaking up old social forms and laying the foundations for new social developments.[3] Lavrov thus has been called an individualistic sociologist. The synthesis of solidarity and individualism, with the latter working upon and working over the former, constitutes Lavrov's theory of social progress. "Lavrov sees progress in the development and strengthening of solidarity, so far as it does not hinder conscious processes and motives in the rational activity of individuals." [4]

MIKHALOVSKY

Mikhalovsky (1842–1904) is pronounced the most original of Russian social philosophers. To him sociology is "the science of the laws of intra- and inter-group relations and of the relations between the group and the individual." [5] He developed a theory of the struggle for individuality.

On the psychological side, as well as on the economic, the struggle for individuality goes on. The struggle between the individual and society continues endlessly. Dr. Hecker indicates that Mikhalovsky was "one of the first to apply psychological principles in the study of social phenomena." [6]

Mikhalovsky analyzed the struggle for individualization in connection with (1) the functioning of the hero and the mob, (2) the functioning of love, (3) the functioning of religion, (4) the functioning of libertinism and asceticism, (5) the functioning of division of labor, and (6) the functioning of Russian economic institutions.

[2] *Ibid.*, p. 81.
[3] *Ibid.*, p. 95.
[4] *Ibid.*, p. 100.
[5] *Ibid.*, p. 105.
[6] *Ibid.*, p. 116.

His theory of the hero and the mob refers to the leader and his crowd. He defines the term *hero* as one "who by his example captivates the mass for good or for evil, for noble or degrading, for rational or for irrational deeds," while the *mob* is the mass who is so influenced by example or suggestion.[7] Each individual has a craving for an ideal. This craving may express itself "in following some one who suggests a kind of heroism." Thus, the hero is a product of the social environment. Both the hero and the mob are products of this same environment.

Individuals are suppressed by monotony of social life and by poverty of individual life. Their individuality is infringed upon, and they obtain relief in seeking an ideal and in joining with others in outbursts of energy.

In the next place Mikhalovsky claims that love is a means of completing individuality. "Each one of us is but a half man or a half woman and each half seeks the other half."[8] Hence a happy marriage is a proper selection of two halves of the same whole; an unhappy marriage is based on an unfitting combination of halves. In consequence, man should strive to be manly and woman to be womanly. "The more men are manly and the more women are womanly, the more powerful will love be."[9]

Religion, according to Mikhalovsky, is an inseparable bond which connects the things which are with those which ought to be. Religion "aids individuality to find itself spiritually."[10] Religion supplements specialized thinking, helping the individual to become a whole or complete unit.

Turning to libertinism and asceticism Mikhalovsky asserts that both these tendencies are "the individual's protest against a too rigid control by society."[11] The libertine protests against the infringement upon his personality in active and militant ways. He grows defiant of rules. The ascetic protests in passive and peaceful ways. Both are non-conformists. Both seek "to get away" in order that their hampered spirits may gain freedom. Both are pathological

[7] *Loc. cit.*
[8] *Ibid.*, p. 121.
[9] *Loc. cit.*
[10] *Ibid.*, p. 123.
[11] *Loc. cit.*

reactions to the social and environmental suppression of individuality.[12]

Mikhalovsky favored an economic division of labor up to the point that it begins to harm the integrity of individuality. Beyond that point specialization in the factory or outside is to be avoided. He contended that the modern workman is no longer an independent individuality.

Mikhalovsky objected to the situation in which the workman is usually controlled "by the small trade union which has no sense of solidarity with society at large."[13] He opposed the factory system and large-scale production because they function against individuality. He supported the division of labor trend only so far as it leaves unharmed the integrity of the indivisible.[14] He fought the institutions of autocracy because they crush individuality. He hoped capitalism would not develop and he feared the rise of city proletariats. The function of sociology is to indicate what institutions will best promote the integrity of all individuals.

He advocated private property for labor. He ordered his followers "to fear more than anything else a social order that will divert property from labor." Such a result "will deprive the people of the possibility of individual initiative, of independence and of liberty."[15]

Mikhalovsky was dubious about the maintenance of individuality. Society tends the other way. "His heart beat warmly for his people, whose intellectual leader and guide he was for a generation."[16]

YOUZHAKOV

Youzhakov (1849–1910) believed that society is based on individuals and that social evolution "takes place by means of individuals and for individuals."[17] He attempted to build a system of sociology on this thesis and analyzed five major sets of principles which function in social life. He defines sociology as "the science of the laws controlling group living and accounting for its origins, development, and dis-

[12] *Ibid.*, p. 124.
[13] *Ibid.*, p. 126.
[14] *Ibid.*, p. 125.
[15] *Ibid.*, p. 128.
[16] *Ibid.*, p. 133.
[17] *Ibid.*, p. 135.

integration." [18] Sociology discovers those forms of social life in which the universal laws of interaction and of equilibration are found. It describes the effect of organic life on these laws. It shows how individuality influences these laws.[19]

Individual self-preservation leads to the formation of groups. Group life involves not only the protection of groups but the maintenance of group individuality as well. These two interests may infringe upon each other and lead to conflict between the individual and society. The welfare of the group is the criterion for setting up ethics and ethical standards. However, the efficiency resulting from co-operation and from increased security creates a surplus which may be turned into further socialization and social progress.[20]

The two main struggles of life are the one for individuality and the one for culture. When culture suppresses individuality, culture is thereby lowered in quality. When individuality destroys culture, individuality suffers degeneration. The adapting of life to social existence is the essence of the problems of morality.[21]

Youzhakov pointed out that individuality becomes a personality when its social group regards it as a responsible member of the group. In other words, when the individual is accorded status he becomes a person. This theory of an individual acquiring recognition and becoming a person was expressed by Youzhakov as early as 1896 in his *Sociological Etudes*.[22]

Youzhakov, who acknowledges his indebtedness to Comte and Spencer, shows how socialization is "an equilibration between the inner and outer relations of life and environment.[23] His theory of "the role of surplus" explains how the individual may be freed from too much social control and from the ill effects of overspecialization.

KAREYEV

Nikolai I. Kareyev (1850–1929) declares that society is "a

[18] *Ibid.*, p. 137.
[19] *Ibid.*, pp. 137, 138.
[20] *Ibid.*, p. 140.
[21] *Ibid.*, p. 144.
[22] Vol. II, p. 187, as pointed out by Hecker, *op. cit.* p. 144.
[23] *Ibid.*, p. 147.

living product of art, a harmonious co-ordination of individuals, possessing solidarity without sacrificing their individuality, and remaining individualistic without being to one another antagonistic." [24]   Perhaps this statement pertains to social goals.   The social problem then would become the achievement of this goal.

Progress is the setting up of increasingly integrated goals for mankind, and the attaining of these goals "by the aid of a growing culture and a social organization which makes possible an increasing reaction upon nature." [25]   Progress is the elevation of the standards of living and the changing of conditions so that increasing numbers of people can attain these rising standards.

Kareyev speaks of mental progress, which is developing "the capacity for realizing spiritual interests and improving our views of the life of the world."   To him moral progress involves improving the principles of ethics and developing the power to act according to conviction.   He explains political progress as the increasing of individual freedom within the state.   Judicial progress is found in perfecting the institutions of law and justice.   Economic progress includes the development of solidarity and bettering the ways for "obtaining the means of existence." [26]

Progress includes compromises between individual and social interests.   It means larger individualities.   These create culture which in turn tends to repress individuality. Thus, a never-ending conflict results.   The only reasonable way out is continuous compromise.

Of the four Russians, Lavrov, Mikhalovsky, Youzhakov, and Kareyev, Julius Hecker indicates that they were all indebted to Comte and to a degree to Spencer with whom they tended, however, to disagree.   Lavrov was the earliest and the pioneer of the group.   Mikhalovsky was "the most original."   Youzhakov attempted to develop a synthetic system of sociology.   Kareyev was "the most thorough and extensive scholar."   All emphasized individuality and all opposed the dialectic materialism of Marx.

[24] *Ibid.*, p. 158.
[25] *Ibid.*, p. 166.
[26] *Ibid.*, pp. 168, 169.

CHERNOV

Victor M. Chernov tries to adjust the individualistic ideas of Lavrov and Mikhalovsky to those of the communistic Marx. He urges the use of the functional viewpoint in sociology. His basic concept is "the psychology of interest." [27]

Chernov also criticizes both the subjectivistic ideas of Lavrov, Mikhalovsky and the historical materialism of Marx. He wishes to make subjective thinking more scientific. He seeks additional factors besides those developed by Marx for understanding social change.

Chernov holds that man in his biological make-up is the main dynamic force in history. Man interacts with nature and creates different cultures. These differences in culture are themselves vital aspects of the social process. A social ideal is needed, and sociology is charged with the task of determining this ideal.[28]

Chernov investigated values, re-evaluated values, and attempted to develop a formula of progress. He agreed with the theory that man interacts with his physical environment in the form of culture. He tackles the problem of the strong individual who attempts to dominate social solidarity. He believed in individuality, and supported the concept of strong individualities, but argued that in order that a powerful leader might not use social solidarity to his own ends, it would be necessary for another environment to be developed, an ethical environment that would govern the actions of the strong individual in his dealings with the social group.

Maxim M. Kovalevsky (1851–1916) rejected a monistic or single theory explanation of social ills. Sociology must face "the complex of social phenomena." [29]

Kovalevsky was greatly interested in the ethnological approach to sociology. He gave concrete, historical data as a basis for sociology. He stood for breadth of view both in explanation of social causation and in the origins of social processes.

War affords opportunity for the rise of autocratic leader-

---

[27] *Ibid.,* p. 188.
[28] *Ibid.,* p. 190.
[29] *Ibid.,* p. 202.

ship and of feudalistic types of social organization. Property and government play into the hands of the dictator. Thus whole groups of people fall into subordination.

In summing up current Russian social thought in his *Moscow Dialogues,* Julius Hecker defines dialectic materialism as the study of living phenomena, "not as fixed and permanent, but in a moving continuity of interpreting opposites." It is an evolutionary philosophy which presupposes revolutionary outbursts as integral phases "of the evolutionary process." It is a philosophy that traces its origins to Hegel and Kant but particularly to a third great Dutch philosopher, namely, Spinoza.

Hecker fails to make clear in his clever "dialogues" how a classless society will remain classless. Through "Socraton," a character which he creates, he effectively criticizes mechanistic materialism because it sees only the similarity between nature and society. He asserts that idealism is weak because it sees chiefly the differences between nature and society. He supports dialectic materialism because it accepts the unity of these differences and the idea that revolution is a transitional step to further evolution.

In his *Religion and Communism,* Dr. Hecker asserts that the communist movement "declares itself unreservedly and categorically against every religion, whether orthodox, humanitarian, or philosophical." It goes so far as to emphasize "that reformed, modernized, socialized and every other removed religion is worse than the old orthodox, reactionary religion." He described the "Atheist International" which pursues "the task of organizing freethinkers and atheists all over the world."

How are these attitudes to be accounted for? Partly on the grounds of unpleasant experiences with religion under the czars, which raised no voice against the political and economic slavery of the masses; partly on the grounds of rationalization regarding life. The communist, says Dr. Hecker, suffers as do other people, from logophobia.[30] He has prejudices against unpleasant terminology. He does not want communism called a religion, even though he has a bias, the same as do religious dogmatists. He admits that he has an

[30] Julius Hecker, *Religion and Communism,* p. 12.

ideology, based on scientifically derived data. The communist admits that he and the non-communist and the religionist can meet and understand one another on the basis of common humanity.[31]

On the other hand, Dr. Hecker asserts that the young soviet people have personal longings which today are not satisfied.[32] They reject the existing religious teachings as being
antiquated. Moreover, large numbers of them are also rejecting the anti-religious propaganda. They are seeking a
message with emotional and ethical values not found in
present-day communism. They want a message that will be
more intellectual and "more esthetic in form and sentiment"
than "any of the old institutions of religion." Where will
this message come from? Who will develop it for them?
Or, will they develop it for themselves?

"Modern composers have been unable to create an atheistic music," and Russian communists are still attracted to the
religious symphonies of Beethoven.[33] Moreover, "atheistic
ideology" is too rationalistic. Not only that, but it operates
"in an emotional vacuum which is unsuited to human nature." In other words, man needs both "a guiding philosophy of life" and "some emotional stimuli." Religion is objected to in Russia not so much because it has often lacked
intellectual dignity but because it has failed to make civilization ethical.[34] Therefore, the communist fights for communism, for he believes that his ideology is the only system
that will make civilization ethical.

LENIN

Nikolai Lenin (1870–1924) took the Marxian ideas, and
adapted them to Russia. He held that reality is "independent of human consciousness," and thus he believed in a world
whose laws should be studied objectively. The world is an
"interpenetration of opposite forces" that approach a unity
and then pull apart. The law of change is essentially evolutionary, characterized from time to time by "spontaneous;

[31] *Ibid.*, p. 12.
[32] *Ibid.*, p. 273.
[33] *Ibid.*, p. 268.
[34] *Ibid.*, p. 8.

periodic breaks" or revolutionary outbursts. When feudal aristocracy and clerical orders interpenetrate unduly, a revolution occurs sooner or later and a realignment with new interpenetrations begins to develop.[35]

According to Lenin the producing activities in society underlie all other factors. They control government and even human thinking. The state has always been an agency for the suppression of "the majority by a ruling minority." [36] Lenin conceived that the state would ultimately wither away. When the classes disappear and only the working class survives, when all develop the habit of "communist toil" or of working productively together for all, then the organs of political and other forms of coercion will disappear through lack of use. Ultimately, when all peoples of the world work together in one great collectivity, then armies and navies will be discarded and constructive peace will prevail.[37]

Lenin's thinking has undergone modification in the hands of his two successors, Leon Trotsky and Joseph Stalin. Trotsky has carried forward Marx's thought and Lenin's also, for he has held that one country struggling as a lone exponent of a communist social order cannot make much headway surrounded by hostile, capitalistic nations. A world revolution is the only hope. He has represented the urban point of view and been sympathetic with a working-class philosophy as distinguished from a rural peasant set of attitudes. His is the cosmopolitan outlook, widely sympathetic, and seeking comprehensive action now.

On the other hand, Joseph Stalin has a rural background, being a Georgian peasant's son. He is a strong nationalist. He understands the rural peasant's outlook and reactions to a nationwide collectivism. He has perceived that a rural people, for Russia is largely rural, cannot be changed overnight into urban collectivists. He has held that communism must proceed slowly in changing the culture patterns of a nation, and that it must move by degrees from one stage to the next in social organization. Further, he has concluded that the time is not ripe for world revolution. It is better,

[35] Julius Hecker, *Russian Sociology*, p. 233.
[36] *Ibid.*, p. 244.
[37] *Loc. cit.*

he thinks, to build up communism within a nation first, before attempting to spread it far and wide. Particularly is this true when you have a far-flung territory and 180,000,-000 people with which to work, as in the case of Russia.

Among the recent soviet social thinkers, Alexander Bogdanov (1873–1928) developed the Marxian theories and produced what he called a "tectological" system. He differed from Marx in that he believed that man could construct social laws out of natural, material laws. He became social-psychological in his system and evolved a "science of social consciousness." He found social life responding to changes in the physical environment and described two types of social adaptations. The first includes technical adjustments which in turn produced the second, or the ideological. His concept of a collectivist society includes: (1) control over natural forces, (2) a democratic organization of production with the workers being trained to fairly even mental levels, and (3) freedom of consumption, no coercion, and a full exercise of comradeship by and among all.[38]

Bogdanov did not accept Marx's idea that classes develop out of differences in the ownership and use of the means of production. He found the key to the rise of classes in differences in organizational ability.[39]

Nicolai Bukharin was another soviet social writer who elaborated some of Marx's ideas and who, at the same time, emphasized a social-psychological analysis of society. He developed an occupational psychology in the sense that one's occupation tends to influence the nature of personality. The subtler influences of one's environment upon one are not recognized by the individual. However, these influences will be recognized if a person takes the place of society and views the operation of environmental forces objectively.

Revolutionary socialism has been paralleled in certain ways by anarchism. These teachings first acquired force through the writings of Proudhon. Another leading anarchist was the Russian nobleman and military officer, Michael Bakunin (1814–1876). Although of aristocratic

[38] A summary of the analysis by Barnes and Becker, *Social Thought from Lore to Science*, pp. 1046-1048.
[39] *Ibid.*, p. 1048.

birth, Bakunin became furious when he observed the human misery among the masses which Russian autocracy was producing. He became an agitator. He was confined in dungeons and exiled to Siberia. He escaped from Siberia, and by way of California went to England and then to Switzerland. His chief work is *God and the State*. Vital, vigorous, magnetic, fearless — these are the adjectives which describe the personality of Bakunin.

Bakunin scorned rank, birth, and fortune. He attacked external authority of all kinds. He denied the validity of concepts such as "God" and the "state"; they are parts of systems which enslave the free will of man. Classes must be abolished and the masses of individuals freed from all enslaving institutions, such as marriage, the church, and the state.

In a related way Prince Kropotkin (1842–1921) developed principles of mutual aid. Peter A. Kropotkin was of aristocratic Russian birth and a person of mild, courteous manners. His father was a serf owner; the son could not bear to see the sufferings which the serfs underwent. He threw away the privileges of rank and became a defender of the oppressed. He attempted to correlate the theories of anarchism with those of mutual aid, and fought socialism with its concept of centralized control on the ground that it would destroy individual liberty. In a later chapter, Kropotkin's theory of mutual aid will be analyzed.

Eugene DeRoberty (1843–1915) was a Russian writer who lived in Paris and who wrote chiefly in French. He outlined under twelve headings what he called "hyperpositivism." He attempted to make more accurate and positivistic the ideas of Comte. He urged that method be separated from object; that the transcendent shall be reduced to experience; that reality be conceived a homogeneous whole; that abstract and concrete knowledge be kept separate in thought; that the subject matter of sociology is composed of phenomena that are social and hence ethical; and that four factors be considered paramount in the realm of sociological data: science, philosophy and religion, art, and work. He traced evolution from the organic to the superorganic or the social. The latter began with thinking.

DeRoberty developed the "bio-social hypothesis." According to it a sharp distinction is to be made between the biological and psychological, and social and cultural. As a result of association, man is transformed into a social being. He neglected to include the idea that association alone is not enough. To become truly a social being man must associate with human beings who have a culture.

DeRoberty divided culture into ideas or tools of analysis, tools of synthesis, tools of emotional content, and tools that tend to satisfy "the three preceding evolutions." His ethics was humanistic in the sense that moral behavior is to be evaluated in terms of group and social welfare.

Somewhat related to DeRoberty in his social thought is Jacques Novicow. He was "an anti-Darwinian pacifist and federationist."[40] Because of his criticism of war his ideas will be given further attention in a later chapter on conflict theories.

Pitirim A. Sorokin, a Russian by birth and an American by adoption, offers no one explanation of social change but submits instead an interpretation in terms of the interactions of many social factors.[41] He attacks dialectic materialism and Marxian thought with vigor. He points out the various sources of Marxianism thought and gives the impression not only that Marx contributed little to it, but that it is an unsound conglomeration of thinking. His constructive thought centers around special concepts such as social mobility, a theme to be treated in a later chapter.[42]

Russian social thought runs the gamut from subjectivism to objectivism. It traverses the field of thought from individualism to communism. It has run into difficulty in recent years in the controversies between capitalistic and socialistic ideologies and particularly in the bitter conflict between Bolshevik and Menshevik, and between Stalinism and Trotskyism.

GROUP DISCUSSION TOPICS

1. Origins of Russian social thought.
2. Lavrov's theory of social progress.

---

[40] Julius Hecker, *Russian Sociology*, p. 211.
[41] Pitirim Sorokin, *Contemporary Sociological Theories*.
[42] *Social Mobility*.

3. Mikhalovsky's concept of individualism.
4. Mikhalovsky's attitudes regarding division of labor.
5. Youzhakov's thesis concerning social evolution.
6. Youzhakov's belief about personality.
7. Kareyev's analysis of social progress.
8. The task of sociology according to Chernov.
9. Bakunin's repudiation of social institutions.
10. Lenin's concept of international communism.
11. Trotsky versus Stalin.
12. Hecker's social theories.
13. Bolshevism's objections to religion.

READINGS

Barnes, Harry E., Editor, *An Introduction to the History of Sociology* (Chicago: University of Chicago Press 1948), Chs. 22 and 23.

Bucharin, N. I., *Historical Materialism* (New York: International Publishers Company 1925).

Hare, Richard, *Pioneers of Russian Social Thought* (London: Oxford University Press 1951).

Hecker, Julius, *Russian Sociology* (New York: John Wiley and Sons 1934).

———, *Religion and Communism* (New York: John Wiley and Sons 1934).

———, *Moscow Dialogues* (New York: John Wiley and Sons 1934).

Mirsky, D. S., *Russia, A Social History* (New York: Century Company 1931).

Morkovin, Boris V., *Incipient Revolution in Its Personal and Group Aspects,* doctoral dissertation (University of Southern California 1929).

Novicow, J., *La critique du darwinism sociale* (Paris: Alcan 1910).

Pratt, Helen, *Russia, from Tsarist Empire to Socialism* (New York: American Council, Institute of Pacific Relations 1937).

Proudhon, P. J., *What Is Property?* (Princeton, Mass.: Tucker 1876).

Sorokin, Pitirim A., *Contemporary Sociological Theories* (New York: Harper and Brothers 1928).

———, *The Sociology of Revolution* (Philadelphia: J. B. Lippincott Company 1925).

Webb, Sidney and Beatrice, *Soviet Communism: A New Civilization* (New York: Charles Scribner's Sons 1936).

CHAPTER XIX

BUCKLE AND GEOGRAPHIC SOCIAL THOUGHT

It has long been observed that climate, fertility of soil, rainfall, and similar factors have had a powerful influence upon human nature and upon the development of civilization. The chief founders of this line of thought were Buckle and Ratzel. In recent years Semple and Huntington have become well-known authorities. Many other thinkers have contributed to present knowledge concerning the interactions between geographic factors and human development.

BODIN

One of the first writers to elaborate a climatic theory of social evolution was Bodin (1530–1596). Hot climates, he observed, further the rise of all kinds of superstitious beliefs. Cold climates produce brute will-power. Temperate climates constitute an essential basis for the development of reason. In the ideal commonwealth which Bodin described, all three types of climate are represented.[1] The northern zone furnishes the fighters and the workers. The southern zone produces poets, priests, and artists. The temperate zone is the parent of legislative, judicial, and scholarly leaders.

Bodin's theory of physical and social causation was revolutionary, and while partly ill-founded, because of the lack of development of basic scientific studies, stood for two centuries as the chief representative of geographic human thought. Latitude, longitude, elevation, location, fertility of soil are each given a place in his social causation theories. The psychological results of these geographic factors are remarkable, considering the general lack of psychological knowledge in Bodin's time. Family life, mental growth, temperamental variations, and particularly morals, have explanatory factors in climatic conditions.

Bodin gave the basic place in society to the family, claim-

[1] Jean Bodin, *The Six Books of a Commonweale*, translated by R. Knoles.

ing that society is not necessary to the existence of the family. He distinguished between natural associations of a voluntary nature and the state which rests on force.[2] He urged the abolition of slavery, but did not favor the sudden and complete enfranchisement of slaves. Enfranchisement of slaves should take place step by step and vocational training should be required before complete enfranchisement in any case is granted.[3] If Thaddeus Stevens and the other persons responsible for granting the suffrage to Negroes in the United States in 1868 had taken a leaf from Bodin's notes, they would have saved the Negro, the South, and the nation a great deal of suffering and injustice. It is the business of social philosophy to study the laws of growth and change of societies in order that societal change may be understood and that social planning may go ahead intelligently.

Professor Edward A. Ross quotes a principal of a woman's college in Mysore, India, who does not look forward with ease to a time "when the young people will enjoy freedom of matrimonial choice." Why? Professor Ross quotes the answer: "The climate simply will not allow the deferring of marriage to an age when they can be trusted to select their own mates."[4] Professor Ross has found many illustrations of what he calls a "vertical sun" theory. In other words, "sex thirst is sharpened by the vertical sun." In tropical South America Dr. Ross was told that in a tropical climate conjugal abstinence is difficult.[5]

MONTESQUIEU

In the *Spirit of Laws,* to which reference was made in Chapter XIV, Montesquieu accentuated the importance of environmental influences on social processes. He attempted to show the effects of climate upon social institutions. Montesquieu did important pioneer work in what is now known as the field of anthropo-geography.

Montesquieu sought to define cause and effect, and thus shifted the emphasis from social philosphoy to social science.

[2] Bodin, *ibid.,* B. III, Ch. VII.
[3] *Ibid.,* p. 46.
[4] Edward A. Ross, *Seventy Years of It,* p. 219.
[5] *Ibid.,* p. 214.

His mind was upon both observation and processes, and thus he improved upon Bodin. He attempted to explain the process by which people in cold climates are more vigorous than those in warm regions — "cold air constringes the extremities of the external fibres of the body; this increases their elasticity, and favors the return of blood from the extreme parts to the heart. On the contrary, warm air relaxes and lengthens the extremes of the fibres; of course it diminishes their force and elasticity. People are therefore more vigorous in cold climates." [6]

Climate plays a role in marriage forms. In line with the statement already quoted from Professor Ross, Montesquieu asserted that "women in hot climates are marriageable at eight, nine, or ten years of age; thus, in those countries, infancy and marriage generally go together. They are old at twenty; their reason therefore never accompanies their beauty." [7] He continues: "In temperate climates, where the charms of women are best preserved, where they arrive later at maturity, and have children at a more advanced season of life, the old age of their husband in some degree follows theirs; and as they have more reason and knowledge at the time of marriage, if it be only on account of their having continued longer in life, it must naturally introduce a kind of equality between the two sexes; and, in consequence of this, the law of having only one wife." [8]

Great heat enervates the strength and courage of people, while cold climate creates a certain strength of body and mind, "which renders them patient and intrepid, and qualifies them for arduous enterprises." [9] Even religious attitudes are affected by climatic conditions. North Europe accepted Protestanism and South Europe kept Catholicism because "the people of the North have, and will forever have, a spirit of liberty and independence which the people of the South have not; and therefore a religion which has no visible head is more agreeable to the independence of the climate than that which has one, according to Montesquieu. [10]

6 *Spirit of Laws,* I:7.
7 *Ibid.,* I:270.
8 *Ibid.,* I:271.
9 *Ibid.,* I:284.
10 *Ibid.,* I:114.

Even commerce is affected by climate. Climatic differences lead to different agricultural products, and thus exchange of goods comes about. People of the same climate
have not this same need for trading.[11]

Sometimes the climate is more favorable than the soil ; the
people multiply, and are destroyed by famine ; this is the case
in China.[12] Under these climatic conditions there is no need
of legislation to increase propagation. In these samples of
Montesquieu's thought, the virility, and at the same time,
the error of particularization are evident.

By way of contrast, the viewpoint of Hume, whose contributions to social psychology have already been noted, stands
out sharply. According to Hume, physical causes have no
particular effect on the human mind. No geographic factors
influence either the temperament, disposition, or ability of
people. Hume was led to this extreme position by his
staunch faith in the subjective and psychological factors of
human nature.

The distinguished German scientist, Alexander von Humboldt (1769–1859), traveled extensively throughout the
world, observing the physical geography of many lands in
conjunction with the meteorological conditions of each. At
the same time Von Humboldt was a careful observer of the
customs, manners, and standards of the various peoples with
whom he came in contact. In these travels and studies, Von
Humboldt was careful to note relationships between soils and
civilizations. His contributions to social thought were of
this descriptive nature, based on first-hand observations in
many parts of the world.

BUCKLE

The writings of Henry Thomas Buckle (1821–1862) contain an extensive and detailed explanation of the ways in
which geographic and natural factors modify human life.
Buckle starts with a decidedly dualistic universe — a dualism
which is disjunctive. The dualism consists of nature and
mind, each subject more or less to its own laws. Rejecting

[11] *Ibid.*, II:3.
[12] *Ibid.*, II:90.

both the doctrine of free will and of predestination, Buckle concludes that the actions of men are determined solely by their antecedents and that they have a character of uniform-ity.[13] Man modifies nature, and nature modifies man, but in the past in many parts of the world the thoughts and desires of men are more influenced by physical phenomena than they influence such phenomena. Because of this dominant activity of the physical forces, these should be studied as a basis for understanding the history of man.

FOUR CLIMATIC FACTORS

The physical factors which have powerfully influenced men are four : climate, food, soil, and the general aspects of nature. By the fourth, Buckle refers to those appearances which are presented chiefly through the medium of sight and which produce their chief results by exciting the imagination and suggesting superstitions. The first three factors do not operate on the mind directly.[14]

The first effect of climate, food, and soil upon man that may be noted is that they lead man to accumulate wealth. These accumulations permit that degree of leisure from "making a living" which enables some members of society to acquire knowledge. Upon these acquisitions of knowl-edge, particularly of socialized knowledge, civilization de-pends. This progress in the early stages of civilization rests on two circumstances : "First, on the energy and regularity with which labor is conducted, and second, on the returns made to that labor by the bounty of nature." [15] Both these causes are the results of physical antecedents. The returns which are made to labor are regulated by the fertility of the soil. Moreover, Buckle asserted, the energy and regularity with which labor is conducted will be entirely dependent on the influence of climate.[16] When heat is intense, men will be indisposed and partly unfitted for active industry. Climate also affects the regularity of the habits of laborers. In very cold climates, the weather interferes with regular

[13] H. T. Buckle. *History of Civilization in England*, I:14.
[14] *Ibid.*, p. 20.
[15] *Ibid.*, p. 51.
[16] *Ibid.*, p. 22.

habits and produces desultoriness. In southern countries regular labor is likewise prevented — this time by the heat. Thus in the early stages of civilization the fundamental law may be stated. The soil regulates the returns made to any given amount of labor; the climate regulates the energy and constancy of labor itself.[17]

Of the two primary causes of primitive societary growth, the fertility of the soil is more important than the climatic influences. Only where soil fertility exists can civilization arise at all.[18] But in Europe climate has been more effective than soil fertility. In Europe a climate has existed which has stimulated human activities.

Since the mental powers of man are unlimited, they are more important, once they get started, than the powers of nature, which are limited and stationary. Man has endless capacity, through his dynamic mental tendencies to develop the physical resources of the earth.

The birth rate depends on food supply. In hot countries, where less food per capita is required than in cold countries, and where an abundance of food exists, the birth rate is very high. In cold countries highly carbonized food is necessary, but this food is largely animal in origin and great risk is involved in procuring it. Hence the people of cold countries become adventuresome.[19]

By the study of physical laws it is possible to determine what the national food of a country will be. In India, for example, the physical conditions are decidedly favorable to the growth of rice, which is the most nutritive of all cereals, and which, consequently, is a causal factor in a high birth rate.

Where there is a cheap national food, the increase in population becomes very great. As a result, there are multitudes of people who are able to keep just above the subsistence level. A few persons who understand the operation of these physical laws are able to manipulate the multitudes in such a way as to make themselves immensely wealthy. Since wealth, after intellect, is the most permanent source of

[17] *Ibid.*, p. 33.
[18] *Ibid.*, p. 36.
[19] *Ibid.*, pp. 44 ff.

power, a great inequality of wealth has been accompanied by a corresponding inequality of social and political power.[20] It produces classes and even castes. Poverty provokes contempt. Class conflict results. The poor are ground low, murmur, and are again subjected to ignominy. Under such conditions democracy has a hard struggle. When physical conditions favor one class, that class will constitute itself the government and bitterly oppose the extension of government to all other classes. In Europe there was no cheap national food, no blind multiplication of population, and hence no such disparity between classes as in India. In Europe it has been easier for democratic movements to spread.

Early civilization developed in the Euphrates valley, the Nile valley, and in the exceedingly fertile regions of Peru, Central America, and Mexico. Modern civilization is found largely in fertile river valleys, such as the Thames, Seine, Rhine, Po, Danube, Hudson, Mississippi. But in the Amazon valley the fertility of soil has not invited the growth of a large population. The trade winds have brought in a superabundance of moisture, producing torrential rains, and a luxuriance of plant life and a complexity of virile animal life which thus far have defied the skill of man to overcome.

GENERAL ASPECTS OF NATURE

The fourth physical factor which Buckle presents is the general aspects of nature. Of these the first class excites the imagination and the second stimulates the rational operations of the intellect.[21] In regard to natural phenomena it may be said that whatever inspires feelings of terror, of the vague and uncontrollable, and of great wonder tends to inflame the imagination and to cause it to dominate the intellectual processes. Where nature is continually exhibiting its power, man feels his inferiority. He assumes a helpless attitude. He ceases to inquire or to think. His imagination, rather than his reason, reigns. On the other hand, where nature works smoothly and quietly, man begins to assert himself. He even essays to dominate nature and other men.

[20] *Ibid.*, p. 52.
[21] *Ibid.*, p. 85.

All early civilizations were located in the tropics or subtropics. In these regions nature is dangerous to man. Earthquakes, tempests, hurricanes, pestilences prevail. Consequently, the imagination of man takes exaggerated forms. The judgment is overbalanced; thought is paralyzed. The mind is continually thrown into a frantic state. These reactions turn human life into feeling molds, into poetic rather than scientific forms. Religious feelings are promoted. The leading religions of the world originated in the subtropical and tropical regions of the earth.

East Indian literature and thought illustrate the effect of nature upon the feelings and the imagination. The works of the East Indians on grammar, law, history, medicine, even on mathematics, geography, and metaphysics are nearly all poems.[22] Prose writing is despised. The Sanscrit language boasts of more numerous and more complicated meters than can any European tongue. The East Indian literature is even calculated to set the reason of man at defiance.[23]

The imagination, for example, in India has produced an exaggerated respect for the past; it is this situation which has led poets to describe a Golden Age in the remote past. In the literature of India is recorded the statement that in ancient times the average length of life of common men was 80,000 years. There are reports of poets who lived to be half a million years old.

In Greece, on the other hand, nature is more quiet and the mind of man functioned in a reasoning way. In the North Temperate zone science developed. "The climate was more healthy; earthquakes were less frequent; hurricanes were less disastrous; wild beasts and noxious animals less abundant."[24] Buckle, in other words, insists that everywhere the hand of nature is upon the mind of man.

The work of Buckle, the chief exponent of the influence of physical nature upon mental man, accentuates important phases of the growth of civilization. Buckle over-emphasized his anthropo-geographic observations. However, they constitute a part of the whole picture of human progress, and when

[22] *Ibid.*, p. 95.
[23] *Ibid.*, p. 96.
[24] *Ibid.*, p. 99.

seen in the light of modern mental growth and control of environment they shrink into proper proportions.

SEMPLE

The field which Buckle opened has been developed extensively by Friedrich Ratzel (1844–1904). This German scholar, traveler, and geographer is generally credited with putting anthropo-geography on a scientific basis. Ellen Semple attempted to translate his work on *Anthropo-Geographic* into English, but found the German constructions so difficult to handle accurately that it was necessary for her to put Ratzel's observations into her own words. She also points out in Buckle a lack of system and an undue tendency to follow one generalization with another. Her own *Influences of Geographic Environment* promptly became a standard work on the ways in which physical nature affects mankind.

Miss Semple, following but improving upon Ratzel, has shown in turn the influences of geographical location, area, and boundaries upon people. She indicates the various ways in which oceans, rivers, and coast lines have molded human minds; she distinguishes between the effects of mountains, steppes, and deserts upon mankind. She describes man as a product of the earth's surface. She stresses unduly the physical influences; she considers nature the dominating force. Even where civilized man has developed inventive powers and spiritual prowess, nature is given the credit.[25] Nevertheless, Miss Semple has marshaled facts in powerful array and increased their force by literary skill. No student or teacher can afford to neglect Miss Semple's extensive survey of the interaction between physical nature and human life.

Among the many other writers upon the relation of geographic factors to civilization the investigations of Ellsworth Huntington are significant. He has described the climatic conditions that are most favorable to mental stimulation and growth, and then has classified all districts of the earth according to the degree in which they actually stimulate or arrest mental advance. There is a close relationship, country

25 Ellen C. Semple, *Influences of Geographic Environment*, p. 635.

by country, between the areas which have favorable conditions for mental activity and the areas in which achievements have developed. Even the seasons have their measurable effects upon human activity. By a series of experiments upon different types of workers, Huntington concludes that "both physical and mental activity reach pronounced maxima in the spring and fall, with minima in midwinter and midsummer." [26] On the whole, Huntington takes a more conservative attitude toward the influence of climate upon man than do Buckle and Semple.

Activity varies according to temperature.[27] Lower types of life "seem to reach their optima at higher temperatures than do the more advanced types," but even mental effort has its optimum working temperature. "The law of optimum temperature apparently controls the phenomena of life from the lowest activities of protoplasm to the highest activities of the human intellect." [28] Changes in temperature are beneficial; likewise alternations in sunshine and cloudy weather are helpful. Humidity plays a leading role in effective human activity. In dry weather metabolism is more active. Huntington has attempted with some degree of success to determine what variations in mean temperature from month to month, what temperature variations from day to day, and what variations in humidity are most conducive to physical and mental productivity. Huntington would develop scientific methods in studying the ways in which man is affected by climate.

Huntington has prepared world maps showing the areas most favorable to the expression of human energy. He has also made maps showing the regions in which human leaders and men of ability have developed. Comparative studies of these maps are thought-stirring.[29]

Huntington's most important hypotheses, however, relate to his findings: first, regarding the correlation of the distribution of climatic energy over the earth's surface and the distribution of civilization; and second, to his correlations between the shifting of climatic zones and the shifting cen-

[26] Ellsworth Huntington, *Civilization and Climate*, p. 32.
[27] *Ibid.*, p. 109.
[28] *Ibid.*, p. 110.
[29] *Ibid.*, p. ;

ters of civilization.[30]   He is inclined to take a long-term view of geographic factors.

In this same connection William Z. Ripley has investigated the relation of climate to races.[31]   After analyzing races and distinguishing between them and the geographic influences upon pigmentation, head, form, stature, and other traits, mainly structural, he classifies climatic elements in order of importance, as follows : humidity, heat, and monotony.   A high humidity, excessive heat, and long series of sunshine or of cloudy weather produce mental enervation, stagnation, and retrogression.

Acclimatization of races is a very slow process, according to Ripley.   It requires centuries.   Perhaps the white race can never become truly acclimated in the tropics.   Racial differences, he shows, are due to environmental factors far more than is ordinarily supposed.   C. S. Coon, who has completely revised Ripley's work, and who is cautious regarding the influence of environment, admits that races as entities are always undergoing change.

In conclusion, it may be said that physical forces have operated strongly on man.   But when man has developed modern mental tools, he has been able to escape a part of the enslaving environmental influences.   The history of the relation of geographic factors to human progress indicates a fundamental but a proportionate decrease in those influences. The limited influence of environment is well summarized by R. H. Lowie, who points out how the identical environment is consistent with distinct cultures, and how cultures disappear "when one would least expect it on geographic principles." [32]   To quote further : "Indeed environment is not only unable to create cultural features, in some instances it is even incapable of perpetuating them." [33]   Lowie is discriminating in analyzing geographic influence upon culture.   He thinks : "The environment, then, enters into culture, not as a formative but rather as an inert element ready to be selected from and molded."

[30] *Ibid.*, Chs. XI, XII.
[31] W. Z. Ripley, *Races of Europe*, p. 571.   See the new work by C. S. Coon on *The Races of Europe*, published in 1939 (New York).
[32] R. H. Lowie. *Culture and Ethnology*, p. 6'.
[33] *Ibid.*, p. 62.

Within recent years anthropo-geographic thought has appeared in a new form with new tendencies. Human ecology is the new name. Borrowing its title from plant ecology and holding to certain plant-life tendencies, it has laid a great deal of emphasis on the place of economic and physical resources in explaining the life and structure of human communities. On a strictly biologic and economic basis it is not sociology but a scientific refinement of old forms that gives a more substantial understanding of social processes than has been previously developed. Some carry human ecology to the extreme of making it synonymous with environmental studies of all types, with spiritual environment dominant. Time-and-space-relations concepts are borrowed from philosophy but given new and exact meanings which are helpful. Human ecology, as described in Chapter XXXIV, links up with sociology at the point of community studies, and gives fine promise of making fundamental contributions to sociological understanding.

GROUP DISCUSSION TOPICS

1. The meaning of geographic social thought.
2. Bodin's idea of the influence on man of climatic factors.
3. Hume's reaction to the alleged influence of geographic elements.
4. The four main geographic factors according to Buckle.
5. The relation of food supply to birth rate.
6. The major contributions of E. C. Semple to geographic social thought.
7. Ellsworth Huntington's analysis of climatic influence on man.
8. Huntington's method of approach.
9. Comparisons of Buckle, Semple, and Huntington.
10. Ripley's distinctive viewpoint.
11. Lowie's argument against geographic influence.
12. Environment versus culture.
13. Culture versus heredity.

READINGS

Bodin, Jean, *The Six Books of a Commonweale* (transl. by R. Knolles) (London : Bishop 1606).

Buckle, H. T., *History of Civilization in England* (New York : Appleton and Company 1874).

Coon, C. S., *The Races of Europe* (New York : The Macmillan Company 1939).

Ellwood, Charles A., *A History of Social Philosophy* (New York : Prentice-Hall, Inc. 1938), Ch. XX.

Dunning, W. A., *Political Theories: From Luther to Montesquieu* (New York : The Macmillan Company 1913).

Huntington, Ellsworth, *Civilization and Climate* (New Haven, Conn. : Yale University Press 1915).

Lowie, R. H., *Culture and Ethnology* (New York : Boni and Liveright 1917).

Montesquieu, C. L., *The Spirit of Laws* (transl. by Nugent) (London : Bell and Sons 1894).

Ripley, W. Z., *Races of Europe* (New York : Appleton and Company 1899).

Semple, Ellen C., *Influences of Geographic Environment* (New York : Henry Holt and Company 1911).

Sorokin, Pitirim A., *Contemporary Sociological Theories* (New York : Harper & Brothers 1928), Chs. III, VII.

CHAPTER XX

SPENCER AND ORGANIC SOCIAL THOUGHT

In the second half of the last century social thought passed under biological influence. Society was discussed in terms of biological analogies, that is, it was compared in its structure and functions to organic life. Herbert Spencer was the leader among those writers who attempted to analyze society in terms of biological figures of speech. He also stressed the structural nature of society, and in his *Principles of Sociology* he went into great detail in giving a historical description of social institutions.

The Greek writers, the Hebrews before them, the Founder of Christianity, made references to the likeness between human society and plant and animal life. Mankind has often been compared to a tree or a plant with its manifold, evolving branches and fruit.

Spencer's famous organic analogies were preceded by the studies of biologists, such as Lamarck and Darwin. Lamarck (1744–1829) argued that by activity and use man could develop traits which would be transmitted by inheritance. Although this theory has been undermined by Weismann, it served as a basis for the further study of the biological laws of human evolution.

DARWIN

The thought of Charles Darwin (1809–1882) upon the nature of evolution was stimulated in part by Malthus' doctrine of surplus population and the consequent struggle for existence. He also based his ideas on the principles of natural selection. He developed the concepts of the prodigality of nature and the struggle for existence, which led to the resultant concept of natural selection and survival of the fittest. The process of natural selection accounts for the instincts, imitation, imagination, reason, as well as for self-consciousness, and the esthetic and religious impulses. In this way, according to the Darwinian formula, man has ascended by stages from the lower order of life.

The fittest to survive, concluded Darwin, are those individuals who are best fitted to meet the conditions of their environment. If the environment be competitive, savage, brutal, then the fittest will be the strongest physically and the most vicious. If the environment be co-operative, then the fittest will be the persons who co-operate best. With the development of intelligence and sagacity in early human society, individuals otherwise cruel learned to co-operate. A tribe of co-operating individuals would be victorious in a conflict with a tribe of non-co-operating members. Thus co-operation and a co-operating environment themselves are the result of natural selection.

Unfortunately, Darwin's concept of natural selection has been grossly distorted. Upon this misapprehension, a doctrine of "social Darwinism" has gained recognition. According to a false interpretation of Darwinism, the tooth-and-fang struggle for existence among animals is the normal procedure among human beings. Brutal, cruel, and shrewd men are "fitted" to survive in an environment of physical and mental competition. Likewise, the nations which can marshal together the most powerful armies and navies are the "fittest" to survive in a world where each nation is accountable unto itself alone. Thus it is seen that human society is simply an extension of the animal society and that the fundamental law of social progress is the law of force and might, first physical, and then physical and psychical.

But this interpretation is false to Darwin's own principles. While Darwin did describe and lay great emphasis upon the tooth-and-fang struggle for existence, he noted and stressed the fact that even among animals, modifying influences were at work. He made clear that co-operation exists among many species of animal life, and that this co-operative tendency is an important survival factor. He also saw that among the highest types of animals there were new and complex expressions of co-operation, and that the higher mental activity of these animal types seemed to be a correlate in some way of the greater co-operative spirit. The application of this principle to human progress implies that co-operative attitudes may ultimately become the chief survival force, and that some day the "fittest" to survive will be those persons or groups of persons who co-operate most wisely. This theory will be developed further in the chapter upon "Kropotkin and Co-operative Social Thought."

Darwin made another important contribution to social thought in his theory of sexual selection. This idea is a phase of natural selection. Among the higher animals the females choose their mates. The males, for example, with the singing voice and beautiful plumage, are the most likely to be chosen. These males thus become the progenitors of the next generation of the given species; the less attractive males mate, if at all, with the inferior types of females. Thus signs of male attractiveness come to possess survival value.[1]

Among human beings the principle of sexual selection operates, but in a reversed sexual form. During the earlier centuries of human history the custom developed whereby the males took the initiative in choosing mates. As a result, the females resorted to all sorts of devices to make themselves "attractive" and to get themselves "selected."

HERBERT SPENCER

The social theories of Herbert Spencer (1820–1903) have caused more controversy than those of any other writer in the sociological field. The fact that in these controversies the ideas of Spencer have usually been worsted will not obscure the important role which Spencer took in the field of social thought.

Spencer early developed the habit of causal thinking, that is, he believed in causes, and hence searched everywhere for causes. Because of the acrimonious discussions which took place between his father and mother, and because of his own independent nature, he repudiated the orthodox religious explanations of the universe. He was trained for the profession of civil engineering. His studies in mathematics and mechanics accentuated his precise and somewhat materialistic interpretation of the universe. His social theories are

[1] Charles Darwin, *The Descent of Man*, pp. 229 ff.

an outgrowth in part of his emphasis upon the laws of co-existences and sequences in the physical world.

LAW OF EVOLUTION

In order to understand Spencer's social laws it is necessary further to consider his general law of evolution. He traced everything in the world back through causal chains to two fundamental factors, namely, matter and motion — two aspects of force. As a result of the operation of some First Cause, an integration of matter began to take place, accompanied by a concomitant dissipation of motion. As a result, matter passes from an indefinite, incoherent homogeneity to a definite, coherent heterogeneity. During this process the unexpended motion undergoes a similar change.[2]

The best explanation of this law of evolution can be found in its application to societary phenomena. Suppose that a modern city neighborhood undertakes to organize itself. It possesses physical resources and mental abilities. The "neighbors" are all more or less untrained in community organization activities. In this sense they are homogeneous. At first they are unable to work together; in fact, they do not know what to do; thus they form "an indefinite, incoherent homogeneity." But with experience in community organization activities, the individuals of the neighborhood learn to work together. Each finds the type of work which he can do best. All work toward a definite goal. Thus a definite, coherent heterogeneity arises. Further, the unexpended energies of the people are influenced and transformed by the pattern ideas which experience in community organization measures has taught.[3]

This application of Spencer's law of evolution to human progress has weak as well as strong points. There is not always an original homogeneity. Upon close examination this homogeneity disappears before a variegated conglomeration of heterogeneous experiences and potentialities of all the individuals who are concerned. It is not necessary to point

[2] Herbert Spencer, *First Principles*, Section III:145.
[3] *Ibid.*, I:596, 597.

out additional errors. Spencer deserves credit, however, for developing the concept of social evolution as a phase of natural evolution and for stressing the idea of natural sequences in societary matters.

Spencer began his *Principles of Sociology* with a very elaborate description of primitive man — the original societary unit corresponding to the biological cell. The physical, emotional, and intellectual life of primitive man is given prominence. An analysis is made of the behavior of man, the original social unit, when he is exposed to the various environing conditions — inorganic, organic, and super-organic. The emphasis upon "man" as the primary unit neglects the importance of the "group" in the social evolutionary process. Moreover, Spencer underrated the intellectual nature of primitive man; he denied to early man the qualities involving excursiveness of thought, imagination, and original ideas.[4]

Spencer's discussion of primitive ideas shows widespread reading of volumes of source materials. The "inductions" are often influenced by preconceived ideas of human life, despite Spencer's sincere desire and effort to be scientific. While the horde, the family, and other groups are described, the influences which are the result of the interaction of individual minds and the interactions between a person and his group are scarcely recognized.

In regard to the state, Spencer carried forward the theories which have already been noted, namely, of individual rights. He repudiated the state which is the product of military organization of society. Such a regime is primordial and uncivilized. It is an organization of homogeneous units in which the units, or the individuals, are slaves to the organization.

INDUSTRIAL ORDER

Spencer believed in a new industrial development whereby "individuals" would become differentiated and developed, and whereby they would be shifted from an autocratic maximum to a democratic maximum. To Spencer, man is vastly

[4] *Ibid.*, I:84.

superior to the state. In the coming industrial order Spencer foresaw an era in which the main business of society will be to defend the rights of "individuals." Spencer forecast an epoch of industrial states which have abolished war. In such a day the only conflicts that will take place between states will be natural. These will be only the competitions that arise naturally between states that are building up the best "individuals," that is, those persons who develop their "individuality" most freely and harmoniously.

The rise of industrial states with a minimum emphasis upon government and a maximum emphasis upn "individuality" will produce a world order in which national barriers will slowly melt away and a planetary unity will develop. Spencer's industrialism, however, has fundamental weaknesses. It implies that social organization is more important than social process. It neglects to provide sufficiently for inherent psychical changes. It assumes that an industrial society, *per se,* will be peaceful. It underestimates the importance of socializing motives.

In the changes from a military to an industrial organization of society, the six main sets of social institutions undergo deep-seated changes. Spencer describes at length these six institutional structures — domestic, ceremonial, political, ecclesiastical, professional, and industrial. Two, the political and industrial, have already been mentioned. Spencer's treatment of the other four is accurate to a degree but at fundamental points is unreliable — judged by current conceptions and data.

ORGANIC ANALOGY

Perhaps Spencer is best known for his treatment of the organic analogy. He set up the hypothesis that society is like a biological organism and then proceeded to defend his thesis against all objections with great logical force. But logic was his sociological downfall, for it overcame his scientific insight.

Spencer found four main ways in which society resembles an organism.[5] (1) In both cases growth is attended by aug-

[5] *Ibid.,* Part II, Ch. II.

mentation of mass. (2) In each instance growth is accomplished by increasing complexity of structure. (3) In the organism and in society there is an interdependence of parts. (4) The life of society, like the life of an organism, is far longer than the life of any of the units or parts.

But there are ways in which society and an organism are unlike.[6] These are analyzed by Spencer and determined to be merely superficial differences. There are four of these main differences. (1) Unlike organisms, societies have no specific extensive form, such as a physical body with limbs or a face. (2) The elements of society do not form a continuous whole, as in the case of an animal. The living units composing society are free, and not in contact, being more or less dispersed. (3) The parts of society are not stationary and fixed in their positions relative to the whole. (4) In an organism consciousness is concentrated in a small part of the aggregate, while in society consciousness is diffused. The alleged superficiality in this difference between society and an organism was difficult for Spencer to maintain.

In discussing the organic analogy further, Spencer compared the alimentary system of an organism to the productive industries, or the sustaining system in the body politic. Furthermore, there is a strong parallelism between the circulatory system of an organism and the distributing system in society with its transportation lines; but more particularly, its commercial classes and media of exchange. Then, in both cases there have developed regulating systems.

Spencer's idea of social control is contained in his description of the "regulating system" of society. He explains how permanent submission to government is forced on people, namely, through war.

In an organism there are dominant centers and subordinate centers, the senses, and a neural apparatus. A similar structure appears in society in the form of an adjustive apparatus, or government, for the purpose of adjudicating the differences between the producers and the consumers. These parallelisms throw only a small measure of light upon the nature of society. They appear ridiculous when carried to an extreme; for example, to the extreme to which Spencer himself

6 *Ibid.*, I:457 ff.

went when he compared the King's Council to the medulla oblongata, the House of Lords to the cerebellum, and the House of Commons to the cerebrum.

Spencer uses his analogies very extensively and vigorously, and later refers to them as merely a scaffolding for building a structure of deductions. This conclusion contains contradictory elements. When the scaffolding is removed, society is left standing as a more or less intangible affair. If a society is like an organism, it experiences a natural cycle of birth, maturity, old age, and death. But according to the telic concept of progress that was advanced by Lester F. Ward and developed by later writers, the death of society does not come with organic inevitableness, but depends on the vision, plans, courage, and activities of that society's members. A society need never die.

For many years it has been popular to criticize Spencer. Nearly all the criticisms are justified. Moreover, they have been so numerous that little of worth seems to be left in Spencer's writings. However, Spencer's contributions to social thought are not negligible for several reasons. (1) He emphasized the laws of evolution and natural causation. (2) He described social evolution as a phase of natural evolution. (3) He suggested likenesses and differences between biological organisms and human society. (4) He made the role of social structures, or institutions, stand out distinctly. (5) He stressed the importance of "individuality." (6) He undermined the idea that the State is a master machine to which all the individual citizens must submit automatically.

JOHN FISKE

In the United States, Spencer possessed an able and loyal friend in John Fiske (1842–1901). Fiske built his social thought upon the evolutionary formulae of Darwin and Spencer. In his *Cosmic Philosophy,* or philosophy of the universe, Fiske contended that the evolution of man produced fundamental changes in the nature of cosmic evolution. With the development of man there appears a new force in the universe, the human spirit, or soul. The advent of this psychical entity has produced a subordination of the purely bodily, physical, material forces, and established a control by spiritual forces. Moreover, in human evolution there has been a slowly increasing subordination of the egoistic phases of spiritual life to the altruistic. With the apparent cessation in important bodily changes there have come unheralded and unanticipated psychical inventions, which have released man from the passive adaptation to environment that animals manifest, and given to him an increasingly positive control over the processes of adaptation. Humanity as the highest product of the evolutionary processes has the power to change the whole course of cosmic development.[7] Fiske distinctly emphasized the psychical forces in evolution and the part which they play in making mankind purposeful and in organizing groups on social principles. Humanity is not a mere incident in evolution; it is the supreme factor.[8] The main purpose of man is not the perpetuation of the species, but the development of increasingly more social purposes.

Following the ideas of Maine, Tylor, McLennan, and Lubbock, Fiske concluded that social evolution originated when families, "temporarily organized among all the higher gregarious mammals, became in the case of the highest mammal permanently organized."[9] Gregariousness developed into definite family relationships and responsibilities. Social evolution produced an increased complexity and specialty in intelligence, which in turn required a lengthening of the period "during which the nervous connections involved in ordinary adjustments are becoming organized." Such a transformation requires time, and hence the need for a period of infancy which is not common to the lower animals. Accompanying this period of infancy, there is the expression of strong affection of relatively short duration among higher animals. Among mankind parental love takes on the characteristics not only of intensity but of duration and forgiveness. In this phase of evolution there is a correlative development of three factors, namely, the prolongation of infancy, the rise of parental affection, and increasing intelligence.

[7] John Fiske, *Outlines of Cosmic Philosophy*, III:280 ff.
[8] John Fiske, *Destiny of Man*, p. 12.
[9] John Fiske, *Outlines of Cosmic Philosophy*, IV:127.

The gradual prolongation of the period of infancy is partly a consequence of increasing intelligence, and in turn the prolongation of infancy affords the circumstances for the establishment of permanent relationships, of reciprocal behavior, of sociality.[10]

Fiske was one of the first social philosophers to point out the significance of foresight as a phase of evolutionary development. Perhaps the chief way in which civilized man is distinguished from the barbarian is in his ability "to adapt his conduct to future events, whether contingent or certain to occur." Civilized man has the power to forego present enjoyment in order to safeguard himself against future disaster.[11] This quality is the essence of prudence and is due in large part to civilized man's superior power of self-restraint, one of the chief elements in moral progress. It is equally important as "an indispensable prerequisite to the accumulation of wealth in any community." It is the basic factor in civilized man's elaborate scientific provisions and in his numerous far-reaching philosophic and religious systems.

LILIENFELD

Paul von Lilienfeld (1829–1903) made the organic analogy a definite part of his theory of society. He compared the individual to the cells in an organism; the governmental and industrial organizations, to the neural system; and the cultural products of society, to the intercellular parts of an organism.[12]

Lilienfeld compared the stages of growth of the individual to the stages of racial development: savage, barbarian, and civilized. This analogy was made use of by Fiske. Although somewhat true in a very general sense, this recapitulation theory cannot be carried into minute details.

The concept of "social capitalization" was originated by Lilienfeld. By it he meant the ability of society to store up useful ideas and methods and transmit them from generation to generation. In this way each generation becomes the

---

10 *Ibid.* pp. 360 ff.
11 *Ibid.,* pp. 303 ff.
12 Paul von Lilienfeld, *Gedanken ueber die Sozialwissenschaft der Zukunft,* II, pp. viii ff.

inheritor of all the human experiences that have gone before.

Lilienfeld was one of the first sociological writers to develop the definite concept of social pathology.[13] His treatment of this theme, however, was exceedingly weak. He distinguished between a normal and diseased organism and then, by analogy, between a normal and diseased society. Social pathology, according to Lilienfeld, deals with three sets of diseases, namely, of industry, of justice, and of politics. Lilienfeld carried the organic analogy to a ridiculous and puerile extreme when he compared the diseases of industry to insanity; of justice, to delirium; of politics, to paralysis. He also elaborated a system of social therapeutics to correspond to the diseases.

SCHAEFFLE

In Albert Schaeffle (1831–1903), the organic analogy found another disciple, but a more worthy one than either Spencer or Lilienfeld. In the thought of Schaeffle, society is not primarily a large organism but a gigantic mind. Schaeffle presented a functional analogy rather than a biological analogy. Whereas Spencer was especially interested in social structures, Schaeffle set his attention upon social functions.

In his functional analogies Schaeffle compared the reason with the legislature in society; the will, with the executive officers, and the esthetic judgment, with the judiciary. Schaeffle's psychology is inaccurate and on the whole unscientific; his analogies add little to an understanding of society. Nevertheless, his thought on these subjects represents an advance over the ideas of Spencer.

In the *Bau und Leben des Socialen Koerpers*, Schaeffle undertook to develop a complete sociological system. His teachings follow the principle that "function leads structure and structure limits function." Activities produce developments in bodily structure, and also cause the formation of new social institutions. Bodily structures and social institutions alike limit activities and usefulness. These proposi-

---

[13] Lilienfeld, *Pathologie Sociale*.

tions are a reversal of the emphasis which Spencer maintained. They are fundamentally correct.

Although Schaeffle referred frequently to the "social body," he did not give the concept a specific meaning. He introduced the term "social process," but did not analyze its nature. He repudiated the idea that the individual is the social unit; he considered the group to be the all-important unit in society. Natural selection in social evolution manifests itself in conflicts between the ideals of different groups. René Worms (1869–1926), it may be added, has assumed the existence of a social consciousness apart from the consciousness of "individuals," and argued that the chief difference between biological organisms and social organisms is one of degree.

Schaeffle considered that government justifies itself in protecting the weaker members of society, and in maintaining the highest welfare of all. He pointed out that social responsibility rests upon the best educated and most fortunate members of society. Schaeffle wisely emphasized the development of purposeful activity on the part of both persons and groups.

MACKENZIE

The ideas of John Stuart Mackenzie differ from those of Spencer, Lilienfeld, and Schaeffle. Mackenzie does not use the figure of an organic analogy; he speaks in terms of homologies. According to Mackenzie, society is not like an organism; it is organic.

The organic nature of society is threefold. (1) There is an intrinsic relation between the parts of society and the whole. The individual reflects the culture of the group in which he has been trained. (2) The development of a group is by virtue of intrinsic processes. A group builds on ideas derived both from the past and from other groups, but it does not genuinely grow unless it takes these ideas and makes them over into a part of its own nature. (3) Society develops toward ends which are discoverable in society itself. By analysis of the ideals and motive forces of a group, it is possible to determine in what direction the group is moving.

Mackenzie argues for the inner principle of things and particularly for society. He believes, however, that knowledge concerning this inner principle and the essential unity of mankind cannot be reduced to a science, but will constitute the basis of a social philosophy. Social philosophy does not supply facts, but seeks to interpret the significance of the special aspects of human life with reference to the social unity of mankind.[14]

The family and the state are the two forms of association in which the most intimate bonds of union are nurtured. Language, if it can be called a social institution, is perhaps the most fundamental institution of all, because it produces that community spirit whereby social intimacy can take place and whereby the realization of a common good can be achieved.[15]

According to Mackenzie, there are three main lines of social progress, and hence three main types of social control to be encouraged.[16] (1) The control of natural forces by human agencies. (2) The control of individuals by the communal spirit. (3) Self-control.

The road of social advance is beset with obstacles. The chief are these: (1) The dominance of vegetative needs. These economic factors are so universal and insistent that they are likely at any time to override all other human needs. (2) The insistence of animal impulses, chiefly love and strife. While love promotes unity, it generally produces a limited unity. Moreover, one mode of unity is apt to conflict with other types of unity, and thus lead to intense strife. (3) The mastery of mechanism. Life is easily crushed under the weight of organization; thought, by scholastic pedantry; industry, by economic systems; nationality, by soulless bureaucracy. (4) Anarchism. The remedy for over-organization is not anarchy, for life and society are composed of numbers of conflicting tendencies, which must be controlled by the power of thought. But the exercise of merely individual thought[17] will not suffice. Individual thought is likely to be egocentric, to evade the problems of group life,

[14] J. S. Mackenzie, *Outlines of Social Philosophy*, p. 14.
[15] *Ibid.*, p. 65.
[16] *Ibid.*, p. 243 ff.
[17] That is, thought about "individuals."

or to solve them narrowly. (5) Conservatism. An established and successful civilization is in danger of relying too
much on its past. It often carries within itself the canker of
decay, and frequently lacks any clear vision of higher development.

Mackenzie is committed to internationalism. It is no
longer fitting for anyone to think of his own country as an
exclusive object of devotion. "The earth is our country,
and all its inhabitants are our fellow citizens; and it is only
the recognition of this that entitles us to look for any lasting
security."

Mackenzie advances beyond the organic analogists when
he describes the ways in which society is organic. As a social
philosopher he has contributed important pattern-ideas. He
has escaped from the foibles of the organic analogy and at
the same time indicated the values that lie beneath that concept.

SUPERORGANIC CONCEPT

Spencer's concept of the "superorganic" has commanded
wide attention. After inorganic evolution, or orderly change
in astronomical and geological phenomena, comes organic
evolution, or orderly change in the vegetable and animal
worlds. Superorganic evolution begins with "all those processes and products which imply the co-ordinated actions of
many individuals." These co-ordinated actions achieve results exceeding in extent and complexity those achievable
by individual actions.[18]

Parental co-operation is included under organic evolution. The dividing line between organic and superorganic
evolution is necessarily indistinct, since the latter developed
in an evolutionary way out of the former. The activities of
the social insects are intermediary between organic and superorganic evolution, for each of these societies "is in reality a
large family." Superorganic evolution implies co-operation
between classes of living forms which have "unlike structures and consequent unlike functions."

Picking up this thread of analysis, A. L. Kroeber makes
the superorganic a fourth order of phenomena. His classifi-

18 *Principles of Sociology,* I:2, 4.

cation becomes: (1) inorganic phenomena, (2) vital organic phenomena, (3) mental organic phenomena, and (4) superorganic phenomena. The description of these types of phenomena becomes: (1) astronomy and geology, (2) natural history or biology, (3) biographic history, and (4) culture history.[19]

Spencer pointed out that as a result of superorganic evolution a tremendous amount of superorganic products has accumulated in the course of time. These include material appliances, language, knowledge, customs, mythologies, theologies, cosmologies, literature, and histories. These exert "an immensely-voluminous, immensely-complicated, and immensely-powerful set of influences" on human beings, modifying both individuals and societies.[20]

It is this theme which Clarence M. Case has treated further, claiming that "culture is not the possession, so far as yet shown, of animals, and, on the other hand, no human group was ever found lacking a culture of relatively high complexity." [21] Hart and Pantzer have replied, contending that animals have culture of a simple sort. "Animals have acquired by imitation or tuition not merely human culture through domestication, but also types of behavior from each other and have even shown some evidence of socially accumulative behavior complexes." [22] Case answers by defining culture in terms of tools and symbols, that is, as expressions "of external storage, interchange, and transmission of an accumulating fund of personal and social experience by means of tools and symbols—a process entirely unknown on any level of life below the human." [23] Case challenges the theory of continuous evolution as being all-inclusive. He explains the rise of culture on the human level only in terms of an emergent evolution. Under the heading of "The Culture of Canines," Read Bain contends that animals acquire verbal and motor culture patterns that are "learned" from

[19] A. L. Kroeber, "The Possibility of a Social Psychology," *American Journal of Sociology*, 23:636.
[20] Spencer, *op. cit.*, I:13, 14.
[21] Clarence M. Case, *Outlines of Introductory Sociology*, p. xxix.
[22] Hornell Hart and Adele Pantzer, "Have Sub-human Animals Culture?" *American Journal of Sociology*, 30:709.
[23] Clarence M. Case, "Culture as a Distinctive Human Trait," *American Journal of Sociology*, 32:920.

man. Bain accepts the emergent evolution idea but holds that it occurs as a non-spectacular and an understandable phase of continuous evolution.[24] The argument tapers off into discussions of the nature of culture, the subject of a subsequent chapter.

This chapter deals with a significant period in the history of social thought. The biology of the time was very faulty and the sociological applications of biological knowledge were consequently of no great merit. The early years of the present century were characterized by noteworthy improvements in biological thinking. The facts about the laws of heredity and variation increased in number; a science of heredity was established. The first decade of the present century also marks the rise of the science of eugenics. In a later chapter the contributions of recent scientific biology, and particularly of eugenics, to social thought will be presented. Moreover, recent decades have seen a remarkable development in the field of cultural anthropology. A later chapter will be devoted to cultural evolution and patterns.

GROUP DISCUSSION TOPICS

1. Darwin's meaning of the "fittest to survive."
2. Darwin's "social co-operation" theory.
3. The chief phases of Spencer's law of evolution.
4. The most valid of the four "likenesses" in Spencer's organic analogy.
5. The chief "unlikenesses" in the organic analogy.
6. The meaning of the prolongation of infancy concept.
7. The significance of "foresight" as a social value.
8. An evaluation of Lilienfeld's "social capitalization" theory.
9. The strength and weakness of Lilienfeld's "social pathology" concept.
10. The leading difference between Schaeffle's and Spencer's thought about organic analogies.
11. The most important of Mackenzie's three "lines of progress."
12. The chief of Mackenzie's "hindrances to progress."
13. Do animals have culture?

[24] Read Bain, "The Culture of Canines," *Sociology and Social Research,* XIII:545 ff.

READINGS

Becker, Howard, and Harry E. Barnes, *Social Thought from Lore to Science* (Washington: Harren Press 1952), Vol. I, Chs. 28 and 29.

Bristol, L. M., *Social Adaptation* (Cambridge, Harvard University Press 1915), Ch. II.

Darwin, Charles, *The Descent of Man* (New York: Appleton and Company 1904).

Duncan, David, *Life and Letters of Herbert Spencer* (New York: Appleton and Company 1908).

Ellwood, Charles A., *A History of Social Philosophy* (New York: Prentice-Hall, Inc. 1938), Ch. XXV.

Fiske, John, *Outlines of Cosmic Philosophy* (Boston: Houghton Mifflin Company 1904).

Hofstadter, Richard, *Social Darwinism in American Thought* (Philadelphia: University of Pennsylvania Press 1944).

House, Floyd N., *The Development of Sociology* (New York: McGraw-Hill Book Company 1936), Ch. XI.

Kimball, Elsa P., *Sociology and Education: An Analysis of the Theories of Spencer and Ward* (New York: Columbia University Press 1932).

Lichtenberger, James P., *Development of Social Theory* (New York: Century Company 1923).

Lilienfeld, Paul von, *Pathologie Sociale* (Paris: Girard & Briere 1896).

———, *Gedanken ueber die Sozialwissenschaft der Zukunft* (Berlin: Reimer 1903).

Mackenzie, J. S., *Outlines of Social Philosophy* (New York: The Macmillan Company 1918).

Sorokin, Pitirim A., *Contemporary Sociological Theories* (New York: Harper & Brothers 1928), Ch. IV.

Spencer, Herbert, *Principles of Sociology* (New York: Appleton and Company 1914).

———, *The Study of Sociology* (New York: Appleton and Company 1910).

———, *First Principles* (New York: Appleton and Company 1900).

———, *An Autobiography* (New York: Appleton and Company 1904).

———, *Data of Ethics* (New York: Appleton and Company 1893).

———, *Social Statics* (New York: Appleton and Company 1903).

Tillett, A. W., *Introduction to Herbert Spencer's Synthetic Philosophy* (London: King and Company 1914).

CHAPTER XXI

WARD AND TELIC SOCIAL THOUGHT

The name of Lester F. Ward (1841–1913) stands forth between the old and new eras of social thought. Ward belongs to both the old and the new. He adopted Comtean positivism and built in part upon Spencer's evolutionary principles, but opposed Spencer's *laissez-faire* ideas and his evolutionary determinism, especially in regard to education. Perhaps his most notable work was the way in which he shocked a Spencerian-tinged world of social thought into a new method of thinking.

Ward became the ardent advocate of social telesis. Man can modify, defeat, or hasten the processes of nature. Ward brought the concept of dynamic sociology to the attention of the world. Although he was interested in social statics, his primary concern was in the fact that man through the use of his intelligence can transform not only the natural world but the social world, and that he can harness not only the natural forces to social ends, but even the social forces to social purposes. Hence it is that Ward ranks today, despite his monistic philosophy and his false psychological premises, as one of the world's leading pioneer sociologists.

Lester F. Ward was born in Joliet, Illinois. He received a limited schooling, and early went to work, first on a farm and then as a wheelwright. He manifested an unusual liking for books and to a great extent was self-educated. He entered the employment of the United States Government, where he remained for more than forty years, after he was honorably discharged from service in the Civil War. In the Government service he held the positions of geologist and paleontologist. Despite his strenuous and efficient work for the Government, he found time to think through and write out an elaborate sociological system of thought.

Ward's published works in sociology began with his *Dynamic Sociology* (1883) and ended with the *Glimpses of the Cosmos* (1913) in several volumes, which, with the exception of Volume I, have been published posthumously. The intermediate books of importance in order were: *Pure Sociology, Applied Sociology,* and *Psychic Factors in Civilization.*

Ward was characterized by an impressive command of his subject and "a terrific mental drive." In 1906 he began the unique experiment of teaching sociology at the age of sixty-five. As a professor of sociology he served Brown University until his death — for a period of seven years. He was supported by the indefatigable assistance of his wife, as shown by the many files which she kept of "Reviews and Press Notices," "Autograph Letters," and "Biography."

DYNAMIC SOCIOLOGY

Ward was led to produce *Dynamic Sociology* because of his observation that preceding 1875 there was an essential sterility in social science thinking. Ward observed that the prevalent teachings of Herbert Spencer were largely static, and that the ideas of Spencer's American disciples were only passively dynamic. Ward believed that before the science of society could be truly established the active dynamic factors must be described. A science which fails to benefit mankind is lifeless. To save sociology from the lifelessness which it was manifesting, Ward wrote *Dynamic Sociology.* He contemplated social phenomena "as capable of intelligent control by society itself in its own interest." [1] His main thesis in *Dynamic Sociology* is "the necessity for universal education as the one clear, overshadowing, and immediate social duty to which all others are subordinate." He argued for a truly progressive system of popular scientific education.[2] He declared that not one-hundredth of the facts which original research has already brought forth are today obtainable by a one-hundredth of the members of society, and hence not one truth in ten thousand is fully apprehended.[3]

The development of two cardinal principles is declared by Ward to make possible the organization systematically of

[1] Lester F. Ward, *Dynamic Sociology,* Vol. I, pp. xxv ff.
[2] *Ibid.,* I:22
[3] *Ibid.,* I:23.

all human knowledge. One of these principles is the interdependence of all phenomena; the other relates to the improvability of the human race.

The highest function among the sciences falls to sociology. By its very nature it is the basis of all efforts to improve the race. "The high utilitarian motive, focalizing all considerations in the good of man, can have no other effect than to establish as the ultimate science, for the perfection of which all other sciences exist, the science of human life, which takes the form and name of sociology." [4]

The prevailing doctrine in social thought, that of *laissez faire*, as championed by Spencer, drew forth Ward's best intellectual efforts as a challenger. Ward protested against the teaching that natural forces are operating only as elements in the all-powerful evolutionary process. He pointed out that man is distinguished from the animals by the development of his psychical nature, i.e., of his foresight and reason. He demonstrated that by this development man is able to master and regulate the operation of the blind evolutionary forces. Hence the doctrine of *laissez faire* is not only false but pernicious. It defeats social progress. The truth is, said Ward, society is able to improve itself, and it should set itself scientifically at once to the opportunity.

Passive, or negative, progress is represented by the social forces operating in their natural freedom, subject only to general evolutionary laws. [5] Active, or positive, progress is represented by the social forces guided by conscious social order; social dynamics treats of the laws of social progress. Social dynamics concerns itself with two types of studies. One line analyzes and describes what is going on in society under the influence of natural laws — this is pure sociology. It is pure diagnosis; it has nothing to do with what society ought to be. It describes the phenomena and laws of society as they are. [6] The other procedure discusses the application of human purpose to the natural social forces — this is applied sociology. It studies the art of applying the active, or positive, forces to the natural evolution of society. This

4 *Ibid.*, I:9.
5 *Ibid.*, I:56, 57.
6 *Ibid.*, I:60, Ward, *Pure Sociology*, p. 4.

method is distinctly a human process and "depends wholly on the action of man himself." Applied sociology treats of social ends and purposes.

Pure sociology describes the spontaneous development of society; applied sociology deals with the artificial means of accelerating the spontaneous processes in society.[7] Pure sociology treats of achievement; applied sociology, of improvement. But applied sociology is not social reform; "it does not itself apply sociological principles, it seeks only to show how they may be applied." It lays down principles as guides to social action. The carrying of these principles into social and political practice is social reform.

The distinction between natural and artificial progress is made clear.[8] The former is a blind growth; the latter, a purposeful manufacture. One is a genetic process; the other, a teleological process. One is characterized by increasing differentiation; the other, by a process of calculation. Artificial progress is considered superior to natural progress.

Ward was a monist. He believed in the absolute unity of nature, from the revolutions of celestial orbs to the vicissitudes of social customs and laws.[9] He held that "life is a property of matter," and naïvely declared that "it is simply the result of the movements going on among the molecules composing a mass of protoplasm."[10] Psychic phenomena are "the relations which subsist among the material molecules of the brain and nervous system and between these and the material objects of the outside world . . ." Since mind is relational, it is immaterial, but it has matter for its basis. Relations, however, constitute the properties of matter, and hence mind, as well as life, is a property of matter.[11] The logical length to which Ward goes in supporting his monistic doctrine is in itself an indication of his error.

HUMAN ORIGINS

Unlike Comte, Ward believed that man originally was antisocial and completely egoistic. In the earliest stage of

---

[7] Lester F. Ward, *Applied Sociology*, pp. 5 ff.
[8] *Dynamic Sociology*, I:72.
[9] *Ibid.*, 1:143.
[10] *Ibid.*, I:320.
[11] *Ibid.*, I:408, 409.

numan existence, man lived a life almost solitary, or at least in small groups.[12] He was surrounded by destructive forces, both inorganic and organic. Against the world and ferocious beasts he found himself almost physically helpless. Some of his number overcame their physical defenselessness by using their "wits." Through sagacity and cunning they were able to withstand the attacks of the wild beasts, to survive, and to propagate their young. Along with increased cunning there went an increased brain size in proportion to size of body, and also an improved brain structure.

This brain development is the essential prerequisite for perceiving the advantages of association.[13] Man early recognized the merits of association, and moved up from the solitary, or autarchic, stage of social life to the second, or constrained aggregate stage. This second stage does not contain the elements of permanency because of its forced nature. The tendencies toward association are often counteracted and at times destroyed by fierce contests for the limited natural foods. In contending that man's early ancestors were very irascible and quarrelsome beings, Ward went beyond the limits of scientific induction. In believing that altruism is an outgrowth of egoism, Ward again violates the best scientific thought. The probabilities are that both egoism and altruism have developed *pari passu,* and in part from different causes. Ward asserted that altruism is a higher but a less influential force than is egoism. "Egoism is the feeling which demands for self an increase of enjoyment and diminution of discomfort. Altruism is that which demands these results for others." [14]

Ward considered that feelings are the most dynamic of all human elements. They are far more powerful than is the intellect, as shown by the fact that "all great movements in history are preceded and accompanied by strong feelings. And it is those persons whose feelings have been most violent that have exerted the greatest influence upon the tone and character of society. Purely intellectual feeling is never sufficient directly to sway the multitude." [15]

[12] *Ibid.,* I:464.
[13] *Ibid.,* I:452.
[14] *Ibid.,* I:14.
[15] *Ibid.,* I:11.

Practical illustrations of the dominance of the feelings over intelligence are legion. Sometimes the result is disastrous, and again needed reforms are to be accounted for in this way.

The use of the rudiments of an established government marks the beginning of the third period in human society. For protection, tribes unified themselves under central controls. Through compulsion or interest, and for protective reasons, tribes united; the spheres of social organizations thus were enlarged. But government, which was established for the purpose of securing peace, became one of the chief causes of external wars. Governments, autocratic control, and territory hunger led peoples into destructive war. The world is still in this third stage.

But some day, according to Ward, wars between nations will cease, national prejudices will soften, diversity of language will be overcome, and all governments probably will be consolidated into one. This picture represents the fourth, or ideal, level of societary life, and may not be attained for ages to come. Ward cherishes the strong belief that the present national stage will be succeeded by the cosmopolitan, or pantarchic, age. Ward perceives an ultimate triumph of humanitarian sentiments, which will be also "a triumph of practical interests, that shall sweep away the present barriers of language, national pride, and natural uncongeniality, and unite all nations in one vast social aggregate with a single political organization." [16]

SOCIAL FORCES

Ward's analysis of social evolution rests on his conception of the social forces. The primary social force is desire. Desire is the expression of any of the native impulses which, at the given moment, has not been gratified. This striving for gratification constitutes desire and the moving force in the societary world. "Desire is the essential basis of all actions."

The desires are numerous and complex, but upon examination lend themselves to classification. There are two

[16] *Ibid.*, I:467.

fundamental and primary sets of desires, the nutritive and the reproductive. The end of the first is to preserve the individual; and of the second, to preserve and maintain the race.

"The first desire of all creatures is for nourishment." This desire remains dominant throughout life. The human race, Ward summarizes, spent its infancy — thousands of years — in the single pursuit of subsistence.[17] When the natural food supply failed, man was forced to be inventive and to labor or die. Too many individuals in one place meant either the migration of some individuals or that others must compel nature through labor to increase her normal yield of subsistence.[18]

The nutritive desire has led man to labor. Labor, however, is not the natural condition of man.[19] Work, according to Ward, is unnatural and irksome. The constant spur of hunger transformed man into a working man. To be useful, however, work must be continuous and applied steadily to a given object until that object is attained. This process is the essence of invention, the highest and most useful form of labor. Without wings, claws for digging, or valuable weapons of offense and defense, man has had but one line of advance open to him, namely, invention, whereby he could overcome his limitations and master nature.

Ward overlooked what Veblen has called the instinct of workmanship.[20] Man has a desire to do, to achieve, to be active — only so can he escape the terrors of *ennui*. He secures illimitable enjoyment from seeing the crude materials of nature change under the manipulations of his hand and mind into works of art.

Nevertheless, the need of nutrition was probably the chief factor in the invention of tools and in the storing of food against the hungry day. These tools and stores constituted property. Property at once represented power. The law of acquisition soon exerted a great force. Intense rivalries in acquiring property developed. "The grand rivalry was for the object, not the method; for the end regardless of the

[17] *Ibid.*, I:474.
[18] *Ibid.*, I:486.
[19] *Pure Sociology*, p. 270; also *Dynamic Sociology*, II:541.
[20] See *The Instinct of Workmanship*.

means." [21] Through the centuries and until the present hour, the morality of obtaining wealth has rarely risen to the morality of many other phases of life.

SOCIAL DECEPTION

Deception early came into prominence. We deceive an animal in order to catch and domesticate or kill him. We deceive a fellow human being and take his hard-earned property away from him. Society has praised deception even when used by one individual against the welfare of his fellows. Society has honored him who could "drive a bargain."

Ward declared that the desire to acquire property regardless of the method is as strong as ever.[22] The only changes that have come are a mitigation of the harshness of the method and the rise of compulsory laws and codes which force individuals to "drive their bargains" and to practice their deceptions within prescribed limits. The acquisitive impulses have created major social evils, as evidenced by "the exceeding indigence of the poor and the exceeding opulence of the rich," and by a relatively large proportion of nonproducing rich people to the entire number of wealthy." [23] On the other hand, those who are poor because they are indolent are only a small proportion of those who are poor and industrious.

The evils of acquisitiveness cannot be overcome by softening the human heart. Ward would make it impossible for persons to take away the property of others by making it to the interest of all persons not to act in that way. And then he would teach them, through the social sciences, that such conduct is against their own highest development.

Ward pronounced the money-making tendency one of the most useful and at the same time "one of the coarsest and cheapest of all mental attributes."[24] It is useful because it is "the spur of all industry and commerce"; it provides the leisure which makes intellectual pursuits possible; it encourages exploration, discovery, and invention; it is the basis of

[21] *Dynamic Sociology*, I:497.
[22] *Ibid.*, I:516.
[23] *Ibid.*, I:517.
[24] *Ibid.*, I:520

all large business undertakings; and it has been an essential force in the development of civilization. Since civilization is so exclusively artificial, money can buy a vast variety of objects of human desire; hence, the possession of money is strenuously sought.[25]

On the other hand, money-making confers a pleasure which after all is sordid.[26] It often leads to avarice. It has produced a pecuniary inequality of mankind which socially admits of little justification. From a moral viewpoint the great struggle for pecuniary possession has been man's greatest curse.[27] Because of it, many infants have opened their eyes as millionaires in a world of boundless plenty; others (equally worthy) have opened their eyes as beggars in a world of abject poverty. It was Ward's belief that capitalism creates artificial inequalities, and that socialism creates artificial equality.

SOCIAL PARASITES

Society becomes divided into two main classes: the industrials and the non-industrials, or parasites. The non-industrials use their cunning in various ways.[28] The leading non-industrial modes of acquisition are these: robbery, theft, war, statecraft, priestcraft, and monopoly. This list represents the chronological order and history of non-industrial types of acquisition.

Robbery is the coarsest manner of acquisition. Theft represents the lowest order of cunning. Wars of conquest are robbery on so large a scale that they arouse group patriotism. Cunning and treachery in war have given way to strategy. Statecraft has often been characterized by the egoistic attempts of a few shrewd persons, who have devised means for supplying the wants of the many, and appropriated rich rewards for themselves from "the befriended and grateful community." Priestcraft as represented by many of the priests of Brahman, Buddha, Osiris, Ormuzd, Mohammed, and even of Jesus have developed successful modes of acquisition. They have often stood at the gates of death, and for

25 *Ibid.*, II:341.
26 *Ibid.*, I:520.
27 *Ibid.*, I:522.
28 *Ibid.*, I:579.

pay guaranteed to the stricken and fearful friends of a departed loved one a safe journey through the perils following death. Monopoly takes cunning advantage of a scarcity of the means of subsistence, or creates an artificial and false scarcity. Monopoly has organized the fields of transportation, exchange, finance, labor, manufacture.

The non-industrials co-operate better than the industrials. The latter, unfortunately, do not understand the principles of co-operation very well and do not have the intelligence to carry them into practical operation. They receive less education than the non-industrials; the years of their industrial apprenticeship are taken from their school days. After their apprenticeship begins, the fatigue of their labor gives them little time or energy for intellectual improvement. In pronouncing co-operation the product of superior intelligence Ward neglects the role played by the gregarious, parental, and related social impulses. Ward sees only part of the truth when he calls competition a natural law, and co-operation artificial. He wisely observes, however, that those who co-operate thrive at the expense of those who compete.[29] In the same way that individuals co-operate in order to secure their own gain, society must organize to secure the progress of all.

The second primary set of fundamental forces is the reproductive. These operate for the future and for the species. In animals they operate without arousing shame or modesty. Among human beings they are manipulated through the agencies of the reason and the imagination and give rise to the sentiments of shame and modesty.[30] They are so clouded in secrecy that they arouse dangerous forms of curiosity.

Among animals the choice of mates is largely determined by the females. In fact, among the lowest types of animals there are no males. Among certain higher forms of animal life the male appears as a mere adjunct. But among human beings, male sexual selection is developed. This change in sexual selection is one of the differences between the brute and the human worlds. This transition is explained by the fact that the higher a being rises in the scale of development

29 *Ibid.*, I:594.
30 *Ibid.*, I:606 ff.

the more sensitive its organism becomes, and by the correlated fact that the male human being through his reason is able to arouse and satisfy a thousand desires of the female, and thus cause her to look to him for "that protection and those favors which he alone can confer." [31]

FORMS OF LOVE

In the human world the reproductive forces have first produced a crude sexual love, animal in its nature, but far-reaching in its basic implications. Sexual love is an unconscious but dominant factor in courtship. In its refined form, and modified by the addition of genuine but often short-lived affective elements, it becomes romantic love. Romantic love, according to Ward, unfits lovers for the normal pursuits of life. While under its spell they are unable to enjoy anything but each other's presence. "The man is unfitted for business, the woman for social life, and both for intellectual pursuits. The only spur that can make either party pursue other things is the sense of doing something that the other desires." [32]

In the sense that natural, or sexual, love becomes the basis of romantic love, so romantic love in turn represents the genesis of a still higher form of love, namely, conjugal love. The love of a man for his wife or of a woman for her husband is, however, fundamentally different from romantic love. It is more stable, less disturbing to the normal processes of life, and makes the home and the family socially productive institutions. It often reaches a high state of refinement and develops its beauty of content from the sharing together by husband and wife of great joys and sorrows.

Maternal love, an outgrowth of maternity, manifests startling degrees of courage even among animals. Under the spur of the need for defending her young, a mother will often perform miraculous deeds. In its highest form maternal love manifests a remarkable strength throughout life and an extra-human power of forgiveness.

Then there is consanguineal love, which, according to

[31] *Ibid.*, I:615.
[32] *Pure Sociology*, p. 403.

Ward, includes paternal and fraternal affections. It becomes the blood bond or feeling of attachment that exists among the members of a primitive kinship group, and it leads to feelings of race and world solidarity and attachment.

Ward also pointed out that for each of these forms of love there is a correlative hate. This force of repulsion is often greater than the correlative love. Jealousy often leads to violent and destructive actions. Race hatred frequently becomes a vicious, brutal, and widespread sentiment that paralyzes all tendencies toward world progress.

Marriage institutions have developed from the operation of the reproductive forces. Polygamy, polyandry, and a score of other types of marriage have arisen, although monogamy has demonstrated itself to be the superior type of marriage institution.

SEX DIFFERENCES

The reproductive forces have led to numerous sexuo-social inequalities. Men and women have come to occupy separate spheres of activity, and to represent distinct social conditions.[33] Although the two sexes live together and appear to be companions, they are in fact dwelling in separate worlds and on different planes. There are several principal inequalities. (1) There is an inequality of dress, which has loaded woman with ornaments and caused her an enormous amount of disease and suffering. (2) There is an inequality of duties, which has kept woman confined to the house, and made a slave or a pampered pet of her. (3) There is an inequality of education. Society has shut woman, in the past, from all opportunities for gaining knowledge by experience. Moreover, society has seen fit in the past to debar women from the knowledge that is acquired by instruction. (4) There is an inequality of rights which has meant that women have been discriminated against before the law. Without direct representation in legislatures, women have suffered in proprietary matters. (5) There is a general sex inequality which has at times made woman the property or the slave of man. In short, women have been denied, until within recent years, entrance to the higher intellectual forms of activ-

[33] *Dynamic Sociology,* I:641.

ity, and at the same time have been denied social and political opportunities.

Reverting to Ward's classification of desires, we may now proceed to a discussion of the third set of forces, the sociogenetic. In contradistinction to the nutritive and the reproductive desires, or to the ontogenetic and the phylogenetic forces, respectively, the sociogenetic forces lead directly to race, or social, improvement. The ontogenetic forces guarantee individual preservation; the phylogenetic, race preservation; and the sociogenetic, race and social progress. Ward classified the sociogenetic forces as moral, esthetic, and intellectual.[34]

Morality is either racial or individual. Race morality is largely an outgrowth of custom. Duty, according to Ward, is conduct favorable to race safety, while virtue is "an attitude of life and character consistent with the preservation and continuance of man on earth."[35] Individual morality, on the other hand, is based on altruism. Altruism is the expenditure of energy by one person in behalf of other persons, and involves the power of representing the psychic states of others to one's self. Morality leads to humanitarianism, whose aim is meliorism. Meliorism aims to reorganize society so that the minimum pain and the maximum enjoyment may be insured. Meliorism is a non-sentimental improvement or amelioration of the human or social state.[36] Meliorism is a term invented by George Eliot, developed by Comte, accepted and made realistic by Ward.[37]

Ward holds that the esthetic forces consist of a desire for open or deep-seated symmetrical forms. Behind a landscape which at first appears irregular and jagged, there is a fundamental symmetry and balance. Sculpture, painting, and landscape-gardening are largely imitations of nature. Architecture, however, emphasizes straight lines, regular curves, and other symmetrical and geometrical figures.[38] Because of the invention of popular musical instruments, music is open to and enjoyed by the common people. No such invention,

[34] *Pure Sociology*, Ch. XV.
[35] *Ibid.*, p. 420.
[36] Ward, *Psychic Factors of Civilization*, Ch. XXXIV.
[37] F. S. Marvin, *Comte*, p. 125.
[38] *Dynamic Sociology*, I:669, 670.

unfortunately, has taken place in the fields of painting and sculpture. These realms are limited to the highest geniuses and "their choicest productions appropriated by the few who combine wealth with taste." [39]

INTELLECTUAL FORCES

The intellectual forces are chiefly the desires to know. These desires are threefold: (1) to acquire knowledge, (2) to discover truth, and (3) to impart information. [40] The desire to acquire knowledge is perhaps strongest in the young. Youth will often learn anything, without exercising any powers of discrimination. The gratification of the desire to discover new truths yields almost divine thrills of satisfaction. There are four methods of imparting information to others: (1) by conversing, (2) by teaching, (3) by lecturing, and (4) by writing.

In addition to the dynamic forces there is the directive agent in society, namely, the intellect. Ward makes a precarious distinction between the feelings and thought, or between intellect as a seat of emotion, appetite, and motive power, and intellect as the organ or source of thought and ideas. [41] Ward's psychology is admittedly unscientific. The thought or ideational phase of the intellect Ward divorced almost absolutely from the affective aspects of consciousness. He failed to perceive the dynamic character of thought and ideas.

In thought, Ward found the hope of the race. Thought can restrain and control social energy. It can produce telic methods of progress which are immeasurably superior to the blind, ruthless methods of nature. The procedure of nature with unlimited resources is "to produce an enormously redundant supply, and to trust the environment to select the best." [42] Nature secures success through "the indefinite multiplication of chances." Hence the survival of the fittest results in a sacrifice of a great majority—a highly wasteful method. The method of mind is the reverse. Through

[39] Ibid., I:673, 674.
[40] Pure Sociology, p. 438.
[41] Ibid., pp. 457 ff.
[42] Pure Sociology, p. 469.

prevision, mind utilizes all the dynamic forces of society, that is, the human desires, in constructive, orderly ways. Social waste may be reduced, by telic methods, to a minimum. Mind can perceive the best social ends and pursue them, whereas nature works blindly. Thought has in its power the possibility of subjugating natural forces and turning them into contributors to human needs. Education is the open sesame to progress.

SOCIAL DYNAMICS

Ward developed essentially four leading principles or social dynamics and hence of societal progress. (1) The first law he called *difference of potential*.[43] This term, which he borrowed from physics, refers to the difference in potential possibilities of individuals. This difference is manifested also, for example, in the crossing of cultures. It disturbs social stability, and creates social liability. Sex is a device whereby a difference of potential is maintained. While asexual reproduction is characterized chiefly by repetition of forms, sexual reproduction creates changes in the stock in countless directions. The difference of potential which is caused by a crossing of strains is highly dynamic, resulting in unnumbered variations, and hence in providing endless opportunities for progress. In a similar way a cross fertilization of cultures opens many opportunities for social advancement. "Progress results from the fusion of unlike elements."[44] Difference of potential, again, is illustrated in the friction of mind upon mind. Thoughts conflict, and the result is likely to be an invention.

Difference of potential may lead to creative synthesis.[45] When two elements are joined, the result is usually more than the sum of the parts. The combining of hydrogen and oxygen in given proportions produces water, which manifests characteristics that are not possessed by either of the constituents. Likewise, the combining of two ideas by the human mind may result in a new idea, and thus in progress.

[43] *Pure Sociology*, pp. 231 ff.
[44] *Ibid.*, p. 237.
[45] *Ibid.*, pp. 79 ff.

(2) A second dynamic principle is *innovation,* which has its biologic homologue in the sport, or mutant. Throughout nature and society, fortuitous variations occur. Life at times breaks over the bounds of pure heredity — the result is innovation. Variation, in the sense of mutation or innovation, appears to be due to the exuberance of life. At times nature appears to react against being bound by rigid laws of heredity, to defy her own rules, and to become rampant.

Social innovation is invention. New ideas often appear accidentally. The mind in its exuberance coins new phrases, catches new glimpses of reality, and creates ideas which are contrary to all that is established and supposedly true.

(3) Ward's third law of progress is called *conation.* This concept refers to social effort which is carried on naturally to satisfy desire, to preserve or continue life, to modify surroundings. In satisfying normally the gregarious desires, a person advances the cause of social progress. In preserving the life of the child, the mother presumably contributes to the welfare of the race. The sacrifices which parents make in behalf of children are efforts that further the welfare of society. Every constructive modification of either the physical or the spiritual environment benefits mankind. Conation is thus a term which covers a multitude of activities that are performed in the ordinary course of daily life, and which unconsciously to the doers are adding to the sum total of human welfare.

SOCIAL TELESIS

(4) The fourth dynamic principle which Ward described has already been discussed, namely, the principle of *social telesis.* The possibilities in social telesis are illimitable. Social telesis can turn the passions and desires of men into socially useful channels. These passions are bad only when directed to wrong ends. They are like fire — they can destroy or they can refine. If individuals as members of society could develop prevision and work together for societary ends, they would be able to transform the world.

Natural progress still leaves the world half-full of ignorance, poverty, and misery. Society must act intelligently in its own behalf. Millions are overworked and other millions are underworked.

GENIUS

Ward believed that greatness does not rest so much in intellectual power as in emotional force. He had great faith in persons of average intellectual ability who have initiative. It thus becomes the part of wisdom for society to educate wisely the average intelligence. Ward challenged the idea that only a few persons are geniuses and that these individuals, by virtue of their superior abilities, will uniformly overcome their environments. He held that genius is largely a matter of focalization of psychic energy, and that by this process all persons may have the honor of contributing something valuable to civilization.

Ward pointed out that geniuses are as likely to appear in one social stratum as in another, among the poor as among the wealthy, in the hovel as in the palace. He also demonstrated how society allows genius and talent to be ruthlessly destroyed among the lower classes through denial of opportunity. As a solution for this problem, Ward advocated social distribution, that is, the distribution of all useful knowledge to all humanity everywhere. A scientific system needs to be perfected in order to secure a better distribution of the great volume of valuable knowledge which has already been discovered. Ward was a strong advocate of the socialization of education.

In an article which appeared in the month following his death, Ward discussed his idea of social progress under the terms *eugenics, euthenics,* and *eudemics.*[46] He supplemented a theory of sound birth with a theory of sound environment. The practical result in society would be a state of eudemics, or a society of sound people.

Ward was an advocate of *sociocracy.* By sociocracy he did not mean a democracy or a rulership that is likely to be conducted selfishly by the individuals who exercise sovereign power. Sociocracy connotes a rulership of the people in

[46] Lester F. Ward, "Eugenics, Euthenics, and Eudemics," *American Journal of Sociology,* 18:737-54.

which each person is governed primarily not by his own interests but by the interests of society.

"Achievement" was a large concept in Ward's mind. He made achievement one of the chief goals of human life. By achievement in behalf of human progress a person may gain social immortality. The masses of humanity are achieving little or nothing in behalf of society.

In this treatment of Ward's sociological thought it has not been the aim of the writer to enter upon a dissertation regarding the abstract and philosophical implications that are involved in the subject matter. Neither has he attempted a polemic against the weaknesses in Ward's thinking except to note the defective monistic philosophy and the erroneous "faculty" psychology. It has been his purpose to let the strong, constructive elements in Ward's system of sociology speak clearly and effectively for themselves.[47]

GROUP DISCUSSION TOPICS

1. The uniqueness of L. F. Ward.
2. Ward's chief sociological works.
3. The dominant social thought contributed by Ward.
4. Ward's attitude toward the *laissez-faire* doctrine.
5. Ward's concept of "pure sociology."
6. Ward's distinctions between applied sociology and social reform.
7. Work as an "acquired characteristic."
8. Ward's estimate of money-making as a life occupation.
9. The chief characteristic of romantic love.
10. The source of the highest values of conjugal love.
11. The unique characteristic of maternal love.
12. The distinguishing phase of consanguineal love.
13. The major inequalities suffered by women.
14. The nature of duty and virtue.
15. The meaning of meliorism.
16. The leading intellectual desires.
17. The essence of creative synthesis.
18. Conation as a social-thought concept.
19. Ward's concept of "social telesis."
20. The main source of "greatness."

[47] The role that James Q. Dealey played in assisting to bring Lester F. Ward to Brown University to teach sociology is not to be overlooked. Likewise, Dealey rendered a fine service to college students when he condensed Ward's sociological ideas into a compact text — James Q. Dealey and Lester F. Ward. *A Textbook of Sociology*.

21. The relation of eugenics and euthenics to eudemics.
22. The difference between democracy and sociocracy.

READINGS

Barnes, Harry E., Editor, *An Introduction to the History of Sociology* (Chicago: University of Chicago Press 1948), Ch. 7.

Beach, Walter G., *The Growth of Social Thought* (New York: Charles Scribner's Sons 1939), Ch. XIII.

Bernard, L. L., "The Significance of Lester F. Ward," *Social Science*, XVI:372-381.

Bodenhafer, W. B., "The Comparative Role of the Group Concept in Ward's *Dynamic Sociology*" and "Contemporary American Sociology," *American Journal of Sociology*, 26: 273-314, 425-474, 588-600, 716-743.

Bristol, L. M., *Social Adaptation* (Cambridge, Massachusetts: Harvard University Press 1915), pp. 221-226.

Dealey, James Q., "Lester Frank Ward," in H. W. Odum, *American Masters of Social Science* (New York: Henry Holt and Company 1927), Ch. III.

Ellwood, Charles A., *A History of Social Philosophy* (New York: Prentice-Hall Company 1938) Ch. XXIX.

Fleming, James E., "The Role of Government in a Free Society: The Conception of Lester Frank Ward," *Social Forces*, 24: 257-266.

Lichtenberger, James P., *Theory of Social Development* (New York: Century Company 1923), Ch. XIII.

Mihanovich, C. S., *Social Theorists* (Milwaukee: The Bruce Publishing Company 1953), Ch. 5.

Ward, Lester F., *Dynamic Sociology* (New York: Appleton and Company 1911).

———, *Pure Sociology* (New York: The Macmillan Company 1914).

———, *Applied Sociology* (Boston: Ginn and Company 1906).

———, *Psychic Factors of Civilization* (Boston: Ginn and Company 1906).

———, "Eugenics, Euthenics, and Eudemics," *American Journal of Sociology*, 18:737-54.

Young Ward's Diary, edited by B. J. Stern (New York: G. P. Putnam's Sons 1935).

CHAPTER XXII

SUMNER AND CULTURAL SOCIAL THOUGHT

Additional light upon the nature of social thought may be secured by consulting the anthropologists, and particularly, the students of social origins. The last-mentioned group of scholars have been unusually successful in making valuable contributions to sociological thought, because they have used the psychological approach.

For more than a century the anthropologists have been searching for materials and advancing theories concerning the origin of man, of conflict and co-operative tendencies, and of the early ideas and institutions of the human race. They have been aided by the investigations of the geologists and especially of the paleontologists. The ethnographers and ethnologists have also discovered important data. The findings of all these groups of investigators, as far as they relate to the main thread of this book, will be here treated essentially as a unitary contribution. There is not space to deal specifically with the work of such anthropologists as Tylor, Morgan, Pitt-Rivers, Haddon, Frazer, and Keane. Certain of the ideas that have been advanced by Sumner, Westermarck, Hobhouse, Wundt, Boas, Elliott, Smith, Malinowski, Lowie, Kroeber, Goldenweiser, and Thomas will receive special attention, because they are unusually pertinent to the main theme of this volume. Cultural thought will be indicated here under several headings.

SOCIAL ORIGINS

1. There is common agreement among social anthropologists that man is the descendant of a branch of higher animal life, and that the creation of man took place by a slow, evolutionary process. The slowness of this development process does not necessarily lessen the mysterious or miraculous character of it. It places the origin of the human race at a much earlier date than was once supposed — perhaps from 200,000

to 500,000 years ago. The animal inheritance of man does not deny the correlative fact that man possesses spiritual qualities not common to the highest developed animals.[1]

Even the psychic equipment of man can be traced in its origin to the primates with their individual and social behavior traits. The instinctive bases of human conduct are hundreds of thousands of years old. They are so intrinsically a part of human nature that no discussion of current social problems will neglect the imperiousness of the ancient instinct heritage of the human race.

2. There is extensive anthropologic evidence that mankind had a common origin. Many authorities hold to the polygenetic origin of man. Be that as it may, the remains of the earliest human beings are found in regions extending from Java, through India, to England. The Gobi Desert to the northeast and the Nile Valley to the southwest have been claimed as the original centers of the race. From the earliest centers man seems to have migrated in various directions, and finally to the Western Hemisphere. Different climatic and environmental conditions affected the migrating groups in different ways. Those who migrated into the tropical regions were retarded because of the enervating climatic factors. Those who reached the frigid zone were also retarded, or subjected to recidivism for a different reason — a harshness of living conditions and an excess of environmental obstacles. The north temperate zone with its fertile lands and its invigorating climate afforded the proper *milieu* for the development of the race.

3. An important question relates to the alleged potential equality of all races. If a common origin of races is accepted, the question remains open whether, for example, the African races possess the same innate mental abilities as do the Caucasian races. The controversy here is sharply drawn between the environmentalists and the eugenicists. Each side of the debate has collected a large body of evidence. In reality, the question apparently boils down to this: Have the many centuries of living under the enervating torrid zone conditions affected the African races so deeply that under favorable cultural circumstances they have become incapable of develop-

[1] H. F. Osborn, *Men of the Old Stone Age,* Chapter I.

ing beyond a certain mental level which is lower than that attained by the Caucasian races? In the past the answer to this question has been affirmative. The bulk of the evidence that has been collected in recent years indicates that the affirmative answer is incorrect.

4. It is becoming clear that every race is a composite of several races. Ethnological data show that the three grand divisions of the human race [2] may be subdivided into racial stocks, and into races and subraces, until more than 600 races or subraces may be described; and furthermore, that each of the 600 or more races represents an amalgamation of other races. It is evident that no clear line of racial demarcation can be drawn, and that purity of race may be a fictitious term.

RACIAL INTERMARRIAGE

5. Intermarriage of the representatives of races belonging to similar racial stocks seems advisable — according to the ethnologist. Pure bloods apparently die out. The strongest races today are those in which amalgamation has taken place recently — that is, within one thousand or two thousand years, for example, the English, or the Scotch-Irish.

A mooted question of world importance relates to the intermarriage of the representatives of races widely different, such as the white and the yellow races, or the white and the black races. The development of races out of such combinations is now in process, as in Brazil. Race prejudices and social distinctions, however, have been deterring factors nearly everywhere. Very few scientific data are available regarding miscegenation of this type.

Apparently, the interbreeding of whites and blacks leads ultimately to the elimination of the racial characteristics of the blacks and to the complete dominance of the whites. There are some writers who assert that this process takes place to the gain of the lower race and to the loss of the higher race, but the last-mentioned point has not yet been proved. Miscegenation between whites and blacks usually occurs under such abnormal and vicious social conditions that the racial tendencies are definitely obscured.

[2] Caucasoid. Mongoloid, and Negroid.

At this point the problem of "disharmonic" types may be mentioned. The Cro-Magnon type is illustrative, for in this connection a dolichocephalic skull is combined with very broad check-bones.[3] Mental traits may also be crossed in a similar disharmonic fashion. Intermarriage of widely different racial types may produce not only disharmonic physiques but also disharmonic mental types — the latter in particular may mean race inferiority. At any rate the problem is one still subject to research.

6. Conflict between races is primordial; conflict between races today is illustrated in national wars and race persecutions. Weaker races have often combined against a stronger race; from these experiences there has come a growing sense of the value of co-operation. Nations with high moral principles have united against a powerful neighbor nation with bullying tendencies. Out of these temporary combinations there has arisen a sense of need for permanent forms of national co-operation. This common need will ultimately lead, undoubtedly, to a permanent association of nations.

The conflict between the grand divisions of the human race will probably continue for a long time to come. Sometimes it is concentrated in an antagonism between the white and yellow races; and again, it is expressed in the more fundamental struggle between Occidentalism and Orientalism.

7. The origin and development of primitive ways of doing constitute a well-cultivated field of study. Anthropologists have published an endless amount of materials on the origins of languages, religions, occupations, sex distinctions. A portion of this work has been done without an accurate understanding of the psychological principles that are involved, and hence has to be viewed with caution or neglected entirely.

FOLKWAYS

W. G. Sumner, whose argument in favor of individualism and of a *laissez-faire* governmental policy was given in Chapter XIV, published in his *Folkways* a minute and extended account of primitive institutions. In the development of

---

[3] R. Verneau, "La race de Cro-Magnon," *Review Anthropologie*, I:10 ff.

his theories, Sumner began with the needs of primitive peoples and with the attempts to meet these needs. Repetition of these acts leads to established ways of doing, that is, to folkways. Folkways are "the widest, most fundamental, and most important operation by which the interests of men in groups are served."[4]

The way in which folkways spread in influence and became powerful is evolutionary. Small beginnings have mighty culminations. Folkways are at first isolated social phenomena, but without human planning they may become all-powerful. The lower or earlier layers are especially enduring. Only the recent folkways can be changed easily.

The origins of folkways are unknown. They are coming into being now as well as in prehistoric times. Their origins now as earlier are by unconscious means. No great changes in the origins process have occurred through the centuries.

Societal life consists chiefly in making folkways and applying them. Even the science of society might be defined as the study of folkways. Folkways are the product of the trial-and-failure method of meeting needs. They tend to become firmly established and to be passed on from generation to generation. They become traditional. They acquire all the authority which is attached to the memory of respected ancestors. Even the ghosts of ancestors stalk the earth keeping guard over the folkways. The folkways carry with them the conviction that they are essential to human welfare. It is this conviction which gives them the force of *mores*. Thus the folkways are not purposeful methods of securing progress but unconscious ways of meeting current exigencies; they are blindly and rigorously forced upon successive generations.

8. Races are guilty of *ethnocentrism*.[5] Each race considers itself the center of mankind. It judges all other races by its own standards, and not by a higher standard than is determined by data that are representative of the best interests of all races. Ethnocentrism compels each race to exaggerate the importance of its own folkways and to depreciate the folkways of other races. For example, the Romans and

[4] W. G. Sumner, *Folkways*, p. 43.
[5] *Ibid.*, p. 13.

Greeks called all outsiders "barbarians." The Jews considered themselves "the chosen people" and the Romans and
Greeks as "pagans."

Nietzsche's ideas give a basis for thinking in terms of Nordic superiority. However, it was De Gobineau (1816–1882)
who laid the foundations for the doctrine of Aryan and Nordic superiority. He was a literary and historical writer,
whose observations in several countries led him to write an
Essay upon the Inequality of the Human Races (1855). He
started with the hypothesis that the racial question is the
most important one in history. He constructs a thorough-
going doctrine of racial determinism. To him the Aryan
race alone has developed a civilization, and culture is the
product of race. Civilization and culture are determined by
the nerve structure of people. Heredity is the key to social
advancement. The Aryans must keep themselves "pure,"
because admixtures of race always produce degeneracy. He
attributed reason, beauty, and energy to the white race, mediocrity to the yellow race, and passion to the black race; he
put the Germans at the pinnacle of the white race. His ideas
were elaborated upon and popularized in Germany by H. S.
Chamberlain. His position is scientifically untenable. All
races show possibilities of developing a civilization and a culture. Moreover, these characteristics are not alone dependent on social heredity, but also upon learning and opportunity.

In the United States the theory of race superiority has been
advocated by R. M. East, and others. While they have
brought pertinent data to the contentions of a writer like De
Gobineau, they too have increased the feelings of racial prejudice and of race intolerance without scientific justification.
After all, race antagonism has its justification only in personal
aggressiveness and obtrusiveness, in injustices, in destructive
competition on the part of the members of a given race. But
these procedures are not limited to nor characteristic of any
one race.

FOUR BASIC MOTIVES

9. Sumner divided the chief motives of human action into
four classes: hunger, sex passion, vanity, and fear (of ghosts

and spirits). These are considered by Sumner as the basic social forces. Their origins go back a long way in organic history. Out of these motives arise folkways by a process which runs as follows: "It is now the accepted opinion, and it may be correct, that men inherited from their beast ancestors psychophysical traits, instincts, and dexterities, or at least predispositions, which give them aid in solving the problems of food supply, sex commerce, and vanity. The result is mass phenomena; currents of similarity, concurrence, and mutual contribution; and these produce folkways." [6]

Connected with these motives are sets of interests. (1) Hunger led primitive man to invent simple weapons and tools, such as arrows and hoes, and then to produce and hoard more complex forms of wealth. A strange peculiarity of wealth is its effect on its creator; it seems to be stronger than its creator. It often bears him down to a slavish, materialistic, and even self-centered existence. Labor in the struggle for existence is irksome and painful. Wealth and labor, however, are both commendatory when they are used to increase human welfare. In this statement Sumner overlooked the fact that wealth in order to be wholly commendable must also be produced under constructively social conditions, and that labor in order to be praiseworthy must in its exercise be individually helpful. In other words, Sumner's test of the use to which wealth and labor are put is incomplete.

Sumner gave a new meaning to the term slavery. He held that "men of talent are constantly forced to serve the rest. They make the discoveries and inventions, order the battles, write the books, and produce the art." [7] Sumner deplored the tendency to call whatever one does not like by the name of slavery. He felt that marriage slavery, rent slavery, sin slavery, are terms which are coined by a too easily disgruntled people.

(2) The sex passion leads to sex *mores* which cover the relations of men and women to each other before marriage and in marriage, and the obligations of married persons to society. The sex *mores* determine the nature of marriage

[6] *Ibid.*, pp. 18, 19.
[7] *Ibid.*, p. 266.

and of divorce. Sumner derided sex equality. Man has a more stable nervous system than woman, is more self-absorbed, more egoistic, less tactful. Since man has greater physical strength than woman, woman was educated by circumstances in primitive days to adapt herself to the stronger sex, and to win by developing charms where her lack of comparative strength rendered her helpless. Resignation and endurance thus became acquired traits of women.

Neither renunciation nor license is the proper method of control of the sex passions. Both produce unnecessary agony. License, for example, "stimulates desire without limit, and ends in impotent agony." Sumner advocated temperance and regulation — a regulation which comes from knowledge and judgment.

Women by necessity must bear an unequal share in the responsibilities of sex and reproduction. Likewise, men must bear an unequal share of the responsibilities of property, war, and politics. For the latter types of duties women are hampered by a delicately adjusted and cumbersome generative system which men do not possess.[8]

Formerly women yielded to the will of men. Today, according to Sumner, the marital state is one of endless discussion, sometimes a defeat for one party or the other, with unpleasant effects upon life and character. In ancient times women took pride in the supervision which their husbands exercised over them and valued themselves as hidden treasures.[9] This protected position was considered aristocratic. Under polygamy, women looked with pity and disgust upon the man who cannot, or is unwilling to, support more than one wife.

At this point it is interesting to note that W. I. Thomas has distinguished between the sexes on the basis of differences in metabolism — men being katabolic and women anabolic. Man consumes more energy than woman.[10] He is better fitted for bursts of energy, while woman possesses more endurance. Man's structural variability is toward motion; woman's toward reproduction. Hence, man seems to have

[8] *Ibid.*, pp. 343, 362.
[9] *Ibid.*, p. 378.
[10] W. I. Thomas, *Sex and Society,* p. 51.

been assigned in primitive society to tasks requiring violence and exertion, whereas to women fell the work requiring constant attention.

Civilization thus far has largely profited by the intelligence of man. If to this situation it will develop and add the intelligence of woman, it will be supplanted by a higher type of civilization. Under these conditions a large percentage of marriages will represent "the true comradeship of like minds," instead of being frequently an arrangement in which woman is treated as a pet.

(3) The motive of vanity is all-powerful. "One likes to be separated from the crowd by what is admired, and dislikes to be distinguished for what is not admired." [11] To satisfy vanity, barbarian mothers "deform their babies toward an adopted type of bodily perfection." Aristocracies grow up out of appeals to vanity. An aristocracy is a group of persons, closely united, who deify the possession of things for which they are admired and which the masses do not possess. Vanity leads to all types of absurdities and indecencies in dress. Teeth are knocked out for the sake of appeasing vanity. An Indian woman puts a board on the forehead of her baby to make the forehead recede.

(4) Fear as a motive rules the lives of primitives. Fear of ghosts and spirits is peculiarly enslaving. Pestilence, defeat in war, bodily pain were all considered the result of the wrath of the gods.

The mass phenomena of fear are especially pitiful. Manias of various types rule whole masses. Witchcraft thrived for centuries on the strength of fear. Pilgrimages and crusades were partly due to fear; demonism was a product of fear. When fear became firmly established in the folkways, it acted as an ever-ruling tyrant. In the *mores* it became firmly entrenched and was a leading factor in molding character. Through religious practices and dogmas it defined a "hell" and ruled with a fearful hand.

10. Upon simplest analyses, according to Sumner, four societal values stand out with clearness: intellectual, moral, economic, and physical.[12] Each of these, however, is com-

---

[11] W. G. Sumner, *op. cit.*, p. 182.
[12] *Ibid.*, p. 41.

posite. The highest societal value seems to result from a harmonious combination of the four values enumerated. The best member of society is he in whom the intellectual, moral, economic, and physical values are more or less equally and harmoniously represented.

SOCIAL CLASSES

11. Sumner divided society into five main classes :[13] (1) The masses represent social mediocrity. They are of average social usefulness. (2) Then there are the dependent and defective classes — a drag upon society but not harmful or vicious. (3) The delinquent classes are grossly harmful. They are antisocial and a grievous burden. (4) Above the masses there are the people of talent, and (5) above the talented are the geniuses. "A man of talent, practical sense, industry, perseverance, and moral principle is worth more to society than a genius who is not morally responsible, or not industrious." [14]

It is a mistake to think of the masses as being at the base of society; they are located at the core. They are traditional, conservative, and the bearers of the *mores*. The lowest sections of the masses are a dead weight of ignorance, disease, and crime.

12. A social institution is composed of an idea, notion, or interest, and a resultant structure. The primary institutions are property, marriage, and religion.[15] These began as folkways; they became customs. Social institutions can be modified only when the *mores* are changed; they develop rituals which are ceremonious, solemn, and strongest when perfunctory and when exciting no thought.[16]

Sumner boldly asserted that nothing but might has ever made right, and that nothing but might makes right now.[17] The fact that property began in force is not proof that property is a unjust institution. Marriage and religion also began in force, but the element of justice in the existence of

13 *Ibid.*, p. 40.
14 *Ibid.*, p. 41.
15 *Ibid.*, p. 54.
16 *Ibid.*, p. 61.
17 *Ibid.*, p. 65.

these institutions is not seriously questioned today. Sumner, however, did not discriminate between force as an agent or a tool, and force as a primary cause. He did not distinguish clearly between hate and love as the dynamic factors behind action that is decisive. He did not set forth the distinction between harsh, material, immutable force, and a kindly, spiritual, attracting love.

MORES

13. The persistency of folkways and *mores* is illustrated in a thousand ways by Sumner. He described (1) their slow variability under changed life conditions, (2) their sudden variability under revolutionary conditions, (3) the possibility of changing them by intelligent action, (4) the problems involved in adjusting one's self to the *mores* of another group, and (5) the conflicts between the *mores* of different groups.[18]

Folkways, and even more the *mores,* give or take away status. Persons value their status highly and hence are controlled by those influential folkways known as *mores.*

The *mores* are powerful engines of societal selection. The most important fact about the *mores* is the power which they exert over the individual. He does not know their source. He is born into them. He accepts them in his early years uncritically. His habits and character are molded by them. If in adult life he challenges them, he is ostracized by his group, labeled unpatriotic, and even trodden under foot.[19] The *mores* develop powerful watchwords, slogans, and even epithets of contempt and disapproval which only the most independent and courageous individuals dare to face.

14. Ideals are entirely unscientific, declared Sumner.[20] They are phantasies little connected with fact. They are often formed to pacify the restless, or to escape settling a question justly in the present. The "poor" are told to look to the next life for their rewards. The radicals are urged to accept the Christian virtues of meekness and lowliness. Ideals are useful, chiefly, in homiletics, in self-education *via*

18 *Ibid.,* Ch. II.
19 *Ibid.,* p. 76.
20 *Ibid.,* p. 201.

auto-suggestion, in satisfying vanity, in marriage. In these observations, Sumner undoubtedly pointed out genuine weaknesses in ideals. He underestimated the psychological fact that they spring from the very real affective phases of consciousness, and that they can be projected rationally. He was right, however, in deploring the chasm which exists between ideals and practices, and in showing how ideals may become encysted in literature although not in the *mores*. "The Greeks proved that people could sink very low while talking very nobly."

Immorality is conduct contrary to the *mores* of the time and place.[21] Chastity is conformity to the current taboo on the sex relation. "Modesty is reserve of behavior and sentiment." Even "nakedness is never shameful when it is unconscious," that is, when there is no consciousness of a difference between fact and the rule set by the *mores*.

Summer deduced an important principle when he asserted that the "*mores* can make anything right." The *mores* give usages a certain order and form, and cover them with a protecting mantle of propriety. The sanction of the *mores* is utilized by the class in power in order to maintain the established regime, even though it be one of injustice.

Sumner decried the importance which is ordinarily attached to book learning,[22] because it is addressed to the intellect rather than to the feelings which are the springs of action. The real education is that which comes through personal influence and example. It is derived from "the habits and atmosphere of a school, not from the school textbooks."

15. Despite Sumner's failure to appreciate the significance of a thoroughgoing psychological approach to an analysis of folkways, his description of these societal phenomena constitutes a unique and valuable contribution to social thought. Sumner's rigorous attitude toward social life did not permit him to enter into an extensive interpretation of the folkways in the light of folk ideals. He dealt with what *is* to the exclusion of what *ought to be*. He saw the past so clearly, and the present so much as a reflection of the past, that no enheartening forward look was possible. He rested his the-

---

21 *Ibid.*, p. 418; *cf.* W. I. Thomas, *Sex and Society*, pp. 201-220.
22 *Ibid.*, p. 629.

ories on the inexorable work of the laws of biological evolution, modified chiefly by his belief in a strong individualism.
Sumner's fundamental theses have been developed and modified by A. G. Keller, who has projected the Darwinian principles of variation, selection, transmission, and adaptation into societal concepts. In fact, he has done this so well that he has given the Darwinian principles full sway, not allowing sufficiently for the rise and operation of complex psychic principles. He has made the folkways the connecting link between organic and societal evolution, but has not noted fully the new, countless, and often intangible but powerful factors by which societal evolution is characterized.[23]

16. The role that concepts of conduct have played in the evolution of society has been analyzed by E. A. Westermarck and L. T. Hobhouse. The former is usually known as an anthropologist, and the latter as a sociologist. Westermarck has shown that, strictly speaking, a custom is not merely the habit of a certain group of people ; it also involves a rule of conduct.[24] It possesses two characteristics — habitualness and obligatoriness.

Not every public habit, however, is a custom involving an obligation.[25] There may be certain practices which are more or less common in society, but which at the same time are generally condemned. The disapproval of these is as a rule not very deep nor genuine.

Dr. Westermarck has indicated that there is a close similarity between the conscience of a community and that of a person.[26] If a group commits a sin twice, it is likely to be considered allowable. In order to get at the real nature of societal life, the "bad habits" as well as the professed opinions of groups must be examined.

"Society," says Dr. Westermarck, "is the birthplace of the moral consciousness."[7] Emotions which are felt by the community at large tend to take the form of conduct standards.

[23] A. G. Keller, *Societal Evolution,* and *Man's Rough Road.*
[24] Edward Westermarck, *The Origin and Development of the Moral Ideas,* I:159.
[25] *Loc. cit.*
[26] *Ibid.,* I:160.
[27] *Ibid.,* II:740.

The moral emotions lead to a variety of moral concepts. These fall into two main classes: concepts of disapproval, such as bad, vice, wrong; and concepts of approval, such as good, virtue, and merit.

Westermarck is convinced of the tremendous influence that religious beliefs have exerted upon the moral ideas of mankind.[28] This influence has been exceedingly varied. Religion has taught the principles of love and yet has indulged in cruel persecutions. It has condemned murder and yet been a party to child sacrifice. "It has emphasized the duty of truth-speaking, and has itself been a cause of pious fraud." Professor Westermarck has contributed to social thought not only in his valuable descriptions of the rise and evolution of moral ideas, but also in his *History of Human Marriage,* to which reference will be made later.

FOLK PSYCHOLOGY

17. In applying the principles of folk psychology to the anthropologic field, William Wundt has developed a new method and new theories. Folk psychology is the study of "the relations which the intellectual, moral, and other mental characteristics of peoples sustain to one another."[29] The term was originated by Lazarus and Steinthal, whose works will be referred to again in Chapter XXVI. In the masterpiece on the *Elements of Folk Psychology,* Wundt has given a psychological description of the main processes and institutions in society, tracing them from their beginnings in the processes of nature; he has made a survey of human progress. His study opens with a discussion of the processes which produced the digging stick, the club, and the hammer; it ends with an analysis of world empire, world culture, world religions, and world history. The intervening ages are the totemic and the age of heroes and gods.[30]

World empire affected primarily the material aspects of the life of peoples. It led to world intercourse, which in turn multiplied the needs of peoples. These multiplied needs were followed by exchanges of the means of satisfying

28 *Ibid.,* II:745.
29 William Wundt, *Elements of Folk Psychology,* p. 1.
30 *Ibid.,* p. 478.

the needs. The external and material phases of culture are survived by the spiritual phases — thus world culture is a sequence of world empire. It may be said that the vicissitudes of peoples under the rule of the world empire idea brings forth a unified history. World culture in turn creates a common mental heritage of mankind.[31]

In the establishment of a world culture, world religions are the leading forces. They have been foremost in creating the idea of a universal human community. In particular, Christianity is based on a belief in a God who makes no distinction between race or class or occupation. Consequently, "it has regarded missionary activity among heathen peoples as a task whose purpose it is finally to unite the whole of mankind beneath the cross of Christ." [32]

For a long time in human history, religious development was considered to be the main connecting link — such was the contention of St. Augustine. In 1725, Vico argued that the development of language and jurisprudence is of universal import.[33] Finally, world history has become a description of the mental life of peoples, "a psychological account of the development of mankind."

ORIGINAL ABILITY

18. The work of Professor Wundt is similar in many ways, though characterized by a distinctive starting point and by many differences to the contributions of Franz Boas and W. I. Thomas. Professor Boas has declared his belief in man's ability to dominate the laws of organic evolution as expressed in human life. He has brought forward a large amount of evidence in support of the theory that environment has caused differences between races. He has pointed out that race prejudice is largely a product of social environment, and that under changed conditions of life it has little place in the world. Boas is a strong advocate of the theory, already advanced in this chapter, that all races are potentially equal in ability, and that they would demonstrate the truth of this

31 *Ibid.*, p. 514.
32 *Ibid.*, p. 515.
33 *Ibid.*, p. 516.

statement if given a common cultural background and social opportunities. He has advanced the idea that "the organization of mind is practically identical among all races of men." [34]

Hobhouse declared: "While race has been relatively stagnant, society has rapidly developed." Moreover, social progress is determined not by alterations of racial type, but by modifications of social cultures.[35] These modifications are caused primarily by the interactions of social factors.

CULTURE

19. The growth of culture concepts has been rapid. Clark Wissler has done as much as anyone to clarify and standardize meanings.[36] With "culture" as a general term referring to all the ways of doing and thinking of a social group, the term *culture trait* is used to denote a given set of group ways, such as raising maize.

A culture complex, it follows, includes all the sets of group ways that are tied up with any particular culture trait. The raising of maize, for instance, involves ways of soil tillage, of harvesting, of exchange, of food preparation — the whole thing is a culture complex.

Culture traits move; they are diffused. Culture diffusion takes place in both undirected and purposeful ways. In the first instance, persons who migrate carry culture traits into new parts of the earth. In the second case, proselytism, colonization, and conquest account for directed culture diffusion.[37]

There is a universal culture pattern, common to mankind. Wissler finds nine heads or phases to this universal culture pattern, namely, speech, art, religion, property, government, war, mythology, and scientific knowledge, social systems, and material traits (food, clothing, shelter, and occupation habits). All tribes and races possess speech patterns, art patterns, and so forth.

[34] Franz Boas, *The Mind of Primitive Man.*
[35] L. T. Hobhouse, *Social Evolution and Political Theory*, p. 39.
[36] Clark Wissler, *Man and Culture; The American Indian,* and other writings.
[37] Clark Wissler, *Man and Culture*, p. 129.

W. I. THOMAS

20. Noteworthy pioneering in the field of social anthropology and social origins has been done by W. I. Thomas in terms of "crises," "attention," and "control." He has developed the theory that progress results from "crises." [38] As long as life runs along smoothly, a lack of interest is likely to ensue. The result is *ennui*. But a crisis in any of the life processes arouses the attention, that is, produces a concentration of psychic energy. A disturbance of any habit is a crisis. When the exigencies of the crisis are solved through a focalization of consciousness, the situation is said to be controlled by the person, who again lapses into a state of disinterestedness until another disturbance of habit occurs. The new method of control will be imitated. If imitated widely, it will mark a rise in the level of civilization.

It will be observed at once that the power of attention to meet crises is largely an individual matter and that the role of the person is very important. The group level of culture limits the power of the mind to meet crises and to make adjustments. [39] The mind is limited by the psychic fund which the group already possesses. If there is no knowledge of mathematics in the group, then a large banking system is impossible. Crises, attention, control — these are the three leading concepts in Thomas' theory of social origins.

Control is the object of all purposeful activity. [40] It is the end, and attention is the means. An animal differs from a plant in that it has a superior control over a larger environment than does the plant. "It does not wait for food, but goes after it." Man differs from an animal partly in the fact that his fore limbs are free to secure new and varied forms of control. Moreover, man through his mind has a superior instrument of control. By the use of knowledge, mind is effective in controlling factors that are present in neither time nor space. Through its inventions, such as language, religious creeds, mechanical appliances, forms of government, man has risen to what is called civilization.

The main human problem, according to W. I. Thomas, is

[38] W. I. Thomas, *Source Book for Social Origins*, p. 18.
[39] *Ibid.*, p. 20.
[40] *Ibid.*, p. 14.

"one of adjustment, and the forms of adjustive effort are 'behavior.'" In this concept, attitudes and values reflect the personality of the individual and are the result of "a process of conditioning by the influences of the cultural milieu, eventuating in a body of habits." [41]

Adjustment thus becomes both an individual and a group matter, and its scientific study takes into consideration five sets of data: (1) the cultural situations in which individuals must make adjustments. (2) The means, such as social organization and education, by which individuals are adjusted to the cultural situations. (3) The inherited factors and the incentives provided through incentives and status for the adjustment of the individual. (4) The "failure of adaptation" as found in dependency, crime, and so on for the individual, and in decline and subjection for the group. (5) The external changes in the culture situations due to population movements, technological developments, and rise of prejudices. [42]

A logical and succinct analysis of cultural evolution has been given by Charles A. Ellwood. Civilization is the result of active adaptation and intercommunication. The four steps in the cultural process, according to Professor Ellwood, are: (1) usually an exceptional individual by the use of his imagination and reasoning, and under the stress of a crisis, takes the available materials and patterns and creates a new pattern of action. (2) By imitation and communication this new pattern spreads. (3) This pattern becomes embodied in the customs and traditions of the group. (4) The young are taught the new pattern as a part of the traditions. [43]

Another noteworthy treatment of cultural evolution has been offered by F. Stuart Chapin, who speaks of a threefold societal reaction: (1) the group reacts to enforce its mores, but failing, (2) it tries out different expedients, and (3) integrates its trial-and-error efforts into a new pattern of activity. The fundamental processes of cultural change are given as (1) invention, (2) accumulation, (3) selection, and (4) diffusion. [44]

41 W. I. Thomas, *Primitive Behavior,* p. 1.
42 *Ibid.,* pp. 1-2.
43 Charles A. Ellwood, *Cultural Evolution,* Chapters I-IV.
44 F. Stuart Chapin, *Cultural Change,* Part III.

W. I. Thomas summarizes three points of view that have been accepted concerning cultural evolution as follows: (1) cultural evolution emerges and proceeds in "a regular order and invariable unilinear sequence." (2) "The higher cultures are the result of superior inborn mental endowment in the racial divisions which they represent." (3) Cultural progress is due to "more or less favorable geographic positions and economic conditions. This point of view has recently been challenged by Professor S. D. Porteus. As a result of studies in Central Australia, of the Bushmen in Africa, and of other primitive peoples, Dr. Porteus finds by the use of especially devised psychological tests that in some important instances primitive people with a less favorable environment than that possessed by other primitive peoples show superior development.[45]

On the other hand, Thomas advances a threefold explanation of cultural evolution in terms of experiences and resultant habits and culture areas. He argues: (1) "that diversities in behavior and culture are the result of different interpretations of experience, resulting in characteristic behavior reactions and habit systems, and that a uniform course of cultural and behavior evaluation is consequently out of the question."[46] It is the culture area rather than the natural environment that is important. Thomas holds that the theory of differences in "degrees of mental endowment among races" has not been sustained.[47]

CIVILIZATION

21. "Civilization" is a living, tangible thing—a psychical phenomenon that dominates. When an individual arrives at self-consciousness, he finds himself fitted with complete culture paraphernalia. By invention, he may add to civilization, but the new that he may contribute "is never more than a slight ripple on the deep foundation of the old and established."[48]

[45] S. D. Porteus, *Primitive Intelligence and Environment,* pp. 310 ff.
[46] W. I. Thomas, *op. cit.,* p. 7.
[47] *Loc. cit.*
[48] A. A. Goldenweiser, *Early Civilization,* p. 15.

Civilization as a high level of culture, one in which human welfare receives attention on a large scale, is subject to changes. Improvements come as emanations of human minds.

Civilization has marvelous staying power. It persists in and through institutions. Education passes it along from generation to generation. Civilization receives new ideas reluctantly. A great deal of it is dead weight. It is highly conservative. It even determines the nature of the inventions and new ideas that are possible at any given time.

Civilization does not necessarily develop in one race rather than in another. It does not tie itself up with one part of the Caucasian division of the human race. Not the Nordic but the Mediterranean peoples have made the largest contribution to mankind, according to Kroeber. Any one of the present races could drop out of existence and civilization would not necessarily die. Some other race or races would pick up the scepter and "carry on."

"Pre-literate," a term suggested by Ellsworth Faris, has been coming into use in referring to early peoples. "It is neutral, connoting no reflection of inferiority." [49] It is also objective and descriptive. It is far better than "savages," and possibly superior to primitive. Although pre-literate people have not achieved a civilization, they possess cultures that are both complex and comprehensive. They are quite capable of developing a civilization if given favorable environments.

CULTURAL LAG

22. Cultural lag is a concept that has been used extensively in recent years. W. F. Ogburn pointed out that some phases of culture do not change so fast as do others, and hence they "lag." This tendency is particularly true in modern times or in periods of rapid change and growth. Since the "various parts of modern culture are not changing at the same rate," hence adjustments are continually necessary. "A change in industry makes adjustments necessary through changes in the educational system." During the period of

[49] Ellsworth Faris, *The Nature of Human Nature*, Chapter XXIII.

lag of one part of a culture, a maladjustment is said to exist.[50]

The changes in culture which come about in order to make the necessary adjustments are referred to as "adaptive culture." [51] When the cutting down of trees is speeded up to meet modern pulp and paper needs, soil erosion occurs. The conservation measures, as finally adopted, are called *adaptive culture*. As a rule, changes in material culture precede adaptive culture. It is conceivable, however, that under careful social planning, an adaptive culture could be developed and put into effect as soon as changes occur in material culture, and thus a period of maladjustment could be avoided entirely.

W. D. Wallis contends that lag "is almost ubiquitous and moreover, works both ways." Not only does it occur in times of great change but at other times as well. Much depends on what basic factor as the unit of comparison is chosen. "When values are involved, the character of the lag is determined by the observer's standpoint." [52] Or, as Lewis Mumford has shown, the ethics of Confucius lags behind modern warfare; but, on the other hand, it may be that modern warfare represents a backward tendency and that it actually lags behind the ethics of Confucius.[53] Likewise, modern machine production may represent a lag behind the welfare ideas of Mo Ti or a Jesus.

23. "Is a cultural sociology possible?" is a question raised by Theodore Abel. He summarizes the theses of cultural sociology as follows:

1. Sociology is the study of culture.
2. Human behavior must be interpreted in terms of culture.
3. Culture is super-individual.
4. Cultural phenomena are explained if they are adequately described.

Abel criticizes these positions, arguing that each is untenable on the grounds that "the cultural approach does not lead to an adequate understanding and explanation of human be-

[50] W. F. Ogburn, *Social Change*, pp. 220 ff.
[51] *Loc. cit.*
[52] W. D. Wallis, "The Concept of Lag," *Sociology and Social Research*, 19:403-05.
[53] Lewis Mumford, *Technics and Civilization*, p. 317.

havior." His belief is that behavior cannot be understood by a study of cultural facts, but only through a consideration of social processes and relations.[54] Floyd Allport likewise attacks the culture concept. Culture is something which can be described, but people and culture can be understood only when analyzed by the psychologist.[55] Willey has responded that the purely psychological explanation at times offers little aid. Often the psychological analysis is "possible only after the cultural explanation has been given." [56] In one of his last talks, Charles H. Cooley came valiantly to the support of culture study by showing how Sumner's *Folkways* is still one of the outstanding books in sociology despite the fact that it does "not conform to any of the current courses of methodology." [57]

MEASURING CULTURAL CHANGE

24. Can cultural change be measured? F. S. Chapin has suggested the concept of "cultural threshold" as a means of measuring changes in culture. When the cultural lags between different elements necessary to an invention are reduced to a minimum, all enter a zone of potential integration. The "threshold" is low. Another concept for measuring cultural change is "cultural horizon," by which Professor Chapin means that "the process of invention is a function of the stage of development of the science which deals with the natural principles governing the phenomena under consideration, and fundamental to the integration of any new cultural pattern or invention in the field considered." [58] Professor Chapin also suggests the four "type-parts" of institutional structure as a measurement technique. These are: (1) "Common reciprocating attitudes of individuals and their conventionalized behavior patterns," (2) cultural objects of emotional content and hence having symbolic mean-

[54] Theodore Abel, "Is a Cultural Sociology Possible?" *American Journal of Sociology*, 35:737-52.

[55] Floyd Allport, "The Psychological Nature of Political Structure," *American Political Science Review*, 21:211-18.

[56] M. M. Willey, "The Validity of the Culture Concept," *American Journal of Sociology*, 35:204-219.

[57] Charles H. Cooley, "Sumner and Methodology," *Sociology and Social Research*, 12:303-306.

[58] F. Stuart Chapin, *Cultural Change*, p. 349.

ing, (3) cultural objects that satisfy creature wants and that are utilitarian, and (4) language symbols.[59] By application of these standards to various institutions in a comparative way significant results may be obtained.[60]

Under the theme of "measurement of culture levels," L. L. Bernard proposes eight laws of culture levels: (1) "Cultures that habitually radiate more traits, complexes, and patterns to other cultures than they receive from them occupy higher culture levels than those cultures to which they radiate." (2) Cultures that habitually borrow more traits than they transmit occupy lower culture levels than those from which they borrow. Thus "the direction of the flow of culture traits is a rough index of relative culture levels." (3) A culture that is flexible enough to borrow from another culture is higher than the latter. (4) Cultures that are too inflexible to borrow are, other factors being equal, on a lower culture level. Three and four are not contradictory to one and two but subsidiary to them. For example, the culture of the Indians was less flexible than that of the Colonists and as a result the Indians could not take over any of the Colonists' patterns, and therefore lost out in the contact with the Colonists. (5) A migrating people appearing in a new and strange environment must borrow and yet if they can radiate more than they borrow, they can transform the new environment and prove that they occupy a higher cultural level. (6) A migrant people who borrow from an indigenous people and are unable to introduce their own culture will occupy a lower culture level. (7) A culture that modifies its adjustments preferentially by inventing rather than by borrowing occupies a higher culture level than one that adjusts by borrowing. (8) Cultures that are modified by borrowing instead of by inventing are at a lower level than those which reverse the process.[61]

L. L. Bernard classifies culture into four categories, namely: (1) material objects, (2) overt behavior in the form

59 *Ibid.*, pp. 48 ff.

60 In his *Contemporary American Institutions,* Professor Chapin carries his measurement ideas into the field of social institutions and elaborates them considerably. These have an indirect but important bearing upon the measurement of culture change.

61 L. L. Bernard, "The Measurement of Culture Levels," *Sociology and Social Research,* 18:403-419.

of learned or overt responses, (3) symbolic behavior or lan-guage responses, and (4) symbolic cultural objects, such as fetishes, or sacred things and places.[62]

Considerable painstaking work has been done in the field of culture measurement. For example, H. Earl Pemberton's concept of culture diffusion gradients is a case in point. In his discussion of "The Spatial Order of Culture Diffusion," H. Earl Pemberton gives data to show that "early trait adoptions of a new invention are more probable among the adopting units adjacent to the diffusion center and less probable in the more remote regions in ratio to the distance from the point of origin." The reason is found in "the greater probability of culture contact" in the nearer area.[63]

The hypothesis has been outlined by Dr. Pemberton that culture diffusion, an aspect of culture change, "takes place at a rate which may be described by the ogive of the normal frequency distribution." [64] Variations from this curve may occur. One type of variation is that in specific cases a combination of correlation causative elements may pull the curve out of its normal path. A third kind of variation may be due to a social crisis, such as a war, depressions, catastrophic natural occurrences.[65]

ALFRED WEBER

In his *Kulturgeschichte als Kultursoziologie,* Alfred Weber reviews the history of mankind in a realistic way, and ex-amines the concrete evidences of change and growth. His sweep is age-long and culture-wide. He seeks for primary and basic characteristics in this historical view. He looks for data that reveal universal trends. In the first place he de-scribes the *Gesellschaftsprozess,* or social process that under-

---

[62] L. L. Bernard, "Classification of Culture," *Sociology and Social Research,* 15:209-229. In her article on "Culture as Environment," Jessie Bernard in *Sociology and Social Research,* 15:47-55, indicates that the generalizations commonly made regarding natural environment apply equally well to cul-ture. Culture is an important environment of everyone.

[63] H. Earl Pemberton, "The Spatial Order of Culture Diffusion," *Sociology and Social Research,* January-February 1938.

[64] H. Earl Pemberton, "The Curve of Culture Diffusion Rate," *American Sociological Review,* 1:547-556.

[65] H. Earl Pemberton, "The Effect of a Social Crisis on the Curve of Diffusion," *American Sociological Review,* 2:55-61.

lies all other processes. The dynamics of this process is found in impulses that seek order, control, and meaning. Standardized patterns of action recur, such as organization and disorganization, crises and reorganization.

In the next place, Alfred Weber points out a secondary process, which he calls *Zivilisationprozess,* or the civilization process. It refers to the dynamics of reason. Man tries to conquer nature by the use of his reason. Inventions result. Science develops. Technology arises and rules.

The third process is the *Kulturbewegung,* or culture process. It represents an attempt to make emotional adjustments to life. It possesses spontaneous attempts to seek spiritualization of personality. It involves the transcendence of an immanent creativeness.

Alfred Weber's concept of *Anfangskonstellation* or primary constellation refers to that juxtaposition of factors and forces which starts a nation off in a new direction. In other words, Weber emphasizes the importance of the interconnection or interrelationship in the culture field as being of vital importance. Historical sociology takes on a new meaning in Weber's *Kultursoziologie.*

Culture has been divided into three categories: inductive, æsthetic, and control. This distribution is offered as an improvement upon the older and simpler classification into material and non-material. (1) Inductive culture is derived by experimentation; it includes material objects, such as tools, and non-material patterns represented by techniques and bodies of knowledge. (2) The esthetic culture traits, such as paintings or recreational forms, possess not a utility but an enjoyment quality. (3) The control patterns are used to regulate human behavior; they range from the *mores* to rationalized ideologies.[66]

Cultural progress, as defined by Richard C. Thurnwald may be viewed in a threefold way. (1) There is the accumulative process. One device is added to another or to an integration of others, and thus culture patterns grow increasingly complex. (2) There is a linking together of comparatively successive cultures. One begins to decline, another sup-

---

[66] James W. Woodward, "A New Classification of Culture and a Restatement of the Culture Lag Theory," *American Sociological Review,* 1:89-101.

plancs, but in so doing adopts many of the patterns of the preceding culture. (3) There are consecutive changes within a culture, as when a community changes in culture, for example, Russia, in 1917.[67]

At several points in the preceding paragraphs, cultural social thought merged into social psychology. Until twenty-five years ago, anthropology interpreted societary origins largely in terms of the "individual." With the rise of a social psychology such as Cooley represents, "anthropology has given more accurate explanations and has become essentially a social anthropology," or a cultural anthropology.

GROUP DISCUSSION TOPICS

1. The nature of anthropology.
2. The relation of anthropology to ethnology.
3. Anthropological attitudes toward the monogenetic and the polygenetic origins of man.
4. The relative potential ability of African and Caucasian races.
5. The ethnologist's attitudes toward intermarriage of members of widely different races.
6. The meaning of ethnocentrism.
7. Sumner's basic sociological theories.
8. Thomas' theory of the intelligence of women.
9. Vanity as a powerful social factor.
10. Sumner's concept of the "masses."
11. The origin of folkways.
12. The difference between folkways and mores.
13. Sumner's belief in the compensatory nature of ideals.
14. The source of genuine education.
15. The three forces that tend to keep society together.
16. The scope of folk psychology.
17. The leading force in establishing world culture.
18. The "crisis" theory of personality growth.
19. W. I. Thomas' concept of "adjustment."
20. Ellwood's analysis of the "cultural process."
21. W. I. Thomas' concept of "cultural evolution."
22. The meaning of "civilization."
23. Cultural lag in relation to values.
24. Measuring culture changes and trends.
25. Chapin's concepts for measuring cultural change.
26. Bernard's laws of culture levels.

[67] Richard C. Thurnwald, "Progress Viewed as a Component in the Configuration of Culture: A Contribution toward the Analysis of Culture," *American Sociological Review*, I:604-613.

27. Special value of term *pre-literate*.
28. Alfred Weber's "primary constellation" concept.
29. Laws of culture diffusion.
30. The difference between folk psychology and social anthropology.

READINGS

Barnes, Harry E., Editor, *An Introduction to the History of Sociology* (Chicago: University of Chicago Press 1948), Ch. 6.

Bernard, L. L., "The Measurement of Culture Levels," *Sociology and Social Research*, 17:403-419.

Bernard, L. L., "The Social Science Theories of William Graham Sumner," *Social Forces*, 19:153-174.

Calhoun, Donald W., "William Graham Sumner," *Social Forces* 24:15-32.

Case, Clarence March, "A Crisis in Anthropological Research," *Sociology and Social Research*, 12:26-34.

Chapin, F. Stuart, *Cultural Change* (New York: Century Company 1928).

Dixon, Roland B., *The Building of Cultures* (New York: Charles Scribner's Sons 1928).

Ellwood, Charles A., *Cultural Evolution* (New York: Century Company 1927).

———, *A History of Social Philosophy* (New York: Prentice-Hall, Inc. 1938), Ch. XXV.

Faris, Ellsworth, *The Nature of Human Nature* (New York: McGraw-Hill Book Company 1937).

Gillin, John, *The Ways of Man* (New York: Appleton-Century-Crofts, Inc. 1948).

Ginsberg, Morris, "The Life and Work of Edward Westermarck," *Sociological Review*, XXXII:1-28.

Goldenweiser, A. A., *Anthropology, An Introduction to Primitive Culture* (New York: Crofts and Company 1937).

Hobhouse, L. T., *Morals in Evolution* (New York: Henry Holt and Company 1919).

———, *Social Evolution and Political Theory* (New York: Lemcke 1911).

Keller, A. G., *Societal Evolution* (New York: The Macmillan Company 1915).

———, *Man's Rough Road* (Frederick A. Stokes Company and Yale University Press 1932).

Kluckhohn, Clyde, *Mirror for Man* (New York: McGraw-Hill Book Company 1949).

Kroeber, A. L., *The Nature of Culture* (Chicago: University of Chicago Press 1952).

Odum, Howard W., "Folk Sociology as a Subject; Society and the Empirical Study of Human Behavior," *Social Forces*, 31:193-223.

Ogburn, W. F., *Social Change* (New York: Huebsch 1922).

Osborn, H. F., *Men of the Old Stone Age* (New York: Charles Scribner's Sons 1918).

Pemberton, H. Earl, "Culture Diffusion Gradients," *American Journal of Sociology*, 42:226-233.

Porteus, S. D., *Primitive Intelligence and Environment* (New York: The Macmillan Company 1937).

Salomon, Albert, "The Place of Alfred Weber's *Kultursoziologie* in Social Thought," *Social Research*, 3:494-500.

Schneider, Joseph, "Cultural Lag: What is it?" *American Sociological Review*, 11:786-791.

Sumner, W. G., *Folkways* (Boston: Ginn and Company 1907).

——, "Religion and the Mores," *American Journal of Sociology*, LX: 19-33.

Thomas, W. I., *Sex and Society* (Chicago: University of Chicago Press 1907).

——, *Source Book for Social Origins* (Chicago: University of Chicago Press 1909).

——, *Primitive Behavior* (New York: McGraw-Hill Book Company 1937).

Tylor, E. B., *Primitive Culture* (New York: Brentano's 1924).

Wallis, W. D., *Culture and Progress* (New York: McGraw-Hill Book Company 1930).

Weber, Alfred, *Kulturgeschichte als Kultursoziologie* (Leyden, Holland: Sythoff 1935).

Webster, Hutton, "Social Thought of William Graham Sumner," *Journal of Social Philosophy*, 2:327-337.

Westermarck, Edward, *The Origin and Development of the Moral Ideas* (New York: The Macmillan Company 1906).

Wissler, Clark, *Man and Culture* (New York: Crowell Company 1923).

Wundt, William, *Elements of Folk Psychology* (New York: The Macmillan Company 1916).

CHAPTER XXIII

GALTON AND EUGENIC SOCIAL THOUGHT

Eugenic social thought is the child of biological discoveries. Eugenics, the science of good breeding, which did not achieve scientific standing until the closing years of the last century, may be traced back in its incipient forms to Plato, who advocated that strength should mate only with strength, and that imperfect childr͟ should be eliminated from society. In its scientific origins eugenics dates from 1859, when Darwin's *Origin of Species* was first published. Its beginning as a distinct field of human thinking is found in the articles by Francis Galton on "Hereditary Talent and Genius," which appeared in 1865; and in 1869, in book form under the title, *Hereditary Genius*. Later appeared his *Inquiries into the Human Faculty*. In 1904 Galton wrote a paper entitled, "Eugenics: Its Definition, Scope and Aims." In this dissertation the new science of eugenics was formally introduced to the world. Galton's analysis of eugenics became its leading interpretation.

The mantle of the founder fell upon Professor Karl Pearson, whose work has assumed a distinctly statistical nature. Professor Pearson's leaning toward biometry has brought severe criticism upon him. The statistical approach, while exact and thought-provoking, is subject to various errors in interpretation of data. The viewpoint from which Professor Pearson writes, however, is not one-sided. For example, he states that "it may require years to replace a great leader of men, but a stable and efficient society can only be the outcome of centuries of development.[1] He holds that group conscience ought for the sake of social welfare to be stronger than private interest, and that the ideal citizen should be able to form a judgment free from personal bias.[2]

C. W. Saleeby, another English writer, has developed an independent reputation as a eugenicist.[3] In the United

[1] Karl Pearson, *The Grammar of Science*, p. 1.
[2] *Ibid.*, p. 6.
[3] See Saleeby, *The Progress of Eugenics*, Chapter II.

States, such men as C. B. Davenport[4] and Paul Popenoe[5] have made important eugenic contributions. The recent tendency has been to supplement purely statistical studies of heredity by case studies. However, since eugenics is directly indebted to the studies of heredity and since heredity must be investigated for several generations, eugenic social thought has not yet reached its culmination.

EUGENICS

Galton defined eugenics as the science of good breeding. Its aim as a pure science is to study the agencies under social control "that may improve or impair the racial qualities of future generations, either physically or mentally." Galton's program, as outlined by the founder shortly before his death, insisted upon (1) a study of the laws of heredity, (2) a dissemination of knowledge about heredity, (3) a study of the factors underlying marriage, (4) a study of birth rates, and (5) a case study of individual families.

Eugenic social thought holds that heredity among human beings operates according to the same laws that govern heredity among animals. The theory of Mendelian units becomes in practice the theory of *multiple factors*. The unit characters, upon analysis, appear to be complex and to be inherited in complex ways. Multiple factors are inherited from generation to generation directly when pure factors are united with pure factors. But when the pure is united with the hybrid, then the laws of dominance and recessiveness operate. In such combinations certain factors tend to express themselves in greater proportion than do other elements. This failure to secure expression in a given generation, however, means that the specific factor is recessive for the time being. Later, it will likely appear.

Galton stated another important eugenic law, the law of *regression*. Each peculiarity is inherited by the offspring on the average in a slightly less degree than it is found in the parent. Hence, according to Galton, good traits and poor traits alike are inherited in a degree nearer mediocrity by the offspring than by the parents. This law partially explains

[4] See C. B. Davenport, *Heredity in Relation to Eugenics.*
[5] *Applied Eugenics* (with R. H. Johnson).

why gifted men rarely have sons who are equally gifted. The law seems to hold good for large numbers, but not necessarily when considered in relation to single families. It serves as a check upon variation and mutation.

Galton and Pearson advanced another statistical law, the law of *ancestral inheritance.* Galton supposed that the parents contribute to the child one-half of his inherited factors, the grandparents one-fourth, and so on. Pearson has secured statistical evidence which shows that Galton's geometric series is incorrect, and that on the average in a large number of cases the parents together contribute to the child .624 of his traits; the four grandparents, .198; the eight great grandparents, .063; and so on.

The law of *mutation,* described by De Vries and other geneticists, refers to the appearance of mutants, or individuals who do not reproduce to form but represent a new line of heredity. In this way the appearance of genius may often be accounted for. However, the factors which explain the appearance of mutants have not yet been analyzed.

Another fundamental genetic consideration is the law of *selection.* If individuals with worthy traits mate only with individuals who possess worthy traits, a superior stock will be produced. This tendency is very important, since it points the way to a potent method of securing social progress.

Eugenic social thought has been developed in part on the basis of the Weismann theory of *no transmission of acquired traits.* The germ plasm is transmitted from individual to offspring in a direct line of descent. Injuries to the parent rarely change the nature of the germ plasm. Only extreme malnutrition or excessive use of alcohol apparently exerts a definite influence on the germ cells. Nature has thus made provision for the protection of germ plasm, whether strong or defective. Society, then, may encourage the mating of individuals who possess strong physical and mental traits, and discourage the mating of individuals who are defective — thus securing its own positive improvement.

APPLIED EUGENICS

Eugenic social thought follows two courses. Restrictive eugenics advocates the segregation of the so-called dysgenic classes, such as the feeble-minded, the insane, and the grossly defective criminal. Public opinion reacts against sterilization ; injustice that cannot be remedied may be done through sterilization. Segregation by sexes, while involving expense, is a eugenic method of safeguarding society against the reproduction of dysgenic persons.

The other trend of eugenic thought supports the raising of the standards of choice in mating. Constructive eugenics, as distinguished from restrictive eugenics, urges a program of education whereby young people will habitually rate one another by physical and mental standards rather than by wealth and class standards.

Eugenics disapproves of random mating. It favors assortative mating, because, for example, the "marriage of representatives of two long-lived strains ensures that the offspring will inherit more longevity than does the ordinary man." [6] Eugenics thus stresses the importance of teaching young people eugenic ideas, and of training them to be guided by these ideals rather than by caprice and passion.[7] Eugenic ideals include health, paternity and maternity, and pleasing disposition. Education and character are secondary eugenic ideals of importance.

A study of the birth rate shows that the inferior stocks and classes of individuals produce many more children than do the superior groups. Many cultured people do not marry, or if they marry they keep the birth rate very low. As a result, the racial character of a whole people may change within a few generations. The superior strains may be lost and the inferior furnish the entire population.

The low birth rate of the superior stocks is due to several factors : (1) the lengthening period of education and of professional training calls for the postponement of marriage. (2) The desire to give children the best advantages limits the birth rate. (3) The increasing spirit of independence on the part of women causes a postponement of marriage and a limitation of the number of children. These and other causes have produced a *differential birth rate* in favor of the in-

---

[6] Popenoe and Johnson, *Applied Eugenics* (1918 edition), p. 213; also 1933 edition, Chs. XIV and XV.

[7] *Ibid.*, pp. 218, 231.

ferior strains. Eugenic thought urges that the differential be reversed in favor of the superior strains. This conclusion implies that the dysgenic classes must be prevented from producing children, that the poor must be raised to higher educational and economic levels and taught to limit the birth rate, and that the eugenically superior be taught to increase the birth rate.

WAR AND EUGENICS

Eugenics pronounces war to be both dysgenic and eugenic.[8] (1) It is dysgenic in that the bravest and the physically best are killed first. In the case of a long war only the weakest men physically and mentally are left alive to propagate the race. (2) War is dysgenic in that it produces a large number of hurried marriages. Rational choices of mates are supplanted by sudden emotional reactions. (3) War is dysgenic in that sex immorality greatly increases. Prostitution flourishes in the neighborhood of military encampments, unless rigid means of control are established. (4) Again, the dysgenic effect of war is seen in the period of socio-mental unrest which always follows war, and which among other things undermines rational sexual selection.

The chief eugenic effect of war is manifested during the period of training. This preparation period accents the importance of a strong physique and health measures. An insipid, stoop-shouldered population of city young men may be transformed into an army of fit soldiers. However, the conclusions are obvious that the dysgenic effects of war are far more potent than the eugenic gains, and that the eugenic advantages may be acquired in other ways than by promulgating war.

FEMINISM AND EUGENICS

Eugenics looks askance at the feminism movement. Feminism once meant the development of the womanly traits of the sex. It now refers to the elimination as far as possible of sex differences. It would make women as nearly as possible like men. Eugenics objects to this trend, since it underestimates the importance of the fact that women physically are

[8] *Ibid.*, Chapter XVI.

built to be mothers. To the extent that women enter into "heavy" occupants, they will become man-like; and their efficiency as mothers of the race will decrease, and the race will suffer.

The economic equality of the sexes is a satisfactory doctrine to the eugenicist if the doctrine be extended to make motherhood a salaried occupation, like mill work or stenography.[9] "Child-bearing should be recognized as being as worthy of remuneration as any occupation which men enter, and should be paid for (by the state) on the same basis."[10]

Eugenics would throw every possible safeguard around motherhood, especially in the period immediately before and after the birth of the child. The mother, even the expectant mother, "is doing our business, indispensable and exacting business, and we must take care of her accordingly. She is not only a worker but the foremost of all workers."[11]

RACIAL POISONS

Eugenic thought as represented in the writings of C. W. Saleeby has denominated alcohol, venereal disease, and tuberculosis as "racial poisons." While there is some doubt regarding the effects of taking small amounts of alcohol, alcohol when taken in excessive quantities affects the germ plasm and produces a neurotic taint. It appears that alcoholism may be a cause in producing defective children. The verdicts of hygiene and economics that alcoholism is injurious to the race is supported by eugenics.

Venereal disease, another so-called race poison, produces toxins which apparently affect the germ plasm indirectly, if not directly. It lowers the physical and moral tone and causes unfavorable racial tendencies. Venereal disease tends to destroy the generative organs and to cut off the birth rate entirely. It is a result of sex immorality which in itself tends to produce children under such abnormal conditions of vice that it becomes antisocial, if not a dysgenic factor, in society. To the extent, of course, that venereal disease kills off the

9 Popenoe and Johnson, *ibid.*, p. 381.
10 *Ibid.*, p. 380.
11 Saleeby, *op. cit.*, p. 65.

racially useless, it may be considered eugenic.[12] Such a point of view, however, fails to rate properly the invasions which venereal disease is continually making upon normal and superior types of germ plasm.

Tuberculosis weakens the membranous tissues and probably leads in a few generations to an unusual degree of susceptibility to the invasion of tubercle bacilli. It is still a question, however, to what extent tuberculosis may be counted a racial poison. Hobhouse has argued that, by the development of scientific hygiene, it will be possible to center attention not upon eliminating tubercular stock, but upon eliminating the tubercle bacilli.[13]

RACES AND EUGENICS

In regard to race questions the social anthropologist and the eugenicist represent different poles of thought. As was indicated in the preceding chapter, the social anthropologists, such as Boas and Thomas, support the theory of potential race equality. The eugenicist, on the other hand, contends that there are inherently superior and inferior racial stocks, and that the marriages of representatives of inferior stocks with representatives of superior stocks will produce children of a stock distinctly lower than that of the superior stocks. The eugenicists in the United States hold that the immigration of the peoples of southern and eastern Europe will not only supplant through a higher birth rate the native stock of Nordic origin but, where marriages between natives and southern and eastern European immigrants occur, it will lower the racial quality of the population. While eugenic thought in this matter deserves a complete and respectful hearing, it must be considered along with the findings of social anthropology.

Social isolation has played an important part in the development of diverse races. Social interaction is also to be considered in the growth of racial unification. Thus, heredity is seen to be responsive to social conditions.

With current eugenic findings once fully utilized it would

---

[12] Popenoe and Johnson, op. cit., p. 387.
[13] Hobhouse, Social Evolution and Political Theory, p. 45.

be possible to improve upon natural changes and to do some effective racial planning that would be to the advantage of all mankind. Such plans would need to be put into effect with care or they might be misconstrued by the uneducated or the ill-informed.

The differential birth rate which refers to the rapid multiplication of the lower classes and the dying out of the higher classes may be corrected partly by educational measures and partly by securing a more even distribution of wealth. With better opportunities for the masses and less wealth for the few at the top of the social scale a favorable reaction upon racial stock may be expected.

After all, the best racial stocks and biological strains need to be conserved, no matter what means of improving the social environment are utilized. The better the biological material, the greater will be the results that come from the efforts of social reformers.

Why cannot eugenics and social reform work together? Is it not the essence of common sense that they cease poking fun at each other and build a united program of human betterment? If the goal of co-operation is to be reached, then both eugenics and social reform need to take broader views not only of each other, but of social life. They need to make joint studies.

NATURE AND NURTURE

The debate regarding the comparative influences of nature and nurture has been long and bitter. It may be said here that both heredity and environment are more or less equally essential in the development of human personality. Without inherited factors in the individual the environment has nothing upon which to work. Without a stimulating environment the inherited traits will remain dormant. Each human being has inherited factors which, if played upon by certain environmental factors, may lead the individual to try to wreck society or himself or both.

Every person, also, has traits which, if stimulated by the proper environmental elements, may cause him to develop into a useful member of society. While the environment cannot change the inherited potentialities very much, if any, it is a prime factor of vast importance in determining which inherited tendencies will never find expression, which will be expressed in modified ways, and which will reach full fruition.

The eugenic goal, like the intelligence test standards, is often thought of in terms of ability to meet social life conditions. But social standards in an individualistic-capitalistic society may ultimately prove disastrous from the standpoint of securing the "highest" human types. As G. R. Davies has said: "The eugenicist who regards commercial success as the standard toward which society should breed apparently has in mind a nation composed only of cultured bondholders." [14]

In the light of eugenic thought genealogy may become scientific; in fact, it may become a valuable source of scientific materials for eugenics. Heretofore genealogy has been the concern of a few leisure-class people, who have taken pleasure and pride in recounting the fact that some one of a possible thousand or more ancestors several generations back was distinguished in some way or other, and who would have friends or the public believe that they inherited from this ancestor of note the characteristics which made him great. Eugenics points out a wider purpose to which genealogy may be put. It urges that mental and physical traits of every individual in all families be carefully analyzed and accurately and systematically recorded. In this way it will be possible in a generation to have available a large amount of eugenic materials, and in a few generations a reliable body of data for studying racial heredity.

Eugenics insists with increasing force that educational programs shall provide that every child be not only well reared but also well born. A weakness in eugenic thought is that it implies that sound racial stock is sufficient to guarantee progress; it tends at times to overstress an aristocracy of racial stock. It sometimes detracts from the importance of character and personal discipline as essential elements in social progress.

Eugenics really calls for extensive social reform. As noted

[14] G. R. Davies, *op. cit.*, p. 120.

by Clarence Marsh Case, eugenics, in asking for an increase in the percentage of well born, asks for a new economic emphasis.   Its teachings call for an economic system that will yield incomes large enough for the eugenically superior to raise children.   Eugenics "constitutes the most ambitious program of social self-direction the courageous audacity of man has yet conceived." [15]   As long as economic success as such is the highest good, and not eugenically superior children, eugenics is defeated before it starts on its program.   As long as economic goals are put first rather than eugenically sound children, the latter are going to suffer.   As long as people who would like to rear children and who are eugenically capable cannot give such children the opportunities that they need if they are to have a fair chance in the everyday struggle of economic competition, eugenics is helpless.   Eugenically capable parents need an increase of "freedom in their choice of size of family." [16]

"The eugenic predicament," as seen by Samuel J. Holmes, is found in the high correlation today between "success and sterility." [17]   He concludes that "our race is at present in a relatively dysgenic stage of its biological history," and asks, what can we do about it?

GROUP DISCUSSION TOPICS

1.   The leading founders of eugenics.
2.   The chief elements in Galton's program of eugenics.
3.   The reasons why gifted men rarely have sons equally gifted.
4.   The distinction between the law of recessiveness and the law of regression.
5.   The law of ancestral inheritance.
6.   The program of assortative mating.
7.   The nature of "constructive eugenics."
8.   The main dysgenic classes.
9.   Causes of the low birth rate of the superior classes.
10.   War as a dysgenic agency.
11.   War as a eugenic agency.
12.   The attitude of eugenic thought toward feminism.
13.   The meaning of "racial poison.

[15] Clarence M. Case, "Eugenics as a Social Philosophy," *Journal of Applied Sociology*, 7:1-12.
[16] Frederick Osborn, "Development of a Eugenic Philosophy," *American Sociological Review*, 2:389-397.
[17] Samuel J. Holmes, *The Eugenic Predicament.*

14. The distinction between the eugenic and the social anthropological attitude toward the racial equality theory.
15. The leisure-class attitude contrasted with the eugenic attitude toward genealogy.
16. Economic reform as vital to eugenics.
17. The strong and weak points of eugenic thought.

READINGS

Bauer, E., E. Fischer, and F. Lenz, *Human Heredity* (New York: The Macmillan Company 1931).

Carr-Saunders, A. M., *Eugenics* (New York: Henry Holt and Company 1925).

Case, Clarence M., "Eugenics as a Social Philosophy," *Journal of Applied Sociology,* 7:1-12.

Conklin, E. G., *Heredity and Development in the Development of Men* (Princeton: Princeton University Press 1923).

Davenport, C. B., *Heredity in Relation to Eugenics* (New York: Henry Holt and Company 1911).

Davies, G. R., *Social Environment* (Chicago: A. C. McClurg 1917).

East, E. M., *Biology in Human Affairs* (New York: McGraw-Hill Book Company 1931).

Galton, Francis, *Hereditary Genius* (New York: The Macmillan Company 1914).

Guyer, M. F., *Being Well-Born* (Indianapolis: Bobbs-Merrill Company 1927).

Holmes, S. J., *The Trend of the Race* (New York: Harcourt, Brace and Company 1921).

———, *The Eugenic Predicament* (New York: Harcourt, Brace and Company 1933).

———, *Human Genetics and its Social Import* (New York: McGraw-Hill Book Company 1936).

Jennings, H. S., *The Biological Basis of Human Nature* (New York: W. W. Norton Company 1930).

Osborn, Frederick, "Development of a Eugenic Philosophy," *American Sociological Review,* 2:389-397.

Pearl, Raymond, *Studies in Human Biology* (Baltimore: Williams and Wilkins 1924).

Pearson, Karl, *The Grammar of Science* (London: Black 1911).

Popenoe, Paul and R. H. Johnson, *Applied Eugenics* (New York: The Macmillan Company 1933).

Saleeby, C. W., *The Progress of Eugenics* (New York: Funk and Wagnalls 1914).

Schiller, F. C. S., *Social Decay and Eugenical Reform* (London: Constable and Company 1932).

Terman, Lewis M., Editor, *Genetic Studies of Genius* (Palo Alto: Stanford University Press 1926). Three volumes.

CHAPTER XXIV

GUMPLOWICZ AND CONFLICT SOCIAL THOUGHT

The life of mankind on earth has always been characterized by strife, struggle, and conflict. The present troubled
world situation with its fears of impending conflicts is no
exception. Conflict has usually been destructive of life and
property, and has caused untold hatred and misery. It is
natural, therefore, that human thought has sought out the
causes of conflict and has developed theories regarding its
fundamental nature. These theories are both fascinating
and complicated. They can be tested out in any part of the
world by virtue of the universal prevalence of human conflict.

The concept of social conflict has already been introduced
to the reader. In the chapter on "Individualistic Social
Thought" the prolonged struggle between individual rights
and social control was analyzed. Malthus described the
conflict between population and the means of subsistence.
Comte insisted that man is not naturally a social being.
Hence, this unsocial nature of mankind is a fruitful source
of human conflict. Marx pictured the class struggle; and
Darwin elaborated the doctrine of the survival of the fittest.

The slightest grasp of social thought reveals that human
association is characterized at times by deep-seated and subtle conflicts; and at other times by a fundamental co-operative
spirit. Some sociological writers have seen only or chiefly
the conflicts of life; others have sought out the co-operative
activities; still others have tried to discover the relationships
between conflict and co-operation in societal development.
This chapter will deal with the concept of social conflict,
while the next will be centered on the ideal of social co-
operation and upon the relationship of conflict to co-operation in group processes.

GUMPLOWICZ

One of the outstanding believers in the theory that conflict dominates societal life was Ludwig Gumplowicz (1838-1910). He was a Darwinian, believing in the theory of the survival of the fittest. His system of thought begins with the assertion that primitive hordes were the original units of society. Gumplowicz dissented from Herbert Spencer's belief in the individual as the original societary unit, although he accepted the determinism that is inherent in Spencer's theory of evolution. Gumplowicz also repudiated Comte's belief in social amelioration through prevision, but subscribed to Comte's positivism.

According to Gumplowicz, society began with a large number of primitive groups, which were self-sustaining and self-conscious units. Each one of these hordes was a warring group, possessing an instinctive hatred of all other hordes.[1] As these hordes increased in size, the general food supply failed to meet the needs. Consequently, inter-group struggle resulted and the members of the weaker hordes were either destroyed or enslaved. The existence of slaves led to situations of intra-group inequality, which in turn created problems involving injustice.

As a result of continual conflicts between groups there are frequent changes taking place in their personnel. The vanquished are continually being absorbed by victorious groups. In a given successful group two classes are at once established, namely, the victors and the vanquished. Classes are thus continually arising out of new juxtapositions of heterogeneous racial elements.[2]

It was in an intense form of group self-interest that Gumplowicz found the mainspring of social progress. This self-interest leads to an exaggerated group appraisement, a strong degree of group unity, a state of warfare between groups — and perhaps progress. Basic to this group self-interest, there are the material needs and the economic desires. The group is also bound together by various factors, such as a common social life, a common language, religion, and culture.

[1] Ludwig Gumplowicz, *Der Rassenkampf*, p. 64.
[2] Gumplowicz, *Grundriss der Soziologie*, translated by Moore, p. 134.

Gumplowicz advocated a theory of potential race equality. He argued against innate racial superiority and racial inferiority. He doubted the existence of any pure races. Each race is a compound of other races, and hence races are potentially similar in fundamental respects. National progress, therefore, holds no connection with race purity.

GROUP CONFLICT

The conflict between a majority and a minority group works out usually to the advantage of the minority. The majority is less well organized; it is less wieldy and compact.

In group competition, not size, but the number of common interests is the important consideration. Social concentration is more effective than social extension. Social power and influence culminates in the aristocratic few who have pooled their individual power. Custom adds greatly to their strength.

Social groups, like individuals, may experience an increase in desires, in strength, and in actual power. A normal, active group is always wanting more and more for itself. Hence, the chances of clashing with other groups tend to multiply.

Once inaugurated, the conflict between groups becomes inexorable. It is waged on the grounds of group self-interest. It proceeds by the establishing of more institutions within each group. These institutions reflect each group's interests.

The conflict between interests and morals is far-reaching. In conflict a group breaks all the rules of ethics.

Gumplowicz minimized the importance of the individual. Groups rule. Centuries of traditions dominate. The thoughts of the individual are almost, if not entirely, a mere reflection of the social environment. The group develops group pride or group disloyalty in th minds of its members. The distinguished leader is largely the man who expresses the will of the group during the group crisis. Gumplowicz makes only a brief reference to the process of interaction between the individual and the group. An underlying theory of natural determinism vitiates Gumplowicz's ideas concerning the individual.

Inasmuch as society, like individuals, passes through a cycle of growth and decay, subject to unchangeable natural and societary laws, there is no justification for individual interference with social processes. In fact, this theory led Gumplowicz into pessimistic conclusions concerning life. He failed to see that societal life is not necessarily a series of hopeless cyclical conflicts, and that social processes are becoming increasingly subject to human control — for good or ill. He did not appreciate the fact that groups are not subject to laws of cyclical growth and decay after the manner of individuals. Hence, his conflict theory of societal life ended in confusion and pessimism.[3]

NIETZSCHE

A reference was made in an earlier chapter to the theories of Friedrich Nietzsche (1844–1900). This German philosopher developed the idea of social conflict, basing it on the concept of the "will to power." Leaders desire power. They enjoy exercising power and they thrive under that exercise. Jealousy of the leaders arises. The weaker members of society join together against the possessors of power. They develop a will to power, but of a weaker type than that of the leaders. Conflicts ensue between the will to power of the superior and the will to power of the inferior.

The superior and the inferior types each possess a distinctive code of morality.[4] The supermen develop a harsh and rigorous attitude toward themselves and others. They gird and prepare themselves for the crises of life. They strive to augment their power. They become self-contained. They take pride in crushing weakness and in deifying strength. Their morality stresses those factors in life which create power. They feel a condescending pity for the weak. They experience no sense of responsibility for the inferior classes. Since supermen are the supreme goal of nature, supermen feel that all persons and things should contribute to increasing the power of supermen.[5] It is a waste of energy for

[3] Gumplowicz, *Soziologie und Politik*, p. 94.
[4] Friedrich Nietzsche, *Genealogy of Morals*, p. 46.
[5] Nietzsche, *The Will to Power*, pp. 90, 269, 660 ff.

supermen to give their lives in behalf of inferior persons. They are interested only in the welfare of other supermen.

The morality of the inferior is of a type which furthers weakness. It accents sympathy. It emphasizes gregariousness. Inferior persons create a slavish, cringing, meek morality. They sacrifice themselves readily and humbly in behalf of others who may be inferior to themselves.

Nietzsche believed in a eugenics program. He declared that marriages should be arranged with a view to producing supermen. Nietzsche's deterministic view of natural evolution led him to believe, however, that equality of privileges is unattainable. He opposed democracy because its theory of equal opportunities contradicts the tendencies of nature. He was no socialist. He asserted that an aristocracy of power is the only true goal for society. He carried forward the ruthless biological laws of tooth and fang into his conception of the highest types of civilization.

Moreover, the superman is a biological mutant. He appears sporadically. At this point Nietzsche's inconsistency becomes obvious. For example, if geniuses appear sporadically, and without reference to biological laws, why attempt to arrange marriages so as to produce supermen? To get out of this dilemma, Nietzsche postulated cyclical returns of supermen and lost his bearings in trying to interpret an endless circular movement in social evolution, endlessly repeating itself. In an applied form Nietzsche's philosophy has appeared in German political life, but once has resulted in the defeat of Germany.

In starting points, Nietzsche and Gumplowicz were widely different. Nietzsche began with an apotheosis of the man of power and extolled the achievements of supermen. Gumplowicz had little place for the individual, even for the most powerful. Both sets of theories ended in a deterministic philosophy of individual and social despair.

PATTEN

A fundamental delineation of social conflict has been advanced by Simon N. Patten in his *Theory of Social Forces.*[6]

[6] S. N. Patten, *A Theory of Social Forces*, Chapter IV.

Human society is largely the product of a pain economy in which the requisites for survival are determined "by the enemies and pains to be avoided." In a like manner a pain morality and a pain religion develop. The purpose of the pain morality is "to keep persons from committing acts and putting themselves in situations which lead to destruction." The pain religion, likewise, aims to invoke the aid of higher powers in the human conflict with enemies and death. The social forces in a pain economy have been built up in the form of sets of ideals, instincts, and habits.

Society, however, is now in a transition stage — entering a pleasure economy. A large number of the sources of pain have been eliminated through the inventive and administrative phases of civilization. Dangerous beasts and reptiles, barbarous invasions, and superstitious interpretations are uncommon among the advanced human groups.

No nation, unfortunately, has been able to live under a pleasure economy. Its members have not built up sets of instincts, habits, and ideals that withstand the effects of a pleasure economy. Consequently, individuals and nations have fallen into lethargy, vice, and decay. The enemies to a pleasure economy are found within the individual; these are as yet unconquered under the allurements of a pleasure environment.

CARVER

Another type of conflict theory of society is advanced by Thomas Nixon Carver. Professor Carver begins his analysis with a discussion of the conflict of human interests. Originally all conflicts were settled on the basis of might. But conflicts between persons who are beginning to think sometimes lead one or each of the contending parties to a consideration of adjusting the conflict by other than physical strife. At this point the concept of justice begins to take form.

Justice, according to Dr. Carver, is "that system of adjusting conflicting interests which makes the group strong and progressive." [7] Virtue and strength are pronounced identi-

[7] T. N. Carver, *Essays in Social Justice*, pp. 30-34.

cal, and strength is defined "according to its ability to make itself universal."

Conflict arises out of scarcity. Where two men want the same thing, conflict ensues. It is this antagonism of interests which produces moral problems and furnishes a basis for determining justice and injustice. One reason for the lack of supply of things which people seek is that in society human wants are unduly expanded. If wants could be kept low and production high, an adaptation of people to things would take place which would greatly lessen conflict.

Conflicts take place in three different fields: (1) between man and nature, (2) between man and man, and (3) between the different interests of the same man.[8] If there were no such conflicts, there would be no moral problems. The result would be paradise.

The institutions of property, the family, and the state have developed out of antagonism of interests, which in turn, as has been said, is the result of scarcity. If things were not scarce, no one would think of claiming property in anything. In a similar way the kinship group becomes desirous of possessing property and hence acquires unity. In asserting that the unifying principle in the family is an economic one, Dr. Carver espouses a theory of economic determinism. In fact, he holds that "the economic problem is the fundamental one, out of which all other social and moral problems have grown."[9]

Dr. Carver somewhat softens his rigorous social theories when he admits that there may be a few people in the world whose feeling of humanity is strong enough to overbalance an antagonism of interests and to lead them to treat the world as a normal individual treats his family.[10] A world of such people would make a world of communism. But such a world is unthinkable, because world-loving people are social aberrations. The individual whose altruism is such that he gladly gives his body to a tiger is not helping to transform the world into a world of saints but into a world of tigers.[11]

8 *Ibid.*, p. 46.
9 *Ibid.*, pp. 49, 50.
10 *Ibid.*, p. 56.
11 *Ibid.*, p. 56.

Extreme forms of benevolence and meekness constitute the very food upon which selfishness fattens.[12]

Professor Carver, therefore, points out two sources of conflict, namely, scarcity of desirable things and self-centered appreciation. These two bases of conflict are fundamentally natural and normal. Conflicts appear, however, in a great variety of forms. This classification of the methods of struggling for existence is fourfold.[13]

TYPES OF CONFLICTS

(1) There is a group of conflicts which are primarily destructive, such as war, robbery, duelling, sabotage, brawling. These conflicts are all crude, primitive, brutal. They represent man at his lowest ebb. They are militant in character, depending upon the individual's power to destroy, to harm, or to inflict pain and injury.[14]

(2) Deceptive conflicts are of an order slightly higher than the militant. They include thieving, swindling, adulteration of goods, false advertising. They imply a greater degree of intelligence than the purely destructive types of conflict.

(3) Another form of conflict is persuasive in character, for example, political, erotic, commercial, and legal conflicts. Political competition includes seeking governmental appointments, running for office, campaigning for a political party. Erotic conflicts are in the main different forms of courtship. Commercial persuasion utilizes the agencies of advertising and salesmanship. Legal conflicts include litigations in the courts. In all these illustrations the individual strives to further his own interests by his persuasive methods, such as demagogy or political clap-trap. Sometimes the persuasion falls to the level of deception and, occasionally, to destructive depths.

(4) The highest form of conflicts are the productive types. Some productive conflicts refer to rivalries in producing economic goods; others to rivalries in rendering services. In his *Essays in Social Justice,* Professor Carver discusses three

[12] *Loc. cit.*
[13] T. N. Carver, *Principles of Political Economy,* pp. 37 ff.
[14] T. N. Carver, *Essays in Social Justice,* p. 86.

forms of economic competition at length. Here he includes competitive production, competitive bargaining, and competitive consumption of economic goods. The second class has already been referred to as commercial persuasion. Competitive production increases th supply of economic goods and "always works well." Competitive consumption, however, "always works badly." It means "rivalry in display, in ostentation, in the effort to outshine or outdress all one's neighbors, or at least not to be outshone or outdressed by them." It is usually deceptive; it has no productive features about it. It may even assume a form of waste and destruction. The highest type of conflict is friendly rivalry in rendering service to other people.

SOCIAL CONFLICTS [15]

Forms of Human Conflict

Militant	War Rape Duelling Brawling Sabotage	
Gambling		
Persuasive	Political	Courting of royal favors Running for office Campaigning for a cause
	Erotic	Polite social intercourse Courting
	Legal	"Leaving it to the crowd" Litigation before courts
Economic Achievement	Competitive Production Competitive Bargaining Competitive Consumption	
Recreational	Games Sports Dramatics Fiction	

These major forms of conflict are extensive, but not all.

15 *Ibid.*, p. 85.

inclusive. Moreover, they tend to overemphasize unduly the struggle side of life.

A person may utilize more than one form of conflict in order to gain his ends. Generally, if one method fails, he resorts to a more primitive type.

Professor Carver would have self-interest direct its effort toward the welfare of the nation. Since neither law nor government can eliminate self-interest, the next best thing is to connect it with national well-being. Nearly all useful things that are done in a community are undertaken through self-interest.[16] Even co-operation is a form of competition.[17] The purpose of co-operation is to enable groups of individuals to compete more effectively against opposing groups.

The highest type of activity which Carver analyzes and which he heartily approves is competitive-production. Presumably all the participants gain.

The lowest form of activity is competitive consumption. People who engage in outdoing one another in spending in order to make a show and to be approved are to be pitied.

S. R. Steinmetz, the eminent sociologist of Holland, long associated with the University of Amsterdam, attracted attention as early as 1895 in connection with his ethnological studies on the role of war in creating the political state. In his *Soziologie des Krieges,* he pointed out that the tribes that do not fight are not as likely to develop a political organization as are the war-like peoples. In other words, war made necessary the development of political machinery. Moreover, the tribes that were best organized were most likely to win in wars and hence a premium was acquired by political organization. War has played an important part in the development of nationality, causing people not only to become loyal to their nation but to become jealous of that loyalty. War threatens the nation and hence citizens have their patriotism grounded in fears of losing their nation through defeat. As long as man has a deeply pugnacious nature, wars will occur. To stop wars it will be necessary, according to Steinmetz, to change the basic nature of man into something essentially pacific.

[16] *Ibid.,* p. 108.
[17] *Principles of Political Economy,* p. 43.

VEBLEN

Economic and industrial conflict in its subtle social psychological aspects was brilliantly analyzed by Thorstein Veblen (1857–1929). He believed in an instinct of workmanship but pointed out how it is distorted by false social controls. In this connection he dealt with the social psychology of business enterprise, of the machine process, and of the leisure classes. His ideas are well illustrated in what he called "canons."

The Canon of Pecuniary Emulation describes the restless straining of certain persons to outdo one another in the possession of wealth.[18] Such possession is interpreted as conferring honor on its possessor. Wealth becomes intrinsically honorable. The Canon of Pecuniary Beauty refers to the impression that things are· beautiful in proportion as they are costly.[19] The marks of expensiveness come to be regarded as beautiful features.

The Canon of Conspicuous Consumption is a term which describes a method of showing off one's wealth by an elaborate consumption of goods.[20] Conspicuous consumption is seen more in matters of dress than in any other line of consumption. The Canon of Conspicuous Leisure is the rule which some people are following when they live a life of leisure as the readiest and most conclusive evidence of pecuniary strength.[21] Sometimes a man keeps his wife frittering her time away in a doll's house in order to achieve a wealth status.

The Canon of Leisure Class Conservatism is Veblen's label for the conservative tendencies of the wealthy. Those whom fortune has greatly favored are likely to be content with things as they are. Such people are averse to social change, for social innovation might upset their comfortable existence. They have a dominant material interest in letting things alone.

Veblen's Canon of Pecuniary Efficiency means that many persons conceive of efficiency largely in terms of price. The

18 Thorstein Veblen, *The Theory of the Leisure Class,* p. 31.
19 *Ibid.,* p. 169.
20 *Ibid.,* p. 68.
21 *Ibid.,* p. 38.

person who can induce his fellows to pay him well is accounted efficient and serviceable.[22] The man who gains much wealth at little cost is rated high in his neighbor's esteem. The investor who at the turn of his hand reaps $100,000 in a stock or bond deal is praised widely. In other words, there is a common tendency to rate people high in direct proportion to the amount of money that they are able to extract from the aggregrate product.

The Canon of Bellicoseness refers to the enthusiasm for war which the hereditary leisure class displays. The very wealthy, not being obliged to work for a living, find that time drags. Therefore, they seek excitement and relief from *ennui*. They obtain satisfaction in various directions, especially in war.

The Canon of Pecuniary Education covers the tendency to demand "practical" education, which, upon examination, is education that will guarantee individual success. "Success," for which education is to fit young people, turns out to be, in the eyes of the practical man, a pecuniary success. "Practical" means useful for private gain. The test that many persons would give to a course in education is this: Will it help one to get an income? The Canon of Pecuniary Thinking denotes that many occupations lead to habits of pecuniary thought. For numbers of people the beginning and end of their more serious thought is of a pecuniary nature.

The Canon of Machine Process Thinking is that mechanical employments produce a type of thinking that is based more or less on material cause and effect. The Machine knows neither morality nor dignity nor prescriptive right. The machine-process laborers, working in a world of impersonal cause and effect, "are in danger of losing the point of view of sin."

Professor Veblen has developed the concept of the instinct of workmanship at considerable length. According to this contention, it is natural for individuals to do, to construct, to achieve, to work. Through activity the individual expresses himself and, in so doing, develops and attains happiness. Every individual is a center of unfolding impulsive

[22] Thorstein Veblen, *The Instinct of Workmanship*, p. 349.

activity; he is possessed of a taste for effective work.[23]   Labor acquires a character of irksomeness by virtue of the indignity that is falsely imputed to it by a hereditary leisure class.[24]   It was the instinct of workmanship which brought the life of mankind from the brute to the human plane.

The contributions of Veblen to social thought were always of a thought-provoking nature.   Sometimes they gave rise to invidious comparisons, often they antagonized, but as a rule, they were unique.   No brief reference such as is given in the foregoing paragraphs can do justice to Veblen's pungent criticisms of societal foibles.

NOVICOW

It was Jacques Novicow (1849–1912) the Russian sociologist, who laid bare the alleged benefits of war, one of the most destructive forms of conflict, showing that the gains which come from war may be obtained through other methods of social interaction.[25]   Novicow argued forcefully that the real enemies of a group of people are disease germs and death, not the best people of other nationality groups.   Novicow's vision enabled him to perceive the foolishness of men who lock themselves together in destructive conflict, when the real enemies are microscopic disease bacteria and the gaunt, black specter of death.

When will man perceive who his real enemies are?   When will he combine against these enemies instead of engaging in warfare against his own kind?

Albion W. Small has given considerable attention to conflict theories.   These will be presented in a later chapter as a phase of Small's social thought.   They are given a setting by Small largely in relation to co-operation.[26]

Conflict bulks large in the sociology of Edward A. Ross Any interference with the carrying out of the individual's plans and with the satisfying of his interests creates opposition.   The best characteristic of the phenomenon of oppo-

---

[23] Thorstein Veblen, *The Theory of the Leisure Class*, p. 15.
[24] *Ibid.*, p. 17.
[25] J. Novicow, *War and Its Alleged Benefits*.
[26] Albion W. Small, *General Sociology*, Part IV.

sition is that it awakens and stimulates.[27] Competition operates according to psychologic laws; for example, the intensity of competition varies according (1) to the degree of personal liberty, (2) to the rate of social change, and (3) inversely as the efficiency of the selective agents.[28]

One of the most important forms of competition is found in industrialism. The invention and adoption of the power-driven machine has created an industrialism which is molding and transforming society in startling ways, and which is causing "its members more and more to cluster at opposite poles of the social spindle." [29] Professor Ross expresses slight hope that the ownership of industrial capital will be disseminated through the working class according to the conflict rules of the present economic system. His social psychological ideas will be given prominence in a later chapter.

SOCIAL REVOLUTION

Sorokin has analyzed the sociology of revolution, pointing out its changes and arguing for orderly social control and evolution. He defines revolution as "a change in the behavior of the people on the one hand and their psychology, ideology, beliefs and valuations on the other"; it "signifies a change in the biologic composition of population, and of the reproductive and selective processes in the midst"; it involves consequences, "the deformation of the social structure of society," and changes in the "fundamental social processes." [30]

Revolution brings certain psychological types of persons to the top of the "legal and proprietary pyramid," for example, "energetic people with dominating destructive impulses," "narrow-minded people who do not want and cannot foresee all the calamities that are bound to be brought about by unlimited destruction," to "people of a 'single idea,' some of whom are unbalanced maniacs and fanatics, full of unsatisfied ambitions, hatred and exasperations, indifferent to other people's sufferings." On the other hand, "peaceful, compas-

[27] E. A. Ross, *Principles of Sociology*, p. 167.
[28] *Ibid.*, p. 183.
[29] *Ibid.*, pp. 206, 207.
[30] P. Sorokin, *The Sociology of Revolution*, p. 11.

sionate people," creative persons, the sane and broad-minded "are left in the shadow, brought to the bottom and are bound to remain passive." [31]

During the first stages of a revolution social organization sharply veers "in the direction of uncontrolled anarchical autonomy." The movement then shifts in the opposite direction toward "a stage of despotic state intervention surpassing pre-revolutionary despotism." After the revolution is over, the state intervention decreases.[32]

Sorokin has outlined a program to take the place of revolutionary movements. It includes four canons: (1) A reform movement must observe the fundamental principles of human nature and development, (2) it must be preceded by a scientific study of "concrete social conditions," (3) it must be tested first on a small scale in order to see if it will work in a larger way, and (4) it must function within legal and constitutional regulations. A revolution violates all these principles.[33]

In analyzing the origins of the Russian Revolution which culminated in 1917, Boris V. Morkovin developed the concept of *incipient revolution*. Revolution never comes suddenly. It "breaks" suddenly, but it develops through the decades. These antecedent years are characterized by incipient revolution. Dr. Morkovin speaks of the Russian intelligentsia as being the bearers for decades of the incipient revolution. The poets and dreamers reacted against the routine, the materialism, and the corrupt practices of the czars and their governments. The idealism of the philosophers negated the theory of "the old regime." The socially realistic writers "fixed the attention of the public upon the burning evils of Russia." The "nihilists" emancipated themselves "from the old society, mentally, morally, and socially." [34] The summary of the matter is that the social process of incipient revolution involves the rise and functioning of a new social group that proposes to establish a new social order.

In discussing the causes of social revolutions, Professor

[31] *Ibid.*, pp. 280, 281.
[32] *Ibid.*, p. 301.
[33] *Ibid.*, pp. 14, 15.
[34] Boris V. Morkovin, "Incipient Revolution in Its Personality and Group Aspects" (unpublished Doctoral dissertation, University of Southern California 1929).

Raul A. Orgaz of the University of Cordova, Argentina, points out that revolution is an abnormal method of secur-ing social change. Often criticizing adversely the intellec-tualist theories, the struggle theories, and the instinctivist theories, he explains revolution by what he calls the "mutual conditionality and mutual dependence of social phenom-ena." This principle is to be applied to four qualities of the revolutionarily-minded person, namely: (1) discontent with the present, (2) consciousness of right in the revolution-ary mass, (3) ideals of the future expressed by leaders, and (4) consciousness of power.[35] The basic condition is a social unbalance. As a result the revolutionary person develops on the fourfold basis already indicated, and then the revolution develops because of mutual conditionality.

In some ways Franz Oppenheimer is a lineal descendant of Gumplowicz, particularly with reference to the latter's concept of conflict. However, Oppenheimer has made con-tributions more or less distinctive in the field of social thought. An example is his analysis of the evolution of the state in his work, *The State*. In a primitive hunting society there can be no state for there is no storage of property. With herdsmen the situation is different. An accumulation of property suggests its defense against attack. Such defense requires the rudiments of political organization. In order to keep larger herds of live stock, enemies captured in battle are not killed but enslaved. The economic basis of the state is the exploitation of human labor. Social classes develop and economic differentiation takes place. Then comes a "definitely circumscribed territorial limit," and the practice of "dominion" is completed.

Oppenheimer defines six stages in the development of the state. (1) Robbery and killing in border fights. (2) Enemies are no longer murdered but kept as slaves. These peasant slaves accept their lowly status. (3) Peasant groups pay trib-ute. (4) The uniting of the lands of aggressor and of de-feated neighbors. (5) The lord or ruler arbitrates the dif-ferences between his subjects, and "courts" are set up. (6) A sense of "nationality" is achieved. In this rather sordid way

[35] Raul A. Orgaz, "Causes of Social Revolutions." *Sociology and Social Re-search*, XVI:122-114.

the modern state has evolved, if Oppenheimer's analysis be correct.

In summary it may be said that competition is not an evil in itself. The spirit which dominates competition is the important thing. Some people are motivated by the pig-trough philosophy, which emphasizes struggle for the sake of possession and consumption of goods. The workbench phi-losophy accents "action and not possession, production and not consumption."

These theories, excellent in many particulars, apparently do not rate at full value the fact that education and co-operation can and do modify the self-interest of the individ-ual, and at the same time direct the attention of the indi-vidual toward unselfish service. In stressing service through achievement and production, they neglect to emphasize achievement through co-operation and service.

GROUP DISCUSSION TOPICS

1. The meaning of the concept *social conflict.*
2. The mainspring of progress according to Gumplowicz.
3. The relation of the individual to the group, as set forth by Gumplowicz.
4. The nature of Nietzsche's superman.
5. The difference between Gumplowicz's and Nietzsche's atti-tude toward the "individual."
6. The distinction between a pain economy and a pleasure economy.
7. The fatal effects upon a nation of a pleasure economy.
8. The cause of conflicts as indicated by Carver.
9. The chief social cause of economic scarcity.
10. The three fields where conflicts occur.
11. The cause of moral problems.
12. The practical danger of altruism.
13. Types of destructive conflicts.
14. The meaning of deceptive conflicts.
15. The scope of persuasive conflicts.
16. The difference between competitive production and com-petitive consumption.
17. The contrast between pig-trough philosophy and work-bench consumption.
18. The canon of pecuniary emulation.
19. The canon of pecuniary beauty.
20. The canon of conspicuous consumption.

21. The canon of conspicuous leisure.
22. The canon of leisure-class conservatism.
23. The canon of pecuniary efficiency.
24. The canon of bellicoseness.
25. The canon of pecuniary education.
26. The canon of machine-process thinking.
27. The instinct of workmanship.
28. The real enemies of mankind, as seen by Novicow.
29. The useful phases of conflict.

READINGS

Barnes, Harry E., Editor, *An Introduction to the History of Sociology* (Chicago: University of Chicago Press 1948), Ch. 8.

Carver, Thomas N., *Essays in Social Justice* (Cambridge, Massachusetts: Harvard University Press 1915).

Ellwood, Charles A., *A History of Social Philosophy* (New York : Prentice-Hall, Inc. 1938), Ch. XXVII.

Gumplowicz, Ludwig, *Der Rassenkampf* (Innsbruck : Wagner 1928).

————, *Outlines of Sociology,* translated by F. W. Moore (Philadelphia : American Academy of Political and Social Science 1899).

————, *Soziologie und Politik* (Paris: Giard and Briere 1898).

Lerner, Max, editor, *The Portable Veblen* (New York: The Viking Press 1958).

Morkovin, Boris V., "Incipient Revolution in Its Personality and Group Aspects." (unpublished doctoral dissertation, University of Southern California, Los Angeles 1929).

Nietzsche, Friedrich, *Genealogy of Morals* (New York: The Macmillan Company 1924).

————, *The Will to Power,* translated by A. M. Ludovici (London: Allen University 1924).

Novicow, Jacques, *War and Its Alleged Benefits,* translated by Seltzer (New York: Henry Holt and Company 1911).

Patten, S. N., *A Theory of Social Forces* (Philadelphia: American Academy of Political and Social Science 1896).

Rosenberg, Bernard, *The Values of Veblen* (Washington, D.C.: Public Affairs Press 1956).

Small, Albion W., *General Sociology* (Chicago: University of Chicago Press 1905).

Sorokin, Pitirim A., *The Sociology of Revolution* (Philadelphia: J. B. Lippincott Company 1925).

————, *Contemporary Sociological Theories* (New York: Harper & Brothers 1928), Ch. VI.

CHAPTER XXV

KROPOTKIN AND CO-OPERATIVE SOCIAL THOUGHT

Co-operation is a primary social process. It began with earliest mankind. It was a necessary defense against enemies of all kinds. Co-operation has attracted the attention of man as a process to be encouraged. The evidence of its operation is on every hand and hence thought concerning its complicated nature is universal.

One of the first persons to work out a systematic interpretation of co-operation was Giovanni Vico (1668–1744), an Italian philosopher.[1] Vico rejected the social contract idea because he believed that it was a false interpretation of the true principle of co-operation. The concept of a social contract embodied an artificial and metaphysical idea of social life.

VICO

In his chief work, *Principles of a New Science Concerning the Common Nature of Nations,* Vico inaugurated a study of actual social phenomena. He sought to discover possible social laws. He attempted to cast aside the accidental social elements and to organize the regularities of social phenomena into laws. He searched for the laws governing the growth and decay of societies. He undertook to analyze the history of human society.

Although Vico's important treatise was not known outside of Italy until a century and a half after it was originally published, it contained a statement of the factor which is basic to any sound co-operation theory of social progress. Vico was one of the first writers to describe the principle that all human groups have a common nature. His comparative studies of human institutions everywhere led him always to the belief in the common mind of mankind, a concept which in recent years has been elaborated by D. G. Brinton and

[1] *Cf.* S. H. Swinney, "Giambatista Vico," *Sociological Review,* 7:50-57.

others. For this contribution Vico has been called "the father of sociology."

According to Vico, the fundamental social movement is a gradual unfolding or evolution of social institutions in response to the common needs of people. Society owes its development in part to the reflections of the wise, as the social contract theorists have said, but also to the human feelings even of the brutish. This natural sociability of man has furnished the chief basis for the rise and development of the spirit of co-operation.

The natural sociability of human beings has led, more or less consciously on the part of man, to the establishment of necessary social relations and institutions. The purpose of social organization is to produce perfect human personalities. Vico outlined the evolutionary character of society according to the spiral theory: that society does return upon itself, but that, when it completes a cycle, it is upon a higher plane of co-operation than when the given cycle began. Vico also made religion a necessary principle of progress. Although in adjusting himself to the prevailing theological dogmas of his time, Vico may have committed serious errors, he nevertheless is deserving of special credit for his emphasis upon the common nature and natural sociability of mankind.

Hugo Grotius (1583–1645), the celebrated Dutch scholar, gave to social thought the international concept. He advanced the idea of the coming co-operation among the nations — nations which are moved primarily by jealousy and hatred in their relations with one another. Grotius was the originator of a definite set of principles and laws of international co-operation. His work in this regard accentuated the importance of like-mindedness in matters of international polity.

Spinoza, whose contributions regarding the concept of sovereignty have already been stated, declared that the instinct to acquire is naturally stronger than the tendency to share. Hence, man must be educated to perceive the advantages of co-operative living. When this appreciation occurs, when the advantages of co-operation become clear, then man will sublimate his egoistic and self-seeking desires to altruistic communal living. As man comes to understand, step by step, the values of co-operative conduct, he will overcome, degree by degree, his egoistic impulses.

ROCHDALE PIONEERS

The practical experiments in co-operation as represented by the Rochdale Pioneers who organized a consumers' co-operative in 1844 have led to widespread developments in co-operation chiefly in England, in Denmark, and other Scandinavian countries. They have flourished best when a co-operative atmosphere has been first developed. While the experiments in producers' co-operation have often failed and have not yet been outstandingly successful, they have testified to the absence of a developed co-operative spirit rather than to the failure of the principle upon which they are based.

The well-known and highly successful principles of co-operation as adopted at Rochdale are:

1. Membership open to all, irrespective of sex, race, politics, or religion.

2. Each member to receive one vote irrespective of amount of capital invested.

3. Capital to be raised from members only and to receive a fixed and modest rate of interest in place of profit.

4. Cash sales.

5. A small percentage of net returns to go to education and to reserves.

6. The remaining savings to be returned to the consumers or purchasers of goods regularly on a pro rata basis according to the amount of purchases made.

7. Market prices to be charged and honest measure to be given.

The Raiffeisen co-operatives, founded by Friedrich W. Raiffeisen (1818–1888), added another point to the co-operative plan. Instead of returning the profits to the purchasers, the profits are put into a fund, which is used for community betterment enterprises. The marvel of the social principles of the Rochdale co-operative movement is that where they have been modified least since their inception nearly a century ago they have stood the test of time and of use in many countries.

Earlier, Robert Owen (1771–1858) conceived the idea of a Utopian community which he developed in his work entitled, *A New View of Society*, in 1816. His experiments, however, did not succeed. The persons who participated, for example, in the community at New Harmony, Indiana (1825–1827), were poorly prepared and represented too wide a range of miscellaneous individuals possessing pet ideas and panaceas.

KROPOTKIN

Perhaps no names serves quite so well in offering a background for the consideration of co-operative social thought as does that of Peter Kropotkin (1842–1921). He was not the first nor the ablest writer in this field, but he laid far-flung bases for an examination of co-operation as a social concept. His *Mutual Aid; a Factor in Evolution* is a classic in its field.[2]

Kropotkin, a loyal Darwinian, protested against the falsely labeled "social Darwinism." Kropotkin made it plain that Darwin's interpretation of evolution, while stressing the struggle for existence, also pointed out that there is in evolution a powerful tide of co-operation. The logical conclusion of this treatment of evolution, according to Kropotkin, is not an aspect of "social Darwinism" with its emphasis upon a biological struggle in the highest human realms, but a world of human association in which the co-operative spirit has risen to a position of control over physical force and egoistic desire.

Kropotkin studied animal life extensively and concluded that, although there was among animals a severe struggle against a heartless Nature, there was essentially no bitter struggle for existence "among animals belonging to the same species."[3] There is no pitiless inner war for life within this species, and moreover, this alleged war is not a condition of

[2] Valuable for the wealth of data assembled concerning "mutual aid," beginning with the simpler forms of animal life and reaching into complicated human relations.

[3] *Ibid.*, p. vii; *cf.* Kropotkin, *Fields, Factories, and Workshops*, Chapter I.

progress. War, declared Kropotkin, is not a condition of social progress.

Kropotkin is not a one-theory interpreter of society. He perceives the role of self-assertion as a factor in social innovation. Self-assertiveness has received the lion's share of attention. It is necessary, therefore, that mutual aid be given a thorough-going consideration before the two tendencies can be adequately compared.

MUTUAL AID

Mutual aid, being less spectacular, is usually underrated. Self-assertion, by its destructiveness as seen in a single war, cannot be compared as an agency of progress for a moment with mutual aid.

Even in the field of industry where competition is so obvious, the function of mutual aid is outstanding. It rarely receives adequate credit.

When we turn to the technical relations of mankind, there the principle of mutual aid eclipses all else. Thus, mutual aid operates in the most vital phase of human relations in a way that gives it first rank among social forces.

SOCIAL ORIGINS

Kropotkin considered the clan and the tribe rather than the individual or even the family the starting point of society. The tribe itself developed a morale on the basis of beliefs in its common origin and in the worship of common ancestors. Then the possession in common of certain lands served to arouse new tribal loyalties. These loyalties expressed themselves in the form of "con-jurations," sworn agreements, and ultimately in fraternities and guilds for mutual support. Kropotkin believed that primitive man was naturally peaceful, and that he fought from necessity rather than from ferocity.

In primitive communal organization the judge and military chief united for "mutual insurance of domination," drawing to their support the slavish loyalty of the witch-doctor or priest. In the twelfth century, however, the old communal spirit broke forth with "striking spontaneity all over Europe;" it stopped for a time the growth of the despotic monarchies of Europe; it produced endless numbers of communes.

The free cities developed under the shelter of communal liberties, and in them art and invention flourished, producing the beauty of Raphael, the vigor of Michelangelo, the poetry of Dante, and "the discoveries which have been made by modern science — the compass, the clock, the watch, printing, gunpowder, the maritime discoveries, the law of gravitation." [4]

Then, there came the modern State formed by a triple alliance of the military chief, the Roman judge, and the priest. The industrial revolution and the rise of capitalism furthered the interests of the military-legal-priestly triumvirate. When the State and the Church were separated, the money baron took the place of the priest in the triumvirate. With the overthrow of militarism the power of the triumvirate is broken, and the old communal co-operative feelings of man again begin to express themselves. Mutual aid is the main hope of the race and of social progress.

Kropotkin led the way in defining the law of co-operative individualism. He urged decentralization in social control and attacked monopolies of all types, public as well as private. Although he exaggerated the role of mutual aid in primitive society, considering it the main social factor, he nevertheless rendered a valuable service in giving the world a vigorous presentation of a significant concept.

RATZENHOFER

The social process was analyzed in terms of both conflict and co-operation by Gustav Ratzenhofer (1842–1904). He supplemented and corrected some of the ideas of Gumplowicz. The social process is characterized by a continuous reappearance of the phenomena of individualization of structures already extant.[5] Both differentiation and socialization

---

[4] "The State: Its Historic Role," reproduced in *Man or the State*, by W. R. Browne, p. 21.

[5] Gustav Ratzenhofer, *Die soziologische Erkenntniss*, Section 22; see A. W. Small, *General Sociology*, Chapter XIII.

arise out of the operation of human interests. Both are implicit in the nature of man. Certain human interests lead to individualization and some to socialization.

At this point we encounter Ratzenhofer's theory of force. Force and interest are made two primordial principles. These two factors work together in order to secure for the individual the largest possible degree of self-development.

The struggle of pre-primitive men against the harsh phases of nature established a pre-primitive sociality. Struggle has always led to co-operation in the interests of preservation. Similarly, war leads to co-operation. In primitive society institutions arose in response to community needs. Among barbarians the increase in numbers produced an increasing emphasis upon conflict, which was expressed in robberies, wars, and enslavements. Warfare led to the formation of classes and class conflicts. Class interests, as distinguished from individual interests, then began to secure definition. With the rise of capitalism, the interests of capital were asserted; and at once the interests of labor, in opposition, assumed tangible expression. A stage, however, of stable social conditions is coming, in which the whole world will be organized on the basis of a single system of economic and non-competing production and of free international exchange.[6]

Ratzenhofer, whose emphasis on co-operation was pronounced, developed a twofold analysis of the social process into individualization and socialization. These two subprocesses represent two opposing or conflicting tendencies.

The impulse to individualism is set over against the impulse to form communities. One leads to the atomization of society; the other, to its consolidation. Socialization is both restraining and vibrant. It restrains in order to make greater co-operation possible.

To Ratzenhofer, the social order holds in check the struggle for existence. Intelligence and ethics are the factors which keep society orderly and dependable.

Throughout his analysis Ratzenhofer gives "force" a leading place. He also develops a theory of a ruling aristocracy of supermen. Despite these emphases, Ratzenhofer's con-

[6] Ratzenhofer, *Soziologie*, pp. 13-17.

tribution to social thought is his theory of interests as dominating human factors, and his accent upon the rise of an
increasing degree of co-operation.

HOBHOUSE

The sociology of L. T. Hobhouse (1864–1929) is largely an
interpretation of society in terms of increasing co-operation.
Hobhouse defined social progress as the development of the
principle of union, order, co-operation, and harmony among
individuals. He described a certain mutual interest, similar
to Giddings' consciousness of kind, which has served to keep
individuals together, from the lowest groups of savages to
the highest civilized groups. Hobhouse's concept of social
harmony is something more than order established by the
exercise of repression. Repression leads to disharmony.
Moreover, it is an unnecessary disharmony and therefore an
evil. How can social harmony be realized? What must the
individual do? An experimental attitude must be maintained.

The writings of Hobhouse reveal a thorough and comparative study of the conduct rules of mankind. Hobhouse
described the evolution of ethical consciousness as displayed
in the habits, customs, and principles that have arisen in
human history for the regulation of human conduct.[7] He
showed how, in the lowest forms of the organic world, behavior is regulated, and directed to some purpose.[8] This
behavior is somewhat definitely determined by the structure
of the organism itself.

SOCIAL PRINCIPLES

There are three forces which may be called social, or
which tend to keep society together. These social bonds
are: (1) the principle of kinship, (2) the principle of authority, and (3) the principle of citizenship.[9] Kinship is the
moving force in primitive society. The principle of authority becomes prominent when one tribe captures and enslaves

---

[7] L. T. Hobhouse, *Morals in Evolution*, p. 1.
[8] *Ibid.*, p. 2.
[9] *Ibid.*, p. 43; *cf.* Hobhouse, *Social Evolution and Political Theory*, pp.
128 ff.

a weaker group. This principle is also invoked in order to secure an integration of openly diverse attitudes within the group, even of modern national groups. It is exemplified in the various forms of absolutism in government. The principle of citizenship finds expression when certain individuals within the group are delegated to perform as servants and ministers of the public as a whole.[10] Personal rights and the common good are the two reigning ideals. Every person is recognized as having a right to the conditions requisite for the full development of his social personality. The good in life consists "in bringing out into full bloom those capacities of each individual which help to maintain the common life."[11] The third principle, that of citizenship, when carried to its conclusion reveals the possibility of a world state.[12]

It is the contention of Hobhouse that there is a close connection between the growth of law and justice and the prevalent forms of social organization. Organized law has developed out of a sense of community responsibility, which, however, has expressed itself as a rule in crude ways, and without distinguishing between accident and design. This sense of community responsibility in primitive groups tends to hold in check the spirit of anarchy and of self-redress. Sooner or later, the method of community self-redress yields to the authority of a chief or of a council representing the whole community.[13] Ultimately the community develops a special social organ for adjusting disputes and preventing crime. It is then that the ethical idea becomes separated from the conflicting passions of the collectivity. Thus the foundations are laid for true judicial inquiry by evidence and genuine proof, and for a system of scientific public justice.

Hobhouse found the social ideal not in a utopian society, "but in the love of a spiritual life with its unfailing spring of harmonious growth unconfined."[14] The goal above every goal is "the harmonious fulfilment of human capacity."

[10] *Ibid.*, p. 60.
[11] *Ibid.*, p. 64.
[12] L. T. Hobhouse, *Social Evolution and Political Theory*, p. 148.
[13] L. T. Hobhouse, *Morals in Evolution*, pp. 130, 171.
[14] L. T. Hobhouse, *The Elements of Social Justice*, p. 3.

Hobhouse protested vigorously against that co-operation in industry which makes the civilized worker "the slave of a machine where the savage is a hunter or fisherman using his faculties as a whole." [15] He reacts also against a social co-operation whereby "what is one man's luxury is another man's necessity."

The principle of "mutual need" if "carried to completion would yield a harmonious development of humanity." [16] The world has become "one vast society," but unfortunately "it has neither the spirit of unity, nor the clear sense of a common interest, nor an adequate mechanism which might at least maintain the externals of orderly peace." [17] Not constraint in social life but "co-operation resting on mutual need" — such is the Hobhouse formula for social development. [18]

The principle of co-operation lies at the basis of a true democracy. Carried out in full, co-operation requires the extension of democratic government into the international realm. Moreover, it needs a re-interpretation of economic problems in a way so that "each man can find the means of making the best of his own life in the service of the community and in nothing else." [19]

The three basic concepts of Hobhouse, according to one of his pupils, Professor John E. Nordskog, are "development," "harmony," and "rational good." Development can come only through liberty. Harmony extends to all men of good will. It is achieved through sacrifice and co-operation. The rational good is found in humanity itself, which must rank above any national state or international federation of states. [20]

The theories of co-operation are not limited to those presented in this chapter. Special co-operation theories are discussed in the following chapters in connection with such themes as socialization, social understanding, collective representations, and consciousness of kind.

[15] *Ibid.*, pp. 23, 24.
[16] L. T. Hobhouse. *Social Development*, p. 13.
[17] *Ibid.*, p. 30.
[18] *Ibid.*, p. 87.
[19] *Ibid.*, p. 300.
[20] John E. Nordskog, "Leonard T. Hobhouse: Internationalist," *Sociology and Social Research*, 14:382.

GROUP DISCUSSION TOPICS

1. Vico as the father of sociology.
2. Vico's spiral theory of progress.
3. Grotius' international concept.
4. Spinoza's plan for the overcoming of egoistic impulses.
5. The chief reason for the partial failure of producers' co-operation.
6. Kropotkin's attitude toward co-operation.
7. Co-operative individualism according to Kropotkin.
8. The relation of self-assertiveness to mutual aid.
9. Primitive man as a peaceful being.
10. Ratzenhofer's concept of force.
11. Individualization according to Ratzenhofer.
12. Socialization as conceived by Ratzenhofer.
13. Ratzenhofer's idea of the social order.
14. The "social harmony" concept according to Hobhouse.
15. Social forces according to Hobhouse.

READINGS

Bogardus, E. S., *Principles of Cooperation* (Chicago: The Cooperative League of the U.S.A. 1952).

Eaton, Joseph W., "A Conceptual Theory of Cooperation," *American Journal of Sociology*, 54:126-134.

Hobhouse, L. T., *Social Evolution and Political Theory* (London: Lemcke 1911).

——, *Social Development* (New York: Henry Holt and Company 1924).

——, *The Elements of Social Justice* (New York: Henry Holt and Company 1922).

Kropotkin, Peter, *Mutual Aid: a Factor in Evolution* (New York: Doubleday, Page and Company 1902).

——, *Fields, Factories, and Workshops* (New York: G. P. Putnam's Sons 1901).

Nordskog, John E., "Leonard T. Hobhouse: Internationalist," *Sociology and Social Research*, 14:373-382.

Orne, Anders, *Cooperative Ideals and Problems* (Manchester, England: Cooperative Union 1937).

Ratzenhofer, Gustav, *Die soziologische Erkenntniss* (Leipzig: Brockhaus, 1898).

Swinney, S. H., "Giambatista Vico," *Sociological Review*, 7:50-57.

Warbasse, James P., *Cooperative Democracy* (New York: Harper & Brothers 1947).

——, *Cooperative Peace* (Superior: The Cooperative Publishing Association 1950).

CHAPTER XXVI

TARDE AND SOCIAL INTERACTION

A large number of references have already been made to psycho-sociologic thought. In origin it may be traced to the primitive days of the race. The folkways reveal keen phases of psycho-sociologic observations. Undoubtedly, many phases of the psychic nature of group activities were known to the leaders of ancient civilizations. Plato wrote on the importance of custom and custom imitation as a societal force. Aristotle understood the psycho-social nature of man when he observed that property which is owned in common is least taken care of, and when he declared that a fundamental test of good government may be found in the attitude of a people toward public service. In his theory of social attitudes Aristotle made a distinct contribution to psycho-sociologic thought.

Thomas More analyzed the causes of human actions. He was a worthy social psychologist when he protested against heaping punishment upon human beings, without attempting to understand the causes of criminal conduct and without seeking to remove the societal causes of such conduct. Bodin postulated a theory of interests in his explanation of social evolution. He made the common economic, religious, and other interests of man the basis of social organization. These interests, according to Bodin, led primitive families to form a community or organization or government.

It was Hobbes who believed that man originally was a being of entirely selfish interests. Man's interest in others was based on their ability to cater to his own good. This theory still has strong support; there are large numbers of persons who today apparently are living according to this rule. Nations oftentimes seem to be motivated today by no higher principle. On the basis of an introspective psychology, Hobbes made the scientific observation that "he that is going to be a whole man must read in himself — mankind."

Such a person must not simply find in himself this or that man's interests, but the interests of all mankind.

George Berkeley (1685–1753), Bishop of Cloyne and eminent philosopher, in his *Principles of Moral Attraction* attempted to point out the analogies between the physical and social universe. His work was stimulated by the discoveries of Isaac Newton. He tried to apply the Newtonian formulas to society. While his "physical analogies" are of little value, they represent a stage in the rise of psycho-sociologic thought. He made the social instinct, or the gregarious instinct, in society the analogue of the force of gravitation. The centrifugal force in society is selfishness; and the centripetal, sociability. As the attractive force of one mass for another varies directly in relation to the distance between them, so the attraction of persons for one another varies directly in proportion to their resemblances. The physical analogies, however, could not be carried far without being lost in the realm of absurdity.

SYMPATHY

The Scotch philosopher, David Hume, has been called the father of social psychology because of his splendid analysis of sympathy as a social force. "Let all the powers and elements of nature conspire to serve and obey one man, . . . he will still be miserable, till you give him some person at least with whom he may share his happiness, and whose esteem and friendship he may enjoy." [1] "Whatever other passions we may be actuated by, pride, ambition, avarice, curiosity, revenge, or lust — the soul or animating principle of them is sympathy." [2]

But sympathy is not always limited in its operation to the present moment. Through sympathy we may put ourselves in the future situation of any person whose present condition arouses our interest in him. Moreover, if we see a stranger in danger, we will run to his assistance.

Vice was defined by Hume as everything which gives un-

[1] David Hume, *A Treatise of Human Nature,* edited by Selby-Bigge, p. 363.
[2] *Ibid.,* p. 362.

easiness in human actions. By sympathy, we become uneasy when we become aware of injustice anywhere. "Self-interest is the original motive to the establishment of justice; but a sympathy with public interest is the source of the moral approbation which attends that virtue."[3] There is a continual conflict between self-interest and sympathy, both in a person and between persons in society. Although at times this self-interest seems to predominate, "it does not entirely abolish the more generous and noble intercourse of friendship and good offices."[4]

Sympathy causes people to be interested in the good of mankind.[5] But whatever human factor is contiguous either in space or time has a proportionate effect on the will, passions, and imagination.[6] It commonly operates with greater force than any human factor that lies in a distant and more obscure light. This principle explains why people often act in contradiction to their interests, and "why they prefer any trivial advantage that is present to the maintenance of order in society."

In accordance with the analysis of sympathy by Hume, Adam Smith made sympathy a leading concept in his theory of political economy. Smith also carried the concept of self-interest, with the resultant conflict between self-interest and social interest, into nearly all his economic theories.

According to Adam Smith there are four classes of people in modern life. (1) There are those who live by taking rent. They have social interests but are not socially productive; they grow listless and careless. (2) There is the class which takes wages. This group is large, productive, and socially interested, but their widespread lack of education makes many of them subject to the passions of the day, and hence socially useless or even harmful. (3) Those who take profit have interests at direct variance with the welfare of society. Their egoistic interests become unduly developed; their public attitudes are often dangerous to all except themselves. (4) The fourth group is composed of all who derive a living from serving one or more of the three aforementioned

[3] Hume, *op. cit.*, pp. 499, 500.
[4] *Ibid.*, p. 521.
[5] *Ibid.*, pp. 575 ff.
[6] *Ibid.*, p. 535.

classes. The interests of the three first-mentioned groups often clash, leading to destructive social conflicts. Despite this conclusion, Adam Smith was an advocate of *laissez faire*. He urged that natural laws be allowed to express themselves normally.

In 1859, Moritz Lazarus and Heymann Steinthal began to contribute to social thought in the *Zeitschrift für Völker-Psychologie und Sprachwissenschaft*. They applied psychological methods to the study of primitive society. In this journal they made notable contributions concerning the social customs and mental traits of early mankind. It is in this field, which was discussed in Chapter XXII, that the original work of such men as Franz Boas, W. G. Sumner, W. I. Thomas, and L. T. Hobhouse belongs. Fundamental pioneering in psycho-sociologic thought was done by Lester F. Ward (see Chapter XXI). Ward opposed the prevailing belief of his time, and particularly of Herbert Spencer, that society must continue as it now is going on, namely, an exhibition of a blind struggle of competitive forces. He not only perceived the rise of mind out of obscure processes of social evolution, but more important still, he noted the part that mind may play in modifying the course of social forces. Although he considered the human desires to be the dynamic social elements, he gave to mind, through its power of prevision, the prerogative of directing the desires of mankind. Moreover, he pointed out the direction in which mind could best guide the desires. He urged a sociocracy in which the desires of a person are so controlled that they operate only when in harmony with the welfare of other persons. For emphasizing these fundamental considerations, Ward ranks high in the history of psycho-sociologic thought.

TARDE

The chief founder of social psychology was Gabriel Tarde (1834–1904). He wrote the first important treatise in the field of the psychology of society. The *Lois de l'imitation* established Tarde's reputation as a pioneer social psychologist, and at the same time aroused the world of thought to the existence of a new phase of social science. Tarde was a jurist who inquired into the causes of anti-social conduct. He was greatly impressed by the observation that criminal acts are committed in waves. Upon examination of this fact he found imitation to be a potent factor, and began to analyze the laws of imitation. This study soon showed that not all is imitation but that much human conduct arises out of opposition. His analysis of the laws of opposition led him to the conclusion that imitation and opposition are the bases of a third social factor, invention. The social process, as he observed it, is characterized (1) by an ever-widening imitation of inventions, (2) by the opposition of conflicting circles of imitation, and (3) by the rise of new inventions (out o. these oppositions), which in turn become the centers of new imitations. Thus the social process goes on, endlessly and unconsciously or consciously. To understand society, Tarde believed that one must understand how minds act and interact.

There is a universality that is characteristic of Tarde's three laws of societary life that should not be overlooked. Biology helps to explain their operation. Physical process and mental process alike are encompassed by the functioning of these three laws. They furnish the keys for understanding the universe.

Tarde's work, first presented in *Les Lois de l'imitation,* was formally developed in his *Logique sociale,* and summarized in his *Lois sociale* (English translation, *Social Laws*). Together, these books constitute a unique social theory. Although Tarde's approach to the psychology of society was objective and sociological, and although he did not give serious attention to the purely psychological nature of the mind or to the instinctive bases of conduct, he nevertheless made a contribution to social thought which is interesting.

NATURE OF SOCIETY

Society, according to Tarde, is a group of people "who display many resemblances, produced either by imitation or by counter-imitation." [7] Again, he says that society is "a group of distinct individuals who render one another mutual serv-

---

[7] Gabriel Tarde, *The Laws of Imitation,* translated by Parsons, p. xvii.

ices."[8] Societies are groups of people who are organized because of agreement or disagreement of beliefs.[9] "Society is imitation."[10] The outstanding element in social life is a psychological process in which inventions are followed by imitations, which when coming into inevitable oppositions produce new inventions.

Social life is a complicated system, but not a mere accumulation of inventions. Society is not a simple piling up of inventions through endless imitation.

To the degree that a person is social he is imitative. In the way that vital, or biological, resemblances are due to heredity, so human resemblances are caused by imitation. The closer the human resemblances between persons, even though they be occupational competitors, the larger will be the proportion of imitations and the closer the social relationships. The father will always be the son's first model.[11] A beloved ruler will so fascinate his people that they will imitate blindly, yea, even be thrown into a state of catalepsy by him. In such a case imitation becomes a kind of somnambulism.[12]

Imitations are characterized by inclines, plateaus, and declines.[13] The incline refers to the period of time which an imitation requires for adoption. The plateau is the length of time during which an imitation is in force. The decline, of course, has to do with the passing away of an imitation. Each of these phases is of varying length — dependent upon the operation of almost countless socio-psychical factors. It is this career through which all imitations must pass that is the important phase of history.[14]

There are two causal factors determining the nature of imitation: logical, and non-logical.[15] Logical causes operate when the imitator adopts an innovation that is in line with the principles that have already found a place in his own mind. Extra-logical, or non-logical, imitations are

---

8 *Ibid.*, p. 59.
9 *Ibid.*, p. 146.
10 *Ibid.*, p. 74.
11 *Ibid.*, p. 78.
12 *Ibid.*, p. 87.
13 *Ibid.*, p. 114.
14 *Ibid.*, p. 39.
15 *Ibid.*, pp. 141 ff.

those which are determined by the adventitious factors of place, date, or birth of the individual.

LAW OF IMITATION

The fundamental law of imitation, stated in simplest terms, is that the superior are imitated by the inferior; for example: the patrician by the plebeian; the nobleman by the commoner; the beloved by the lover.[16] A more accurate statement of the law of imitation is that "the thing that is most imitated is the most superior one of those that are nearest." The term "superior" in all these cases must be used in the subjective sense, that is to say, that which seems to the specific individual to be superior, not necessarily that which actually is the superior, is imitated.

A country or period of time is democratic if the distance between the highest and lowest classes is lessened enough so that the highest may be imitated freely by the lowest.[17] Democracy will keep the distance between classes reduced to that minimum where imitation may operate.

Imitation tends to create large governing or controlling units in society. It seems to require initiators and large numbers of imitators. At least such is the natural course of events.

An important phase of sociology involves the knowledge and control of imitations.[18] Sociological statistics should determine (1) "the imitative power which inheres in every invention at any given time and place"; and (2) "the beneficial or harmful effects which result from the imitation of given inventions."

TYPES OF IMITATION

Imitation is divided into sets of complementary tendency; custom imitation and fashion imitation, sympathy imitation and obedience imitation, naïve imitation and deliberate imitation.[19] Everywhere custom imitation and fashion imita-

[16] *Ibid.*, p. 213; *cf.* Tarde, *Social Laws*, p. 65.
[17] *Ibid.*, p. 225.
[18] *Ibid.*, p. 111.
[19] *Ibid.*, p. 14.

tion are embodied in two parties, divisions, or organizations
— the conservative and the liberal.[20]

Through custom imitation, usages acquire autocratic
power. They control habit, regulate private conduct, and
define morals and manners with imperial authority. Usages
are frequently extra-logical imitations. Usages are commonly accepted first by the upper classes. They usually are
related primarily to objects of luxury; they stick tenaciously
to the leisure-time phases of life. Their most favorable
milieu is a social and individual status of ignorance.

Fashion imitation rules by epochs, for example: Athens
under Solon, Rome under Scipio, Florence in the fifteenth
century.[21] These epochs of fashion produce great personalities — illustrious legislators, and founders of empire. Whenever the currents of fashions are set free the inventive imagination is excited and ambitions are stimulated.

Fashion imitation has a democratizing influence. A prolonged process of fashion imitation ends "by putting pupil-
peoples upon the same level, both in their armaments and in
their arts and sciences, with their master-people." [22] In fact,
the very desire to be like the superior is a latent democratizing force.

The counterpart of imitation is opposition. Opposition,
however, may be a very special kind of repetition. There
are two types of opposition: interference-combinations and
interference-conflicts.[23] The first type refers to the coming
together of two psychological quantities of desire and belief
with the result that combination takes place and a total gain
is made. The second type refers to the opposition resulting
from incompatible forces. In this case an individual or
social loss is registered.

From another standpoint, opposition appears in one of
three forms, namely, war, competition, or discussion.[24] Conflicts often pass through these three forms, which are obedient to the same law of development, but in order are characterized by ever-widening areas of pacification, alternating,

20 *Ibid.*, p. 228.
21 *Ibid.*, pp. 341 ff.
22 *Ibid.*, p. 369.
23 *Laws of Imitation*, p. 30.
24 *Social Laws*, p. 132.

however, with renewals of discord. War is the lowest, most brutal form of conflict; discussion is the highest, most rational form.

Opposition in human life is society's logical duel.[25] This duel sometimes ends abruptly when one of the adversaries is summarily suppressed by force. Sometimes a resort to arms brings a military victory. Sometimes a new invention or discovery expels one of the adversaries from the social scene.

INVENTION

The logical result of opposition is invention or adaptation. "Invention is a question followed by an answer."[26] Invention, or adaptation, at its best is "the felicitous interference of two imitations, occurring first in one single mind."[27] Inventions grow in two ways: (1) in extension — by imitative diffusions; and (2) in comprehension — by a series of logical combinations, such as the combination of the wheel and the horse in the inventions of the horsecart.[28]

Inventions partially determine the nature of new inventions and new discoveries. A new invention makes possible other inventions, and so on. Each invention is the possible parent of a thousand offspring inventions.

To be inventive, one must be wide-awake, inquiring, incredulous, not docile and dreamy, nor living in a social sleep. The inventor is one who escapes, for the time being, from his social surroundings.[29] Inventing develops from wanting. A man experiences some want, and in order to satisfy his wants he invents. Inventiveness is contrary to sheepishness.

Since an invention is the answer to a problem, inventions are the real objective factors which mark the stage of progress. But invention, according to Tarde, becomes more and more difficult. Problems naturally grow increasingly difficult. Problems naturally grow complex as the simpler ones are mastered. Unfortunately, the mind of man is not capable of indefinite development, and therefore will reach a

[25] *Laws of Imitation,* p. 169.
[26] *Social Laws,* p. 195.
[27] *Ibid.,* p. 204.
[28] *Ibid.,* p. 171; *cf.* Tarde, *La Logique sociale,* Chapter IV.
[29] *Laws of Imitation,* p. 87.

limit in solving problems.[30] At this point, Tarde's argument can neither be proved nor disproved. Apparently, man's ability to solve problems increases with his training and experience in that connection. Moreover, man appears to be at the very dawn of his possibilities in the field of invention. He is only beginning to gather together systematically the materials for inventing, and to understand slightly the principles of inventing.

Inventors are imitative.[31] This statement is but another way of saying that inventions are cumulative, that "they come in droves," that they are gregarious. A new discovery will arouse the ambition of many wide-awake persons to make similar discoveries. "There is in every period a current of inventions which is in a certain general sense religious or architectural or sculptural or musical or philosophical." [32]

Invention and imitation represent the chief forces in society.[33] Invention is "intermittent, rare, and eruptive only at certain infrequent intervals." It explains "the source of privileges, monopolies, and aristocratic inequalities." Imitation, on the other hand, is democratic, leveling and "incessant like the stream deposition of the Nile or Euphrates." At times the eruptions of invention take place faster than they can be imitated. At other times imitations flow in a monotonous circular current.

The contributions of Tarde to social thought have stimulated numerous investigators to enter the field of social psychology. While Tarde's thinking has been severely criticized by the psychologists, and modified by the sociologists, it has opened mines of valuable ores. Not the least important was the impetus which the Tardian thought gave to American writers, such as E. A. Ross.[34] Tarde's name will be long remembered for the way in which he developed the concept of imitation. In recent years, however, much that Tarde called imitation has been more accurately explained in stimulus-response and behavior pattern terms. "Imitation," therefore, plays a role of declining importance in

30 *Ibid.*, p. 138.
31 *Ibid.*, p. 344.
32 *Loc. cit.*
33 *Laws of Imitation*, p. 387.
34 E. A. Ross. *Social Psychology*, p. viii.

psycho-sociologic thought. The current tendency is to think of behavior patterns (systems of neurones connecting affectors, sense organs, and effectors) automatically released by proper stimuli. "Unconscious imitation" as such, is nearly if not entirely eliminated, while "conscious imitation" occupies a greatly reduced and modified rank in present-day social thought.

Imitation is pronounced not only a result, but "an irrelevant result" by Ellsworth Faris.[35] Imitation is not considered an instinct, but "a mere accident of" three quite "distinct types of mechanism." (1) Mob mechanisms release attitudes already existing. Such results are immediate and unwitting. (2) Gradual acquisition of dialects or slow forming of opinions assumes the operation of precedent processes. Not all react in the same way to similar stimuli. (3) There is conscious, volitional, and planned "imitation," such as fashion imitation. Painted lips may be the vogue. Many imitate them, but many do not. And why not? One said to me, "I'm not that kind of girl." And this is the real underlying explanation of all conscious copying. If she is that kind of girl, she will imitate what seems to her to advance her status in the desired direction.[36]

Walter Bagehot, an English publicist, in an epoch-stirring book, *Physics and Politics,* published an important chapter on "Imitation" as early as 1872, thus ante-dating Tarde's *Lois de l'imitation* (1890) by eighteen years. In the United States, Michael M. Davis, Jr., has written an excellent summary of Tarde's socio-psychologic thought.[37]

In 1892, Professor H. Schmidkunz published an elaborate work on the *Psychologie der Suggestion.* This book is an important pioneer work. In the English language, the writings of Boris Sidis on the psychology of suggestion are well known. Professor E. A. Ross has given an intensive treatment of the theme in his *Social Psychology.* In these various discussions, however, the fact is not made clear that suggestion and imitation are correlative phases of the same phenomenon. The point, also, is not developed that suggestion-imitation

[35] "The Concept of Imitation," *American Journal of Sociology,* 32:367-78.
[36] *Ibid.,* p. 377.
[37] M. M. Davis, Jr., *Psychological Interpretations of Society.*

phenomena are natural products of social situations in which like stimuli normally produce like responses.

In 1895, the first book by Gustave Le Bon (1841-1931) on crowd psychology was published. Le Bon has also written on the psychology of revolutions, of wars, and of peoples. He gave a limited definition to the term *crowds,* and then applied the term to nearly all types of group life. He conceived of crowds as "feeling phenomena." They are more or less pathological. The subconscious minds of the individual members, charged with emotions, dominate the crowd. Since the proletariat are subject to crowd psychology, they are untrustworthy and to be regarded perpetually with suspicion. A sounder, more synthetic, and historical position concerning the psychology of groups and of society is taken by G. L. Duprat in *La Psychologie sociale.*

Italian contributions in the field of crowd and group psychology are represented by Paolo Orano's *Psicologia sociale,* which includes only a partial treatment of the subject that is indicated by the title ; and by Scipio Sighele's *La Foule criminelle* and *Psychologie des sectes.* Permanent groups, according to Sighele (following Tarde), are either sects, castes, classes, or states.[38] The sect is a group of individuals which possesses a common ideal and faith, such as a religious denomination or a political party. The caste arises from identity of profession. The class is characterized by a strong unity of interests. States possess common bonds of language, national values, and national prestige.

E. A. ROSS

Professor E. A. Ross began his pioneering in social psychology at least as early as 1894. At that time he delimited the field which is now called "social control." In his *Seventy Years of It,* he says in his inimitable way that in the fall of 1894, "I kept looking for the linch-pins which hold society together" and that about Christmas, in an alcove in Stanford University, "I set down as they occurred to me thirty-five distinct means by which society controls its members." These

---

[38] Gabriel Tarde, *L'opinion et la foule,* pp. 177 ff; also S. Sighele, *Psychologie des sectes,* pp. 45 ff.

thirty-five means of social control were worked over for six years, and emerged first in twenty articles in the *American Journal of Sociology,* and finally in 1901 in the well-known treatise called *Social Control.* At the time that Professor Ross was developing his thought on social control he was also active in the field of "social influence" or of "unintended domination"; in 1897, an article from his pen appeared in *Popular Science* entitled "Mob Mind." It and other materials were published eleven years later in June 1908, under the title of *Social Psychology.* Professor Ross is not far removed from current conceptions of social psychology when he makes references to the larger phase of the study as of "the moulding of the ordinary person by his social environment." Substitute the term *conditioning* for molding and the term *social processes,* which Professor Ross has long used, for the way in which social environment conditions the individual, and you have a definition that is akin to that given in a current work in the field, namely, *Social Psychology,* by LaPiere and Farnsworth.

Moreover, in his pioneer volume of 1908 on social psychology, Professor Ross declares that social psychology should precede rather than follow the study of sociology, inasmuch as "coming into planes and currents of uniformity precedes the establishing of new groups and structures." Here again, the general line of thought is not unsound. In his work as a pioneer in social psychology Edward A. Ross has made original contributions to knowledge concerning the means of social control — or intended social dominance, and of the means of social influence, or unintended social dominance.

In *Social Control,* he defined social psychology as the study of "the psychic interplay between man and his environing society." [39] This interplay is two-fold: the domination of society over the individual (social ascendancy); and the domination of the individual over society (individual ascendancy). Social ascendancy may be either purposeless (social influence) or purposeful (social control). Social psychology, according to Professor Ross, deals chiefly with psychic planes and currents. The psycho-sociologic grounds of control are found in such factors as sympathy, sociability, an elemental sense of

[39] E. A. Ross, *Social Control,* Chapters VII, VIII.

justice, and particularly in group needs. There are individuals whose conduct exasperates the group. "In this common wrath and common vengeance lies the germ of a social control of the person." [40]

PROBLEMS OF SOCIAL CONTROL

Perhaps the best part of Professor Ross' discussion of social control is his analysis of the agents of control.[41] Public opinion and law are the two most important means of controlling individuals. The weakness of one, in this connection, is its fitfulness; of the other, its rigidity. Personal beliefs and ideals function widely and effectively because of their subjective character. An individual may escape the operation of law; he can hide away from the winds of public opinion; but he cannot get away from his own ideas and conscience. It is for this reason that religious convictions are powerful. Art as a means of social control is commonly underrated. It arouses the passions, kindles sympathies, creates a sense of the beautiful and perfects social symbols, such as Columbia, La Belle France, Britannia.[42]

Systems of social control are political or moral.[43] The political form is more or less objective, is likely to be in the hands of a few, is apt to be used for class benefit. The ethical arises from sentiment rather than from utility; it is more or less subjective; it permeates hidden recesses of life. The ethical system is usually mild and enlightening, "rather than bold and fear-engendering." Individuals are ordinarily aware of political control, but the far-reaching influences of ethical control they little suspect.

The two most difficult problems for society to solve in connection with social control are these: (1) what measures of control may be best imposed; and (2) how these measures should be imposed.[44] The variety of disciplines which society may use varies from epithets to capital punishment. The methods vary from the democratic one of social self-

[40] *Social Control*, pp. 49 ff.
[41] *Ibid.*, Part II.
[42] *Ibid.*, pp. 257 ff.
[43] *Ibid.*, pp. 411 ff.
[44] *Ibid.*, Chapter XXXI.

infliction to a direct autocratic procedure. Too much control produces either stagnation or revolution, depending on the amount of energy the rank and file may possess. Too little control leads to anarchy, or at least to a reign of selfishness. A paternal social control may cause resentment or a crushing of self-respect.

Suggestion and imitation are social elements that Professor Ross has described in detail.[45] He has demonstrated that the more gregarious species are more suggestible than the species whose members are more or less solitary; that southern races are more suggestible than northern races, because of the different climatic effects upon temperament; that children are more suggestible than adults, because children possess a small store of facts and an undeveloped ability to criticize; that people of a nervous temperament are more suggestible than persons who are phlegmatic, because of difference in sensibility; that women are more suggestible than men, because they have not had the broadening influences which men have enjoyed, such as "higher education, travel, self-direction, professional pursuits, participation in intellectual and public life."[46]

The laws of imitation, particularly of fashion imitation and rational imitation, which M. Tarde was the first to outline, have been elucidated and illustrated by Professor Ross. He has cut boldly into the shams of fashion, convention, and custom, and made a strong plea for rationality in these fields. He has shown how mob mind, the craze, and the fad sweep not simply foolish and light-headed persons off their feet, but also those who are sane and sensible. In fact, he has made clear that even the most level-headed are blindly or slavishly governed by custom or fashion or both. He does not develop, however, the fact that imitation is largely a result of like-mindedness and common social stimuli. He implies an individual rather than a group origin of suggestion-imitation phenomena.

It is in discussion that Professor Ross sees one of the main hopes of progress.[47] Discussion brings conflicts to a head,

[45] E. A. Ross, *Social Psychology*, Chapter II.
[46] *Ibid.*, p. 70. *Cf.* William McDougall, *Introduction to Social Psychology*, Chapter IV.
[47] E. A. Ross, *Social Psychology*, Chapter XVIII.

and leads to group progress. Discussion changes a person's opinions. Adequate discussion leads to the settlement of a conflict and the creation of an established public opinion, which remains in force until a new invention occurs, a resultant conflict ensues, and a new public opinion comes into power.

In 1920 Professor Ross made his largest and most important contribution to social thought in his *Principles of Sociology*. The original social forces are the human dispositions, impulses, drives. The derivative social forces are societal complexes which tend to satisfy instinctive cravings.[48] Professor Ross' classification of the derivative social forces, or interests, is primarily fourfold. These fundamental interests are wealth, government, religion, and knowledge. This classification contains only two, or at best three, of the six groups of interests which are found in Professor Small's exhibit.

Professor Ross' analysis of the process of socialization centers around the idea of developing a "we-feeling" among individuals. It is "the development of the we-feeling in associates and their growth in capacity and will to act together." Then there is ossification, which is the hardening of social life into rigid forms.[49] Groups often become unduly solidified. The salvation of such a situation lies in "individuation," which is a process of pulverizing social lumps and releasing the action of their members.[50] Any movement that develops the spirit of personal liberty leads to individuation.

"Commercialization is the increasing subjection of any calling or function to the profits motive."[51] The various factors which hold the profits motive in check are: (1) pleasure in creative activity; (2) pride in the perfection of one's product; (3) the desire to live up to accepted standards of excellence; (4) abhorrence of sham in one's work; (5) interest in the welfare of the customer; (6) the social service motive. The profits motive, however, receives support from many social tendencies, notably: (1) the increasing distance between producer and consumer; (2) the growing differentia-

[48] E. A. Ross, *Principles of Sociology*, p. 42. Professor Ross has published three editions of his *Principles*. All references here are to the first edition (1920). This analysis will be discussed further in Chapter XXX.

[49] *Ibid.*, Chapter XLII.

[50] *Ibid.*, Chapter XXXVI.

[51] *Ibid.*, Chapter XXXVIII.

tion between principals and subordinates; (3) the increasing importance of capital in the practice of an art or occupation.

SOCIAL RECONSTRUCTION

Professor Ross has set forth a valuable exhibit of the canons of social reconstruction.[52] (1) Reforms must not do violence to human nature. (2) They must square with essential realities. (3) They should be preceded by a close sociological study of the situation which it is planned to change. (4) Reforms should be tried out on a small scale before being adopted on a large scale. (5) A reform should be the outcome of a social movement. (6) Under a popular government, reforms should move according to legal and constitutional methods.

In regard to the improvement of social institutions, Professor Ross rests his argument on the importance of standards. "Standards are, perhaps, the most important things in society."[53] Although invisible and intangible, they reveal, better than anything else, the quality of a society.

The current standards of the family may be improved through imparting sound ideals of marriage, through fixing these ideals everywhere in social tradition, and through making "the social atmosphere frosty toward foolish and frivolous ideals of mariage."[54] Young people may well be taught to look upon divorce as a moral shipwreck. Loyalty to the state or society has its origin in the obedience of children to parents in the family. A sound family life, thus, is rated by our author as the bulwark of society.

In regard to industry, it is pointed out that the principle of the soviet is associated in an entirely accidental way with Bolshevism.[55] The soviet may well be judged on its own merits. The principle upon which citizens may be grouped for purposes of securing representation in government is not yet settled. Is a given geographical area a better unit for securing representation than occupational areas?

State socialism is objected to by Professor Ross on the

[52] *Ibid.*, pp. 549 ff.
[53] *Ibid.*, p. 564.
[54] *Ibid.*, p. 590.
[55] *Ibid.*, p. 626.

grounds that it leaves the citizen so remote "from that which most vitally concerns him, viz., the regulation of the industry in which he works, that his yearly vote may be a mere fribble and he little better than a state serf." [56]   Guild socialism, on the other hand, urges that each branch of industry shall organize itself democratically, and that the state shall be organized not with provinces and localities as semi-autonomies but with industries exercising a degree of autonomy.   Our author endorses the general shift which is occurring at the present time from the coercive side to the service side of industrial life.

SOCIOLOGICAL PRINCIPLES

Professor Ross has deduced several important sociological principles of general import.   These he calls the principle of anticipation, the principle of simulation, the principle of individualization, and the principle of balance.   By the principle of anticipation, he means that a known policy of an institution will come to be anticipated by the members of the institution and will result in modifying behavior.[57]   Unfair advantage is often taken of people on the basis of this principle.   For example, children frequently count on favor and leniency.   The false beggar's whine is often effective.   It is in this connection that genuine social reform differs from a common conception of charity, for the former method fits people to run, clears their course, and incites them to make the race,[58] while the latter fails to render assistance of permanent value.

The principle of simulation refers to the common tendency of "the unworthy to simulate every type or trait which has won social approval, in order to steal prestige from it." [59] Commercial competition has produced adulterations, misbrandings, counterfeiting.   There is the professional athlete, who sometimes poses as a sincere enthusiast for physical development.   Politicians are often expert dissemblers.

The principle of individualization refers to giving individuality a reasonable chance for growth.   As society grows

56 *Loc. cit.*
57 *Ibid.*, p. 632.
58 *Ibid.*, p. 652.
59 *Ibid.*, p. 653.

more complex, institutions more ossified, and life more standardized, the average person is increasingly in danger of being
crushed; at least, his opportunities for self-expression become fewer. There is need of constant vigilance in education in allowing for individual differences, in industry for
safeguarding the laborer in expressing his personality in his
work, in government in permitting free discussion.

The principle of balance is stated by Professor Ross as follows : "In the guidance of society each social element should
share according to the intelligence and public spirit of its
members and none should predominate." [60]   There has been
in the past, and even now there is in all countries, a bitter
struggle taking place between classes, apparently on the basis
that some one class should rule all the other classes. Society
has suffered immeasurably in this way. Sometimes society
has been the victim of the rulership of the dead, of the rulership of masculinism, of clericalism, of militarism, of commercialism, of legalism, of leisure class ascendancy, of intellectualism, of proletarianism, but always by one class lording
it over the weaker classes until some one of the weaker classes
acquires strength enough to overthrow the class in power.

Professor Ross never felt called upon to penetrate backward into the psychological nature of the individual or of
persons. He has left it to others to define attitudes and behavior patterns and to explain the details of what happens
when the social processes produce and condition human attitudes and patterns of behavior. When this segment is developed and related to the means and processes of social influence and social control, Professor Ross doubtless will be
found to have contributed as much if not more than any of
his critics to the discipline called social psychology.

The autobiography, *Seventy Years of It,* is unique from
the dedication at the beginning to his daughters-in-law, to
the anthropometric data concerning himself at the end.
Throughout this tale, as he says of "25,000 days," is revealed
the author's "passion to know." The urge to understand
"the causes and significance of current trends" is at the center of his life work. He reports that he has saved his aca-

[60] *Ibid.,* p. 693.

demic life by getting off to the hinterlands "of the world."
He arrives at the significant conclusion that "some of the
ugly developments among us are but the attending shadow of
certain shining social gains." Not an extremist, agitator, or
demagogue, he has aimed to do something of importance for
his fellow men, aspiring modestly to constitute "a twenty-
thousandth of the forces shaping our age." He is a champion
particularly of economic justice, and once assured that he is
right, he does not falter in "showing up" big business, the
press, or any other agency that is engaged in deceiving the
people. He protests against narrow conceptions of patriotism and declares that "red baiters" either are deluded, or
else more loyal to their class than to their country. At the
time that his autobiography was written, Professor Ross had
published 75,000 pages of materials in book form, not to
mention 200 or more articles. *Mirabile dictu!* there is not a
dull page in the voluminous array. Not only has systemiza-
tion in sociology been his job, as he says, but many are his
original contributions in concepts, such as "race suicide,"
and the countless number of his brilliant phrases. The
unique descriptions and analyses of social life that illuminate
his system of thirty or more social processes, as found in his
Principles, are among his notable achievements.

The socio-psychological thought of Professor Ross has penetrated the farthermost reaches of human life. It has been
stated in lucid, stimulating language. It has commanded
the attention of socially-thinking persons in many lands. It
has defined the field of sociology, emphasizing the processual
approach, and it has reflected Professor Ross' unique personality.[61]

A contribution of note to the theory of social interaction is
found in the treatment of social actions by Emile Waxweiler
of Belgium whose work will be summarized in Chapter
XXX. Waxweiler found that social actions are ninefold:
(1) Conjunctive actions accompanying physical proximity,
(2) protective or harmful actions, (3) competitive actions, (4)
evocative actions, (5) spontaneous gregarious actions, (6) re-

61 John L. Gillin, "The Personality of Edward Alsworth Ross," *American
Journal of Sociology,* 42:534-542.

petitive actions, (7) initiative actions, (8) acquisitive actions, and (9) selective actions.[62] To Waxweiler, interaction is composed of reciprocal actions. In turn these are explained in terms of action and reaction.

The analysis of social interaction has been contributed to recently by Florian Znaniecki of the University of Poznan in his most elaborate work entitled *Social Actions*. The analysis of social interaction in this volume varies greatly from the viewpoint of E. A. Ross, and it marks a notable advance over Tarde's initial contribution to the field. *Social Actions* is based on reading that involves 3000 or more references in several languages, and on careful, analytical thinking that is far-reaching in its implications, logical in its reasoning, and challenging in the problems that it raises for the social psychologist.[63]

Social actions are "actions which have as objects conscious beings, individually or collectively, and which purpose to influence those beings."[64] The origins of social actions are found in individual interests in individuals, in individual interests in collectivities, in collectivities as they bear upon individuals, and in collectivities as they bear upon collectivities.[65] These four sets of origins represent in the main an ascending degree of complexity in interaction.

It assumes the existence of interests and attitudes that are themselves complex products of hereditary reflexes, incessant conditioning, and daily experience together with a person's favorable and unfavorable reactions to these experiences.

Social actions are divided, in the first place, into those characterized by "a positive subjective prejudice toward" their objects. These are denominated under the somewhat doubtful title of "accommodation."[66] They fall into sub-

[62] Emile Waxweiler, *Esquisse d'une sociologie,* quoted from Becker and Barnes, *Social Thought from Lore to Science,* p. 874.

[63] Professor Znaniecki achieved widespread recognition not only in the United States but elsewhere when he associated himself with W. I. Thomas in the publication of *The Polish Peasant in Europe and America* in 1918. His later work on *The Laws of Social Psychology,* published in 1925 by the University of Chicago Press, is well-known.

[64] *Ibid.,* p. 65. At this point the question may be raised whether conscious purpose is necessary in order to make an action of one person that involves another a social action.

[65] "Interests" are identified as "a combination of objects and of attitudes toward them," p. 54.

[66] *Ibid.,* p. 134.

patterns of invitation, propitiation, enticement, co-operative guidance of various sorts, such as magical guidance, verbal guidance, guidance by authority, and educational guidance.[67]

The other side of this active process of influencing people relates to the subject, as distinguished from the agent, and refers to the way persons respond to social stimuli. This is a twofold response, involving either participative submission or purpose submission. One is found in the case of the person "who actively and spontaneously submits to being led without waiting to be influenced into submission."[68] The other type of response is illustrated by the person who, in attaining a purpose of his own, joins with other persons who have similar aims, or by the person who seeks to achieve a purpose by acting the same (imitation) as someone else who has a similar purpose.[69]

In the second place, social actions may start from a negative purpose against their objects. These may be labeled "opposition" in order to distinguish them from the activities called "accommodation." The primary expression is self defense. Then there is group defense, as found in the repression of criminal behavior, and individual defense, as expressed through revolt. Further, one social group may develop an elaborate defense against another social group.[70] Crime is defined as "an objectively evil act, a violation of social validity, an offense against the superior dignity" of a collective system.[71] Crimes are negative social values. The criminal outsider does not belong to the collectivity, for example, the unbeliever who is thought to profane a religious ceremonial by his very presence.[72] The criminal outsider is often viewed as one who is to be annihilated. The criminal insider is treated differently. He is a different kind of social object.[73] His offense is serious because it strikes from within the group. No loyalty is expected from the outsider, but the insider who attacks the group is likely to break the group

---

[67] *Ibid.*, pp. 134-230.
[68] *Ibid.*, p. 239.
[69] *Ibid.*, Chapters IX, X.
[70] *Ibid.*, Chapters XI to XIV.
[71] *Ibid.*, p. 351.
[72] *Ibid.*, p. 369.
[73] *Ibid.*, p. 380.

asunder and destroy its unity. He may be treated with (1) "a compulsory training in righteousness," (2) "a regenerating penance," or (3) he may be excommunicated.[74]

Revolt as one of the forms of negative social action is ancient and universal. Its most persistent pattern is the re volt of youth.[75] This particular pattern arises from conflicts between an adolescent's own "systems of values and the behavior complexes of individual adults," such as father, mother, or other adults. Youth revolts against an individual adult, against injustice, and against adult civilization. Some youths accept social control by resignation, and others end in a "matter-of-fact transgression." [76]

A beneficial aspect of revolt is that it "tends to bring innovations into the cultural life of the collectivity" involved.[77] In fact, revolt in this sense may be "the main factor of cultural progress."

Then, there is a special phase of opposition, where the agent spontaneously performs an act of aggression.[78] Although he is not being interfered with in any way, he deliberately sets out to interfere with the possessions or the welfare of others. From the individual angle, robbery is an example; from the collective approach, state depredations and confiscations are samples. Also, there is aggressive competition, and coercive exploitation, such as child labor and enslavement.

A third class of social actions are those that for the lack of a better term Dr. Znaniecki calls "altruistic." "Disinterested love" is too specialized a term; "friendship" is too broad; both are too psychological. Every altruistic action may be viewed as an attempt to overcome a difference between the values and activities included within the range of the agent and those within the range of the special object, by producing between them a conscious community where there was none before, and thus increasing the interpenetration of their spheres of experience.[79]

[74] *Ibid.*, pp. 286-408.
[75] *Ibid.*, p. 410.
[76] *Ibid.*, p. 432.
[77] *Ibid.*, p. 440.
[78] *Ibid.*, p. 462.
[79] *Ibid.*, p. 451.

ALTRUISTIC ACTIONS

There are four classes of altruistic actions: (1) making the social object share certain experiences with the agent, or synesthetic communion as when one person endeavors to make another share his pleasant experiences in beholding a work or art; (2) making another share attitudes or sympathetic communion, which involves "agreement in valuation," as when a scientist makes other scientists accept a new theory; (3) making another share active tendencies, or synergetic communion, or getting others to "co-operate for a common objective purpose"; (4) making the social object actively identify himself with the agent, or altruistic substitutions, as when one "solves for another a painful situation which the latter is incapable of solving for himself." [80]

In the fourth instance, social actions include those of hostility, which parallel the altruistic actions: (1) avoiding common experiences (avoidable); (2) eliminating attitudes of the social object from the agent's sphere of valuation (aversion); (3) frustrating activities of the social object (hostile fighting); and (4) actually "destroying the social object's system of values" (revenge).[81]

Altruistic actions are side developments of those called *accommodation,* and hostility actions are side lines of those called *opposition.* In the fifth category are those social actions that represent a compromise between accommodation and opposition. They grow out of an egoistic interest to obtain some object (egoistic compromise), such as trade or employment.[82]

In addition to social actions, there are many other kinds of human actions: technical, economic, religious, intellectual. The social actions and the nonsocial ones are variously connected, and the social sciences are likewise joined together. The study of social actions is sociology, which thus has a clear field of its own.[83] In this way Professor Znaniecki identifies sociology with social psychology.

Irrespective of labels, however, Znaniecki has evolved a

[80] *Ibid.,* pp. 519-67.
[81] *Ibid.,* p. 569.
[82] *Ibid.,* Chapter XVIII.
[83] *Ibid.,* p. 620.

system of social psychologic thought which suggests phases of the conflict and co-operation theories of Gumplowicz, Ratzenhofer, and Small. The analysis involves much more, however, than new names for well-recognized processes. It offers a detailed picture of one whole phase of life, namely, that in which a person influences other persons and groups, and in which he is influenced by others and by groups.

The gamut from Tarde's early ideas about interactions to Znaniecki's analyses of social actions is a long one, marked by the scintillating work by Ross, and manifesting an increasing degree of penetrating thought. Tarde awakened an interest in an aspect of social life and thought that proved to be a fertile field for cultivation by deeper thinkers.

GROUP DISCUSSION TOPICS

1. Aristotle's test of a good government.
2. More as a social psychologist.
3. Hobbes' idea of a good citizen.
4. Hume's role as the father of social psychology.
5. Adam Smith's fourfold classification of people.
6. Tarde's claim to being the founder of social psychology.
7. Tarde's conception of the social process.
8. The meaning of imitation plateaus.
9. The difference between logical and non-logical imitation.
10. The essence of a democratic nation-group.
11. The complementary tendencies of imitation.
12. The democratizing influences of fashion imitation.
13. The three forms of "opposition."
14. The nature of invention.
15. Methods by which imitation grows.
16. The relation of an invention to future inventions.
17. The relation between inventiveness and sheepishness.
18. Le Bon's suspicion of the masses.
19. Social psychology as conceived by E. A. Ross.
20. The distinctions between social ascendancy and individual ascendancy.
21. The two most difficult problems of social control.
22. The evils of too much control versus those of too little control.
23. Ossification versus individuation.
24. The checks upon the profits motive.
25. The stimuli of the profits motive.
26. The three canons of reconstruction, as stated by Ross.
27. The principle of anticipation.

28. The principle of simulation.
29. The principle of individualization.
30. The principle of balance.
31. Four sets of social actions according to Znaniecki.
32. Revolt as a form of negative social action.
33. The concept of altruistic social actions.

READINGS

Barnes, Harry E., Editor, *An Introduction to the History of Sociology* (Chicago : University of Chicago Press 1948), Ch. 25.

Davis, Jr., M. M., *Psychological Interpretations of Society* (New York: Longmans, Green & Co. 1909).

Ellwood, Charles A., "David Hume and Scientific Scepticism," *Sociology and Social Research*, 21:114-119.

Faris, Ellsworth, "The Beginnings of Social Psychology," *American Journal of Sociology*, L:422-428.

Hume, David, *A Treatise of Human Nature*, edited by Selby-Bigge (London: Oxford University Press 1896).

Ross, Edward A., *Social Psychology* (New York: The Macmillan Company 1908).

Sighele, Scipio, *Psychologie des sectes* (Paris: Giard and Briere 1898).

———, *La Foule criminelle* (Paris: Alcan 1901).

Simon, A., "A Formal Theory of Interaction," *American Sociological Review*, 17:202-211.

Sorokin, Pitirim A., *Contemporary Sociological Theories* (New York: Harper & Brothers 1928), Chs. XI, XII, XIII.

Tarde, Gabriel, *Social Laws*, translated by H. C. Warren (New York: The Macmillan Company 1907).

———, *The Laws of Imitation*, translated by E. C. Parsons (New York: Henry Holt and Company 1903).

———, *La Logique sociale* (Paris: Alcan 1898).

———, *L'Opinion et la foule* (Paris: Alcan 1901).

Znaniecki, Florian, *Social Actions* (New York: Farrar and Rinehart 1936).

CHAPTER XXVII

DURKHEIM AND COLLECTIVE
REPRESENTATIONS

The social interaction theory of Gabriel Tarde stands in opposition to the collective-representations concept of Emile Durkheim (1858–1917). If Tarde made a contribution to social psychology, then Durkheim penetrated further beneath the surface of current social interaction and examined the structure and functions of societal life, past and present, and evolved sociological considerations of importance.

Durkheim was in part a positivist and a believer in applying the methods of physical science to the study of social actions. As a believer in the scientific method he sought to deal chiefly with empirical data and to avoid value-judgments. On the other hand, he did not subscribe to an individualistic theory of society. His interest in social ends led him to develop the idea of societary integration of component parts. A society actively at times determines what is best for its own good and definitely promotes that judgment. Hence such societary activity must be studied. Social values may definitely be stated and treated as objective realities. The study of ends and values may be done scientifically, but the promotion of them is a matter of social control or reform or propaganda.

In his discussion of methods, Durkheim urges that all considerations of sentiment be avoided, that the personal equation be kept out of the picture, that objects of study be carefully defined in advance, and that the normal data or data as they are be distinguished from those that ought to be. He puts special emphasis on the method of "concomitant variations."[1] Pure correlation is not enough, for concomitance in variations may not necessarily be causal. Concomitant variations must show logical as well as statistical reasons for their relationship before causal connections can be assumed.

[1] Emile Durkheim, *Les Regles de la methode sociologique,* pp. 159 ff.

Durkheim makes "social facts" central in his methods. A 'social fact" is a phase of behavior (thinking, feeling, or act ing) which is objective to the observer and which has a coercive nature.[2] Social facts are of two kinds, the normal and the pathological. Both have a constraining influence over the individual mind while remaining exterior to it. They involve rules and regulations, systems of procedure, and sets of customary beliefs.

Social facts have a moral aspect, for they affect the wel fare of individuals. They are products of the collective con sciousness that relate to individual behavior. The collective consciousness thus is considered as the ethical authority. So cial facts imply duties that must be performed by the indi vidual. Presumably by virtue of their pragmatic origins these duties are desirable, or as desirable as anything that the individual can know at the given time. Social facts have super-individual value.[3]

COLLECTIVE REPRESENTATIONS

Collective representations is a concept which is a leading contribution to be found in the social thinking of Durk heim. Some would call it his major contribution. Out of the interplay of minds come symbol-products which are mutually owned and mutually proclaimed. These collective symbolizations have force because collectively created and developed. The flag is a political representation; sacred writings are often a religious representation; heroes de velop mythical qualities that are partly the result of collec tive reactions. Collective representations offset the growth of specialization and the increasing opportunities for con flict. They "save the day" for a society beset by conflict. Unscientifically derived as they often are, and frequently exercising control long past their usefulness, they possess tre mendous social force, and constitute a vital phase in a sub ject discussed in an earlier chapter, namely, co-operation.

[2] *Ibid.*, pp. 59, 142 ff.
[3] For a concise, critical treatment of Durkheim's sociological method with its emphasis on "observation" and its implications for collective psychology, see Ethel M. Wilson, "Emile Durkheim's Sociological Method," *Sociology and Social Research*, 18:511-518.

To Durkheim, collective representations are objects or factors of social value. This theory therefore is virtually one of social values. He distinguishes between two meanings of value and shows how the public uses these somewhat interchangeably and to the confusion of its own thinking. He shows that we make judgments of fact and judgments of value. The first are judgments of observation; the second, of appreciation. One is objective; the other is partly subjective in that one's own feeling reactions are included. One refers to the relation of things; the other, to the relation of things to persons.[4] It is this second class of value-judgments which is of interest to the sociologist.

Durkheim proclaimed that the collective representations, social values, and the ideals created by society are imperative in nature. Individuals are more or less irresistibly inclined to respond to them. Because they are collectively derived they possess this imperative nature. The individual reacts to them above almost all other stimuli that come to him.

Because these social values are the product of collective action and not of individual action, they are objective in nature. They come to the individual as objective imperatives. They are objective because they originate not wholly nor chiefly in conscious utility to the individual but in their collective imperative nature.

A high place is assigned by Durkheim to society. He sees it as "the most powerful combination of physical and social forces of which nature offers us an example." The most elevated forms of thought emanate from society. The collective consciousness, "the highest form of the psychic life," being outside of individual and local affairs, "sees things only in their permanent and essential aspects." Sociology or the science of the collective consciousness is "destined to open a new way to the science of man."[5]

Durkheim found socialism unsatisfactory. His objections have been summarized by Marcel Mauss. He objected to its reliance upon class. Its proletarian-class limitations seem narrow. Its emphasis on class warfare and its political char-

---

[4] Cf., Charles Bouglé, The Evolution of Values, pp. 10, 88.
[5] Emile Durkheim, The Elementary Forms of the Religious Life, pp. 444-447.

acter are questionable. Durkheim was interested in the welfare of society as a whole and not simply of one of its parts.[6]

DIVISION OF LABOR

Another type of conflict theory of far-reaching and fundamental importance is Durkheim's theory of division of labor. The earliest division of labor was that involving hoe culture and the care of children on one hand, and hunting and fighting on the other — in other words, the division of labor between the sexes. With the progress of the centuries, labor became repeatedly subdivided until today occupational specialization is outstanding. Its social meanings, however, are not clear.

Increasing density of population has made specialization necessary. Survival has required specialization. With this division of labor has come division of interests — and conflicts. Industrial conflicts are due in part to division of labor. Occupational specialization, moreover, has resulted in a decline of mechanical solidarity, or likemindedness. Increase in organic solidarity, that is, in organized and coordinated solidarity, does not keep pace with the decrease in mechanical or likeminded solidarity caused by increasing division of labor and specialization. Hence, Durkheim developed the concept of constraint as being society's only recourse in order to meet the increasing conflict nature of societary life.

Durkheim made increasing density of population the major key to the development of division of labor. Many exceptions can be given to what amounts to a single theory. At times density of population operates as Durkheim contended, but not always. Other factors may also be cited, such as an inventive atmosphere, the interstimulation of inventors, the recognition of needs coming in conjunction with a flock of geniuses.

Durkheim distinguishes between division of labor and disintegration. The latter phenomenon is illustrated by industrial failures and crises, by conflicts between capital and labor, by the development of crime. All these are patholog-

6 Marcel Mauss, Le Socialisme, p. viii.

ical. In these forms the division of labor ceases to bring forth solidarity and hence represents an "anomic division of labor," not a true expression.[7] However, division of labor in society is to be distinguished from occupational division of labor in the factory, as Marx pointed out, but as Durkheim failed to notice.[8]

Durkheim's theory of socialization involves first the unconscious, and second, a recognition of need. His own statement puts individuality over against sociality, with the latter being the stronger, which of course is not always the case.

The two basic principles operative in society are division and cohesion. These are in continuous conflict. The division of labor principle is the more dynamic, the more disturbing, the more progressive; and yet the stabilizing factors are equally essential though less spectacular.

Durkheim's concept of division of labor includes an original or mechanical solidarity that subordinates the individual, as in the case of a hive of bees. The concept moves on to describe the supplanting of this subordination by the ise of voluntary or organic solidarity in which the individual is influenced by a comprehension of social values. It is also true that society is characterized by an increasing degree of functional organization. This theory is paralleled by Tönnies' *Gemeinschaft*-to-*Gesellschaft* interpretation, and by MacIver's community-to-association description of social evolution.

SOCIAL RELIGION

In his *Elementary Forms of the Religious Life,* Durkheim presented a comprehensive treatment of religion in social terms. He defines religion as "a unified system of belief and practices relative to sacred things; that is to say, things set apart and forbidden — beliefs and practices which unite into one single moral community, called a *church,* all those who adhere to them."[9] It bifurcates life into the profane and the sacred. Religious meetings are set off from other kinds of meetings. Places of worship acquire a sacredness not to

---

[7] *Emile Durkheim on the Division of Labor in Society,* translated by George Simpson, pp. 336, 337.
[8] *Ibid.,* pp. 353 ff.
[9] Emile Durkheim. *The Elementary Forms of the Religious Life,* p. 47.

be invaded by secular things. Life is divided into good deeds and sinful ones.

Again in correcting past ideas about religion originating in beliefs in ghosts and in dreams and the like, Durkheim finds all sources in society. The Kingdom of Heaven is a glorified society. God is an all-powerful and the perfect loving father of a large family group. Religion promotes social solidarity among the "saved." Durkheim seems also to have failed to consider the role of thought in religion, particularly in the expressions that represent current origins of religion, even current elementary developments and modifications.

Evil in society is reflected in the concept of "devil" in religion. The emphasis on a "paradise" in heaven is brought about by experiencing a "hell" on earth. Religion, in short, expresses a collective ideal.[10]

Again, the sociology of religion implies the role of group consciousness in religious professions. To the extent that a religious group gives a person status and recognition it has an effective appeal.

Human beings need an ideal and tend to create an ideal society. Religion may set up such an ideal world in which pain and sorrow exist no more. Religion may stand for collective sentiments. It may symbolize some of society's ideas. It results in ceremonies, reunions, and celebrations.

THEORY OF SUICIDE

Durkheim repudiated most of the accepted theories of suicide. His monographic study demonstrated that heredity, for example, is not a sufficient explanation of suicide. Climatic factors are equally insufficient as explanatory factors. Likewise, waves of imitation are inadequate explanations.

He classified suicides into three main types, namely, egotistical, anomique, and altruistic. All occur as an expression of a group breakdown of some sort. Suicide is a kind of index to decay in social solidarity. Suicide in the main is due to negative social causes. It results from loneliness, from the feeling that nobody cares, and from excess individualism.

[10] *Ibid.*, p. 423.

When people generally are engaged each in his own enterprises to the extent that some individuals feel that they are
outside the pale of human interest, their suicide is fostered.
Egotistical suicide is the type due to the tendency of individuals to shut themselves up within themselves. This situation takes place when other individuals and associates are
so busy with their own activities that some individuals feel
slighted, affronted, "hurt," and ignored. Introvertive traits
thus gain the upper hand and the ego builds a wall around
itself until it feels entirely cut off from the social world.

"Anomique suicide" is the type that follows catastrophic
social changes. Social life all around seems to go to pieces.
Without the social backing to which one is accustomed, life
is judged to be not worth continuing. Durkheim did not
take into consideration that the ability "to take it" as found
in one's character or configuration of personality might be
as important as the social upset itself.

"Altruistic suicide" is taking one's life for the sake of a
cause. Japanese sometimes illustrate this type when they
take their own lives for the sake of a larger social unity that
threatens to be broken if they do not engage in self-destruc-
tion.

In attempting to correct previous explanations of suicides,
Durkheim committed the error of overstatement of the social causes. He left no room for any factors save the social.

BOUGLÉ

In his *Evolution of Values,* Charles Bouglé, a successor to
and follower in some ways of Durkheim, specializes on the
processes by which values evolve and are transmitted. It is
in behavior together, or in collective behavior, that key ideas
arise and become commonly accepted and hence become
values. Moreover, out of attachment of these group values
individuals are raised from a lower to a higher plane. Society itself becomes stabilized by means of these symbols or
collective representations.

These commonly accepted ideas, the center of social organization in the functional sense, are not necessarily true.
Some of them are generally false. Their force comes, how-

ever, from the fact that people believe them to be true. Further, many of these jointly-accepted ideas are inconsistent with reference to each other. They may be contradictory, and yet accepted and served. The reasons for this are that they express to a degree what individuals are interested in, and indicate that the ideas and behavior of a given individual are rarely consistent.

It should be noted that when a group evolves a new value, it is always some individual within that group who through personal insight originates the new idea. Also, it is true that many new ideas are never, or only belatedly, accepted by the group. In fact, many new ideas are often fought by the group, and the persons who advocate them are persecuted or punished.

It is in the recognition by individuals of the need for group action that new ideas and modifications in values arise and are accepted by the group.[11] Social reformers often neglect this fundamental principle which Bouglé stressed and which has validity.

Following up Durkheim's discussion of the division of labor and of the resulting reorganization and tying together of specialized units into new organic wholes, Bouglé argues that religion will tend to lose its force as an agency of social control. In the reorganization process, viewpoints from a variety of specialized directions come together and serve to neutralize the convictions, religions for example, of any one unit. Bouglé claims that art and science will tend to furnish more and more the controls needed by society.[12]

Bouglé frequently mentions what he calls "polytelism." Society is characterized not only by an increasing division of labor, but also by a concomitant differentiation in social values. This is the spiritual aspect of the division of labor. First, there arises a multiplicity of meanings, or *polysemy*, and then a multiplicity of ends, or *polytelism*. Let it be noted that values are not only being differentiated, but that the opposite process is also taking place, namely, the differentiated values are continually coming together again. The conjunction of values is of equal significance with the differ-

11 Charles Bouglé, *The Evolution of Values*, p. 84.
12 *Ibid.*, pp. 145, 146.

entiation of values. Polytelism "plays its role of preserving and reconciling." It keeps diversities associated.[13]

In discussing the "projection of values," Bouglé suggests an idea similar to a step in the growth of personality as outlined by J. Mark Baldwin. Values are not only objective (because imperative) but also unconsciously subjective, having come from a pooling of individual actions and reactions. This individual element in them enables a person to have meanings for them and hence to project their significance out into the lives of other persons. "A country or a principle, an ensemble of institutions or a system of beliefs, is invested with limitless value if we see, therein, permanent possibilities of satisfaction for a whole people." [14]

SOCIAL VALUES

Social values may be classified. They become differentiated. In fact, there is a law of differentiation operative among both immaterial and material values. Moreover, this differentiation "corresponds to the progress of culture." Still more significant, the differentiation of value, like the division of labor, can "specialize souls and imprison them in one zone." [15]

Most values are unilateral. Each claims only a part of life. Moral values are an exception. "Morality is determined to have its say as to the whole of life." [16]

One of the highest values is reason, but there are two kinds: (1) the kind that carries on scientific research in the accepted fashion; and (2) the type that acts as a "guide to evolution." There is reason, for example, which is engaged in working out a harmony among differentiated values. This harmonization function is accompanied by a "moral resonance." It detaches the reasoner from himself and attaches him to social causes. There is a moral thrill in leading the direction of social evolution.[17]

Each nation not only glorifies its own values, but tends to

13 *Ibid.*, pp. 84, 257, 260.
14 *Ibid.*, pp. 20, 37.
15 *Ibid.*, pp. 56, 60, 63.
16 *Ibid.*, p. 60.
17 *Ibid.*, pp. 219, 220, 225.

identify them with civilization itself.   In time of war the
nation uses propaganda to get its people to believe that in
fighting for its values they are about to save the world from
destruction.   The most popular slogan in the United States
during the World War was "To make the world safe for
democracy," and in 1937 the Japanese people were told by
their leaders that in sending their sons to fight in China
they were saving civilization itself.[18]

The concept of "social complication" as developed by
M. Bouglé, carries the idea that the viewpoints of several different social groups are expressed in the thought life of each
individual.   In this way the tendencies toward "division of
labor" and of differentiation are offset.

Bouglé is a moral rationalist.   While he is fully aware of
the processes of differentiation, he points out that many
values are being internationalized and that the "circle of
common civilization, intellectual and material, is enlarging."
He finds the hope of the future in a moral rationalism which
leads both to democracy within nations and to internationalism between nations.[19]

Clarence M. Case has analyzed social values in terms of
"life levels."   He defines values as "the selected objects of
living things." [20]   They are objects selected by the eval-
uators themselves.   Four major life levels are distinguished
by Dr. Case : organic, species, social, and socio-cultural.   Each
level is characterized by more or less distinctive sets of values.
These values may be objects that are sought for or those that
are avoided, that is, either positive or negative.   Illustrations
of organic values are fire, corrosive substances, heavy crushing masses.   An example of species' values is found in the
pond of water which is a positive value to a duck but a negative value to a hen.   Social values are found in (a) associates,
(b) the group, (c) status, (d) habitat, (e) perhaps mutual aid,
and (f) the common weal.   Socio-cultural values are all the
tools and symbols that man has invented and passed down
from one generation to another ; they are characterized by

[18] *Ibid.*, pp. 253, 254.
[19] C. Bouglé, "Social Differentiation and Assimilation," *Sociological Review,*
29:154-174.
[20] Clarence Marsh Case, "The Value Concept in Sociology and Related
Fields," *Sociology and Social Research,* XXIII:410.

being true, beautiful, good, and useful. Dr. Case suggests a scale for measuring the values on his final socio-cultural level in terms of three qualifications: imperativeness, universality, and inclusiveness.[21]

LÉVY-BRUHL

Lucien Lévy-Bruhl accepts Durkheim's concept of "collective representations" and examines primitive people in terms of these representations. He defines them as follows: "They are common to the members of a given social group; they are transmitted from one generation to another; they impress themselves upon the individual members, and awaken in them sentiments of respect, fear, adoration, and so on."[22]

The collective representations of primitive people are different from ours. One of the chief characteristics of such representations is that of "mystical perception." Primitive people believe that some influence emanates from the collective representations, an occult power, as it were. The primitive person lives in a mystical world, a world of spirits; any object may have a spirit or special force residing in it. Each of their collective representations possesses mystical qualities. Since they see objects as mystical, they ascribe mystical characteristics to their collective representations.

Another characteristic of the primitive mind is that it emphasizes the "principle of participation." The primitive man believes himself to be human and at the same time to possess characteristics, for example, of some of his collective representations. For example, the Bororos, a tribe of northern Brazil, insist that they are araras or parakeets. How they can be men and parakeets at the same time does not bother them. They are not aware that they are illogical, and illustrating the law of contradiction. However, as we move up the scale from primitives to scientific persons, the collective representations and their interconnections gradually lose their mystical quality and attain the level of true "concepts."[23]

[21] Ibid., pp. 414 ff.
[22] L. Lévy-Bruhl, How Natives Think, p. 13.
[23] Ibid., pp. 76, 361, 368, 375.

Mystical perception and the law of participation, and ignoring the law of contradiction are all evidences, according to M. Lévy-Bruhl, of the pre-logical thinking of primitive people. Their failure to distinguish, for instance, between the power of a fetish and a poison is further evidence of pre-logical thinking. They do not think in terms of the physical properties of a poisonous substance. They are not illogical; they are not yet appreciative of the logical.[24]

While M. Lévy-Bruhl considers primitive mentality as being of a different kind from civilized mentality, Franz Boas has amassed considerable evidence in support of the theory that basically there is no real difference. He showed in his work on *The Mind of Primitive Man* that, in the matter of inhibition of impulses, of power of attention, of ability to do original thinking, primitive people compare favorably with civilized people. His conclusion logically follows that, inasmuch as the social environment is powerful and education is effective in making over social environments, education can raise all races to the same high level, and at the same time unify them upon the same knowledge bases.

There is considerable truth in the positions of both Lévy-Bruhl and Boas. The latter is dealing with mental processes and the former with the results of these processes. Let the primitive child be born into a civilized environment and carefully trained and he probably would show about the same mental traits as civilized children. In one case there is a scientific heritage; in the other a mystical heritage which melts away slowly before the increase in scientific teachings.

Somewhat outside the sequence of French sociologists discussed in this chapter is the name of René Worms (1869–1926). He was a lineal sociological descendant of Comte, although his ideas ran far ahead of Comtean concepts. He conceived of sociology as a general science, in fact, as Case and Woerner have suggested, in a sense similar to that developed by Albion W. Small.[25] Prolific writer that he was, he founded (1892) the *Revue Internationale de Sociologie* and edited it for thirty-three years. In 1894 he founded the International Institute of Sociology.

[24] *Ibid.*, pp. 65, 67, 71, 78.
[25] See Clarence M. Case and Fred Woerner, "René Worms: An Appreciation," *Sociology and Social Research*, 8:403-425

Worms distinguished between a general psychology or psychology of mankind, an individual psychology, or psychology of persons, and a psychology of social groups. When people talk about using the wrong psychology or "the psychological moment," they speak as though they mean individual psychology; but actually they are thinking in terms of the general psychology of mankind, that is. social psychology.[26]

G. L. Duprat of the University of Geneva has elaborated Durkheim's concept of social facts. He begins with the scientific observation that a social fact must first of all "be established by a sufficient number of informed observers." It has a control nature which, if felt through the feelings, makes it a subjective fact, and if experienced through corresponding behavior, it becomes an objective fact. Relationship is a characteristic of a social fact. Moreover, a social fact involves a social distance relationship, that is, a closeness or farness in relationship. The essence of a social fact is found in two sources; namely, in psychic processes and in visible behavior. They include all the relationships of a social group or collective entity.[27]

As Durkheim noted, a social fact results from the influence of the collective consciousness on the individual. It is a process growing out of the solidarity of human beings.[28]

WALLAS

A philosophical counterpart to the idea of "collective representations" appears in the concept of "the great society" that was developed by Graham Wallas (1859–1932). The Great Society is a name of current human society, the product of mechanical inventions, industrial production, commercial expansion, democratic evolution — highly organized and intricately complex. It is ruled, in the main, by men "who direct enormous social power without attempting to form a social purpose," and it is composed to a surpassing degree of persons who recognize the power of society but

[26] *Ibid.*, p. 421.
[27] G. L. Duprat, "Social Facts," translated by M. J. Vincent, B. V. Morkovin, and M. Devron, *Sociology and Social Research*, 19:3-17.
[28] *Ibid.*, pp. 13, 14.

dimly and who often treat society with distrust and dislike.[29]

Wallas substituted organization for organism as a fundamental social concept. He made a distinction between thought organizations, will organizations, and happiness organizations. Thought organizations are those institutions in society whose main function is the organization of thought, such as discussion groups, ranging from a philosophical club to an ordinary committee that is called together to plan new legislation. At this point Wallas asserted that he has attended perhaps 3000 meetings of municipal committees, of different sizes and for different purposes, and that he was sure that at least half of the men and women with whom he has sat "were entirely unaware that any conscious mental effort on their part was called for." [30] They attended in the same spirit that many persons attend church — in the spirit that if they merely attend they are doing their duty, and that some good must come of it.

Will organizations come into existence because of imperfect social machinery. In industry three types of will organizations are striving for mastery — the institution of private property, represented by the individualists; the state, represented by collectivists; labor organizations, represented perhaps by syndicalists. There is urgent need for "the invention of means of organizing the conflicting wills of individuals and classes within each nation more effective than reliance upon any single 'principle,' whether representation, property, or professionalism." [31]

The organization of happiness has not yet made much progress. Efficiency has supplanted happiness as a modern god. The ideal of making money has shadowed the ideal of making people happy. A social system organized on the basis of happiness avoids both destitution and superfluity, employs the Mean as the standard for the representation of all social interests as well as for all faculties of individuals, and avoids the Extreme in all things.[32]

Wallas has given new life to the concept *social heritage.* It apparently comprises a large portion of a mature per-

[29] Graham Wallas, *The Great Society*, p. 11.
[30] *Ibid.*, p. 270.
[31] *Ibid.*, p. 319.
[32] *Ibid.*, p. 268.

sonality. Nurture as distinguished from nature has two aspects: that which we acquire for ourselves and that which has been handed down to us. The second part is our social heritage. If this were suddenly to be taken away from mankind we should be helpless. We could not read nor do business nor meet each other's needs. "The white races would probably become extinct everywhere." [33]

The concept of "social heritage" is at once more concrete and more general than the term *collective representations*. It is more objective and less processual.

HALBWACHS

Maurice Halbwachs, a member of the Durkheim school, has received favorable comment for his studies of social classes. He connects socia' classes with social values. He sees these values as collective representations that create social differentiations. Long years of group life produce a gradation of values, which in turn accounts for the gradations in classes.

In studying the working classes, Halbwachs found that they spend a smaller proportion of their income for rent than do people who have more income. They do not seem to have so great an appreciation of their homes, judging by the rents they pay, as do people of greater income. This condition is a result, according to Halbwachs, of the degenerating influence of unskilled work and of hours of routine labor.[34]

Halbwachs does not find that prosperity is so important a cause of suicide as Durkheim believed to be the case. Halbwachs developed the thesis that the complexities of modern urban life are the chief factors in increasing the suicide rate. Many persons cannot withstand repeated blows from a heartless urban environment.

Halbwachs' theory concerning the sociology of knowledge goes back to the role of groups and collective representations. He carries this theory so far as to imply that social patterns not only affect the content of knowledge but also

[33] *Ibid.*, p. 17.
[34] Maurice Halbwachs. *La classe ouviere et les niveaux der vie.*

the origin of the mental processes. He upsets the psychologist's contention that the mental processes which are usually referred to as "memory" are socially made more than they are biological. It is collective representations which enable us to remember! We remember within the framework of our social experiences. We remember in terms of experiences with individual friends and with, or as a part of, society as a whole. Freed from such experiences, our memories merely contain the stuff out of which incoherent dreams are made.[35]

Closely connected with Durkheim's social thought are the ideas of Marcel Mauss of Paris. The science of "social morphology" as conceived by Mauss deals with the substrata of society, such as connections with the land, and the density and distribution of population. It includes the cultural organization and even the moral ideas of a people. For example, as a result of winter conditions the Eskimos have one type of social living, and in consequence of summer factors another type of life prevails. Social unity in winter gives way to social isolation in summer. Religion is stronger in winter than in summer (when the Eskimos wander far and wide).

Durkheim included the educational process within the swing of his social thought. He defined education as the socialization of the young. Education "brings the child into contact with a definite society," and not with society in general.[36] In his lectures on *l'Education Morale à l'Ecole Primaire*, Durkheim emphasized the nature of moral civilization which is to be transmitted to the child, and the nature of the child who is to acquire these moral doctrines. The first field is viewed as sociological, and the second as psychological. The basic elements in the first are the spirit of discipline, of self-denial, and of autonomy.[37] Discipline includes regularity, limitation of desire, and effort. Self-denial carries these ideas further, and autonomy refers to "the attitude of a will that accepts rule because it recognizes it as being rationally founded." In other words, sociology is to de-

[35] Maurice Halbwachs, *Les Cadres sociaux de la memoire.*
[36] Paul Fauconnet, "The Pedagogical Work of Emile Durkheim," *American Journal of Sociology*, 28:533.
[37] *Ibid.*, 28:540.

fine the desirable intellectual types, psychology is to determine what resources are available in the child toward achieving this goal, and education is to realize the product.

Durkheim's "collective representations" and "division of labor" theories are likely to be viewed for a long time as basic contributions to social thought. Doubtless they will be modified, and imperfections in them will be corrected, but they testify to the penetrating analyses of society by the leading French contributor to sociological thinking, Emile Durkheim.

GROUP DISCUSSION TOPICS

1. Relation of Durkheim's ideas to those of Comte.
2. Durkheim's emphasis on methods.
3. The nature of social facts.
4. Duprat's concept of social facts.
5. The meaning of "collective representations."
6. The theory of the "division of labor."
7. Density of population and division of labor.
8. Durkheim's views of the nature of religion.
9. Durkheim's social explanation of suicide.
10. Bouglé and "evolution of values."
11. Bouglé's "polytelism."
12. Lévy-Bruhl's idea about the "mystical perception" of primitive people.
13. The "principle of participation" as developed by Lévy-Bruhl.
14. "The Great Society" according to Wallas.
15. The role of the "social heritage."

READINGS

Alpert, Harry, "Celestin Bouglé (1870–1940)," *Journal of Social Philosophy*, 5:270-273.
———, *Emile Durkheim and his Sociology* (New York: Columbia University Press 1939).
Barnes, Harry E., Editor, *An Introduction to the History of Sociology* (Chicago : University of Chicago Press 1948), Ch. 27.
Becker, Howard, and Harry E. Barnes, *Social Thoughts from Lore to Science* (Washington : Harren Press 1952), Vol. I, Ch. 22.
Bouglé, Charles, *The Evolution of Values*, translated by Helen S. Sellars (New York: The Macmillan Company 1926).
Case, Clarence M., and Fred Woerner, "René Worms: An Appreciation," *Sociology and Social Research*, 13:403-425.

Case, Clarence M., and Fred Woerner, "The Value Concept in Sociology and Related Fields," *Sociology and Social Research,* XXIII: 403-430.

Durkheim, Emile, *De la division du travail social* (Paris: Alcan 1893).

——, *The Elementary Forms of the Religious Life,* translated by J. W. Swain (Glencoe, Ill.: The Free Press 1954).

——, *Les règles de la méthode sociologique* (Paris: Alcan 1901).

——, *Le suicide* (Paris: Alcan 1897).

——, *On the Division of Labor in Society;* being a translation of his *De la division du travail social,* with an estimate of his work, by George Simpson (New York: The Macmillan Company 1933).

——, *The Rules of Sociological Method,* edited by G. E. G. Catlin (Glencoe, Ill.: The Free Press 1950).

——, *Socialism and Saint-Simon,* edited by A. W. Gouldner (Yellow Springs, Ohio: The Antioch Press 1958).

——, *Sociology and Philosophy,* translated by D. F. Pocock (Glencoe, Ill.: The Free Press 1953).

Fauconnet, Paul, "The Pedagogical Work of Emile Durkheim," *American Journal of Sociology,* 28:529-553.

Friedman, Georges, "Maurice Halbwachs, 1877-1945," *American Journal of Sociology,* LI: 509-517.

Gehlke, C. E., *Durkheim's Contribution to Sociological Theory* (New York: Columbia University Press 1915).

Gurvich, Georges, "The Sociological Legacy of Lucian Lévy-Bruhl," *Journal of Social Philosophy,* 5:61-70.

Halbwachs, Maurice, "Individual Consciousness and the Collective Mind," *American Journal of Sociology,* XLIV: 812-822.

Lévy-Bruhl, Lucian, *Les fonctions mentales dans les sociétés inférieures* (Paris: Alcan 1910).

Merton, Robert K., "Durkheim's Division of Labor in Society," *American Journal of Sociology,* 40:319-328.

Mihanovich, C. S., *Social Theorists* (Milwaukee: The Bruce Publishing Company 1948), Ch. 8.

Nisbet, Robert A., "The French Revolution and the Rise of Sociology in France," *American Journal of Sociology,* XLIX: 156-164.

Simpson, George, "Durkheim's Social Realism," *Sociology and Social Research,* 18:3-11.

Wallas, Graham, *The Great Society* (New York: The Macmillan Company 1914).

Wilson, Ethel M., "Emile Durkheim's Sociological Method," *Sociology and Social Research,* 18:511-518.

CHAPTER XXVIII

SMALL AND THE SOCIAL PROCESS

Social thinkers have long been probing for the ultimate in social life. They have been delving deeply into the meanings of the life that is going on around them. It was natural that someone should sooner or later lead the way in this search for the basic concept in human society. Perhaps this concept is *social process*.

It was Albion W. Small (1854–1926) who thought and talked in terms of the social process more definitely and consistently than any before him, and perhaps since his day. A characteristic phrase of his was "the ongoing of the social process."

Small was an American pioneer in sociology. A product of the stirring years of the last half of the nineteenth century, conditioned early by the ethics of Christianity, trained at Johns Hopkins University in a broad social science point of view, and stimulated by long and careful studies of German social scientists, Small was well fitted to be a sociological pioneer.

Not only as a voluminous writer, or as an able teacher, or as an indefatigable editor, but also as a personality, Small will be long remembered. He was dynamic, alert, polemic yet friendly, subject to criticism yet not given to taking himself too seriously.

Small's sociological thought arose out of his times and his training. From Gumplowicz and Ratzenhofer he gained the idea of social process. From them also he received a content for the term. This content grew out of the different types of "interests," of the "conflicts" between these interests, of the expression of these interests in social groups as well as in persons, of the adjusting of interests and the "cooperation" of persons representing different interests. Thus the phrase "the ongoing of the social process" begins to give out definite meanings.

HUMAN INTERESTS

"In the beginning were interests," says Professor Small.[1] An "interest" is defined as an unsatisfied capacity, an unrealized condition of the organism, a tendency to secure satisfaction of an unsatisfied capacity.[2] In its subjective phase an interest is a desire, and in its objective phase, a want. An interest is developed when the individual knows something, feels something, or wills something. Consequently, the whole individual or social process consists in developing, adjusting, and satisfying interests.

The six groups into which Small divides all interests are as follows: (1) The health interest arises from the sheer interest in keeping alive. It is expressed in the food interest, the sex interest, the work interest, and includes all the desires which find satisfaction in the exercise of the powers of the body. (2) The wealth interest is encompassed in the desire for mastery over things. (3) The sociability interest is represented at its best by the appetite for personal interchanges of stimulus of a purely spiritual nature. (4) The knowledge interest arises from the curiosity impulses. The limits of its possibilities are expressed in the terms *nescience* and *omniscience*. (5) The beauty interest secures satisfaction through an appreciation of the symmetrical phases of material and spiritual phenomena. (6) The rightness interest traverses the gamut of all other interests. It results in enjoyment when it secures the sanction of the individual's ideal self or of his whole self.

Each of these interests tends to be absolute.[3] Each seeks satisfaction regardless of the others. In consequence, there is a universal conflict of interests. Moreover, there is a universal conjunction of interests. The conflict, however, is more spectacular than the conjunction. In the history of mankind this conflict has been the predominating relationship. The social process has resolved itself into a series of reactions between persons some of whose interests comport, but others of which conflict. Furthermore, the social process

[1] Albion W. Small, *General Sociology*, p. 196.
[2] *Ibid.*, pp. 433 ff.
[3] *Ibid.*, pp. 201 ff.

is a continual formation of groups and institutions around interests. It is a perpetual equating and adjusting of interests;[4] it is a rhythm of differentiations and integrations.

SOCIAL CONFLICT

Small is now ready to state his theory of social conflict. It is found in the conflict of the six sets of interests. This conflict boils itself down into a continuous contest between those who believe that social institutions are supreme and those who would hold institutions accountable to human beings. This basic conflict among conflicts resolves itself into a struggle regarding the present social and economic system. Millions would preserve it at all costs; other millions would destroy it.

Small puts the fundamental conflict in another way. It is the conflict between the intellectual interest and all the other interests. Hence the basic problem of all problems is that of intellectualizing the other interests. How can all human interests be directed toward intelligent social betterment?

CO-OPERATION

Along with the rise of conflict there develops the practice of co-operation. The manner of its growth is illustrated by Small: "A few men dedicate themselves to causes which they regard as greater than themselves." They speak of these ends as "country," "humanity," "science," "art," "literature," "reform," "God." Not all of these men, by any means, actually reinforce the co-operative impulse which we assert, but some of them do. There spreads among the multitude a certain contagion of this collective spirit.[5]

This spirit of co-operation acquires momentum. It expresses itself through an ever-widening sense of community. "Our thesis is that along with out-and-out struggle, i.e., self-assertion of the extremest type — and along with the externally socialized self-assertion which recognizes the self-interest of pooling issues with others; a factor quite different in

4 *Ibid.*, p. 217.
5 *Ibid.*, p. 370.

temper develops in the course of the social process.   We have called this the co-operative or civilizing factor." [6]

In other words Small put co-operation on a par with conflict as an important phase of the social process.   Perhaps it is more important because of its civilizing nature.

In the mind of Small the social process turns out to be two social processes, namely, conflict and co-operation, with the latter playing an increasingly influential role.[7]

Small pointed out that struggle and co-operation are always to a certain extent functions of each other.[8]   Moreover, in the social process viewed historically, there is a movement "from a maximum toward a minimum of conflict, from a minimum toward a maximum of helpful reciprocity."   The social process, thus, is a perpetual adjustment between the forces which "tend backward toward more socialization."   By a minimum of conflict, Small does not mean absence of conflict, for he recognizes that stagnation would result in a society in which conflict was eliminated.   By a maximum of co-operation he does not refer to a state of complete social solidification, which in turn would mean stagnation and death.

The fundamental social problem is to give free scope to those interests which require the fullest rational development of all other interests.   The social problem is to intellectualize all the interests, and moreover, to intellectualize the conflict of interests.   Hence the fundamental conflict today is between the knowledge interest and all other interests.[9]   Socialization, then, becomes the process of transforming conflict into co-operation.

Sociology may be said to be the study of human interests, together with their conflicts and reciprocities.   It is an interpretation of human association in terms of the effective interests of man.   It focalizes within one field of vision all human activities so that the persons who have the benefit of this outlook may rate their own activities in relation to the whole.

[6] *Ibid.*, p. 569.
[7] *Ibid.*, p. 370.
[8] *Ibid.*, p. 325.
[9] *Ibid.*, pp. 389, 390.

INDUSTRIAL DEMOCRACY

In a concrete, specific way Small has presented his theory of the social process in the book *Between Eras, From Capitalism to Democracy*. Here is a vivid picture of the conflict between labor and capital, with the resultant misunderstandings and injustices. A young lady, Hector, observes the essential activities of labor and capital, and as a representative of capital perceives the relationship which actually exists between herself and one of the working girls. She receives large dividends, for which she puts nothing into the productive activities of the corporation. The working girl is paid low wages, but is giving her life to the industrial concern from which Hector's liberal dividends are pouring forth. The main end of the discussion is an argument for the establishment of the principle of industrial democracy. Professor Small urges that the employees, *per se*, be given representation on boards of directors. While this representation at first will necessarily be a minority one, it will serve the useful purpose of providing for regular meetings of representative employees and employers around the same council table. These meetings will enable the representatives of either party in the bitter labor-capital conflict to become acquainted with the problems which the opposing group faces. In this interchange Small sees the rise of a spirit of co-operation which will melt many of the difficulties that have sprung up in the controversy between capital and labor.[10] Although Dr. Small's *Between Eras* was published in 1913, the idea of industrial representation was not considered seriously in the United States until some years later. The initial steps which have thus far been taken toward industrial representation in the management of business and in the determination of wages, hours, and conditions of labor, have produced noteworthy co-operative results and have fully justified Small's prophetic recommendation for the solution of a world-disturbing social situation.

In addition to *General Sociology* and *Between Eras*, which represent the extremes of his sociological thinking and of his style, Small wrote *The Cameralists*, a scholarly work deal-

[10] *Between Eras, From Capitalism to Democracy*, Ch. XXIII.

ing with the German movement that was a counterpart to a degree of the Mercantilist Movement in England. His book on *The Meaning of Social Science* is a set of lectures, written in a serious yet delightful vein, pointing out the dangers of departmentalism of the social sciences. His *Origins of Sociology,* published two years before his death, selects a number of interesting factors in the development of nineteenth-century social science in Germany. His editorship of the *American Journal of Sociology* from its founding in 1895 for about three decades, and the many articles that he wrote are not the least important of his attainments. The sixty and more Doctors of Philosophy in Sociology, who were trained under his guidance at the University of Chicago during the course of a long period, beginning with the founding of the Department of Sociology at that University in 1892, represent his most significant achievement for the cause of sociology.

HAYES

Trained first for the ministry and then coming under the influence of Small at Chicago, Edward C. Hayes (1868–1928) carried forward the concept of ethics into sociological thought. He began with the social process. He shifted attention somewhat from interests to activities, and while not forgetting the former, he thought of the social process in terms of conflicts between and adjustments of activities. The central activity of sociology for Hayes is to explain social activities. Social activities result in social problems. In analyzing social activities, Hayes inquired into the factors that condition and modify human actions. In his thinking sociology shifted attention from causal forces to explanatory conditions.

To Hayes the all-important social conditions are to be found in the form of human relations which he classified at some length. These are largely psychical processes, such as suggestion, and psycho-social processes, such as competition or co-operation. Thus Hayes is known for his attention to the psychological approach. Finally, the ethical aspects of all social activities, conditions, relations, are immanent.

Sociology cannot avoid ethical or value judgments. It must evaluate methods of research, evaluate facts, evaluate the generalizations of its own scholars, evaluate the application of its findings, and evaluate society.

Some of the special aspects of society in which Hayes was interested were : social control, education, public opinion, and democracy. The nature of social control, according to his analysis is "to secure the completed and most harmonious realization of good human experience, regarded as an end in itself.[11] Social control should prevent activities which do not bear the test of reason, and should elicit those which stand that test, when judged by their own intrinsic value and by their effect upon other values. This statement of the purpose of social control is similar to that of other standard interpretations of the process.

There are two types of social control. The first is control by sanctions, and the second by social suggestions, sympathetic radiation, and imitation. Social sanctions refer to proffered rewards and threatened punishments. Hayes, however, made not law but personality the ultimate basis of social order. Repression of crime is a correct social procedure but of a distinctly lower grade than the movement to raise the moral character of those who never go to prison. The problem of social control is to take the instinctive tendencies of each individual when he is young and make them over into a disposition that is characterized by the four following traits : (1) reliability, or honesty ; (2) controlled animalism, or temperance regarding eating, drinking, and other animal propensities ; (3) steadiness in endeavor ; (4) the social spirit, or justice.[12]

Hayes' statement of the agencies of social control is similar in purport to the list that Professor Ross has given. Education is considered the chief agency of social control. Education can determine the direction of ambition ; education can shift the emphasis in social valuations. Hayes recognizes the import of heredity and how the degree of individual achievement is "more dependent upon heredity than upon the directions of effort." Society, however, has the power to

---

[11] E. C. Hayes, *Introduction to the Study of Sociology*, p. 586.
[12] *Ibid.*, pp. 586 ff.

decide which of its members shall develop as far as their potential abilities will permit, and also the power to determine the direction the activities of its members shall take.[13]

Among educational agencies of control the family ranks first.[14] The power of the family at its best in building personality is comparable to the influence in this connection of all other agencies combined. The profession of motherwork is more important to society than any other profession.[15]

The formation of public opinion is centered in the newspaper, but the newspaper is tied up with the power of wealth. Hence it must be viewed critically, or it may mislead people.

Closely rivaling wealth as a social power are ideas. But democracy requires that ideas have free avenues for expression. The secret ballot promotes democracy. Another aid is found in the chance for the average person to receive the facts through unbiased avenues.

Hayes defined democracy as a social organization not of special interests competing against each other, but of the interests of the welfare of all. In this connection Hayes urged the establishment of a free and untrammeled press. He asked for a press that would print the news from each of several political angles.

ELLWOOD

Another of Albion W. Small's early and eminent pupils is Charles A. Ellwood, who, while accepting the social process concept, developed it in social-psychological directions without separating it from its ethical aspects. Professor Ellwood defines a society as "a group of individuals carrying on a collective life by means of mental interactions."[16] As a result of mental interactions, co-ordination or co-adaptation of the activities of the members is effected.

The psychological basis of social interactions is found in such characteristics of the individual as spontaneity, instincts,

---

[13] *Ibid.*, pp. 664 ff.
[14] *Ibid.*, p. 669.
[15] *Loc cit.*
[16] C. A. Ellwood, *Sociology in its Psychological Aspects*, Ch. IX.

emotions, consciousness, mind. Organisms possess spontaneity; that is, movements are set up in them without apparent aid of external causes.[17] The organism, however, is dependent largely upon the environment for the development of its potentialities, "but the essential ground for the beginning of its activities lies within — in its own organic needs." Instincts, the product of natural selection, represent preformed neurological pathways that developed "in response to the demands of previous life conditions." The emotions, also hereditary, are complexes of feelings and sensations. The desires are complex combinations of feelings and impulses which are accompanied by an awareness of the objects that will satisfy the impulse.[18] Consciousness develops to solve problems which the instincts cannot meet. At first, consciousness is largely a selective activity. It develops, however, into a highly complex agency for mastering the problems of life and the universe. Mind is a product of the social life-process. It has arisen under conditions of association.

Communication, says Professor Ellwood, is "a device to carry on a common life-process among several distinct, though psychically interacting, individual units."[19] This definition probably emphasizes unduly the "individual units," which are doubtless a product, in part, of the stream of social life. Suggestion is an elemental, but quick form of communication related in its simpler phases to sympathetic emotion. Imitation is a common mechanism whereby actions and ideas spread. Communication in the form of oral and written language is the chief mechanistic factor in securing social change.

The contention of Ward that primitive man was antisocial is refuted by Professor Ellwood, who points out that according to social anthropology the so-called antisocial traits of earliest man are not found fully developed among "savages" but among people of later ages. Primitives were characterized by a narrow sociality, confined largely to the family and small groups.[20]

[17] *Ibid.*, p. 100.
[18] *Ibid.*, p. 117.
[19] *Ibid.*, p. 153; *cf.* Ellwood, *Introduction to Social Psychology*, p. 149.
[20] Ellwood, *Sociology in its Psychological Aspects*, p. 138.

SOCIAL CHANGE

Professor Ellwood's theory of social change is of twofold character : unconscious and conscious — the former being characteristic of the lower stages of social evolution, and the latter, increasingly characteristic of the higher stages.[21] The forms of unconscious social change are manifold.

Natural selection tends to crush and destroy the weaker individuals and the weaker groups. Another type of unconscious social change is that which comes through gradual disuse of certain cultural elements. One generation fails to copy the preceding in all particulars. Another set of sources of unconscious social change is found in the shifting of relationships between individuals that is produced by "the increase of population, a new physical environment, a new cultural contact, a new discovery or a new invention." In fact, Professor Ellwood states that all social changes start in an unconscious way.[22]

Conscious change begins with the awareness on the part of one or more persons that some social habit is not functioning well. Through communication this awareness spreads from person to person. Discussion ensues. At first, discussion is largely critical of the unsatisfactory social situation. The useless or harmful elements in the situation receive first attention. As discussion proceeds, it takes on a more constructive nature, that is, it becomes projective, planful, positive. It suggests a change to be made. It becomes transformed into a more or less stable public opinion, demanding a substitution of a proposed way of doing for the old. The chief elements in guaranteeing conscious re-adjustments are free communication, "free public criticism, free discussion, untrammeled formation of public opinion, a free selection of social policies and social leaders." [23] The selective process in conscious social change is public opinion, whose social function it is to mediate in the transition from one social habit to another. "The psychological conception of human

---

21 Ellwood, *Introduction to Social Psychology,* p 149.
22 *Ibid.,* p. 147.
23 *Ibid.,* p. 151.

social life has more than a mere theoretical value. As soon as we understand that human life is a behavior process, we begin to understand how it may be modified. We understand that such a behavior process is not so much the result of inborn traits plus the influence of physical environment as of the mental patterns in the minds of the individuals in the group." [24]

Professor Ellwood elaborates still further his ideas about social change. To effect change it is necessary to change culture. "The problem of modifying the social life, according to the psychological view, is essentially a problem of modifying habits and beliefs in vast masses of individuals." [25]

Conscious social change in Western Civilization is endangered on one hand by an excessive individualism, and on the other by a socialism which threatens to suppress individual initiative and to underemphasize the role of mental and moral character. Professor Ellwood urges the importance of an education which will socialize the individual and at the same time develop a high type of personal character.

Social change, also, takes place under socially abnormal conditions, so long as societies fail to keep "a high degree of flexibility in their habits and institutions." [26] Autocratic rulers, propertied classes, ecclesiastical classes, special groups in power, a general intellectual stagnation, are factors which tend to resist institutional flexibility. If this adaptability does not exist, then social conditions will produce revolutions. If the ruling autocracy is so powerful that the lives of all objectors are snuffed out, then revolution is indefinitely postponed. If the energetic forces within a society are hampered greatly in securing constructive opportunities for expression, they become forces of discontent and agents of revolt. If a revolution comes, then much that is worthy in social organization will be obliterated along with the unworthy, confusion will reign and a reversion to the brutal stages of societal life is easily possible.

[24] Charles A. Ellwood, "The Cultural or Psychological Theory of Society," op. cit., X:15.
[25] Ibid., X:16.
[26] Charles A. Ellwood, Introduction to Social Psychology, p. 170.

THE SOCIAL PROBLEM

In his discussion of "the social problem," Professor Ellwood points out that the good fruits of the World War are in danger of being destroyed by "the blindness and selfishness of some in our socially privileged classes, the fanatic radicalism and class hatred of some of the leaders of the non-privileged." [27] The forces which are combining against making the world safe for democracy today are national imperialism, commercialism, materialistic standards of life, class conflicts, religious agnosticism, and a reckless attitude toward marriage and the family.[28] The social problem, from one angle, becomes the problem of training people to live together justly, constructively, and co-operatively.

As Turgot indicated, the only way to avert social revolution is through suitable and well-timed reforms. Today the reforms most urgently needed are threefold: the substitution of an unselfish internationalism for a selfish nationalism, of a spiritual civilization for a rampant materialism, and of a socialized human race for individualized peoples. To bring about these changes is a gigantic task, namely, *the* social problem.

Civilization is a complex of social values. According to Professor Ellwood, Western Civilization is represented by the following groups of social values historically derived: (1) a set of spiritual and ethical values, described by the ancient Hebrews; (2) a set of esthetic and philosophic concepts from the Greeks; (3) a set of administrative and legal forms of Roman origin; (4) a set of personal liberty beliefs of early Teutonic derivation; (5) a scientific spirit and technique, originating during the Renaissance; (6) economic efficiency, born of the industrial revolution; and (7) an extensive group of humanitarian values, the product of the nineteenth century. This vast and complicated Western Civilization needs, however, to remove from its structure the three "rotten pillars" of hyper-individualism, materialism, and selfish nationalism, substituting for each its spiritualized and socialized counterpart.

[27] Charles A. Ellwood, *The Social Problem*, p. 2.
[28] *Ibid.*, p. 4.

Human nature is the most modifiable thing that we know. Ordinary human behavior is an indefinite compound, and hence is subject to change by changing the elements of the compound. "Through science, man will be enabled more and more to master nature and to control his own behavior," is Ellwood's belief as stated in his book, *The Psychology of Human Society*, which contains a refinement and a mature statement of the major psycho-sociologic points advanced in earlier treatises by the same author.

In his *Man's Social Destiny*, Ellwood discusses the future of science, government, education, and religion. A need is for science to perfect its "controls over culture." Autocracy in government is backward, for it "keeps the people politically children," and "does not favor the development of personality." To survive, democracies must secure a better distribution of wealth and a more equal opportunity than now occurs. Education is moving toward the materialistic; women are securing emancipation but growing indifferent spiritually. Religion will aid all men of good will everywhere in the work of redeeming men "from ignorance, impoverishment, hate, irrational fear, foolish pride, brutal lusts, vice, crime, and self-will."

In the writings of Small, and of his pupils, such as Hayes, Ellwood, and many others, we see sociological thought taking shape in terms of a general process. This process is viewed increasingly in psychological terms with more and more attention being paid to stages and aspects of the process. In the main, the ethical aspects are recognized as being tied up closely with the scientific and purely descriptive.

GROUP DISCUSSION TOPICS

1. The nature of the social process.
2. The meaning of "the ongoing of the social process."
3. The reasons for Small's interest in the social process.
4. The meaning of "interests."
5. The relation of interests to conflicts.
6. The connection between interests and co-operation.
7. Explain : "A minimum of conflict."
8. Explain : "A maximum of conflict."
9. The nature of "the fundamental social problem."
10. The differences between the social thought of Small and of Hayes.
11. The types of social control according to Hayes.
12. The major contribution of Ellwood to social thought.
13. Ellwood's theory of social change.
14. "The social problem" according to Ellwood, and its relation to Small's definition of "the fundamental social problem."
15. The social values in Western Civilization.
16. The "rotten pillars" of Western Civilization.
17. The social destiny of man.

READINGS

Barnes, Harry E., "The Place of Albion W. Small in Modern Sociology," *American Journal of Sociology*, XXXII:15-44.

Edlefsen, John B., "Albion Woodbury Small," *Sociology and Social Research*, 39:217-23.

Ellwood, Charles A., *The Psychology of Human Society* (New York: Appleton and Company 1925).

———, *The Social Problem* (New York: The Macmillan Company 1919).

———, *The Reconstruction of Religion* (New York: The Macmillan Company 1922).

———, *Man's Social Destiny* (Nashville: Cokesbury Press 1929).

———, *A History of Social Philosophy* (New York: Prentice-Hall, Inc. 1938).

Goodspeed, T. W., "Albion W. Small," *American Journal of Sociology*, XXXII:1-14.

Hayes, Edward C., *Sociology* (New York: Appleton and Company 1930).

———, *Sociology and Ethics* (New York: Appleton and Company 1921).

———, "Social Process, Social Relation, and Social Structure," *Sociology and Social Research*, XII:403-410.

Hiller, E. T., "The Sociology of Edward Cary Hayes," *Sociology and Social Research*, XIV:204-210.

House, F. N., "A List of the More Important Published Writings of Albion Woodbury Small," *American Journal of Sociology,* XXXII:49-58.

McLean, Annie M., "Albion Woodbury Small: An Appreciation," *American Journal of Sociology,* XXXII:45-48.

Page, Charles H., *Class and American Sociology: From Ward to Ross* (New York: The Dial Press 1940), Ch. 4.

Small, Albion W., *General Sociology* (Chicago: University of Chicago Press 1905).

————, *Between Eras, From Capitalism to Democracy* (Kansas City: Intercollegiate Press 1913).

————, *Origins of Sociology* (Chicago: University of Chicago Press 1924).

————, *The Meaning of Social Science* (Chicago: University of Chicago Press 1910).

————, *The Cameralists* (Chicago: University of Chicago Press 1909).

————, "Fifty Years of Sociology in the United States," *American Journal of Sociology,* XXI:721-864.

————, "Some Researches into Research," *Journal of Applied Sociology,* IX:3-11, 98-107.

————, "The Church and Class Conflicts," *American Journal of Sociology,* LX, Part Two: 54-74.

Sutherland, E. H., "Edward Cary Hayes, 1868–1928," *American Journal of Sociology,* 35:93-99.

CHAPTER XXIX

GIDDINGS AND CONSCIOUSNESS OF KIND

It was Franklin H. Giddings (1855–1931) who startled the social-philosophical world in 1896 with his *Principles of Sociology* and his theory about "consciousness of kind." Although his contributions to social thought were not limited by any means to this theory, yet it still stands out in the minds of many persons when his name is mentioned.

That Giddings was a sociological pioneer no one can deny. He brought to the field of social thought a wealth of data about civilization and its history. He also represented a striking type of personality, vigorous, determined, forceful. He had new ideas and he fought for them. As F. H. Hankins has said, Giddings "greatly enjoyed the thrill of departing from the serene objectivity of the scientist in order to become the preacher, the advocate, or the denouncer."[1]

Influenced by Ward and Sumner, he began as a disciple of Herbert Spencer. Along with Ward and Sumner and Small he became one of the four outstanding pioneers in American sociology. He was a Spencerian evolutionist. While remaining philosophical throughout his life and while exhibiting a flair for the unusual which perhaps was developed during his ten years as a journalist before becoming a sociologist, he demanded scientific procedures. He adopted the inductive method and urged a statistical approach. Most important of all was his psychological attack which culminated in his consciousness-of-kind theory. The evolution of his sociological thought, described by John L. Gillin,[2] is seen in his books and is revealed in his latter-day writings on "pluralistic behavior" and "societal variables."

As a professor at Columbia University the list of those who received their Ph.D. in sociology under his teaching is formidable, as in the case of Small's repertoire in the same con-

[1] F. H. Hankins, "Franklin Henry Giddings, 1855–1931: Some Aspects of his Sociological Theory," *American Journal of Sociology*, 37:349-367.

[2] J. L. Gillin, "Franklin Henry Giddings," in H. W. Odum, editor, *American Masters of Social Science*, Ch. VII.

nection. "Giddings men" are to be found throughout the United States and in foreign lands. They represent a wide range of social thought and, like their master-teacher, have proved loyal to sociology.

CONSCIOUSNESS OF KIND

The concept of "consciousness of kind" was developed by Franklin H. Giddings in his *Principles of Sociology* (1896). Consciousness of kind is the original and elementary subjective fact in society.[3] Professor Giddings defines this term as "a state of consciousness in which any being, whether low or high in the scale of life, recognizes another conscious being as of like mind with itself." In its widest meaning, consciousness of kind marks the difference between the animate and the inanimate. Among human beings it distinguishes "social conduct" from purely economic or purely religious activity. Around consciousness of kind, as a determining principle, all other human motives organize themselves.

People may be classified according to the development of the consciousness of kind in them. Roughly speaking, there are four such types.[4] (1) The non-social are persons in whom the consciousness of kind has not yet developed — in whom it finds imperfect but not degenerate expression, and from whom the other classes arise. (2) The antisocial, or criminal, classes include those persons in whom the consciousness of kind is approaching extinction. They detest society. (3) The pseudo-social, or pauper, classes are characterized by a degeneration of the genuine consciousness of kind. (4) The social classes are noted for a high development of the consciousness of kind; they constitute the positive and constructive elements in society. At the head of the list are the preeminently social. These people devote their lives and means to the amelioration of society; they are called the natural aristocracy of the race, the true social élite.

Consciousness of kind is made possible in part by the operation of physical factors. Fertility of soil is one of the sources

---

[3] F. H. Giddings, *Principles of Sociology*, p. 17.
[4] *Ibid.*, pp. 71, 126 ff.

of human aggregation. Favorable climate makes aggregation possible. Aggregation of population is either genetic (due to the birth rate) or congregate (due to immigration). Aggregation leads to association — the proper *milieu* for the growth of consciousness of kind.

Aggregation guarantees social intercourse which, however, is a mode of conflict. Conflict, according to Giddings, is related to social growth. Primary conflicts are those in which one adversary is completely outdone, and hence likely to be crushed, by the other. Secondary conflict refers to the contests between more or less evenly balanced forces. Primary conflict is conquest; secondary conflict is growth. Among people secondary conflict leads to the development of consciousness of kind through the successive steps of communication, imitation, toleration, co-operation, alliance. The supreme result is the production of pre-eminently social classes. Of these various functional factors, Giddings particularly stresses imitation. "It is the factor of imitation in the conflict that gradually assimilates and harmonizes." [5]

Association reacts upon individuals and produces self-consciousness, which in turn creates social self-consciousness, or group awareness of itself. Social self-consciousness is characterized by rational discussion. With the rise of discussion social memory, or traditions, becomes possible. Moreover, a sense of social values arises. Public opinion springs from the passing of judgment by the members of the group upon any matters of general interest. [6]

Social memory, or traditions, becomes highly differentiated. [7] It consists of impressions concerning the tangible world, the intangible world, and the conceptual world. The traditions in any field, plus current opinion in that field, form the standards, ideals, faiths, "isms," of the time. For example, the integration of economic traditions with current economic opinions is the general standard of living of the time and the place. The integration of the esthetic tradition with current criticism is taste, and the modification of a traditional religious belief by current religious ideas is a faith.

---

[5] *Ibid.*, pp. 101 ff. *Cf.* Giddings, *Descriptive and Historical Sociology*, Ch. III.
[6] *Principles of Sociology*, p. 109; *Descriptive and Historical Sociology*, pp. 157 ff.
[7] *Principles of Sociology*. p. 138.

Inasmuch as consciousness of kind is the psychological basis of social phenomena, it is natural that the chief social value is the kind itself, or the type of conscious life that is characteristic of the society.[8] The social cohesion is another important social value. Social cohesion is vital to the unity of any group; therefore the group is usually willing to make many sacrifices in its own behalf. The distinctive possessions and properties of the community, such as territory, sacred or historic places, heroes, ceremonies, constitute the third class of social values. A fourth group is found in the general principles which promote the growth of the group; for example, the principles of liberty, equality, and fraternity. The social values largely determine the social choices of groups and the nature of social organizations.

STRUCTURAL DUALISM

Giddings develops an interesting theory of the dualism in social structures. Civilization is marked by the contemporaneous existence of public and private associations. Civilized society affords four main sets of dualistic associations: political, juristic, economic, and cultural. In the political field there are private political parties and the public association, namely, the government or the political party in power. Among juristic associations there are the privately organized vigilance committees and the public associations, such as the police, the courts, the prisons. In the realm of economics there are private individual entrepreneurs, partnerships, corporations; and on the other hand, there are the governmentally-owned railroads, postal service, the water systems, the coinage systems. In regard to cultural associations we may note the privately endowed universities and state universities, privately organized churches and state churches, private charities and public charities. This dualism in social structure is supported by Giddings on the grounds that private associations are needed for purposes of initiation, experimentation, and stimulation; and the public associations serve the useful purposes of regulation and maintenance of balance among various contending factors.

[8] *Ibid.*, pp. 141 ff.

The highest test of social organization is the development of social personality. An efficient social organization is one which makes its members "more rational, more sympathetic, with an ever-broadening consciousness of kind." [9]

Giddings developed the concept of pluralistic behavior. "Any one or any combination of behavior-inciting stimuli may on occasion be reacted to by more than one individual." [10]

The character of pluralistic reactions, whether similar or dissimilar, simultaneous or not, equal or unequal, is determined by two variables : (1) the strength of the stimulation ; (2) the similarity or dissimilarity of the reacting mechanisms. Thus Giddings considers pluralistic behavior the subject matter of the psychology of society, or sociology.

Giddings explains further the nature of pluralistic behavior in terms of its own conditions and nature. These differ distinctly from the laws that govern individual behavior. "Whether they are dissimilar or similar, rivalistic or combined, simultaneous or not, equal or unequal, pluralistic reactions to a common stimulation make a strictly individualistic struggle for existence impossible." [11]

In *The Mighty Medicine,* published about two years before his death, Giddings made an effective and characteristic attack upon superstition and occultism. Natural science proceeds serenely in the laboratory, but the supernaturalist "tom toms and taboos. He carries his tom-tomery into legislative lobbies and gets his tabooery into statute law. He formulates creeds and demands subscription to them by the teachers, professors, and college presidents." He assigns a sense of mystery and of sacredness to many things in order to protect them. "To millions of voters the flag is more sacred than the country which flies it, and a written Constitution is more sacred than the rights and liberties it defines and guar-

---

[9] *Descriptive and Historical Sociology,* p. 541. *Cf.* Giddings, *Inductive Sociology,* Part III.
[10] *American Journal of Sociology,* XXV:387.
[11] *Loc. cit.*

antees." [12] In other words, Giddings criticized civilized man for still maintaining in a modified way the habits of "mystical perception" which Lévy-Bruhl found to be so characteristic of primitive man.

BALDWIN

To understand Giddings' early thought, special stimuli are found in the writings of J. Mark Baldwin, whose ideas Giddings pondered over considerably. In 1897 *Social and Ethical Interpretations*, by J. Mark Baldwin, was published; it bears the subtitle of "A Study in Social Psychology." This was the first time that the term *social psychology* had appeared in the title of a book in America, though three years earlier, in 1894, one of the leading parts of Small and Vincent's *Introduction to the Study of Society* was designated "social psychology" and included a discussion of social consciousness, social intelligence, and social volition. Baldwin's *Social and Ethical Interpretations* and Giddings' *Principles of Sociology* appeared almost simultaneously, one by a psychologist and the other by a sociologist. One was written from the genetic viewpoint, and the other from the objective viewpoint; one dealt primarily with social psychology, and the other with a psychology of society; one was built around the concept of the social self, and the other around the concept of consciousness of kind. They both hastened the development of social psychology.

BIPOLAR SELF

Baldwin demonstrated that the self is largely a product of the give-and-take of social life. A child becomes aware of his *self* by setting himself off from other selves. It is in group life, that is, in contact with other selves, that the child develops a self-consciousness.

Moreover, the self is bipolar. One end of the self-pole is characterized by what one thinks of himself, and the other end by what he thinks of other persons.[13] "The ego and the alter are to our thought one and the same thing."[14]

---

[12] F. H. Giddings, *The Mighty Medicine*, pp. 8, 10.
[13] J. M. Baldwin, *Social and Ethical Interpretations*, p. 15.
[14] *Ibid.*, p. 18.

A person comes to think of himself as composed of many behavior traits which he once considered as being characteristic of other persons. The growth of personality, thus, becomes a subtle process of borrowing and appropriating.

PERSONALITY GROWTH

Baldwin formulated an interesting theory of personality growth. He postulated three stages. These are the projective, subjective, and ejective. The first is largely contemplative; the second is experimental and imitative; the third is social, in that the individual is able to understand other persons' experiences.[15]

People are so much alike because they are imitative. It is imitation which keeps people alike. Imitation is either (1) a process whereby one individual consciously or unconsciously copies another individual, or (2) the copying of a model; that is, adopting a model which arises in one's own mind.[16]

Baldwin found the law of social growth in the particularization by the individual of society's store of material, and by the generalization on the part of society of the individual's particularizations. The essence of the first phase of this process is invention and of the second, imitation. Baldwin considered invention and imitation the two fundamental processes of social growth.

In this chapter the importance of the psychological approach to an understanding of societary processes has been demonstrated. In the chapter which follows, the reader will find further materials showing the tremendous vitality of psycho-sociologic thought.

Along with Baldwin, and others, there were several writers who sought a psychological theory of society. By way of contrast, the instinct theory of William McDougall may be cited. Later this was supplemented by a group-mind theory, an explanation decidedly different from Giddings' consciousness of kind, and Durkheim's "collective representations."

15 J. Mark Baldwin, *Mental Development in the Child and the Race*, first edition, p. 335.
16 J. Mark Baldwin, *Social and Ethical Interpretations*, pp. 529 ff.

McDougall's ideas also stand in sharp contrast to those of E. A. Ross and of Gabriel Tarde.

MCDOUGALL

The year 1908 is a red letter year in the history of socio-psychologic thought. In that year two important treatises appeared, both bearing in their titles the term *social psychology;* one was written by William McDougall (1871–1938) and the other by Edward A. Ross. Professor McDougall considers social psychology largely as a study of the social instincts of individuals; Professor Ross concentrates attention upon the suggestion and imitation phases of societal life. In a sense Professor Ross begins his analysis where McDougall concludes.

McDougall treats the instincts as the bases of social life. He makes them the foundation of nearly all individual and social activities.[17] Instincts are biologically inherited; they cannot be eradicated by the individual. Instincts constitute the materials out of which habits are made. Consciousness arises only when an instinct or a habit (that is, a modified instinct) fails to meet human needs.

The primary instincts are the sex and parental, the gregarious, curiosity, flight, repulsion. Each is accompanied by its peculiar emotion; for example, the instinct of flight by the emotion of fear, the instinct of curiosity by the emotion of wonder. This instinct-emotion theory is, however, drawn out until it seems to become academic rather than actual in its details.

Professor McDougall points out that the instincts are the basic elements upon which all social institutions are built. For example, the sex and parental instincts are the foundations of the family; the acquisitive instinct is an essential condition of the accumulation of material wealth and of the rise of private property as an institution. Pugnaciousness leads to war.

This emphasis upon the instincts reaches an extreme form in W. Trotter's *Instincts of the Herd in Peace and War,* where the herd instinct is made all-dominant. According to

[17] *Introduction to Social Psychology,* pp. 23 ff.

Mr. Trotter the herd instinct arouses fear in the individual and rules him through rigorous conventional means — in a large percentage of cases to his detriment.

In conjunction with his theory of instincts, Professor Mc-Dougall has advanced a noteworthy conception of the sentiments. The three leading expressions of sentiment are love, hate, and respect. Sympathy is regarded as an elemental sentiment, in fact, as an emotion in its simplest form. A sentiment is "an organized system of emotional tendencies centered about some object." The sentiments comprise an important phase of the self, and function powerfully in determining social conduct.

McDougall held that each of the nations is "in process of developing a group mind." "Group spirit" and "nationalism" are somewhat synonymous. Another closely related term is "collective psychology."

Professor McDougall explains that group psychology is engaged in discovering the most general principles of group life and in applying these to "the study of particular kinds and examples of group life." [18] While rejecting the idea of a "collective consciousness" in the sense of "a unitary consciousness of the society over and above that of the individuals comprised within it," he still contended that a society that has had a long life and become highly organized "acquires a structure and qualities which are largely independent of the qualities of the individuals who enter into its composition and take part for a brief time in its life." [19]

Although group psychology as expressed in the form of crowds and mobs is characterized by degrading elements, yet organization of the higher types "renders group life the great ennobling influence by aid of which man alone rises a little above the animals and may even aspire to fellowship with the angels." [20] What, then, are the major characteristics of the group mind? The answer is: "A common object of mental activity, a common mode of feeling in regard to it, and some degree of, reciprocal influence between the members of the group.".[21] The group spirit results in pulling

---

[18] William McDougall, *The Group Mind*, p. 9.
[19] *Ibid.*, p. 12.
[20] *Ibid.*, p. 28.
[21] *Ibid.*, p. 33.

each person out of the narrow circle of his own friends, "in inspiring him to postpone his private to public ends, in enabling the common man to rise at times . . . to lofty heights of devotion and self-sacrifice." [22] To obtain this group spirit the individual must become versed in the knowledge of the group and conditioned to feel some sentiment of attachment to the group for its own sake.

While the mantle of Giddings fell upon no one person in particular, his chair at Columbia was assigned to Robert M. MacIver, whose thinking is rich in social-philosophical backgrounds. One of his basic concepts is that of "community," and another is "association," which refers to an interest-group within a community. A third is "institutions" which are "the established forms or conditions of procedure characteristic of group activity." [23] Institutions are systems of controls that extend "beyond personal relations"; they are bonds between the past and the present, and between the present and the future. Hence "we belong to associations, but not to an institution." [24] An organized group is an association; a mode or means of service is an institution.[25]

Society is a system of relationships that provides traditions and institutions and a changeful order of life arising from physical and psychical needs of human nature. Within this *milieu* human beings fulfill themselves and transmit the faculties of living to the generations that follow.[26] Tönnies' concepts of *Gemeinschaft* and of *Gesellschaft* bear an interesting relation to MacIver's "community" and "association."

Professor MacIver holds to the idea that nationality is "a type of community sentiment, a sense of belonging together, created by historical circumstances and supported by common spiritual possessions, of such an extent and so strong that those who feel it desire to have a common government peculiarly or exclusively their own." [27] The keynote is sentiment. McDougall's group spirit seems to give a large

[22] *Ibid.*, p. 119.
[23] R. M. MacIver, *Society: A Textbook of Sociology*, p. 14.
[24] *Ibid.*, p. 15.
[25] *Ibid.*, p. 17.
[26] *Ibid.*, p. 45.
[27] *Ibid.*, p. 155.

place for knowledge. Giddings' consciousness of kind stresses more an awareness of kindred interests.

GROUP DISCUSSION TOPICS

1. Giddings' place among sociologists.
2. Relation of Giddings' thinking to that of Herbert Spencer.
3. The concept of consciousness of kind.
4. Social classes according to Giddings.
5. Structural dualism in Giddings' system.
6. The concept of pluralistic behavior.
7. The bipolar self as conceived by Baldwin.

READINGS

Baldwin, J. Mark, *Social and Ethical Interpretations in Mental Development* (New York : The Macmillan Company 1906).

Elwood, Charles A., "The Social Philosophy of James Mark Baldwin," *Journal of Social Philosophy*, 2:55-68.

Giddings, Franklin H., *Principles of Sociology* (New York : The Macmillan Company 1896).

———, *Descriptive and Historical Sociology* (New York : The Macmillan Company 1911).

———, *Studies in the Theory of Human Society* (New York : The Macmillan Company 1922).

———, *The Scientific Study of Human Society* (Chapel Hill : University of North Carolina Press 1924).

———, *The Mighty Medicine* (New York : The Macmillan Company 1929).

Gillin, John L., "Franklin Henry Giddings," in H. W. Odum, editor, *American Masters of Social Science* (New York : Henry Holt and Company 1927).

Hankins, F. H., "Franklin Henry Giddings, 1855-1931 : Some Aspects of Sociological Theory," *American Journal of Sociology*, 37:349-367.

Jensen, Howard E., "William McDougall's Doctrine of Social Psychology," *Journal of Social Philosophy*, 6:206-219.

McDougall, William, *The Group Mind* (New York : G. P. Putnam's Sons 1920).

———, *Introduction to Social Psychology* (Boston : Luce and Company 1908).

Pastore, Nicholas, "A Social Approach to William McDougall," *Social Forces*, 23:148-152.

Sewny, Vahan D., *The Social Theory of James Mark Baldwin* (New York : Kings Crown Press, 1945).

Tenney, Alvan A., "Franklin Henry Giddings, 1855-1931," *Sociology and Social Research*, 16:103-110.

CHAPTER XXX

SIMMEL AND SOCIALIZATION

While Albion W. Small discussed "the social process," it was Georg Simmel (1858–1918) who gave it a concrete name. If one social process is more significant than another, that one is socialization.

Simmel's intellectual backgrounds included the teachings of Kant and Treitschke. He taught at the Universities of Berlin and Strassburg. His intellectual interests were broad, being philosophical rather than scientific. He was concerned with philosophy both as a critic of science and as a synthetic treatment of scientific findings. He was at home in the fields of metaphysics and epistemology as well as in sociology.

Simmel's sociological thought begins with the process of social becoming. He studied the descriptive data of history in search for generalizations. The social process first of all springs out of social interaction. As stated in his *Soziologie,* Simmel attempted to set forth the "forms of socialization," which have their bases in interaction.

To Simmel sociology studies the ways in which social interaction recur over and over. The major recurring social "form" is the process of socialization.

Simmel defines socialization as "the growing into a unity." [1] There are circles of socialization — of identification with wider interests and larger groups. To Simmel sociology is essentially the science of socialization or of the forms of unity under which people live. The most important system of relationship in the social world is that of the leader and his followers, or of the superior and his subordinates. Without this "form" of socialization no social life would be possible. [2]

The subordinate, according to Simmel, is an influential partner in the leadership-subordinate relationship. The leader can never ignore his followers entirely. They always have the choice of submitting to or of refusing to take orders and of being punished.

[1] *The Social Theory of Georg Simmel,* by Nicholas Spykman, p. 79.
[2] *Ibid.,* p. 95.

Behind leadership is the question of authority. There are two major sources of leadership; one is achieved and the other is conferred.

There are three kinds of superior relationships. The authority may be found in any one of three centers. "The superiority may be exercised by a single individual, by a group, or by an objective principle in the form of a social or ideal superindividual power."[3]

OPPOSITION

Opposition, according to Simmel, plays a necessary role in socialization. Conflict makes for social unity and contributes to socialization.[4] It is "a positive form of interaction" between human beings and therefore is a form of socialization. Conflict brings in socializing factors, if only in terms of restraint.[5]

The effects of conflict are subtle. They may even include unification; certainly they produce concentration of each of the conflicting elements. Opposition from without causes socialization within.

SOCIALIZATION

Many writers have analyzed the process of socialization. By way of comparison, the ideas of E. A. Ross, L. M. Bristol, and of Park and Burgess will be considered here.

Socialization, in content, is the development of a we-feeling in a number of persons, and "their growth in capacity and will to act together."[6] A very simple causal factor of this process is the age-long custom of giving a banquet, that is, of eating and drinking together. A consciousness of kind arises, which, as Professor Ross believes, is not the perception of a general resemblance but "an awareness of likeness or agreement in specific matters."[7] Nationalism, or

[3] *Ibid.,* p. 112.
[4] *Loc. cit.*
[5] "The Sociology of Conflict," by Georg Simmel, translated by A. W. Small, *American Journal of Sociology,* 9:490.
[6] *Principles of Sociology* (first edition 1920), p. 395.
[7] *Ibid.,* p. 405.

the process of creating a spirit of national patriotism, illustrates the meaning of the socialization concept.

Origins of the we-feeling are found in many types of experiences. These include expansion of feelings which, however, may be short-lived.

Ross emphasizes the significance of feeling and acting alike in the same situation. Persons who do not feel and act alike in the same situation do not grow socialized toward each other.

The common meal is a simple but effective means of promoting socialization. The banquet has a socialization validity. Community of interest is a basic factor in socialization. It promotes the we-feeling without the expenditure of effort.

The primordial social group, according to Professor E. A. Ross, is a band of mothers and their children. In such groupings preliminary socialization took place. In earliest societies definite principles of human action made themselves evident.[8] Domination was one of the ruling principles. Note, for example, the domination (1) by parents over offspring, (2) by old over young, (3) by husband over wife, (4) by men over women, (5) by the military over the industrial classes, (6) by the wealthy over the poor. The chief purpose in dominating is to exploit, that is, to use other individuals as means to one's own ends.[9]

Simmel's idea of socialization has been supplemented by many similar but non-parallel concepts. Sometimes the concept of social adaptation has been used to cover an idea germane to socialization. L. N. Bristol had made an extensive analysis of social adaptation theories.[10] Passive adaptation comprises the process of biological evolution, and passive spiritual adaptation includes psychic evolution or the non-purposeful development of language, mores, and particularly of education. Active material adaptation includes the process of industrial development, and active spiritual adaptation not only comprises the purposeful adjustment of the individual to his spiritual environment, but also social reform, and purposeful social control.[11]

8 *Ibid.*, p. 121.
9 *Ibid.*, p. 135.
10 L. M. Bristol, *Social Adaptation.*
11 *Ibid.*, p. 9.

Socialization, or social adaptation, runs the gamut of toleration, compromise, accommodation, and amalgamation. The
simplest form of co-operation is mutual aid, which, however,
is more popular among the lower classes than among the
higher. Socialization, it may be noted here, has been shown
by E. W. Burgess to be the fundamental process in the determination of social progress.[12] Socialization has two aspects.
"From the standpoint of the group, we may define it as the
psychic articulation of the individual into the collective activities. From the standpoint of the person, socialization is
the participation of the individual in the spirit and purpose,
knowledge and methods, decision and action of the group." [13]
Socialization of a person means that he "consciously modifies
his behavior and shapes his purposes to promote more efficient co-operative activity and to realize the higher welfare
of the group."

This discussion may be supplemented by reference to the
socialization of a group. This process has two phases. One
phase relates to the organization and functioning of the
group whereby "the members change from a loose heterogeneity to an organized homogeneity, with authority distributed to each, with each functioning fully in the group enterprises." [14] The other phase involves the relation of the
group to other groups whereby the main purposes of the
group become centered outside itself and harmonized with
the welfare of all democratically organized groups and with
the welfare of the world itself.[15]

An interesting phase of socialization is organization. Organization of effort results (1) in the accomplishment of ends
which are unattainable otherwise, (2) in arousing a common
interest intermittently in all, (3) in dividing a task into its
natural parts, (4) in securing a degree of expertness, (5) in
producing a co-ordinated, intelligent plan, (6) in eliminating
needless duplication of effort.[16] On the other hand, organization leads to wastes and abuses, which are : (1) overhead ex-

12 E. W. Burgess, *The Function of Socialization in Social Evolution.*
13 *Ibid.,* p. 2.
14 E. S. Bogardus, *Fundamentals of Social Psychology* (Century Company
931), Chapter XXIII.
15 *Ibid.,* p. 292.
16 E. A. Ross, *Principles of Sociology,* pp. 257 ff.

penses, (2) undue time devoted to making out reports and similar routine work, (3) a loss in personal contacts, (4) a tendency to formalism and red tape, (5) an inflexibility of machinery, (6) a misapplication of power to personal ends, (7) too much specialization, and (8) the organization becomes an end in itself.

SOCIAL PROCESSES

Park and Burgess in their *Introduction to the Science of Sociology* conceive of a single social process, namely, social interaction, which includes, first, competition and conflict, and then as may be the case, accommodation and assimilation. Taken together, accommodation and assimilation are roughly equivalent to co-operation, but represent a more accurate and scientific usage of terms. Competition may be viewed as a process basic to the more distinctly sociological ones of conflict and accommodation, and with the latter two bearing a definite relation to socialization.

Since competition is explained as "interaction without social contact," it can hardly be called a sociological process, for the interaction is unconscious. In this sense competition takes place without any of the parties experiencing any meaning for the process, in fact, without anyone being aware of its taking place.[17]

Conflict involves contact and communication. When persons are aware that they are competing, the competition becomes conflict. "Conflict is always conscious, indeed, it evokes the deepest emotions and strongest passions and enlists the greatest concentration of attention and effort."[18] Conflict takes various forms, such as war, rivalry, political strife, race antagonism, and cultural clashes.

Accommodation relates to "changes in habit, which are transmitted, or may be transmitted, sociologically, that is, in the form of social tradition."[19] It is to be distinguished from adaptation, which applies chiefly to organic modifications. Domestication is a form of adaptation; taming, an illustration of accommodation. "Accommodation is

[17] Park and Burgess, *Introduction to the Science of Sociology*, p. 507.
[18] *Ibid.*, p. 574.
[19] *Ibid.*, p. 663.

the natural issue of conflicts." [20]   Acclimatization is a subtle form of accommodation.   Naturalization in its essence is another expression of accommodation.   Simmel's terms, subordination and superordination, are accepted as phases of personal accommodation.

Assimilation is an unconscious "interpenetration and fusion" of memories, sentiments, and attitudes.   "The person is incorporated into the common life of the group before he is aware" of what has been taking place.   Assimilation involves participation and resultant "thorough-going transformation of the personality."   Acculturation, as the term implies, is a fusion of cultures.

Socialization may be used either as a descriptive term, involving chiefly participation, or as an appreciative or evaluative concept.   In the latter sense, socialization sets up "as the goal of social effort a world in which conflict, competition, and the externality of individuals, if they do not disappear altogether, will be so diminished that all men may live together as members of one family." [21]

THE STRANGER

Simmel's discussion of the "stranger" suggests nearness and farness in social relationships.   The stranger, in moving out of one social circle and striving to secure acceptance in another, illustrates both nearness and farness at the same time.   When he is geographically far from his old home, he may be socially near, especially if he experiences homesickness.   On the other hand, when he arrives in a new location and is not at first accepted, he illustrates physical nearness and social remoteness.   Thus he represents in himself a union of nearness and remoteness.   Even the stranger is near us if we feel that between him and us are similarities of nationality, of social or professional position, or of common personal traits.   On the other hand, a person may belong to our own nationality or profession and still seem far from us simply because he is one out of a countless multitude.[22]

Robert E. Park speaks of "distance" as coming into use "in

[20] *Ibid.*, p. 665.
[21] *Ibid.*, p. 496.
[22] Georg Simmel, *Soziologie*, third edition, p. 511.

an attempt to reduce to something like measurable terms the grades and degrees of understanding and intimacy which characterize personal and social relations generally." [23] Democracy is supposed to keep social distances at a minimum, yet it maintains them. Some persons, however, accept the whole world within the scope of social nearness.

In a recent study of the "stranger," Margaret M. Wood finds that "the new relationships which are formed when strangers meet are not governed wholly by fortuitous circumstances, but that they are closely correlated with social relationships that are already present in the group which the stranger has entered." [24] The conclusion is that the newcomer to any group is a stranger to the degree that he does not share the basic sentiments and values of that group. He is rated by the group as an asset or a liability according to how he is adjudged as a help or a hindrance in the promoting of the group's values. [25] Margaret Wood has made extensive studies interpreting the role of the stranger in terms of the differing community patterns that exist in immigrant communities, in foreign colonies, in frontier settlements, in retarded districts, in the rural community, in the small town, and in the large city. New light thus is thrown on the varying conditions underlying social distance.

SOCIAL DISTANCE

Simmel's study of the "stranger" naturally leads to a consideration of "social distance," which refers to the degrees of sympathetic understanding that exist between persons, a person and his social groups, and between social groups. It may be either horizontal distance, that is, between peers, or vertical distance, that is between leaders and their followers.

Social distances are of two kinds. One is due to faulty perception and communication. The other a recoil from acquaintance and intimacy in which differences in attitudes, sentiments, and beliefs are discovered and in which conflicts are developed. Conflicts thus may arise from an

[23] Robert E. Park, "The Concept of Social Distance," *Journal of Applied Sociology*, 8:339.
[24] Margaret M. Wood, *The Stranger*, p. 7.
[25] *Ibid.*, pp. 283, 284.

absence of knowledge of the other person's attitudes, or from a feeling or an awareness of difference.

Viewed from a social distance an individual takes on the characteristics of his group or groups. His traits are not distinguished from his group's tastes. "All Chinese look alike to me" — when they are socially distant. On the other hand, a person upon close acquaintance reveals his individuality, or his distinguishing marks. But this individuality may produce either favorable or unfavorable attitudes. Intimacy may lead to arousal of disgust or to *ennui* caused by repetition of tiresome stimuli. Where there is no caste system, individuals are continually getting "out of place" from the standpoint of somebody, and hence arousing unfavorable reactions on the part of the "somebody." [26]

Social distance is a measure of actual or potential social conflict. It reveals the location of actual or incipient social problems.

All social problems may be thought of in terms of social distance, and applied sociology in terms of the principles involved in the necessary decreasing of social distance. Social distance accounts for the rise of misunderstandings and hence for the real underlying factors which create social problems. The capitalist in denouncing the labor unionists displays social distance traits. The wealthy landlord condemning the tenants of his unsanitary and congested tenements is maintaining social distance. The survey of any untoward conditions, no matter how objective and concrete, such as the wage problem, strikes, race prejudice, juvenile delinquency, requires an analysis of the social distances involved before the situation is fully understood. In fact, the analysis of social distance in all of its aspects makes clear why any given problem exists.[27]

Causes of social farness are found in unfavorable personal experiences. These generate what are relatively lasting negative sentiments. Nearness originates in favorable experiences.

Unpleasant sense impressions personally experienced in childhood and adolescence are many. Sometimes fear is

[26] E. S. Bogardus, *The New Social Research,* p. 209.
[27] *Ibid.,* adapted, pp. 200, 201.

aroused; and again, disgust. Fear is the more dynamic and predominant factor. In either case there is a sensory image that is often described as "horrifying." The fact that these images were experienced in childhood gave them a more or less permanent character.[28]

Derivative experiences, hearsay reports, traditions are also causes of social farness. In fact, derivative experiences may be as effective as direct ones, especially if the sources are closely identified with one's own personal life.

A large grouping of materials offered by life history data of the persons expressing the greatest social farness reactions is composed of tradition and accepted opinion. It is clear that hearsay evidence coming from both one's personal friends and relative strangers is widely influential in creating social farness.[29]

"All my store of unpleasant reactions against the Turks is not based on any personal knowledge of them. I do not even know a representative of this people; never have glimpsed a Turk in gentle or savage mood, never, except in imagination. But I have much secondhand knowledge. I have derived it from the lurid headlines of newspapers, from magazine articles on revelations of pseudo-political intrigue, from the stories dealing with the exotic life behind the mysterious veil and barred window. In church I have heard of Turkish atrocities to helpless missionaries. I have heard of the Turkish aversion to our culture and ideals talked of at dinner, at club meetings, and on the street. Nowadays I hear of the young Turk, with his intellectual veneer but who is the same unspeakable old Turk underneath." [30]

Social farness is deliberately fostered, sometimes in order to maintain status, sometimes to keep oneself or the group in power, sometimes to maintain self-respect. Both persons and groups will fight for status.[31]

[28] *Ibid.*, p. 204.
[29] *Ibid.*, p. 202.
[30] *Ibid.*, pp. 203, 204.
[31] The close relation between social distance and personal status has been emphasized by Jessie R. Runner who has diagrammed distance relationships of adolescent girls in the form of concentric circles. "Social Distance in Adolescent Relationships," *American Journal of Sociology*, 43:428-439.

Other variations in the social distance test are being developed. For example, see Stuart C. Dodd, "A Social Distance Test in the Near East," *American Journal of Sociology*, 41:194-204.

Social distances are deliberately maintained by an auto-cratic society. The people in authority maintain personal "reserves" and social conventions which hinder the rank and file from becoming intimate with them, and from entering imaginatively into the minds of the leaders. Democracy, on the other hand, theoretically strives to overcome the factors which create or support social distance.[32]

Social distance results from the maintenance of social status, that is, of the *status quo* in social relationships. By keeping others at a distance a person maintains his standing among his friends. One can more easily bear the loss of almost anything in life than loss of social status, hence, the *raison d'etre* for maintaining social distances.[33]

Closely related to the ideas of vertical distance are those dealing with "social mobility" and with the "circulation of the élite." The latter concept will be treated later in the discussion of Pareto, who has developed the term at length. Social mobility will be considered here. P. A. Sorokin, who has written extensively on social mobility, interprets it in terms of horizontal and vertical movements of individuals. Vertical mobility is the more significant, for it involves changes in the control of one person by another. More mobility, particularly of the vertical sort, obtains in demo-cratic than in autocratic societies. Stratification prevents mobility except with each stratum. Mobility, particularly vertical, is controlled extensively in and by institutions, such as the church, school, and state. Rigid rules for vertical mobility are maintained in the army as a social institution. When incapable persons accumulate too greatly in any one level of society, then revolution occurs and people are re-distributed.[34]

Everett W. DuVall has made an interesting inquiry into the nature or child-parent distance, following up the earlier work of Meyer F. Nimkoff ("Parent-Child Conflict," *Sociology and Social Research*, 8:446-458), and ob-taining a rank difference correlation of .76 ± .15 in one phase of his study. The social distance tests thus are being perfected until a reasonable degree of reliability is being obtained (Everett W. DuVall, "Child-Parent Social Dis-tance," *Sociology and Social Research*, 21:458-463).

[32] *Ibid.*, p. 210.

[33] *Ibid.*, p. 217.

[34] Pitirim A. Sorokin, *Social Mobility* (New York: Harper and Brothers 1927).

Leopold von Wiese begins with certain realistic aspects of Simmel's social thought, particularly with social processes, and develops an extensive classification. He explains human society in terms of "relations through actions." [35] He examines concrete social relations, seeking out the processes by which they are characterized. The particular subject matter of sociology, the *specificum sociologicum*, is found in the three classes into which all social relations may be classified : (1) associative relations, (2) dissociative relations, and (3) those relations which fall in part in both (1) and (2).[36]

Von Wiese draws frequently from the writings of Max Weber, particularly with reference to the latter's analysis of social relations and processes. He seeks out concrete social actions. A social action is carried out "according to the intention of the acting person or persons, with reference to the behavior of others and is orientated toward the behavior of those others throughout its course." [37] Thus Weber's emphasis upon "meaning," explained further in the next chapter, is included in von Wiese's system.

In analyzing social relations von Wiese has collected several hundred sociological terms dealing particularly with different phases of social processes. Moreover, he has sought to classify these processes into main ones and sub-processes. He has arranged them according to the degree of generality that each represents, to the extent of associating or dissociating that each includes, and to the type of social relation that is revealed.

While von Wiese finds E. A. Ross' long series of social processes valid to a large degree, he goes further and elaborates a set of sub-processes that accompany each of the main processes. Von Wiese's thought is noteworthy because of the extent to which he has analyzed the sub-processes.

The two main social processes of associating and dissociating continually undergo change. The former moves toward

---

[35] Leopold von Wiese, *Allgemeine Soziologie*, p. 3.

[36] Leopold von Wiese, *Systematic Sociology*, adapted and amplified by Howard Becker, p. 37.

[37] Quoted by von Wiese, *op. cit.*, p. 56.

what amounts to socialization. The steps of the process are four : (1) approach, (2) adaptation, (3) equalization, and (4) unification ; or (1) advance, (2) adjustment, (3) accordance, and (4) amalgamation.[38] "Approach" is represented by escorting, adoring, or enticing. "Adaptation" refers to giving credit, covenanting, or coming to terms. "Equalization" has to do with interceding, forming friendships, and sharing burdens. "Unification" involves betrothing and forming close unions.

On the other hand, the social process of dissociating has three phases : (1) competition, (2) opposition, and (3) conflict. "Competition" is characterized by both rivalry and striving. "Opposition" refers to repulsing, depreciating, or frustrating. "Conflict" signifies attacking, abhorring, and maligning.

Plurality actions and plurality patterns are central concepts in von Wiese's sociology. These are expressed in three types of interhuman structures : (1) crowds, (2) groups, and (3) abstract collectivities. "Crowds" are plurality patterns of the "lowest power." They are either active or latent, natural or artificial, leaderless or led, concrete or abstract.[39]

Groups begin with dyads, tryads, tetrads, and continue on into large collectivities. Typical dyadic groups include sexual pairs, generation pairs (such as father-son), and friendship pairs. Atypical dyadic groups are either superior-subordinate, aider-aided, teacher-pupil, and pairs conditioned by the economic order.

The abstract collectivities "are plurality patterns just as are crowds and groups, and consequently are constituted in and through social processes in substantially the same way." Of all the types of groups the state most clearly typifies the abstract collectivity. The church is "a plurality pattern devoted to the collective gratification of religious needs." [40] Other primary social collectivities are "station, class, the economic order, aesthetic and scientific bodies." [41] Von Wiese has urged the measuring of social relations and the analysis

38 *Ibid.*, p. 194.
39 *Ibid.*, pp. 445 ff.
40 *Ibid.*, p. 613.
41 *Ibid.*, p. 646

of plurality patterns. He has suggested the use of concrete, specific, and quantitative yardsticks wherever possible.[42]

Emile Waxweiler (1876–1916), to whom Von Wiese and others express indebtedness, defined sociology as the study of "the processes of reaction resulting from the mutual stimulation of individuals of the same species." [43] Waxweiler, director from 1901 until his death of the *Institut de Sociologie Solvay*, insisted that the concept "social" should be relieved of ethical responsibilities and be limited "to denote observable actions and reactions as they are manifested by individuals in their reciprocal relations." [44] He repudiated organic analogies although favoring a biological approach. He made "social affinity" a basic concept, contending that association arises out of feelings of identity or at least of similarity. His classification of social actions [45] under nine categories was presented near the close of Chapter XXVI. Waxweiler's natural science approach to the study of social relations was, despite its weaknesses, his major contribution. His social-evolutionary point of view is also significant as shown in his sequence of actions, repetition of actions, formation of personal habits, formations of institutions, culminating in the formation of the social organization of a society.[46]

The discussion in this chapter has emphasized the importance of socialization, particularly, the "forms of socialization," that is, the social processes. Simmel's basic contributions are far-reaching. He virtually made sociology the science of the forms of socialization, that is, of social processes.

GROUP DISCUSSION TOPICS

1 Simmel's sociological backgrounds.
2. Socialization according to Simmel.
3. Subordination and superordination as explained by Simmel.

[42] Social psychology has received widespread attention in Germany, beginning with Johann Herbart and including folk psychologists such as William Wundt, or recently, Richard Thurnwald. For a critical review of this development see L. H. Ad. Geck, "Social Psychology in Germany," *Sociology and Social Research*, 8:504-516 and 14:108-129.

[43] Emile Waxweiler, *Esquisse d'une sociologie,* quoted from Von Wiese and Becker, *Systematic Sociology,* p. 80.

[44] *Ibid.,* p. 79.

[45] *Ibid.,* p. 179.

[46] Emile Waxweiler, "Avant-propos," *Bulletin Mensuel,* Solvay Institute of Sociology, No. 1, 1910.

4. The concept of authority.
5. Simmel's concept of conflict.
6. The significance of "the singing dual."
7. Comparison of Simmel's and Ross' concepts of socialization.
8. Comparison of Simmel's and Bristol's concepts of socialization.
9. Burgess' explanation of socialization.
10. The concept of organization.
11. Park and Burgess' statement concerning competition.
12. The nature of conflict as defined by Park and Burgess.
13. The concept of accommodation.
14. Distinctions between accommodation and assimilation.
15. The concept of the "stranger."
16. Social distance as a sociological concept.
17. Two origins of social distance.
18. The relation of social distance to social problems.
19. Horizontal and vertical social distance.
20. Causes of social farness.
21. The meaning of social mobility.
22. Von Wiese's development of a "systematic sociology."
23. Classification of social structures by von Wiese.
24. Types of groups as classified by von Wiese.
25. "Abstract collectivities" according to von Wiese.
26. Waxweiler's classification of "social actions."
27. An estimate of Simmel's sociological thought.

READINGS

Abel, Theodore, *Systematic Sociology in Germany* (New York: Columbia University Press 1929), Ch. I.

Bogardus, Emory S., *The New Social Research* (Los Angeles: J. R. Miller 1926).

Bristol, Lucius N., *Social Adaptation* (Cambridge: Harvard University Press 1915).

Burgess, Ernest W., *The Function of Socialization in Social Evolution* (Chicago: University of Chicago Press 1916).

Coser, Lewis A., "Georg Simmel's Style of Work," *American Journal of Sociology*, LXIII:635-41.

Geck, L. H. Ad., "Social Psychology in Germany," *Sociology and Social Research*, XIII:504-516 and XIV:108-192.

Hawthorne, H. B., "A Test of Simmel on the Secret Society," *American Journal of Sociology*, LXII:1-7.

Naegele, K. D., "Attachment and Alienation: Complementary Aspects of Durkheim and Simmel," *American Journal of Sociology*, LX:1-18.

Newman, K. J., "Georg Simmel and Totalitarian Integration," *American Journal of Sociology*, 55:254-261.

Park, R. E., and E. W. Burgess, *Introduction to the Science of Sociology* (Chicago: University of Chicago Press 1921).

Rosenthal, Erich and Kurt Oberlaender, "Books, Papers, and Essays by Georg Simmel," *American Journal of Sociology,* LI:238-247.

Ross, Edward A., *Principles of Sociology* (New York: Century Company 1923).

Simmel, Georg, *Soziologie* (München: Duncker und Humboldt 1923).

———, "The Sociology of Conflict," translated by A. W. Small, *American Journal of Sociology,* 9:490-525; 672-689; 798-811.

———. "Fashion." *American Journal of Sociology,* LXII:541-58.

———, "Contribution to the Sociology of Religion," *American Journal of Sociology,* LX:1-18.

Sorokin, Pitirim A., *Social Mobility* (New York: Harper & Brothers 1927).

———, "Social Mobility," *Journal of Applied Sociology,* 11:21-32.

Spykman, Nicholas, *The Social Theory of Georg Simmel* (Chicago: University of Chicago Press 1925).

Von Wiese, Leopold, *Systematic Sociology,* translated and adapted by Howard Becker (New York: John Wiley & Sons 1932).

———, *Allgemeine Soziologie* (München: 1924 and 1929).

Waxweiler, Emile, *Esquisse d'une sociologie* (Brussels: Misch and Thron 1896).

Wolfe, Kurt H., editor and translator, *The Sociology of Georg Simmel* (Glencoe, Ill.: The Free Press 1950).

———, "The Challenge of Durkheim and Simmel," *American Journal of Sociology,* LXIII:590-96.

Wood, Margaret M., *The Stranger* (New York: Columbia University Press 1934).

CHAPTER XXXI

WEBER AND SOCIAL UNDERSTANDING

Another German thinker who has left a deep imprint upon sociology was Max Weber (1864–1920). A scholar of erudition and a man interested in the practical affairs of government and politics, Weber combined the theoretical and the practical viewpoints in a way which led him to insist upon concrete, meaningful interpretations of human behavior.

DEFINITION OF SOCIOLOGY

On the first page of his *Wirtschaft und Gesellschaft*, Weber defines sociology as "a science which aims to understand clearly social behavior and thus give a causal explanation of its course and results." Since attitudes and motives explain social behavior, it is important to search out the nature and operation of these factors. Moreover, the attitudes of a person are affected by and changed by the motives and actions of other persons.

Sociology seeks out the characteristic recurrences in social relations. It assumes that these are deep-seated, far-reaching, and of universal import. It develops laws on the basis of these recurrences. A sociological law thus describes a series of social recurrences and generalizes upon this series.

W. I. Thomas' reference to behavior as a test of an attitude is related to Weber's contention that the meaning of human life can be determined only by studying the actions of human personalities. Activity of the person in his relations with other person discloses patterns and categories of sociological validity.

If science cannot tell a person what his conduct should be, is it therefore helpless from a practical viewpoint? Weber would give a negative answer and proceed to show that science can make clear to a person what he desires to do. It can go further and describe what a person needs to do if he wishes to attain a certain goal. It can indicate whether a given means is the appropriate one to use if one wishes to reach a given end. It can show how the achievement of a value-goal will affect other values.[1]

If sociology or any other social science would be scientific it must (1) study the unique and distinguishing phases of the historical evolution of human relations; (2) determine the causal series of events and of functions in the fundamental trends of social life; and (3) provide explanations of the interplay of the various culture elements. This analysis must be exact enough to demonstrate how one social event leads to one result and not to another. It must be precise enough to show how under similar conditions one event will always lead to a certain result and to no other.

Weber divided social behavior into four main categories. (1) Traditional behavior is merely behavior in conformity to past traditions. (2) Emotional behavior is current response to the behavior of others expressed in terms of loyalty or antagonism. (3) Valuational behavior is acting in accordance with what is expected of one by other persons who possess ethical or esthetic standards. (4) Rational-purposeful behavior is acting according to a plan devised in relation to the expected behavior of others.[2]

In this analysis it will be noted that motives and intentions are important. We often act socially in relation to what others intend to do. Social understanding requires that the sociologist be an expert in diagnosing the meaning or the intention behind the behavior of individuals.

SOCIAL UNDERSTANDING

The intention of some behavior is very clear, self-evident, as it were; but very deep-seated and subtle in other cases. Reflex action has no meaning at all. Behavior is the key to intentions and to a person's understanding of a social situation. Social understanding thus involves an analysis of what effects human beings intend to achieve.

There are two ways in which "understanding" may be secured. (1) The intellectual method follows the logic of a

[1] Max Weber, *Gesammelte Aufsätze zur Wissenschaftslehre*, p. 150.
[2] *Ibid.*, pp. 11 ff.

series of actions in order to arrive at the intention. (2) The empathy method follows the emotional sequence and arrives at the intention. By putting one's self into the irrational behavior through empathy, understanding may be attained.[3]

Weber suggests two kinds of "understanding." (1) Actual understanding is based on a knowledge of the overt behavior of others which discloses the immediate or direct intention with reference to the particular object. (2) Explanatory understanding reaches into the wider field of motives which may have their origins far removed in time and space.[4]

Weber, in opposition to Vierkandt's "phenomenal" method, to be discussed presently, built up a sociological method in "typological" terms. He sought to use physical science methods as far as possible and hence to describe reactions of persons to situations and to abstract from these the general types. He seeks "type-patterns" of behavior.[5] These "ideal types" become the governing concepts in sociology. They are to be used for purposes of comparison and even of social measurement. They may be general and hence complex or they may be more localized and more easily understood. Unfortunately Weber did not live to carry out his system of sociology to its natural conclusions.[6]

Max Weber's contribution to methodology was to distinguish between the scientific approach to social data and the value-judgment approach. He insisted that these two considerations must not be allowed to mix in studying human relations. In his own way he laid a foundation for the development of a science of sociology.

Weber did not hesitate to discuss social norms and ethical standards. He pointed out the conflict between politics and ethics, claiming that the politician rather naturally sacrifices ethics for the standards of the state whenever the two conflict. If the ethics of the state are lower than the ethics of smaller groups to which the politician belongs, he follows the lower rather than the higher.

Personal ethics is of two varieties, individual and group. The first type is grounded in personal convictions. It is car-

3 *Ibid.,* p. 2.
4 *Loc. cit.*
5 *Ibid.,* p. 9.
6 *Ibid.,* pp. 188 ff., 276.

ried out in action with great personal earnestness. The second type is related to one's obligations to other persons. It is relative and subject to change as one's relation to the welfare of others changes. Science, however, is helpless in attempting to evaluate the relative worth of these two ethical patterns.

Weber wrote extensively on the subject of religion. He perceived a close connection between religious and economic forces. Neither one comes first and dominates the other. They are interactive. His concept of religion is more ethical than theological. Religion is a vital influence in everyday life. Weber examined at length the influence of each of the major religions upon the life of the people concerned.

Weber claimed that capitalism is a product of Protestant Christianity's emphasis on the individual's worth. This viewpoint led to the development first of individualism, and then of an economy, built around powerful individuals, or capitalism. Weber saw a close relation between the ethics of Christianity, and honest, efficient toil. The attitudes and habits of individuals fostered by Christianity were picked up and made the basis of a capitalistic system of industry. Thus Weber as a functionalist contradicts Weber as a pluralist in religion and economics.

Weber wrestled with the concept of personal liberty. He considered the slavery of the individual in the past and the reign of autocrats as well as of customs, but he was more concerned about the relation of the individual and the future. He perceived the rise of a new autocracy growing out of the use of scientific techniques and totalitarian principles. He saw man growing more and more systematic and bureaucratic under the ægis of science. Organization in the factories makes robots of men, and organization in society leads to annihilation of persons.

Weber was jealous of opportunities for heroic action by individuals. He wished to guarantee the rise of heroes. But with society growing more and more mechanized, where are the chances for the common man to be heroic? Where will lie the chances for individuals to touch the sky in a mechanized social order?

Weber believed in science but deplored the arrival of a

day when we have "experts without spirit, sensualists without heart." When everyone becomes an automaton, trained to be such from birth, the soul dies both in the individual and in society. Deplorable indeed will be society when all are taught from birth to be mental automatons, so that no one, when he grows up, can or will be permitted to think anything about anything except what he is told to think.

No one need fear "democratic individualism." In its very nature lie the elements of correction of human behavior. No one can go far astray when the many are free to express themselves. Democratic individualism will provide for enough authority and aristocracy, so that it will not be necessary to resort to an authoritarian state.

The problem is not so much that of getting freedom "from" something arising in the past, as to guarantee freedom "for" those who come after us. We are headed toward the annihilation of individual freedom under scientifically controlled political autocracies. How can we prevent our children's children from becoming systematized puppets, acting and speaking only as strings are automatically pulled?

The greater the development of reason, the more the individual will plan and rationalize, and at the same time the more will society be transformed by man. With an increased growth of reason, hero-worship will decline. Charismatic leadership, or the imputing of greatness to a person, results in an overturn of traditional beliefs and customs as social controls. Reason tends, however, to unfrock the mystical leader.

It was an irrational social world in which Weber saw human beings endeavoring to achieve personalities. He perceived irrational things happening throughout history to human life. He recognized the conflict between action and thought, between the militant and the democratic, between force and ethics, between war and Christianity. He understood how two far-reaching sets of values, those of force and those of Christian love, are contending with one another for priority in social position. Out of this and other conflicts, Weber was anxious for the individual to rise, triumphant and in a heroic mold.

The social contest is one in a capitalistic order, according

to Weber, in which a last stand against a bureaucratic sys-
temization is being made by and under the caption of liberalism. A revolutionary socialism will merely plunge the
individual from one bureaucratic situation into another;
and yet man, if he is to develop a personality, must breathe
the air of at least a reasonable degree of freedom.

Human behavior is determined by the interplay of two
sets of factors. One of these emanates from within the individual's storehouse of motives and attitudes. The other set
of causal factors are the non-human ones that are involved in
the particular social situation. A person's behavior under
such conditions takes on a meaning, then, in relation to a
third set of factors, namely, the goals which he has adopted.
His reaction in his various social situations are performed
in relation to those far-flung "ideal types" of his.

A person thus has a "qualitative existence." This qualitative element is found in the meaning that each item in one's
experience possesses for one. Can we say that this meaning
varies according to the richness of content of the goal?

Weber's mental reach was widespread. He carried out
extended research. He had genuine political interests. He
helped to found the German Sociological Society. His work
as editor of the *Archiv für Sozialwissenschaft und Sozialpolitik* is well-known. His mind reached around the world, also
back to the beginning of human history. The aid that he
rendered the rise of sociology as a science is outstanding.

TÖNNIES

Another name of primary importance in sociology is that
of Ferdinand Tönnies (1855–1936). He conceived of social
relations in terms of *Gemeinschaft* (community) and *Gesellschaft* (society). *Gemeinschaft* is characterized by *Wesenwillen,* or the actions of basic life-forces or urges. *Gesellschaft*
is motivated by *Kurwillen,* or action based on deliberation
and conscious choice. "Community" emphasizes natural
processes; "society," artificial, telic ones. Community is a
form of primary grouping, and society of secondary grouping.

Tönnies was descended from a peasant farmer stock which
had known something of a real community of spirit and

genuine co-operation. His *Wesenwillen* is an expression of universal feelings. Tönnies' early thought was based in part on Marx's economic materialism, showing that man's early social relations were normal expressions of satisfying the food and other material necessities of life.

Tönnies was also indebted to Thomas Hobbes, whose writings he greatly appreciated. He took Hobbes' statement of modern social relations under capitalism, a system of uniting to exchange in order to gain special ends, and evolved a theory of *Gesellschaft*, or "society," motivated by *Kurwillen*, or "arbitrary will." Tönnies made concrete studies of social problems, pointing out social trends and using statistical methods. From *Gemeinschaft* to *Gesellschaft*, and then to a combination of the two types of social relations governed by a rational ethics, such will be the course of social evolution, a logical process in a vast historical sequence. Justice is natural rather than arbitrary, law is based on morals, and society becomes socialistic.[7]

Pure sociology with its system of social concepts includes a theory of social norms. These norms are the rules and regulations by which any group lives. According to these rules individuals are judged. There are three classes of norms; order, will, and morality. "Order" is conventionalized rule by facts; "law" is control by custom and legislation enforced by judges; "morality" is control by personal conscience and belief in a Higher Power. The first norm is based on the "order" represented by nature; the second, on the laws arising out of man-made practices and interpretations; and the third, on the dictates of an "inner judge."

In these analyses, Tönnies seems to underestimate the power of thought and ideas. Appeals for improvements apparently are to be made not to higher ethical considerations but to special interests of everyone who may be concerned. His defense concerning this criticism would be that he is describing what has been and is the case and not what might happen.

Although Tönnies reached the age of eighty, his greatest

---

[7] It may be noted (P. A. Sorokin, *Contemporary Sociological Theories*, p. 491), that Durkheim's concepts of mechanical and organic solidarity are similar to Tönnies' "community" and "society," but that the labels are used with reverse meanings.

work is his earliest, namely, his *Gemeinschaft und Gesellschaft,* published when he was thirty-two. In that work he set forth the three types of sociology, namely, pure, applied, and empirical. He also thought of a general sociology, larger in scope and including the social aspects of all society.

"Pure sociology" consists of an integrated set of concepts of society and of normal human relations, goals, and processes. "Applied sociology" is the application of the concepts of pure sociology within the field of historical social evolution. While pure sociology gives a cross section of social processes, applied sociology offers a longitudinal picture of society in action. In applied sociology man is seen on the move from "community" to "society." These divisions of pure and applied sociology suggest a similar classification by Lester F. Ward, whose main work antedated Tönnies' analysis by several years.

Empirical sociology is the collecting by direct and objective methods of facts about social life. To these the concepts of pure sociology must be applied if one would obtain an understanding of social evolution.[8]

Soziale Wesenheiten, or social entities, represent the keynote to Tönnies' social thought. By these he meant products of the human will, or better, processes of willing that arise in the individual's tendencies to action. They range from *Wesenwille* to *Kurwille* and culminate in associations ranging from communities to societies. The simplest origins of the *Wesenwille* are found in organic and biologically derived similarities in response. The complex origins reach up to similar established adherences to commonly accepted symbols, suggesting the "collective representations" of Durkheim. The upper level of origins of the *Soziale Wesenheiten* is represented by *Kurwille,* or in some degree of rational choice regarding association.

Moreover, the social entities are of three sorts: social relations, social *Samtschaften,* and social corporations. Each involves some degree of recognition of social relationship. A "social relation" in its simplest form is the conscious interaction of any two persons. Social *Samtschaften* are large

8 Based on "The Sociology of Ferdinand Tönnies," by Rudolf Heberle. *American Sociological Review,* 2:9-25.

groups whose recognized unity is based on some degree of cultural and psychic similarity. A social corporation is a social group that has an organization. This organization is thought of as being a person possessing a will and functions of its own.

Somewhat related to *Gemeinschaft* is the concept of "universalism" advanced by Otto Spann, whose writings are not so well known as they deserve to be, because of his heavy and difficult style. He begins with society rather than with the individual. His is in part a *gestalt* sociology. Every individual can be understood only as a part of the whole, and of a moving social whole. He has little sympathy for the "self-made man" theory. He tends to repudiate the adequacy of natural science methods in the field of social relations. In his emphasis on the social whole he considers the social relationships between the units of the whole as being very significant. His concept of *Gezweiung* means something akin to a feeling and emotional acting together on the basis of similarity in interests.[9] He is opposed to individualism. His universalism leads him into totalitarianism, although logically it postulates merely a universal or supersociety which may be viewed as objective standard for evaluating current social behavior.

Alfred Vierkandt analyzed social life in terms of the common nature of human nature. As a result of this universal nature of mankind, it is natural for one person to put himself into the experiences of others. The concept of sympathy lies at the heart of his thinking. Not only will one person sitting on the bleachers lean and shove in the direction in which he wants his football team to carry the ball, not only will he, when watching a friend who is pole-vaulting, go through some of the bodily motions of his friend; but, more than this, he will personify material objects and reproduce in his actions the motion and direction that he wishes the object to take. In these ways he illustrates *empathy*.

Vierkandt put special emphasis on *einfühlung* or living one's self in the experiences of others. By so doing one comes to understand the experiences of others and if he proceeds far enough and long enough, he can interpret society

---

[9] Otto Spann, *Gesellschaftslehre* (1930 edition), pp. 10 ff.

itself. The corollary follows that unless one does develop *einfühlung* he cannot correctly interpret social relations. He who remains entirely objective to the social situation which he would study is likely to miss the main elements in his research analysis. Here is an argument similar to that research method which has recently been called "participant observation." Here is a hint in support of social case analysis.

Vierkandt accepted and developed the "phenomenal method" of investigation. He studied psychic-phenomena which, by their nature, reveal the pattern according to which they function. These patterns or inner abstractions become the concepts of sociology. These patterns, however, need to be explained in terms of further examination and appreciation of the universal elements in them. Again, a single case that is being analyzed carries in its make-up and functioning something of universal meaning. Through one's ability to put himself into the human situations that he is considering, one can grasp the inner, deeper, and comprehensive meaning of social situations and of the nature of man.[10]

Vierkandt's doctrine of "inner furtherance" relates to the effects of personal interaction. Interstimulation gives in and of itself an inner enjoyment that possesses stability in a concomitant inner bond. Here Vierkandt's idea is close to Giddings' "consciousness of kind" and Cooley's concept of "primary group relationship." [11]

The essence of this inner *Gemeinschaft,* or community of interests "similar to Tönnies' concept of the same name," is found not only in primary-group relationships but also in secondary connections. For example : (1) It exists in *agreements* mutually kept. The validity of an agreement ranges from the overt observance of rules that have been agreed upon to an inner tying together of purposes. (2) The dominance-subordination relationship may suggest a dovetailing together of aims and interests. A hierarchy of performances is mutually accepted. One party accepts responsibility for action and the other for obedience. (3) It is found in conflict conducted according to established or previously agreed

[10] Alfred Vierkandt, *Gesellschaftslehre,* pp. 19 ff.
[11] *Ibid.,* pp. 287 ff.

upon rules. For instance, in war there may be an agreement that non-combatants shall not be destroyed by bombing. Here is a recognition of human kinship.

In primary groups, Vierkandt recognized (1) *Gemeinschaft;* and in secondary groups, (2) democratic agreement, (3) dominance, and (4) conflict. The last three types of relationships are found in *Gesellschaft*. In this analysis Vierkandt would claim that he had made an advance over Tönnies' social thought.

SOCIOLOGY OF KNOWLEDGE

From a different angle, Karl Mannheim has made basic contributions to our understanding of human behavior, particularly of our understanding of the origins of knowledge. An excellent sociology of knowledge has been written by Karl Mannheim. He holds that "knowledge is from the very beginning a co-operative process of group life, in which everyone unfolds his knowledge within the framework of a common fate, a common activity, and the overcoming of common difficulties (in which, however, each has a different share)." [12] Most thought arises out of collective actions, and hence out of the "collective unconscious." The control of the collective unconscious thus is seen as a problem of our age.

Mannheim divides systems of thought into two: one he terms ideologies; the other utopias. By ideologies he means ways of thinking which direct activities in the maintenance of the prevailing social order. Utopias are treated as systems of thought that direct activities toward changing the present social order. Research, then, needs to be directed toward concrete social situations in which thought takes place. The sociology of knowledge is the study of it as produced in social situations.

Mannheim distinguishes between five political ideologies and four types or stages of utopian systems of thought. The ideologies are: bureaucratic conservatism, conservative historicism, liberal-democratic bourgeois thought, socialist-communist conceptions, and fascist thought. Bureaucratic ideologies in time of social crises try "to find a remedy by means

[12] Karl Mannheim, *Ideology and Utopia*, p. 26.

of arbitrary decrees rather than to meet the political situation on its own grounds." [13] Bureaucratic thought identifies the science of politics with the science of administration, and thus greatly limits itself. The historical ideology recognizes the phase of political control that lies outside of the purely administrative, but does this in terms of socially inherited forces, working silently, namely, the folk spirit, or the *Zeitgeist*. It justifies government by the aristocratic class, by those "who know," and by the political "instinct." Bourgeois intellectualism calls for "a scientific politics" and "a thorough-going rationalization of the world." The socialist-communist ideology is intuitional, for "it denies the possibility of exact calculations of events in advance of their happening," and yet it is rationalistic in that it fits every new happening into a planned scheme of things. Fascist thought is "activistic and irrational." Not programs, not the desires of the masses, but an "unconditional subordination to a leader" is important.

The utopian mind is "incongruous with the state of reality within which it occurs." A utopian state is one that seems to be unrealizable only from the point of view of a social order which is already in existence. The four types of utopian thinking are: orgiastic, liberal-humanitarian, conservative, and socialist-communist. The orgiastic thought conceives of a catastrophic change that will bring in a millennium. It represents a closed system of thought. The liberal-humanitarian "is characterized by a positive acceptance of culture and the giving of an ethical tone to human affairs." Conservative utopian thought suggests a new order feasible "here and now." The socialist-communist utopian would "radicalize the liberal utopia" and yet guard itself against the anarchistic elements in its own structure.[14]

SOMBART

The hope of current German Socialism is to escape from the domination of economic interests and to accept the domination of political goals, according to Werner Sombart.

[13] *Ibid.*, pp. 105 ff.
[14] *Ibid.*, pp. 173 ff.

The various modern trends of thought not only in Germany but in the world are: (1) intellectualization or despiritualization, (2) objectification and (3) unification of divergencies. Today there is taking place a submerging of individuals, a lowering of the average level of achievement, a loss of connection with and appreciation of nature, particularly by city people, a domination by "a robust, practical materialism," and a dehumanization. These tendencies emanate from "the monarchical rule of the economic interests under which we stand." [15]

Socialism has arisen to combat economic evil by political means. Sombart finds, however, that the term *socialism* is used in the German language alone in 187 different senses. He refers to Griffith's collection of 261 different definitions, chiefly in English.[16] He admits the bitter conflict between various types of socialism, particularly between Marxian or Proletarian Socialism and German or National Socialism. He suggests goals for German Socialism, such as: (1) The competitive principle in industry must be eliminated. Competition for quality may be kept, provided it is adapted to a system of national social planning. (2) Advertising, "one of the most unfortunate phenomena of our times," should be done away with, for it promotes harmful competition. (3) The profit-account, thought of as synonymous with money-making and often including the principle of profit-making, is "one of the basest inventions with which the devil has yet deceived mankind." [17] As a result of the modern acceptance of current ideals, such as (1) veneration for bigness, (2) rapid movement, and (3) the ever new, "the life of mankind has become meaningless." What is needed is fundamental knowledge, a unified plan, and the carrying out of a planned economy under state control. Just how such a program will bring growth and expansion and creativeness to personality is not made clear.[18] Sombart's contention that a planned economy "must always be a national economy" neglects other possibilities such as regional, even an international, economy. He suggests "a supreme council of cul-

---

[15] Werner Sombart, *A New Social Philosophy*, pp. 18, 28 ff.
[16] Dan Griffith, *What is Socialism?*
[17] Werner Sombart, *op. cit.* pp. 275 ff.
[18] *Ibid.*, p. 252.

ture," to determine what new inventions shall be accepted in the national economy, which calls for almost super-human wisdom.[19]

The point of view of Max Weber and of the other German scholars whose social ideas have been presented in this chapter might be summed up in terms of philosophic insight. Many of the social interpretations distinguish between the ethical and the objective viewpoints. In connection with both content and methods Max Weber ranks high among European social thinkers.

GROUP DISCUSSION TOPICS

1. Max Weber's sociological backgrounds.
2. The subject matter of sociology according to Weber.
3. Weber's categories of social behavior.
4. The concept of "understanding."
5. The "typological" method.
6. Weber's concept of personal liberty.
7. The theory of "ideal types" or "types of behavior."
8. Contrasts in the thinking of Weber and Simmel.
9. The concepts of *Gemeinschaft* and *Gesellschaft*.
10. The concepts of *Wesenwillen* and *Kurwillen*.
11. Tönnies' theory of "pure sociology."
12. The concept of "social entities."
13. Otto Spann's theory of "universalism."
14. Vierkandt's "phenomenal method."
15. The concept of "inner furtherance."
16. Mannheim's sociology of knowledge.
17. Differences between ideologies and utopias.
18. Types of utopian thought.
19. The "utopian mind."
20. Sombart's defense of "German socialism."
21. Differences between "proletarian socialism" and "German socialism."
22. A "supreme council of culture."

[19] *Ibid.*, p. 244.

READINGS

Becker, Howard, and Harry E. Barnes, *Social Thought from Lore to Science* (Washington : Harren Press 1952), Vol. I, Ch. 23.
Bendix, Reinhard, "Max Weber's Interpretation of Conduct and History," *American Journal of Sociology*, LI:518-526.

Blum, Fred H., "Max Weber's Postulate of 'Freedom' from Value Judgments," *American Journal of Sociology*, L:46-52.

Constas, Helen, "Max Weber's Two Conceptions of Bureaucracy," *American Journal of Sociology*, LXIII:400-409.

Cox, Oliver C., "Max Weber on Social Stratification: A Critique," *American Sociological Review*, 15:223-227.

Gerth, H. H., and C. W. Mills, *From Max Weber: Essays in Sociology* (New York: Oxford University Press 1959).

Heberle, Rudolf, "The Sociology of Ferdinand Tönnies," *American Sociological Review*, 2:9-25.

Honingsheim, Paul, "Max Weber as Rural Sociologist," *Rural Sociology*, II:207-218.

Lynd, R. S., *Knowledge for What?* (Princeton: Princeton University Press 1939).

Mannheim, Karl, *Ideology and Utopia* (New York: Harcourt, Brace and Company 1936).

Munch, Peter A., "Empirical Science and Max Weber's *Verstenden Soziologie*," *American Sociological Review*, 22:26-32.

Salomon, Albert, "Max Weber's Methodology," *Social Research*, I:147-168; and II:60-73.

———, "Max Weber's Political Ideas," *Social Research*, 2:368-384.

———, "In Memoriam Ferdinand Tönnies (1855-1936)," *Social Research*, 3:348-363.

Sombart, Werner, *A New Social Philosophy*, translated by K. F. Geiser (Princeton: Princeton University Press 1937).

Sorokin, Pitirim A., *Contemporary Sociological Theories* (New York: Harper & Brothers 1928).

Spann, Otto, *Gesellschaftslehre* (Leipzig: Quelle and Meyer 1923).

Tönnies, Ferdinand, *Community and Society* (East Lansing: The Michigan State University Press 1957).

———, "The Concept and Law of Human Progress, translated by K. J. Arndt and C. L. Folse, *Social Forces*, 19:23-29.

Vierkandt, Alfred, *Gesellschaftslehre* (Stuttgart: Enke 1928).

Weber, Max, *The City*, translated by D. Martindale and G. Neuwirth (Glencoe, Ill.: The Free Press 1958).

———, *The Methodology of the Social Sciences*, translated by E. A. Shils and H. A. Finch (Glencoe, Ill.: The Free Press 1949).

———, *The Protestant Ethic and the Spirit of Capitalism*, translated by T. Parsons (New York: Charles Scribner's Sons 1956).

———, *The Theory of Social and Economic Organization*, translated by A. M. Henderson and T. Parsons (New York: Oxford University Press 1957).

Wirth, Louis, "The Sociology of Ferdinand Tönnies," *American Journal of Sociology*, 32:412-422.

Znaniecki, F., *The Social Role of the Man of Knowledge* (New York: Columbia University Press 1940).

CHAPTER XXXII

COOLEY AND COLLECTIVE BEHAVIOR

"Collective behavior" is another vital concept in social thought. It is developed in one direction by Tarde and Ross, in another direction by Giddings, in yet another way by Simmel and von Wiese, in still other but related ways by Weber and Vierkandt. The sharpest analysis was probably made by Charles Horton Cooley (1864–1929). Cooley was an informal, unostentatious thinker who made vital contributions to social psychology without coining an elaborate terminology.

In 1902 Cooley's *Human Nature and the Social Order* was published. This book was at once accepted as an authority on the integral relationship of the individual self and the social process. It was followed in 1909 by *Social Organization,* and in 1918 by *Social Process.* The three books constitute a chronological development of a logical system of psycho-sociologic thought.

The first volume treats of the self in its reactions to group life; the second explains the nature of primary groups, such as the family, playground, and neighborhood, the nature of the democratic mind, and of social classes; the third analyzes the many elements in the processes by which society is characterized. The chief thesis of the three volumes is that the individual and society are aspects of the same phenomenon, and that the individual and society are twin-born and twin-developed.[1]

An individual has no separate existence. Through the hereditary and social elements in his life he is inseparably bound up with society.[2] He cannot be considered apart from persons. Even the phenomena which are called individualistic "are always socialistic in the sense that they are expressive of tendencies growing out of the general life."[3] It

[1] C. H. Cooley, *Social Organizations,* p. 5.
[2] C. H. Cooley, *Human Nature and the Social Order,* p. 3.
[3] *Ibid.,* p. 5.

is not only true that individuals make society, but equally true that society makes individuals.

LOOKING-GLASS SELF

Cooley gave an excellent presentation of what he called the looking-glass self. There are three distinct psychic elements in this phenomenon : (1) the imagination of one's appearance to another person ; (2) the imagined estimation of that appearance by the other person, and (3) a sense of pride or chagrin that is felt by the first person. The looking-glass self affects the daily life of all individuals. "We are ashamed to seem evasive in the presence of a brave one, gross in the eyes of a refined one, and so on." [4] Even a person's consciousness of himself is largely a direct reflection of the opinions and estimates which he believes that others hold of him.[5]

Cooley made a lucid distinction between self-consciousness, social consciousness, and public consciousness. The first is what I think of myself ; the second, what I think of other people ; and the third, a collective view of the self and the social consciousness of all the members of a group organized and integrated into a communicating group.[6] Moreover, all three types of consciousness are parts of an organic whole. Even the moral life of persons is a part of the organic unity of society. Social knowledge is the basis of morality. An upward endeavor is the essence of moral progress.

The three types of groups which Cooley called primary were so labeled because through them the individual gets "his earliest and completest experience of social unity." [7] The family, play groups, and neighborhoods remain throughout life as the experience bases from which the more complex phases of life receive their interpretation.

A primary group is one that is primary in importance in developing a person's ideals, in giving a person a sense of belonging to the social group. While this concept of primary groups has been criticized, it has achieved wide acceptance.

An unbounded faith in human nature was enjoyed by

4 *Ibid.*, pp. 152 ff.
5 *Social Organization*, p. 11.
6 *Ibid.*, p. 12.
7 *Ibid.*, p. 26.

Professor Cooley. Human nature comprises those senti-ments and impulses which are distinctly superior to those of the higher animals, such as sympathy, love, resentment, ambition, the feeling of right and wrong.[8] The improve-ment of society, according to Cooley, does not involve any essential change in human nature but rather "a larger and higher application of its familiar impulses."[9]

COMMUNICATION

Communication is a fundamental concept in Cooley's sys-tem of social thought. Communication is "the mechanism through which human relations exist and develop."[10] Cooley has pointed out that not only does language constitute the symbols of the mind, but that in a sense all objects and actions are mental symbols. Communication is the means whereby the mind develops a true human nature. The symbols of our social environment "supply the stimulus and framework for all our growth." Thus the communication concept furnishes a substantial basis for understanding the psycho-sociologic phenomena which are ordinarily called suggestion and imitation.

Personality has its origin partly in heredity and partly "in the stream of communication, both of which flow from the corporate life of the race." A study of communication shows that the individual mind is not a separate growth, but an integral development of the general mind.[11]

The means of communication developed remarkably in the nineteenth century, chiefly in the following ways: (1) in expressiveness, that is, in the range of ideas and feelings they are competent to carry; (2) in the permanence in re-cording; (3) in swiftness of communication; and (4) in dif-fusion to all classes of people.[12] Thus society can be or-ganized on the bases of intelligence and of rationalized and systematized feelings rather than on authority, autocracy, and caste.

A free intercourse of ideas, that is, freed and unimpeded

[8] *Human Nature and the Social Order*, p. 28.
[9] *Ibid.*, p. 37.
[10] *Ibid.*, p. 61.
[11] *Ibid.*, p. 63.
[12] *Ibid.*, p. 80.

communication, will not produce uniformity. Self-feeling will find enlarged opportunities for expression. An increased degree of communication furnishes the bases for making the individual conscious of the unique part he can and should play in improving the quality of the social whole. On the other hand, freedom of communication is tending to produce "the disease of the century," namely, the disease of excess, of overwork, of prolonged worry, of a competitive race for which men are not fully equipped.[13]

Public opinion, according to Cooley, is not merely an aggregate of opinions of individuals, but "a co-operative product of communication and reciprocal influence."[14] It is a crystallization of diverse opinion, resulting in a certain stability of thought. It is produced by discussion. Public opinion is usually superior, in the sense of being more effective, than the average opinion of the members of the public.

The masses make fundamental contributions to public opinion, not through formulated ideas but through their sentiments. The masses in their daily experiences are close to the salient facts of human nature. They are not troubled with that preoccupation with ideas which hinders them from immediate fellowship. Neither are they limited by that attention to the hoarding of private property which prevents the wealthy from keeping in touch with the common things of life.

The striking result of the social process is the development of personalities. The social process affords opportunities which individuals, ambitious and properly stimulated, may accept. Education may perform a useful function in adjusting individuals to opportunities. But education often fails because it requires too much and inspires too little; it accents formal knowledge at the expense of kindling the spirit.[15]

SOCIAL PROCESS

The social process, as Cooley analyzed it, is not a series of futile repetitions or brutal and wasteful conflicts, but an eternal, onward growth which produces increasingly humane,

[13] *Ibid.*, p. 103.
[14] *Ibid.*, p. 121.
[15] Cooley, *Social Process*, pp. 68 ff.

rational, and co-operative beings. While the element of conflict is useful, in that it awakens and directs human attention
and thus leads to activity, it is limited by a superintending
factor of co-operation and organization to which the con-
testants must adjust themselves if they would succeed.

Social stratification hinders.[16] It cuts off communication.
It throws social ascendancy into the hands of a stable, communicating minority. The majority are submerged in the
morass of ignorance. Degrading neighborhood associations,
vicious parents, despised racial connections — these all serve
to produce stratification and to hinder progress.

Cooley held that in the social process the institutional element is as essential as the personal.[17] Institutions bequeath
the standard gifts of the past to the individual; they give
stability. At the same time, if rationally controlled, they
leave energy free for new undertakings. Vigor in the individual commonly leads to dissatisfaction on his part with
institutions. Disorganization thus arises from the reaction
against institutional formalism manifested by energetic persons. It may be regarded as a lack of communication between the individual and the institution. Formalism indicates that in certain particulars there has been an excess of
communication.

The economic concept of value has long been analyzed in
individualistic terms — the economic desires arise out of "the
inscrutable depths of the private mind." To this explanation Cooley replied that economic wants, interests, and values
are primarily of institutional origin; they are socially created. Pecuniary valuations are largely the products of group
conditions and activities.

It was in a rational public will that Cooley saw the salvation of the social process. While he repeatedly expressed a
large degree of faith in human nature as it is, he looked forward to a day, rather remote, when communication and education would enable all individuals to take a large grasp of
human situations and on the basis of this grasp to express
effectual social purposes. Unconscious adaptation will be
superseded by the deliberate self-direction of every group

[16] *Social Organization,* Chapters XVIII, XXV-XXVII.
[17] *Ibid.,* p. 320; *cf. Social Process,* p. 297 ff.

along lines of broadening sympathy and widening intellectual reaches.

Many sayings of Cooley appear in his *Life and the Student*. In these "Roadside notes on human nature, society, and letters," appear a great variety of wise observations which reflect Cooley's incisive style of thinking and writing better than any descriptive words can do. At one point he says: "Is there not a kind of emptiness in the upper stories of society, too much room and equipment for the life that inhabits it?" At another point he remarks: "It is a good plan in any study to observe for a while carefully but with no definite purpose." Or again: "In the eye of each, if you look for it, you may see an individual spirit, a self, often only partly at home with its fellows."

As George H. Mead pointed out, Cooley's style was that of Emerson.[18] He utterly lacked "combative dogmatism." Democracy to Cooley, according to Arthur E. Woods, was more than a way of life; "it was an intellectual disposition." A student characterized him as a sage who never spoke unless he had something to say "and whatever he said was important."[19] Appreciative of statistics, he felt that to limit one's self to the methods of physical science in the study of human relations was to blind one's self to the heart of the theme.[20] And at his death, Charles A. Ellwood said: "A light is out in sociology. Some of us think that it is the greatest light that has yet shone in our science."[21] Not the least of his traits was "the life of quiet serenity" which he lived. "For those who knew him well, there is the vivid realization that the stream of life will forever flow more splendidly and beautifully because he lived."[22]

Cooley earned the title of a sound, sane, and deep sociological thinker. His contributions to social thought are found in his lucid descriptions of the social process from

[18] George H. Mead, "Cooley's Contribution to American Social Thought," *American Journal of Sociology*, 35:693-706.

[19] Arthur E. Woods, "Charles Horton Cooley: An Appreciation," *American Journal of Sociology*, 35:707-717.

[20] Charles H. Cooley, "The Roots of Social Knowledge," *American Journal of Sociology*, 32:59-79.

[21] Charles A. Ellwood, "Charles Horton Cooley, Sociologist," *Sociology and Social Research*, 14:3-9.

[22] Roy H. Holmes, "Charles Horton Cooley: Scholar," *Sociology and Social Research*, 14:104-107.

which personalities and social organizations arise, in his keen analysis of communication as the fundamental element in progress, and in his emphasis upon rational control through standards.

ATTITUDES AND VALUES

The social process has been analyzed by W. I. Thomas in terms of social attitudes and social values — and thus a new emphasis has been given to psycho-sociologic thought. An *attitude* is a process of individual consciousness that determines "the real or possible activity of the individual in the social world." [23]

Thomas' concept of social value includes any datum that has an empirical content accessible to the members of a social group and a meaning which may make it an object of activity. Activity is thus the bond between a social attitude and a social value. The value is the meaning which a material or spiritual datum may have.

Another important psycho-social concept is *status*. It involves the attitudes of other persons toward a given person. It gives personality to the individual, as emphasized by R. E. Park and E. W. Burgess.

One's status is affected by countless factors. Many of them are entirely external to a person. Moving from one place to another, for example, affects one's status and has its practical significance.

Personality sometimes gets caught between two cultures. At least it may not belong sufficiently to either of two cultures to be entirely at home in either. The man "without a country" is an extreme expression of this dilemma. Robert E. Park's concept of "the marginal man," and Everett V. Stonequist's explanations of the many ways in which personality suffers as a consequence of belonging to more than one culture while not being fully accepted by either, are worthy of further study. The racial and cultural hybrids are notable and notorious illustrations. Through no fault of their own, they are buffeted about until personality conflicts become chronic. [24]

[23] Thomas and Znaniecki, *The Polish Peasant in Europe and America*, I:22.
[24] Everett V. Stonequist, *The Marginal Man*.

Sometimes conflicts between cultures are viciously paralleled by inner conflicts in the lives of the marginal persons. Sometimes these conflicts are so sharply drawn that a person cannot be assimilated or nationalized. He remains an outcast, and personality adjustment is impossible except as the individual receives sympathy and understanding from other marginal persons or from non-marginal persons who as individuals will befriend him. In these ways he obtains a measure of satisfying status.

The social process, according to Park and Burgess in their *Introduction to the Science of Sociology*, is normally composed of four stages: (1) competition, or unconscious struggle, (2) conflict, or open struggle, (3) accommodation, or conscious adaptation, and (4) assimilation, or unconscious unification. Social interaction is the starting point of the social process.

MEAD

George H. Mead (1863–1937) has given a thoroughgoing discussion of communication, language, and the consciousness of meaning.[25] He began with a social situation, where the actions of one person serve as stimuli to other persons, whose responses in turn act as stimuli to the first person. Thus life is a series of actions, stimulations, responses, resultant stimulations — these activities constitute gestures or symbols with meanings. Symbols and the consciousness of meaning of these symbols are the main elements in communication.

The consciousness and origins of meaning play a large role in Mead's thinking. Meaning arises only "in the relation and responses to the activities which they ultimately mediate." The consciousness of meaning consists chiefly "in a consciousness of attitude, on the part of the individual, over against the object to which he is about to react." [26] The consciousness of meaning may be discovered in the readiness to respond.

Language is a highly specialized form of gesture. By one's

[25] George H. Mead, "Social Consciousness and the Psychology of Meaning," *Psychological Bulletin*, 7:405.
[26] *Ibid.*, VII:399.

own responses to another's gestures, one can interpret the attitudes of another person. Moreover, these responses contain one's own values, which in turn become stimuli to the conduct of other persons. Thus language takes place, thus meanings rise to the level of consciousness, and thus the materials are provided out of which selves are constructed.

Mead's analysis of social consciousness and of its relation to the consciousness of meaning includes three factors. (1) First, there is a social situation, where another's act arouses responses in one's self. These responses in turn become stimuli to the other person, and so on. (2) Second, there arises a consciousness of relationships and hence meanings between acts and responses. In this way values develop. (3) Response and imagery and resultant response — these are the processes by which thought is stimulated.[27]

SYMBOLS AND MEANINGS

Special attention to the analysis of "the genesis, integration, and functioning of symbols" is given by J. F. Markey. He utilizes behavioristic methods for the analysis of speech reactions, of thinking or "reflective behavior," and of the symbolic process, or the reflective and ideational process. The meanings of the symbols that a child, for example, develops are found in his responses to his environment. The origin of thinking is found in the mediate response. The origin of meaning is located in "sequential or functionally dependent relationship existing between parts of behavior." Personality is realized in the integrating of symbolic behavior.[28]

A social group may manipulate the symbols (a young boy, for example, fears being called a "sissy" by his group), and thus the symbolic process is a generic phase of social control. "The symbolic process furnishes a most remarkable means of determining group unity, morale, and control."[29]

Gestures were originally expressions of emotion with reference to disturbing factors in one's environment. They began as outflows of nervous excitement, and when viewed in

[27] *Ibid.*, VII:405.
[28] John F. Markey, *The Symbolic Process.*
[29] *Ibid.*, p. 177.

relation to the acts which called them out, they acquired meaning. Thus, "the consciousness of meaning is social in its origin." [30] Out of these meanings one's intellectual life flows. When responses become standardized, they are symbols. They are beginnings of acts and language is a conversation of acts and appropriate responses. The birth of the symbol occurs at this point and here arises thought.

The woof of personality is a series of reactions to the lives of other persons. One plays as many different "roles" as there are other persons to whom he responds. Out of all these "roles" taken with reference to others' behavior one develops a synthetic self, or, as Mead said, a "generalized other." [31]

Mead developed a functional theory of the self in which one's social consciousness antedates his physical consciousness. We recognize selves before we develop a reflective experience of things that are purely physical.[32] The self includes the "I," or ego, which is an active agent, or activity itself, and an empirical self, or "me," which is constructed out of one's experiences in the social environment.

Moreover, a human being can stimulate himself as well as be stimulated by other persons.[33] A person thus becomes a social world to himself. In acting out the role of others to himself, he becomes aware of himself. One organizes himself in terms of "the social organization of the outer world."

A synthetic presentation of psycho-sociologic thought has been made by L. L. Bernard, who describes the organic bases of behavior, the nature of behavior patterns, of habit mechanisms, and of the functional organization of consciousness. Personality is integrated under the influences of the psycho-social environment. Social pyschology is defined as "the science which studies the development of collective or social adjustment patterns in the individual as the result of his contacts with his various environments, especially with

[30] George H. Mead, "Social Psychology as Counterpart to Physiological Psychology," *Psychological Bulletin*, 6:406.
[31] T. V. Smith, "The Social Philosophy of George Herbert Mead," *American Journal of Sociology*, 37:378.
[32] G. H. Mead, "What Social Objects Must Psychology Presuppose?" *Journal of Philosophy*, 7:180.
[33] G. H. Mead, "The Mechanism of Social Consciousness, *Journal of Philosophy*, 9:404.

the most important of all of these environments, the psycho-social." The concept of "instinct" in the traditional sense is annihilated. After showing that it has been used in several hundreds of different senses, and hence made valueless as a tool, Professor Bernard contends that much which has been labeled "instinct" is habit formation. He substitutes for an instinct theory a theory of environmental processes acting upon highly sensitized protoplasm that can respond, and a theory based on biological formulae combined with concepts of objective social control.[34]

In the analyses of social psychologists, such as Cooley, Baldwin, Mead, Thomas, and others, the concept of personality is given a superior ranking. W. I. Thomas emphasized the origin of personality in four basic wishes: for security, for new experience, for response, and for recognition. A fifth wish has been suggested, namely, the wish to aid others.[35] This wish expresses itself when other persons, not always one's friends or chums, but sometimes strangers, are in imminent danger. The four wishes are egoistic in nature; the fifth altruistic.

A sixth basic wish may be added to Thomas' list, namely, the *wish for freedom*.[35a] This seems to be innate in human nature, for without opportunity for its expression, personality does not reach its full development. No one reaches maturity without seeking freedom, particularly from some of the restraints of human customs and traditions. The abandon of children released from the schoolroom is evidence of the wish for freedom. The joy that comes to anyone when he feels "free as a bird" is another bit of proof. The adverse reactions of human beings who suffer regimentation is negative proof.

The Thomas list may be supplemented by a seventh basic wish—the *wish to be treated fairly or justly*. Any child will illustrate this wish many times in a day. Preliterate people are equally good illustrations. No man is so humble or so ignorant that he does not appreciate just treatment. Hatred based on a sense of having been treated unjustly is

---

[34] L. L. Bernard, *Introduction to Social Psychology*.
[35] E. S. Bogardus, "The Fifth Wish," *Sociology and Social Research*, 16:75-77.
[35a] Louis Petroff, *Solitaries and Solitariness*, p. 12.

universal. The fact that unjust treatment separates more blood relatives, creates more feuds, and perpetrates more wars probably than any other single factor in life indicates how far-reaching is the wish for fair play.

If personality acquires status from social groups and if groups possess different sets of values, then one has personality selves, with a self for every social group of which one is a member. E. E. Eubank goes further and says that personality is composed of many "situation selves." Every person has a self for every social situation by which he is affected.[36] Taking a cue from Richard Thurnwald, we may say that personality is representative of social function. For every social function that is performed, personalities develop. Personality stands for social function.[37] Whatever our concept of personality, the role of personality in society is outstanding and noteworthy.

GROUP DISCUSSION TOPICS

1. The chief contribution of Cooley to sociologic thought.
2. The meaning of the statement : An individual has no separate existence.
3. The difference between self-consciousness and social consciousness.
4. The significance of the concept, primary group.
5. The importance of communication.
6. The disease of the century, according to Cooley.
7. The superiority of public opinion to personal opinion.
8. The contribution of the masses to public opinion.
9. Reasons for the sometime failures of education.
10. The weakness of social stratification.
11. Cooley's attitude toward economic determinism.
12. The tenor of Cooley's sayings.
13. The social process according to W. I. Thomas.
14. The nature of attitudes and values.
15. The concept of status.
16. The social origins of meaning.
17. The gesture as the basis of communication.
18. The use of "symbols" as a form of social control.
19. Bernard's substitute for "instinct."

[36] E. E. Eubank, "The Concept of the Person," *Sociology and Social Research*, 12:354-364; also E. E. Eubank, *The Concepts of Sociology* (Boston: D. C. Heath and Company 1932), pp. 106-110.
[37] Richard Thurnwald, "The Social Function of Personality," *Sociology and Social Research*, 17:203-218.

READINGS

Bernard, L. L., *Introduction to Social Psychology* (New York: Henry Holt and Company 1926).

Bittner, C. J., "G. H. Mead's Social Concept of the Self," *Sociology and Social Research*, 16:6-22.

Bogardus, Emory S., *Contemporary Sociology* (Los Angeles: University of Southern California Press 1932), Ch. V.

Cooley, Charles H., *Human Nature and the Social Order* (New York: Charles Scribner's Sons 1902).

———, *Social Organization* (New York: Charles Scribner's Sons 1909).

———, *Social Process* (New York: Charles Scribner's Sons 1918).

———, *Life and the Student* (New York: A. A. Knopf 1927).

Eubank, E. E., *The Concepts of Sociology* (Boston: D. C. Heath and Company 1932).

Gutman, Robert, "Cooley: A Perspective," *American Sociological Review*, 23:251-56.

Kolb, W. L., "A Critical Evaluation of Mead's 'I' and 'Me' Concepts," *Social Forces*, 22:291-296.

Levin, S. M., "Charles Horton Cooley and the Concept of Creativeness," *Journal of Social Philosophy*, 5:356-359.

Markey, John F., *The Symbolic Process* (New York: Harcourt, Brace and Company 1928).

Mead, George H., *Mind, Self and Society from the Standpoint of a Social Behaviorist* (Chicago: University of Chicago Press 1934).

———, "Social Consciousness and the Psychology of Meaning," *Psychological Bulletin*, 7:397-405.

———, "Social Psychology as Counterpart to Physiological Psychology," *Psychological Bulletin*, 6:401-408.

———, "National-Mindedness and International-Mindedness," *International Journal of Ethics*, 39:385-407.

———, "Scientific Method and the Moral Sciences," *International Journal of Ethics*, 33:229-247.

———, "The Genesis of the Self and Social Control," *International Journal of Ethics*, 35:251-277.

Smith, T. V., "The Social Philosophy of George Herbert Mead," *American Journal of Sociology*, 37:368-385.

Thomas, W. I., and Florian Znaniecki, *The Polish Peasant in Europe and America* (Chicago: University of Chicago Press 1918).

———, "The Mechanism of Social Consciousness," *Journal of Philosophy*, 9:401-406.

Troyer, W. L., "Mead's Social and Functional Theory of Mind," *American Sociological Review*, 11:198-202.

CHAPTER XXXIII

PARETO AND FASCIST THOUGHT

While fascist social thought as such has developed largely since the death of Vilfredo Pareto (1848–1923), and while it is still in the process of development, yet Pareto's social thought offers a better background for it than do the ideas of any other philosophically-minded person. While fascism has some of its roots in Nietzsche's concepts and other roots in Machiavellianism, yet Pareto's ideas come even closer to giving an adequate basis. However, some may contend that fascism is entirely the product of the minds of its immediate leader and his associates, and others may believe that its origins are to be sought in the imperial dictatorships of the past. Probably there is truth in each of these arguments. But let us examine Pareto's thinking, even though not all of it may be appropriate to the fascist picture.

PARETO'S BACKGROUNDS

Pareto was born of Italian parents who had been exiled and who were living in Paris at the time. His father was an admirer and supporter of Mazzini. He was a humanitarian, idealist, and advocate of democratic justice, but met with failure and was exiled. He returned from exile in France to Italy when Vilfredo was ten. The son thus received part of his education in Paris and part in Turin.

Vilfredo Pareto turned against his father's ideals and became a rabid opponent of humanitarianism and of the doctrines of Mazzini. He virtually contended, it is said, that the killing of humanitarians is a service to the state.

For a time he became interested in politics and economics. His ideas in support of free trade were not pleasing to the government. He fell into disfavor governmentally and withdrew to private life. The failure of his liberal economic program accounts to a degree for his turning to force as the best means of getting needed things done. He fought hu-

505

manitarianism, liberalism, and socialism. His negative ideas with reference to crushing out these programs were later carried out by the fascists when they came into power in Italy.

When fascism went on to set up a state capitalism it carried Pareto's ideas to a point where he would not have approved. He wanted freedom for himself but not for the masses. His doctrines, however, are the logical precursors of fascism, even of state capitalism.[1]

An engineer, a mathematician, a member of the faculty of the University of Lausanne, Switzerland, an erudite man, these terms indicate some of Pareto's characteristics and activities. As a university professor he had Mussolini as one of his pupils.[2] Mussolini appointed him to office, but his death in 1923 prevented him from rendering fascism any direct service. Many passages from Pareto are quoted by fascists[3] in justification of their system. His writings give, in the main, an excellent background for understanding the authoritarian state.

MIND AND SOCIETY

His *Trattato di Sociologia Generale* is ponderous. It has been translated into French, and in four English volumes under the title of *Mind and Society*. To read these four volumes once is not enough; to read them rapidly is inadequate. It is necessary to read and reread portions of them with a great deal of care. The style at times is heavy and abstruse, but the editor and translators have clarified rather than confused Pareto's thinking.[4]

One does not read far before being impressed that Pareto is a master logician. He thinks in terms of syllogisms and is continuously pointing out errors in the rationalizations

[1] Franz Borkenau, *Pareto*, p. 20.
[2] Homans and Curtis, Jr., *An Introduction to Pareto*, p. 9.
[3] *Ibid.*, p. 10.
[4] This translation, the editor reports, had its inception fifteen years ago; it "has consumed some 9000 hours in preparation, spread over the last five years." The editor apparently has mastered Pareto's bibliographic notes more fully than did Pareto himself. Not the least valuable phase of this translation are these voluminous notes. The painstaking work of the editor and translators is indicated by the index and bibliography which cover a total of 100 pages of small type in double columns.

of mankind. He must have had an "error complex," for he discovers so many errors in the thinking of the common people, of leaders, and of scholars, that one wonders whether or not it is possible to avoid error in thinking.

Another reaction is that Pareto's knowledge, especially of classical history and legend, of the writings of the Middle Ages, and of the modern history of southern Europe, particularly of Italy, knows no limits. He was obviously weak in his acquaintance with American and Asiatic history. Although his was no Spenglerian mind, he had a remarkable command of Grecian, Roman, and Italian literature.

Pareto is primarily interested in the relationships between social facts. He looks for uniformities in these relationships, which to him constitute sociological laws. He follows in the main the inductive method of describing social facts, of classifying them, and of looking for uniformities between them. He fails, however, in living up to the scientific standard of having no preconceptions and "no *a priori* notions." At times he gives the impression of having very definite *a priori* notions that he wishes to prove. His marshaling of data from Grecian and Roman history comes dangerously near to conveying the idea that he has brought materials together for purposes of proving rather than of examining a hypothesis.

Pareto demonstrates by the piling up of evidence how sentiments directly and indirectly dominate society, not only the common man but leaders in all walks of life as well, and particularly in the religious field. These sentiments are closely related to the "desires" that Lester F. Ward emphasized as the dynamic elements in society; and to the "interests" that Albion W. Small showed were so dominant in human life.

RESIDUES

Pareto next undertakes to analyze the nature of the sentiments; he arrives at a theory of residues. The residues are not the sentiments but the manifestations of them. Six classes of residues are analyzed and described at length. Class I : "Instinct" for combining similars or opposites. For example, the homeopathic principle combines similars. Class II : Group persistences or persistences of aggregates, or persistence of combinations. A political theory or combination of ideas, for instance, may have developed first among the Greeks and in different guises be handed down from generation to generation. Class III : Need of expressing sentiments by external acts. The sentiment of religion calls forth certain acts of worship among peoples of every religion. Class IV : The living together in society and maintaining a disciplinary structure. Under this heading occur such phenomena as pity and cruelty, self-sacrifice for the good of others, sentiments of superiors and of inferiors. Class V : The integrity of the individual and of his appurtenances and possessions. To this end the individual often resists alterations in the social equilibrium, and also engages in acts restoring his integrity when it declines. Class VI : Sexual appetite influences theories and modes of thinking which are often dissembled "especially among modern peoples." Incidentally, Pareto questions whether the emancipated women of the United States are any less moral than the Roman matrons in the heyday of the Republic and refers to the United States as being of all countries "the paradise of sex hypocrisy."

Accepting this classification of six residues at its face value the question arises : It is well done ? The answer is difficult to give because it is not always clear what Pareto means to include under each of the headings. While some of the categories remind one of factors in Sumner's fourfold classification of motives of human action or of phases of Thomas' four wishes, the ensemble is at least distinctive and unique. However, it suggests elements that function on different planes. The first and second residues obviously belong together : combinations and persistence of combinations represent a logical unity. The third item, manifestations of sentiments through actions, appears to be in a class by itself and to refer to the generic nature of muscular-neural mechanisms. The fourth and fifth residues, those of sociality and of individuality, bear a relation to each other by virtue of being opposites with an underlying unity. The sixth residue, the sexual, holds a direct relation to the third and an indirect to the fourth. Further refinement of the sixfold classification of residues is needed.

DERIVATIONS

Supplementing the manifestations of sentiments, man attempts to justify these manifestations or residues. He feels called upon to explain his actions. Evidently he sees inconsistencies between his actions and social demands, hence he argues himself into believing that his behavior is logical and hence justifiable. This widespread procedure, by virtue of its nature, might have been called a residue, making seven instead of six. Pareto divides these justifications into four; he defines four "derivations." These derivations occur between the level of instinct, on the one hand, and of logico-experimental science, on the other.

The four classes of derivations or justifications according to Pareto are: (1) assertions, (2) authority, (3) accords with sentiments, and (4) verbal proofs. (1) Assertions are easy to make. They are dogmatic statements that are not to be contradicted. The force with which they are uttered seems to give them reliability. (2) Assertions, if accepted logically, become authority. A person who is actually an authority in one field tends to be erroneously accepted as an authority in other fields. Authority survives long after it has lost any real claim to that distinction. (3) Justification is often found simply in the identification of behavior with one's own sentiments. However, such identification is quickly expanded to rest on the sentiments of mankind, and therefore it must be corrected. Identification with sentiments may involve the support of pleasurable feelings, of supernatural sanctions, or of personal and national interest. For instance, politicians, suggests Pareto, are in favor of birth control when they are afraid of the increase of proletarians; they are against it when there is danger that the population will prove inadequate for their designs. (4) Logical sophistries and "terms of indefinite, doubtful, equivocal meaning" that do not correspond to reality are in common use as means of justifying behavior.[5]

---

[5] Pareto thus may be interpreted as giving a large place to what R. E. Park has discussed as social myths, sometimes created by people with vested interests of any kind who wish to maintain themselves and their ideas in control.

The question may be raised whether the classification of "derivations" is accurate and complete. The first two, namely, assertions and those assertions that become widely accepted as authority, are clearly related. The third, accords with sentiments, is in a class by itself, and underlies the first derivation directly and the second indirectly. It is sometimes explanatory of the first and to a degree of the second. The fourth, verbal proofs, represents another category. It arises out of logical thinking or reasoning, and hence is different in nature from the first and second, and also from the third, although often complementary to the third derivation.

Pareto has developed a number of special or subsidiary theories, such as theory of utility, the élite, class circulation, revolution, and demagogic plutocracy. These will now be succinctly treated in order.

COMMUNITY UTILITY

The theory of utility involves utility as meaning usefulness, or ophelimity, that is, the power to give satisfaction. Utility, however, means different things to different persons. The utilities of the materialistic and luxury-loving capitalist are quite different from those of the ascetic. There are direct utilities, and indirect ones, or those which are derived through mutual relationships. There are utilities for the individual and utilities for the community, with conflicts existing between some of these according to differences in the sentiments of individuals. An influential question is: "What form of society best fits my sentiments?"

One of the subtlest of the warping sentiments is ophelimity. The tendency of certain observations or of certain experiences, or of certain inferences from observation and experiences to give one a sense of satisfaction needs to be guarded against carefully. If the hardest-boiled sociologist in the world were to read Pareto faithfully, he would probably discover that some of the things that he has been saying under the name of sociology have grown not out of logico-experimental thinking but out of the satisfaction he has received from shocking other sociologists, or the public, or out of being in the limelight.[6]

Paraphrasing Pareto's discussion of community utility we may say (1) that we "ought to stop at a point beyond which no 'advantage' would accrue to a society as a whole, (2) that no 'useless' suffering should be inflicted on the public as a whole or even in part, (3) that the benefit of a society should be obtained without sacrificing its ideals 'for the public good,' and (4) that efforts should be proportionate to purposes, in other words, that burdensome sacrifices for slight gain should be avoided." [7]

Pareto recognizes the appearance of a difficult problem, namely, that in matters of reform and new social objectives, different reformers disagree as to what is a utility for their community; that is, what is best for their society. They fall into disagreement among themselves and thus defeat the attainment of new objectives. The reason for this unfortunate result is that reformers as a rule usually allow the data to be deeply colored by their own feelings and sentiments. "They say and believe that they are solving an objective problem: 'What is the best form for a society?' Actually they are solving a subjective problem: 'What form of society best fits my sentiments?'" [8]

THE ÉLITE

The theory of the élite is that in every society there are

[6] Moreover, the maker of social objectives will safeguard himself not only against sentiments and residues, but against "derivations," or rationalizations and justifications of his thinking. References to authority are to be examined critically before being advanced argumentatively.

Even social uniformities or sociological laws derived from facts by the logico-experimental method are to be treated at any moment, chiefly as hypotheses. The best social laws that we know today are but "hypotheses serving to epitomize a more or less extensive number of facts and so serving only until superseded by better ones." (Pareto, *op. cit.*, I: 35.)

Since Pareto would hold the sociologist to rigid adherence to impersonal logico-experimental thinking, it may be inquired whether a complete limitation to natural science methods is adequate in the social sciences. The logico-experimental or natural science method is doubtless to be accepted with one reservation, namely, that after one has secured as complete an understanding as possible of human actions in this way, one may well keep in mind that there may be important phases of human behavior which require super natural-science methods for their comprehension.

[7] *Ibid.*, IV:1417.

[8] *Ibid.*, IV:1477.

"people who possess in a marked degree the qualities of intel·
ligence, character, skill, capacity, of whatever kind"; that
there are two classes of élite; that the two groups are disjunc·
tive at any given time; and that there is an up-and-down circulation of the élite. But aristocracies, with the governing
élite at the top, do not last. The Athenian aristocracy of the
élite passed away without leaving descendants. "In Germany
the aristocracy of the present day is very largely made up of
descendants of vassals of the lords of old." The élite are
repleted both in numbers and in quality "by families rising
from the lower classes." The élite are élite in everything
except in replenishing their numbers from their own stock.

A phase of the theory of the élite is the circulation of the
élite, or of class circulation. The élite may fall; some of the
nonélite become élite. The élite are not like thoroughbreds
among animals, "which reproduce themselves over long periods of time with approximately the same results." Hence
a society that maintains itself is characterized by a circulation of the nonélite upward to take the places of the élite or
of the descendants of the élite who have become nonélite.
Thus Pareto has evolved a "societal cycle" theory of consid·
erable merit.

A variation from Pareto's concept of the circulation of the
élite and from Sorokin's social mobility theories is found in
the thinking of Roberto Michels (1876–1936), an Italianized
German. Michels emphasized the tendency of the older
leaders, who are in the first stages of being discredited, to
call upon new blood. Moreover, the older often permit, reluctantly to be sure, a number of changes in their policies.
In this way they may fool the public and maintain themselves at the top.[9]

Obviously, a natural and fundamental social objective
would be the determination of how many superior persons
there are in each phase of every normal activity of a society
from time to time, of providing the superior with freedom
of expression, of stimulating the élite in each phase of social
activity opportunities to contribute their superiorities in be-

[9] Dino Camavitto, "Roberto Michels — In Memoriam," *American Sociological
Review,* 1:797-799. See Roberto Michels, "Social Mobility in General with
Special Reference to Post-War Mobility," XII International Congress of
Sociology, Rome, 1936

half of social well-being, and of seeking out and training the potentially superior among the nonélite, so that a given society may have the full advantage of all its developed and latent talent at the points of their greatest efficiency and its greatest need. A corollary is that a natural social objective would be to keep the superior functioning in a superior way. It was this point that Plato many centuries earlier recognized as the most difficult social objective to maintain.

Pareto's emphasis upon the way in which people generally and even the élite most of the time are subject to their sentiments rather than to the logico-experimental thinking suggests a social objective that may be basic to all other concrete and practical objectives. What social objective could be more significant than that of conditioning and training the great majority to free their thinking from their feelings, sentiments, and rationalizations; that is, from residues and derivations? How can any set of concrete objectives become firmly rooted if most people accept them or develop them in terms of what they feel that they want, in terms of personal interests, in terms of ophelimity, that is, of their power to give personal satisfaction? Not until the vast majority in a democracy are conditioned and educated to be objective, to think of human welfare first of all, will there be any use in thinking out and putting into operation concrete social objectives.[10]

Can we go Russia, the communist state, one better? Can we go Italy, the fascist state, one better? Can we go Germany, or national socialism, one better? Can we go Japan, the emperor-loving state, one better? Can we go all the authoritarian states one better? If they are successful in conditioning their respective peoples to think first in terms of national welfare and only secondarily in terms of self, could not they and we of a democratic state condition each generation to think first in terms of human welfare? When such a practical social objective becomes realized, all other needed social objectives are likely to follow.

Pareto's theory of revolution is based on the fact that dis-

---

[10] It is this enslavement of people generally to feelings and rationalizations which doubtless led Pareto to believe that democracies may easily be victimized and turned into demagogic plutocracies, and that under such conditions autocracies are better than democracies.

turbances occur in the social equilibrium as a result of "the accumulation of superior elements in the lower classes and, conversely, of inferior elements in the higher classes." Revolutions occur, according to Pareto, through accumulations of decadent elements in the governing classes, or because the latter shrink from using force, while at the same time elements of superior quality are coming to the fore among the lower strata. A way to prevent revolutions, suggested by Pareto, is for the élite to absorb from time to time a few of the superior persons among the nonélite. In this way the nonélite can be kept helpless. On the other hand, if the subject class is disposed to use force and has capable leadership, it can project a successful revolution. If the governing class is humanitarian, it is especially vulnerable and insecure. A governing class that is "adept in the shrewd use of chicanery, fraud, corruption" is difficult to overthrow. Especially is it safe from the subject class if it will "absorb only a small number of new individuals in order to keep the subject class deprived of leadership."

Pareto's theory of demagogic plutocracy involves the weaknesses of democracies. Pareto speaks of the fiction of "popular representation." In democracies there is increasing resort to artifice and to the political machine "as against the instrument of force." In certain situations those who govern must "grant favors and protect the interests of financiers and promoters of economic production, and, in their turn, must receive favors and patronage from them." Moreover, this relationship between rulers and promoters will be kept in the dark.

LOGICO-EXPERIMENTAL FACTORS

The third class of social phenomena, in addition to residues and derivations, is the logico-experimental. A small number of persons for a small part of the time are strictly scientific in their thinking. They proceed only on the basis of experience, of discovery of experimental uniformities, of laws derived from noting uniformities.

Pareto thus would limit sociology to the methods of the natural sciences, namely, "of reducing highly complicated concrete phenomena to simpler theoretical phenomena, being exclusively guided all the while by the intent to discover experimental uniformities." A logico-experimental person guards against "intrusions of personal sentiments," and against "what ought to be in order to fit in with his religious, moral, patriotic, humanitarian or other sentiments." The quest for uniformities in social relationships is the sociologist's main if not only goal.

Pareto's contention brings to mind Bacon's four idols which must be avoided before thinking can become scientific. Logico-experimental thinking involves three things, namely, observation, objective experiences, and logical inferences drawn from observation and experience; these three, and no more. It has no dogmas and rests on none, "not even the dogma that experimental facts can be explained only by experience." [11] It rests on no principles excepting those which are "abstract propositions summarizing the traits common to many different facts." It keeps sentiments entirely out of thinking, although at the same time it directs most of its thinking toward sentiments and their manifestations, for these provide the bursts of energy by which social action is characterized. It avoids at all costs in its thinking the influences due to the manifestations of sentiments, or in Pareto's terminology, to residues, whose six classes or types have already been reviewed.

Applying his objective approach somewhat rigidly to social life, we would not expect Pareto to be concerned about social objectives, at least insofar as the term implies Ward's concept of social telesis. The inference is correct, for Pareto specializes on describing what has been and what is in society; he says little regarding what will be and still less about what ought to be. Being a social describer, not a social planner or a prophet, he insists on looking for uniformities in social life or for sociological laws. Hence, while he does not speak of social objectives, he stands firmly for what every sociologist needs to keep continually in mind when considering social objectives, namely, what social laws are supporting the proposed objectives?

Does not any consideration of social objectives require that

[11] *Ibid.*, I:26.

considerable attention be directed to a better understanding and formulation of social uniformities or laws in descriptive terms? Can any social objective stand the test of validity if it does not grow out of social laws? In positing a social objective can we state at the same time what social law or laws it is in harmony with?

Pareto is ranked high by many persons because of his objective approach to the study of society. His mathematical mind led him to disown a subjective and philosophical system of social thinking. His viewpoint was that of a pragmatist, a practicalist, an opportunist, a realist.

Pareto's popularity in certain quarters is connected with the current trends away from liberal-democratic ideas and toward Machiavellism and fascism, for his own theories are of similar stripe. Like Le Bon he sees the populace subject almost entirely to their sentiments and illogical as thinkers.

Pareto would have sociology proceed after the fashion of the natural sciences, reducing highly complicated concrete phenomena to simpler theoretical phenomena, being exclusively guided all the while by the intent to discover experimental uniformities, and judging the efficacy of what one has done only by the experimental verifications that may be made of it.[12] He does not seem to take into full consideration the fact that the subject matter of sociology contains human, psychical variables not present in the subject matter of the physical sciences and that methods supplementary to those used by the physical sciences are needed to cope with the new variants. He deplores the attempt of modern sociologists to create systems of thought which turn out to be new religions. He regards religions as largely the products of superstitious thinking, and humanism as a blindfolder of true thinking in sociology. His skepticism regarding the possibilities of predicting "the social effects of any change in a given order of facts" has been undermined somewhat by recent studies in predictability such as those by E. W. Burgess.[13] He is doubtless sound, however, when he insists that a great sociological need is "to discover experimental uniformities." On the other hand, he appears to overlook the

12 *Ibid.*, IV:1739.
13 *Ibid.*, IV:1738, footnote.

other great sociological need of searching for the meanings of personal and social uniformities and variations.

Pareto's conception of a pyramidal society has long since been supplanted by Sumner's diamond-shaped conception. Pareto's view coincides with the contention of certain intelligence testers which places four per cent of the population at the top and the remaining ninety-six per cent at the bottom, instead of putting, as does Sumner, a small proportion at the bottom and another small percentage at the top, and according to the great mass a place between the two extremes.

He also seems to ignore the developmental nature of human nature, for he gives no place to the education and training of socialized attitudes or to a belief in a real democratic society. He gives little consideration to the possibilities of developing the social intelligence of the rank and file.

Pareto falls a victim at times to his own insistence on classification. To divide people into two disjunctive classes at a given time and to label one class élite and the other nonélite overlooks the fact that the persons called élite may be nonélite at the same time in a number of particulars, and that those called nonélite may be élite in many ways.

Pareto's weakness as a sociologist appears to arise from the fact that he was rather limited in his studies to Greek and Roman history, and in his firsthand knowledge of people, to his acquaintance with Latin races and cultures. A wider, more open-minded acquaintance with peoples elsewhere in the world might have enabled him to overcome some of his evident shortcomings.

Professor Ellsworth Faris finds an extraordinary correspondence between fascism and Pareto's ideas. "Pareto is bitterly scornful of the very word morality and equally contemptuous of truth, right, justice, and democracy." While he is concerned with the élite, he identifies the élite with the strong and successful.[14]

FASCISM

Fascism as a system of social thought is based partly on theories such as Pareto described and partly on the results

[14] Ellsworth Faris, "An Estimate of Pareto," *American Journal of Sociology*, XLI:667.

of opportunist measures. Its central theme is a powerful nationalism rather than hero-worship. One of its slogans is that "everyone shall work, but no one shall work against the state."

Fascism is based first and foremost on nationalism, next on militarism, third on autocracy, and fourth on state capitalism. Fascism makes the state supreme and the individual insignificant. Fascism's greatest strength in Italy is in its appeal to national loyalty and patriotism, to a revival of the glories of ancient Rome, and to the possible future greatness of Italy.

Fascism is a boon to the national state. It personifies the state. It enthrones the state above every name. Today the individual sacrifices for the state, and nationalism waxes strong, whereas immediately prior to the fascist regime in Italy dissident elements threatened to wreck both the state and the individuals that compose the state.

Fascist thought includes the military machine. It relies upon force to make its will supreme. Little boys and girls are trained to think in military terms.

The autocracy of fascism centers in one person, who rules from the top down. Even the Grand Council in Italy has acted largely in an advisory capacity. New ideas can originate with the people and be sent up through the various fascist organizations, but they do not advance far unless they are in line with the principles of fascism. Freedom of speech, of assemblage, of the press, of the radio, are not tolerated except within fascist limits.

Capitalism has undergone modifications under fascism. "Corporations" composed of workers and employers "in each industrial activity are created as legal units," and hence are directly controlled by the government. If a business enterprise is conducted in a way judged detrimental to the state, it receives first a warning, and then an order to cease the questionable practices. Both strikes and lockouts are forbidden by law. All individuals who do not belong to the "corporations" of employers and employees are ignored.

Fascist thought thus includes a corporate state, that is, a state composed of corporations. The members of the corporative state have status as workers, but not as citizens as that term is understood in democratic countries.

The private promoter as such, the real estate "shark," the blatant advertiser are suppressed. Prices may be regulated. Private property and capitalism still exist but under public control.

Fascist thinkers claim a number of advantages for fascism. For example, it is opportunist. More than once its original leader has changed the course of fascism. He has prided himself on being free to change the rules and regulations whereby fascism and Italy may progress. He has bound himself to no past except the past glories of Rome. He refrains from future commitments except those which he thinks will make his country great. Fascism in practice has shown considerable resiliency. Within the limits of fascist principles experimentation goes on.

Fascism is an antidote to the evils of social irresponsibility, of exploitation by private interests, of an individualism grown defiant. It is a natural turn for a people to take who have allowed individualism to go uncontrolled but who are not ready to exercise democratic control.

Fascist thought supports a strong social organization and believes in getting things done. It puts people to work. It substitutes order for chaos, and efficiency for inertia. It supplants a rabid, uncouth, antisocial individualism with an organized autocracy. Aside from the individual or individuals who may be exercising authority, it puts a heavy foot on individualism wherever the latter begins to manipulate the public good to its own gain.

Fascist thought stands for action, and if occasion requires, for quick action. It does not believe in waiting on long debates by incompetent but talkative congressmen. It knows no deadlocks. Its slogan is "Action" and not "Words." It believes in moving quickly to gain its aims. It boasts of action and speed and efficiency. It supports the idea of building needed roads, putting hospitals into operation, and draining swamps without debate.

On the other hand, fascism in practice is charged with serious defects by its democratic opponents. Its very con-

centration in the hands of one or of a few makes it dangerous. Its future acts are uncertain. Its international policy
is likely to take a sudden and dangerous turn at any moment.
Fascism is a makeshift. It is doing its work, even its good
work, at a tremendous sacrifice to personal liberty and freedom. Says one observer : "Fascism secures the welfare of the
state at the expense of all the political liberties that our
fathers have fought and died for."

Fascism thrives on power, physical power, in short, on the
army. The safety and continuance of the state are maintained not by good will but by military force and by the
power to imprison and exile.

Fascism contains the seeds of its own destruction in its
autocracy. Any so-called democratic society that has allowed
material values and self-centered interests to dominate it,
must pay the price of fascism or of something more drastic.
A so-called democracy that allows special interests to thrive
at the expense of the public good must suffer the fiats of
fascism or of a proletarian dictatorship, unless it can develop
a democracy of socially responsible citizenry.

It is not political democracy and popular government that
is being repudiated in the world today, but too much individualism. There have been so many different kinds of individualists that they have gotten in each other's way. Where
self-centered individualism rules, the national welfare is
eclipsed. Where individualism dominates, call it rugged or
ragged, as you will, national progress has been obstructed.

The choices before the world today are three. There is a
practical individualism that is headstrong and self-centered,
an individualism that tends to result in a dictatorship by
the economically powerful. A second choice is communism
or a dictatorship of the proletariat, of the economically helpless, of the unemployed, of the hopeless, and of the disillu-
sioned. A third choice of a real democracy of socially intelligent citizens, of socially motivated citizens, of citizens who
are willing to think and act in behalf of the public welfare
morning, noon, and night. To the extent that all the people will actually put the common weal ahead of individualistic scheming, dictatorships are unnecessary. But if people
still insist on getting something for nothing, or every man

having a racket, or trying to crowd the weaker to the wall, then a dictatorship, either a fascist one or a proletarian one, will result. On the other hand, there is the third concept, a democracy composed of only socially motivated citizens.

The fascist state has become a totalitarian state, and as such has developed a social ideology more or less distinctive. As pointed out by Luigi Sturzo in discussing the totalitarian state, we may arrive at six conclusions concerning the social principles expressed by the fascist state. (1) The fascist state carries administrative centralization to an extreme. The executive dominates all, and the legislative and judicial bodies are rubber stamps. (2) The military forces are allied with the executive to the point that everyone has become a unit in the military organization. (3) State education dominates all education if it has not become a monopoly. Propaganda has been elevated to the status of education. (4) A controlled economic policy operates in behalf of the state. (5) Personal liberty is permitted only in line with the promotion of totalitarian principles. (6) The ethics of Christian civilization is either suppressed or destroyed in favor of the ethics of the state. Whatever is best in promoting the ends of the state is ethical. Religion as far as it deals with social life is subordinated to the ends of the state.[15]

GROUP DISCUSSION TOPICS

1. Comparisons of Pareto's ideas with those of Machiavelli.
2. Explanations of Pareto's ideas in terms of his early experiences.
3. The role of sentiments in society according to Pareto.
4. The nature of the "residues" and their significance.
5. Contrasts between Pareto's "residues" and Thomas' "wishes."
6. Relation of "derivations" to "residues."
7. Pareto's theory of community utility.
8. Connections between ophelimity and useful thinking.
9. The theory of élite and its merits and demerits.
10. Social objectives according to Pareto.
11. Pareto's theory of revolution.
12. The concept of demagogic plutocracy.
13. The logico-experimental method in relation to scientific method.
14. The strong and weak points in Pareto's social thought.

[15] Luigi Sturzo. "The Totalitarian State," *Social Research*, III:222-235.

15. Similarities of and differences between Pareto's thought and fascism.
16. Merits and weaknesses of fascist social thought.

READINGS

Barnes, Harry E., and Howard Becker, *Social Thought from Lore to Science* (Boston : D. C. Heath and Company 1938), Ch. XXV.

Borkenau, Franz, *Pareto* (New York : Wiley and Sons 1936).

Ascoli, Max, "Society through Pareto's Mind," *Social Research,* 3:78-89.

Bongiomo, A., "Study of Pareto's Treatise on General Sociology," *American Journal of Sociology*, 36:349-70.

Davies, G. R., "Pareto—The Darwin of Social Sciences," *Social Science,* 10:117-22.

Einandi, M. M., "Pareto as I Knew Him," *Atlantic Monthly,* 156:336-46.

Faris, Ellsworth, "An Estimate of Pareto," *American Journal of Sociology*, XLI:657-668.

Ginsberg, Morris, "The Sociology of Pareto," *Sociological Review*, XXVIII:221-245.

Homans, G. C., and C. P. Curtis, *An Introduction to Pareto* New York : Knopf 1934).

Keller, A. G., "Pareto," *Yale Review* (new ser.), 24:824-828.

Moore, Harry E., and Bernice M. Moore, "Folk Implications in Pareto's Sociology," *Social Forces*, 14:293-300.

Northington, R. V., "Pareto : The Karl Marx of Fascism : A Scientific Sociologist," *Economic Forum*, 1:311-15, 460-66.

Pantaleoni M., "Pareto — Obituary," *Economic Journal*, 33:582-90.

Pareto, Vilfredo, *The Mind and Society,* edited by Arthur Livingston, 4 volumes (New York : Harcourt, Brace and Company 1935).

———, "Future of Europe," *Living Age,* 315:447-50.

Rocca, V., "Working with Pareto," *Virginia Quarterly Review,* 11:375-82.

"Symposium on Pareto's Significance for Social Theory," McDougall, William, "Pareto as a Psychologist," Murchison, Carl, "Pareto and Experimental Social Psychology," Tufts, J. H., "Pareto's Significance for Ethics," House, F. H., "Pareto in the Development of Modern Sociology," *Journal of Social Philosophy*, I:36-89.

Timasheff, N. S., "Law in Pareto's Sociology," *American Journal of Sociology*, XLVI:239-249.

Wilson, Francis G., "Social Objectives of Fascism," *Sociology and Social Research*, XX:322-327.

CHAPTER XXXIV

ROSS AND SOCIAL CHANGE

The phenomenon of social change is receiving attention today from nearly everyone, social philosophers, social scientists, statesmen, the man of the street. Current conditions of turmoil in many countries around the world are compelling people to think about the nature of changing world conditions. People are asking: Whither is the world bound? Is civilization headed for destruction?

In the field of social thought the questions take on a deep-seated note. What factors produce social change? What is it basically? How can the people of any one nation control the international conditions that make for destructive change, and what can they do to promote constructive change? Is social change beyond human control, or can the individual citizen do something about it? Will people of all countries be obliged to unite in order to control social change?

Edward A. Ross (1866-1951) pioneered in many fields of social thought, but at all times he was gathering data regarding social conditions and analyzing them in thoughtful terminology. He travelled extensively in the United States and widely throughout the world. He was a sharp observer of social life and took copious notes wherever he went. The titles of a number of his books indicate his interest in the changing social conditions in many countries: *Changing America, The Changing Chinese, Russia in Upheaval, The Social Revolution in Mexico, The Social Trend, World Drift.* The data recorded in these books are already of historical importance and many of the inductions that Ross made from them are of current significance.

Ross strove to describe social conditions exactly as he saw them. He specialized in asking questions about whatever he saw that he did not understand. He sought people in all walks of life who might have the answers, and on both major sides of every question that he considered. After the data were in hand, he subjected them to analysis and drew incisive conclusions from them. He adopted high standards of social welfare and discussed his factual materials in the light of these standards. He did not hesitate to express value judgments and to condemn those social trends which he believed against the common good. In one of his first books, *Social Control* (1901), he advanced what he considered to be the foundations of a sound social order. These foundations were fundamentals on the basis of which social change might well take place. Any other bases would lead to dangerous social change. After discussing the grounds of social control, the means of control, and the system of social control, he asks : "Is there any prospect that humanity, having sown its wild oats, will now settle down and be good?" He concludes that probably there is no reason to believe that in the years to come a change will occur making social control less necessary than now.[1]

A major reason for social control is that society has grown faster than the spirit of community or the we-feeling has grown. In fact the larger that society grows and the more the secondary groups increase in size, the less the relative amount of community spirit and the less the social responsibility. Thus, the social change represented by the rise of Big Society calls for an increasing amount of social control to offset the failure of social responsibility to keep pace with this bigness.[2]

Another social change which calls for more and improved social control methods is the result of the use of new inventions in communication and transportation. The world is shrinking because of the increasing ease of making social contacts. Ethnic and other groups having provincial or localized standards are coming into close relationships before they have come to understand one another and before they have developed adequate means of working together. Hence, the need for social control measures on a large scale.

Ross opposed change brought about by the increasing conflict of classes. He deprecated the class-struggle development

---

[1] Edward A. Ross, *Social Control* (New York: The Macmillan Company, 1901), p. 432.

[2] *Ib d.*, p. 435.

whether brought about by natural economic trends or by definite Marxian teachings. "When class spirit has sapped social spirit and rent society in twain, the first effect is a weakening of social control and a drifting toward disorder." [3] Ross favored social change that would lessen the extremes between the rich and the poor, and that would keep the middle class ideology as the controlling way of life.

As far back as 1905, Ross proclaimed that we "are entering a tumultuously dynamic epoch." [4] His words sound as though they were uttered but yesterday. The reason for the far-reaching changes that were predicted is the rise of "a new economic civilization" which is destined "to work in the world a transformation such as the plan works among nomads." [5] Ross saw great social changes coming first in Western civilization and then spreading to the ends of the earth. This cycle of change would take, he thought, two or three generations to make over the world. Then a new uniformism will set in for a time in which "self-reliance will be at a discount." Culture is becoming cosmopolitan, complex, and sophisticated.

The change from a rural civilization to one dominated by "the great glittering cities" has its advantages for mankind, but "the cities constitute so many blast furnaces where the talented rise and become incandescent, to be sure, but for all that are incinerated without due replacement." [6] If the gospel of the simple life cannot be maintained modern social change will mean that "the afternoon spirit is sure to creep upon us at last."

In *Sin and Society* (1907) Ross carried forward what was to be a life-long campaign against any form of social change that created wrong-doing on a large scale. In a letter received by him in 1907 from President Theodore Roosevelt, the latter said: "You show that the worst evils we have to combat have inevitably evolved along with the evolution of society itself." [7] Large-scale wrong-doing has evolved faster

[3] *Ibid.*, p. 403.
[4] Edward A. Ross, *Foundations of Sociology* (New York: The Macmillan Company, 1905), p. 365.
[5] *Ibid.*
[6] *Ibid.*, p. 394.
[7] Edward A. Ross, *Sin and Society* (Boston: Houghton Mifflin Company, 1907), p. x.

than a controlling public opinion. Theodore Roosevelt put the idea this way: "You war against the vast iniquities in modern business, finance, politics, journalism, due to the ineffectiveness of public opinion in coping with the dominant types of wrong-doing in a huge, rich, highly complex industrial civilization like ours."[8] To meet evidences of large-scale wrong-doing, Ross pleaded for honest, courageous, active achievement on the part of leaders of all types of big social organizations.

Negative or destructive social change does not just happen but comes about through the planning of persons who seek gain of wealth, of political power, of other forms of control by putting activities into operation which militate against the general welfare. Sometimes it comes about from the efforts of socially well-meaning individuals who are misguided, ill informed, or emotionally blinded. It may result from sins of omission and failure to safeguard hard-won advances in the direction of the commonweal.

The change which is represented by what Ross called "social sinning" lacks "the familiar tokens of guilt."[9] The child-beater is condemned vigorously "but the exploiter of infant toil" may feel no guilt and even may continue to be recognized as a pillar of society. The petty shoplifter is abhorred more than the stealer of a franchise.[10] Big and formidable sinners against society have developed into menaces of the first rank, while at the same time maintaining status and respectability among people generally.

In small groups offenders are singled out for chastisement but the change from small groups to Big Society has developed what Ross called the "criminaloid."[11] This new development has more recently been referred to as "white collar crime."[12] It is Sutherland's contention that in the course of social change a new type of crime has become prevalent, namely, crimes committed by a person of respectability and

[8] *Ibid.*
[9] *Ibid.*, p. 9.
[10] *Ibid.*, p. 16.
[11] *Ibid.*, Ch. III.
[12] E. H. Sutherland, *White Collar Crime* (New York: The Dryden Press, 1949).

social prominence in the course of his occupation. The rise of bigness seems to be a major explanatory factor, for in bigness moral responsibility sometimes fails to function, and impersonal relationships develop and spread in large groups, industrial, political, civic, and so on.

Why has this change for the worse come about? Ross would give three answers. First, the development of large groups creates the opportunity. Second, individuals trained to repudiate offenses against a person are not necessarily trained to refuse to participate in offenses against society. Third, public opinion has not kept pace with the rise of social sinning and has not developed the appropriate moral standards or the will to support those standards.

Another type of far-reaching social change was extensively discussed by Ross in his *Social Psychology* (1908). This is the change from a tradition and custom dominated society to one in which fashion plays outstanding roles. Intensive analysis was made of the nature and fields of custom and of the conditions affecting its sway.[13] The rise of fashion and the appeal of the new in a democratic society shifts the center of attention from custom to all kinds of new patterns of apparel, of material inventions, of ideas, even of philosophies. The wide sweep of fashion development seems to overshadow the role of the stable elements in society. Instability supplants a portion of the stability represented by custom and convention. In a study by the writer of those striking forms of fashion known as fads, it was found that a small percentage, perhaps two or three, survived long and were adopted as parts of changing culture patterns.[14]

In the changes from the old to the new Ross pointed out how discussion is one of the major factors.[15] Open discussion subjects old ideas and customs to crucial tests. Can the old face free discussion or must it hide behind the cloak of authority? If it does the latter it incriminates itself — in a democracy. No custom can long stand the light of general

---

[13] Edward A. Ross, *Social Psychology* (New York: The Macmillan Company, 1908), Chs. XII-XV.
[14] E. S. Bogardus, *Fundamentals of Social Psychology* (New York: Appleton-Century-Crofts, Inc., 1950), pp. 305, 306.
[15] Ross, *op. cit.*, Ch. XVIII.

scrutiny unless it can demonstrate that it has a current as well as a past value. The procedure of retiring one generation after another at a certain age is due in part to the desire to give the younger generation a chance to put new ideas into operation. As a result social changes, often subtle ones, are daily taking place.

The emphasis on the role of discussion in bringing about change was inaugurated by Bagehot about 1870.[16] He pointed out that "a government by discussion if it can be borne, at once breaks down the yoke of custom" and opens doors to a variety of social changes. Discussion brings new ideas to the surface and proposes a multitude of changes. Because open discussion may mean the status quo will have to give way to change, it is widely opposed. "One of the greatest pains to human nature is the pain of a new idea" because it suggests change.[17]

Six or seven decades after Bagehot's chapter was written, democratic countries have seen a great outburst of emphasis on discussion groups, particularly small discussion groups as a means of bringing needed changes to pass. More recently Lasker has defined discussion as a "social dynamic" and analyzed a reasonable discussion procedure as having five phases : (1) concern with a situation, (2) clarification of issues, (3) defining elements of conflict, (4) presentation of larger values and additional facts, and (5) dynamic agreement.[18] Herein is found a basis for rational social change. Williams refers to discussion as "a shortcut to social action"[19] and as a means "to take the American people into partnership in the actual organization of the great struggle to save democracy."[20] Thus, organized discussion groups may be viewed as one of the best available means of bringing about intelligent social change.

In his *Changing America* (1912), Ross describes a related expression of social change, namely, the movement "toward

16 Walter Bagehot, *Physics and Politics* (New York: D. Appleton-Century Company, 1873), Ch. V.

17 *Ibid.*, p. 163.

18 Bruno Lasker, *Democracy through Discussion* (New York: The H. W. Wilson Company, 1949), Part III.

19 Chester S. Williams in Emory S. Bogardus, *Democracy by Discussion* (Washington, D.C.: American Council on Public Affairs, 1942), p. iii.

20 *Ibid.*, p. v.

democracy," which is "world-wide and tidal." [21]   He explained this aspect of social change as due to several causes.
For example, "light is flooding the social deeps," and people
are becoming informed.   As they acquire education they
resist being treated as the "masses," in fact, formally educated
or not, the masses are demanding a voice in the control of
their lives.

The advent of the machine is another factor that has stimulated the movement toward democracy.   As the machine
multiplies output and increases the leisure hours, people are
laying claim to speak and act for themselves rather than
through an "upper class."   People are asking for democracy
faster than they are being educated to exercise it efficiently.

As people without means become aware of the economic
and social chasm between themselves and the wealthy, they
grow restless.   If they cannot get enough goods with which
to meet the necessities of life, some may turn to socialism or
communism.   They are willing to give the state some of their
freedom in return for the aid the state will give them in security and in obtaining more of this world's goods.   According to Ross, "the spread of socialism, then, is but the latest
phase of the universal tendency for the people to endeavor
to control government for their own benefit." [22]

Another expression of social change that interested Ross
greatly is the falling birth rate in the most intellectually advanced countries.   He objected to the tendency to shirk
duties to the race, to put self-centered living ahead of chil-
dren-centered living.   He was a forerunner in a way of persons who pointed out as East did that the world is at the
crossroads, that is, will the least developed be allowed to
propagate and replenish mankind and the more fit cease to do
so through a birth rate that falls to or even below the death
rate ? [23]

Ross approved that emancipation of women which led to
their revolt "against the needless anguish and mortality" that

[21] Edward A. Ross, *Changing America* (New York: The Century Co., 1912),
p. 3.
[22] *Ibid.*, p. 31.
[23] Edward M. East, *Mankind at the Crossroads* (New York: Charles
Scribner's Sons, 1923).

"excessive child-bearing inflicts upon them." [24] At the same time he protested against the fact that five-sixths of mankind was maintaining an excessive birth rate. The five-sixths are on the whole the least in need of a high birth rate. He outlined such dangerous subsidiary movements as were taking place in Japan, a country with a cultivatable area one-seventh the size of California, which not only had a population at the time Ross wrote, of fifty million, but whose population was increasing by more than half a million a year. This tendency seemed to be furthered by the military leaders, for it was accompanied by a demand by them for more territory that Japan could conquer or at least control. Here were subtle developments that suggested foreboding social changes.

Another change that Ross deplored is the increasing divorce rate.[25] Several explanatory factors are given. "An inevitable by-product of the liberation of women from men, and of both from tradition, is a rank individualism which makes a lasting union impossible, and thus defeats the end for which marriage exists." [26] Bad marriages are cited as major factors in an increasing divorce rate. More careful marriages based on a period of acquaintance and courtship are urged, for courtship gives a couple an opportunity to learn about each other's likes and dislikes, strong points and weak points. The fact that intemperance figured "in nearly a fifth of the divorces ought to invigorate the temperance movement in all its branches." [27]

Immigration to the United States was seen as furthering democratic change, change from harsh old-world conditions to free new-world ones, change from little or no opportunity to extensive opportunities of many kinds. Ross perceived immigration as a leveling up of economic conditions, of increasing the homogeneity of the human race, of improving the possibilities for wider understanding, of extending democracy. However, he saw in unlimited immigration of the poor of other countries a future defeat "for the invisible children of our poor," that is, for the unborn children of a submerged

[24] Edward A. Ross, *Standing Room Only* (New York: The Century Co., 1927), p. vii.
[25] Ross, *Changing America, op. cit.*, pp. 49 ff.
[26] *Ibid.*, p. 60.
[27] *Ibid.*, p. 63.

tenth in the United States.[28]   The change that he advocated,
and that conveys a timely suggestion for today, is that the
United States develop "high standards of living, institutions,
and ideals" which other countries may adopt or adapt and
thus bring themselves up to our level.   There is great room
for improvement in institutions and in putting ideals into
general practice in the United States, and in the crowded
countries a basic need to restrict a birth rate that keeps people
ground down in a state of impoverishment.

Although a sociologist Ross was also a eugenicist and feared
the changes that would come from the multiplication or immigration of low-grade stock biologically speaking.   The
descendants of the colonists and the early immigrants he
considered as not keeping up a reasonable birth rate and
low-grade stock as multiplying too rapidly and thus diluting
the quality of the general level of the genes in the people of
the United States.   If the best biological stock does not add
to the population, the low-grade will, and a nation that so
proceeds "deserves the distinction that surely awaits it." [29]
Thus Ross depicted a downward change in biological worth
as an accompaniment of a rise in intellectual individualism,
and of the tendency for the least developed to have the most
children.

Ross studied social change in the making in Russia, China,
South America, Mexico, India, and elsewhere.   He wrote
three books on social change in Russia in the following order :
Russia in Upheaval (1918), *The Russian Bolshevik Revolution* (1921), and *The Russian Soviet Republic* (1923).   As
revolution is a violent form of social change it affords an
opportunity to examine change in its most sudden and most
costly form.   Ross found the Russian revolutions of 1917
costly in lives, costly in good will, costly in organization, costly
in security, and for a long time costly in welfare.[30]   The
November revolution in 1917 was not so much the work of
leaders as it was an expression by leaders of "the background
of experience of the Russian common people."   The soldiers

[28] Edward A. Ross, *The Old World in the New* (New York: The Century
Co., 1914), p. ii.
[29] *Ibid.*, p. 304.
[30] Edward A. Ross, *Russia in Upheaval* (New York: The Century Co., 1918),
p. 344.

were ready to quit fighting for the Tsar, the peasants were ready to seize the estates, and "the robbed and oppressed masses — a hundred millions of men and women — moved toward the goal of their long unfulfilled desires like a flow of molten lava that no human force can dam or turn aside. It was a majestic and appalling social phenomenon — as elemental almost as an earthquake or a tidal wave."[31] Rarely has even a poet been able to describe revolutionary social change in such virile and compelling language.

The conclusion is that where evolutionary change is repeatedly thwarted for a period of time, revolutionary change is in the making. Ross concluded that "the real security of the possessing classes in other countries is not their hysterical and malevolent measures to throttle free speech" but in seeing that "production for profit really subserves the general welfare," in making capitalism "in very truth, serve society as it professes to do — instead of plotting to dominate and exploit it."[32] Evidently the revolution that came about in Russia in 1917 affords much food for thought, even for all who are opposed to revolution. Revolution is evidently the most costly form of social change and one that can be avoided by man if he will use his intelligence in line with social justice.

Social change has not always occurred overnight but historically it has come about at a snail's pace. After visiting slow-moving China, Ross fell into an historical view and reports how it required 280 years after the Crucifixion before Christianity "won toleration in the Roman Empire." It took 120 years after Luther issued his defiant theses before the Protestant Reformation was assured. It needed 115 years after the discovery of the New World before "the first English colony was planted here."[33] When Ross was in China several decades ago he found not only countless evidences of China's domination by tradition, but impacts that were being made by Western cultures in China and the resultant conflicts that were causing China to stir. Although he did not predict

[31] Edward A. Ross, *The Russian Bolshevik Revolution* (New York: The Century Co., 1921), p. v.

[32] Edward A. Ross, *The Russian Soviet Republic* (New York: The Century Co., 1923), pp. 394 ff.

[33] Edward A. Ross, *The Changing Chinese* (New York: The Century Co., 1911), p. 344.

the Communist revolution of 1948 he did state that "the renaissance of a quarter of the human family is occurring before our eyes." [34]

In South America Ross found social change taking place very slowly. Moreover, his prediction (1915) still seems to hold true that substantial change caused by "such modern forces as industry, democracy, and science will be delayed." He finds the reason in the past when "the masterful whites simply climbed on the backs of the natives and exploited them." [35] Other factors have been the pride of the white man and his adverse reactions to doing manual labor. Additional explanations are found in an extended parasitism and authoritativeness that was fastened upon South American society. Abuse of political and economic power often prevents those who work with their hands to receive recognition but is "the shortest road to wealth." [36] The upper class maintain a heavy hand and the children of the masses "are growing up in darkness." The masses seem to be kept backward and public welfare receives attention in many places as a means to increase the authority of those in control. As a result social change occurs sporadically. Revolutions occur but they do not involve or affect the people. They are limited largely to political leaders and the army. They represent political change or superficial and transitory social change, not real social change.

In Mexico Ross again found social change taking place very slowly, especially among the Indians, because of lack of education and of stimuli to do better.[37] The government under far-sighted leaders, like Vasconcelos, inaugurated a federal school system but the peons have responded very slowly because of having become more or less "insensible to the hopelessness of their lot." [38] Social change is supposed to be taking place through a century and a half long revolution that began with Hidalgo and Morales in the early part of the nineteenth century. They led people to revolt against the

[34] Ibid., p. 345.
[35] Edward A. Ross, South of Panama (New York: The Century Co., 1915), p. ii.
[36] Ibid., p. 368.
[37] Edward A. Ross, The Social Revolution in Mexico (New York: The Century Co., 1923), p. 154.
[38] Ibid.

Spanish yoke, and from time to time to revolt against political Mexican dictators. Popular education as predicted by Ross is proving to be "the key to the regeneration of Mexico." [39] The Revolution that began in 1810 and that was followed by lesser revolutions of a political nature is now turning into a slow evolution. Thus social change is undergoing an evolution through the increase in education of the peons who were formerly serfs on the haciendas.

The effect of martial inventions on social change concerned Ross greatly. He saw them as bending "the stream of social history." They are used for two purposes, defense and attack, but unfortunately those made for defense may turn into weapons for attack. Thus, arming for defense inspires "suspicion, fear, and counter-arming in other nations." [40] The submarine torpedo boat was at first built for protection but it soon became a distance sea-going invention that "converted it into an offensive arm of great deadliness." [41] Soon after heavy coast defense guns were developed, they were loaded on giant superdreadnoughts and carried destruction thousands of miles away from the home coast. Ross foresaw (1922) changes whereby "the hand of Mars will be heavier upon us in the future."

Inventions in communications "wipe out those distances which formerly gave the nations a sense of security." At the same time many nations are becoming immensely dynamic and hence engage in acts which are interpreted as menacing gestures by insecure nations. Population pressure increases demands for more opportunities at home and for more markets abroad. Hence dynamic events lead to "outbursts of human energy" that shock mankind and lead to the adoption of resolutions that "this is to be the last war." But after a major portion of the horrified generation passes on, social conditions arise which may lead to a war on a still vaster scale of destruction. How could this downward social change be halted and reversed? Through religion? Through the peace movement? Through an awareness of the great economic waste by commercial minds?

[39] *Ibid.*, p. 155.
[40] Edward A. Ross, *The Social Trend* (New York: The Century Co., 1922), p. 230.
[41] *Ibid.*

The propaganda changes, and leading nations carry on the destructive armament race under the rubric of "needed for defense." Moreover, the nation that takes the lead in disarming "runs the risk of being thwarted or beaten."[42] In stark language: "The men of Mars set the pace for the rest of the world." This trend in destructive change can be reversed, according to Ross, by creating "an organization provided with the means of adjudicating disputes and enforcing awards" between nations.[43]

In South Africa Ross found little real social change. He found those in economic control reluctant if not definitely unwilling to improve the lot of the natives who are in the large majority, except in minor ways, but not from the standpoint of granting them political democracy in the government.[44] The problem is difficult from the standpoint of planned social change, for if the European minority who are in control help the non-European majority to become educated and give them the ballot in the Union as fast as they qualify, the latter will ultimately take over, and the white people will lose their political power. Hence, the whites consider that any major change from the status quo will be disastrous for them. Current reports from South Africa indicate few changes in the situation as Ross reported it, except that the government is furthering *apartheid,* or separateness, of the non-Europeans, and determined that the latter shall not vote in the white man's government. As a result of many factors there is a growing unrest among the non-Europeans.

In Portuguese Africa Ross found little change and for the same reason as in South Africa,[45] namely, "the privileged ruling classes" were accredited with protecting status quo and holding back the forces that make for change. But in so doing, tendencies leading to violent outbreaks were gathering underground strength.

Ross tackled a major practical aspect of social change,

---

[42] *Ibid.,* p. 232.
[43] *Ibid.,* p. 234.
[44] Edward A. Ross, *Seventy Years of It* (New York: D. Appleton-Century Company, 1936), Ch. XXI.
[45] *Ibid.,* Ch. XX.

namely, is the world growing better or worse?[46] After weighing both tendencies he favored the first probability. Why? Because the average age is increasing, and "if life is a good thing then to have more of it is to be better off."[47] Because there is "a brightening outlook for babies," due to a decreasing infant mortality rate. Because there is "more generous public provision for education." Because there is an equalization of freedom of men and women with discriminations against women being slowly wiped out. Because marriage and the family are becoming more democratic. Because of the increased opportunities for children. Because of the gains being made by industrial wage earners. Because of medical gains over many types of disease. Because of the spread of new freedoms.

The evidences that the world is growing worse are found in the high birth rates in overpopulated countries and among the least able in all countries, in the continuing exploitation of the underprivileged by the overprivileged for the love of power or of money, and in the increasing range and destructiveness of weapons of war.

Ross finally arrived at what he called "a world view"[48] and proclaimed that "there is no foretelling where the finer human traits will crop up." He admitted that he finally "awoke to the fallacy of rating peoples according to the grade of their culture," while still believing that it may be difficult for a people to rid themselves of their socially inherited culture and adopt another. His world outlook however did not lead him to take "a rosy view of the near future." He saw social change for the worse in population pressures in many countries and in the procedure of nations "in being 'prepared' to loose upon one another the most frightful agencies of mass murder."[49] In his portrayal of negative social change he found that thanks "to the holders of investments, scheming munitions makers, rabid nationalists and warped militarists, at humanity's feet yawns a veritable hell." He decried dictatorships of all types, dictatorships of the proletariat, of the money-classes, of the political bureaucrats.

[46] Edward A. Ross, *World Drift* (New York: The Century Co., 1928), Ch. I.
[47] *Ibid.*, p. 3.
[48] *Seventy Years of It, op. cit.*, Ch. XXVII.
[49] *Ibid.*, p. 279.

In his development of a system of sociological principles he utilizes his widespread and firsthand observations of social change. In fact he begins his system of principles with population make-up and population changes.[50] He draws upon "the cityward rush" and the "decadence of the countryside." He builds upon social conflicts everywhere and on their possible outcome, forward or backward, as far as change is involved. He sees regress in such phases of social life as "the rise of gross inequalities, in industrial strife, in religious strife, in exploitation, in international war, in estrangements in the family and elsewhere, in ossification and the crystalization of the status quo, in the power of commercialized vice." He concludes that social change in the sense of development is not unilinear. Society "is not moving in a predetermined path."[51] From time to time new social forces appear that change the direction of change. These usually appear in the form of localized social movements that are tested and if accepted tend to spread until they effect far-reaching modifications in the direction of social change.

In the foregoing discussion of Ross and Social Change it may be evident that Ross covered an unusual range of social problems in an unusual varieties of countries around the world. In this study he made firsthand observations, he asked a multitude of questions of people on both sides of controversial issues. In his descriptive accounts he burst forth with unusually picturesque phrases, as illustrated by the quotations in this chapter, in order to drive home his observations. Upon a wealth of data he brought to bear certain sociological approaches and principles as illustrated to a definite degree in a preceding chapter. More than anyone else in the field of social thought he succeeded in making social changes vivid and significant. He made other contributions to social thought but in no case with more vigor than in his portrayal of social change. He was a past master in making social reconnaissances.

---

[50] Edward A. Ross, *New-Age Sociology* (New York: D. Appleton-Century Company, Inc., 1940).
[51] *Ibid.*, p. 523.

READINGS

Bagehot, Walter, *Physics and Politics* (New York: D. Appleton Company, 1873).

Becker, Carl, *Progress and Power* (New York: Alfred A. Knopf, Inc. 1949).

Bogardus, Emory S., *Democracy by Discussion* (Washington, D.C.: American Council on Public Affairs 1942).

——, "Social Change in Alaska," *Sociology and Social Research,* 36:183-89.

Borgatta, E. F., and H. J. Meyer, editors, *Social Control and the Foundations of Sociology, Pioneer Contributions of Edward A. Ross to the Study of Society* (Boston: Beacon Press 1959).

Chase, Stuart, *Roads to Agreement* (New York: Harper & Brothers 1951).

East, Edward M., *Mankind at the Crossroads* (New York: Charles Scribner's Sons 1923).

Fellows, Erwin W., "The Sociologist and Social Planning," *Sociology and Social Research,* 36:220-26.

Girvetz, Harry K., *From Wealth to Welfare* (Stanford: California: Stanford University Press 1951).

Hertzler, J. O., "E. A. Ross: Sociological Pioneer and Interpreter," *American Sociological Review,* 16:597-613.

Kolb, William L., "The Sociological Theories of Edward Alsworth Ross," in Harry E. Barnes, *An Introduction to the History of Sociology* (Chicago: The University of Chicago Press 1948), Ch. XLII.

Landis, Paul H., *Rural Life in Process* (New York: McGraw-Hill Book Company, Inc. 1948).

Lasker, Bruno, *Democracy through Discussion* (New York: The H. W. Wilson Company 1949).

Ogburn, William F., *Social Change with Respect to Culture and Original Nature* (New York: The Viking Press 1950).

——, "How Technology Changes Society," *Sociology and Social Research,* 36:75-83.

Ross, Edward A., *Social Control* (New York: The Macmillan Company 1901).

——, *Foundations of Sociology* (New York: The Macmillan Company 1905).

——, *Sin and Society* (Boston: Houghton Mifflin Company 1907).

——, *Social Psychology* (New York: The Macmillan Company 1908).

——, *The Changing Chinese* (New York: The Century Co. 1911).

——, *Changing America* (New York: The Century Co. 1912).

——, *The Old World and the New* (New York: The Century Co. 1914).

——, *South of Panama* (New York: The Century Co. 1915).

Ross, Edward A., *Russia in Upheaval* (New York : The Century Co. 1918).
——, *The Russian Bolshevik Revolution* (New York : The Century Co. 1921).
——, *The Social Trend* (New York : The Century Co. 1922).
——, *The Russian Soviet Republic* (New York : The Century Co. 1923).
——, *The Social Revolution in Mexico* (New York : The Century Co. 1923).
——, *Standing Room Only* (New York : The Century Co. 1927).
——, *World Drift* (New York : The Century Co. 1928).
——, *Seventy Years of It* (New York : The Century Co. 1936).
——, *Principles of Sociology* (New York: D. Appleton-Century Company 1938).
——, *New-Age Sociology* (New York : D. Appleton-Century Company 1940).
——, "Uniqueness of the Social Sciences," *Sociology and Social Research*, 16:3-5.
——, "Watchman, What of the Night?" *Sociology and Social Research*, 18:110-14.
——, "Some Contributions of Sociology to the Guidance of Society," *American Sociological Review*, 1:29-32.
——, "Recollections of a Pioneer in Sociology," *Social Forces*, 20:32-35.
——, "Fifty Years of Sociology in the United States," *American Journal of Sociology*, 50:489-92.
——, "How Sociology Is Becoming a Science," *Sociology and Social Research*, 29:339-42.
——, "Capsules of Social Wisdom," *Social Forces*, 27:187-227.
Sims, Newell L., *White Collar Crime* (New York : Thomas Y. Crowell Company 1939).
Sorokin, Pitirim A., *The Reconstruction of Humanity* (Boston : The Beacon Press 1948).

CHAPTER XXXV

THOMAS AND SOCIAL ATTITUDES

The role of attitudes in the field of social thought has greatly increased in importance in recent years. Whereas desires engaged the thinking of Lester F. Ward and instincts the attention of William McDougall and other psychologists, the concept of wishes as developed by William I. Thomas became the basis for the concept of attitudes which Thomas and sociologists after him have generally adopted. Psychologists have likewise found attitudes a useful concept, so that today we find a wide usage of the concept by sociologists, psychologists, and social psychologists. Very few mental constructs today enjoy the wide acceptance of all three disciplines. It might be said that the concept of attitudes is the main meeting ground at present of sociology, psychology, and social psychology.

Preceding his discussion of attitudes, Thomas described the basic factors as wishes, and named four. His original plan was to use the term, desires, but following Freud's stress on "wish," he decided to use the latter term, although he did not accept Freud's use of the term. However, the recognition given "the Freudian wish" obscured Thomas' usage for many people, and confused others. Hence, the term did not prove to be a fortunate choice. Thomas' main concern was to supplant the term, instinct (with its definite biological connotations), and develop a concept with indefinite biological origins and with possibilities of specific application in countless ways to the social life of persons, according to the individual's responses to environmental stimuli.

It is interesting to note that Thomas' first elaboration of the four wishes began with (1) the desire for new experience and for fresh stimulations. He placed next (2) the desire for recognition, which ranges from sexual response to general social appreciation secured by such devices as the display of ornaments or the proclaiming of one's scientific attainment by one's friends. Third, interesting enough, is (3) the desire for mastery or the will to power as found in ownership, domestic tyranny, political despotism. Fourth is (4) the desire for security which is based on fear and which may be exemplified negatively in the person who withdraws from social participation and lives in solitude.[1]

A revision of these desires took the form of wishes for new experience, for security, for social response, and for recognition.[2] (1) New experience means heightened states of stimulation, physiological expansion, change, adventure, thrill. Interest in reports of the sensational, hunting game, pursuit in any of its various forms contain the pattern. (2) Security is the opposite of new experience. This contrast is often seen in work as against play, in utility as against pleasure, in saving as against spending. Youthfulness seeks new experience ; old age, security. (3) Desire for response is found in love, in intimate privileges, in companionship. (4) Desire for recognition is satisfied in the achievement of status, of fame, in approval in a large way.[3]

In the form of attitudes, wishes become tangible and stable. In attitudes wishes realize countless ends. Thomas was the first person in any social science to give the concept of attitudes a vital role. Since his initial emphasis on attitudes the concept has come to be a leading one in any carefully considered discussion of personality. In some ways an attitude and its correlative, a value, have become the most important pair of concepts for understanding personality.

Thomas originally defined an attitude as "a process of individual consciousness which determines the real or possible activity of the individual in the social world."[4] It is a tendency to action "whether this action is a process of mechanical activity producing physical changes in the material world, or an attempt to influence the attitudes of others by speech and gesture, or a mental activity which does not at

[1] William I. Thomas and Florian Znaniecki, *The Polish Peasant in Europe and America* (New York: Alfred A. Knopf, Inc., 1927), I:73.

[2] William I. Thomas, *The Unadjusted Girl* (Boston: Little, Brown and Company, 1923), p. 4.

[3] *The Unconscious, A Symposium* (New York: Alfred A. Knopf, Inc., 1927), pp. 145, 146.

[4] *The Polish Peasant in Europe and America, op. cit.,* I:221.

the given moment find a social expression or even a mere process of sensual apperception.[5]

Every attitude has an objective counterpart in a value. A social value is defined as "any datum having an empirical content accessible to the members of some group and a meaning with regard to which it is or may be an object of activity."[6] Values thus are the objective data which have their counterparts in attitudes. Neither comes first. Neither causes the other. Each is at one and the same time an antecedent of the other. The interrelationship may be explained by saying that a value is the result of "an attitude acting upon or influenced by some preexisting social value."

The connection link between subjective attitudes and objective values is behavior. "Activity in whatever form is the bond" between an attitude and its related value. Activity is an attitude being expressed with reference to some value.

Thomas' emphasis on attitudes led to widespread acceptance of this concept as central to social psychology. In 1931, for example, appeared a volume, edited by Kimball Young, which bore the inscription: "To William I. Thomas whose concept of social attitudes has been so significant in the contemporary analyses of human behavior, this volume is dedicated by former students and colleagues." The book included fifteen papers by as many different sociological writers on as many different aspects of attitudes. A few of these topics were: the concept of social attitudes (Faris); human nature, attitudes, and the mores (Park); attitudes and the redirection of behavior (Bernard); and social attitudes of superior boys in an interstitial community (Thrasher). In the discussion by Faris, the idea expressed by Thomas to the effect that there is an attitude-value-attitude sequence is criticized. Faris claims that the attitude and the value (or object as Faris would say) seem to exist always "as two aspects of a single unity or organization." In other words neither precedes the other, but Faris does not indicate what precedes both the attitude and value. Could it be another attitude-value unity of relationship?[7]

5 *Ibid,* I:27.
6 *Ibid.,* I:21 ff.
7 Kimball Young, Editor, *Social Attitudes* (New York: Henry Holt and Company, 1931), p. 10.

The test of an attitude is behavior, according to Thomas. One might add that a complete test would be behavior over a period of time, for an individual might fake an attitude for a given length of time. An interesting question arises here, namely, how long can a person fake an attitude without it becoming in a way an aspect of his personality. Since an attitude is a construct for a subjective phenomenon, it can be analyzed or measured only by the behavior including the ideational behavior to which it may give expression.

There is always a tendency to rationalize an attitude, that is, to adjust its expression to the social situation in which a person finds himself. A person may boast of his wealth among his friends but play it down when interviewed by an assessor. Which of these two expressions of his represents his real attitude toward his wealth? Or does he have two, or more, contradictory attitudes regarding his wealth? A bystander may conclude that the man of wealth is a hypocrite, judging by his two contradictory expressions. If accused of being a hypocrite to his face, what will be his attitude? Will he display irritation and anger, admit the allegation, or attempt to explain away the seeming contradiction?

It is doubtless true that persons are not aware of all their attitudes. It is only when called upon to express themselves in a social situation that an attitude becomes defined by its possessor. Sometimes a person will express an attitude signifying idealism but when called on suddenly to act will behave materialistically. Which is his real attitude, or does he have only one attitude which when tested by circumstances underwent a mutation? Or was the materialistic attitude the real one all the time, while its idealistic one was a fake one for public appearance sake?

An attitude is defined in various ways at the present time, but this vital aspect of personality may be summed up by saying that it is an acquired, established tendency to act with reference to some aspect of the environment or of the reacting organism. If it is acquired, then it is not an instinct although it may have instinctive bases. Since it is acquired, it is learned during the lifetime of its subject. If it is learned, then it can be modified, changed, and perhaps even unlearned unless it has become too integrally a part of personality.

Since an attitude is a mental construct that involves being established it is distinguished from an impulse. Because of being established it gives stability to personality. Possibly it is the main stabilizing aspect of personality, and its nature and how it developed become very important. Of course it may become so stabilized that it in connection with related attitudes may prevent personality from making needed changes. Many a person has developed attitudes when he was young which were called liberal, but as time went on these attitudes resisted change. Ultimately this person became known as a conservative, because the standards of his social groups had moved on while his ruling attitudes had stood still.

An attitude is a tendency to act, not an act, although an act, or better, a series of acts over a period of time may be necessary in order to indicate its nature. An attitude has been compared to a trap that has been set. The appropriate stimulus will release the spring. An attitude is some stored-up energy ready to be expressed by the appropriate stimulus.

An attitude is a tendency to act toward a given aspect of the environment. If this aspect be a material object, a physical attitude is involved. If the aspect be a person, then a social attitude has developed. Social attitudes may include person toward person, person toward group, group toward group, and even person toward himself.

If the tendency to react is favorable the object toward which the attitude is directed becomes a value, and in this case, a positive value. If the tendency is unfavorable, the result is a negative value. A number of well-knit favorable attitudes together with their accompanying positive values constitute a general viewpoint. Likewise unfavorable attitudes and their negative values comprise another type of general viewpoint. The integration of one's general viewpoints represents the essence of a philosophy of life, of an optimist, of a pessimist, or of a frustrated person.

Attitudes comprise a large portion of the inner core of personality. If personality is the whole person acting in a social situation, then the acting discloses the nature of one's attitudes. There could be no personality without attitudes. One's attitudes may become expressed in one of three major types of life organization, that is, in "a set of rules for definite situations which may be even expressed in abstract formulas."[8]   These are : (1) One type of life organization of attitudes is the Philistine, whose set of attitudes may be such as practically "to exclude given conditions of life, because the reflective attitudes of an individual have attained so great a fixity, that he is inaccessible to only a certain class of influences — those constituting the most permanent part of his social milieu."[9]   The Philistine type usually accepts "social tradition in its most stable elements."

(2) The Bohemian type of person has not completely formed his character.   His behavior depends at least at times on his momentary reactions which in turn may be determined either "by some outburst of a primary temperamental attitude or by some isolated character-attitude which makes him subject to some indiscriminately accepted influence."[10]   The Bohemian type is unorganized in a number of aspects of personality and is undergoing considerable change in his attitudes.   His "possibilities of evolution are not closed."

(3) The creative type of personality is one whose character is organized to a definite extent but which may undergo further evolution because "the reflective acts constituting it include a tendency to change, regulated by plans of productive activity."[11]   He continues open to such development as will be in line with his openmindedness.   The term, "creative type," is somewhat misleading, for it suggests originality and inventiveness, even creativeness, which the definition does not necessarily include.   Thomas is careful to state that no one of the three aforementioned types of personality is ever "completely and absolutely realized by a human individual in all lines of activity."[12]

Attitudes are a vital part of one's character.   If they are well integrated and organized with reference to the major aspects of life, one is said to have a strong character.   He knows what he wants.   He stands four square for certain policies and procedures.   If his attitudes are relatively un-

8 *The Polish Peasant in Europe and America, op. cit.,* II:1853.
9 *Ibid.*
10 *Ibid.*
11 *Ibid.,* II:1855.
12 *Ibid.,* II:1854.

organized and not integrated, he acts in a wishy-washy fashion, he is not dependable and is said to have a weak character. This classification of character is psychological.

If one's attitudes are organized around what are considered goodness and rightness, he is said to have a good character. If they are organized around cheating, lying, robbing, his is described as a bad character. This classification is ethical. All persons represent combinations of psychological and ethical character.

The character of a person, according to Thomas, may be viewed from four different angles. (1) Character may be determined on the ground of temperament. "Theoretically any possible character might be involved out of any temperament." [13] An individual may have an aspect of his temperament suppressed in order "to attain a character that he wants." An individual may be isolated from or isolate himself from all experiences that may give stimulation "to endeavors to define situations by the undesirable tendency."

(2) Character may be found in the constitution of a life-organization which permits a more or less objective expression of the various constituent attitudes. (3) Character may develop out of the indirect or direct social demands placed upon personality. In each group specific characters develop in line with the group's particular interests, e.g., a family person, a religious person, a sportsman, a drunkard. [14] (4) Character also develops as an adaptation of the individual's life-organization to social organization. There is a growing difficulty of maintaining a stable social organization "in the face of the increasing importance which individual efficiency assumes in all domains of cultural life." [15]

Attitudes vary from temporary to permanent. The temporary relate to objects on the periphery of one's personal objects of attention and interest. They involve no special feeling or emotional elements. At the other pole are the attitudes that are set and fast in strong emotional reactions. They are held firm in sentiment. Attitudes set in sentiments of hate or genuine love are hard to change.

[13] *Ibid.*, II:1863.
[14] *Ibid.*, II:1886.
[15] *Ibid.*, II:1898.

Attitudes may be chiefly cognitive, or refer to ideational reactions.   They may be affective, that is highly charged with feelings, emotions, sentiments.   They may be primarily conative, or ready to burst into action, without much thought being involved and with or without emotional manifestations.[16]   Some attitudes may express cognitive, affective, and conative responses, all three combined in somewhat equal proportions.

Attitudes bear a relation to motivation.   In other words, what sets off or releases an attitude and produces action? The answer depends on the set of the attitude, that is, what stimulus is it set to respond to?   The answer depends too on the appearance of the appropriate stimulus.   If it does not appear, the given attitude is not released, and the person is not motivated.

Attitudes may explain a great deal of social perception. Since one perceives only a very small proportion of his social environment, it makes a difference what part he perceives and to which he responds.   If he has attitudes to respond to certain social stimuli, and not to others, he will perceive the first type of stimuli and not the second.[17]   In forming one's attitudes one goes a long way in fashioning his social perceptive tendencies.

DEFINING THE SOCIAL SITUATION

Attitudes have their sources in original biological forces, in reactions to past experiences and the life organization of these reactions, and in a person's reactions to his experiences in current social situations.   Thomas brought the concept of social situation to the center of social thought.   "The situation is the set of values and attitudes with which the individual or group has to deal in a process of activity and with regard to which this activity is planned and its results appreciated."[18]   The situation involves three types of data.

[16] Robert F. Bales, *Interaction Process Analysis* (Cambridge, Massachusetts: Addison-Wesley Press, Inc., 1951), pp. 52, 53.

[17] See Jerome S. Bruner and Leo Postman, "An Approach to Social Perception," in Wayne Dennis, Editor, *Current Trends in Social Psychology* (Pittsburgh: University of Pittsburgh Press, 1948), pp. 71-118.

[18] Kimball Young, *Social Attitudes*, Editor, *op. cit.*, p. 10.

First, there are "the objective conditions under which the individual or society act, that is, the totality of values... which at the given moment affect directly or indirectly the conscious states of the individual or the group." Second, there are the preexisting attitudes of the individual or the group which at the given moment have an actual influence upon his behavior. Third, the definition of the situation, that is, "the more or less clear conception of the conditions and consciousness of attitudes." [19] In this explanation it will be noticed that the definition of the situation is very important. To understand a person's behavior in any situation it is necessary to know how he defines that situation, that is, what attitudes does it arouse in him, what values if any function in it for him, in short, what meanings does it have for him? "It is these meanings which determine the individual's behavior." [20]

Thomas summarizes the functional and processual aspects of defining the situation as follows: "An adjustive effort of any kind is preceded by a decision to act or not act along a given line." Further, this decision is preceded by a definition of the situation, that is to say, "an interpretation or point of view, and eventually a policy and behavior pattern." [21] Thus, the definition of the situation is seen to play a vital role in every human decision involving interpersonal relationships.

In order that one may develop social attitudes one learns how to relate personal meanings to the needs of society. This adaptation of personal meanings to social needs involves the development of what is called ethical character, while the parallel development of intellectual methods of controlling social reality leads to a life-organization or to character in the psychological sense. It is assumed that a social system "which the individual voluntarily helps to realize must acquire gradually in his eyes a much greater importance and desirability than a system which is imposed on him." [22] The cooperative method thus is much sounder than the coercive methods used

[19] *The Polish Peasant in Europe and America, op. cit.,* I:68.
[20] *Ibid.,* II:1849.
[21] William I. Thomas, *Primitive Behavior* (New York: McGraw-Hill Book Company, 1937), p. 8.
[22] *The Polish Peasant in Europe and America, op. cit.,* II:1429.

by totalitarianism. Although the applications of the co-operative ideal have been limited and imperfect this ideal "is eminently capable of becoming the leading principle of a social order whose possibilities of expansion and improvement are practically unlimited." [23]

DISORGANIZATION OF SOCIAL ATTITUDES

Considerable importance is attached by Thomas to the concept of disorganization of social attitudes. This disorganization is due to "a decrease in the influence of existing social rules of behavior upon individual members of the group." [24] It is a universal phenomenon because "always and everywhere there are individual cases of breaking social rules which exercise some disorganizing influence on group institutions and if not counteracted are apt to multiply and to lead to a complete decay" of these institutions. [25] Some social disorganization cannot be avoided when a community comes in contact with outside communities and when its members learn of standards different from its own.

Social disorganization involves (a) the decay of group opinion, (b) the decay of community solidarity, and (c) the causal explanations of these decaying tendencies. Vital questions are : Why do individual members neglect community obligations ? Why do individual members engage in antagonisms with other members to the extent of breaking the community solidarity ?

Social disorganization may be regarded as a breakdown of group attitudes. It is a universal phenomenon because "always and everywhere there are individual cases of breaking social rules, cases which exercise some disorganizating influence on group institutions and if not counteracted are apt to multiply and to lead to a complete decay" of these institutions. [26] Social disorganization reflects the disorganization of the attitudes of individual members, particularly of attitudes of group loyalty and of group morale.

Social disorganization involves (a) the decay of group at-

[23] *Ibid.*
[24] *Ibid.,* II:1128.
[25] *Ibid.,* II:1130.
[26] *Ibid.,* II:1129.

titudes and opinion, (b) the breakdown of group organization of attitudes or solidarity, and (c) the factors that explain these decaying tendencies. Attitudes develop that conflict with the group aims and organization, and the question arises of how to handle these challenging forces so as to maintain a vital and yet flexible social organization.

Universal causes of social disorganization, or laws, cannot be found. "We can only hope to determine causes which always and everywhere produce certain definite attitudes." [27] These are the attitudes which explain the objective, superficial evidences of disorganization. A social group in its attempt to resist disorganization will try to reorganize the attitudes of some or many of its dissatisfied members. It will at least develop attitudes that will counterbalance the new divergent, discordant ones.

A revolution involves the demand for new values for a whole group — community, class, nation.[28] A revolt does not aim at a complete change in a traditional system of attitudes, but a revolution is inclusive in its demand for a change in the traditional system. A revolution seeks a more or less complete and apparently sudden change in the established attitudes of the members.

METHODOLOGY

Thomas made a major contribution to social thought in the field of methodology, particularly in connection with documentary materials that reveal the sources and nature of social attitudes. He began with social psychological interpretations of concrete, ethnological materials but later changed to the analysis of data obtained from various sources "in terms of a conceptual framework." He developed one concept after another, which look toward the formation of a social-psychological conceptual system.[29] He continually sought concrete data and empirical evidence. He interpreted the behavior and attitudes of persons as reported in human documents. He worked with human documents of five

[27] *Ibid.*, II:1132.
[28] *Ibid.*, II:1265.
[29] Ernest W. Burgess, "William I. Thomas as a Teacher," *Sociology and Social Research*, 32:762.

kinds : (1) Letters, thousands of them (particularly with the aid of Znaniecki). He interpreted the contents of letters in terms of a conceptual framework that gave them meaning. (2) Life histories. The life history is a free and frank and personal uncovering not only of a person's experiences but also of his reactions to his experiences. It is valuable in that it observes the whole process of a personality evolution, ascertains the nature of social personality and characterizes it as a type.[30] (3) Intimate newspaper accounts. (4) Court records. (5) Records of social agencies. Undoubtedly Thomas made the most of the first three types of materials. Of these, the second or life-history yielded the most significant results under Thomas' analytical procedures.

In introducing the lengthy and now almost classical life history of a Polish peasant the following explanation is made. "We shall presently follow the life-history of an individual who living amidst this process of change, finds in his environment no place for himself, because his fundamental attitudes correspond entirely to the old type of social organization whereas by his social status he no longer belongs to this organization and is thrown without any permanent guidance into various new conditions to which he can adapt himself always only partially and imperfectly." [31]

Thomas gave life-histories a high rating. He spoke of them, when they are as complete as possible, as constituting "the perfect type of sociological material." [32] Even in searching for abstract laws "life-records of concrete personalities have marked superiority over many other kinds of materials." For the characterization of attitudes and values "personal life-records give us the most exact approach." They enable one "to trace the career of an attitude and follow its evolution through a series of experiences." [33]

Thomas faced the practical difficulty of how to recognize the data which are important. He analyzed his data into their elements and systemized the elements. He worked with two kinds of data : (1) "the objective cultural elements of

[30] Herbert Blumer, *Critiques of Research in the Social Sciences* (New York: Social Science Research Council, 1939), p. 41.
[31] *The Polish Peasant in Europe and America, op. cit.*, II:1117.
[32] *Ibid.*, II:1832.
[33] Blumer, *op. cit.*, p. 40.

social life" and (2) "the subjective characteristics of the members of the social group." [34] The first mentioned he considered as values and the second as attitudes. The values are stimuli and the attitudes are action tendencies. [35]

Since a life-history of one person when fully recorded is an extended document requiring hours and days to obtain and record, it is necessary to limit this type of research to "a few representative documents whose study will yield results as nearly applicable as possible to all other types concerned." [36] Thomas recognized the difficulty in selecting representative cases in the social science field. He never used statistical procedures in order to do so, although in his later life he showed an appreciation of social statistics.

Thomas endorsed the idea that the ultimate object of scientific study is prediction, for as he said, "with prediction we have control." However, he held that the sociologist cannot set up experiments with the precision found in the chemical laboratory. It is not possible for the sociologist to hold the various factors consistent "while he measures the influences of the variation of some particular factor and everywhere the complications of the data have led to difficulties in the way of objective analysis." [37] While supporting the method of verification through statistics in most fields of human behavior, Thomas urged the "continual and detailed study of case-histories and life-histories." Any behavior reaction can be studied only in connection with the whole context, that is, "the situation as it exists in verifiable, objective terms." [38] But the total situation cannot be defined satisfactorily, for it is too complex. It involves "the interaction of language and gesture and gossip and print and symbols and slogans and propaganda and imitation," and so on. [39] Thomas used the term measurement in a special sense as indicated in his statement that by "comparing the histories of personalities as determined by social influences and expressed in various schemes of life we can establish a measure of given influ-

[34] The Polish Peasant in Europe and America, op. cit., I:20.
[35] The Unconscious, A Symposium, op. cit., p. 144.
[36] The Polish Peasant in Europe and America, op. cit., II:1835.
[37] William I. Thomas, The Child in America (New York: Alfred A. Knopf, Inc., 1928), p. 563.
[38] Ibid., p. 572.
[39] Ibid., p. 575.

ences." [40]   He summed up his idea of scientific method in the social sciences in the processes of analyzing, comparing, and interpreting (in terms of the total social situation that is involved).

Social psychology was defined by Thomas as being "precisely the science of attitudes and that while its methods are essentially different from the methods of individual psychology its field is as wide as conscious life." [41]   In social psychology the importance of an attitude is "proportionate to the number and variety of actions in which this attitude is manifested."   In other words, "the more generally an attitude is shared by the members of a given social group and the greater the part which it plays in the life of every member," the greater is social psychology interested in it. [42]   Thus, social psychology is viewed as performing the role of "a general science of the subjective side of social culture."   Thomas even referred to it as "the science of consciousness as manifested in culture." [43]   The field of social psychology comprises the attitudes of the individual toward all cultural values of a given social group, while sociology may be viewed as the science of social organization in its relation to individual attitudes.

READINGS

Asch, Solomon, *Social Psychology* (New York: Prentice-Hall, Inc. 1952), Chs. 18, 19.

Barnes, Harry E., Editor, *An Introduction to the History of Sociology* (Chicago: The University of Chicago Press 1948), Ch. XL.

Blumer, Herbert, *An Appraisal of Thomas and Znaniecki's The Polish Peasant in Europe and America* (New York: Social Science Research Bulletin 44, 1939).

Bogardus, Emory S., "The Sociology of William I. Thomas," *Sociology and Social Research*, 34:34-48.

———, "William I. Thomas and Social Origins," *Sociology and Social Research*, 43:362-69.

Burgess, Ernest W., "William I. Thomas as a Teacher," *Sociology and Social Research*, 32:260-64.

Faris, Ellsworth, "William I. Thomas (1863-1947)," *Sociology and Social Research*, 32:755-59.

---

[40] *The Unadjusted Girl, op. cit.,* p. 250.
[41] *The Polish Peasant in Europe and America, op. cit.,* I:27.
[42] *Ibid.,* p. 29.
[43] *Ibid.,* p. 31.

Hinkle, Gisela J., "The 'Four Wishes' in Thomas' Theory of Social Change," *Social Research,* 19:464-84.

Locke, Harvey J., "Research Methods of William I. Thomas," *Sociology and Social Research,* 32:907-10.

Newcomb, Theodore M., *Social Psychology* (New York : The Dryden Press 1950), Chs. 3-7.

Shrag, F. James, "Measuring Basic Community Attitudes," *Sociology and Social Research,* 35:338-45.

Thomas, William I., and Florian Znaniecki, *The Polish Peasant in Europe and America* (New York: Alfred A. Knopf, Inc. 1927).

Thomas, William I., *Source Book for Social Origins* (Chicago : The University of Chicago Press 1909).

———, *The Unadjusted Girl* (Boston : Little, Brown and Company 1923).

———, *The Child in America.* With Dorothy S. Thomas (New York: Alfred A. Knopf, Inc. 1928).

———, *Primitive Behavior* (New York : McGraw-Hill Book Company, Inc. 1937).

———, "The Province of Social Psychology," *American Journal of Sociology,* 10:445-55.

———, "The Psychology of Race Prejudice," *American Journal of Sociology,* 9:593-611.

———, "Race Psychology," *American Journal of Sociology,* 17:725-75.

———, "The Problem of Personality in the Urban Environment," Publications of the American Sociological Society (Chicago : The University of Chicago Press 1926), 26:30-38.

———, "The Configurations of Personality" in *The Unconscious : A Symposium* (New York: Alfred A. Knopf, Inc. 1927), pp. 143-77.

———, "The Behavior Pattern and the Situation," in E. W. Burgess, Editor, *Personality and the Group* (Chicago : The University of Chicago Press 1929).

Volkart, Edmund H., Editor, *Social Behavior and Personality.* Contributions of W. I. Thomas to Theory and Social Research (New York: Social Science Research Council 1951).

Young, Kimball, Editor, *Social Attitudes* (New York : Henry Holt and Company 1931).

Znaniecki, Florian, "William I. Thomas as a Collaborator," *Sociology and Social Research,* 32:765-67.

CHAPTER XXXVI

PARK AND SOCIAL PROCESSES

The contributions to sociology of Robert E. Park (1864–1944) were tied up primarily with the rising social consciousness of the time and secondarily with the social conditions as he observed them. In 1914, at the age of fifty, he was persuaded by W. I. Thomas to become a sociologist, and at the invitation of Albion W. Small he joined the faculty of the University of Chicago. This choice at a relatively late age for entering a new profession was no accident and, as later developments proved, it was no mistake.

The choice was a logical decision. Park was essentially an iconoclast. He was quick to perceive weaknesses in sociological thinking and to react against the inadequate results. He protested against sociology as social philosophy and armchair philosophizing based on previous armchair philosophizing. He recognized that sociology had unlimited possibilities if it would only begin with people where they are and with what they are doing and thinking and feeling.

Park sought to penetrate the masks that persons wear in order to get at their true reactions and beneath the surface of their words. He became a sociologist partly because he felt that the discipline was wasting its time in philosophizing before its representatives had studied sufficiently the meaning of human behavior. When he became a teacher of sociology the field was still largely in the control of social philosophy, and when he left it, thirty years later, sociology had made great progress in becoming an inductive science, and he had played a major role in bringing about the change.

Small developed the concept of "social process" and one of his stirring phrases was "the on-going of the social process." Park began his studies from the opposite pole, namely, with human experiences. He treated these in a realistic way, classified them, and arrived not at the social process but at a series of social processes, beginning with social interaction and running the gamut of competition, conflict, accommodation, and assimilation.

JOURNALISTIC BACKGROUND

Park's background always stood him in good stead as a sociologist. As a boy he was free from many of the conventionalities of the time and learned to view human nature realistically and with a degree of common-sense objectivity. He early recognized social shams and desired to pierce them. In college he turned further toward a philosophy of independent realism in his examination of social life.

As a journalist his experiences, which ranged from those of a newspaper reporter to those of a city editor, helped to give him a direct, unaffected approach to human nature. On one hand he specialized in exposing social and personal foibles; on the other hand he perceived the modern city as a social entity exerting powerful influences upon people and transforming their lives for better or for worse. Hence, it is no surprise that he sought out those factors that make for environmental influence, and through them the nature of social and personal change.

Always restless in spirit Park perceived that journalistic efforts did not plough deep enough. Through them he could arouse attention, he could stir up transient disgust for things as they are, but only superficial changes would result. Thus, he was stimulated to return to university studies. To his undergraduate days at the University of Michigan he added advanced work at Harvard University, the University of Berlin, Heidelberg University. Among his American mentors were James, Royce, Dewey, Mead, and in Europe he came under the influence of men such as Simmel and Windelband.

A FRAME OF REFERENCE

It was a long mental stretch from making a newspaper report of a tragedy in some person's life to interpreting the events leading up to a tragedy in terms of a sociological frame of reference. Park made the effort and achieved his goal of thinking of events in terms of process and of interpreting them with reference to a sociological frame of thought. He repeatedly indicated that concrete social research is of little moment unless it is perceived first within a social frame of

reference and then in a sociological frame of reference.   The
first frame is essential because every act of a human being
is an aspect of personality, and personality is an aspect of
social interaction.   No act, no tragedy, no thrilling event
ever stands alone.   No thousand of human experiences
added up and statistically treated disclose their real meanings.   Research may begin with the experiences of human
beings but that is only a beginning.

The social frame of reference itself has a larger and more
meaningful sociological frame of interpretation.   This all-
significant frame is a conceptual system for which Park began
to search when, as a young man, he discovered that newspaper reporting in itself is but the beginning of something
very important, namely, the significance of what is reported
to those who are involved.   He also seemed to feel that reform efforts, in which he never engaged, arrived nowhere
unless they took into account the processes of social change.
Park's great teachers impressed him with the importance of
having an adequate frame of reference for studying human
life, and he proceeded to formulate one.   All the remainder
of his life he struggled to develop an adequate system of sociological concepts, but never succeeded in satisfying himself.
Always, however, he used the best system of concepts that he
had mustered at any given time and made full use of it, but
with the qualification that it would be improved when more
research data were at hand.   To him all research had its
meaning within some such conceptual system of reference.
The first major expression of his system of sociological concepts may be found in *The Introduction to the Science of
Sociology,* published in 1921.[1]

INTERACTION

Park's conceptual system began with the social process of
interaction.   If there is no interaction there is no awareness,
no understanding, in fact, no mental life or social life or
growth.   But interaction, being general and all-inclusive,
does not help much in analyzing human behavior.   One

[1] Park and Burgess, *Introduction to the Science of Sociology.* (The University of Chicago Press 1921).

specific expression of interaction that Park found of great significance is communication. In fact, he refers to communication as the typical social process.[2]

COMMUNICATION

Communication is more than the psychologist has found in the process. It is more than stimulus and response. Such an explanation unduly simplifies the process and also misses its essence. To Park, communication is "expression, interpretation, and response," [3] and of these three the greatest is interpretation. A not only recognizes the stimulus as coming from B, but he also interprets it in the form of an attitude toward B. To use Park's illustration : If when a brick falls near A he looks up and sees B grinning maliciously from the wall from which it was dropped, A will think of the falling brick as evidence of an unfriendly attitude on the part of B. In return he develops a hostile attitude toward B. Thus, the process of communication may be viewed as expression, interpretation, and response. Instead of dropping a brick on A, B might have leaped from the wall and given A a hearty greeting, and A would have responded with words of welcome. Again, the sequence of communication was : expression, interpretation, and an appropriate response.

Communication is also a process of transmission. It is the chief process for transmitting news. Park recognized great possibilities in news reporting and its circulation. For instance, he once pointed out that the conclusion of the Russian-Japanese War in 1905 in which a nation of "white people" was defeated by a nation of "yellow people" probably "circulated farther and more rapidly than any other report of events had ever travelled before." [4]

If news does not circulate there can be no interpretations and no responses, and hence no understanding of what is going on. Park suggested that there are gradients in the circulation and in the influence of news. For example, he

[2] "Reflections on Communication and Culture," *American Journal of Sociology*, XLIV:192.
[3] *Ibid.*, p. 196.
[4] *Ibid.*, p. 199.

pointed out there was a circulation of 91.2 newspapers per 100 population in Chicago; 78.1 per 100 population at a radius of 40 miles from Chicago; 49.1 per 100 at a radius of 80 miles ; and 42.9 at a radius of 120 miles.[5]   In other words, the farther one lives from a metropolitan center the less subject he is, other things being equal, to the newspaper as a source of communication with the world.

The role that "news" plays in communication was put by Park as follows.   The usual reaction of any person to news is to repeat it, that is, to tell it to several other persons as soon as possible.   "This makes conversation, arouses further comment, and perhaps starts a discussion." [6] Thus, news greatly stimulates communication.   It multiplies communication. As a result of this free-for-all communication of news, clashes of opinion and even of sentiment occur.   Communication augments the interpretation of news and makes possible the development of public opinion.   Without communication there could be no public opinion, and without public opinion, developed through the channels of free communication, there could be no democracy.

The process of communication can be and is used to authoritarian ends.   Censorship can stop free communication.   Propaganda and coloration of the news can abuse the privileges of communication.   Communication itself is amoral.   The citizens of democracy need to see to it that the channels of free communication are kept as nearly open as possible.   It is important that news be communicated spontaneously and without restraint, or else, rumors of all sorts, entirely unfounded rumors, vicious rumors, will be spread.

The nature of communication is fostered by news interest. Persons communicate most readily what they are most interested in, and they "forget" to report at home or to their friends a great deal of what is communicated to them in the course of a day or a week, simply because they do not think that such news is important.

---

[5] "Urbanization as Measured by Newspaper Circulation," *American Journal of Sociology,* XXXV:62.

[6] Robert E. Park, "News as a Form of Knowledge : A Chapter in the Sociology of Knowledge," *American Journal of Sociology,* XLV:677.

Communication is said to be "catching," as for example, in a crowd; and lightning-like in a mob. Communication may take the form of "contagious excitement," as in the herd. The pervasive social excitement of the crowd may be a major factor in facilitating the communication of news.[7] When a group of people are in rapport or in a state of general excitement, particularly when ruled by fear, communication functions at its greatest speed if not at its best social efficiency.

The dimensions of a person's world depend on "the direction and the distances from which the news comes" to him.[8] A person's potential development is related to the number of channels of communication that are open to him or that he keeps open through the newspapers, magazines, and books that he reads, through his conversations and correspondence, and through news broadcasts. His opinions and attitudes are changed in the degree that his avenues of communication reach into thinking and cultures other than his own. Everyone lives at the center of a world whose boundaries are determined by the nature and cultural length of his lines of communication.[9]

The phrase "area of orientation" of a person or of a community had special importance to Park.[10] The area of orientation, of course, refers to the reaches of a person's or a community's avenues of communication. A provincial person is one who communicates only with people in his own province, and a provincial nation is one whose people do not communicate beyond the boundaries of their own nation. Today the problems of one nation are the problems of all nations, and the problems of Abyssinia, of Greece, of Argentina are problems that sooner or later will affect all nations. The social problems originating in the invention of the atomic bomb are problems of all people. But most people in one nation are not in regular communication to any extent with the peoples of other nations. This international communication is a first essential to the development

[7] *Ibid.*, p. 683.

[8] Robert E. Park, "Morale and the News," *American Journal of Sociology*, XLVII:371.

[9] *Loc. cit.*

[10] "A Memorandum on Rote Learning," *American Journal of Sociology*, XLII:34.

of world-wide understanding and of a world-wide government.

COMPETITION

Competition is considered to be one "of the four great
types of interaction." [11] The other types are conflict, accommodation, and assimilation. Competition was viewed by
Park as a process characteristic of animal life in general, and
of human life when people are not in contact with each other
but are unconsciously struggling, each against the other—
man with man or group with group. Competition becomes
conflict when it is consciously engaged in by people in contact ; however, it continues to function in unconscious ways.
Competition is also involved in accommodation even though
the latter be a conscious process. Moreover competition
operates, in a way, even in assimilation.

If competition be "interaction without social contact,"
then the nature of social contact requires explanation. Social contacts are not limited to "contacts of touch or sense or
speech," [12] but include communication where meaning is
transferred and hence where there is mutual influence of
mind on mind. Consequently, wherever news travels, "social contacts" occur and communication operates and one
or more social processes are functioning.

Competition, being a subconscious process, is the dominant
one among plants and animals. It is the central ecological
process. It "determines the distribution of population ter-
ritorially and vocationally." [13] It explains "the division of
labor and all the vast organized interdependence of individuals and groups of individuals characteristic of modern
life." [14]

Park is usually recognized as "the father of human ecology." Not only did he coin the name, but he laid out the
patterns, offered the earliest exhibit of ecological concepts,
defined the major ecological processes and stimulated more
advanced students to cultivate the fields of research in ecol-

[11] Park and Burgess, *Introduction to the Science of Sociology* (The University of Chicago Press, 1921), p. 507.
[12] *Loc. cit.*
[13] *Ibid.*, p. 509.
[14] *Loc cit.*

ogy than most other sociologists combined. Perhaps R. D. McKenzie might be considered as Park's leading student of ecology.

Human ecology was defined by Park as "an attempt to investigate the processes by which the biotic balance and the social equilibrium (1) are maintained once they are achieved and (2) the processes by which, when the biotic balance and the social equilibrium are disturbed, the transition is made from one relatively stable order to another." [15] As may be anticipated Park thought in terms of processes, and isolated a number in this field, such as symbiosis and succession. He stimulated the use of "social base maps" that show the layout of "natural areas," such as the physical factors of a district that hinder population movements, for example, rivers and hills, and the artificial factors that also impede the movements of people, for instance, railroad tracks and factory-covered sections of a city. They also exhibit the occupational and residential zones of a city, and other economic and social conditions that facilitate and hinder the freer movement of people.

Park did not consider human ecology a branch of sociology but rather a separate discipline operating largely in the field of unconscious competition. It is, however, one of the branches of knowledge that logically precedes sociological research. Human ecology furnishes materials that can throw light on the nature of social problems and of human conflicts.

On its most developed levels as conceived by Park, human ecology "seeks to investigate the processes and mechanisms of social and cultural change." [16] In Park's hands such an ecological concept as "succession" becomes a study of the causes of social change. This study may begin with social base maps but it finally arrives at attempts "to make change intelligible, so that it can eventually be controlled by technical devices or political measures." [17] The study of succession gives attention to the natural history of social change,

---

[15] "Human Ecology," *American Journal of Sociology*, XLII:15.

[16] "Succession, An Ecological Concept," *American Sociological Review*, 1:179.

[17] *Ibid.*, p. 178.

that is, it is concerned "not only with the form which change takes but even more with the circumstances and events which precede, accompany, and follow change." [18] Park's treatment of the concept of succession is true of his handling of of other basic concepts, namely, he was prone to develop each until it seemed almost all-inclusive.

CONFLICT

The concept of conflict is noteworthy in Park's conceptual system. He seems to have considered it as the most important of the social processes, or at least one of the two or three most important. Conflict is a contest in which social contact and awareness are indispensable conditions.[19] If competition is unconscious activity, conflict is conscious struggle between persons and between groups. Conflict is of vital importance, for it determines a person's place in society, his status, and the expressions of social control. It is also important for it determinates a nation's place in the world of nations, its status, and the controls to which it will be subject. Park found the beginnings of conflict in unconscious competition. He gave attention to rivalry as a subtle form of conflict. He gave extensive consideration to race prejudice as an aspect of conflict. He declared that war is the most outstanding form of conflict.

Conflict may be viewed as conscious competition. Out of social contacts and conscious competition develop many of the characteristics of personality. Park enumerated these as "pride and humility, vanity and self-respect, modesty and arrogance, pity and disdain," as well as "race prejudice, chauvinism, class and class distinctions." [20] Conscious competition arouses and sharpens a person's self-consciousness. It may lead him to identify his desire for security and for recognition with the welfare of his group, and hence arouse in him many kinds of prejudices.

Rivalry is an important type of conflict. It is likely to be subtle in its operation, for it tends to hide behind polite

[18] *Loc. cit.*
[19] *Ibid.*, p. 575.
[20] *Ibid.*, p. 576.

social relations. In the rivalry of groups the welfare of the individual members is subordinated to the control of the respective groups. A personal conflict within a group makes behavior conscious; it indicates the need for thought-out activities.

An especially important form of conflict is involved in race relations. Race conflicts arise from differences in cultures and in color. After Park completed his formal graduate studies at Harvard, Berlin, and Heidelberg he did not accept at once a university position as might have been expected. For several years he associated himself with Booker T. Washington at Tuskegee Institute. He was fundamentally impressed by Washington and often expressed his deep indebtedness to the able leader of Tuskegee. Park's years at Tuskegee made lasting impressions upon his sociological thinking. The concluding eight years of his life, after he retired from the University of Chicago, were spent at Fisk University where he continued research in race relations. In fact, after meeting Booker T. Washington he never ceased to study race relations.

War is conflict in its most destructive form and yet with non-destructive accomplishments of great moment, such as, "the amazing energies and resources released in peoples organized for military aggression or defense" and "the colossal losses and sacrifices endured for the glory, the honor, or the security of the fatherland." [21] Park emphasized the ease with which the feelings and emotions of people, the world around, may be organized for fighting. He recognized that traditions play a major role in war. He doubted whether economic factors alone account for wars, but thought that these factors are definitely related to prestige, honor, and social position.

War defies precedents. War creates no principles by which it abides. As war comes to involve more and more powerful forces and as the importance of the stakes increase, war becomes a type of conflict in which respect is not shown for anybody or anything. War makers no longer bother even to declare war. They begin their attacks surreptitiously and show little or no concern for non combatants.

[21] *Ibid.*, p. 577.

Atom bombs fall or are dropped on little children and the helpless aged, on nurses and doctors, on ministers and priests of religion. "We do not know what to expect of war any more." [22]

Park suggested a conjunctive theory of war, although he did not use this phrase. He suggested that when three factors occur together in time and place, the fighting pattern becomes a reality. The first factor includes the pugnacious tendencies in human nature. The second refers to the forces of tradition such as honor of one's Country and chauvinism. The third involves "the exigencies of the situation," such as an insult to the flag of one's country, or an unannounced attack upon a nation's territory or people. Of course this theory assumes that there is no international legal authority to which the troublesome "exigencies" can be referred and by which they can be handled.

War leads to a reorganization of society. The victorious nation is never the same after a war as it was before. Not only its social organization has been changed but the ideologies of its people have been modified. The defeated nations also must revamp their social life to meet the demands imposed on them by the victors. They usually suffer the greatest losses proportionately, in people killed and in property destroyed, and they must adjust to paying heavy reparations. Even a victorious nation that fights for "democracy" and wins, suffers a tremendous loss in morals. War, no matter how worthy its objective, gives people practice in killing with impunity ; in fact those who kill most may be honored most. The pattern of regarding human life (of the enemy) as something to be destroyed has its ruthless effects, especially if the war be prolonged. The defeated nation suffers even greater losses of its morals, for if it fights stubbornly on, any acts that contribute to survival are justified.

War may be a struggle for land, oil, or resources, but at the same time it is also an ideological contest. It may start out as ideological but before it is over, or by the time the treaty is signed, vast material resources are likely to be involved and even to change hands. In its ideological aspects

[22] Robert E. Park, *op. cit.*

war becomes a procedure to establish a new or a different political and social philosophy of life.[23] It is important, therefore, that conflicting ideologies be submitted to the world, that their underlying meanings be brought to the surface and thoroughly explained, and that their merits and weaknesses become generally understood. It may be possible, thus, to work out accommodations without recourse to war. In a recent discussion of ideologies the prevailing conflicts are analyzed, and accommodations are indicated as being feasible on the basis of widespread and general understanding. Current ideological conflicts such as the conflict between the Eastern and Western civilizations, between traditional American individualism and current Russian collectivism, between theistic and non-theistic religions of the world, between Anglo-Americans and Latin-Americans, between Catholics and Protestants, between Arabs and Jews, between labor and capital may be resolved, according to F. S. C. Northrop, by developing in each culture a truly inclusive cultural idea in which each of the conflicting parties may find support. By this means they may work together instead of trying to destroy each other by engaging in conflict.[24] Each party needs to accommodate itself to the other, to allow it a place in which to function and to be respected. The members of the two conflicting groups may acquire mutual respect by working together first on matters of secondary importance. When mutual trust is developed on this basis, the conflicting groups may proceed to take up questions of primary significance. If each is careful to be worthy of confidence in this connection, satisfactory accommodations may be worked out and put into operation.

ACCOMMODATION

Park distinguished accommodation from adaptation in that the latter refers to "organic modifications which are transmitted biologically," whereas accommodation involves

[23] Robert E. Park, "The Social Function of War," *American Journal of Sociology*, XLVI:556.

[24] *The Meeting of East and West* (New York : The Macmillan Company, 1946), p. x.

"changes in habits or attitudes and their correlative culture patterns which are transmitted socially," that is, through changes that they call for in the social environment.[25] In fact, in this sense, all culture patterns are viewed as accommodations in themselves. They represent personal adjustments to environment.

Conflicts result in accommodations of one kind or another. Whether one group is victorious in war with another group, or whether war ends in a stalemate, the results are the same in one sense, namely, accommodations. Of course the kinds of accommodations in the two afore-mentioned situations are markedly different, but they are still accommodations, and thus the world of life is full of strife and resultant accommodations and temporary equilibriums. Social equilibrium is in itself expressive of temporary accommodations.

Even if conflict results in accommodation it does not end there. Potential conflict remains beneath the surface of accommodation, and may break forth in overt action. Accommodations, as such, are rarely temporary. When the balance, represented by accommodations, is upset for any reason, a new set of accommodations are needed in order to prevent overt conflict in the form of riots, wars, and the like. These, in turn, involve new accommodations. A socially intelligent society would anticipate conflicts by making necessary accommodations as needed in recognition of underlying social changes.

In a practical sense naturalization of immigrants is an interesting form of accommodation. Herein is involved changes in certain habits and attitudes, and likewise in certain culture patterns of the immigrant. These accommodations usually relate to changes in working habits; changes in eating habits come later, for they involve organic functions. Naturalization also calls for accommodations that are difficult to make, for they require that the immigrant give up his loyalty to his fatherland. If such accommodations run counter to deep-seated sentiments, they are exceedingly hard to make ; for instance, the English immigrant foreswears his loyalty to the Union Jack with great reluctance. Of course if the immigrant has suffered persecution in the land of his

[25] *Ibid.*, p. 663.

birth, as in the case of many Jewish immigrants, the process of naturalization in its political aspects functions easily.

A universal form of accommodation is that which Park discusses under the heading of subordination and superordination. These terms refer to various relationships such as submission and domination, slave and slave owner, follower and leader, football player and coach, child and parent, parishioner and priest. Sometimes these pairs of roles are mutually satisfactory, but often the subordinated are unhappy in the relationship and seek readjustments. If an authoritarian order obtains, then the dissatisfied individuals usually must seek inner adjustments through sublimation of their energies. If the prevailing ideology is democratic, then dissatisfied persons may work to change the rules of the game and to obtain a social order that will give them more leeway for personal expression and development.

ASSIMILATION

Accommodation logically and sociologically leads to assimilation, the next social process that is treated at length by Park. He conceives of it as "a process of interpenetration and fusion, in which persons and groups acquire the memories, sentiments, and attitudes of other persons or groups, and by sharing their experience and history, are incorporated with them in a common cultural life."[26] In one sense he views assimilation as the central cultural process, for it denotes a sharing of traditions and customs and "an intimate participation in common experiences." If accommodation reduces the problems of conflict, assimilation likewise reduces the problems of accommodation. Park's close association at Tuskegee led him to formulate his statements regarding assimilation largely on the basis of race relations.

If conscious conflict begins in unconscious competition, then conscious accommodations end in unconscious assimilation and acculturation. Assimilation is "the fusing of cultures," whereas acculturation is "the tranmission of cultural elements from one social group to another."[27] While ad-

[26] *Op. cit.,* p. 735.
[27] *Ibid.,* p. 737.

mitting that assimilation may be viewed as a result, Park gives his attention to assimilation as a process—a process based on prolonged and favorable social contacts. Assimilation is a social-psychological process and means "the growing alike in character, thoughts, and institutions." Assimilation is not necessarily limited to the incorporation of one social group with all its ideas and culture into another social group. Assimilation may be a process of mutual give and take, both groups undergoing modifications. The process is essentially one of developing a somewhat new type of group that represents an integration of both the participating groups.

In the case of immigrants, assimilation means both denationalization and renationalization. It requires the immigrant to give up one set of political loyalties and to accept another set but may not disturb all his ways of living. He may hold on to many of his sentiments connected with his boyhood days. He may contribute freely many of his early ideas to the land and people of his adoption.

Park pointed out that assimilation is natural and easy in primary groups. If an outsider is actually accepted as a member of a primary group, assimilation automatically operates. Unconsciously he adopts the ways of the group that accepts him freely. Only when he is opposed or ridiculed does he become irked or ashamed and hence intensely conscious of his alien origins.

It is in secondary groups that assimilation is slow. As long as an immigrant is a member of a secondary group he lacks the stimuli "to become like the others." In fact, if there are many people in his situation, a solidarity may develop among them and a new social entity may develop. It is in this way minority groups, as functioning entities, come into being. Park also contends that a new nationality may have its beginnings in this way.[28]

It is necessary to distinguish between assimilation that is only manners-deep and that which involves the making over of personality. The former takes place more or less easily, but does not mean much. In fact, it may be grossly misleading. The latter brings about basic changes in attitudes.

[28] Robert E. Park, "Racial Assimilation in Secondary Groups," *American Journal of Sociology*, XIX:620 ff.

in philosophies of life, and even in ideologies. If people have similar cultures, they will not necessarily assimilate. People who are alike in cultures may compete vigorously if not viciously and develop mutual hatreds. Assimilation is a matter of sentiments as well as of ideas.

Park distinguished sharply between Negro neighborhoods and Slavic colonies in the United States. "In one case the Negro has his separateness forced on him ; in the other situation the Slavic colonies have segregated themselves in order to avoid assimilation and to escape racial extinction in the large cosmopolitan states." [29] Even if the Negro in the South is promised and given equable segregation he does not like it, because he is segregated or set apart and hence set down by the dominant group. People generally like segregation if they can do the segregating, but they oppose it if the other fellow orders it. Forced segregation paralyzes assimilation; it makes the segregated group self-conscious and even belligerent. It prevents mutually accepted accommodation.

The first step in assimilation of immigrants living in cities is that "the immigrant ceases to be a provincial and becomes a nationalist." [30] One reason for this step is found by Park in the fact that "cities crush immigrant colonies together," and do not allow them to live in isolated provinces as many of them did in their home countries. In rural districts in the United States, by contrast, the rural immigrant colony "emphasizes local differences, preserves memories, and continues sentimental interest" in the home country.

Nationalist newspapers hold back the assimilation of immigrants. They tend to keep alive homeland contacts and to stir up afresh with each issue some of the old time sentiments. They help to keep the immigrant community active as a separate entity in American life. Through this community the immigrant moves slowly on the road to assimilation. Were it not for the immigrant community, many immigrants would become disorganized rather than assimilated.

[29] *Ibid.*, p. 621.
[30] Robert E. Park, "Immigrant Heritages," *National Conference of Social Work*, 1921, p. 494.

The latter process takes time, for it involves a reorganization of sentiments.

The "hyphenated American," as the term has been used, refers to the immigrant who comes almost to a standstill on the way to assimilation. Naturally, he gives up his old sentiments slowly, and naturally he is accepted slowly in the strictly American community. In the meantime he continues to function in his immigrant community, for as a person he must have status, and a long time must ensue before he can be accepted in the American community. He is delayed in the assimilation process, for he sees the United States "through the immigrant colony's eyes." On the other hand, it may be kept in mind that the assimilation of the immigrant usually begins before he comes to the United States.[31] Through letters from his friends and relatives who have already migrated to the United States he has learned many interesting things about the new land across the Atlantic, and in some ways he has become interested in obtaining the benefits of living here.

The assimilation of the immigrant is delayed often because of the race prejudices and antipathies of the average American citizen. It is natural to have prejudices, even race prejudices, according to Park, for "a man without prejudices is a man without conviction, and ultimately without character."[32] To these strong words, Park adds the remark that common sense is "a tissue of hunches and prejudices that have not been and, in most cases, cannot be justified on general and rational grounds." Race prejudices are widespread attitudes that arise out of powerful desires to maintain status. These prejudices of the native get in the way of the assimilation of the immigrant. The immigrant can anticipate race prejudices on the part of natives and accommodate himself to them or he can conduct himself so as not to arouse them, and in either case his assimilation may take place at a fair rate of progress.

Race prejudice arises partly out of race consciousness,

---

[31] *Ibid.*, p. 496.
[32] "The Bases of Race Prejudice," *Annals of the Academy of Political and Social Science,* 140:11.

which is an acquired trait, and partly out of "a sense of insecurity in the presence of the strange," which has inherited bases. It is important, therefore, that the immigrant who is in process of being assimilated and who desires to avoid being stung by the race prejudices of other persons shall not invade an established community too suddenly, or in too large numbers. Moreover, he will not act "in outlandish or incalculable ways." [33]

ACCULTURATION

Assimilation is closely and integrally related to acculturation, according to Park. The latter is "the process by which one group or people learns from another, whether the culture or civilization be gotten by imitation or by inculcation." [34] In the simplest sense it is the transmission of culture patterns from one group to another. More often it is the mutual intertransmission of culture patterns. Acculturation, also, is the interadoption of culture patterns by two or more cultural groups.

The actual connection between assimilation and acculturation has been suggested by Park's reference to culture as "the set of attitudes and values which we call the immigrants' heritage." [35] One might say that culture patterns are the values, and attitudes are their subjective aspects. Acculturation calls for changes in culture patterns ; and assimilation, for changes in attitudes. Attitudes and values are different aspects of an assimilation-acculturation process, which functions widely because "the fundamental patterns of life and behavior are everywhere the same, whether among the ancient Greeks, the modern Italians, the Asiatic Monguls, the Australian blacks, or the African Hottentots." [36] Moreover, the nature of man is everywhere essentially the same and tends to express itself everywhere in similar sentiments and institutions.[37] Then, why is there need for so much accommo-

[33] *Ibid.*, p. 16.

[34] Robert E. Park and Ernest W. Burgess, *Introduction to the Science of Sociology* (University of Chicago Press 1921), p. 135.

[35] Robert E. Park and Herbert A. Miller, *Old World Traits Transplanted* (New York : Harper & Brothers 1921), p. 267.

[36] *Ibid.*, p. 1.

[37] *Ibid.*. p. 2.

dation and why so much conflict between peoples? Park and Miller suggest the answer when they indicate that one group attaches values to one thing, and another group to another thing, and perhaps "different values to the same thing." These assignments of values arise out of the all-important course of experiences of each group and out of the feelings that are aroused by these experiences. Out of these differences in reactions, arise misunderstandings and sometimes conflicts. It is also true that conflicts develop where competition for the same values becomes strong and prolonged.

AMALGAMATION

Assimilation and acculturation are closely related to amalgamation, which is a biological process, but amalgamation is not necessary for assimilation, but follows somewhat naturally, more or less slowly. Members of different racial backgrounds in the United States learn to think alike on many phases of life long before they become amalgamated into one blood. They can think alike without looking alike.

Amalgamation accompanies and follows miscegenation, which includes both intermarriages and race mixtures outside of marriage. Wars greatly speed up miscegenation both of the legal and the illegal forms. Race intermixture outside of marriage has played a major role in amalgamation, but it usually takes place under circumstances of great disadvantage to the large numbers of children who are born out of wedlock. These products of intermixture usually have the care of only one parent; they may have the handicap of not being wanted ; they may receive very poor training ; they may become the victims of the social frowns conveyed by the term "illegitimate children."

Park sometimes referred to amalgamation as hybridization. In this connection he concluded that hybridization does not proceed everywhere and always with the same facility at the same rate.[38] He pointed out that in the United States assimilation and amalgamation are taking place at different speeds in different groups; that, according to one study, the

[38] "Mentality of Racial Hybrids," *American Journal of Sociology*, XXXVI: 536.

intermarriage rates for Jews and Negroes in New York are less than those of any other national-racial group, that miscegenation apparently takes place more rapidly "on the frontiers of an advancing civilization," particularly in seaport cities and large commercial centers.[39]   In these places customs are relaxed, a certain degree of anonymity obtains, and persons of many different cultures meet "under more than usual freedom." Park even considered amalgamation as "one of the indices, perhaps the ultimate index, of the extent to which cultural fusion in any given case has actually taken place." [40]

The role of romantic love in furthering amalgamation is also stressed by Park. Romantic love defies customs and taboos. It responds to the exotic. It may not lead to a large percentage of stable marriages, but it produces children, and thus results in amalgamation.

The mentality of the mixed blood greatly interested Park. For example, he found that generally speaking the mulatto is superior to the Negro, but that this difference is due largely to "the situation in which his mixed origin inevitably puts him." [41] He is both a cultural and racial hybrid, being the product of different traditions and of divergent racial stocks. The mulatto child in the United States has thirty or more times as great a chance of becoming a leader of his race as does a Negro child, according to Park's investigations.

The mixed blood is a somewhat distinct personality type. Again Parks draws his conclusions from his studies of the Negro in the United States. In this connection the mulatto on the whole is more restless, aggressive, and enterprising than is the Negro.[42] He is often more sensitive and self-conscious. He lives under higher tensions, he is more stimulated, and he takes himself more seriously. He has more intimate associations with the superior cultural group. Since he shares extensively in the life-experiences of two racial groups which are unassimilated with each other, he

39 *Ibid.*, p. 534.
40 *Ibid.*, p. 535.
41 *Ibid.*, p. 540.
42 *Ibid.*, p. 545.

cannot identify himself freely with either, and thus he be comes what Park gave special attention to—a marginal man.

THE MARGINAL MAN

The marginal man is one who is emerging from one cultural group and is entering another culture, who has not given up all his old attachments, often based on deep-rooted sentiments, and who is only partially accepted in the new group. He is generally the product of migration. He leaves an old cultural situation that is governed more or less closely by traditions. He enters a group where greater freedom in some ways exists. By virtue of migrating, he necessarily gives up some of his customary ways of doing and ultimately of thinking. To a degree, he is emancipated from old ways, but in becoming an emancipated person he also becomes, in a sense, a lost person, for he is not fully accepted in his new environment. Moreover, he repeatedly longs for his old attachments, but he cannot return to them. He also longs to establish new attachments but is often prevented from doing so. In this emancipation from old customs, however, personal energies are released and the marginal man is likely to embark on new adventures.

Thus, the marginal man may play the role of a social innovator—by being freed from limiting connections and by accepting and developing new opportunities. In this way immigration may bring about a social evolution ; it may "secularize relations which were formerly sacred." [43] The arrival of an invading population may release in them new forces that will change greatly the social order of the native peoples. It may lead to historic changes. It makes fundamental changes in the personalities of the immigrants and may change the complection of establish communities.

At this point, Park shows how racial problems "grow out of situations in which assimilation and amalgamation do not take place at all, or take place very slowly." [44] If the newcomers are not accepted, then the natives become more de-

---

[43] Robert E. Park, "Human Migration and the Marginal Man," *American Journal of Sociology*, XXXIII:888.

[44] *Ibid.,* p. 890.

fensive and the invaders become more aggressive. As a result a long-term race conflict develops with race riots likely to break out and race prejudice taking vicious turns, at times.

In discussing the Jews Park declares that "when the forward, outward movement of the race has been too rapid, it has invariably provoked a racial reaction in the outer Gentile world, and Jewish life has been thrown back upon itself." [45] The Jew tends to return to his Jewish community and obtains inspiration and strength from the old traditions for a time, but having obtained a taste of emancipation, he again ventures into the Gentile world. If enough time has elapsed the latter receives him, providing he has learned to invade the Gentile community slowly and non-aggressively. If this lesson has not been learned, an outward Jewish surge will bring about another wave of anti-semitism. Racial invasions may take place slowly or rapidly, depending in part upon the understanding and observance of the processes of acculturation of the invaders.

If the culture of the immigrants is not too different, if they are not too aggressive, and if they do not "invade" too rapidly, the unconscious assimilation process takes place and acculturation results ultimately in the development of a culture that is a modification of that of the newcomers and that of the natives. In this way, social change and progress peacefully take place. The mind of the marginal man when he is changing his habits, attitudes and sentiments is one of the best laboratories in which to study "the processes of civilization and of progress." [46]

The marginal man may be a frustrated person. If the distance between his original culture and that of the culture in which he seeks admission is great, he may fall into an abyss of frustration. He is a divided self—one part loyal to the old and the other loyal to a new way of life. He needs to be understood by at least a few friends or else he may suffer personality disorganization and possibly disintegration, as in the case of the often-defeated and isolated immigrant who takes his own life on the lonely prairies of the Dakotas

---

[45] "Behind Our Masks," *Survey Graphic*, IX:136.
[46] *Ibid.*, p. 893.

or on the equally lonely prairies of an anonymous district in Chicago.

The marginal man has the opportunity of being educated in two cultures. As a bilingualist, if he becomes such, he can maintain a communication system in each of two cultural worlds. He may become "a superior, though sometimes a superficial intellectual type," [47] by virtue of attempting to maintain status in two worlds at the same time.

The marginal man may play a leading role in the acceleration process. He can help in transmitting culture patterns from one cultural unit to another. He can become an educator in carrying the culture of one group into the life of another, and in stimulating the members of the group into which he goes, to recreate their culture patterns in the light of those that he brings to them.

In his discussion of methods of studying race relations Park gave a primary place to the measurement of social distances. He defined social distance as "the grades and degrees of understanding and intimacy which characterize personal and social relations generally." [48] Race prejudice he defined as a "more or less instructive and spontaneous disposition to maintain social distances." [49] But social distance goes further, for it aims to measure "those vaguer, subtler taboos and inhibitions which persist even in so mobile and changing an order as our own, and represent the stabilizing, spontaneous, and instinctive and conservative forces upon which social organization rests." [50]

THEORY OF PERSONALITY

An important theory of personality was developed by Park. He suggested a two-fold expression of personality. One is represented by the masks that a person wears. "Everyone is always and everywhere, more or less consciously, playing a

[47] Robert E. Park, "Education and the Cultural Crisis," *American Journal of Sociology*, XLVIII:729.

[48] "The Concept of Social Distance," *Journal of Applied Sociology*, VIII: 339.

[49] *Ibid.*, p. 343.

[50] *Ibid.*, p. 344.

role." [51]   A person wears one kind of mask in his group of intellectual friends and another among his nightclub friends (if he has such).   He wears one mask when visiting his bank and another when the assessor calls on him ; one among his staid and conventional associates and another when associating with emancipated persons.   The mask type conforms to the type of personality and group life that one wishes to impersonate.[52]   The mask may represent a person's ideal self, the self he would like to be, the self toward which he is moving.   On the other hand, the mask may indicate a self which, on occasion, a person is ashamed of, but one that he assumes for the time being because it will bring him status among certain people.

When a person lives to a great extent behind his mask, or when his mask is allowed to misrepresent his personality, he may expect to be misunderstood.   False reports about him will naturally be spread.   He cannot expect to be accepted at his real worth.   The introvert is likely to hide behind a mask, and hence be misunderstood ; as a result of such misunderstanding, he tends to hide still farther behind his mask, and thus the vicious circle continues.   The extrovert is more likely to reveal his real self in frank and open masks and at times to antagonize by his frankness.

Socialization is a social process with which Park toyed a great deal but which he never fully analyzed.   It begins in interaction and essentially ends in assimilation.   It is in a different category from the other social processes, for it functions in and through them all—through competition, conflict, accommodation—and reaches its end in the unity represented by assimilation.   Its goal is a world in which competition, conflict, and accommodation and "the externality of individuals" tends to disappear, and in which all individuals tend to live as one family.[53]   Socialization involves "the more or less complete incorporation of the individual into the existing moral order."   In this sense every child, as he grows into adulthood and maturity, moves up through one gradation

[51] Robert E. Park, "Behind Our Masks," *Survey Graphic*, IX:137.
[52] *Loc. cit.*
[53] Robert E. Park and Ernest W. Burgess, *Introduction to the Science of Society* (University of Chicago Press 1921), p. 496.

after another of socialization until he may be completely at home in the given moral order. Historically, the sociologist can see "the progressive socialization of the world" and the development of a world-wide moral order.[54] The socialization of individuals may develop at pace with the socialization of the world.

A THEORY OF SOCIOLOGY

In developing a theory of sociology, Park differentiates sociology from history. He states that when events are considered in their historical sequence of occurrence, in their time and place relationships, when unique events are described, the treatment comes under the heading of history. By contrast, sociology takes events out of their historical setting, in order to compare and classify them, to see them in processional forms, to put them into conceptual frameworks, and to emphasize the typical and representative. Sociology "seeks to arrive at natural laws and generalizations in regard to human nature and society irrespective of time and place." [55] Sociology is interested in the nature of the social processes reflected in events and experiences.

Sociology emphasizes description. It assumes that what is being done can be done again. It formulates natural laws and is a natural science, in that it describes, and then classifies what it describes. It sets up hypotheses for testing and it arrives at tentative conclusions that it treats as hypotheses for further testing. It assumes that these hypotheses can be proved or disproved by additional observation and experimentation. It compares, classifies, makes generalizations and concepts, and eventually formulates social laws. [56] It considers "the experiential aspects of human life," treats them as events, and transforms them into generalizations and concepts, that is, into knowledge, and indicates how this knowledge may be applied to useful social ends.

Sociology is distinguished from ethics in that it describes

[54] Robert E. Park, "Symbiosis and Socialization," *American Journal of Sociology*, XLV:23.

[55] Robert E. Park, "Sociology and the Social Sciences," *American Journal of Sociology*, XXVI:411.

[56] *Ibid.*, p. 416.

what has been done and hence what can be done, while ethics tells what ought or should be done. Often ethics, with its concern for the "oughtness," makes its pronouncements without adequate sociological support concerning what can be done.[57] When sociology reports what can be done and what effects follow given efforts, then ethics has a groundwork for the pronouncements of what should be done, and for passing judgments of good and bad on behavior and hence on persons.

Sociology is the study of collective behavior.[58] Collective behavior is the behavior of individuals; it is "the result of interaction, or of impulses that are common to a number of people.[59] It seeks to find the sequences and uniformities in such collective behavior and to state these in terms of processes and, eventually, of laws in such a way that they can be tested and verified.

Closely related is Park's concept of social control. It is the mutual subordination of individual members of a social group to that group's expression of its united impulses to action. It has various forms of expression, for example, spontaneous forms as found in the crowd; more explicit forms as found in gossip, rumor, news, and public opinion, and more formal expressions as in law, dogma, and political decrees.[60] The control exercised by the crowd is the most elementary form of group action. It is exercised "by the mere play of elemental forces." Control by gossip and rumor is also quite elemental and at times unpredictable, while control by public opinion is likewise fitful. Control by law, or by other stabilized institutions is definite and predictable.

Control in the popular sense is illustrated by "the arbitrary intervention of some individual—official, functionary, or leader—in the social process, as when a policeman arrests a person and a judge sentences him to prison. Such procedures represent social control because these intervenors

---

58 Robert E. Park and Ernest W. Burgess, *Introduction to the Science of Sociology* (University of Chicago Press 1921), p. 42.
59 *Ibid.*, p. 865.
60 *Ibid.*, p. 788.

are acting in behalf of socially authorized or accepted mores, laws, and public opinion.[61]

A practical problem in connection with social control is due, in part, to the fact that "the number of competent persons in a community is no measure of the competence of the community itself.[62] Many of the able persons who might be expected to take an interest in sane social control are so specialized and so wrapped up in their own specialties that they are not concerned in the welfare of the community as a whole. Moreover, incompetent persons often have an interest in social control, particularly in manipulating such control to their own gain.

The development of increased leisure time does not necessarily give people more time for problems of social control. Instead, many of them use this extra time in "a restless search for excitement." When the day's job is done, many rush away from the city and from their social responsibilities. In seeking escape from the wear and tear of their work they neglect their obligations to society.

SOCIAL RESEARCH

As Ernest W. Burgess has stated, Park had a "great drive for scientific investigation and an extraordinary gift for stimulating and guiding the research of his students."[63] Burgess goes on to say that Park devoted his life from the time that he began teaching in 1914 to his death in 1944 "with rare singleness of purpose to research." He was "prodigal of his time with students, partly because he deemed each topic significant in a total program of sociological research."[64] He was continually busy in charting new fields of research and an outstanding by-product was the way in which "his research zeal" was impressed upon his students. Moreover, it should be noted that "Park's investment of his time in his students

61 *Ibid.*, p. 789.
62 Robert E. Park, "Community Organization and the Romantic Temperament," *Social Forces*: 673.
63 "Contribution of Robert E. Park to Sociology," *Sociology and Social Research*, XXIX:256.
64 *Ibid.*, p. 261.

produced high dividends," in two ways, first in the relatively large number of "first-class research men who took as their life-work" a special problem of research which Park had mapped out "in its main conceptual outlines." [65] The writer recalls hearing Dr. Park relate some of his experiences after taking one of his most extensive trips, and the account was a description of going from one foreign city to another and visiting one after another of his former research students. In each city it seemed as though Park had a research scholar at work and that Park's main interest in travelling was to see how each of these persons was getting along and, more particularly perhaps, how the given research project was unfolding.

According to Ellsworth Faris, Park believed that it was better "to induce ten men to write ten books than to take time off to write one himself." [66] Erle F. Young brings out a related point, namely, that Park "in his research attacks cuts squarely through current preconceptions, conventional clichés, and closed systems of thinking." [67] This social research attack began "with an opening of the student's mind to new possibilities to new points of view, and to new methods." [68] To Park all social research findings were essentially tentative ; the research process was continuous ; no findings were ever "in any sense conclusive" to him. All the results of his studies were never more than tentative findings, hypotheses for verification and restatement, a means of improving the conceptual system or the frames of reference for interpreting human behavior, social problems, and the like.[69]

Park's classrooms were really seminars in discussion of research topics, of research methods, of the nature of concepts. Never were they cut and dried. He refused to abide by conventional methods in both research and in teaching. He followed the procedure of those whom he called his most

[65] *Loc. cit.*

[66] "Robert E. Park, 1864–1944," *American Sociological Review*, 9:324.

[67] "A Sociological Explorer: Robert E. Park," *Sociology and Social Research*, XXVIII:436.

[68] *Loc. cit.*

[69] "Sociology and the Social Sciences," *American Journal of Sociology*, XXVI:26-412.

inspiring teachers, namely, those who employed "the most unconventional and the least formal methods." [70] In the classroom Park sometimes seemed to be finding his way in experimental thinking. At times he would pick up what was a casual statement of a social situation by a student, and follow that out to many of its major implications.

No findings of a student report in class were ever "in any sense conclusive" to him. Although Park was not a teacher in the conventional sense, he was "one of those great teachers who can draw out of students the best of which they are capable ; and the lines of thought which he suggested to them, the meanings which he was able to infer from their scattered observations, have flowered in a whole series of diverse publications in the field of social science," [71] particularly in the field of community studies, of race relations, and of sociological concepts.

Park's interest in urban studies began with his work as a journalist. In 1915 appeared his first and well-known paper on the city. It set forth some of the things that needed to be done in studying urban communities and the process of urbanization. These communities were his laboratories and from 1914 on he was continually at work in them exploring for new ideas. In some of them he found fascinating materials, year after year, on the subject close to his thinking, namely, race relations. Throughout his studies of urban communities and of race relations he was mentally at work in making over and perfecting his conceptual framework, for after all, no social research findings are complete until they are interpreted within as accurate a conceptual system as possible. The subtitle of this initial article on the city is especially significant : "Suggestions for the Investigation of Human Behavior in the City Environment." [72] In this document he proposed one set of questions after another for investigation. Some of these sets of questions were answered ten or more years later in that intensely interesting set of research volumes known as the Sociological Series of the Uni-

[70] "Methods of Teaching: Impressions and a Verdict," *Social Forces*, 20:36.
[71] Charles S. Johnson, "Robert E. Park : In Memoriam," *Sociology and Social Research*, XXVIII:357.
[72] *American Journal of Sociology*, XX:577.

versity of Chicago, dealing, for example, with *The Gold Coast and the Slum, The Ghetto, The Taxi-Dance Hall, The Gang,* and so on.

In his conclusion to this pioneer statement on research of the city, Park sagely observed that "a great city tends to spread out and lay bare to the public view, in a massive manner, all the characters and traits which are ordinarily obscured and suppressed in smaller communities." [73] Park justified his use of the city as "a laboratory or a clinic in which human nature and social processes may be most conveniently and profitably studied" on the ground that "the city, in short, shows the good and evil in human nature in excess." [74]

In his research studies Park emphasized the "natural history" of persons. In considering human behavior he wanted to know not simply the opinions, creeds, and doctrines of persons, but primarily the experiences out of which these opinions and beliefs have arisen. We become intelligent about a person's behavior when we know the process by which it has reached a particular point of expression. We cannot know this process unless we obtain a free and full account of what has happened to a person, by virtue of which he has acted in a certain way.[75] Moreover, it is necessary to know a person's philosophy of life, that is, his framework of reference which explains his interpretations of what has happened to him. It is not enough to know what a person's physiological reactions are ; we must also know the nature of the physiological act.[76]

The natural history of a person's behavior may best be understood by the life history and personal interview methods to which W. I. Thomas as well as R. E. Park gave far-reaching thought. The aim of these documents is "to reproduce the circumstances" under which a person's attitude arose, and to do it so thoroughly "that the observer can enter imaginatively into the situation and the experience of which

[73] *Ibid.,* p. 612.
[74] *Loc. cit.*
[75] Robert E. Park, "Human Nature and Collective Behavior," *American Journal of Sociology,* XXXII:729.
[76] *Ibid.,* p. 741.

the attitude is a part." [77] The life history is an important research document, for it gives the explanations of why a person acts the way he does, the origins of his attitudes, and defines his motives and the process of motivation. "Ordinarily the behavior of another individual becomes intelligible as soon as we are able to reproduce all the circumstances, including perhaps the previous history of the individual involved." [78]

Another research concept that Park referred to repeatedly was the "social situation," a term which W. I. Thomas also has used a great deal. The social situation differs for every person, for each person defines or understands an event in terms of his own frame of reference. A social situation is a person's account of an event or of what is happening that is interesting. He sees the event in terms of his own frame of reference, which is different from everyone else's frame of reference.

The life history makes clear the nature of a person's frame of reference at the time of a given crisis in his life and explains how he developed this particular frame or scheme of interpretation. According to Park, a life history in a race relations survey is "the account which one individual is able to give of his own first-hand encounter, in a problematic situation, with members of another race." [79] In a life history, in this connection, it is important to obtain an account of first contacts, early impressions, later opinions and attitudes, reflections, and conclusions.

In his article on "A Race Relations Survey" Park gives four types of materials needed in a race relations study, namely, geographical distribution of racial groups on the land and in the cities, the nature and extent of occupations of the immigrant groups and the native groups, the nature and degree of the current competition, conflict, and accommodation, and the type of public reactions or the public opinions including the sources of irritation that are found in each

[77] Robert E. Park, "Experience and Race Relations," *Journal of Applied Sociology*, IX:21.

[78] *Ibid.*, p. 23.

[79] "A Race Relations Survey," *Journal of Applied Sociology*, VIII:202.

group.[80] Statistics will answer a number of these questions but they alone cannot give the main or explanatory information that is needed concerning the attitudes that are in conflict—only life histories and interview documents can give the real answers.

Another concept to which Park gave wide currency is "universe of discourse." By it he meant something "which has come into existence to enable individuals associated in any one of the several sciences or associated for any common purpose, to think consistently and to act understandingly, and in some sort of concert.[81] It has two uses, scientific and practical. Scientists cannot work together or even do teamwork if they do not understand the terminology of each other. Unless they have a common universe of discourse they will work in divided worlds. Statesmen cannot achieve commonly accepted agreements if they think in different universes of discourse. Likewise, any two persons are bound to misunderstand each other and to grow apart unless they think in one universe of discourse.

GROUP DISCUSSION TOPICS

1. In what way was it a logical decision for Robert E. Park to enter into the profession of teaching sociology at the age of fifty?
2. What factors in Park's background were especially valuable to him as a sociologist?
3. Wherein does social research find its meaning?
4. In what ways is social interaction the basic social process?
5. What is the essential element in the concept of communication?
6. Explain what is involved in urbanization?
7. What is meant by "the dimension of one's world"?
8. Illustrate a person's "area of orientation"?
9. What are the characteristics of a provincial nation today?
10. What is the relation of competition as a sociological concept to competition as an economic concept?
11. In what ways is conflict a very important concept sociologically?

[80] *Ibid.*, pp. 198-205.
[81] Robert E. Park, "Methods of Teaching: Impressions and a Verdict," *Social Forces*, 20:45.

12. Evaluate what is called in this chapter Park's conjuncture theory of war.
13. Account in three ways for Park's interest in race relations.
14. Give three concrete illustrations of accommodation.
15. Compare nationalization with naturalization.
16. What is the relation of the process of renationalization to denationalization?
17. In what ways can accommodations between nations avoid war?
18. How is accommodation different from appeasement?
19. Can you suggest a general pattern for resolving a conflict between two different ideologies?
20. Explain how accommodation logically leads to assimilation?
21. Is assimilation a one-way process or a mutual process as far as two different peoples in contact are concerned?
22. What does Park mean by social contacts?
23. Compare assimilation in primary groups and in secondary groups.
24. What are the objections to "equitable segregation"?
25. What is meant by "hyphenated Americans"?
26. In what sense is a person without prejudices "ultimately a person without character"?
27. What are the origins of race prejudice?
28. Contrast assimilation and acculturation.
29. What is the relation of acculturation to transmission of culture?
30. Does amalgamation naturally follow assimilation?
31. What is miscegenation and its relation to amalgamation?
32. What are the relations of hybridization to amalgamation?
33. How does romantic love sometimes play havoc in miscegenation?
34. Why is the mixed blood a somewhat distinct personality type?
35. What are the characteristics of the "marginal man"?
36. What is the normal role of the marginal man in acculturation?
37. How does race forwardness and ambitiousness arouse race prejudices?
38. Criticize Park's two-fold interpretation of personality.
39. Why do persons wear masks?
40. What is the relation of socialization to all the other major social processes?
41. Give as many differences as you can between sociology and history.
42. What are the relations of sociology to ethics?
43. Is social control a social process?
44. How is "natural history" different from history?

45. What are the strong points of life histories as research documents?
46. What are the main factors involved in every social situation?
47. How does social distances explain social conflicts?
48. What is distinctive about the ecological approach?
49. In what ways was Park "the father of human ecology"?
50. What are the connections between "universe of discourse," "frame of reference," and "area of orientation"?
51. In what ways would you attribute greatness to Park in the field of social research?

READINGS

Burgess, Ernest W., "Contribution of Robert E. Park to Sociology," *Sociology and Social Research*, XXIX:255-261.

Faris, Ellsworth, "Robert E. Park, 1864-1944," *American Sociological Review*, 9:322-325.

Johnson, Charles S., "Robert E. Park : In Memoriam," *Sociology and Social Research*, XXVIII:354-358.

Park, Robert E., and Ernest W. Burgess, *Introduction to the Science of Sociology* (Chicago : The University of Chicago Press 1921).

Park, Robert E., Ernest W. Burgess, and Others, *The City* (Chicago : The University of Chicago Press 1925).

Park, Robert E., and Herbert A. Miller, *Old World Traits Transplanted* (New York : Harper & Brothers 1921).

Park, Robert E., Editor, *An Outline of the Principles of Sociology* (New York : Barnes & Noble 1939).

Park, Robert E., *The Immigrant Press and Its Control* (New York : Harpers & Brothers 1922).

———, "Racial Assimilation in Secondary Groups," *American Journal of Sociology*, XIV:606-623.

———, "The City : Suggestions for the Investigation of Human Behavior in the City Environment," *American Journal of Sociology*, XX:577-612.

———, "A Race Relations Survey," *Journal of Applied Sociology*, VIII:195-205.

———, "Relation of Social Research to Social Service," *Journal of Applied Sociology*, VIII:263-273.

———, "Concept of Social Distance," *Journal of Applied Sociology*, VIII:339-344.

———, "Experience and Race Relations," *Journal of Applied Sociology*, IX:13-24.

———, "Methods of a Race Survey," *Journal of Applied Sociology*, X:410-415.

———, "The Yellow Press," *Sociology and Social Research*, XII: 3-11.

Park, Robert E., *Race and Culture,* Edited by E. C. Hughes and Others (Glencoe : The Free Press 1950).

——, "Bases of Race Prejudice," *Annals of the American Academy of the Political and Social Science,* 140:11-20.

——, "Immigrant Heritages," *National Conference of Social Work,* 1921:492-497.

——, "Foreign Language Press and Social Progress," *National Conference of Social Work,* 1920:493-500.

——, "Community Organization and the Romantic Temper," *Social Forces,* III:673-677.

——, "Sociology and the Social Sciences," *American Journal of Sociology,* XXVI:401-424, XXVII:1-21, 169-183.

——, "The Natural History of the Newspaper," *American Journal of Sociology,* XXIX:273-289.

——, "Human Nature and Collective Behavior," *American Journal of Sociology,* XXXII:733-741.

——, "Human Migration and the Marginal Man," *American Journal of Sociology,* XXXIII:881-893.

——, "Urbanization as Measured by Newspaper Circulation," *American Journal of Sociology,* XXXV:60-79.

——, "Mentality of Racial Hybrids," *American Journal of Sociology,* XXXVI:534-51.

——, "Succession : An Ecological Concept," *American Sociological Review,* 1:171-179.

——, "Methods of Teaching : Impressions and a Verdict," *Social Forces,* 20:36-46.

——, "Industrial Fatigues and Group Morale," *American Journal of Sociology,* XLII:1-15.

——, "A Memorandum on Rote Learning," *American Journal of Sociology,* XLIII:23-36.

——, "Reflections on Communication and Culture," *American Journal of Sociology,* XLIV:182-205.

——, "Symbiosis and Socialization : A Frame of Reference for the Study of Society," *American Journal of Sociology,* XLV:1-25.

——, "News as a Form of Knowledge," *American Journal of Sociology,* XLV:669-686.

——, "The Social Function of War : Observations and Notes," *American Journal of Sociology,* XLVI:551-570.

——, "News and the Power of the Press," *American Journal of Sociology,* XLVII:1-11.

——, "Morale and the News," *American Journal of Sociology,* XLVII:360-377.

——, "Education and the Cultural Crisis," *American Journal of Sociology,* XLVII:728-736.

Young, Erle F., "A Sociological Explorer : Robert E. Park," *Sociology and Social Research,* 28:436-439.

CHAPTER XXXVII

ELLWOOD AND SOCIAL RECONSTRUCTION

On the basis of his concepts of culture and cultural evolution Charles A. Ellwood (1873-1945) developed a theory of social reconstruction. In order to direct cultural evolution and social change in the direction of social improvement, it is necessary to change the culture patterns that prevail in a societary group. These culture patterns are expressed in habits, beliefs, and group practices and hence are all learned. In order to change them in socially desirable directions education will be utilized. As Ellwood developed his sociological thinking he became more and more interested in what he called the adjustment of human relations.

In his thinking about human relations he developed the ideas of Lester F. Ward concerning social telesis, or the reconstructing of human society in desirable directions. He opposed the use of force in the adjustment of inter-human relations and laid great stress on the importance of understanding and sympathy in these relations.

Ellwood's interest in social reconstruction was aroused by what he referred to time after time in writings and teachings, namely, the social problem. In fact he delivered a set of lectures and published a book on the subject. To him, the social problem "is now, what it has been in all ages, namely, the problem of the relations of men to one another," in short, "the problem of human living together." [1] His interest in human living together centered in all the failures of human behavior, and he proposed educational measures of reconstructing the living together process. He strove to give "a scientific basis for progressive, in distinction from revolutionary or reactionary, social reconstruction." [2]

Ellwood found the need for social reconstruction (1) in the prevalence of a materialistic philosophy which "denies the

---

[1] Charles A. Ellwood, *The Social Problem* (New York: The Macmillan Company, 1915), p. 13.
[2] *Ibid.*, p. viii.

reality of the spiritual values" necessary for civilization, in an individualistic philosophy which "denies the reality of the common life" and hence the need "for social responsibility and obligation," and (2) in a national egoism which "denies the reality of the common life of humanity and the unlimited obligation of nations to humanity." [3]

Not only Hobhouse with his evolutionary philosophy but Schmoller's historical emphases appealed greatly to Ellwood. [4] Hobhouse's evolutionarism was given priority over Dewey's pragmatism which Ellwood at first accepted. Paulsen's ethical analyses were accorded a large place in Ellwood's sociological thought, and Rauschenbusch's "social religion" was elaborated by Ellwood. Marett of Oxford led Ellwood to feel that his psychological analyses of culture were inadequate. As a result the latter gave a larger and larger place to culture and culture evolution and in 1927 his *Cultural Evolution* was published. In this work many pages were devoted to a comprehensive description of the historical role of culture in human relations. While he continued to stress "mental attitudes and conscious values of individuals" as the essence of social life, he believed that they could not be understood apart from their rootage in social tradition. [5]

Ward's emphasis on improvement through social telesis, or socially planned education, gave a framework to Ellwood's sociology throughout his life. Since he believed that human nature is composed largely of attitudes and values which are learned, he saw great hopes for social reconstruction through planned educational procedures. While admitting temporary defeat he never lost faith in the underlying correctness of his theory that human society could reconstruct its traditions and institutions if its leaders and its masses were socially intelligent and if adequate social planning and educating were followed.

Ellwood's theory of social reconstruction is based on the third of the following theories of the meaning of social life. (1) In which the goal and purpose is the happiness of the

[3] *Ibid.,* p. 44.
[4] See Howard E. Jensen, "Development of the Social Thought of Charles A. Ellwood," *Sociology and Social Research,* 31:341-51, for an excellent summary of the persons who influenced Ellwood extensively.
[5] *The Social Problem, op. cit.,* pp. 48 ff.

individuals. This hedonistic, individualistic, ego-centered theory has wide support in actual practice. (2) In which self-realization or the self-development of individuals is also largely individualistic. This highest-development-of-the-self theory involves both constructive and destructive contributions to roles in human life. (3) In which there is the development of a harmonious society of human beings, requiring an others-centered and a humanity-welfare-centered motivation of all persons.[6]

Inasmuch as Ellwood believed that social reconstruction begins with culture and with directing cultural evolution, these subjects will be considered first. But social reconstruction also involves social education and social religion as aspects of its motivation. It also calls for continuous research by methods that Ellwood referred to as humanized social science. Hence, there follows in this chapter a discussion of (1) culture and cultural evolution, (2) social education, (3) socio-religious education, and (4) humanized social methodology as bases for social reconstruction.

CULTURE AND CULTURAL EVOLUTION

Since Ellwood believed that social reconstruction deals with the nature and evolution of culture, he gave considerable attention to the composition of cultural change. The substance of culture is custom and tradition, with custom being practically always "supported by traditions, that is, by the knowledge, ideas, beliefs, and standards of the group." [7] Customs and traditions may be viewed as "the objective and subjective aspects of the same process." [8] Traditions may come to be valued so highly that a group may make them "hard and fast and unchangeable and oppose any change whatsoever in them," no matter how great the need for the change may be. This set of attitudes is called "traditionalism" and applies to institutions as well as to traditions.[9]

Culture is the differential factor between human groups

---

[6] Charles A. Ellwood, *The Psychology of Human Society* (New York: D. Appleton and Company, 1925), pp. 475, 476.

[7] *Ibid.*, p. 195.

[8] *Ibid.*, p. 197.

[9] Charles A. Ellwood, "Starting Points in Sociology," *Social Science*, 19:162.

and all other groups. Ellwood might have added that culture is the differential factor between human groups, ethnic, religious, political, and so on. Animal groups have no way of storing up what each generation learns from its own experiences. Culture whether tool-making, ritual-making, institution-making or idea-making is "all a process of learning and communication." [10] It evolves by laws of its own which "are only indirectly affected by the laws of organic evolution" or of physical evolution, and hence the methods of studying it involve different or special techniques.[11] The statement that, "organic evolution furnishes the capacity but social evolution develops the capacity," is an excellent summary of Ellwood's position.[12] Culture is "an appreciation of values brought about through the accumulation of experience." [13] Culture is invention or achievement; it is a means of social control. It is "a collective learning process produced by the interaction of human minds," [14] and thus is fundamentally a psycho-social process. The method of culture is "invention, appreciation, diffusion, and accumulation." [15] Ellwood's summary of culture is that it consists of "behavior patterns socially acquired and socially transmitted by means of symbols." [16] Perhaps he should have added "and by their appropriate meanings."

Ellwood developed what he tentatively called the parabola of culture development. He thought of culture patterns as changing very slowly during the first thousands of years in human history as a result of becoming enmeshed in static forms of traditions and customs. Then, with the development of incipient reasoning ability or some catastrophic happening a period of sudden and marked changes occurred. This period was followed by one in which we still live, where the early, the primitive, the irrational contend for domi-

[10] Charles A. Ellwood, *Cultural Evolution* (New York: The Century Co., 1927), p. 6.

[11] *Ibid.*, p. 14.

[12] See Howard E. Jensen, *op. cit.*, 31:344.

[13] *Cultural Evolution, op. cit.*, p. 42.

[14] *Ibid.*, p. 73.

[15] Charles A. Ellwood, *Man's Social Destiny in the Light of Science* (Nashville: The Cokesbury Press, 1929), p. 67.

[16] Charles A. Ellwood, "Culture as an Elementary Factor in Human Social Life," *Social Science*, 10:33.

nance with rational and carefully planned procedures. For example, according to the parabola of the development of property, primitive man had "little sense of private ownership and few private belongings." Then came inventions, and the day of communal property was followed by the reign of private property. Then, with the growth of the sense of social responsibility property was bound "to be limited to its rational, individual, and social utility, and state or common ownership arose." Hence, a parabola-like development may be discerned in the communalism of primitives being balanced in recent times by public ownership trends.[17]

Another parabola of cultural development consists of the slow development of science in the early forms of religion, a rapid rise of scientific methods, and now a slow development of humanized science.[18] Likewise the parabola of the development of morality may be noted. First, for long centuries there was almost no development in custom-made morality. Then, through a development in education the morality of individual power arose, followed by the current slow development of humanitarian morality.[19]

There are several theories of the causes of cultural evolution, for example, (1) the geographic-environmental, (2) the racial-biological, (3) the psychic-accident-imitation, (4) the habit-environmental, (5) the instinct-habit-environmental, and (6) the psycho-social. The sixth as held by Ellwood is "a process of active adaptation on the part of individuals and groups, carried on by the human brain as an active adaptive organ and by means of intercommunication among the members of human groups,"[20] and constitutes a basis of Ellwood's theory of social reconstruction.

SOCIAL EDUCATION

In reconstructing society by means of a humanized social science Ellwood banked a great deal on his faith in social education and socio-religious education. He elaborated

---

[17] *Cultural Evolution, op. cit.*, p. 191.
[18] *Ibid.*, p. 249.
[19] *Ibid.*, p. 224.
[20] *Ibid.*, p. 76.

Lester F. Ward's concept of social telesis [21] and urged a dynamic view of education, that is, an education that goes beyond simply conserving the social order; it aims at "the initiation and control of social progress." [22] He wanted an education that would produce efficient members of society, good citizens, who would not only take their places in groups but would "add something to the life of the group." [23] It is not enough for education to "emancipate the individual and develop his capacities." [24] It is not enough for education to be based on individual psychology, for the result is not always consistent with social survival or social progress." [25] Education based on the science of sociology could make a normal individual "many times more effective socially than he is at the present time," and could make much more harmonious the relations between individuals. [26]

Ellwood changed Wells' statement about civilization being a race between education and catastrophe to read that civilization is a race not between education in general and catastrophe but between social, political, moral, and religious education and catastrophe. These are "just the kinds of education which we have been neglecting." [27] But education of a social nature functions very slowly, for its task is that of making over the mores or those folkways which are judged essential to the welfare of the group. Social education is slow to the extent that the schools "are controlled by the mores of their time and place from which they cannot escape even if they would." [28] The socially needed education will develop and will spread those principles which underlie all human progress, all justice and fair play, freedom of the individual for thinking, investigating and discussing the welfare of each human group as a part of humanity and of humanity itself. [29] It is that phase of the cultural process which not

[21] Lester F. Ward, *Dynamic Sociology* (New York: D. Appleton and Company, 1915), II:90 ff.
[22] Charles A. Ellwood, *Methods in Sociology* (Durham: Duke University Press, 1933), p. 179.
[23] *Methods in Sociology, op. cit.,* p. 183.
[24] *Ibid.*
[25] *Ibid.*
[26] *Ibid.,* pp. 206, 207.
[27] *Man's Social Destiny in the Light of Science, op. cit.,* p. 81.
[28] *Ibid.,* p. 155.
[29] *Ibid.,* p. 161.

only transmits culture but more important, may enhance and enrich culture.

Education that will function well in social reconstruction will do four things. (1) It will free and train the mind of the individual. (2) It will impart definite social information and acquaint students "with our human world." (3) It will give social studies "the central place in the curriculum of our schools, flanked on one side by language and on the other by the natural sciences." [30] The social studies will "not only train the imagination but awaken emotion." [31] (4) It will control the learning of all individuals in regard to their ideas, attitudes, and emotions, as they come on the stage of life. In this way it will be possible to modify "the whole complex of our social life, or our civilization within the comparatively short space of one or two generations." [32] When education includes all classes and social conditions within one horizon, then "our sympathy, and so our love may be taught to go out to all mankind." [33] If religious leaders sometimes forget to include knowledge in their procedures, Benjamin Kidd failed to emphasize the need for intelligence "along with love or good will in our human world." [34] But Ellwood does not make clear the procedures involved in educating the emotions, except to say that indirectly "we can control our emotions through the control of ideas," [35] and then he turns from education to religion as "the great means of promoting faith, hope, and love in human society." [36] Ellwood had faith that love can be cultivated and controlled in human society just as well as intelligence can. [37] When people have learned to identify themselves with all of their fellows, "even with the lowest and meanest," they have entered fully into that larger life which is at once true education and true religion." [38] Thus, Ellwood sees social education and social religion as

[30] Ibid., pp. 166 ff. ; also Charles A. Ellwood, Sociology: Principles and Problems (New York: American Book Company, 1943), pp. 367 ff.
[31] Ibid., p. 175.
[32] Christianity and Social Science, op. cit., pp. 13 ff.
[33] Ibid., p. 121.
[34] Ibid., p. 127.
[35] Ibid., p. 130.
[36] Ibid., p. 132.
[37] Ibid., p. 134.
[38] Ibid., p. 149.

inseparable Siamese twins for meeting the social problem inherent in human relations.

Social reconstruction involves social planning and hence social progress. Ellwood was deeply interested in "rationally planned progress and collective achievement." This comprehensive undertaking involves these procedures: (1) To find and train efficient intellectual leaders; (2) to organize and make available all the tested knowledge that can be obtained; and (3) to diffuse the scientific attitude and general social intelligence throughout the group. The masses must be taught "to appreciate intellectual achievement," the scientific attitude and value of intellectual guidance.[39]

Social planning may be expected to result in "a certain freeing of the individual so that he can have fullest opportunity for normal development."[40] Ellwood did not seek "supermen" of the Nietzschean formula, who are "beyond the need for social control" but the socialization of attitudes of everyone organized under the direction of socially responsible leaders. It is the function chiefly of the schools, particularly of the universities, to find and train these leaders. But "a scientifically-trained leadership along non-material lines" will avail little "if the general cultural level of the people has not been raised to the point where they can appreciate such leadership.[41] Ellwood challenged schools and colleges especially to make social studies fundamental in their curricula.

Ellwood was interested in changing the motivation of people by socio-educational processes. Instead of obtaining or possessing something as a motive, he would set before all young people as the main motive of life the devotion to the welfare of other people and the contributing of something of value to the welfare of mankind by constructive or creative means. He inveighs against what he calls our "semicriminal civilization" which over-stimulates "the lust of possession and which dwarfs personal attitudes because of the "exploitation and deprivation" which it perpetrates on helpless people. An education that can save civilization is "one which will effect a psychological revolution, and lead us to see that men

39 *Ibid.*, p. 338.
40 *Ibid.*, p. 471.
41 *Man's Social Destiny*, p. 81.

cannot live together upon the bases of selfish aggrandizement, exploitation, or violence; that men can live together only upon a basis of mutual service, mutual sacrifice, and mutual good will." [42]

SOCIO-RELIGIOUS EDUCATION

Ellwood conceived of religion as "that phase of culture which is concerned with the highest personal and social values. It is a valuing attitude toward life and toward the universe." [43] In its best developed expressions religion "is perhaps the most intimate and personal form of culture, because in it all the hopes, fears, loves, and aspirations" of the human spirit are centered." [44] Because of its highly subjective nature religion is perhaps "the vaguest element in culture" and yet at the same time it is probably "the most vital element because it concerns the supreme values of life." [45] Religion helps persons "to confront the world with hope and courage and faith, and with loyalty, good will, and devotion to their fellows." [46] It gives man a connection with "a reality which lies behind both him and physical nature."

Ellwood contended that "the social reconstruction of the future must wait largely on the teaching and activities of the church," but the need is for a church that is "effective socially." [47] He decries theological and ecclesiastical systems as well as emotional mysticisms, but he pays little attention to all the prejudices and hatreds that have been expressed in the name of religion. [48] He bases his arguments on the social teachings of Jesus and gives socio-philosophical support to Rauschenbusch's analyses of the social gospel.

The Christianity of Jesus is "a new set of 'pattern ideas,'

[42] Charles A. Ellwood, "The Function of the Church-Related College in Our System of Education," *Religion in Life*, 7:71.
[43] Charles A. Ellwood, *The Psychology of Human Society, op. cit.*, pp. 271, 272.
[44] Charles A. Ellwood, *Man's Social Destiny in the Light of Science, op. cit*, p. 185.
[45] *Ibid.*, p. 187.
[46] *Ibid.*, p. 190.
[47] Charles A. Ellwood, "The Social Function of Religion," *American Journal of Sociology*, 19:307.
[48] "Religion and Democracy," *Proceedings of the American Sociological Society*, 14:132.

marking the dawn of a new civilization, a civilization with non-predatory morality on a humanitarian basis." [49] It endeavors "to transcend predatory, individual, class, tribal, and national ethics" with "a universalized, social international humanitarian ethics." [50] It is this type of religion which can be viewed as "the supreme embodiment of the values of life." [51]

If the spiritual values of Christianity do not control, the animal lusts of man will do so.[52] Today God or gods are not ignored, but it is the social teachings of Jesus which are neglected.[53] Moreover, Western civilization "has never been Christian." Today humanity is losing its hope and its radiance because faith in it and in the teachings of Jesus has waned in the lives of so many people. The great need is for "a revival of faith" in Jesus and in his teachings about peace-making, the brotherhood of man, and the cooperation of people everywhere "in the realization of a kingdom of spiritual values." [54]

Ellwood places a major responsibility upon Christianity's main institution, the church. He asked that the church develop techniques for teaching "effectively the Christian way of life to all mankind." [55] A major social function of the church is "to propagate moral ideals in society." [56] Its "higher work" is to create a "public conscience," in other words, "an effective public opinion regarding the conditions under which persons and groups of persons may live together peacefully and constructively." [57]

A concrete program for the church was proposed by Ellwood. If the church is to reconstruct civilization it may undertake (1) to combat "the increasing sensate character of our civilization" and get "body-mindedness and thing-minded-

---

[49] *The Reconstruction of Religion* (New York: The Macmillan Company, 1922), p. 85.
[50] *Ibid.*
[51] *The World's Need of Christ* (New York: Abingdon-Cokesbury Press, 1940), p. 153.
[52] *Ibid.*, p. 49.
[53] *Ibid.*, p. 20.
[54] *Ibid.*, p. 54.
[55] *Ibid.*, p. 179.
[56] "The Social Function of Religion," *American Journal of Sociology*, 19:306.
[57] Charles A. Ellwood, "The Formation of Public Opinion, *Religious Education*, 15:73.

ness" subordinated to "spiritual-mindedness," [58]   (2) to teach the need for universal love, or active good will, among all men as a means of developing a Christian civilization, and (3) "to arouse and organize enthusiasm for the Christian cause among its members." [59]   Ellwood greatly deplores what Sorokin has called sensate culture; he deprecates the easy-going hedonistic philosophy which is so common today; he condemns "group selfishness which probably has had more to do with causing the disorders of our world than individual selfishness." [60]

Ellwood's religious views are largely ethical in nature.   His bachelor's thesis in 1896 was on "The Social Sciences as a Basis for the Science of Ethics," [61] and the influence on him of persons like Paulsen and Rauschenbusch was considerable. To no small extent his was an ethico-psychical theory of sociology.   He held that "mere intelligence is futile in the solution of the social problem," that is, in effecting better human relations among people, and that intelligence "must be supplemented by the wide diffusion of altruism among the masses." [62]   Intelligence is "the capacity to improve upon natural tendencies through profiting by prior experience." [63] In order that intelligence may assist in bettering human relations it must be socialized, that is, made dynamic by moral motivation.

The conception of morality among primitive people was that "it was simply a matter of sharing customs," and immorality was "the breaking of the rule of custom." [64]   Morality today may be viewed as "the sharing of a social ideal," and anything may be considered moral "which works toward the establishment of an ideal social order or a perfect human society." [65]   Moreover, moral values are "explicable only through the psychic life of society as a whole," [66] and ethical

[58] *The World's Need of Christ, op. cit.,* p. 194.
[59] *Ibid.,* p. 196.
[60] *Ibid.,* p. 45.
[61] Howard E. Jensen, *op. cit.,* p. 344.
[62] *Ibid.,* p. 345.
[63] *The Psychology of Human Society, op. cit.,* p. 98.
[64] *Cultural Evolution, op. cit.,* p. 216.
[65] Charles A. Ellwood, "Social Development of Morality," *Sociology and Social Research,* 12:23.
[66] Charles A. Ellwood, "Prolegomena to Social Psychology," *American Journal of Sociology,* 4:664.

ideals are derived genetically from the social life. Ellwood prescribes for the solution of conflicts in human relations a humanitarian ethics supported by a social religion. By the latter he means "that which will exalt the service of humanity over and above the service of any individual, class, nation, or even race, as the highest end and value." [67] It is the self-development and self-sacrifice of people "not as ends in themselves but for the sake of the service of humanity" that Ellwood urges in a dozen different ways.[68]

Ellwood sees no change in the problem of living together, of human behavior, for it is "essentially the same today as it was 2000 years ago." [69] The solution likewise is the same, for as St. Paul said, "We are members of one another," and "whatever we do to the lowliest of our fellow human beings we have done to God himself." [70] The problem arises with every social contact: Will the participants understand one another and will they come to agreements regarding differences?

SOCIAL METHODOLOGY

Ellwood based social reconstruction upon what he considered a sound methodology. He remonstrated against making a god out of statistics and measurement in the physical science sense. He believed that such methods would greatly restrict the development of socially useful knowledge. He advocated the use of measurement methods "whenever and wherever they can be employed," [71] but not exclusively or predominantly. When sociology uses physical science methods exclusively, "it cannot guide us because it will miss the non-material aspects of culture and end in negation." [72] In keeping with Sorokin's line of thought, Ellwood declared that "sensate science cannot deal with the intangibles and imponderables in human relations," because "it cannot see the social process,

[67] Charles A. Ellwood, *The Social Problem* (New York: The Macmillan Company, 1915), p. 210.
[68] *Ibid.*, p. 221.
[69] *The World's Need of Christ, op. cit.,* p. 84.
[70] *Ibid.*, p. 75.
[71] *Methods in Sociology, op. cit.,* pp. 15, 85.
[72] Charles A. Ellwood, "The Future of Science," *The Scientific Monthly,* 28:545, June, 1929.

the process of interaction between individuals and between groups, but sees only the results of such interaction in the experiences of individuals." [73] Moreover, psycho-social data are not primarily spatial and temporal in nature, and hence "they can make little use of mathematical methods," [74] and "most of the important problems in human social evolution cannot be solved by narrow scientific methods." [75]

Ellwood advocated "objective thinking," or "impersonal detached thinking" not colored by one's subjectivity or objectivity. [76] To the methods of the natural sciences, that is, to observation, experiment, and the use of instruments and of measurement, he added logical reasoning, logical criticism, and synthesis. [77] He repeatedly emphasized the use of "scientific imagination in methods of research," since imagination is "the basis of all culture, of religion, of good citizenship." [78] Scientific imagination enables persons "to identify themselves not only in thought but also in feeling" with their fellow men everywhere. [79] Social imagination is the basis of an "intelligent social sympathy." [80] The training of the imagination in a social direction and the awakening of a social sympathy are fundamental to social education.

A subject closely related to social research is "participant observation" which is "the use of imagination to put ourselves in the place of the group described, backed up, however, by our actual experiences as members of groups" and "by our experiences with the class of individuals described." [81] The historical method as developed by Ellwood along the line of Schmoller's use of it, gives knowledge of the trends "of the cultural development of any people." It assists the research worker in understanding "the forces and factors, the possibilities and the probabilities, of any social movement or condition." [82] The case study may have important historical

[73] *The World's Need of Christ, op. cit.,* p. 61.
[74] Howard E. Jensen, *op. cit.,* p. 348.
[75] Charles A. Ellwood, *A History of Social Philosophy* (New York: Prentice-Hall, Inc., 1938), p. 557.
[76] *Methods in Sociology, op. cit.,* p. 28.
[77] *Ibid.,* p. 68.
[78] *Man's Social Destiny, op. cit.,* p. 170.
[79] *The Psychology of Human Society, op. cit.,* p. 332.
[80] Charles A. Ellwood, *Christianity and Social Science, op. cit.,* p. 199.
[81] *Methods in Sociology, op. cit.,* p. 74.
[82] *Ibid.,* pp. 80 ff.

aspects but as a rule it is "too narrow to throw any light upon the larger sociological problems connected with social evolution and cultural changes." [83]   The survey method is weak unless it becomes a study of processes and tendencies.   It too often neglects the non-material aspects of human relations, such as traditions, standards, values, opinions, beliefs.   Empirical research requires "breadth of scholarship to redeem it from futility." [84]

Behavioristic methods likewise offer "no adequate basis for dealing scientifically with the non-material aspects of culture." [85]   They do not show "the true nature of the social process," nor of "adult behavior which is essentially cultural nor of human institutions which are grounded in values and valuing processes."   Since the social sciences are more definitely studies of culture than of nature, and since culture is so distinct from nature, research regarding it must be conducted differently.

The social researcher cannot get away from value judgments.   He studies them as objects of research and he makes them too.   "Even the physical sciences are filled with relative value-judgments as to the utility or disutility of certain adjustments." [86]   The concept of value, according to Ellwood, "may prove the key that will eventually release all of the human sciences from their present position of pathetic if dignified futility." [87]   Since socially recognized values are products of human interaction and explain many of the human relations problems, an emphasis on them in social education is natural and necessary.

READINGS

Barnes, Harry E., Editor, *An Introduction to the History of Sociology* (Chicago: The University of Chicago Press 1948), Ch. XLIV.

Bogardus, Emory S., "The Sociology of Charles A. Ellwood," *Sociology and Social Research,* 34:365-73, and 34:451-58.

Dewey, Richard, *The Development of Human Behavior* (New York: The Macmillan Company 1951), Ch. XXV.

[83] *Ibid.,* p. 91.
[84] See Howard E. Jensen, *op. cit.,* p. 350.
[85] *Methods in Sociology, op. cit.,* pp. 54 ff.
[86] "Sociology," *The Americana Annual* (New York: American Corporation, 1943) , p. 665.
[87] *Methods in Sociology,* p. xxxiv.

Ellwood, Charles A., *The Social Problem* (New York : The Macmillan Company 1915).

———, "The Social Function of Religion," *American Journal of Sociology,* 19:289-307.

———, *The Reconstruction of Religion* (New York : The Macmillan Company 1922).

———, *Christianity and Social Science* (New York: The Macmillan Company 1923).

———, *The Psychology of Human Society* (New York : D. Appleton and Company 1925).

———, *Cultural Evolution* (New York: The Century Co. 1927).

———, "Social Development of Morality," *Sociology and Social Research,* 12:23.

———, *Man's Social Destiny in the Light of Science* (Nashville : Cokesbury Press 1929).

———, *Methods in Sociology* (Durham: Duke University Press 1933).

———, *Sociology : Principles and Problems* (New York : American Book Company 1943).

———, *A History of Social Philosophy* (New York : Prentice-Hall, Inc. 1938).

———, *The World's Need of Christ* (New York : Abingdon-Cokesbury Press 1940).

Hobhouse, L. T., *Morals in Evolution* (New York : Henry Holt and Company 1919).

Jensen, Howard E., "Development of the Social Thought of Charles A. Ellwood," *Sociology and Social Research,* 31:341-51.

Roder, Melvin, *Ethics and Society* (New York : Henry Holt and Company 1950).

Sorokin, Pitirim, A., *Man and Society in Calamity* (New York : E. P. Dutton and Company 1942).

———, *The Crisis of Our Age* (New York : E. P. Dutton and Company, Inc. 1940).

———, *Society, Culture, and Personality* (New York : Harper & Brothers 1947).

CHAPTER XXXVIII

MANNHEIM AND SOCIOLOGY OF KNOWLEDGE

Within the last three decades a new development of social thought has occurred under the label of sociology of knowledge, or *Wissensoziologie*. German writers have made the chief contributors to this expansion of thought. Karl Mannheim (1893-1947), who was born in Budapest, educated for the most part in Germany, and spent his concluding fourteen years in England, was the main developer of this field of social thought. His first extensive formulation of the sociology of knowledge appeared in his *Ideologie and Utopie* (1929). This work was preceded by five years by Max Scheler's *Versuche zu einer Soziologie des Wissens* (1924), in which considerable groundwork was laid. William Dilthey in the early part of the second half of the nineteenth century seems to have made initial contributions to this field. J. J. Maquet, a Belgian scholar, currently has made a critical analysis of Mannheim's sociology of knowledge and followed this analysis with a discussion of the role of Pitirim A. Sorokin in this field.[1] Paul Kecskemeti has also contributed a valuable discussion of the six essays by Mannheim that he has edited.[2]

But what is the sociology of knowledge? Mannheim defines it as "a discipline which explores the functional dependence of each intellectual standpoint on the differentiated social group reality standing behind it, which sets itself the task of retracing the evolutions of the various standpoints."[3] Stated briefly the sociology of knowledge is the study of the ways that social factors influence mental products, or knowledge.

Maquet arrives at the conclusion that the sociology of knowledge is "the study of mental productions as related to social or cultural factors." This gives a somewhat broader

[1] Jacques J. Maquet, *The Sociology of Knowledge* (Boston: The Beacon Press, 1951).
[2] *Essays on the Sociology of Knowledge* by Karl Mannheim. Edited by Paul Kecskemeti (New York: Oxford University Press, 1952).
[3] *Ibid.*, p. 190.

scope to the sociology of knowledge than the definition by Mannheim. F. S. C. Northrop concludes that Sorokin's works support the broader interpretation, namely, that the sociology of knowledge deals with the relationships between society and knowledge.[4] The opposite approach may also be made: How far do the mental products or ideas affect social relations? This is a vital question and is as important as that with which the sociology of knowledge deals, namely, how do social factors affect the origin, development, and expression of ideas? In fact it might well be considered in juxtaposition to the sociology of knowledge. At least it may be kept continually in mind when considering the ways that social factors influence ideas.

Ideas may not be viewed as wholly the result of social influences if they are considered to be self-perpetuating in any way. An idea may have in it the germs of a new idea which will secure expression without being stimulated by social factors. However, Mannheim contends that different social conditions do not necessarily produce systems of ideas "in a crude, materialistic sense," but in the sense "that social groups emerging within the social process are always in a position to project new directions of that 'intentionality,' that vital tension, which accompanies all life." [5] In considering the history of ideas the social factors may be viewed as having something to do with calling forth the expression of new ideas that lie germinal and dormant within old ideas, hence the reason for studying the sociology of knowledge.

PURPOSE OF SOCIOLOGY OF KNOWLEDGE

The purpose of the sociology of knowledge is "to show how the life plans of individuals depend on the sociological structure of the groups to which they belong." [6] As an extreme case, the ambition of individuals is said to be determined by the different areas of modern industrial society. In other words, economic factors influence the nature of ideas, the choice of ideas to be expressed, and the ideas that will be

---

[4] Maquet, *op. cit.,* p. xv.
[5] *Essays, op. cit.,* p. 188.
[6] *Ibid.,* p. 26 ("Introduction" by Kecskemeti).

accepted. Styles of thought are evidenced by economic and social groups; they vary from group to group, and influence the thinking of those who grow up in each group. Every development of a set of ideas occurs within the thinking of a group and subject to a group's approval.

The idea that "the economic system forms men, that society moulds us" is strongly emphasized by Mannheim, while at the same time he expresses the belief that "under certain circumstances men can also form their economic and social systems." [7] Mannheim thus escapes from social determinism, and accepts a theory of personal freedom. This is not an abstract freedom, but a freedom that can be achieved "only by exact observation of the field of activity within which freedom can be achieved." [8] A study of social determinism may be made in order to understand its interplay with the forces making for personal freedom. In this way the interplay of social forces may be put "at the service of an educational work in personality formation which one can pursue consciously in full freedom and responsibility." [9] A potentiality of freedom "grounded in mind" may be granted.

The wish of education has always been "to mould the rising generation according to some conscious or unconscious idea." It has "always sought to control every factor of personal formation." [10] Mannheim puts foremost the function of personal contact between human beings. "The personality of teacher, parents, friends in certain circumstances exercises a more profound effect on a child than his institutionalized cultural surroundings." [11] The vital effect of the personality of a teacher "cannot be replaced by mere objective cultural products." [12] A second group of educational factors is composed of objective products and achievements of a culture, which include knowledge and skills, and also moral and aesthetic values. A third aspect of educational procedure is to develop "automatic habits" which may give more stability to personality than ideas as such.

[7] Essays, op. cit., pp. 274, 275.
[8] Ibid., p. 275.
[9] Ibid.
[10] Ibid.
[11] Ibid., p. 230.
[12] Ibid.

The problem of *Wissensoziologie* as stated by Kecskemeti is "that of the insight which participants in a process of social interaction can have into that process." [13] A person has an advantage by being a functioning unit in a social process, and a disadvantage because of the difficulty of viewing it objectively and impartially. A still greater problem is this : May it not be that one's way of judging the results of social reality is in itself one of the results of that process? If so, how can one achieve a needed objectivity in his analysis of this or any social process? At least he can be cautious in making absolute judgments.

METHODS OF SOCIOLOGY OF KNOWLEDGE

The methods of the sociology of knowledge as developed by Mannheim accept those of natural science only in part. A mechanistic method that breaks up the whole into minute parts is unsatisfactory for social science.[14] The static concepts of natural science and mathematics on the one hand are contrasted with "the dynamic concepts of historic and social sciences on the other." [15] Social science involves the study of the meanings of experience to the persons involved. The natural sciences have no such problem to deal with because the atoms, for example, do not experience meanings when atomic experiments are conducted.

The significance of meanings ranks high in the sociology of knowledge. A modification of Mannheim's objective, expressive, and documentary or evidential meanings [16] may be modified and presented as: objective meanings or what can be seen and observed; subjective or the current meanings to the individual who is acting; and depth meanings, or the meaning hidden in past experiences of the individual himself. If the subjective meaning of a gift to a beggar is sympathy as far as one donor is concerned and the desire to get rid of the beggar as far as another man is concerned, then the depth meaning refers to the hidden factors which cause one man on

13 *Ibid.*, p. 32.
14 *Ibid.*, p. 188.
15 Kecskemeti in *Essays, op. cit.*, p. 5.
16 *Essays, op. cit.*, pp. 44 ff.

the sight of a beggar to be sympathetic and another man to want to get rid of said beggar.

Mannheim emphasizes the gestalt approach to understanding social action.[17] We do not understand a part unless we understand the whole. Hence, to understand a person's action, we must make our approach from the total human viewpoint. Nothing less than a world outlook[18] (*Weltanschauung*) is necessary if one would understand the action of any part of the world. From the world outlook we can begin to study the postulates of different conflicting groups in the world. We can trace these postulates to the nature and aims of the groups holding these postulates.[19]

To understand the postulates of any one of several conflicting groups it is also necessary to make a historical approach, and find out what dynamic factors have entered into the formulation of the given postulate, under what conditions the dynamic factors developed, and under what conditions and at what time changes occurred in the nature and the direction of these dynamic factors. No particular line of thought can be understood unless its social origins are brought to light. It is essential to investigate "the concrete setting of an historical-social situation out of which individually differentiated thought only very gradually emerges."[20]

One does not think as an individual alone or very far by himself. He begins with the thoughts of others and either thinks them over or thinks in terms of modifications of them or in terms of substitutes for them in order to meet new developments in social situations. He is first of all an integral part of an intellectual continuum which he may modify in a few particulars. A person belongs to a group not only because he was born into it, not only because he professes to belong to it, not only because he has a loyalty to it, but also because he sees life and the world in terms of the meanings that have been acquired by or developed in the group or groups in question.[21] Therefore, in order to understand

17 *Ibid.*, p. 305.
18 *Ibid.*, Ch. II.
19 *Ibid.*, pp. 184 ff.
20 Karl Mannheim, *Ideology and Utopia* (New York: Harcourt, Brace and Company, 1936), p. xxvii.
21 *Ibid.*, p. 19.

fully a person's behavior or facts about a person's behavior one must study the system of meanings that his groups possess and to which such a person is basically loyal. One life-history is not enough as bases for adequate sociological research, for "the individual life history is only a component in a series of mutually interviewed life-histories" which together have their origins in preceding life-histories.[22] To life histories of several contemporaries in a given social group it may be suggested that life histories of members of at least two or three generations of given families are a minimum essential for an understanding of why the members of a social group act in certain ways and with certain meanings. Thus, Mannheim makes an important contribution to the life-history procedures as developed by Thomas and Znaniecki.

Mannheim considered the development of knowledge as a social aspect of group life, and hence as a kind of social process in itself. More particularly it is a cooperative process in which the knowledge of everyone develops within the framework of common activities in which persons play a related but somewhat different role.

Inasmuch as knowledge develops out of collective activities, it is important to note that much of this knowledge develops out of "the collective unconscious." Thus, one of the functions of the sociology of knowledge is that of investigating and bringing to light "the irrational foundations of rational knowledge."[23] A related problem is that of finding out the connections between the irrational foundations and the resultant rational knowledge. Methods of defining and of understanding the collective unconscious suggest the problems of controlling the current collective unconscious. Mannheim suggests an approach through the study of the ideologies that govern the collective activities of people.[24]

[22] *Ibid.*, p. 25.
[23] *Ibid.*, p. 28.
[24] Cf. Ernest Grunwald, *Das Problem einer Soziologie des Wissens* (Leipsig: Braumueller, 1934) ; R. K. Merton, "The Sociology of Knowledge," *Isis*, XXVII: 493-503; Hans Speier, "The Social Determination of Ideas," *Social Research*, V: 182-205.

IDEOLOGIES AND UTOPIAS

Mannheim's contributions to a sociology of knowledge include his analyses of ideologies and utopies, referred to in an earlier chapter.   He conceived of an ideology as a group's system of ideas which is interest-bound.   If these interests do not change, then the group thinking will remain static and hence fall behind the needs of new times.   A group's ideology may be so interest-bound that the members are able to think only what the group wants them to think.   Interest-bound ideology prevents individuals from seeing all sides of a current problem and from being objective.   It encourages them to condemn what they do not understand or whatever seems to be against the group's particular interest.   In other words, they may be moved by propaganda and by their "collective unconscious" to act shortsightedly and narrowly.   The influences of special-interest propaganda and of totalitarian propaganda often blind people to the best interests of the larger whole of which they are a part and hence to their own best interests in the long run.

The people in most groups do not recognize how their behavior "is determined by their interest," [25] or how their conduct is influenced by the interest-colored lens with which they view all social situations.   This conception is an expansion of Francis Bacon's discussion of "idols," which are an individual's preconceptions that influence and shape his thinking regarding new situations as they arise.

The major ideologies which exert powerful influences upon large numbers of peoples, as already noted, are: (1) bureaucratic conservatism which issues arbitrary decrees;   (2) historical conservatism which puts the controlling social influences in the hands of an aristocratic class; (3) liberal democracy which stresses "scientific politics" and carefully planned procedures of justice for all; (4) socialist-communist thinking which is dialectual and which culminates in a blind irrationalism that resorts to violence; and (5) fascism which uses an action-psychology and demands unconditional responses of the individual to the controlling powers.

Mannheim asserts that in modern times the real intellectual

[25] Ideology and Utopia, *op. cit.,* p. 43; also see p. 328.

activity does not come from a ruling class with closed minds but from a social group not attached to any one social class but recruited from the several social classes. This intellectual activity is dynamic, in a state of flux, and continually facing and trying to solve new problems in new ways.[26] Mass action, too, is coming more and more into the current picture, partly because the masses are obtaining education, partly because they are becoming desperate with reference to improving their conditions of life, and partly because they are becoming convinced that massed action is their only weapon of obtaining an improved social order.

Utopian thinking is considered incongruous in the social situation in which it occurs. It seems out of place because it is not traditional. For example, the idea of Christian brotherly love is incongruous in a society dominated by cutthroat competition.

In contrast with ideologies which attempt to make people satisfied with the present, the status quo, and the past, there are utopias or dreams of the future, which arouse many people to new hopes, sometimes fantastic hopes, sometimes to great dissatisfaction with what is or has been. Utopian thinking tends to rise from frustrations and dissatisfactions and perhaps from unrealized needs. While ideologies rise out of attempts to maintain security, utopias spring from the wish for change. The ideologies are realized thinking on the part of the secure and the utopias are unrealized thinking by the insecure and dissatisfied. The four forms of utopian thinking as referred to in an earlier chapter are: orgiastic-chiliasm, liberal-humanitarian, conservative, and socialist-communist. Sooner or later one or the other forms of utopian thinking make an impact on the masses of mankind, and also on the ideologies themselves, which may as a result undergo modification. Both utopian thinking and ideologies play an extensive role in molding the ideas of work-a-day people.

THE PARADE OF GENERATIONS

Another aspect of *Wissensoziologie* relates to the influences that affect people because of what might be called the passing

26 *Ibid.*, p. 139.

parade of generations. A member of the younger generation repeatedly contacts members of the older generations having values developed a third of a century earlier, as well as members of his own generation. A continual interplay takes place between two sets of values as seen from the viewpoint of the younger generation. Likewise and at the same time the interplay takes place between these values as seen through the eyes of the older generation.

Wilhelm Dilthey nearly a century ago pointed out the significance for the sociology of knowledge of the co-existence of generations in constituting influential environments, each for the other. Mannheim carried the analysis further and pointed out how new participants in the social process are continually emerging and older participants are continually disappearing, how the cultural heritage is being continually transmitted, and how the transition from generation to generation is a continuous process.[27] Within each generation are "generation units" having an identity of purpose and exerting social influence as a group as well as by individuals.[28] In periods of rapid social change, new centers of social influence form and a new generation style or entelechy develops and constitutes a powerful influence in the social environment.[29] The fact of generation and of generation change constitutes an important aspect of the way social factors influence mental products. Znaniecki succinctly says: "The old generation insists right now that the young be molded as uniformly as possible in accordance of what an educated human person ought to be and demands that educators mold them that way."[30] On the other hand, the younger generation in a free society continually balks and wants to experiment. When the stubbornness of the old is pitted against the recklessness of the young, then the generation problem appears in its most difficult form. But when the older and the younger generation each has a viewpoint large enough to include the other, adjustments are feasible.

27 *Essays, op. cit.*, pp. 292 ff.
28 *Ibid.*, p. 306.
29 *Ibid.*, p. 309.
30 Florian Znaniecki, "Sociological Ignorance in Social Planning," *Sociology and Social Research*, XXX:96.

THE CHANGING OF SOCIAL RELATIONS

The sociology of knowledge is concerned with ways of changing those mental products which function as social values. To the extent that values are affected by social factors, these subjective forces may be changed by changing social relations, that is, by social reform. Social reconstruction by changing social conditions, by regulating economic institutions, by the use of measures affecting external conditions, does not preclude the use of methods that would directly change the spirit of man. The sociology of knowledge deals with external systems for bringing about needed social change. It favors not an authoritarian or a laissez faire but a democratic type of society.

The democratic society involves "a theory of power aimed at defining ways of distributing and controlling communal power for maximum security, efficiency, and freedom." [31] Democracy condemns abuses of power and emphasizes functional power, not arbitrary power. Democracy faces a problem because pressure groups develop and exert tremendous power on individuals. The sociology of knowledge is tremendously interested in pressure groups and how they influence the minds of the individual members of society, for the exercise of pressures and counterpressures is an undemocratic way of securing social change or of maintaining social stability. Social influence exerted through violence, revolutions, wars, works against a democratic way of life which calls for "orderly patterns of human interaction" [32] that are produced by free decision.

SOCIAL PLANNING

For a society to exert constructive influences on its members there must be social planning, that is, planning "for freedom, subject to democratic control." [33] It is planning "not for a classless society but for one that abolishes the ex-

---

[31] Karl Mannheim, *Freedom, Power, and Democratic Planning* (New York: Oxford University Press, 1950), p. 45.
[32] *Ibid.*, pp. 45, 48.
[33] *Ibid.*, p. 29.

tremes of wealth and poverty," planning for new culture patterns without discarding what is valuable in tradition, "planning for gradual transformation of society in order to encourage the growth of personality," planning for coordination, not regimentation, planning for free choices.[34] While the sociology of knowledge stresses the influence of environment on man's thinking, yet its exponents grant that its subject matter is but a part, shall we say a half, of the total picture, the other part being the way man's thinking has affected environment.

Religion is given an interesting place in social planning by the sociology of knowledge. It can play a role in bringing about needed human integration. Mannheim, for instance, assigns to religion "freed from authoritarian and superstitious admixtures, the task of an ultimate integration of all human activities."[35] In addition to the functioning of conduct and character, there is needed "the integrating function of ideological or spiritual inspiration chiefly represented by religion."[36] Religion may answer man's craving for "a more fundamental oneness relating all his scattered activities to a common purpose" than man's daily and mundane contacts provide for him. In other words, man's deepest needs are not satisfied by living entirely on "the pragmatic level of daily activity."

If religion is to fulfil "certain indispensable functions in this age of transition" its leaders must keep up with the needs of the changing social order and with the latest developments in psychology and sociology. Religion has the vital role of helping to keep personality in equilibrium. It can assist to keep personality unified in an environment which influences personality to become disrupted, disorganized, meaningless, and to develop into a split personality.

A dilemma faced by any religion professing brotherhood doctrines arises when it tries to apply "the virtues of a society based upon neighborly relationships to the world at large."[37]

[34] *Ibid.*, pp. 113, 176.
[35] E. K. Bramsted and Hans Gerth in "A Note on the Work of Karl Mannheim," in Mannheim, *Freedom, Power, and Democratic Planning, op. cit.,* p. xiv.
[36] *Ibid.*, p. 19.
[37] Karl Mannheim, *Diagnosis of Our Times* (New York: Oxford University Press, 1944), p. 21.

It is hard for one to be a good citizen in a world "where the basic rules are against the spirit of Christianity." [38] If the family exerts ethical influences and "the laws of the market compel us to become self-assertive, the consequence of these conflicting demands will be a kind of neurosis." [39] It is asserted that the Christian principles of moderation and restriction are overwhelmed by "the endless stimulation of desires originating in a competitive system, where the producers try to outdo each other by creating cravings for new kinds of goods." [40]

Fascist influences on human thinking try to produce "an external harmony" by the use of compulsion. They seek to obtain change in ideas by the maximum use of external force. Dictators resort to the rise of purges as a means of influencing the thinking of their followers, but purges are irrational forces, for they usually liquidate the persons with new ideas and with the virility to carry forward needed reforms. [41]

In creating social influences a variety of social planning is expressed. There is bad planning as well as good, and there is planning by and for special interests that work against the common good as well as special interests that work for the well-being of all. There is planning that leads to dictatorship, but the best planning involves the good of the whole of human society. A *Weltanshauung* is essential for the best planning. Moreover, the best planning is that in which the largest percentage of a group have a voice in the planning, provided they are trained in planning goals and procedures. Social planning can have a socially constructive influence when "it is based on the creative tendencies in societies," when it can stimulate and direct "living forces without suppressing them," [42] and when its aim is "the democratization of society."

An important question in social planning is whether it shall work for the "mass transformation of external behavior" or the transformation of individuals. The latter method is

[38] *Ibid.*, p. 34.
[39] *Ibid.*, p. 91.
[40] *Ibid.*, p. 11.
[41] *Ibid.*
[42] Karl Mannheim, *Man and Society in an Age of Reconstruction* (New York: Harcourt, Brace and Company, 1940), p. 106.

slower because it begins with individuals and uses the evolutionary methods of education, but it may be too slow in an atomic age. The former method may change only the outward behavior "without really transforming men." Its emphasis may lead to brow-beating, emotional appeals, crowd psychology, violence.[43] In general the sociology of knowledge gives major support to the use of indirect methods rather than to direct ordering and forbidding procedures. It would influence human thinking through discussion groups, through the use of procedures based on the interdependence of groups, through changing the nature of social situations.[44] It would so direct social influences that freedom of the individual will be furthered, the Four Freedoms will be expanded to include the human race, that all may have freedom from want, freedom from fear, freedom of expression, and freedom of religion, as well as other freedoms.

Robinson brings before the sociology of knowledge its ultimate question: Who plans the super-planners?[45] If one answers that no one does, then one ignores the past influences on them, the historical process, the field of social forces. If one answers that existing groups influence the super-planning, then one has succumbed to the environmental theory. Perhaps the correct answer involves both the environmental forces and innate creativeness. McClenahan defines social planning "as that planning which affects the activities and institutions of social groups and the functioning of human beings in relation to each other and thus ultimately tends to provide a mold for the shaping of personality through limiting or enlarging opportunities."[46]

Perhaps Mannheim should be given a concluding word. He contended that when "spontaneous mutual adaptation of groups and individuals does not work," then social planning "becomes inevitable."[47] He believed that social forces when left to themselves "can produce only extremely undesirable

43 *Ibid.*, p. 275.

44 *Ibid.*, p. 42.

45 Daniel S. Robinson, "Karl Mannheim's Sociological Philosophy," *The Personalist*, XXIX:137 ff.

46 Bessie A. McClenahan, "The Sociology of Planning," *Sociology and Social Research*, XXVIII:184.

47 *Essays on Sociology and Social Psychology.* Edited by Paul Kecskemeti (New York: Oxford University Press, 1953), p. 7.

or even intolerable results." [48]   A function of social planning is to forestall what goes on perpetually in unplanned societies, a social conditioning (indirect social planning) that may have disastrous results for human freedom.[49]   He objected to planning by the totalitarianism of either the communist or the fascist type because both types destroy human freedom.   He did not think of "developing a blue-print of a new social order and reshaping society to its specifications," [50] but of the fostering of the freedom of the individual as a test of acceptable social planning.

In summing up the development of the sociology of knowledge one may say that Mannheim has so far played the major role.   While he has stressed the role of social influences on personal thinking, he has done so in order to clarify that role, being aware all the time that the role of personal freedom in influencing human thinking is equally important.

The sociology of knowledge will give one of the major bases for social reconstruction.   It will serve as one aspect of a framework within which flexible social planning will proceed. Its *Weltanschauung* gives an adequate frame of reference for working out world policies that will build peaceful relationships between nations and well-oriented personal freedom within nations.

GROUP DISCUSSION TOPICS

1. The main contributors to the sociology of knowledge prior to Mannheim.
2. Criticize the definition of the sociology of knowledge as given by Mannheim.
3. Compare Maquet's definition of the sociology of knowledge with that of Mannheim.
4. The influence of the areas of society in which individuals live on the "ambition of individuals."
5. The contradictory elements of determinism and freedom in the theory of the sociology of knowledge.
6. The relation of the sociology of knowledge to educational procedures in the schools.
7. The role of "meanings" in the sociology of knowledge.

---

48 *Ibid.*
49 *Ibid.*, p. 294.
50 *Ibid.*, p. 9.

8. The relation of gestalt psychology to the sociology of knowledge.
9. The connection between "ideologies" and "utopias."
10. The significance of "the passing parade of the generations."
11. The bearing of the sociology of knowledge on social planning.
12. "Who plans the superplanners?"

READINGS

Bogardus, Emory S., "Mannheim and Social Reconstruction," *Sociology and Social Research,* 32:548-55; also "Democratic Planning according to Mannheim," *Sociology and Social Research,* 36:110-15.

Grunwald, Ernest, *Das Problem einer Soziologie des Wissens* (Leipzig: Braumueller, 1934).

Lorwin, Lewis L., *Time for Planning* (New York: Harper & Brothers 1945).

Mannheim, Karl, *Essays on the Sociology of Knowledge,* edited by Paul Kecskemeti (New York: Oxford University Press 1952).

———, *Essays on Sociology and Social Psychology,* edited by Paul Kecskemeti (New York: Oxford University Press 1953).

———, *Ideology and Utopia* (New York: Harcourt, Brace and Company 1936).

———, *Man and Society in an Age of Reconstruction* (New York: Harcourt, Brace and Company 1940).

———, *Diagnosis of Our Times* (New York : Oxford University Press 1944).

———, *Freedom, Power, and Democratic Planning* (New York : Oxford University Press 1950).

Maquet, Jacques J., *The Sociology of Knowledge* (Boston : The Beacon Press 1951).

Merton, Robert K., "The Sociology of Knowledge," *Isis,* XXVIII:493-503.

McClenahan, Bessie A., "The Sociology of Planning," *Sociology and Social Research,* XXVIII:182-93.

Robinson, Daniel S., "Karl Mannheim's Sociological Philosophy," *The Personalist,* XXIX:137-148.

Speier, Hans, "The Social Determination of Ideas," *Social Research,* V:182-205.

Znaniecki, Florian, "Sociological Ignorance in Social Planning," *Sociology and Social Research,* XXX:87-100.

CHAPTER XXXIX

ODUM AND FOLK SOCIOLOGY

Although the nature of folk sociology had been discussed by William Wundt, William G. Sumner, Charles Bouglé, and a host of cultural anthropologists, it remained for Howard W. Odum (1884-1954) to raise the theme to a high level in the field of social thought. While accepting some ideas from each of his predecessors in this sector of social thought, Odum took exception to the thought of each in one or more particulars and then developed an up-to-date system of folk sociology. Odum was born in Bethlehem, Georgia, taught and conducted research for many years at the University of North Carolina. He was one of Franklin H. Giddings' outstanding students.

While Odum took cognizance of Wundt's position that folk psychology examines the relations between "the intellectual, moral, and mental characteristics of peoples,"[1] he disagreed with Wundt's assumption of collective minds.[2] He accepted a part of Sumner's concept of folkways,[3] but did not agree with Sumner that folkways arise out of mass instincts and that no one knows specifically where or how they arise. Odum would not limit the term "folkways" to ethnic or primitive fields but claimed that it could be applied "equally well to the synergy of social forces and processes in New York City."[4]

Odum spoke of folk society as transcending organized social control. It may "abound in any stage of culture or civilization whenever the major conditioning factors are extra-organizational or when a synergy of conflicting forces and necessities results in an integrated transitional society, the transition featuring change from one culture to another, from individual and group development to social organization."[5]

[1] William Wundt, *Elements of Folk Psychology* (New York: The Macmillan Company, 1916), pp. 2-10.
[2] Howard W. Odum, "Folk and Regional Conflict as a Field of Sociological Study," *Publication of the American Sociological Society*, XXV:4.
[3] William G. Sumner, *Folkways* (Boston: Ginn and Company, 1907)
[4] Odum, *loc. cit.*
[5] *Ibid.*, p. 5.

Odum perceived folk society as developing into a national or state society, a *Gemeinschaft* developing into a *Gesellschaft*, after the concepts of Tönnies,[6] or as "a component society" developing into "a constituent society" in terms used by Giddings.[7]   He wrote of folk society as "the normal transitional, extra-organizational, and non-technological social process." He called it, therefore, "the definitive, comparative society itself."[8]

Robert Redfield's views coincide to a degree with Odum's that "in every city there is the folk society."[9]   He refers to the city as "an assemblage of part-folk societies: the neighborhoods, the immigrant groups, the religious communities, indeed the little personal and moral part-worlds that we now come to discover to exist even among factory workers beneath the formal organization of the technology and the administration."[10]   The folk, in other words, involves personal interaction and a social becoming.

Sumner centered attention on folkways and never said much directly about the nature of folk.   Likewise, Odum wrote much about folk society, folk culture, and folk sociology, but did not seem to come to grips with a thoroughgoing analysis of folk as a basic concept in a folk-regional system of thought.   Perhaps both Sumner and Odum were making what amounts to an operational explanation, that is, explaining the term "folk" by describing what a folk creates in the form of folkways and folk-regionalism.

In the past, many social anthropologists have limited themselves in their discussions of folk societies to primitive or preliterative peoples.   Odum was one of the first writers to extend the concept of folk society to include societies intervening between primitive people and modern urban societies, and also the part-folk societies to be found in current metropolitan areas.

To Odum the folk have a way of informal personal think-

6 Ferdinand Tönnies, *Fundamental Concepts of Society* (New York: American Book Company, 1940) .

7 Franklin H. Giddings, *Readings in Descriptive and Historical Society* (New York: The Macmillan Company, 1911) , pp. 433 ff.

8 Odum, *op. cit.*, p. 7

9 Robert Redfield, "The Natural History of the Folk Society," *Social Forces*, 31:225.

10 *Ibid.*

ing and doing in addition to being a formal organization of people acting in technicways and by administrative rules. It is a group of people groping toward the light regarding its own nature and ways of meeting its needs, reaching out from its current social structure for new meanings for life and building "more stately mansions" in which to live. It is a group striving for some of the desired intangibles of life that its current social organization does not provide.

The folk, according to Odum, is "a universal constant in a world of variables," that is, an ongoing of the "basic elements of new cultures." When old civilizations succumb to their social forms, "new cultures arise from the folk," [11] the imperishable, perhaps we might say. The folks are "not just the people, not just population, but they represent the dominating pattern of the behavior and culture of any particular society at any time." A folk is "characterized by homogeneity of traits" and a unity of behavior. The folk is found in "family life, religion, education, industry, and the community in contrast to a single dominating institution of the state." [12]

Odum suggested a more liberal use of the term "folk" when he proposed that it be substituted for the term "race," especially since the latter term is used in different and confusing senses. He argued that many race traits are really folk attributes, and that some peoples called races are "more nearly folk societies." [13] He thought of the culture of the Jews, for example, as representing not a race but a folk society, and of the Germans under nazism as being "a powerful folk society" rather than a super race.

Further light on Odum's concept of the folk is thrown by his references to *folk culture*. Folk culture is characterized "by primary relationships and institutions, kith and kin in ethnic relationships and primary occupations." [14] Folkways are matured into folk culture as an informal social institution in itself. The folk culture exhibits a closely knit, cohesive

[11] Howard W. Odum, *Understanding Society* (New York: The Macmillan Company, 1947) , p. 261.

[12] *Ibid.*, p. 262.

[13] *Ibid.*, p. 261.

[14] Howard W. Odum, "Folk Sociology as a Subject Field for the Historical Study of Total Human Society and the Empirical Study of Group Behavior," *Social Forces*, 31:204.

behavior that is "primarily spontaneous, personal, traditional, yet strongly integrated through its institutional growth and moral order." [15]   The folk culture, in brief, is "the supreme product of the folk society," and the folk society is "the basis from which all societies develop." [16]

CONCEPT OF FOLK SOCIOLOGY

This discussion of folk, folk society, and folk culture is rounded out in an analysis of *folk sociology*. Odum's concept of folk sociology developed out of his experiences in the Southern states where he was born, received his bachelor's and master's degrees, where he lived, taught, served on commissions, and achieved national and international acclaim. When at the University of Mississippi he developed his interest in collecting and analyzing the folk songs and folk poetry of Negroes. He analyzed the nature of this folk literature and produced a number of books in this field.[17]   At Clark University where he received a Ph.D. degree under G. Stanley Hall and at Columbia University where he received another Ph.D. degree under Franklin H. Giddings he applied analytical methods to the Negro folk poetry and began to develop a folk sociology. At the beginning of the dissertation accepted at Columbia he says: "To know the soul of a people and to find the source from which flows the expression of folk-thought is to comprehend in large measure the capabilities of the people." [18]

Odum thought of folk sociology as "a theory of the continuum of society developing from the folk culture to the state civilization." [19]   His folk sociology developed out of his studies of folk society. In one of his last statements on the

---

[15] *Ibid.*

[16] Odum, *Understanding Society*, p. 260.

[17] For example: *Rainbow Round My Shoulder* (Indianapolis: The Bobbs-Merrill Company, 1928) ; *Cold Blue Moon* (Indianapolis: The Bobbs-Merrill Company, 1931); *Wings on My Feet* (Indianapolis: The Bobbs-Merrill Company, 1929); *Negro Workaday Songs* (Chapel Hill: The University of North Carolina Press, 1926); H. W. Odum and Guy B. Johnson, *The Negro and His Songs* (Chapel Hill: The University of North Carolina Press, 1925).

[18] Howard W. Odum, "Religious Folk Songs of the Southern Negroes," *American Journal of Religious Psychology and Education*, III:265.

[19] Howard W. Odum, *American Sociology* (New York: Longmans, Green and Company, 1951).

subject, he summarized all that he had done by calling folk sociology "a general sociology," that is, a body of social theory having hypotheses and a series of concepts that would be adequate for studying scientifically "the interacting causal factors of cultural evolution and the cumulative products of social change." [20]

CONCEPT OF FOLK-REGIONALISM

Odum projected his ideas of folk society into the larger world of regionalism and, as a result, perfected a theory of folk-regionalism. He defines the *region* as "the smallest unit for study that combines all the factors of time, geography, and folk behavior essential to complete analysis." [21] Regionalism is defined as "the study and planning of each region with special reference to the integration of all regions into the societal whole." Regionalism is viewed as a framework for both scientific research and social planning. Folk attitudes, for example, can be studied better in a region than in its subunit, the community, for the latter "does not comprehend all the factors of time, area, and cultural conditioning." [22]

The region includes several local districts which in turn include several zones or neighborhood areas. The United States might be divided into metropolitan and rural regions,[23] and these in turn into different kinds of urban regions and different types of rural regions.

While no sharp lines can be drawn between regions in the United States, Odum divided the nation into six regions, which he called the Middle States and their "Middle West," the Northeast and its New England, the Southeast and its "Old South," the Far West and its California, the Northwest and its Great Plains, the Southwest and its Texas. He separated these regions on the map by shaded state lines to indicate a lack of sharp division. However, the placing of each state

[20] Odum, "Folk Sociology as a Subject Field for the Historical Study of Total Human Society and the Empirical Study of Group Behavior," *op. cit.*, p. 193.
[21] Odum, *Understanding Society*, p. 98.
[22] *Ibid.*, p. 99.
[23] Howard W. Odum and Harry E. Moore, *American Regionalism* (New York: Henry Holt and Company, 1938), Part III.

of the Union in one or another of six regions has its draw-backs, particularly because the states are political units with boundaries determined long ago and lacking distinct meaning for current economic and social developments.

The standards that Odum set up in prescribing regional boundaries were as follows: (1) a region must be "large enough to comprehend the large number of values specified for applying to the present and to future trends," (2) a region must possess "physiographic homogeneities, historical development, folk culture and institutions," [24] and special characteristic features, and (3) a region must show statistical indices of a socioeconomic nature. These criteria, however, need further refinement.

Odum thought of a region as "at once an extension and a subdivision of the folk society." It has definitive traits derived through "action and behavior processes rather than through technological functions and areas." [25] In other words, a region is an enlarged and expanded folk society with all its personal and informal expressions of human desires, aims, functions. On the other hand, because of its size and development of needs, it possesses some of the extra-folk society characteristics, such as technological and administrative machinery. Thus, a region is a folk society that is large enough to constitute a comprehensive unit for sociological research. It furnishes that regional environment which is necessary for an adequate study of a folk society.

While a region may have a geographic size and a history, a past cultural development, and population characteristics, as well as economic, educational, and other social resources, yet it is not self-sufficient but reliant on other regions, and on the over-all government of the various regions of which it is one. Odum envisaged a reasonable balance between regions "in the sharing of goods and services and other regional resources." [26]

Odum recognized that regions overlap. Moreover, they are in a state of flux. His was an evolutionary concept of

[24] *Ibid.*
[25] Odum, "Folk and Regional Conflict as a Field of Sociological Study," *op. cit.,* p. 9.
[26] George L. Simpson, Jr., "Howard W. Odum and American Regionalism," *Social Forces,* 34:104.

region. For example, the United States began with two regions, North and South, and then a West developed, which became a Middle West, a Southwest, a Northwest, and a Far West. The North receded into a Northeast and the South into a Southeast. Regions are even subject to change in geographic limits in natural resources, in people, in culture.[27]

Following up the criticism that Odum's classification of regions of the United States by using state boundaries for dividing lines is unrealistic, Zimmerman and Du Wors set forth a sevenfold regional division of the United States on the basis of curving lines demarcating regions according to the major types of economic production characteristic of each. The dividing lines weave in and out of the states and freely cross state boundary lines. A rough order of historical development is presented as follows: the South, the Urban-Northeast, the Appalachian-Ozark, and later, the Cornbelt, the Wheat belt, the Arid West, and the Pacific Mediterranean regions. The authors suggest that a given type of mentality is characteristic of each region. Each of these seven regions is a geosocial entity—"each with its own peculiar social system." While economic production as a test of regional size may have some merits over Odum's approach, this emphasis, too, seems incomplete. Moreover, the idea of sustaining mentalities for each region has apparent weaknesses.[28]

Odum reacted against sectionalism and distinguished sharply between sectionalism and regionalism. To him, the concept of sectionalism had inherent in it "the idea of separatism and isolation, of separate units with separate interests." Sections have a self-seeking, divisive power which is quite different from "the integrating power of coordinate regions built into a social whole. Perhaps the most striking sectionalism in the United States has been the North-South sectionalism with all its animosities and divisiveness. Historical sectionalism may become so deeply ingrained in a nation's life that it can be integrated only with the greatest skill over a long period of time. On the other hand, regionalism is "in reality the opposite of its most common interpretation, namely,

---

[27] Odum and Moore, *American Regionalism*, p. 449.
[28] Carle C. Zimmerman and Richard E. Du Wors, *Graphic Regional Sociology* (Cambridge, Mass.: Phillips Book Store, 1952).

localism, sectionalism, or provincialism." [29] To Odum, sectionalism was a form of "regional imbalance." Many years before Odum's treatment of sectionalism Ross had analyzed some of its weaknesses, such as political strife, economic exploitation, personal ill will.[30]

The concept of folk sociology included what Odum called a composite regionalism and a societal wholeness. But he distinguished the composite regionalism from the technological state society. While the latter may contain a good deal of "folk quality," its technicways and its administrative machinery tend to circumscribe and inhibit the functioning of the folkways. However, new folk cultures will arise from crushed state-civilizations and thus kindle human aspirations and hopes anew.

State ways become characterized by technology, robotism, mechanical gadgets, and political power. State society tends to foster an artificial way of life, a modernized tempo, and countless frustrations. State civilization brings "to focus the frustrations and pathology of individuals isolated from primary associations and from the feeling of belonging to the group." [31]

Folk society, then, as conceived by Odum, begins in a study of local societies, reaches its climax in folk-regionalism, and tapers off in the personal aspects of a state-wide civilization. It has a distinct dynamic quality, an evolutionary aspect of important proportions, and is described as "a constant process which gains power in the form of the gradual development of conditioned, comparative society, evolving from one stage to another, merging now into formal or organized society, now gradually being transformed, as old cultures break up, into another folk society which again transcends organized social control." [32] The folk society, according to Odum, comprehends "the definite constant social processes" of Giddings' natural society "conceived as a phenomenon of evolution." [33]

[29] Odum and Moore, *American Regionalism*, pp. 14, 35 ff.

[30] Edward A. Ross, *Roads to Social Peace* (Chapel Hill: The University of North Carolina Press, 1925).

[31] Odum, "Folk Sociology as a Subject Field for the Historical Study of Total Human Society and the Empirical Study of Group Behavior," *op. cit.*, p. 200.

[32] Odum, "Folk and Regional Conflict as a Field of Sociological Study," *op. cit.*, p. 5.

[33] *Ibid.*, p. 7.

A folk society is viewed "essentially as a directive process between different stages" of organized society, maintaining an informal social force and regulating "current generations more powerfully than formally organized society." [34]

Odum posited the integration of all regions first into a national whole and then into a societal whole. Odum and Jocher asserted that "the most dynamic problem in postwar America" is "the achievement of the regional quality and balance of America." [35] This problem is a part of the need for "a better regional balance of people and resources everywhere." [36] There is a need for complete state, regional, and national planning under the auspices of governmental and voluntary programs, adopted and enacted through the consent of the people and through new reaches in the effectiveness of education." [37]

Odum believed in social action as a natural companion for tested social theory. He saw a major culmination of his folk sociology in social planning. He posited "physical planning, economic planning, and social and cultural planning." He recommended a United States planning agency supported by an amendment to the Constitution, having both research and planning specialists. He suggested a planning agency for each state of the union, and also regional planning agencies to tie together the state agencies and to act as liaison with the national agency.[38] Moreover, he took active part in many social planning programs in his state and the South,[39] while at the same time making important contributions as sociologist, folklorist, teacher, administrator, and prose poet to the concept of folk sociology.

[34] *Ibid.*, p. 4.
[35] Howard W. Odum and Katharine Jocher, *In Search of the Regional Balance of America* (Chapel Hill: The University of North Carolina Press, 1923) , Foreword.
[36] *Ibid.*
[37] Howard W. Odum, "The Regional Quality and Balance of America," *Social Forces*, 23:42.
[38] Simpson, *loc. cit.*
[39] For a partial list of these activities see Rupert B. Vance and Katharine Jocher, "Howard W. Odum," *Social Forces*, 33:203-17. Also see this same article for an eight-page listing of Odum's books and articles.

GROUP DISCUSSION TOPICS

1. The nature of a "folk."
2. The nature of a "folk society."
3. The differences between folk psychology and folk sociology.
4. Wundt's contributions to folk psychology.
5. Sumner's contributions to folk sociology.
6. Odum's early interest in folk sociology.
7. Explain: A folk society is a modern phenomenon as well as one of the past.
8. Explain: There is a folk society in every city.
9. The reasons for substituting the term "folk" for the term "race."
10. The meaning of "the soul of a people."
11. The definition of a region.
12. Odum's evolutionary concept of region.
13. The meaning of regionalism.
14. The relation of region to folk society.
15. The differences between the major regions of the United States.
16. The meaning of regional balance.
17. The differences between regionalism and sectionalism.
18. The natural culmination of a folk society.
19. The world as a folk society.
20. The basic principles of a folk sociology.
21. The next steps in the culmination of folk sociology.

READINGS

Brooks, L. M., "Some Contributions of Howard W. Odum to Sociology," *Sociology and Social Research*, 39:224-29.

Odum, Howard W., *American Sociology* (New York: Longmans, Green and Company 1951).

——, "Folk and Regional Conflict as a Field of Sociological Study," *Publication of the American Sociological Society*, XXV:1-17.

——, "Folk Sociology as a Subject Field for the Historical Study of Total Human Society and the Empirical Study of Group Behavior," *Social Forces*, 31:193-223.

——, *Negro Workaday Songs* (Chapel Hill: The University of North Carolina Press 1926).

——, *Rainbow Round My Shoulder* (Indianapolis: The Bobbs-Merrill Company 1931).

——, "Religious Folk Songs of the Southern Negroes," *American Journal of Religious Psychology and Education*, III:265 ff.

——, *Understanding Society* (New York: The Macmillan Company 1947).

Odum, Howard W., "The Way of the South," *Social Forces,* 23:258-68.
———, *Wings on My Feet* (Indianapolis: The Bobbs-Merrill Company 1929).
Odum, Howard W., and Katharine Jocher, *An Introduction to Social Research* (New York: Henry Holt and Company 1929).
———, *In Search of the Regional Balance of America* (Chapel Hill: The University of North Carolina Press 1923).
Odum, Howard W., and Guy B. Johnson, *The Negro and His Songs* (Chapel Hill: The University of North Carolina Press 1925).
Odum, Howard W., and Harry E. Moore, *American Regionalism* (New York: Henry Holt and Company 1938).
Redfield, Robert, "The Natural History of the Folk Society," *Social Forces,* 31:224-28.
Simpson, George L., Jr., "Howard W. Odum and American Regionalism," *Social Forces,* 34:101-6.
Sumner, W. G., *Folkways* (Boston: Ginn and Company 1907).
Vance, Rupert B., and Katharine Jocher, "Howard W. Odum," *Social Forces,* 33:203-17.
Wundt, William, *Elements of Folk Psychology* (New York: The Macmillan Company 1916).
Zimmerman, Carle C., and R. E. Du Wors, *Graphic Regional Sociology* (Cambridge, Mass.: Phillips Book Store 1952).

CHAPTER XL

MUKERJEE AND SOCIAL VALUES

In the first chapters of this book, the social thought of the early Hebrew, East Indian, Chinese, and related thinkers of the East was given primary attention. Then came a series of discussions of social thought as presented by leading European and American contributors to the field. We come now to the social thought of an outstanding Oriental sociologist and social philosopher of the present day—Radhakamal Mukerjee of India.

Mukerjee presents in a notable way a treatment of social values that is not only representative of both East and West, but is the result of an integration of Eastern and Western social thought viewed in the light of a world-wide universe of social discourse. He has gone further than most of his contemporaries and any of his predecessors in orienting the nature of social values within a general theory of society.

Mukerjee was born in 1889 in India. His father was an Indian lawyer, and he grew to manhood in a house filled with books from both the East and the West and where his older brothers were "humming over books." He was well grounded in Indian social philosophy, but his education did not stop there. He studied history with deep interest but he reports that "the face-to-face contact with misery, squalor, and degradation in the slums of Calcutta decided my future interest in economics and sociology." [1] He early acquired practical experience in the adult evening schools that he set up as early as 1906 and in which he has maintained a lifelong participation. He has also maintained continued contact with social welfare work of various kinds, including rural credit societies and other types of village cooperatives.

Another important background in Mukerjee's analysis of values is his understanding of *mysticism*.[2] At this point he

[1] Baljit Singh, (ed.), *The Frontiers of Social Science* (London: Macmillan & Co., 1956), p. 4.
[2] R. Mukerjee, *The Theory and Art of Mysticism* (New York: Longmans, Green and Company, 1937).

brings to bear a basic Oriental approach to the study of values that many Western thinkers tend to ignore. To this "primary and indispensable sympathy," as Hocking points out, Mukerjee adds "a threefold objectivity: that of the scholar scientifically trained, that of the reader widely familiar with Western literature on his subject, and that of the sociologist concerned with the bearing of religion upon the health of human institutions." [3]

The role of Oriental and especially Indian mysticism in an understanding of social values is indicated by Mukerjee who rejects the escapist theory about mysticism and indicates that it effects a quieting of the mind, it develops "an ethical neutrality," it provides "a searching self-analysis, a strenuous and patient self-discipline and an ultimate self-transcendence," it produces "a freedom from all contingencies and references, even from the accidents of life and death"; in short, it posits the common man as the universal man, and it sees the universal man as "the true, eternal expression for human freedom and equality, for justice and goodness in all human relations and institutions, and for sharing, service, and solidarity of all groups and classes. . . . Between mysticism and society there is a reciprocity which has an end." [4] True mysticism, according to Mukerjee, "discovers a configuration of the self, expanding its circumference indefinitely, establishing itself as the center of the world of values." [5]

Mukerjee pays tribute to the influence on his thinking of Professor Benay Kuman Sarkar, "a man of great sacrifice and idealism," interested in social education and in the rehabilitation of rural village life. This contact was made more real by a visit to south India, "still the home of the self-governing village, where Mukerjee's concepts of regionalism and social ecology began to take shape." [6] In later years, Robert E. Park visited Mukerjee in India and brought home an emphasis on community studies. E. A. Ross was another visitor who was impressed by Mukerjee's studies of regionalism. Mukerjee in recent years visited a number of American universities

3 W. E. Hocking in B. Singh, *op. cit.*, p. 409.
4 Mukerjee in B. Singh, *op. cit.*, pp. 12, 13.
5 *Ibid.*, p. 14.
6 *Ibid.*, pp. 6, 9.

and profited by contacts in the United States with Park and Ross; earlier, Mukerjee had been a careful student of the writings of Ward and Giddings, as well as of Comte, Spencer, Bagehot, Hobhouse, Ricardo, Mill, Marshall. Thus, it is seen that Mukerjee's thinking represents an unusual combination of Eastern and Western thought. Perhaps no other sociologist has been so fortunate in the breadth of his mental contacts and in his approach to the interpretation of human values.

The writing of this chapter is stimulated by the recent appearance of a volume issued "in honor of Radhakamal Mukerjee," containing a summary, "A General Theory of Society," by Mukerjee.[7]

REGIONAL BASES OF VALUES

Mukerjee's theory of social value is based to a degree on his thinking regarding regionalism and ecology, prompted in part by studies in south India, and in part by a study of the proposals of Patrick Geddes who visited India in 1914 and 1915. Mukerjee was also influenced by the ideas of Park, of Lewis Mumford, and of Odum. He accepts the concept of "natural region," but claims that Park, McKenzie, Burgess, and others "do not give adequate consideration to the unity of region built up by social habits, traditions, and values."[8] He agrees with Odum's emphasis on social-psychological factors in the latter's discussion of "folk regionalism." He conceives of the region "as an intricate network of interrelations" and as exhibiting "a complex pattern of adaptations between the environmental factors and the plant and animal communities including human societies."[9] Mukerjee proclaims the region as an "ecological aggregate of persons," "an economic framework and a cultural order," a coordinate set of stimuli, eliciting a similarity of responses, habits, and feelings that are moulded into a "characteristic neutral type and pattern

---

[7] *Ibid.*, pp. 3-74.
[8] *Ibid.*, p. 16.
[9] R. Mukerjee, *The Regional Balance of Man* (Madras: University of Madras, 1938), Intro. p. 1.

of living"; hence "the fundamental unit of study for sociology is the region." [10]

In regional research, Mukerjee found the social sciences to have a basic relation in common. In studies of regions "the walls which keep the different social sciences in watertight compartments crumble down." [11] Mukerjee, after coming to the faculty of the University of Lucknow in 1921, introduced "an integrated approach in economics, sociology, and anthropology." [12]

In his studies of regions, Mukerjee found a regional balancing of the different forces at work. One study of this regional balance he called social ecology, which he defined as "a synoptic study of the balance of plant, animal, and human communities, which are systems of correlated working parts in the organization of the region." [13] Social ecology considers human communities as an integral part of the organization of all life—plant, animal, and human—in a region. [14] It has three tasks. One is "to trace the adaptations of interacting human beings and of interrelated human institutions to the region, including in the latter term not merely soil, climate, and land form, but also plant and animal communities." A second task is to investigate "the spatial and food relations in which human beings and activities are organized in a natural area in terms of the ensemble of ecologic forces." The third task is "to measure the balances and mutual pressures of human along with other living and non-living communities in the region and discover whether these prove favorable or unfavorable for man's dominance and permanence." [15]

According to Mukerjee, it is necessary for man in order to control nature to follow nature, for "she has her own wisdom." It is not wise for man seriously to disturb "the balance and rhythm in which nature delights" or vengeance may

[10] R. Mukerjee, *Social Ecology* (New York: Longmans, Green and Company, 1945), p. viii.
[11] R. Mukerjee, "Foreword," *Indian Sociological Review*, August, 1923.
[12] Mukerjee in B. Singh, *op. cit.*, p. 10.
[13] R. Mukerjee, *Regional Sociology* (New York: Century Company, 1926), p. vi.
[14] R. Mukerjee, "The Concepts of Balance and Organization of Social Ecology," *Sociology and Social Research*, XVI:504.
[15] *Ibid.*, p. 505.

follow quickly.[16]   Mukerjee develops the concept of "applied ecology" as well as of "synecology."   The former envisages man's manifold development as being "in harmony with the ecologic balance of population and resources as well as of vegetation and animal life."[17]   The latter is ecology working in cooperation with human geography, human biology, economics, social psychology and technics.[18]   Man lives in a multidimensional environment, that is, "in the ecological area, in the institution, in the class, in the state, in the communion (of people), and at the same time internalizes the region, the institution, the class, the state, and communion."[19] Mukerjee's theory of social values emerges from the study of interactions involved in man's multidimensional environment.[20]

VALUES AND SYMBOLS

Out of his multidimensional environment, man develops "values and symbols," which are synthetic products of the human mind that enhance, elevate, and refine social relations and processes and bind men together in ever-expanding, ever-deepening participation and communication."[21]   Values are defined as "socially approved desires and goals that are internalized through the process of conditioning, learning or socialisation and that become subjective preferences, standards, and aspirations," and society is "an organization and accumulation of values."   There is a hierarchy of values ranging from "immediate, specific, and instrumental to ideal, universal, and intrinsic values."[22]

Values have an "absolutism" which is "an embodiment of the universal human craving for order and harmony," and

---

[16] R. Mukerjee, "The Broken Balance of Man and Region," *Sociology and Social Research,* XVII:407.

[17] *Ibid.,* p. 408.

[18] Mukerjee in B. Singh, *op. cit.,* p. 17.

[19] *Ibid.,* p. 30.

[20] James A. Quinn (in B. Singh, *op. cit.,* p. 267) credits Mukerjee with having published "the first constructive, systematic, theoretical book on social ecology." Although Park, Burgess, McKenzie made basic contributions earlier, and Bews and Alihan published books on certain aspects of ecology before Mukerjee's *Social Ecology* (London: Longmans, Green and Company, 1945) appeared, he was the first to "systematize constructively the theoretical concepts and principles of social ecology."

[21] Mukerjee in B. Singh, *op. cit.,* p. 21.

[22] *Ibid.,* p. 23.

"with his values man actualizes his desires and goals with zest and persistence." Values can be inferred from the manner in which "man spends his time, income, and energies." The patterns of social life, relations, and institutions emerge from the "differentiation and the hierarchy of normal value experience."[23]

By their nature "all human relations and behavior" are values. Values play an important role in the integration and fulfillment of man's basic impulses and desires "in a stable and consistent manner appropriate for his social living." They are "generic experiences in social action made up of both individual and social responses and attitudes." They build up societies, integrate social relations, "mould the ideal dimensions of personality and the range and depth of culture."[24]

Values have "condensed epitomised expressions," namely, symbols. A symbol may be defined as "a vehicle of communication and regulation of human relations, a pregnant, epitomised expression of meanings and values shared in human life." Human relations are largely symbolic; man "competes and struggles with [his] fellowmen even for sex, food, and living space symbolically." Symbols not only bring one nearer than values to the experiences of individuals, but as vehicles of "communication, stratification, and control are also more amenable to scientific, objective analysis."[25] Symbols make a part of the values of life "visible by patternising and stereotyping these," and hence make it possible for man to understand and experience these values.[26]

A gradation of values is found in four basic types of social integration. (1) In the crowd, there may be an outburst by brute force of moral feeling that aims to correct some act adjudged to be wrong. (2) In the economic-interest group, certain elemental values may be expressed, such as reciprocity, integrity, consideration, fairness. There may be "individual assertion and reciprocal service" or "impersonal conflict and

23 *Ibid.*, p. 24.
24 *Ibid.*, p. 35.
25 *Ibid.*, pp. 35, 53.
26 R. Mukerjee, *The Social Structure of Values* (London: Macmillan and Company, 1949), p. 183.

retaliation." [27]   (3) In "society" or "community," equity and justice find expression. (4) In "commonality," the chief values are "spontaneous love," social responsibility, solidarity, and cooperativeness. It is values such as these which "can alone supply the sure moral foundation of world reconstruction of the future." [28]   On this high value level, life is shared. The human person ascends "from the superficial, egoistic, and evanescent self to the deep, altruistic, and universal self." [29]

Disvalues as well as values are found "in all dimensions of behavior." On the personality side of life there are lapses, denials, and perversions of values. These are accompanied by "a sense of guilt, shame and loss of self-esteem or self-status." On the societary side there are "disharmonious, haphazard, inequitous, and exploitative social relations and anti-social group formations." [30]   Disvalues have their origins "in the lack of coherence or dissociation between the biological, the social, and the ideal phases of human satisfaction." They are expressed in institutions which "evade laws and social codes." [31]   Mukerjee's emphasis is on the side of treatment of disvalues. He would reintegrate deviant individuals and groups by working on the total social situation and on the social adaptability of persons and groups.[32]

Mukerjee distinguishes between goals, ideals, normative ideals, and values. Out of man's basic needs and tensions goals arise and are selected to meet needs and reduce tensions. But goals become competitive and it is necessary to select the best or the ideal. Ideals, however, are at first incomplete and do not give "stability, harmony, and coherence, which may be secured by means of norms (normative ideals) which are imperative." "Norms incarnate man's strivings and aspirations for self-realization and growth that his life and his society present." [33]   Norms become values when they are internalized as man's "conscience and faith, and projected in

[27] *Ibid.*, p. 119.
[28] *Ibid.*, p. 189.
[29] R. Mukerjee, *The Dynamics of Morals* (London: Macmillan and Company, 1950), pp. 407-8.
[30] Mukerjee in B. Singh, *op. cit.*, p. 24.
[31] S. Chandra in B. Singh, *op. cit.*, p. 504.
[32] *Ibid.*
[33] Mukerjee in B. Singh, *op. cit.*, p. 66.

his concrete social relations and institutions, in his freedoms, laws and rights, and duties." [34] In Oriental culture, norms and values constitute both man's "deepest self and the essence of an eternal, spiritual, teleological order of the cosmos." [35]

PERSONALITY AND VALUES

Values and value systems "define and govern the structure of personality," and a person in turn "seeks a qualitative refinement and enrichment of his value insight and experience." In so doing a person conserves and maximizes "values without which he cannot find harmony with himself and society." This "reciprocity between the person and environment via community keeps values ever changing, lapsing, or augmenting." [36]

The command, love thy neighbor as thyself, really means "love thy neighbor as thyself because in essence thou art thy neighbor." It is possible for a person to lead society toward that full harmony and perfect concord which he obtains from his experience of God, "for God is the supreme good." [37] Man possesses a superiority over society and nature, as "shown by the world of values which his philosophy creates and his religion makes dynamic in his heart." [38]

The person passes from one level of behavior to another. There are three main dimensions (levels) of behavior within which an individual finds expression "in the improvement of his social relations, the enrichment of values and personality, as well as of his moral life." The first dimension is the bio-social. A person prepares himself for living in society "by learning to obey coercive rules and regulations that arise out of the constant threat and pressure of the external environment and the inadequacy of his nature." The second dimension is that of psychic integration in society. For his inner growth and fulfillment, he "must live in harmony and intimacy with [his] fellowmen." The third dimension is the spiritual, wherein a person may achieve self-poise and com-

34 *Ibid.*, p. 67.
35 *Ibid.*
36 *Ibid.*, p. 24.
37 Mukerjee, *The Theory and Art of Mysticism*, p. 3.
38 *Ibid.*, p. 221.

petence by achieving a rapport with the cosmic order and God (spiritual at-homeness).[39]

A person develops prudence in his biosocial environment, loyalty in his psychosocial environment, and reverence in his spiritual environment. There are "no social relations that are not moral" and no spiritual relations that are not reverent. There is more than a passing relationship between Mukerjee's emphasis on "reverence" and Schweitzer's concept of "reverence for life."[40]

The moral progress of the person "builds up and communicates itself in reverence." Reverence "proclaims the majesty and dignity of the common man." It seems to guard, integrate, and order "the varied social relations and goals" of life, and it provides "the true meaning of man's social nature and values and the staying-power for a wholeness and integrity in self, society, and cosmos."[41]

"A society in order to persist must regularly fulfil the supreme values of personality." This statement suggests why great civilizations have fallen, and it suggests why some current civilizations may not long survive. They will rise or fall according to their emphasis on personality development.[42] It is suggested that civilization needs a social-science theory "of full and integrated personality and of free and universal society."[43] The highest search of personality is for "higher spiritual values of beauty, goodness, and love," for the creation and re-creation of social relations and institutions based on beauty, goodness, and love. An enduring world order calls for an appreciation of the continuity between personality and universe, between the social order and the cosmic order. In no other way is it possible to unite mankind and save beauty, goodness, and love.[44]

[39] Ibid., pp. 38, 39.
[40] Albert Schweitzer, Out of My Life and Thought (New York: Henry Holt and Company, 1949), p. 185.
[41] Mukerjee in B. Singh, op. cit., p. 39.
[42] Ibid., p. 46.
[43] Ibid., p. 73.
[44] Cf. ibid., pp. 73, 74.

A GENERAL THEORY OF SOCIETY

On the basis of social value systems as created, developed, and changed by persons, Mukerjee develops a general theory of society. To attain this theory he calls for a close integration of the social sciences. He deplores the development in the past of the different social sciences in watertight compartments. Only through the close collaboration of the sciences of life, of the mind, and of society can a general theory of society be soundly based and developed. Society "is not divisible" and an understanding of it can be obtained only from studying "the habits, values, and symbols of society as a totality." [45]

Society is "the sum of the structures and functions through which man orients himself to the three dimensions or levels of his environment, ecologic, psychosocial, and telic-moral." In so doing he "fulfils his basic requirements of sustenance, status, and value-fulfilment," [46] according to the three moral levels of prudence, loyalty, and reverence. In the ecologic world, a balance and rhythm of growth takes place for all; in the psychosocial world, a kind of balance or equilibrium occurs for all the institutions and the culture found therein. Here culture becomes the guardian that assures a true equilibrium not merely "between different institutions" but also "between the divergent statuses, expectancies, and values of man." [47] Culture is defined by Mukerjee as "the aggregate of beliefs, values, and behaviors of the members of a society and the aggregate of symbols which express and communicate such beliefs, values, and behaviors." [48] In the telic-moral and spiritual world an equilibrium occurs among all the values functioning therein.

Mukerjee's general theory of society considers society as an open system, which means "an essentially self-directed and active organization that tends toward increased heterogeneity, wholeness, and macroscopic orderliness." It involves the uniqueness of each person's "feelings, emotions, and learned trends." It is this uniqueness of each personality "that con-

[45] *Ibid.*, pp. 11, 19.
[46] *Ibid.*, p. 33.
[47] *Ibid.*, p. 31.
[48] *Ibid.*, pp. 31, 32.

tinually renews culture and changes its course." [49]   Social structure and functions comprise "an expanding universe of symbols, eidos, and ethos."   Social evolution moves from the "immediate, specific, and instrumental to ideal, universal, and intrinsic values." [50]

Social controls are necessary if a society is to maintain its identity and self-sufficiency.   Hence, society "prevents and regulates conflicts of groups and individuals."   It uses physical restraint and coercion to safeguard its status-power-prestige system.   It uses laws to see that values are "protected and shared and at the same time are scaled and ordered."   The personal interiorization of values through experience becomes the chief means of control.

Mukerjee adopts the "field" concept because it is "interactional, emphasizing dynamics within a unified system and self-direction toward a specific coordinated unity of structure and activities." [51]   He repudiates a "closed system" of society, a naturalistic philosophy, and dialectical materialism.   He develops social optima and population optima for the different dimensions of society.   The essence of his general theory of society is "the identification of the way to individual perfection with the general progress of society and humanity in terms of values and ideals exercised in rational direction and control." [52]

Mukerjee envisages a master science of society.   It includes "the human ecological theory, the sociological theory, and the theory of values and symbols" with each standing on its own footing," with each borrowing from and lending to the others."   Together they form what may be called a macroscopic "general theory of society" that unites the various social sciences and "fills the gaps between the various islands of theoretical knowledge." [53]   It is broader "than the science of sociology itself." [54]

[49] *Ibid.*, p. 62.
[50] *Ibid.*, p. 23.
[51] *Ibid.*, p. 63.
[52] *Ibid.*, p. 51.
[53] *Ibid.*, p. 56.
[54] Talcott Parsons, "The Position of Sociological Theory," *American Sociological Review*, 13:156 ff.

The science of sociology is defined by Mukerjee as "an aspect of the general theory of society which is connected with the social relationships of communication and status within the frame-work institutions."[55] Sociology deals with the fundamental complementary status relationships between persons, such as kinship, reciprocity, dominance, deference, distance, proximity, competition, and cooperation within the communicative structure of the institutions of society.[56] It is the function of sociology "to cultivate a dispassionate, objective attitude" toward values without viewing present values as sacrosanct, and "to seek to explore and analyze emerging values and validate all values, new and old, with reference to the social situation, need, and experience."[57]

A unity of the social sciences is pointed out by Mukerjee. Such a unity is needed to speak for "the reality of the manifold human relations as life expressions, as discoveries of, and strivings toward greater fullness and richness of value experience and clarity of meaning in man's ever-expanding life."[58] But a social science theory is needed today "of full and integrated personality and of free and universal society" by which social values themselves may be measured.

There is "a unity of human nature which transcends ethical and cultural relativity and binds mankind in a teleological world order." There is "a continuity and solidarity between man and universe, between the social order and the cosmic order" that must be recognized before there will be "any possibility of uniting mankind."[59] A scientific humanism is not enough, for it cannot arouse "flagging human enthusiasms without these latter being oriented and channeled in an infinite, superhuman, supersocial frame of reference."[60]

There is need for a master science of society, for "the great unanswered questions of mankind" are those which a master social science might be expected to answer. It will include more than sociology, although the field of sociology is developing to include "the sociology of knowledge, the sociology of

[55] Mukerjee in B. Singh, *op. cit.*, p. 27.
[56] *Ibid.*
[57] *Ibid.*, p. 66.
[58] *Ibid.*, p. 41.
[59] *Ibid.*, pp. 73, 74.
[60] Mukerjee, *The Dynamics of Morals*, p. 428.

values, the sociology of symbols, the sociology of arts, and the sociology of religion."[61]   All these fields "have just begun to be assiduously tilled."

A master science of society will be "global in its outlook"; it will tackle "the problems of world community"; it will respect "the common values of mankind, even when revealed in diverse schemes of life in different countries and epochs." It will include a philosophy that will "examine and reconstruct the presuppositions underlying the various social sciences" in the context of changing social-environmental relations and values.   It will sustain "self-correcting methods."[62]

This master science of society will tackle the problems of how "to obtain solidarity, security, freedom, poise, and sharing."   It will clarify "the relations between the social and ethical spheres of human relations."   It will define the processes by which the ideal values of a particular culture are reshaped or destroyed by technology and "diffused widely or circumscribed narrowly by the class system and status-power structure."[63]

It will recognize God as the perennial symbol of the unity of truth, beauty, and goodness coalesced with "wholeness" or holiness.   It will recognize that "God dwells in the heart of every finite creature and leads mankind steadily and steadfastly to universal freedom and perfection."

The master science of human society will accept the belief that the indwelling of God engenders the intense love, sharing, and compassion of the humble, sensitive, and worshipful spirit . . . and leads to the identity of the ends of society, religion, and metaphysics."[64]   It accepts the idea that religion is faith in the "permanence of values."

A general theory of society will include "an indispensable place for both empirical and scientific viewpoints on one hand, and the philosophical and artistic on the other hand." Values can be controlled by the relative constancies in human nature and revealed by symbols.[65]   Social philosophy may "bridge the gulf between biological and moral man and society" and between the philosophy of science and the science of values.[66]

[61] *Ibid.*, p. 70.
[62] *Ibid.*, p. 72.
[63] *Ibid.*

[64] *Ibid.*, p. 15.
[65] *Ibid.*, p. 22.
[66] *Ibid.*, p. 176.

A general theory of society utilizes great art, for it is "the great binder." The great arts of the world "immortalize the collective visions and values of historical cultures and the essential oneness of mankind." Great arts reveal "the perfectibility of man," and "the enduring essence of society that transcends the barriers of class, race, or epoch." [67] The culmination of art is found in music which is "the only adequate, final, and impeccable utterance of man's unutterable ecstasy of concord of Being and Becoming." [68]

Mukerjee's social thought has a universal tone. It is both humanly and cosmically universal. It brings the social sciences into one functioning unit of study and research and application. It brings the science of sociology and the philosophy of science together. Moreover, it views all races of peoples as one. It considers each individual and human society as one. It envisages one world community. It makes values supreme in the human universe, and the human universe an aspect of the cosmic purposeful universe, and it calls for a master science of society that will include all social science, philosophy, and religion.

GROUP DISCUSSION TOPICS

1. The meaning of "social values."
2. Bouglé's concept of "evolution of values."
3. Mukerjee's East Indian heritage.
4. Mukerjee's European and American sociological backgrounds.
5. Mukerjee's "threefold objectivity."
6. Mukerjee's theory of social value.
7. Comparison of Mukerjee and Odum on regional sociology.
8. The concept of "synecology."
9. The relation of values to symbols.
10. The gradation of values.
11. The meaning of "disvalues."
12. The relation of norms to values.
13. The relation of value systems to the structure of personality.
14. The meaning of "value-orientation patterns" (Parsons in *The Social System*).
15. Mukerjee's general theory of human society.
16. Mukerjee's "master science of society."
17. The unity of the social sciences.
18. The relation of science and social philosophy.

[67] *Ibid.*, pp. 394, 405.   [68] *Ibid.*, p. 398.

19. The social role of the great arts in human society.
20. The role of values in a world community system.

READINGS

Bouglé, Charles, *The Evolution of Values* (New York: The Macmillan Company 1926).

Case, Clarence M., "The Value Concept in Sociology and Related Fields," *Sociology and Social Research*, XXIII:403-30.

Lin Yutang, editor, *The Wisdom of India* (London: M. Joseph, 1954).

Mukerjee, Radhakamal, "A General Theory of Society," in B. Singh, editor. *The Frontiers of Social Science* (London: Macmillan and Company, Ltd. 1956), pp. 21-74.

——, "A Theory of Symbols," *Sociology and Social Research*, 39:145-50.

——, "The Broken Balance of Man and Region," *Sociology and Social Research*, XVII:403-8.

——, "The Concepts of Balance and Organization of Social Ecology," *Sociology and Social Research*, XVI:503-16.

——, *The Dynamics of Morals* (London: Macmillan and Company 1950).

——, "Faiths and Influences," in B. Singh, editor, *The Frontiers of Social Science* (London: Macmillan and Company, Ltd. 1956).

——, *The Regional Balance of Man* (Madras: University of Madras 1938).

——, *Regional Sociology* (New York: Century Company 1926).

——, *Social Ecology* (New York: Longmans, Green and Company 1945).

——, *The Social Structure of Values* (London: Macmillan and Company 1949).

——, "Sociology and Mysticism," *Sociology and Social Research*, XV:303-10.

——, *The Theory and Art of Mysticism* (New York: Longmans, Green and Company 1937).

——, "Toward a Sociological Theory of Ethics," *Sociology and Social Research*, 34:431-37.

Parsons, Talcott, "The Position of Sociological Theory," *American Sociological Review*, 13:156 ff.

——, *The Social System* (Glencoe, Ill.: The Free Press 1951), pp. 36-45, 101-12, 180-200.

——, *The Structure of Social Actions* (New York: McGraw-Hill Book Company 1937), pp. 167 ff, 256 ff, 400 ff.

Articles Featuring the Works of Talcott Parsons, *Alpha Kappa Deltan,* Winter, 1959.

Singh, Baljit, editor, *The Frontiers of Social Science* (London: Macmillan and Company 1956).

CHAPTER XLI

DEVELOPMENT OF SOCIOLOGICAL THOUGHT

The rise of social thought has culminated in several scientific thought movements synonymous with the social sciences. One of these culminations has been the development of sociological thought. Despite its youth, inchoateness, and naïveté, sociological thought is exerting a vital influence in the world. It is giving a new rating to the established values of life, undermining some, strengthening others, and creating still others. As distinguished from social thought, sociological thought is the analysis of the meanings to persons of social experiences and the stating of laws and the description of processes that underlie and explain all social life.

The chief values in sociological thought are : it constitutes a center of all worthwhile thought; it exposes prejudices and social intolerance; it smites egoistic living; it rivets attention to the essential human values; it stimulates personal development in harmony with group and societary welfare. At the same time, it postulates group advancement, not upon paternalistic or autocratic grounds, but upon a constructive projection of personalities that harmonizes with co-operative group participation.

RISE OF SOCIOLOGY

For centuries genuine social thinking was confined largely to a few of the intellectually élite. These few lived, and did even their social thinking, in a more or less isolated way. It was not until the first decades of the last century that social thought began to be scientific in character, that is, became sociological. Sociological thinking, however, was isolated and uncorrelated for many years. In the last decade of the nineteenth century, sociology began to develop a considerable group of thinkers and a new morale. There were many disagreements that tended to break the new science asunder. The opening decades, however, of the twentieth century witnessed a development of sociological thought that was followed by the establishment of the teaching of sociology as a profession.

Sociology's rise to recognition has been achieved, but as in the case of newcomers generally it has had to withstand many shafts of ridicule, some of which doubtless were deserved. George Elliott Howard was one of its ablest defenders, at a time when it needed defense.[1]

In a practical way, sociology as well as all the social sciences have both indirectly or directly stimulated a great deal of social investigation. More important, the social sciences have furnished the tools and manned the investigations.[2] Sociology is credited by Dr. Howard with stimulating three "socialization" movements. The first is in the field of education. "Through the 'socialization of education' our schools and colleges, freed in part from the hindering fetters of the 'classical' and other superstitions, are beginning in new and more enlightened ways to minister to the real needs of men."[3] The second involves the practice of religion. "The rising call for the 'socialization of religion and the church,' which is winning encouraging response, may eventually, let us hope, effect a new Reformation in these fields. Aroused to its ethical responsibility, the church is beginning to take a direct hand in efforts for the betterment of world conditions." There is a third development, namely, that represented in the United States by a socialized jurisprudence.[4]

Charles Horton Cooley, another sociological pioneer, speaks from inside the field, and describes three generations of sociologists. Since 1890 sociology has been undergoing a rapid transformation. Cooley was an unusually careful observer of the changes that have occurred.[5] The first generation, going back to 1890, represented armchair and wishful thinking. The second felt that a correct start had not been made and naturally therefore occupied themselves "for the most part with somewhat extensive studies, rather than in-

[1] George Elliott Howard, "Sociology: its Critics and its Fruits," *Journal of Applied Sociology*, VI, No. 4:1.

[2] *Ibid.*, pp. 2, 3.

[3] *Ibid.*, VI:7-9.

[4] *Loc. cit.*

[5] Charles Horton Cooley, "Now and Then," *Journal of Applied Sociology*, VIII:259 ff.

tensive, at the same time endeavoring, by first-hand and dis-interested study of facts, to ensure that their generalizations should have the character of working scientific hypotheses." [6] The third generation found fault with its elders and con-tinues the study of problems and of research methods.   Not content with localized community studies, it is now groping for a larger framework within which to interpret its studies.

Scientific method in sociology goes back to social statistics. Jacques Quetelet (1796—1875) is usually considered the founder of statistical science.   He gives 1820 as the birth year of his science.   He not only applied the method of counting to the study of the members of human society (the census method in its common form), but he tried to get at the problem of causation, and to indicate rules of procedure for making studies in statistics.   Although this celebrated Belgian statistician tabulated and analyzed facts ranging from the astronomical to the societary fields, his ideas can be mentioned here only so far as they contributed to the subject of social thought.   Quetelet pointed out certain of the pit-falls in the way of gathering accurate data.   He improved the methods of census taking, and undertook the difficult tasks that are involved in qualitative human studies.

Among the results of Quetelet's work, the concept of "the average man" is well known.   Quetelet defined the law of averages and described types, especially the average indi-vidual.   Although it is very important and useful to know about the "average man," the term is practically fictitious, since no one even in a large group exactly fits the description. All individuals are either "above" or "below" the average.

The contributions of Quetelet in the field of social statis-tics were admirably supplemented by the achievements of Frederic Le Play (1806—1882).   This French sociologist and mining engineer applied the methods of physical science to social science.   He insisted upon observation of data and the use of induction in making generalizations.   His method is illustrated by his studies in family budgets.   In order to se-cure accurate data he lived with individual families, studying at firsthand the conditions by which they made a livelihood. Le Play opposed *laissez-faire* theories and urged programs of

[6] *Loc. cit.*

reform through the journal which he founded, namely, *La Réforme Sociale*. He rejected socialism, and advocated the method of conciliation and sympathy for effecting agreements among employers and employees. Similar methods in statistics were evolved by German investigators, such as Engels.

The statistical method has been carried forward by a large number of social investigators. With averages, modes, and medians, and so on, it is now possible to make accurate quantitative studies. Current statistical methods include the use of index numbers, frequency tables, discrete series, deviations, skewness, correlations, probable error, measures of reliability. Statistics has thrown a flood of light upon important phases of societary life, such as the economic, where wage scales and price levels are significant concepts. Statistics has been widely utilized in the study of crime and poverty. The various methods of graphic presentations are valuable in interpreting tables of statistical data to the lay mind.[7]

Twelve fields in which social statistics is a functioning method today have been outlined by R. Clyde White. These are: (1) employment and unemployment, (2) poverty, (3) old age dependency, (4) neglected and dependent children, (5) divorce, (6) crime and delinquency, (7) birth and death rates, (8) morbidity, (9) insanity, (10) mental deficiency, (11) education, and (12) the interrelationships among social problems. Social statistics is also "of primary importance to scientific work and to efficient administration."[8] Social statistics is a method that avoids the use of unreliable personal generalizations.

F. H. Giddings gave a far-reaching impetus to the statistical method in sociology. His *Scientific Study of Human Society* is built on the statistical method. Societal patterns are to be sought first, and then societal variables. Behavior is pluralistic, involving "the approximately simultaneous reaction of a considerable number of individuals that happen to be in the same situation or circumstance."[9] Thus "every

7 M. C. Elmer, *Social Statistics*, p. 17.
8 R. Clyde White. *Social Statistics*, pp. 5 ff.
9 Franklin H. Giddings, *Scientific Study of Human Society*, p. 50.

observable phase of human society is statistically a pleuralistic field," [10] with sampling being necessary because of the multiplicity of factors. Most difficult of all the tasks of the sociologist is that of measuring social energies. These must be considered in terms of "what they do." "Relations of toleration, the reactions of conflict, and the reactions of adjustment are notoriously contingent upon forms of association, and these contingencies in a great number of instances admit of quantitative determination." [11]

A practical point in the use of social statistics has been made by Otakar Machotka. He shows how "averages" in two parallel series of social data must be considered in the light of the distribution of all the items in the two series. In a study of 11,982 needy families in Prague the skilled families and the unskilled families were compared. While the average monthly income, for instance, of the skilled families was larger than that of the unskilled families, yet further comparisons by income units showed that the lowest-income families in the unskilled group was much greater in number than the similar-income families in the skilled group, and that at the top for each income group the number of skilled families greatly outnumbered the unskilled. The ratios "crossed" near the points of highest ratios. Dr. Machotka suggests that social differences be studied not in terms of averages but in terms of the crossing of social series and of all the conditioning.[12] Dr. Machotka finds that the less two series of social data are similar, the less likely is the "crossing" to occur "between the greatest frequencies." This result indicates a method for studying social differences, social gains and losses, and for planning for the future according to the verdict of the inventory.

The social survey is one of the most extensive sources today of social thinking. By it, large quantities of social facts are being collected. Urban and rural surveys, specific and general surveys alike, are bases at the present time for inductive social thinking.

[10] *Ibid.*, p. 80.
[11] *Ibid.*, p. 240.
[12] Otakar Machotka, "Social Stratification," *Sociology and Social Research,* XXII:3-13.

CLASSIFICATION METHODS

The nature of the classificatory method has already been indicated. The Greeks classified the various fields of knowledge under three heads : physics, ethics, and politics. Francis Bacon classified knowledge according to his understanding of mental operations. He divided mental fields into three : feeling, memory, reasoning ; and made a corresponding division of knowledge into art, history, and science. Auguste Comte classified the social elements into four groups : the industrial, the esthetic, the scientific, and the philosophical (previsional). His hierarchal classification of the sciences into mathematics, astronomy, physics, chemistry, biology, and sociology has been discussed in an earlier chapter.

Guillaume de Greef (1842—1924) may be considered the leading exponent of the classificatory method. De Greef accepted Comte's hierarchy of the sciences with its basic principles of decreasing generality and increasing dependence of parts, assented to Spencer's evolutionary dictum of increasing coherence and heterogeneity, and added his own concept of volitional contractualism.

De Greef argued that social progress is characterized by an increasing degree of volitional activity and freedom. This volitionalism is the basis of rational social control. The telic factors, however, are not well developed by De Greef. His social thought rests upon a certain logical but inaccurate classification of social factors.

The basis of this classification is increasing volitionalism and particularism. De Greef gives the following classification : economic, industrial, genetic, artistic, scientific, moral, juridical, and political. In holding that the economic elements in society represent the least volitionalism, and the political the most volitional activity, with graded degrees of volitional activities represented by the intermediate factors, the weakness of De Greef's analysis becomes evident. While an improvement over Comte's classification and superior to Spencer's mechanistic order, De Greef's contribution possesses only a relative degree of logical merit. It is far from being objectively correct, and is indicative of the difficulties in the way of classifying social elements in an evolutionary or filial order. There is no doubt that any classification of merit would have to be arranged according to some correlative plan, which would serve the purposes of an exhibit but would not be of much scientific value. Moreover, the classifications that are most useful are classifications of societary forces; these are psychical in nature and may be illustrated by reference to the "four wishes." [13]

Classification is now used in social research as a phase of case analysis. In this sense classification refers to the methods used, for example, by the biologist in "classifying" his data. In studying a new specimen the zoologist refers as many items as possible to well-known categories, and then proceeds to examine the items that cannot be so classified. As a result he may find it necessary to create new categories. By this procedure he comes to understand the specimen under examination.

CULTURAL-HISTORICAL APPROACH

Culture-history refers to the nature of and trends in the customs and traditions of a people. It gives an account of the origins and development of culture patterns, traits, and complexes. It depicts the scene of feeling, thought, and action into which each human being is born and within which he is conditioned to meet life's problems. It portrays the age-old as well as the more recent folkways and mores with which a growing child or adolescent is surrounded.

The close relation of culture to social interaction and to the frustration of personal wishes has been pointed out by J. K. Folsom. If culture channels human actions and molds personality, then it is important to study the culture patterns involved in any conflict situation. "The processes of interaction are channelized, so to speak, by the culture of the people involved. Every culture has its own patterns as channels through which it encourages activities to take place. It discourages other forms of activity which do not follow these channels." [14]

---

[13] By W. I. Thomas.
[14] J. K. Folsom, *Social Psychology*, p. 506.

ECOLOGICAL METHODS

Human ecology is developing sociologically useful concepts for use in research. These concepts begin with spatial relationships. Every aggregation of people has a spatial relationship or pattern of its own. Certain similarities in all may be found; likewise certain peculiarities also operate. Human spatial distribution possesses known characteristics that may be studied. *"Human ecology* is the science which deals with the changing spatial distribution of all organisms, plant and animal as well as human, in which the individual units bear a sustenance or semi-organic relationship to one another. The relationship may be that of mutualism, parasitism, competition, or combination of these. The organic nature of plant and animal communities has been studied for some time in the special disciplines of plant and animal ecology. We are just begining to study human spatial distribution from the same objective standpoint." [15]

Natural area is a term that has a definite meaning to all ecologists, and hence it is a useful concept in research. It is an area in which it is easier than elsewhere for certain types of social conditions, situations, and problems to develop.

Dr. U. G. Weatherly has defined what he called "interest areas." The interest area is one in which the people have bonds of loyalty to a common-social concern, not necessarily related to geographical regions. [16]

Concentration is an ecological term which refers to the results of mobility. Concentrations of population make interesting units for social analysis. [17]

Closely related is *centralization.* A concentration of people is usually undergoing important changes within itself. A special form of concentration is *segregation,* or the gathering of a group of people either freely or under compulsion in a place apart, by themselves. Special attributes run uniform in segregation. It is "the tendency of like units to concentrate within a specific area."

But population does not stay in one place within a given

15 R. D. McKenzie, *Journal of Applied Sociology.* "The Scope of Human Ecology," X:316.
16 U. G. Weatherly, *Journal of Applied Sociology,* X:404.
17 R. D. McKenzie, *op. cit.,* X:317, 318.

concentration. It moves on, to somewhere else, and in so doing illustrates the concept of *succession*. When a given land area is occupied today by Jews and a few years later by Italians, succession is illustrated. When a residence area changes into a business district, succession has occurred.

When people move into an area already occupied by a group that calls itself "native," then *invasion* has taken place. When the invaders supplant the natives, invasion changes into succession.

The *social base map* is a valuable asset in studying the ecological aspects of a community. It portrays many important social relationships and serves a number of research functions. It is "a device for studying the spatial distribution and movement of social phenomena. The location and movement in space at any given moment of peoples and institutions are the resultant of mutually modifying social forces plus the effect of geographic forces. Like iron filings under the influence of a magnet they behave in characteristic ways and assume characteristic forms and patterns. A study of these social patterns is at once a clue to the character of the social forces in question and to the effect of geographic forces." [18]

PARTICIPANT AND NON-PARTICIPANT OBSERVATION

The *participant observer* is a research person who lives in a community, takes part in the activities and functions of the various constituent groups. In this way he gets the "feel" of what is going on. He discovers what the various processes mean to the regular participants. This discovery could never be his if he remained wholly objective.

On the other hand, the participant observer must play a dual role. He must take an objective position after he has performed as a participant, or else his subjective reactions will distort his findings. After taking an active part in the situations which he is studying, the participant observer then withdraws into a scientific and objective role. The studies of *Middletown* and of *Middletown in Transition* are notable examples. [19]

[18] Erle F. Young, *Journal of Applied Sociology*, IX:202.
[19] By Robert and Helen Lynd.

The participant observation method is meritorious in that it gives the investigator insight into what has been described objectively. It is a way of securing meaning and understanding. It reveals what social processes are at work.

Non-participant observation, on the other hand, is wholly objective. The observer takes a position where his presence is not disturbing. He charts and describes what happens, for example, when a group of kindergarten children come together morning after morning. The non-participant observer may follow in detail the behavior of one child only, whether he plays a dominant or quiescent role, whether he plays alone or with others, whether he performs in a clique, and so on. In this way a great deal can be learned about particular personalities and their growth. The method is most effective where groups are small and the conditions are somewhat subject to control.[20]

Non-participant observers sometimes operate mechanized processes for recording behavior. They gather immense quantities of data which may be treated by statistical machines and formulae. The observations of one investigator are measured against those of another of the same moving set of conditions and thus the relative accuracy of several observers may be recorded.

The variations in the observations of reliable observers are startling. Thomas, Loomis, and Arrington report that "four observers do not constitute a stable observational norm." Moreover, "three consecutive observations are not a large enough number to permit the isolation of consistency from reliability."[21]

It appears that observational errors vary with the type of situation studied. Observer inconsistency is a definite factor. Distortion of reality repeatedly occurs.[22] In other words, accuracy of research rests on overcoming the inaccuracies of observation even on the part of trained observers.

PERSONAL INTERVIEW AND LIFE HISTORY METHOD

In the social case analysis field the interview and life his-

---

[20] Thomas, Loomis, and Arrington, *Observational Studies of Social Behavior* (New Haven: Yale University, Institute of Human Relations 1933).

[21] *Ibid.,* p. 246.

[22] *Loc. cit.*

tory procedures are challenging methods of research. Not formal facts but human experiences are the subject matter. In experiences we find many of the explanations of social conflicts.

The research interview has methods that are all its own. It aims to make objective and available research materials that are highly subjective in nature. Despite the difficulties involved, it has made tangible progress.

Interviewing is a social process that involves a series of interacting relationships, usually between two persons known as interviewer and interviewee. At every state of the process the interviewer-interviewee situation changes; the reactions of both interviewer and interviewee tend to change from moment to moment according to each successive stimulus in the process.

This process may be called *spiral response,* because after each round the interviewer and the interviewee occupy a more advanced position of knowledge about each other and about the social situation under consideration than they did at the beginning of each round of interaction. The interviewer does not act as questioner but becomes an associate and joint-student with the interviewee. Together they strive to obtain data and to seek meanings.[23]

Personality research is an intensive boring-in process. Heavy layers of defense reactions, and of "too-personal-to-tell" factors must be penetrated. No complete personal life history has ever been written. Some things are bound to be withheld.

Personal experiences are the first stratum. These and accompanying opinions are near the surface. They are fairly easy to obtain. Beneath are the persons' real attitudes. Influencing all are the basic wishes. Complete personality research gives a cross section of all the major personality elements. Extensive and representative sampling of all the personalities in a given social conflict situation offers meaningful interpretations of social problems.

Charles A. Ellwood, while accepting the interpretation of "objective," which means that the scholar should keep his

[23] E. S. Bogardus, "Interviewing as a Social Process," *Sociology and Social Research,* XIX:70-75.

own ideas and feelings out of his research, protests against "objective" in the behavioristic sense. To use purely natural science methods is to be blind to a very real part of the subject matter of sociology. Human life cannot be reduced entirely to habit and environment. Social facts cannot be studied "apart from the conscious subject in whose minds they exist." Feelings, sentiments, and values are valid data for sociological study. The true nature of human relations involves values and these must be included in a sociological analysis. The older methods of the natural sciences are described as: (1) observation, (2) experiment, and (3) measurement; the newest methods of the social sciences are: (1) scientific imagination, (2) psychological analysis, and (3) historical interpretation. The quantitative stage of science "appears to be merely transitional," and both physical and social science will turn toward: (1) logical reasoning, (2) synthesis, and (3) logical criticism of theories.[24]

A similar position is held by Robert M. MacIver, for he contends that "the range of the measurable is not the range of the knowable." The most important phases of life, such as happiness or pain, cannot be measured. Science, when limited to the measurable, is "a means to power, not to understanding." We can measure only the external and know only the internal. "It is only quantity we can measure, but it is only quality we can experience."[25]

Concepts are important tools in social research. Without accurate usage of such concepts no progress in research can be expected. At the present writing the following classification of representative sociological concepts is offered as a basis for discussion.

SOCIAL RESEARCH

Social research may be thought of in terms of (1) agencies participating, (2) methods of gathering data, (3) types of materials that are collected, (4) methods of treatment of the collected data, (5) products that result from the methods of treatment, and (6) finding in terms of community and personality.

---

24 *Ibid.*, pp. 82, 83.
25 R. M. MacIver, *The Elements of Science*, pp. 15, 16.

1. Agencies participating
   (a) Social science departments
   (b) Psychology, biology, and related departments
   (c) Social research societies and foundations
   (d) Research divisions of private and public enterprise
   (e) Independent and lone investigators

2. Methods of gathering data
   (a) Non-participant observation and notation
   (b) Participant observation
   (c) Making social surveys and community studies
   (d) Experimentation, projects, and control group studies
   (e) Personal interviewing and securing life histories
   (f) Complete case studies

3. Types of materials
   (a) Ecological data
   (b) Culture-history facts
   (c) Current social facts, objective in type
   (d) Attitudes, values, opinions

4. Treatment of materials
   (a) Statistical
   (b) Logical and comparative
   (c) Case analyses
   (d) Classification and interpretation

5. Products of treatment
   (a) Averages and trends
   (b) Coexistences and sequences
   (c) Social processes and laws

(1) There is particular need for the agencies taking part in social research to co-operate. The future bulks large when the results of co-operative sociological research are anticipated. Individual research, however, even within university departments, is still the rule.

(2) The methods of gathering social research data are still inchoate. Common agreement has not yet been reached. Experimentation with methods is the rule. In fact, much social research involves the search for better tools with which to work.

(3) The types of materials of research value are limitless in variety. The ecological data are far-removed in content from interview and life history documents. Culture-history backgrounds are different from current social facts. None

can be ignored if a total picture of a conflict situation is sought.

(4) The methods of treatment of research data are so varied that sometimes one method does not recognize the validity of another type of procedure. Probably each of the several methods has something worthy to contribute. Co-ordination of methods is needed.

(5) If the products of social research are expressed in terms of averages and trends or of coefficients of correlation and probable error, they do not seem to be related to a statement of social processes and laws. In between come findings in terms of coexistences, sequences, and possible causal relationships.

(6) Social research may be reviewed as culminating in both community or group studies and in personality studies. The first are more objective and formal; the second, more subjective in content and meaningful.

6. Findings

    A. *Community*
    (a) Natural areas and spatial relationships
    (b) Material resources and utilization
    (c) Cultural traditions and trends
    (d) Psycho-social conflicts and adjustments

    B. *Personality*
    (a) Experiences, direct and derivative
    (b) Feeling reactions and opinions
    (c) Attitudes and values
    (d) Behavior patterns and configurations

A goal of social research is to formulate laws about social life and processes. In social psychology Florian Znaniecki distinguishes between (1) laws of evolution, (2) laws of finality, (3) laws of motivation, (4) laws of suggestive social interaction, and (5) quantitative laws.[26] K. D. Har analyzes laws into four types: (1) teleological laws, (2) logical laws, (3) positive laws, and (4) statistical laws.[27] He sums up a complicated problem by concluding that a law is "a statement of

[26] Florian Znaniecki, *The Laws of Social Psychology* (Chicago: University of Chicago Press 1925), Ch. I.

[27] K. D. Har, *Social Laws* (Chapel Hill: University of North Carolina Press 1930), Ch. II.

relations." Positive and statistical laws are scientific, and scientific laws are of three kinds : (1) "Those which describe invariant causal relations, (2) those which describe invariant associations, and (3) those which describe varying degrees of correlations." [28] The essence of a scientific social law is found in "a description of an invariant pattern of social phenomena." Even such a definition is subject to qualifications, and the discovery of such laws in social life still baffles social research. How can invariant patterns be reliably defined in a changing world that is characterized by so many variant factors as is ours?

TEACHING OF SOCIOLOGY

For a long time sociology was considered only as a postgraduate study. In the last few years, however, sociology has been making its way downward in college and university curricula, until it is being widely taught to college freshmen and sophomores. In this connection there is a variety of textbooks that have been written to meet the needs of beginning students. Some teachers would introduce sociology through anthropological studies, beginning with the origins of man. Others would give a survey or prospectus of social institutions, processes, and problems. Still others would deal only with social problems. Then there are those persons who would build a textbook around a central theme, tracing it through a series of social relationships. One of the more advanced approaches is the conceptual. Park and Burgess' *Introduction to the Science of Sociology* made this approach, dealing with "human nature," "isolation," "social contacts," "social interaction," "competition," "conflict," "accommodation," "assimilation," and so forth.

For high schools, the technique of sociological teaching is in the beginning stages. The importance of teaching social science in high schools is generally recognized, but there has been great difficulty in effecting an agreement among the various social science branches. Some high school teachers prefer a "social problems" course, although the demand is growing for "social science" courses, dividing the time more

28 *Ibid.*, p. 12.

or less evenly between human geography, economics, sociology, and civics. There are other high school teachers who contend that sociology can be taught best in a general "citizenship" course. One of the specific difficulties is that the high school curriculum is full, and that the representatives of none of the established courses are willing to see the subjects in which they are interested crowded out. Another difficulty is the power which the self-culture and self-development concepts possess. The equal importance of the social culture and social development concepts is being recognized, but with amazing slowness.

In the grades the teaching of social science is gaining ground. In the sense that there is an advanced group of mathematical studies for university men and women and an elemental mathematics for the grades, so there is advanced sociology, and also an elemental sociology centering around the activities of the primary groups, such as the family, play, neighborhood, and school groups. A child who is old enough to learn to obey is old enough to begin the study of elemental sociology; in fact, when he learns to obey, he is already beginning to experience the meaning of social, if not sociological, concepts.[29] Simple social studies are being prepared for the grades, even beginning with the first grade.

The dissemination of sociological thought is a practical question to which in the last score of years special attention has been given. The universities and colleges began to establish chairs of sociology in the closing years of the last century. The movement has acquired a remarkable momentum in the United States. Normal schools and high schools have adopted the movement. Sociological journals have multiplied.

THE SPAN OF SOCIAL THOUGHT

From the social proverbs of primitive man to treatises such as Ross' *Principles of Sociology*, Park and Burgess' *Introduction to the Science of Sociology*, or von Wiese's *Systematic Sociology*, with their careful analyses of significant societal processes — this is the main span of social thought.

---

[29] Such as superordination and subordination (according to Simmel).

Social thought began in the simplest form of observations about social relationships between individual and individual, between chieftain and tribal member, between master and servant. It experienced various stages of denunciation of social wrongs. It produced perspectives of perfect societies. It moved profoundly forward in the form of social philosophies. Now it is proceeding either as the investigator of new social facts, or the social-psychological interpreter of these facts in terms of social processes. It is assuming a scientific procedure, although a portion of the results of its undertakings finds expression in social philosophy. It is beginning to formulate sociological laws. It is pointing out techniques for preventing the maladjustments that produce social evils; it is also establishing a teaching technique. Although the masses of the human race are beginning to feel blindly the meaning of social values, they have not yet been able to make their highest social aspirations rationally articulate. Until that time comes, democracy will remain an experiment, and world progress a toy of autocratic forces.

A history of social thought is essentially a review of a slow, irregular, but positive acceptance of social thought concepts. Individual after individual, leader after leader, profession after profession, group after group, have felt and accepted the challenge of the sociological viewpoint. In so doing and living they have found enrichment of personality and contributed to the advancement of society. Since the days of Comte in particular, the social sciences have been increasing in variety, and they number a score or more, and sociological influence has been widening until the related sciences are inviting sociology, which is the scientific study of collective behavior, to define their objectives for them. In fact, sociological concepts are permeating the fathermost reaches of personal living and societal control. A history of social thought is a history of the processes involved in the socializing of human attitudes and values, presaging a human society in which personal achievement and group progress are equally and supremely sought.

To some sociological thought began in France with Auguste Comte; to others, in England with Herbert Spencer; and to still others in the United States with Lester F. Ward. In France the name of Comte, who coined the term *sociology* about 1838, and who developed "positivistic" foundations, has been followed by the name of Durkheim. It is Durkheim who is credited with teaching the first courses in sociology in France beginning in 1887 (in the University of Bordeaux). Many other French writers have contributed to sociology but none excels in importance or perhaps equal the achievements of Durkheim. His emphasis upon separating the descriptive and analytical phases of social life from value-judgments has given French sociology an objective trend.

The influence of French sociology has been felt in England, Germany, and the United States, but has exercised a more dominating force in other countries perhaps, such as Russia, Belgium, Italy, Turkey, and Argentina. Many Russian writers came to France to live. Many sociological studies in other countries than France have been produced in France. The ideas of Durkheim have been noticeable in all.

Belgian sociology has been closely allied with the French. It has been written largely in French, and it has shown French trends. However, De Greef and other Belgian sociologists have attained the level of making independent studies and of achieving original contributions.

Likewise, Italian writers have felt the impact of French sociological thought. Even Pareto lived many years in France and Switzerland and owed much to French thinkers, although developing his ideas independently. The Italian flair for criminology centers around the studies of Lombroso and gives to Italy prominence in this field of sociology.

French sociology appears in Turkey in many writers. The "real founder of Turkish sociology" is Ziga Gokalp (1875–1924) who translated some of the works of Durkheim into Turkish and who developed a system of his own, "founded on Durkheim's works." He developed a "dualism of civilization and culture, with cultures being more or less of national group significance, and with civilization being an inter-group achievement."[30] Other sociologists have been affected by

---

[30] Niyazi Berkes, "Sociology in Turkey," *American Journal of Sociology*, 42:242ff.

the works of Simmel and Weber, but Durkheim has been the most important sociological force.

In Argentina, the first sociological name of importance has been that of Dr. Ernesto Quesada, whose teaching at the University of Buenos Aires began in 1904.[31] In the University of Cordova, the achievements of Dr. Paul A. Orgaz have been influenced by American writers, particularly in the social-psychological field. Orgaz has been doing important work in gathering a group of associates about him; Alfredo Poviña illustrates this development.

In Brazil sociology is represented by a number of scholars. The *Principios de Sociologia* by Fernando de Azevedo, a member of the faculty of the University of São Paulo, was published in 1935, and is but one of many volumes by the same author. In the main Dr. Azevedo builds upon French sociology; however, he is well versed in the writing of other European sociologists, and pays tribute to the sociologists of the United States. He centers his analyses around "social facts" and their nature. He takes cognizance of the synthetic and historical methods of German writers and of the analytical procedures of North American sociologists.

In Rio de Janeiro, Dr. Delgado de Carvalho has been an outstanding sociological leader. His interest in educational sociology is well known and his *Sociologia Educational* begins with a discussion of primary, intermediate, and secondary groups. It then discusses social values at some length. Social groups and social values serve as a basis for an analysis of the educational process. In this discussion the influence of Dewey is noticeable. His *Sociologia Aplicada* is a noteworthy contribution. An elementary text has been prepared by Dr. Carvalho for use in the "curso complementar," or two-year liberal arts course required in Brazil of persons entering the professional schools. It will prove very useful and is entitled *Praticas de Sociologia*. One other outstanding Brazilian name may be mentioned, that of Arturio Ramos, whose work in the field of social research, particularly of research in race relations, has attracted wide attention. His best-known studies are: *O Negro Brasilein, O*

31 Alfredo Poviña, "A Brief History of the Teaching of Sociology in the Argentine Republic," *Sociology and Social Research*, 17:505.

Folk-Lore Negro do Brasil, and the *Culturos Negros no Novo Mundo.* His point of view is psycho-sociological and is developed in his *Introducção á Psychologia,* published in 1936.

Augustin Venturino's work in Chile is worthy of consideration. He has made analyses of the customs and traditions of the Indians of Chile, showing how the physical environment has played a role. The conflicts between the Indian and the Spanish invader are described, particularly in terms of differing cultures and of cultural accommodations. Venturino describes the dominance of the city in Chile over rural life. Other ecological as well as cultural processes are emphasized. Venturino thus stresses first of all physical influences in social life, then, the cultural, particularly the cultural importance of the city is made evident. Beneath Venturino's literary style are many valuable social observations.

From Peru has come the important synthetic work of Mariano H. Cornejo. Spanish, French, English, and American social thought emerge in Cornejo's writings. He considers the social life of man and of higher animals to be phases of the same process. He divided physical factors into external and internal; for example, climate, and heredity. Also there are two types of social factors, that is to say, primary and secondary. The first are represented by language, and the second by education.

Herbert Spencer's role as a sociologist in England has been far less fruitful in producing successors than might be expected. Critics have been numerous enough, but English sociology has been largely expressed in social philosophy, culture history, or social investigation. The recent outstanding figure of Leonard T. Hobhouse is known best for his contributions to political philosophy. Ethnological contributions by noteworthy English sociological writers have had most influence in France, Germany, and the United States. A stimulus to sociology in India has been given, and Indian sociology colored by mysticism has been developing.

In Germany sociology of a philosophical nature has produced a galaxy of well-known writers. There is plenty of room for disagreement, but probably Simmel has had the greatest influence. Tönnies, Max Weber, Vierkandt, von

Wiese, Mannheim, and others have made a great impression on sociological thought. Their erudition has made important additions to sociology. Their thinking has penetrated French, English, Russian, and Japanese thought and has been widely acclaimed in the United States. Simmel has stood at or near the top of the list of German writers who have influenced American sociology.

It has remained for the United States to make the most extensive contributions to a science of sociology. Lester F. Ward, opposed to the individualism of Herbert Spencer, developed social telesis and socioeducational theories. Sumner gave folkways a lasting connotation. Small produced ethical and social-philosophical interpretations of "the social process." Giddings built up the concept of consciousness of kind. Ross pioneered in analyzing social control and laid foundations for a social-psychological approach to the study of human relations.

In the past two or three decades American sociology has made rapid strides in developing departments of sociology in many colleges and universities. Nearly a hundred of these institutions offer "majors" leading to the degree of Doctor of Philosophy in sociology. Thousands of college students are annually taking courses in sociology and graduates in sociology are finding employment in many fields, including industry and government service. Moreover, as sociology has come to be better understood as a basic social science, it has been rising in public esteem.

Recent years have seen a great upsurge in research in the various fields of social science. As empirical research and the use of social statistics in sociology have increased, the emphasis on making value judgments has shifted into the fields of ethics and social philosophy. Research into the nature of small groups has been surging forward. Industrial sociology has been coming to the fore. Marriage and the family are subjects receiving more and more intensive research. Deviant behavior is calling forth basic research, and the sociology of the uses of leisure time is receiving widespread research attention. Social stratification is being analyzed by an increasing number of sociological investigators.

A number of special social fields are arousing research

interest, such as the sociology of aging, the sociology of mental health, the sociology of law, the sociology of religion, the sociology of knowledge.

The growth in sociological interest is illustrated by the development of national sociological societies, not only in the United States but in several European countries and the Orient. The American Sociological Society at its Fifty-second Annual Meeting in 1958 offered a program that included 65 sessions with 350 designated participants as compared with the Annual Meeting ten years earlier in 1948 that offered 21 sessions and had 90 assigned participants. Several regional sociological societies in the United States meet annually and present noteworthy programs.

In the field of social theory, current attention centers on such themes as problems of concept formation, theory construction, models in social science, operationalism in social research, levels in social theory, values in social science, deviant modes of social adaptation. Moreover, a master social science has been proposed which will include not only sociology and the other social sciences but all scientific knowledge, religious thought, and philosophy as a frame of reference within which to conduct specific pieces of research regarding the nature of social relations.

GROUP DISCUSSION TOPICS

1. The chief method, historically, of social investigation.
2. The strong and weak points of the statistical method.
3. The "classification" method.
4. The "natural history" method.
5. The life history of a community.
6. The meaning of personality research.
7. The significance of culture factors.
8. Basic ecological concepts.
9. The social base map procedure.
10. Participant observation.
11. Non-participant observation.
12. Comparisons of statistical and case analysis.
13. A complete research pattern.
14. The chief values in sociological thought.
15. Major reasons for the downward movement of social thought courses in school curricula.

16. A summary of three or four main phases of the history of social thought.
17. The rise of sociology in France.
18. The influence of French sociology on other countries.
19. The failure for the rise of sociology in a widespread way in England.
20. Reasons for the prominence of German social philosophers.
21. The scientific trend in sociology in the United States.
22. Present status of sociology in the world.
23. Future possibilities of sociology.

READINGS

Armstrong, L., "The Influence of American Sociology in the Middle East," *Sociology and Social Research*, 42:176-84.

Barnes, Harry E., *Historical Sociology: Its Origins and Development* (New York: Philosophical Library 1948).

———, editor, *An Introduction to the History of Sociology* (Chicago: University of Chicago Press 1948).

Becker, Howard, and Harry E. Barnes, *Social Thought from Lore to Science* (Washington: Harren Press 1952).

Bogardus, Emory S., *Fundamentals of Social Psychology* (New York: Appleton-Century-Crofts, Inc. 1950).

———, *The Making of Public Opinion* (New York: Association Press 1951).

———, "Sociology as a World-wide Social Science," *Sociology and Social Research*, 39:409-14.

Brim, O. G., Jr., *Sociology and Education* (New York: Russell Sage Foundation 1958).

Burgess, Ernest W., "Seven Significant Changes in Sociology," *Sociology and Social Research*, 40:385-88.

Ellwood, Charles A., *A History of Social Philosophy* (New York: Prentice-Hall, Inc. 1938).

Gitler, Joseph B., *Social Dynamics* (New York: McGraw-Hill Book Company 1952).

Hartley, E. L., and Ruth, *Fundamentals of Social Psychology* (New York: Alfred A. Knopf, Inc. 1952).

Hawley, Amos H., *Human Ecology* (New York: Ronald Press Company 1950).

House, Floyd N., *The Development of Sociology* (New York: McGraw-Hill Book Company 1936).

Kilzer, E., and E. J. Ross, *Western Social Thought* (Milwaukee: The Bruce Publishing Company 1954).

Madge, John, *The Tools of Social Science* (New York: Longmans, Green and Company 1953).

Merton, R. K., *Social Theory and Social Structure* (Glencoe, Ill.: The Free Press 1957).

Mihanovich, C. S., *Social Theorists* (Milwaukee: The Bruce Publishing Company 1953).
Morioka, K. K., and Jesse F. Steiner, "American Sociology in Japan," *American Journal of Sociology*, LXIV:606-9.
Odum, Howard W., *American Sociology* (New York: Longmans, Green and Company 1951).
Ogburn, W. F., *Social Change with Respect to Culture* (New York: The Viking Press 1950).
———, "Trends in a Half Century of Sociology," *Sociology and Social Research*, 40:399-400.
Parsons, Talcott, *Essays in Sociological Theory* (Glencoe, Ill.: The Free Press 1954).
Quinn, James A., *Human Ecology* (New York: Prentice-Hall, Inc. 1950).
Rapport, V. A., and others, "Sociology in Italy," *American Sociological Review*, 22:441-48.
Rose, Arnold M., *Theory and Method in the Social Sciences* (Minneapolis: The University of Minnesota Press 1954).
Roucek, J. S., and Associates, *Social Control* (New York: D. Van Nostrand Company 1947).
Sorokin, Pitirim, *Society, Culture, and Personality* (New York: Harper & Brothers 1947).
———, *Contemporary Sociological Theories* (New York: Harper & Brothers 1928).
Steiner, Jesse F., "Present Trends in Sociology," *Sociology and Social Research*, 41:87-92.
Von Wiese, Leopold, and Howard Becker, *Systematic Sociology* (New York: John Wiley & Sons 1933).
Williams, Melvin J., *Catholic Social Thought* (New York: Ronald Press Company 1950).
Williamson, Robert C., "Sociology in Latin America," *Sociology and Social Research*, 40:24-30.
Young, Pauline, *Scientific Social Surveys and Research* (New York: Prentice-Hall, Inc. 1949).

SELECTED BIBLIOGRAPHY

PRIMARY SOURCES

Aristotle, *Politics,* translated by Jowett (London: Oxford University Press 1905).

Augustine, Saint, *The City of God,* translated by Watts (New York: G. P. Putnam's Sons 1912).

Aurelius, Marcus, *Meditations of* (London: Dent and Company 1935).

———, *Thoughts* (London: Frowde, n. d.).

Baldwin, J. Mark, *Social and Ethical Interpretations in Mental Development* (New York: The Macmillan Company 1906).

Barnes, H. E., and Howard Becker, *Social Thought from Lore to Science,* two vols. (Boston: D. C. Heath and Company 1938).

Bodin, Jean, *The Six Books of a Commonweale* (London: Bishop 1606).

Borgatta, E. F., and H. J. Meyer, editors, *Social Control and the Foundations of Sociology, Pioneer Contributions of Edward A. Ross to the Study of Society* (Boston: Beacon Press 1959).

Bouglé, Charles, *The Evolution of Values,* translated by Helen S. Sellers (New York: The Macmillan Company 1926).

Buckle, H. T., *History of Civilization in England* (New York: Appleton and Company 1874).

Carver, T. N., *Essays in Social Justice* (Cambridge: Harvard University Press 1915).

Cooley, Charles H., *Human Nature and the Social Order* (New York: Charles Scribner's Sons 1902).

———, *Social Organization* (New York: Charles Scribner's Sons 1909).

———, *Social Process* (New York: Charles Scribner's Sons 1918).

Comte, Auguste, *Positive Philosophy* (London: Bell and Sons 1913).

Durkheim, Emile, *De la division du travail social* (Paris: Alcan 1903).

———, *Education and Sociology,* translated by S. D. Fox (Glencoe, Ill.: The Free Press 1956).

———, *The Elementary Forms of the Religious Life,* translated by J. W. Swain (Glencoe, Ill.: The Free Press 1954).

———, *On the Division of Labor in Society;* being a translation of his *De la division du travail social,* with an estimate of his work, by George Simpson (New York: The Macmillan Company 1933).

———, *The Rules of Sociological Method,* edited by G. E. G. Catlin (Glencoe, Ill.: The Free Press 1950).

———, *Sociology and Philosophy,* translated by D. F. Pocock (Glencoe, Ill.: The Free Press 1953).

Ellwood, Charles A., *A History of Social Philosophy* (New York: Prentice-Hall, Inc. 1938).

671

Ellwood, Charles A., *Method in Sociology* (Durham: Duke University 1933).

——, *The Psychology of Human Society* (New York: Appleton and Company 1925).

Epictetus, Discourses of (New York: Scott-Shaw 1903).

Eubank, E. E., *Concepts of Sociology* (Boston: D. C. Heath and Company 1932).

Galton, Francis, *Hereditary Genius* (New York: The Macmillan Company 1914).

George, Henry, *Progress and Poverty* (New York: Doubleday 1916).

Giddings, Franklin H., *Principles of Sociology* (New York: The Macmillan Company 1896).

——, *The Scientific Study of Human Society* (Chapel Hill: University of North Carolina Press 1924).

——, *Studies in the Theory of Human Society* (New York: The Macmillan Company 1922).

Gumplowicz, Ludwig, *Der Rassenkampf* (Innsbruck: Wagner 1928).

——, *Grundriss der Sociologie* (Philadelphia: American Academy of Political and Social Science 1899).

——, *Outlines of Sociology,* translated by F. W. Moore (Philadelphia: American Academy of Political and Social Science 1899).

Halbwachs, Maurice, *The Psychology of the Social Classes* (Glencoe, Ill.: The Free Press 1958).

Henri, Comte de Saint-Simon, edited and translated by F. M. H. Markham (New York: The Macmillan Company 1952).

Hobbes, Thomas, *Leviathan* (New York: G. P. Putnam's Sons 1904).

Hobhouse, L. T., *Morals in Evolution* (New York: Henry Holt and Company 1919).

——, *Social Development* (New York: Henry Holt and Company 1924).

——, *Social Evolution and Political Theory* (London: Lemcke 1911).

Keller, A. G., *Societal Evolution* (New York: The Macmillan Company 1929).

Kropotkin, Peter, *Mutual Aid: A Factor in Evolution* (New York: Doubleday, Page and Company 1902).

Langland, William, *The Vision of Piers the Plowman* (New York: E. P. Dutton and Company 1912).

Lassalle, Ferdinand, *Science and the Workingman* (Chicago: Kerr 1903).

Lévy-Bruhl, Lucian, *Les fonctions mentales dans les sociétés inférieures* (Paris: Alcan 1910).

——, *The Philosophy of Auguste Comte* (New York: G. P. Putnam's Sons 1903).

Lilienfeld, Paul von, *Gedanken über die Sozialwissenschaft der Zukunft* (Berlin: Reimer 1903).

Locke, John, *Two Treatises on Government* (London: Routledge, n. d.).

Machiavelli, *The Prince* (London: Routledge, n. d.).

Mackenzie, J. S., *Outlines of Social Philosophy* (New York: The Macmillan Company 1918).

Malthus, Thomas, *An Essay on the Principle of Population* (London: Reeves and Turner 1878).

Mannheim, Karl, *Essays on the Sociology of Culture,* edited by Ernest Manheim and Paul Kecskemeti (New York: Oxford University Press 1956).

———, *Essays on the Sociology of Knowledge,* edited by Paul Kecskemeti (New York: Oxford University Press 1952).

———, *Essays on Sociology and Social Psychology,* edited by Paul Kecskemeti (New York: Oxford University Press 1953).

———, *Freedom, Power, and Democratic Planning* (New York: Oxford University Press 1950).

———, *Ideology and Utopia* (New York: Harcourt Brace and Company 1936).

———, *Systematic Sociology,* edited by J. S. Eros and W. A. C. Stewart (New York: Philosophical Library 1958).

Maquet, Jacques J., *The Sociology of Knowledge* (Boston: The Beacon Press 1951).

Marx, Karl, *Das Kapital,* translated by Moore and Aveling (Chicago: Kerr 1909).

McDougall, William, *Introduction to Social Psychology* (Boston: A. C. Luce and Company 1908).

Merton, R. K., *Social Theory and Social Structure* (Glencoe, Ill.: The Free Press 1958).

Montesquieu, Charles L., *The Spirit of Laws* (London: Bell and Sons 1894).

More, Thomas, *Utopia* (London: Bell and Sons 1910).

Mukerjee, Radhakamal, "A General Theory of Society," in B. Singh, editor, *The Frontiers of Social Science* (London: Macmillan and Company 1956).

———, *The Dynamics of Morals* (London: Macmillan and Company 1950).

———, *The Social Structure of Values* (London: Macmillan and Company 1949).

Nietzsche, Friedrich, *The Will to Power,* translated by A. M. Ludovici (London: Allen 1924).

Novicow, Jacques, *War and its Alleged Benefits* (New York: Henry Holt and Company 1911).

Odum, Howard W., "Folk and Regional Conflict as a Field of Sociological Study," *Publication of the American Sociological Society,* XXV:1-17.

Odum, Howard W., "Folk Sociology as a Subject Field for the Historical Study of Total Human Society and the Empirical Study of Group Behavior," *Social Forces*, 31:193-223.

Ogburn, W. F., *Social Change with Respect to Culture and Original Nature* (New York: The Viking Press 1950).

Pareto, Vilfredo, *The Mind and Society*, edited by Arthur Livingston, four volumes (New York: Harcourt, Brace and Co. 1935).

Park, Robert E., *Race and Culture*, edited by E. C. Hughes and others (Glencoe: The Free Press 1950).

Park, Robert E., and Ernest W. Burgess, *Introduction to the Science of Sociology* (Chicago: University of Chicago Press 1921).

Parsons, Talcott, *The Social System* (Glencoe: The Free Press 1951).

Ratzenhofer, Gustav, *Die soziologische Erkenntniss* (Leipzig: Brockhaus 1898).

———, *Soziologie* (Leipzig: Brockhaus 1907).

Ross, Edward A., *Principles of Sociology* (New York: D. Appleton-Century Company 1938).

———, *Social Control* (New York: The Macmillan Company 1901).

Rousseau, J. J. *Contrat social* (Paris: Garnier, n. d.).

Seneca, *Moral Essays*, translated by J. W. Basore (New York: G. P. Putnam's Sons 1928).

Simmel, Georg, *Soziologie* (München: Duncker und Humboldt 1923).

Small, Albion W., *The Cameralists* (Chicago: University of Chicago Press 1909).

———, *General Sociology* (Chicago: University of Chicago Press 1905).

———, *Origins of Sociology* (Chicago: University of Chicago Press 1914).

Smith, Adam, *The Wealth of Nations* (New York: G. P. Putnam's Sons 1904).

Sombart, Werner, *New Social Philosophy*, translated by K. F. Geiser (Princeton: Princeton University Press 1937).

Sorokin, P. A., *Contemporary Sociological Theories* (New York: Harper & Brothers 1928).

———, *Social Mobility* (New York: Harper & Brothers 1927).

Spencer, Herbert, *Principles of Sociology* (New York: Appleton and Company 1914).

———, *Social Statics* (New York: Appleton and Company 1903).

———, *The Study of Sociology* (New York: Appleton and Company 1910).

Stark, Werner, *The Sociology of Knowledge* (London: Routledge & Kegan Paul 1958).

Sumner, W. G., *Folkways* (New York: Ginn and Company 1907).

Sumner, W. G., *What Social Classes Owe Each Other* (New York: Harper & Brothers 1920).

Sumner and Keller, *The Science of Society,* four volumes (New Haven: Yale University Press 1929).

Sun Yat-sen, San Min Chu I, *The Three Principles of the People* (Shanghai: China Committee, Institute of Pacific Relations 1927).

Tarde, Gabriel, *La logique sociale* (Paris: Alcan 1898).

———, *The Laws of Imitation* (New York: Henry Holt and Company 1903).

———, *Social Laws* (New York: The Macmillan Company 1907).

Thomas, William I., *Primitive Culture* (New York: McGraw-Hill Book Company 1937).

———, *Source Book for Social Origins* (Chicago: University of Chicago Press 1907).

Thomas, William I., and Florian Znaniecki, *The Polish Peasant in Europe and America* (Chicago: University of Chicago Press 1918).

Thomas William I., and Dorothy S. Thomas, *Child in America* (New York: Knopf 1928).

Todd, A. J., *Theories of Social Progress* (New York: The Macmillan Company 1918).

Tönnies, Ferdinand, *Community and Society* (East Lansing, Mich.: The Michigan State University Press 1957).

———, *Gemeinschaft und Gesellschaft* (Berlin: Curtius 1926).

Tylor, E. B., *Primitive Culture* (New York: Brentano's 1924).

Veblen, Thorstein, *The Nature of Peace* (New York: The Macmillan Company 1917).

———, *The Portable Veblen,* edited by Max Lerner (Washington, D.C.: Public Affairs Press 1958).

———, *The Theory of the Leisure Class* (New York: The Macmillan Company 1912).

Vierkandt, Alfred, *Gesellschaftslehre* (Stuttgart: Enke 1928).

Von Wiese, Leopold, *Systematic Sociology,* translated and adapted by Howard Becker (New York: Wiley & Sons 1932).

Wallas, Graham, *The Great Society* (New York: The Macmillan Company 1914).

———, *Our Social Heritage* (New Haven: Yale University Press 1921).

Ward, Lester F., *Applied Sociology* (Boston: Ginn and Company 1906).

———, *Dynamic Sociology* (New York: Appleton and Company 1915).

———, *Psychic Factors in Civilization* (Boston: Ginn and Company 1906).

———, *Pure Sociology* (New York: The Macmillan Company 1914).

Waxweiler, Emile, *Équisse d'une sociologie* (Brussels: Misch and Thron 1896).

Weber, Alfred, *Kulturgeschichte als Kultursoziologie* (Leyden, Holland: Sythoff 1935).

Weber, Max, *Aufsätze zur Soziologie und Sozialpolitik* (Tübingen: Mohr 1924).

———, *Aufsätze zur Wissenschaftslehre* (Tübingen: Mohr 1922).

———, *The City*, translated by D. Martindale and G. Neuwirth (Glencoe, Ill.: The Free Press 1958).

———, *The Methodology of the Social Sciences*, translated and edited by Edward A. Shils and Henry A. Finch (Glencoe, Ill.: The Free Press 1949).

———, *The Protestant Ethic and the Spirit of Capitalism*, translated by Talcott Parsons (New York: Charles Scribner's Sons 1958).

———, *The Theory of Social and Economic Organization*, translated by A. M. Henderson and Talcott Parsons (Glencoe, Ill.: The Free Press 1957).

Westermarck, Edward, *History of Human Marriage* (London: Macmillan and Company 1894).

Wissler, Clark, *Man and Culture* (New York: Crowell Company 1923).

Znaniecki, Florian, *Social Actions* (New York: Farrar and Rinehart, 1936).

SECONDARY SOURCES

Alihan, M., *Social Ecology* (New York: Columbia University Press 1938).

Alpert, Harry, *Emile Durkheim and His Sociology* (New York: Columbia University Press 1939).

Abel, Theodore, *Systematic Sociology in Germany* (New York: Columbia University Press 1929).

Barnes, Harry E., and Howard Becker, *Social Thought from Lore to Science* (Boston: D. C. Heath and Company 1938).

———, *Society in Transition* (New York: Prentice-Hall, Inc. 1939).

Beach, Walter G., *The Growth of Social Thought* (New York: Charles Scribner's Sons 1939).

Bernard, L. L., *Social Control* (New York: The Macmillan Company 1939).

Bogardus, Emory S., *Contemporary Sociology* (Los Angeles: University of Southern California Press 1932).

———, *The Making of Public Opinion* (New York: Association Press 1951).

———, *The Principles of Cooperation* (Chicago: The Cooperative League of the U. S. A. 1958).

———, *Social Distance* (Yellow Springs, Ohio: The Antioch Press 1959).

Borkenau, Franz, *Pareto* (New York: Wiley & Sons 1936).

Bristol, L. M., *Social Adaptation* (Cambridge: Harvard University Press 1915).

Carver, Thomas N., *Sociology and Social Progress* (Boston: Ginn and Company 1905).

Chugerman, Samuel, *Lester F. Ward, the American Aristotle* (Durham: Duke University Press 1939).

Daugert, Stanley M., *The Philosophy of Thorstein Veblen* (New York: King's Crown Press 1950).

Durkheim, Emile, *On the Division of Labor in Society;* being a translation of his *De la division du travail social,* with an estimate of his work, by George Simpson (New York: The Macmillan Company 1933).

Ellwood, Charles A., *A History of Social Philosophy* (New York: Prentice-Hall, Inc. 1938).

Gehlke, C. E., *Durkheim's Contribution to Sociological Theory* (New York: Columbia University Press 1915).

Harper, F. R., *The Code of Hammurabi* (Chicago: University of Chicago Press 1904).

Hecker, Julius, *Russian Sociology* (New York: John Wiley & Sons 1934).

Hertzler, J. O., *The History of Utopian Thought* (New York: The Macmillan Company 1923).

———, *The Social Thought of the Ancient Civilizations* (New York: McGraw-Hill Book Company 1936).

Hexter, J. H., *More's Utopia, The Biography of an Idea* (Princeton: Princeton University Press 1952).

Holland, Francis, *Seneca* (New York: Longmans, Green and Company 1920).

House, Floyd N., *The Range of Social Theory* (New York: Henry Holt and Company 1929).

———, *The Development of Sociology* (New York: McGraw-Hill Book Company 1936).

Jacobs, P. P., *German Sociology* (Lancaster: Steinman and Foltz 1909).

Jarrett, Bede, *Social Theories of the Middle Ages* (Boston: Little, Brown and Company 1926).

Kent, Charles F., *The Social Teachings of the Prophets and Jesus* (New York: Charles Scribner's Sons 1917).

Kilzer, E., and E. J. Ross, *Western Social Thought* (Milwaukee: The Bruce Publishing Company 1954).

Lichtenberger, James P., *Development of Social Theory* (New York: Century Company 1923).

Maquet, Jacques J., *The Sociology of Knowledge* (Boston: The Beacon Press 1951).

Marvin, F. S., *Comte* (New York: John Wiley & Sons 1937).

Mihanovich, C. S., *Social Theorists* (Milwaukee: The Bruce Publishing Company 1953).

Motwani, Kewal, *Manu, a Study in Hindu Social Theory* (Madras, India: Ganesh and Company 1934).

Mumford, Lewis, *The Story of Utopias* (New York: Boni and Liveright 1922).

Odum, Howard W., *American Sociology* (New York: Longmans, Green and Company 1951).

Roe, Frederick W., *The Social Philosophy of Carlyle and Ruskin* (New York: Harcourt, Brace and Company 1921).

Rosenberg, Bernard, *The Values of Veblen* (Washington, D.C.: Public Affairs Press 1956).

Sorokin, Pitirim, *Social and Cultural Dynamics* (New York: American Book Company 1937).

Spykman, Nicholas, *The Social Theory of Georg Simmel* (Chicago: University of Chicago Press 1925).

Wallis, Louis, *A Sociological Study of the Bible* (Chicago: University of Chicago Press 1912).

Wolfe, Kurt H., editor and translator, *The Sociology of Georg Simmel* (Glencoe, Ill.: The Free Press 1950).

INDEX